Peter H. Weinrich has contributed to numerous books and magazines and is author of *Select Bibliography of Tim Buck*. He is executive director of the Canadian Crafts Council.

This select bibliography lists materials published in English and French on social and political protest from the left in all areas of Canada (except Quebec, for which a similar bibliography exists). The chief criterion for inclusion is that the document advocate social or political reform which, by the standards of the time in which it was published, would have seemed revolutionary, drastic, or far-reaching.

The author has included publications of the CCF, NDP, and Communist parties, the Socialist and Labour parties, and trade unions that encouraged political action. Also listed are those of 'ban the bomb,' pacifist, secularist, native rights, and feminist movements and documentation on riots, rebellions, and strikes. Only major, or little known but important, government documents are listed.

Entries are arranged chronologically by year of publication and alphabetically by author within each year. A list of serials, with place of publication, publisher, and date of first and last issue, is presented in alphabetical order by title.

PETER WEINRICH

Social Protest from the Left in Canada 1870–1970

University of Toronto Press
Toronto Buffalo London

©University of Toronto Press 1982
Toronto   Buffalo   London
Printed in Canada

ISBN 0-8020-5567-2

077548

Canadian Cataloguing in Publication Data

Weinrich, Peter, 1932-
    Social protest from the left in Canada 1870-1970

    Includes indexes.
    ISBN 0-8020-5567-2

    1. Radicalism - Canada - Bibliography. 2. Canada -
    Social conditions - Bibliography.   I. Title.

    Z1387.S66W44   016.3205'3   C82-094366-5

To R.S.Kenny who started it all

Contents

Introduction

I started this bibliography for my own pleasure and plea-
santly unaware of the eventual extent of the work involved.
I like old books, and I particularly like old pamphlets,
even not-so-old pamphlets. They have an immediacy and a
vigour about them wholly absent from the more qualified
judgements of maturity. Indeed, it may well be that within these covers are listed many youthful indiscretions
which their authors would repudiate with a shudder in later
life. However, *quod scripsit, scripsit.*
Apart from their charms of directness and brevity,
pamphlets are also a prime source for the social and political movements of the last two hundred years, although
the heyday of the religious controversy has long passed.
An anonymous reviewer wrote in the *Times Literary Supplement*
in 1970 'In Canada the power-seekers and election-winners
have for many generations depended for success on approp-
riating the ideas of the intellectual left and inventing
lures for the working class.' Many of those ideas were
originally expressed in pamphlets and since I believe the
quotation to be essentially correct this bibliography is
intended to help those who may also wish to document that
thesis. It is not, however, restricted to pamphlets.
The extent to which that thesis may be true has been
difficult to investigate because of the lack of a bibliography such as this. The material recorded here has rarely
survived; it is often still in private hands, from where
it is fortunately now being deposited in public collections, though usually of archives rather than libraries;
hence much of it remains uncatalogued and hard to find.
Public libraries did not collect it when it first appeared,
it was seldom available through booksellers, it is often
printed on poor paper, fragile and ephemeral in nature.
But it remains a prime source of information.
Of course it was not meant for posterity. Further-
more it was often dangerous to have. Very few people in
Canada would have risked being caught with Communist party
publications in the 1930s, certainly not in the later years
of that decade in Québec when the notorious Padlock law
was in force. No doubt much material was thrown out or
burned; some was quietly removed to rural houses and barns,
but I am afraid that the stories of undiscovered caches of
rarities are part of the folklore of the intrepid book
hunter. If such caches survive at all today it is as a
pulpy mass or the shredded lining of a mouse nest.
Thirteen thousand copies of Tim Buck's pamphlet *The
road ahead* were printed between 1934 and 1937. In the course of nearly ten years of specialized dealing in the kind

of material listed here I handled about six copies and
know of a dozen or so more. Let us be generous and say
that fifty, even one hundred, survive. One hundred out
of thirteen thousand! The survival rate bears no relation whatever to its distribution and impact at the time
of publication. Small wonder that another reviewer noted
recently that the part played by the Communist party in
the labour movement of the 1920s and 1930s is frequently
underestimated. Many writers are simply unaware of the
extent of the material available, as I was myself, since
I considerably underestimated the size this bibliography
would eventually assume.

This bibliography lists published material on social
and political protest from the left in Canada from 1870
to 1970. Why 1870 to 1970? I started work in 1970, cou-
nted back one hundred years and found 1870 a convenient
date to start from: just at the end of the Fenian movement, just before Louis Riel and landmarks such as the
Toronto typographers strike. Industrialization was beginning, confederation was under way, the west was being col-
onized and Canada beginning to take a form familiar to us
today; it seemed as good a date as any and I claim no more
significance for the dates than that.

What is social and political protest from the left?
This is more difficult to answer. Something that spelt
red revolution in 1870 might not raise an eyebrow on the
Tory front bench in 1970. My guidelines have essentially
been: does this document advocate social or political reform which, by the standards of the time when it was published, would have seemed revolutionary, drastic or far-
reaching? To a limited extent I have included material
that was contemporary if it refers to, or was descriptive
of, events and policies that fall within my guideline or
that later became left-wing 'causes'. Louis Riel is the
prime example. With the best will in the world it is hard
to classify Riel as a dangerous left-wing revolutionary,
but he has certainly been hailed as a hero by much of the
later left. What is to be done? Because of the mass of
material about him, much of dubious value, I have listed
only material contemporary with Riel himself. This also
includes material that was opposed to him, and it is included mainly because of the equivocal position he himself
holds. This is the only time I have followed this course.
The great controversies of free trade and reciprocity, the
Jesuit estates, the Manitoba schools, Orangeism, temperance and the like, while giving rise to social protest of
a sort, have been largely omitted.

What this means in practice is that I have attempted
to list all the publications of the CCF, NDP and Communist
parties, the Socialist and Labour parties, most of those
of the trade unions (certainly those that encouraged political action), publications of movements such as 'ban
the bomb' and pacifism, secularism, native rights, feminism and similar movements, and documentation on riots,
rebellions and strikes. I have also included co-operatives. Some of these subjects present difficulties - not
all were always left-wing; the trade unions, for example,

frequently published material that was conservative in outlook.

It is also often difficult to say what constitutes publication. This is especially true of mimeographed documents, and on the odd occasion when I have been compelled to consult microfiche or microfilm there has never been any indication whether or not the document I am peering at is mimeographed or simply a typescript. In general I have assumed 'publication' of anything that appears to have found its way intentionally outside a restricted group. Thus mimeographed documents of the executive of the CCF are excluded (unless there is evidence that wide distribution was authorised) whereas mimeographed convention reports are included. Federations of labour, trade unions, and many organizations often presented annual briefs to their provincial or federal government, sometimes printed and distributed widely, sometimes not. Similarly, reports of annual conventions are sometimes found only in typescript, sometimes printed, sometimes in full, sometimes abbreviated, sometimes mimeographed.

Secondary works have been included selectively (and hence somewhat subjectively). One main criterion has been if they include documentation or material not available elsewhere or include other primary research. It is partly for the latter reason that I have attempted an extensive listing of theses which are unpublished in the strict sense.

It is as well to point out what is not included, if only for the benefit of the cursory viewer, who need look no further. The first major omission is material relating to Québec. This was excluded because there is already one major published bibliography covering Québec relative to my topic, and a second which also reprints selected documents, and more are planned. It seemed needlessly expensive of time and money to duplicate this excellent work which is recorded here in the list of bibliographies consulted.

Canada is not an isolated country. It is impossible to study this field adequately without a knowledge of events and conditions elsewhere, especially in the United States and the United Kingdom. Ties to these countries, particularly the United Kingdom, were strong. J.W.Buckley, M.J.Coldwell, Harold Winch, William Irvine, James Simpson, T.C.Douglas, Tom Moore, Irene Parlby, R.B.Russell, Tom McEwen, Tim Buck, Percy Bengough, Bill Bennett, E.T.Kingsley, W. Lefeaux, Victor Midgley, William Pritchard, H.E. Spencer and Norman Priestley, to name but a handful, were all born in the United Kingdom, and many of them retained their contacts there. But it is clearly beyond the scope of this bibliography to include relevant works from every country that were circulated in Canada and which may have been influential.

For example, the publications of Charles Kerr in Chicago were extensively studied and except when banned were freely available. Material from the Fabian Society, the Labour Party and Gollancz' Left Book Club was circulated. In an appendix I have listed a couple of sample groups of such publications; those banned during the period 1916-20 and those seized at the time of the arrest of the Communist party leaders in 1931. There is a certain intrinsic interest in these events anyway, and they do crystallize a group of publications at a particular period.

As noted above I have not attempted to list all secondary works, nor have I attempted to list all such things as election leaflets - that is, multiple reproductions of party statements, often with different candidates pictures and sometimes with different titles - issued in connection with national, provincial or local elections or some sort of campaign, unless they are the only published source of policy statements.

Government documents have also required selective exclusion. It is obviously absurd to list all the publications of the CCF government in Saskatchewan for example, especially since bibliographies of government documents already exist for many provinces. Similarly it is not necessary to list all the publications of departments of labour because they may relate to trade unions. What I have done is compromise, and hence satisfy nobody. I have listed major documents together with those that seem to be less well-known than they should be, and those that specifically relate to other material listed - reports of riots for example.

With regard to works in languages other than English or French I have, in the end, reluctantly decided to omit them (except in the section on serials). My knowledge of Finnish is nil and the Finnish socialist movement in Canada an important one; the same might be said of Yiddish. And while I have some smatterings of Russian, German and so forth, it seemed invidious to include some of these while excluding others. I hope that the various specialized ethnic studies now being carried out will ultimately produce a more comprehensive listing than I can manage. In fact, many foreign language publications were only translations of documents such as the Regina manifesto or the leaflets of the One Big Union, although there was definitely much original material as well.

A single entry in the first year of publication has been made for most constitutions with dates of amendment (if known) listed under the same entry. And, as noted above, annual events did not always leave a published record. Changes of name have made it difficult to track some of these down since cataloguing procedures vary, and archives are often incomplete. However, the locations cited for known published reports should enable researchers to track down 'missing' years that may only exist in typescript in archival collections.

The bibliography is arranged chronologically by year of publication and alphabetically by author within each year. If an item is not dated, a date can often be assigned accurately from other evidence. No special note has been made in these cases. However, where a date is conjectural the entry is under the conjectured year but recorded after the pagination as being c. (for circa) that particular year.

Where there is multiple authorship all known names
are listed and each will appear in the author index, the
entry itself being under the name of the author mentioned first on the title page. Works not identified as being by an author or authors are listed in the same alphabetical sequence but under the name of the organization
responsible. Completely anonymous works where the publisher cannot be identified either are listed by the first
word of the title (excluding 'the') and in the same alphabetical sequence.

Each entry is numbered consecutively throughout the
book. The suffix a,b etc is given where different forms
of the same titles are listed, for example in translation
or with added material. When the number is enclosed within brackets it means that the item has not been seen by
me, but that its existence (or former existence) is not
in doubt.

In the entry proper the author's name comes first,
followed by given names or initials as recorded on the
item itself. Thus William Irvine will sometimes appear
as Irvine, William and sometimes as Irvine, W. The auth-
or's name is followed by the main title and full sub-title.
It is not always easy to decide what the title is. Sometimes the cover carries one title and the title page (if
any) another; sometimes there is no title page and only
a bold face heading immediately preceding the text; sometimes there is only a cover which for decorative reasons
carries the gist of a title in no apparent order other
than the use of large or small or more decorative type
faces. It has proved impossible to be consistent about
transcribing these. In general I have tried to proceed
from the first words at the top to the last words at the
bottom, but where this would make nonsense of the entry
I have had to use common sense.

Where the author's name reappears in the title, this
has been silently omitted in the transcription. For example *Speech of the Hon Edward Blake on the disturbances in the
North-West* becomes *Speech on the disturbances in the North-West*.
Capital letters, italics and other typographical niceties
have been ignored, other than for proper names. The abbreviation CCF for Cooperative Commonwealth Federation has
been used consistently regardless of title page usage.
Ampersands have been consistently expanded to 'and'. I
have been cowardly and refused to take a stand between
'labor' and 'labour' and have left these in the version
in which they appear on the title page - which is not always consistent either.

Place of publication, publisher and pagination follow. Brackets are used around any of these to indicate
that they are not cited in the work but are assumed or
calculated. A query - '?' - is used in addition if the
assumption may be questionable. If no publisher is cited
then the author is the publisher. If the publisher is
unknown then the abbreviation 'np' is used. Suffixes to
the publishers principal name (eg 'and Sons', 'Company
Limited' etc) are omitted in the interests of economy.

This is followed by locations. Libraries and archives

have been coded using the National Library's *Symbols of Canadian Libraries*, eighth edition.   However, as this does not always distinguish between archives and general and special collections, I have had to use additional letters for precision and in two cases establish a new code using the same principles.   These codes are all listed under location codes and collections examined.   I have listed all the collections examined even though some of them are not cited in the main bibliography as I found nothing in them. I have done this so that other researchers may know that I have examined them.

The locations cited first are derived from the National Union catalogue and are simply there to provide an added guide.   Locations cited after the asterisk * are to collections where I have actually examined the item. As most of the works cited are in archives it has not been possible to move these around the country and so make side by side comparisons of texts, so no research of this kind has been undertaken.

With the exception of those derived from the National Union catalogue (when a card in the catalogue of the originating library is assumed) the location entry gives first the library/archive code followed by additional references. If there is no additional reference in the codes after the asterisk it means the item can be found in the card catalogue of the library in question.   In some cases the added reference is to a call number, but most are to collections in archives.   Clearly it makes no sense to list OOA for the Public Archives of Canada or even OOA/CCF when there are several hundred boxes in this collection, any one of which might contain the item.   The entry therefore reads something like OOA/CCF365, meaning box 365 of the CCF collection in the Public Archives.   I have chosen this method rather than citing call numbers since these may be (and already have been) changed.   Unfortunately I have to record that some box numbers have also been changed since the work was started, but the new numbers are cross-referenced by the archives responsible which enables the researcher to identify the new box number.   Occasionally I have not been able to give a box number because I was privileged to examine some collections before they had been properly classified, notably at the University of British Columbia, McMaster University and the International Institute for Social History in Amsterdam.   It was nonetheless worthwhile recording these items even though it may take a subsequent researcher somewhat longer to find them.

Where an item is available in many libraries across Canada (more than ten or twelve anyway) I have only given the locations where the work was actually examined.   No one should have any difficulty in locating a copy of *Make this your Canada* for example.   I assume some previous knowledge on the part of users so that they can separate a genuinely rare work with only one location cited from one which has only one location cited because of its ready availability.

Finally there is the problem of private collections and booksellers' stocks.   I have only cited these (and collections outside Canada) when I have not been able to find an item elsewhere. Both classes have been assigned a single code letter in the location codes. The booksellers' names and addresses are given, but not those of the private collector. Should a private collection finish up in the public domain it can then be readily identified.

Finally any other relevant information follows the location. If the title and sub-title are not self-explanatory (or liable to create confusion) a note explains the content of the work or gives a further quotation from it. This section also includes the reference numbers used by Peel and Hann et al (see the list of bibliographies consulted) for ease of cross-referencing. I have done this since these are the two largest bibliographies containing the kind of works cited here, and my entries are generally somewhat fuller than those in Hann and there are a number of items here that are not in Peel.

After the main bibliography of monographs there is a listing of serials. These are in alphabetical order of title, cross-referenced where the title changes. Place of publication, publisher, date of first and last issue and locations are given when known. It has been particularly frustrating trying to compile this information, since apart from the fly-by-night nature of many of these serials, a good many are now on microfilm and usually no effort has been made during microfilming to record essential information such as missing issues, changes of frequency etc etc. I have no doubt that there are many lacunae in this section. A letter from W.T.Burford, Secretary-Treasurer of the Canadian Federation of Labor dated 4th December 1946 and cited by Robbins Elliott in his thesis reads in part: 'I have your letter of the 1st instant, requesting to be furnished with a list of publications of unions...There is no such list available, as we do not keep a record of such matters, nor would it be of any conceivable value to anybody'. With such an attitude it is small wonder that it is difficult to track them down today.

I have tried to examine every work listed here. I believe this is of critical importance. The examination of the sometimes inadequate card catalogues of libraries -the kind that list the League of Social Reconstruction under Communism and fail to distinguish the violently anti-socialist tracts of people like Gladstone Murray from genuine CCF publications - can easily give rise to problems. I have not confused this bibliography by listing antagonistic material (except in the case of Riel for reasons already given). If this bibliography is to have the value and use I hope it will have, then the user deserves, and should expect, that each item will have been examined with some care and that the finished work is reliable to the best of the author's ability. Of course this work can never be complete; items identified but not found by me will be found by others, and many new items will turn up. I welcome any users' amendments, corrections or additions.

In conclusion, I cannot do better than quote from Samuel Johnson's preface to his dictionary: 'In hope of

giving longevity to that which its own nature forbids to
be immortal, I have devoted this book, the labour of years,
to the honour of my country...I look with pleasure on my
book, however defective, and deliver it to the world with
the spirit of a man that has endeavoured well. That it
will immediately become popular I have not promised myself;
a few wild blunders, and risible absurdities, from which
no work of such multiplicity was ever free, may for a time
furnish folly with laughter...but useful diligence will at
last prevail, and there can never be wanting some who distinguish desert...What is obvious is not always known, and
what is known is not always present; sudden fits of inad-
vertency will surprize vigilance, slight avocation will
seduce attention, and casual eclipse of the mind will dar-
ken learning; and...the writer shall often in vain trace
his memory at the moment of need, for that which he knew
yesterday with intuitive readiness, and which will come
uncalled into his thought tomorrow.

'In this work, when it shall be found that much is
omitted, let it not be forgotten that much is likewise
performed; and though no book was ever spared out of ten-
derness to the author, and the world is little solicitous
to know whence proceeded the faults of that which it con-
demns; yet it may gratify curiosity to inform it, that...
it was written...not in the soft obscurities of retirement,
or under the shelter of academick bowers, but amidst incon-
venience and distraction, in sickness and in sorrow...'

The cadences may not be mine, but the sentiments are.

Peter Weinrich
Ottawa, 1981

Acknowledgements

I must express my thanks first to the Social Sciences and
Humanities Research Council of Canada for a grant which
enabled me to travel to the collections listed in this
work. I am very grateful for their support without which
the work could not have been finished.
My thanks must go next to all the archivists and librar-
ians who put up with my inquiries with courtesy and understanding. To list them all would be impossible, but I
must mention Nancy Stunden formerly of the Public Archives
of Canada, who provided help and encouragement beyond the
call of duty.
I must also thank those who kindly allowed me access to
collections otherwise restricted: the National Office of
the New Democratic Party for permission to search in their
own and the National CCF collection; the New Democratic
Party in Manitoba for similar permission for that province;
Dr J.G.Endicott; the Hon.T.C.Douglas, whose archives are
now all in public hands. To the private collections of
Mr R.S.Kenny (now in the University of Toronto Rare Books
Library); Mr Ross Dowson; Mr Don Stewart; Mr Don Lake;
and the Communist Party of Canada (now being transferred
to the Public Archives of Canada).
I have also consulted the antiquarian book catalogues of
Joseph Patrick Books, Toronto; October Books (now D.& E.
Lake Ltd), Toronto; Northland Books, Saskatoon; and David
Mason Books, Toronto. The late Bernard Amtmann's catalo-
gues are recorded in the list of bibliographies under his
Short title catalogue...
I should also like to acknowledge with thanks the help I
have generally received from my former colleagues in the
antiquarian book trade, and the encouragement from many
people, particularly in the academic world, who have spur-
red me on with judicious inquiries as to my progress.
Last but not least I must thank Mr R.I.K.Davidson of the
University of Toronto Press who has provided valuable
advice and much encouragement since the beginning.
    For all faults I have only myself to blame.

Abbreviations

Abbreviations for locations and collections cited are
listed separately.

CCF   Cooperative Commonwealth Federation

mimeo Mimeographed, cyclostyled or some similar method
of reproduction.

np   no publisher or place of publication

pp   Pages. Unfortunately pagination by publishers is
far from consistent. Some publishers have preliminary pages unnumbered followed by preliminary pages
numbered in small roman numerals, followed by the
text in arabic numerals which may number straight
on from the preliminary pages, or start afresh.
Some omit numbering the sub-title pages in the body
of the text, some omit the number of the last page,
some number pages of advertising at the end, some
do not. Some even number each chapter afresh, starting with a 1 each time, some do not number anything
at all. Brackets around the page number(s) indicate
numbering supplied, small roman numerals for preliminary pages, arabic for text. The terminal number is either that recorded by the publisher or
silently supplied, but numbers have not been supplied for advertising or blanks at the end (unless
so numbered by the publisher). Recording the first
page of each section has been omitted. A sample
entry might therefore read (ii),viii,354pp, meaning
two unnumbered preliminary pages, plus eight numbered preliminary pages, plus 354 numbered pages of
text, including index, appendices etc.
An added difficulty concerns mimeographed publications where the printing may be on one or both
sides of the page. The script letter el (for leaves)
is often used for typescripts, but this is not universal and the printed el is easily confused with
the numeral 1. I have therefore used the abbreviation pp whether the work is printed on both sides
of the page or not. Thus a mimeographed item recorded as being 16pp may be sixteen pages printed on
one side only or eight pages printed on both.

Location codes and collections examined

Alberta

ACG   Glenbow-Alberta Institute, Calgary
ACGA   Glenbow-Alberta Institute Archives
     /CCF: Alberta CCF records (BE.21.C776)
     /Coote: C.G.Coote papers (A.C779)
     /Hutchison: A.N.Hutchison papers (A.H976)
     /Smith: Walter Norman Smith papers (A.S663)
     /Spencer: H.E.Spencer papers (A.S745)
     /UFA: United Farmers of Alberta collection
        (BE.24.U58A)
     /UMWA: United Mineworkers of America collection
        (BL.U58G)
     /USWA: United Steelworkers of America collection
        (BL.U58F)
ACGL   Glenbow-Alberta Institute Library - political and
     agrarian pamphlet collection
ACU   University of Calgary
AEP   Alberta Legislature Library, Edmonton
AEPAA   Provincial Archives of Alberta, Edmonton
     /Alta: Information file, Alberta politics
     /Brown: Ernest Brown papers
     /Farmilo: Alfred Farmilo papers
AEU   University of Alberta, Edmonton
AEUS   University of Alberta Special collections
     /CCF: CCF collection
     /PSSA: Prairie School for Social Advance collection
     /Rutherford: Rutherford pamphlet collection

British Columbia

BVAA   Vancouver City Archives
BVAS   Simon Fraser University, Burnaby
BVAU   University of British Columbia Special collections
     /Garrison: Lindsay Garrison papers
     /IWW: Industrial Workers of the World collection
     /Mac: Angus MacInnis memorial collection
     /Pam: General pamphlet collection
     /Shepherd: A.Shepherd papers
     /Smith: Evelyn Smith papers
     /Steeves: Dorothy Steeves papers
     /Turner: Arthur Turner papers
     /WB: William Bennett memorial collection
     /Webster: Arnold Webster papers
     /Young: Rod Young papers
BVIP   Legislative Library, Victoria
BVIPA   Provincial Archives, Victoria
BVIV   University of Victoria

Manitoba

MWP   Legislative Library, Winnipeg
MWPA Provincial Archives of Manitoba, Winnipeg
     /AG: Attorney-General's records, Manitoba (RG3.Cl)
     /Brigden: B.Brigden papers (MG14.C19)
     /CCA: Canadian Council of Agriculture collection
       (MG10.B25)
     /CCF: CCF-NDP collection (MG14.D8)
     /CCO: Citizens Committee of 1000 collection
       (MG10.E2)
     /Eliason: M.Eliason papers (MG14.B64)
     /Dixon: F.J.Dixon papers (MG14.B25)
     /Gray: C.F.Gray papers (MG14.B18)
     /ILP: Independent Labor Party of Manitoba coll-
       ection (MG14.D4)
     /Ivens: William Ivens papers (MG14.B31)
     /Kardash: W.A.Kardash papers (MG14.B19)
     /ManNW: Manitoba and North West Farmers Union
       collection (MG10.E14)
     /Manning: R.A.C.Manning papers (MG14.B36)
     /Norris: T.C.Norris papers (MG13.H1)
     /OBU: One Big Union collection (MG10.A3)
     /PEL: Political Equality League collection
       (MG10.C30)
     /PH: Patrons of Husbandry collection
     /PRU: Political Reform Union collection (MG14.D1)
     /Pitblado: Isaac Pitblado papers (MG14.C64)
     /Puttee: A.W.Puttee papers (MG14.B50)
     /RCR: Royal Commission on Rebellion Losses records
       (MG3.C14)
     /RRD: Red river disturbances collection (MG3.A1)
     /RvIvens: Manitoba Court Records: Kings Bench:
       Rex v. Ivens (RG4.A1)
     /Rigg: R.A.Rigg papers (MG14.B43)
     /Russell: R.B.Russell papers (MG10.A14-1 & 14-2)
     /Salton: H.G.A.Salton papers (MG7.F8)
     /Stinson: L.G.Stinson papers (MG14.B62)
     /Summers: Summers Labor Church collection (MG9.B4)
     /Thompson: F.G.Thompson papers (MG14.C46)
     /UFM: United Farmers of Manitoba collection
     /WTLC: Winnipeg Trades and Labor Council coll-
       ection (MG10.A12)
     /Winnipeg: Winnipeg General Strike collection
       (MG14.A18)
     /Wiseman: Wiseman political history of Manitoba
       CCF-NDP collection (MG9.B6)
MWU   University of Manitoba, Winnipeg

New Brunswick

NBFL   Legislative Library, Fredericton
NBFU   University of New Brunswick, Fredericton
NBSAM Mount Allison University, Sackville

Newfoundland

NFSM   Memorial University, St John's

Nova Scotia

NSHD Dalhousie University, Halifax
NSHDS Dalhousie University special collections (Pamphlet file)
NSHP Nova Scotia Public Archives, Halifax
NSWA Acadia University, Wolfville (principally Eric Dennis collection)

Ontario

OH Hamilton Public Library
OHM McMaster University, Hamilton
OHMA McMaster University special collections (principally the radical archive)
OKQ Queens University, Kingston
OKQS Queens University special collections
OLU University of Western Ontario, London
OOA Public Archives of Canada, Ottawa
  /Avison: H.R.C.Avison papers (MG30.D102)
  /BCFL: British Columbia Federation of Labour records (MG28.I-104)
  /Bengough: Percy Bengough papers (MG30.A47)
  /CCF: National CCF-NDP records (MG28.IV-1)
  /CCJC: Cooperative Committee on Japanese Canadians records (MG28.V-1)
  /CFAW: Canadian Food and Allied Workers Union records (MG28.I-186)
  /CFL: Canadian Federation of Labour records (MG28.I-110)
  /CLC: Canadian Labour Congress records (MG28.I-103)
  /CPA: Community Planning Association records (MG28.I-14)
  /CU: Cooperative Union records (MG28.I-15)
  /Censor: Dept of the Secretary of State: Chief Press Censor (RG6.E-1)
  /Coldwell: M.J.Coldwell papers (MG27.III.C.12)
  /Endicott: James G. Endicott papers (MG30.C130)
  /Farrer: Edward F.Farrer papers (MG30.A4)
  /Forsey: Eugene Forsey papers (MG30.A25)
  /Frontier: Frontier College papers (MG28.I-124)
  /Good: W.C.Good papers (MG27.III.C.1)
  /Gray: Charles F.Gray papers (MG30.A83)
  /Harper: Henry Harper papers (MG30.A28)
  /Heaps: A.A.Heaps papers (MG27.III.C.22)
  /IUE: International Union of Electrical, Radio & Machine Workers records (MG28.I-264).
  /KWLC: Kitchener and Waterloo Labour Council records (MG28.I-166)
  /Kangas: Victor Kangas papers (MG30.C138)
  /Kaplansky: Kalmen Kaplansky papers (MG30.A53)
  /Keen: George Keen papers (MG30.A15)
  /Klein: A.M.Klein papers (MG30.D167)
  /Lucas: Louise Lucas papers (MG27.III.D.6)
  /MacInnis: Grace MacInnis papers
  /McIntee: Ralph McIntee papers (MG30.A87)
  /MacPhail: Agnes MacPhail papers (MG27.III.C.4)
  /Man: Henri de Man papers (MG30.A50)

/Moore: Tom Moore papers (MG30.A31)
/Morrison: J.J.Morrison papers (MG27.III.D.3)
/ODLC: Ottawa and District Labour Council records
        (MG28.I-236)
/OFL: Ontario Federation of Labour (MG28.I-195)
/OPEU: Office and Professional Employees Union
        records (MG28.I-163)
/Parlby: Irene Parlby papers (MG27.III.D.4)
/Priestley: Norman Priestley papers (MG27.III.D.7)
/Rhodes: Henry G.Rhodes papers (MG30.A55)
/Riggs: Richard Riggs papers (MG30.A45)
/Spencer: H.E.Spencer papers (MG27.III.C.5)
/Sudeten: Sudeten Club 'Forward' records (MG28.V-6)
/TUA: Trade Union Advocate (MG28.I-112)
/Underhill: F.H.Underhill papers (MG30.D204)
/VOW: Voice of Women records (MG28.I-218)
/VS: Vapa Sana (MG28.V.42)
/Woodsworth: J.S.Woodsworth papers (MG27.III.C.7)

OOAL	Public Archives of Canada Library, Ottawa
OOAG	Dept of Agriculture Main Library, Ottawa
OOCC	Carleton University, Ottawa
OOL	Dept of Labour, Ottawa
OONL	National Library, Ottawa
OOP	Library of Parliament, Ottawa
OOU	University of Ottawa
OPAL	Lakehead University, Thunder Bay
OPET	Trent University, Peterborough (principally Gainey collection)
OTAR	Archives of Ontario, Toronto
	/CPC: Dept of the Attorney-General: Communist Party of Canada records
OTCPA	Communist Party of Canada Archives, Toronto (now being transferred to the Public Archives)
OTMCL	Metropolitan Toronto Library
OTP	Toronto Public Libraries
OTPB	Metropolitan Toronto Public Library Baldwin room
	/Buckley: J.W.Buckley papers
	/Simpson: James Simpson papers
OTU	University of Toronto
OTUAR	University of Toronto Archives
OTURS	University of Toronto Rare Books and Special collections
	/Mavor: James Mavor papers
	/RSK: R.S.Kenny collection
	/Salsberg: J. .Salsberg collection
	/Woodsworth: J.S.Woodsworth collection
OTV	Victoria University, Toronto
OWA	University of Windsor
OWTU	University of Waterloo

Prince Edward Island

PCU	University of Prince Edward Island, Charlottetown

Québec

QMBM	Bibliothèque de la ville de Montréal
QMBN	Bibliothèque nationale du Québec
QMM	McGill University, McLennan Library

QMU	Université de Montréal
QQL	Legislature du Québec, Québec
QQLA	Université Laval, Québec

Saskatchewan

SRA	Saskatchewan Archives, Regina
	/CCF: CCF Saskatchewan records
	/Douglas: T.C.Douglas papers
	/Riot: Regina Riot Commission records
SRL	Legislative Library of Saskatchewan, Regina
SRU	University of Regina
SSA	Saskatchewan Archives Office, Saskatoon
	/CanHist: Canadian History collection
	/Communism: Communism collection
	/Coops: Cooperatives collection
	/Dunning: E. Dunning papers
	/Eliason: M. Eliason papers
	/Endicott: Endicott papers
	/McNaughton: McNaughton papers
	/Motherwell: Motherwell papers
	/NCWC: National Council of Women of Canada records
	/NDP: New Democratic Party collection
	/PO: Peace organizations collection
	/Suffrage: Womens suffrage collection
	/SDPC: Social Democratic Party of Canada collection
	/UWV: United Women Voters collection
	/VOW: Voice of Women collection
	/WILP: Womens International League for Peace and Freedom collection
	/Winnipeg: Winnipeg General Strike collection
SSU	University of Saskatchewan, Saskatoon
SSUS	University of Saskatchewan Special collections
	/Coops: Cooperatives collection
	/Labour: Labour collection
	/Shortt: Shortt collection
	/UFC: United Farmers of Canada collection

Other

D	David Mason Books, Toronto
E	Private collection
f	appearing in a collection code means file or folder number within the box
G	Library of the Labour Party, Transport House, London, England
HI	International Institute for Social History, Amsterdam, Netherlands
J	Joseph Patrick Books, Toronto
K	Northland Books, Saskatoon
T	Private collection

Bibliography of monographs
1870–1970

1a Canada, Governor-General. Correspondence and papers
   connected with the recent occurences in the North West
   Territories. Ottawa: I.B.Taylor. 129pp. *OOAL
   Peel 295

1b Same source, title, and text but 157pp. *ACGL

2 Canada, Senate. Report of the Select Committee of the
  Senate on the subject of Rupert's Land, Red river and
  the North-West Territory, together with minutes of
  evidence. Ottawa: I.B.Taylor. 38pp, map. *OOAL
  Peel 296. Contains some evidence on Riel.

3 Corbett, G.O. An appeal to the Right Honourable W.E.
  Gladstone, M.P., Her Majesty's Prime Minister, respecting the suppression of certain papers by the government,
  the 'Red river rebellion' and the illegal transfer of
  the North West Territories to the Canadian government,
  1870. London (Eng.): (author). 12pp. BVIPA *ACGL
  Peel 299

4 Corbett, Griffith Owen. 'The Red river rebellion': the
  cause of it. In a series of letters to the British government on the importance of opening the overland route
  through Rupert's America from Canada to British Columbia
  for the introduction of means for the administration of
  justice therein; the promotion of emigration; and earn-
  est appeals to stay bloodshed in the Red river settlement, by extending righteous rule to that country.
  London (Eng.): for the author by Cassell, Petter and
  Galpin. 36pp. OTMCL BVIPA SRL *ACGL Peel 300

5 Great Britain. (No title). Official journal. Part 1,
  57pp and Appendix 32pp (incomplete). *OTAR/1870/27.
  Part 1 consists of correspondence, the appendix contains
  a diary of the Red river expedition. Extensive note
  attached to OTAR copy by D.Russell, archivist, on the
  sources and origins of this work.

6 Halifax Typographical Union. Local 130. Constitution,
  by-laws and rules of order. Halifax: J.Bowes. 20pp
  *NSHPL. Organized 21 September 1869.

7 Hurlbert, J. Beaufort. Field and factory side by side;
  or, how to establish and develop native industries.
  Montreal: John Lovell. 63pp. AEU OH OTP QMBN QQL
  *OOAL. Hann 2081. Basically an anti-free trade tract.

8 MacDougall, Wm. The Red river rebellion. Eight letters

to Hon. Joseph Howe, in reply to an official pamphlet. Toronto: Hunter, Rose. iv, 68pp. *OOAL. Peel 307. OOAL is Howe's copy of this pamphlet, heavily under- lined and annotated by him, frequently with numbered comments (e.g. 'a lie', of which there are 29). The 'official' pamphlet referred to is no. 11 below which was issued anonymously but, according to MacDougall, under Howe's direction 'by one of your colleagues who has seldom, hitherto, lacked the courage to affix his name to his productions'.

9 **Mills, David.** Speech at St Thomas on the 12th Novem- ber 1869, on the present and future political aspects of Canada, with an appendix containing the letters of the Rev. St. George Caulfeild (*sic*) on the Irish ques- tion with Mr Mills' replies thereto. London (Ont.): John Cameron. 38pp. QMBM *OOAL. The letter is signed Caulfield but the spelling otherwise is Caulfeild.

10 **(Red river expeditionary force).** Standing orders. Tor- onto: np. *OPTB/1870/RR. Long broadside dated 14 May 1870 and signed G.J. Wolseley. There are thirty-five standing orders, including 'Reveille will sound at 3 a.m. every morning'.

11 **Red river insurrection.** Hon. Wm. McDougall's conduct reviewed. Montreal: John Lovell. 69pp OONL OTP SSUS *ACGL OOAL. Peel 289. See 8 above.

12 (Riel, Louis.) Aux habitants du Nord et du Nord-Ouest. Fort Garry: Maison du Gouvernement Provisoire. *OOAL

13 (Riel, Louis.) Liste des droits revendiqués par le peuple de la Terre de Rupert et du Nord-Ouest, et con- ditions sous lesquelles ce peuple consentirait à entre dans la Confederation Canadienne. Fort Garry: Maison du Gouvernment. *MWPA OOAL. Peel 291(m)

(14) (Riel, Louis.) Ordonnances du Gouvernement Provisoire de la Terre de Rupert. Fort Garry. Peel 291(k)

15 **Riel, Louis.** Pour prouver aux nations sauvages que le peuple de la Riviere Rouge ne veut pas laisser maltrait- er par le Canada. Fort Garry: Maison du Gouvernment. *OTPB/1870/Riel. Peel 291(n) Dated 23 mars 1870.

16 **Riel, Louis.** Proclamation aux peuples du Nord-Ouest. Fort Garry: Maison du Gouvernement. *OTPB/1870/Riel Dated 9 avril 1870.

17 **Riel, Louis.** Proclamation to the people of the North- West. Fort Garry: Government House. *MWPA/RR25. Peel 291(p). English version of 16.

18 **Riel, Louis.** Protestation des peuples du Nord-Ouest. (Fort Garry): (Maison du Gouvernement). 2pp *OOAL Peel 291(q)

1871

19 Begg, Alexander. The creation of Manitoba; or, a history of the Red river troubles. Toronto: Hunter Rose. vi, 408pp. *OONL Peel 319.

(20)Brockett, Linus P. Paris under the Commune. Toronto: Hovey. 170pp SRU

21 Canada, Secretary of State. Return to an address of the House of Commons, dated 30th March 1871, for copy of the report of Mr S.J. Dawson; upon the Red river expedition of 1870; also copy of any document submitted by him in reference to the strictures published in England by an officer of the Expeditionary Force. Ottawa: 31pp. *ACGL Note at end: 'In accordance with the recommendation of the Joint Committee on printing that portion of Mr Dawson's report having reference to the strictures...is not published'.

22 Canada, Secretary of State. Statement of claims made on the Dominion government, consequent upon the insurrection in the North-West Territories. Ottawa: I.B. Taylor. 57pp *AEUS/Rutherford. Peel 323.

23 (Fisher, Wm. N.) The memorial of the Chippeway tribe of Indians, some of whom reside on their reserves near Sarnia, and others on Walpole island, together with other documents praying that they may be allowed to form themselves into one tribe as they were prior to 1831, and to hold their lands and moneys in common, and that the foreign Indians may hereafter be excluded from participating in the annuity. Sarnia: Canadian Power Press Plant. 18pp *OOAL. Contains the affidavit of Chief Joshua Wawanosh, 1870, and various treaty articles of 1836, 1838, 1820, 1808, 1829, list of surrenders and report.

24a Great Britain, War Office. Correspondence relative to the recent expedition to the Red river settlement: with journal of operations. Presented to both Houses of Parliament. London (Eng.): Harrison and Sons. 96pp. *ACGL Peel 327

24b the same work with maps but without correspondence. 11p. *ACGL

25 Huyshe, G.L. The Red river expedition. London and New York: Macmillan. xii, 275pp, maps, illustrations. *OOP Peel 329

26 Mills, D. The blunders of the Dominion government in connection with the North-West Territory. A speech at London, January 17th, 1871. London (Ont): Advertiser Steam Job Office. 9pp BVAU *OOAL. Peel 332.

27 Moncrieff, W.G. Party and government by party. Toronto: Copp Clark. 76pp OTP *OOAL. An attack on party voting and party discipline.

28 Riddell, H.S.H. The Red river expedition of 1870; a

paper read before the Literary and Historical Society of Quebec, 15th March 1871. np. (40pp). *OOAL Peel 335 Separately bound as Paper V of the Society.

29 Sulte, Benjamin. L'expedition militaire de Manitoba 1870. Montréal: Eusèbe Senécal. 50pp. ACG ACU BVIPA MWU OTP QMBM QMU QQL *OOAL. Peel 337

1872

30 Brown, William. The labour question. Thoughts on paper currency and lending on interest; as affecting the prosperity of labour, commerce and manufactures. Montreal: Dawson Bros. 240pp plus advts. BVIV OKQ OOA OOP OOU OTP QMU SSU *OONL. Hann 2104. 'Our legalized banking system...cannot, in its very nature, do anything but oppress labour'.

31 Canada. Return to an address of the House of Commons for copies of all dispatches and correspondence between the Dominion and Imperial governments, relative to the claims arising from the Fenian invasion of Canada and of the account of the Fenian brotherhood drawn up by Lord Tenterden. Ottawa: I.B. Taylor. 14pp. *OTAR/ 1872/8. (Sessional paper 26).

32 (Griffin, Justin A.) From Toronto to Fort Garry: an account of the second expedition to Red river: diary of a private soldier. Hamilton: Evening Times. 64pp ACG MWP MWU OH OTP QMBN *OOAL. Peel 346

(33) Lanctot, Médéric. Association du capital et du travail. Montréal: Wilson. 46pp. QMBN.

34 MacKelcan, F.P. Labor and capital: how to unite them and produce universal industry and prosperity. Addressed to the Dominion and provincial governments, to capitalists and to workingmen. Montreal: Gazette. 19pp. OTU QMBM QQL *OOAL Hann 2094. Essentially a proposal to establish a Dept of Manpower.

35 Newcomb, D.B. How to win: or, the dignity of labor. Suggestions to young men in three lectures, for the encouragement of agriculture and the industrial arts. Halifax: Nova Scotia Printing Co. 69pp. BVAS NSHPL *NSHDS. Hann 2096.

36 (O'Hanly, J.L.P.) Electors of Russell, read this and reflect. Extracts from a pamphlet entitled *The political standing of the Irish catholics in Canada* written by J.L.P.O'Hanly, and now being circulated in the county of Russell, in the interests of Hon Malcolm Cameron. (?Ottawa): np. (4pp) *OOAL. See next item.

37 O'Hanly, J.L.P. The political standing of Irish catholics in Canada: a critical analysis of its causes, with suggestions for its amelioration. Ottawa, np. 67pp. AEU BVAU OKQ OTP OTU QMBMM QQL SSU *OOAL. Hann 2097

38 (Shannon, James.) Hard times in Ontario: a pretty
   story, certainly. Kingston: Daily News Office. 36pp
   plus inserted postscript. NSHD *OTAR/1872/22 OTP
   Hann 2092

39 **Temporary home** for young women seeking employment.
   Third annual report...171 Lockman St, Halifax, Nova
   Scotia. Halifax: T. Chamberlain. 8pp *NSHD/F6.1

1873

40 **Bradford, Robert.** Addresses delivered at Agincourt,
   April 2nd and May 7th, 1873. An able exposition of
   the causes of the hard times. The banks, loan companies
   and importing merchants are to blame. Toronto: Morton
   and McLean. 30pp *OOAL Hann 2146. Includes a phren-
   ological character of Bradford by Prof. O.S. Fowler.

41 **Canada, Dept of Agriculture.** Labour wants of Canada.
   Ottawa. 79pp *OOAL Hann 2816. Details by province
   and county with wages, costs of living and price of land.

42 **Canadian Labor Union.** Proceedings of the first annual
   session held in the Trades Assembly Hall, in the city
   of Toronto on the 23rd, 24th and 25th September, 1873.
   Toronto: Ontario Workman. 28pp. *HI Uncatalogued C300.
   Includes constitution.

43 **Cunningham, Robert** and **Donald A. Smith.** Speeches on
   the Indian difficulties in the North-West delivered in
   the House of Commons April 1st, 1873. Ottawa: Free
   Press. 14pp. ACGL BVIPA *OKQS. 'The whole thing
   (treaty) was a solemn farce...and the terms of the
   treaty, meagre as they were, had not been complied with'.

44 **Lacroix, Henry.** The un-pacific scandal at the Custom-
   House of Montreal. Montreal: author. 16pp NSHPL OOA
   OOP OTP OTU QMBM QMBN SSU *OONL (defective, lacking
   pp 5-12).

45 **Macrae, D.** Sermon preached after the Drummond colliery
   explosion of May 13th, 1873 at St Columba, Hopewell, on
   May 25th, 1873. Halifax: James Bowes. 16pp NSHPL
   *NSHDS/B5 Hann 2101.

46 **Mott, Henry.** Shall capital punishment be abolished?
   An essay read at a meeting of the Trinity Young Men's
   Association, February 10, 1873. Montreal: Daniel Rose.
   13pp plus 6pp appendix. OKQ *OTAR/1873/36. Against
   capital punishment.

47 **Ontario.** Election pamphlets 1873-1934. Microfilm of
   661 items most of which have been subsequently destroyed.
   *OTAR, not examined in detail.

48 (Thompson, T. Phillips.) The political experience of
   Jimuel Briggs, D.B. at Toronto, Ottawa and elsewhere.
   Toronto: Flint, Morton. iv, 126pp. *OONL

49 Brown, William. The labour and money questions: a new catechism on political economy. Montreal: J. Lovell. 68pp. NSWA *SSUS Hann 2104.

50 Canada. (Secretary of State.) Acts respecting the administration of justice and for the establishment of a police force in the North-West Territories: as consolidated for the purpose of reference. Ottawa. 19pp. *OOAL/1872/24 Peel 384.

51 Canada, House of Commons. Report of the Select Commitee on the causes of the difficulties in the North-West Territory in 1869-70. Ottawa: I.B. Taylor. ix, 208pp. *OTAR/1874/42 Peel 385

52 L'Evénement. Au pilori: la trahison des chefs conservateurs démontrée par les témoignages recueillis devant le Comité du Nord-Ouest. Québec: L'Evénement. 22pp. *ACGL Peel 388.

53 Foran, Thomas. P. Trial of Ambrose Lepine at Winnipeg for the wilful muder of Thomas Scott. Question of jurisdiction. Montreal: Lovell. 15pp. ACU QMBN QMU *OKQS Peel 391

54 Galbraith, Thomas. Bensalem; or, the new economy. A dialogue for the industrial classes on the financial question. New York: Thomas Galbraith, Jr. 70pp. OH QMU *OOAL Hann 2108. Galbraith is described on the cover as being from Port Hope, Ontario. The pamphlet concludes 'End of first part' but no second part has been traced, unless we include the later works of Prof. J.K. Galbraith.

55 Grainger, Allendale and Maria S. Rye. Charges made against Miss M. Rye before the Poor Law Board at Islington and her reply thereto. np. 16pp. *OKQS Hann 2109. Relates to the immigration to Canada of pauper children: 'If there is so great need of cheap labour, why...should Canadians not import coolies and negroes instead of orphan girls?'

56 The Leader and Patriot. The history of the Lake Superior ring. An account of the rise and progress of the Yankee combination, headed by Hon Alexander Mackenzie, Premier of Canada, and the Browns, for the purpose of selling their interest and political power to enrich Jay Cooke and Co and other American speculators, changing the route of the Canada Pacific railway, with a view to breaking up our great Dominion, and severing our connection with the British Empire. Thorough expose of Mackenzie and Brown's treachery to their country. This pamphlet is stereotyped so that generations to come may look back with contempt upon a government that has united with the Republicans of the United States

to destroy our prosperous country. Toronto: The Leader and Patriot, James Beaty proprietor. 14pp. ACU BVIP *OOAL Peel 378.

57 Lewis, John W. 'The Proton outrage:' or, a clear exposition of the difficulties arising out of the South Grey election, December 1871. The documentary evidence in the case. The action of the Mowat government in the matter. The innocent vindicated. The real criminals exposee (sic). np. 16pp. *OOAL

58 McLachlan, Alexander. Poems and songs. Toronto: Hunter Rose. viii, 9-223pp. *NSHDS SSUS/Shortt.

59 Patrons of Husbandry. Manual of subordinate granges: adopted and issued by the Dominion Grange. First edition. London (Ont). 63pp plus 8pp headed 'Copies of this are only furnished to the M., O., S., A.S., L. & A.S'. (i.e. Master, Overseer, Steward, Assistant Steward and Lecturer). *OTURS Hann 2114.

60 Pictou Presbytery. Statement and correspondence of the Pictou Presbytery PCLP respecting the Antigonish riot. Pictou: William Harris. 76pp. *NSHDS/C135

61a Riel, Louis. L'amnistie aux Métis de Manitoba: mémoire sur les causes des troubles du Nord-Ouest et sur les négociations qui ont amené leur règlement amiable. Ottawa: np. 43pp. BVAU OOP SSU *OOAL Peel 399.

61b ------ L'amnistie: mémoire sur les causes des troubles du Nord-Ouest et sur les négociations qui ont amené leur règlements amiable. Montréal: Nouveau Monde. 22pp AUE BVAU OKQ OONL QMBM QMBN SSU *OOAL (Même texte)

62a Taché (A.A.) L'amnistie. Montréal: Le Nouveau Monde. 72pp *OOAL Peel 400.

62b ------ A translation of the above into English was published as a special Times Extra of the Ottawa Times, a single sheet, printed both sides in eight columns.

62c ------ The North-West difficulty: on the amnesty question...The Times, 6th, 7th and 8th April, 1874. (Ottawa): (Ottawa Times). 36pp. *OOAL(xerox copy). Same text as 62b.

1875

63 Canada, Governor-General. Despatches regarding commutation of Lepine's sentence and North West amnesty. Ottawa: Maclean, Roger. 42pp *ACGL OOAL/1875/73 Peel 409.

64 Elliott and Brokovski,(compilers). Preliminary investigation and trial of Ambroise D. Lepine for the murder of Thomas Scott. Being a full report of the proceedings in this case before the magistrate's court and the several courts of Queens Bench in the province of Manitoba.

Montreal: Burland-Desbarats. 127pp, illus, errata.
*ACGL Peel 397. (Dated 1874 on title page).

65 (**Great Britain**). Correspondence relating to the disturbances at Red river 1869-70. London(Eng.): Sir Joseph
Cawston and Sons. 11pp *ACGL

66 **Great Britain**, Colonial Office. Correspondence relating
to the question of an amnesty for acts committed during
the disturbances in the Red river settlement in 1869-70.
London (Eng.). 57pp *ACGL Probably Peel 368.

67 **Montgomery, James F.** An experiment in communism and
its results: a letter to the Right Honorable the Earl
of Carnarvon, Secretary of State for the Colonies, on
the Prince Edward Island Land Commission. Charlottetown: Bremner Bros. 14pp. *OOAL Hann 2123. 'It would
be an insult to Her Majesty's government to assume that
they share in the communistic views of some of the radical sections of the Liberal party, that *property in land
is a crime against society...*' In fact, Montgomery is comp-
laining that under a new act no one can own more than
1,000 acres of land in PEI or 500 acres if let to tenants - this is the 'expériment in communism'.

68 **Norris, William.** The Canadian question. Montreal:
Lovell. 90pp. AEU OTP QMBM QMM QQL SSU *OKQS 'It is
independence and independence alone that will enable
Canada to fulfil her destiny, to be the asylum for the
oppressed and down-trodden peoples of Europe'.

69 Un ouvrier sans travail. L'appel au peuple; droit du
travail; les conservateurs; crise; famine; mandat con-
tractuel. Montréal: (L'auteur). 8pp. QMBN *OONL

70 **Les rouges** et les bleus devant le pays: quelques pages
de politique. Montréal: np. 101pp. BVAU OTP QMBM
QMBN QQL SSU *OOP Incl: La question du Nord-Ouest:
Mgr Taché et l'amnistie: La corruption des purs etc.

71 Taché, A.A. The amnesty again; or charges refuted.
Winnipeg: The Standard. 31pp. *ACGL Peel 431.

1876

72 **Burns, R.F.** Our modern Babylon: a discourse delivered
in Fort Massey church, Halifax, N.S. on the evening of
the 12th March, the Sabbath succeeding the 'Chiniquy
riot': with an appendix. Halifax: Nova Scotia Printing.
22pp *NSHDS/B5 Hann 2129.

73 **Canada.** Report of the Select Committee on the causes
of the present depression of the manufacturing, mining,
commercial, shipping, lumber and fishing interests.
Ottawa: Maclean, Roger. 290pp, tables. *OOAL
Evidence from many owners, but including some information on labour.

74 Dominion Grange. History of the Grange in Canada, with hints on the management of subordinate Granges, rules for Patrons' Co-operative Associations, list of masters and secretaries of Dominion, division and sub-ordinate Granges. Toronto: Belford. 32pp. AEU OTAR *OTU Hann 2131.

1877

75 Davison, Thomas and Richard Lewis. Mechanics' Institutes, and the best means of improving them. Prize essays. Toronto: Hunter, Rose. 24pp *OOAL Hann 2140 Davison pp 1-4; Lewis pp 4-19 with a synopsis of other essays pp 19-24.

76 Munro, John. The place and work of women in the church. Halifax: Nova Scotia Printing. 12pp *NSHDS/B5 Hann 2141. (See also No. 79)

77 Patrons of Husbandry. Recommended constitution and by-laws of division and subordinate Granges. Welland. 20pp *OOAL

1878

78 Daily Mail. The election campaign. A summary of the public records of the past five years; for the use of the people. Toronto. 78pp. *OOP Includes 'Extravagance and corruption; On the make' etc.

79 David, Joseph. A reply to 'The place and work of women in the church'. Pictou: William Harris. 11pp. NSHDS/B5 (See No. 76).

80 Mackenzie, Alexander. Address to the Toronto working-men on the 'National Policy'. Toronto: The Globe. 32pp NSHPL OKQ QMBM QQL *OTAR/1878/3 and 19. Hann 2145 Mainly on protection and addressed to the 'Liberal workingmen'.

81 ------ Workingmen's demonstration at Toronto, Thursday, May 30th 1878. Speech of Hon Mr Mackenzie. Cornwall: The Freeholder. 16pp *OOAL. This is probably the same text as No. 80 but it has not been possible to compare them.

82 Patrons of Husbandry. Constitution and by-laws of the Dominion Grange, Patrons of Husbandry organized June 2nd, 1874. Welland. 16pp *OOAL OTP 7th edition. Includes 'Declaration of principles'.

83 Workingmens Protective Association. Constitution, by-laws and rules of order. Victoria: M'Millan. 8pp *BVAA

1879

84 **Patrons of Husbandry.** Manual of subordinate Granges
   adopted and issued by the Dominion Grange. Welland.
   75pp *OTP 5th edition.

1880

85 **McCormick, John.** The conditions of labour and modern
   civilization. Toronto: Bell. 51pp. *OOAL OTAR/1880/24
   Hann 2159. On monopoly and usury with a dialogue on
   'Usury vs Labour' reprinted from the issues of the
   Irish Canadian. 'We do not hesitate to aver, that the
   plutocracy and shoddy aristocracy...comprise within
   their unholy confines the only really dangerous crim-
   inal class on American soil'. Contains text of the
   Platform of principles adopted at the International
   Conference of the Socialistic-Labor Party of the United
   States, January 1880, pp 43-46.

86 **Morris, Alexander.** The treaties of Canada with the
   Indians of Manitoba and the North-West Territories,
   including the negotiations on which they were based,
   and other information relating thereto. Toronto:
   Belfords, Clarke. 375pp. *OONL Appendices of texts
   of treaties.

87 **Pringle, Allen.** Ingersoll in Canada: a reply to
   Wendling, Archbishop Lynch, 'Bystander' and others.
   Toronto: Belford. 61pp. OTP *OHMA275 OOAL Hann 2161.
   Second edition. The 'others' are 'A rationalist',
   the Rev. Bray and with a concluding section on 'The
   oath question (to Canadian freethinkers)'.

1881

88 **(Begg, Alexander.)** Letters on the situation in the
   North-West as they appeared in The Montreal Gazette,
   by 'Julius'. Montreal: The Gazette. 24pp *OOAL
   Peel 561. n.b. Not the same man as the author of
   No. 19 above.

89 **Co-operative Supply Association.** Abridged prospectus.
   Montreal. *OKQS Hann 2165. Includes letters from
   William P. Lockwood to the Gazette explaining the
   principles of co-operative distribution, the shoppers'
   rebellion and by-laws.

90 **(Fuller, William H.)** Flapdoodle: a political encylo-
   paedia and manual for public men. Edited by an ex-
   minister. Illustrated by Bengough. Toronto: np. 28pp.

AEU NSHPL OOP OTP QMBM QMBN *OOP SSUS/Shortt.
'Politician: a person of small means but great assurance, who, declining or failing to make a living by
honest industry, takes up the profession of politics
as a quack doctor takes up that of medicine, with a
view to making money out of the credulity of his fellow
men'.

91 Klotz, Otto. A review of the special report of the
Minister of Education of the Mechanics' Institutes,
Ontario. Toronto: Willing and Williamson. 18pp.
*OTAR/1881/20 Hann 2165.

92 A workingman. A reply to the Rev. Father Graham's
lecture on modern infidelity. Montreal: Cosmopolitan
Press. 38pp. *NSWA/Dennis Hann 2169. Quotes from
Tyndall, Huxley etc.

1882

93 Artigue, Jean d'. Six years in the Canadian north-
west. Translated from the French by L.C. Corbett and
S. Smith. Toronto: Hunter, Rose. viii, 9-206pp.
*OONL Peel 595.

94 'Castor'. Le pays, le parti et le grand homme. Montréal: Gilbert Martin. 108pp. *OOP. Possible that
the author is F.X.O. Trudel. 'Le grand homme' is J.A.
Chapleau.

95 Counter, Charles A. Woman's rights: being the celebrated lecture delivered by Canada's own orator. With
an autobiography of the author. Kingston: Daily News.
8pp *OOAL Hann 2174. 'Having endowed these terres-
trial angels with intellectual faculties, why, sir,
should they not possess their rights and privileges
monopolized by the selfish man.'

96 Johnson, William Wickliffe. Sketches of the late depression; its cause, effect and lessons, with a synop-
tical review of leading trades during the past decades.
Montreal: J. Theo. Robinson. iv, 5-258pp. *OOAL
Hann 2177.

97 (?Liberal Party). The Dominion land policy: speculators and land grabbers taken under the protection of
the government: the rights of the settler disregarded:
the speculator can have land at half price - the hardy
son of toil to be handed over to his tender mercies..
(?Ottawa): np. 20pp *OOAL

1883

98 Blackeby, A.H. Report of the Commissioner appointed
to enquire into and report on the system of laws reg-

ulating labor in the State of Massachusetts. (Ottawa): (Queens Printer). 8pp. *OOAL Hann 2948. The ten-hour day, children's employment etc. The system is recommended for Canada.

99 **Winter, William.** Call to the farmers! Brandon: np. (1p). *MWPA/ManNW. Notice for a convention of farmers (26 November 1883) 'to take into consideration the political situation of Manitoba and the North-West Provinces, and to adopt such measures as may be deemed expedient to secure redress of the grievances under which those provinces are suffering'.

1884

100 **Carleton Place Mechanics Institute.** By-laws of the library and reading room with a catalogue of books in the library. Carleton Place. 18pp. *OKQS

101 **Le Sueur, W.D.** A defence of modern thought. In reply to a recent pamphlet, by the Bishop of Ontario, on 'Agnosticism'. Toronto: Hunter, Rose. 40pp OTP *BVAA OTV Hann 2201.

(102)------ Evolution and the positive aspects of modern thought, in reply to the Bishop of Ontario's second lecture on agnosticism. Ottawa: Woodburn. 43pp. QMSS

103 **Lowe, John.** Population, immigration and pauperism in the Dominion of Canada. np. 32pp. BVIPA OHM QMBM *OKQS Hann 2202. Reprinted from *Canadian Economics*; paper read before the British Association meeting in Montreal.

104 **Manitoba and North-West Farmers Union.** Resolutions adopted at the farmers' convention held in the City of Winnipeg, 19th and 20th December 1883. Instructions as to the formation of branch unions etc. (Brandon): 13pp *MWPL Peel 758.

105 **Le scandale Mousseau:** révélations complètes. L'accusation, le contrat. Québec, L'Electeur. 58pp ACU OTP QMBM QMBN QMU *OOP (regarding Chapleau).

106 **Stone Masons' Union.** Constitution, by-laws and rules of order adopted May 1884. Toronto. 31pp. *OTURS/RSK Signed by a Committee: Ed. Farthing, G. Beer, W. Langman.

1885

107 **Adam, G. Mercer.** From savagery to civilization. The Canadian North-West: its history and its troubles from the early days of the fur-trade to the era of the railways and the settlers; with incidents of travel in the region and the narrative of three insurrections.

Toronto: Rose. viii, 9-390pp. NSHP *OTURS Peel 782.

108 Amey, Edward. Farm life as it should be; and farm
labourers' and servant girls' grievances. Also rules
of the proposed agricultural labourers' union. Toronto:
Ellis and Moore. 46pp, errata slip. *OTAR Hann 2207.
Rules of the proposed union pp 33-35.

109 Bell, F.H. The poor of Digby; official enquiry. Commissioner's report: in the matter of certain charges
affecting the treatment of the poor in the County of
Digby. (Halifax): (Provincial Secretary). 48pp including Minutes of evidence. *NSHP photocopy. Hann 2217.

110 Bellerose, (Joseph-Hyacinthe.) Assemblée à Saint-
Hyacinthe le 8 décembre 1885 pour protester contre
l'exécution de Riel; discours de L'Hon. M. Bellerose.
np. 8pp QMBM *OTPB Peel 785.

111 Blake, E. and others. Debate of the North-West Mounted
Police Force, Ottawa June 9th, 1885. Ottawa: Maclean,
Roger. 17pp. *OOAL

112 ------ Speech on the disturbance in the North-West,
Ottawa, May 20th 1885. Ottawa: Maclean, Roger. 17pp.
ACG QMM *OOAL OTAR/1885/6 SSUS/Shortt Peel 787.

113 ------ Speech on the disturbance in the North-West,
Ottawa July 6th 1885. Ottawa: Maclean, Roger. 36pp.
*OOAL

114 ------ Speech on the Franchise Bill delivered in the
House of Commons, Ottawa, Friday, April 17th, 1885.
(Ottawa): (Maclean, Roger). 31pp. *OKQS

(115) British Columbia. Metlakatlah inquiry, 1884. Report
of the Commissioners, together with the evidence.
Victoria: Richard Wolfenden. 6, lxxxii pp. BVAU

116 Campbell, Sir Alexander. In the case of Louis Riel,
convicted of treason, and executed therefor. Memorandum. Ottawa: Maclean, Roger. 10pp. *OTAR/1895/8
SSUS/Shortt Peel 793. Edition française *OHMA/518

117a Chapleau, J.A. La question Riel: lettre aux Canadiens-
français. Ottawa. np. 14pp. AEU BVAU MWU OKQ OPET
QMBM SRU SSU *OONL Peel 802. 'Un vent de révolte
souffle, en ce moment, avec violence sur la province
du Québec'.

117b ------ The Riel question. (Ottawa): np. 14pp. ACG
AEU MWU OOA OONL OTP OTU QMSS *OTAR/1885/9

118 Deriares, Jules. Riel: patriotisme vs loyauté.
Montréal: np. 11pp. *OONL 'Nous n'aimons pas les
Anglais. Leur morgue insipide, leur dédaigneuse fierté,
leur orgueil, leur égoisme, n'a jamais été ni peut
aller au tempérament canadien, ouvert, franc, joyeux
et libéral'.

119 Forin, J.A. Diary. No.3 Coy. QQR. 1 January 1885 to
31 December 1885. np. 37pp. *ACGA/Cassels/BG3Q3
Undated, published at some later date unknown.

120 Haultain, T. Arnold. A history of Riel's second reb-
    ellion and how it was quelled. The souvenir number of
    The Canadian Pictorial and Illustrated War News. Toronto: Grip.
    2 parts, 44pp, illus. *OOAL Peel 820.

121 Laidlaw, Alexr. From the St Lawrence to the North
    Saskatchewan; being some incidents connected with the
    detachment of 'A' battery, Regt. Canadian Artillery,
    who composed part of the North-West Field Force in the
    rebellion of 1885. Halifax: (author). 43pp. *OOAL
    (photocopy). Peel 823.

122 Manitoba and North-West Farmers Union. Statement of
    the claim of the province of Manitoba and North West
    Territories to the constitutional rights of a province
    under the British North America Act 1867. np. xxii,
    90pp. ACU *MWPL Peel 829.

123 Middleton, F. Copy of official reports (116th) from
    Major-General Middleton concerning engagements at Fish
    creek, on the 24th April, 1885; Poundmaker's camp (near
    Cree's reserve) 2nd May, 1885; Batoche, 9th, 10th, 11th
    and 12th May, 1885. Ottawa: Maclean, Roger. 17pp.
    *OTMCL

124 Le Monde. L'insurrection du Nord-Ouest 1885. Montréal:
    Le Monde. 40pp, illus. AEU MWP OONL OTP QMBM QMU QQL
    SSU *OTAR/1885/1 Peel 832. A second edition was pub-
    lished in 1886 AEU MWP OTP QMBM QMU QQL *SSUS/Shortt.

125 Montpetit, A.N. Louis Riel à la Rivière-du-Loup.
    Levis: Imp. Mercier. 111pp. *SSUS/Shortt Peel 833.
    The story of a hoax.

126 La Presse. Louis Riel, martyr du Nord-Ouest. Sa vie-
    son procès-sa mort. Montréal: Imp. Générale. 96pp.
    AEU BVAU OTP QMBM QMBN *ACGL Peel 840.

127 Ryan, Matthew. Neglect of the federal government to
    meet the lawful demands of the half-breeds of the North
    west. (?Winnipeg). np (4pp). *OTPB/1885/Ryan

128a Taché, Alexandre. La situation. St Boniface. 10pp.
    *OONL SSUS/Shortt, damaged copy. Peel 848.

128b ------ La situation au Nord-Ouest. Québec: J.O. Fil-
    teau. 22pp. AEU OPET *OONL

129 Town of Selkirk. (Manitoba). To Gen. Middleton and
    the soldiers of the North-West Expeditionary Forces.
    Victorious soldiers! Heroes of Fish creek and Batoche!
    Citizen soldiers of Canada! np. 1p *OTPB/1885/Selkirk.

130 Tremblay, Ernest. Riel: réponse à Monsieur J.A. Chap-
    leau. St Hyacinthe: 'L'Union'. 80pp BVIPA OKQ OONL
    OOU OTP QMBM QMBN *OOAL SSUS/Shortt Peel 851.

131 The Witness. The Riel rebellion. Montreal: The Wit-
    ness. 44pp ACG AEU BVIPA MWP OH OKQ OOAL OTP SSU
    *NSHPL Peel 858.

1886

132 Beauregard, George. Le 9me bataillon au Nord-Ouest.
(Journal d'un militaire). Québec: Jos-G. Gingras.
100pp, illus. *OOAL   Peel 873.

133 **Belleville Mechanics Institute and Library Association.**
Alphabetical and classified catalogue of books: yearly
subscription $3.00 admitting members to library, read-
ing room, billiard room - gymnasium. Belleville.
84pp. *OKQS General literature, reference and fiction;
newspapers. Over 2,000 titles (listed by title) including works by Darwin, Spencer, Huxley, Tyndall, Ruskin
etc etc.

134 **Blake, E.** Dominion election: campaign of 1886. Speeches
No. 1 (First series). (London banquet, January 14th/86)
- General review - Riel (Owen Sound) - North West mal-
administration - Riel No. 12 (First series): (Toronto)
- The interests of labour: (Belleville) - Legislation
for labour: (Deseronto) - The Knights of Labour:
(Hamilton) - Who released the printers? No.14 (First
series) North-West affairs. Neglect, delay and mis-
management. Race and creed cries. Toronto: Hunter,
Rose. Paged 1-48; 329-375; 397-424. *OOAL   Hann 2221.

135a ------ Ministers on trial. Was the execution of Riel
necessary or proper? Mr Blake's great judgements, delivered in the House of Commons of Canada on the 19th
March 1886. (Ottawa): 61pp. BVIPA OH OTP QMBN *OTAR
OTP   Peel 881.

135b ------ also printed in: Speeches and a synopsis of
the debate on the Home Rule resolutions. Toronto:
Blackett Robinson. 106pp.

136 ------ Speech on the execution of Louis Riel, Ottawa
March 19th, 1886. Ottawa: Maclean, Roger. 29pp
*OOAL   Peel 879. Also printed in 135a above.

137 ------ Speeches on the North-West rebellion, Ottawa,
April 5th, 1886. Ottawa: Maclean,Roger. 6pp. *OOAL
Peel 883.

138 **Boulton, C.A.** Reminiscences of the North-West rebellions with a record of the raising of Her Majesty's
100th Regiment in Canada, and a chapter on Canadian
social and political life. Toronto: Grip. 531pp,
illus, maps. *SSUS/Shortt   Peel 884.

139 **Canada, Dept of Militia and Defence.** Report upon the
suppression of the rebellion in the North-West Territories, and matters in connection therewith, in 1885.
Presented in Parliament. Ottawa. xii, 128pp, 17
coloured plates, map. *SSUS/Shortt SSA/X21   Peel 896.

140 ------ Report upon the suppression of the rebellion
in the North-West Territories, and matters in connection therewith, in 1885. Ottawa. xii pp plus

16

Appendices as follows:
Appendix No. 1 pp2-15: Special report by Major General Sir Frederick D. Middleton upon the military operations ...1885 (see No. 123 above):
Appendix A pp17-21: General report by Middleton
Appendix B pp23-26: Battleford and Poundmaker by Lt Col Otter
Appendix C pp27-37: Fighting at Batoche by Middleton
Appendix C.1 pp 39-41: Batoche by Capt Smith
Appendix D pp43-44: Fort Pitt by Major General Strange
Appendix E pp45-47: Swift Current to Battleford by Lt Col Otter
Appendix F pp49-50: Jackfish lake after Big Bear by Lt Col Otter
Appendix G pp51-60: Report of Alberta Field Force by Maj General Strange
Appendix 2 pp61-63: Organization of company and stockade at Yorkton
Appendix 3 pp65-66: Special report on stores by Lt Col Macpherson
Appendix 4 pp67-69: Preliminary report of Commissioners on war claims
Reports 1-111 of the War Claims Commission, pp71-304
Index of names to reports of the War Claims Commission pp305-325
Appendix 5 pp327-335: Report of the Surgeon-General (D. Bergin)
Appendices A to G pp337-384 on hospitals, supplies, instructions and report of the Deputy Surgeon-General James Bell
Continuation of Appendix No. 4 to the report of the 18th May 1886 on matters in connection with the suppression of the rebellion in the North-West Territories in 1885: Final report of the War Claims Commission pp 1-180. Together with:
(43) Return for a copy of the report of the medical men appointed by the government to enquire into the mental condition of Louis Riel after his conviction pp 1-2
(43a) Memorandum respecting the case of The Queen v. Riel pp 2-11
(43b) Return for copies of all commissions, letters, telegrams or instructions whatsoever, given to His Honour Mr Justice Hugh Richardson, in relation to the trial of Riel at Regina. pp 11-12
(43c) Return for copies of all documents forming the record in the case of Her Majesty against Louis Riel pp 12-233
(43d) Return for copies of the shorthand notes of the application to postpone the trial of Louis Riel pp 233-34
(43e) Petitions that the sentence passed upon Louis Riel be not disturbed in any way pp 235-39
(43f) Return for copies of all petitions in favour of the commutation of the sentence of Louis Riel pp 239-87
(45a) Return showing number of half breeds and claims pp 289-316

(45b) Supplementary return for copies of all correspondence relating to claims of inhabitants of Prince
Albert pp 316-336
(45c) Detailed report upon all claims to participate
in North-West half breed grant pp 336-353
(52a) Return, supplementary, partial for copies of
all documents relating to Her Majesty against different parties in connection with the late rebellion
pp 354-371
(52b) Return, supplementary, final for copies of all
documents relating to Her Majesty against different
parties in connection with the late rebellion pp 371-80
(52c) Message...the Governor General transmits copies
of letters of a confidential character pp 380-389.
*OOP

141 Canada, Dept of Secretary of State. Epitome of parliamentary documents in connection with the North-West
rebellion, 1885. Ottawa: Maclean, Roger. 389pp.
Contains following documents from No. 140 above:
43, 43a, b, c, d, e, and f; 45a, b, and c; 52a, b,
and c. Note, however, that 45c is not the same document as 45c in No. 140. *OTAR/1886/32 Peel 903.

142 Canada, Auditor General. Expenditure under appropriation of $2,300,000 to defray expenses and losses
arising out of troubles in the North-West Territory
from 1st July, 1885, to 15ty March, 1886. (Ottawa):
(Maclean, Roger). 60pp *OOP Peel 888.

143 Canada, Dept of Indian Affairs. The facts respecting
Indian administration in the North-West. Ottawa.
74pp *OOP Peel 892

144 Canada. The Queen vs. Louis Riel, accused and convicted of the crime of high treason. Report of trial
at Regina - Appeal to the court of Queens Bench, Manitoba, - Appeal to the Privy Council - Petition for
medical examination of the convict - List of petitions
for commutation of sentence. Ottawa: Queens Printer.
207pp *OTAR/1886/3 SSUS/Shortt Peel 961.

145a Canada, Secretary of State. Return (in part) to an
address of the House of Commons dated 5th March 1886
for copies of all documents forming the record in the
cases of Her Majesty against the different parties
tried in connection with the late rebellion...in short,
of every document whatever relating to the said trials.
Ottawa. 408pp *SSUS/Shortt Peel 897.

145b ------ also issued as: Trials in connection with the
North-West rebellion, 1885. Ottawa: Maclean, Roger.
408pp *OTAR/1885/5

146a Caron, Adolphe. Discours sur la question Riel pron-
oncé le 17 mars 1886, à la Chambre des Communes.
Ottawa: Maclean, Roger. 32pp, illus. BVIPA OKQ OONL
OTP QMBM QMBN SRU *SSUS/Shortt Peel 910.

146b ------ Speech on the execution of Louis Riel. Ottawa:
Maclean, Roger. 12pp *OOAL

147a Chapleau, J.A. Discours à l'occasion de la motion
     censurant le ministère pour avoir permis l'exécution
     de Louis Riel. (Comte-rendu officiel), séance du 24
     mars. Montréal: Imp. Générale. 39pp OONL OOU SRU
     *SSUS/Shortt Peel 911.

147b ------ Discours sur l'exécution de Louis Riel: Chambre
     des Communes, 24 mars 1886. Ottawa: Maclean, Roger.
     50pp OPET *OHMA516 SSUS/Shortt

147c ------ Speech on the motion made before the House of
     Commons on the 11th March 1886, to blame the govern-
     ment for having allowed the execution of Louis Riel
     (from the official debates): House of Commons, March
     24th, 1886. Montreal: Imp. Générale. 40pp MWP OKQ
     OOA OOP QMBM SRU *OONL Peel 911.

147d ------ Speech on the execution of Louis Riel (from
     the official debates). House of Commons, March 24th
     1886. Ottawa: Maclean, Roger. 50pp BVAS BVIPA OKQ
     OOA OOP OTP QMBM *NSHD/Hist2 OOP

 148 Comité de Collaborateurs. La mort de Riel et la voix
     du sang. Montréal. 20pp *SSUS/Shortt Peel 916.
     'La voix du sang de notre frère crie vengeance'.

 149 Curran, J.J. Debate on Louis Riel: speech in the
     House of Commons, Ottawa on Monday, the 15th March,
     1886. Ottawa. 16pp. BVIPA OKQ OTP QMBM *OOAL
     Peel 918.

 150 Daoust, Charles R. Cent-vingt jours de service actif.
     Récit historique très complet de la campagne du 65ème
     au Nord-Ouest. Montréal: Eusèbe Senécal. 242pp,
     illus. *SSUS/Shortt Peel 919

 151 L'Etendard. Documents officiels constatant les nom-
     breuses plaintes et reclamations des Métis du Nord-
     Ouest. Montréal: L'Etendard. 32pp *SSUS/Shortt
     Peel 923. Apparently incomplete, but so issued.
     (See No. 152 below).

 152 ------ Polemiques et documents touchant le Nord-Ouest
     et l'exécution de Louis Riel. Premier fascicule se
     rapportant principalement aux événements antérieurs
     à 1885. Montréal: L'Etendard. iii, 1-(10), 1-(8),
     1-(14), 1-57, 1-35, 1-55, (ii), 1-32 pp. viz. La sit-
     uation par Mgr Alexandre Taché: Les Métis: Le peuple
     vs. Sir John!: Un auguste document - histoire et
     origine des troubles du Nord-Ouest racontées sous
     serment par sa Grandeur Mgr. L'archeveque de St Bon-
     iface (i.e. Alexandre Taché): Affaires du Nord-Ouest:
     Question national au Nord-Ouest: Documents officiels
     constatant les nombreuses plaintes & reclamations des
     Métis du Nord-Ouest. *SSUS/Shortt Peel 927. The
     last item lacks some text, but so published.

 153 Facts for Electors. Reform, race and revenge; the
     rise and progress of the Riel movement in Quebec and
     Ontario. (?Toronto), np. 8pp *OOAL

 154 Facts for the electors, consisting of extracts from

speeches recently delivered upon questions connected with the administration of the Dominion government. (Ottawa): np. 72pp. Includes Blake on Riel; Charlton on the land grabbers and Somerville on printing scandals etc.

155 Flynn, E.J. Affaire Riel: discours prononcé devant l'Assemblée législative le 29 avril 1886, pendant le débat sur la motion présentée par l'Honorable M.P. Garneau, touchant l'exécution de la sentence de mort contre Louis Riel, accusé de haute-trahison. Québec: Imp. Générale. 16pp. ACG AEU OTP *SSUS/Shortt Peel 929.

(156) Girouard, (Désiré). Discours sur l'exécution de Louis Riel. Otttawa: Maclean, Roger. 21pp. BVIPA MWV QMBN Peel 933

157 Hodgins, Thomas. The Canadian Franchise act, with notes of decisions on the Imperial acts relating to registration, and on the provincial franchises of Ontario, Quebec, Nova Scotia, New Brunswick, Manitoba, British Columbia and Prince Edward Island. Toronto: Rowsell and Hutchison. iv, 220pp. *OONL.

158 Laurier, Wilfred. Speech on the Riel question delivered in the House of Commons at Ottawa, March 16th, 1886. Ottawa: (Maclean, Roger). 24pp. *SSUS/Shortt Peel 944.

159 Louis Riel and the North-West rebellion. A review: compiled from public records and other authentic documents. Questions and answer. (?Ottawa): np. 16pp. *ACGL Peel 826

160 Macdonald, John A. Speech to the Workingmen's Liberal Conservative Association of Ottawa and Le Cercle Lafontaine, delivered in Ottawa on the 8th of October, 1886. (Ottawa). 23pp. ACU BVAS NSHPL OTP QMBM SSU *OOP Hann 2223. On trade unions, relief, convict labour, Chinese labour, establishment of the Royal Commission etc.

161 Moffat, Christina. To the members of the Grange Patrons of Husbandry of Canada, these essays - Flora, Ceres and Pomona - are respectfully dedicated. Cannington (Ont): 33pp, errata slip. *OTAR Hann 2224.

162 Le mot de la fin. Voici le vote! Conspiration armée contre les Métis français. Le chief Métis sacrifié aux Orangistes! Sa pretendue vénalité. Légitimaté du Provisoire. Ce meutre de Scott! L'opinion de quelques evêques sur le débat. Celle du missionaires. Evêques et missionaires. Nouvelles indignités! Nouveaux griefs! La folie de Riel. np. 40pp. OKQ OTP QMBM QQL *OOAL SSUS/Shortt Peel 865. 'L'attaque inconsiderée faits contre eux, au lac des canards, fut une déclaration de guerre'.

163 Mulvaney, Charles Pelham.assisted by a well-known journalist. The history of the North-West rebellion of 1885. Comprising a full and impartial account of the

origin and progress of the war, of the various engage-
ments with the Indians and half-breeds, of the heroic
deeds performed by officers and men, and of touching
scenes in the field, the camp and the cabin: including
a history of the Indian tribes of North-Western Canada.
Toronto: A.H. Hovey. 440pp. *SSUS/Shortt Peel 834.

164 **One who knows.** The gibbet of Regina: the truth about
Riel. Sir John A. Macdonald and his cabinet before
public opinion. New York: Thompson and Moreau. 200pp,
illus. *OTURS/RSK Peel 954. Preface signed Napoléon
Thompson.

165 **La question Riel:** les griefs des Métis. np. 67pp.
*SSUS/Shortt Peel 867.

166 **Riel, Louis 'David'.** Poesies religeuses et politiques.
Montréal: L'Etendard. 51pp plus certificat. *OONL
Peel 960.

167 **Tassé, (Joseph).** La question Riel prononcé devant le
'Cercle Lafontaine' d'Ottawa le 19 février 1886.
Ottawa: np. 13pp. BVIPA OTP QMBN *SSUS/Shortt
Peel 974.

168a **Thompson, D.** Discours sur la question Riel, prononcé
le 22 mars 1886, à la Chambre des Communes. np. 54pp.
*OTAR

168b **------** The execution of Louis Riel: speech of the
Minister of Justice delivered March 22, 1886. (Ottawa).
31pp. *OOAL Peel 976.

1887

169 **Blake, Edward.** Dominion election. Campaign of 1887.
Speeches on political questions of the day delivered
in the province of Ontario, subsequent to the prorog-
ation of the federal Parliament, June 1886, and previous to its dissolution, January 1887. Toronto:
Hunter, Rose. 424pp, index. OKQ OLU OOL QMG QMU SSU
*OOP. Contains speeches on Riel, the boodle brigade,
Indian starvation policy, Canadian Pacific railroad,
labour question and the printers' strike.

170 **Bryant, Wilbur F.** The blood of Abel. Hastings (Neb):
169pp, appendices. AEU BVIPA MWU OKQ OTP QMBM *OOAL
Peel 990. In three parts: I. Ultima Thule, a history
and description of the North-West. II. Civis anglicanus
erat - rebel Riel. III. Civis americanus fuit - citizen
Riel. Appendices include indictment of outlawry, US
naturalization, open letter of Riel to *The Irish World*
21 November 1885, and various letters.

171 **Canada, Dept of Militia and Defence.** Continuation of
Appendix No. 4 to the report of 18th May 1886, on
matters in connection with the suppression of the rebellion in the North-West Territories in 1885. Final

report of the War Claims Commission; Presented to
Parliament. Ottawa: Maclean, Roger. iv, 80pp.
*SSA/X21 Peel 993. (See also No. 140 above).

172a **Canada, Dept of the Interior.** Facts for the people:
the North West rebellion. The question of the half-
breeds and the government's treatment of them. Ottawa.
18pp. *OOAL SSUS/Shortt Peel 855 and ?996. Includes
Mr Laurier's statement in Ontario.

172b ------ La rebellion du Nord-Ouest; faits pour le
peuple. La question des Métis et leur traitement par
le gouvernement. Ottawa. 18pp. *ACGL Peel 982.
(See also 185 below).

173 **Canada, Dept of Militia and Defence.** Report of Lieu-
tenant-Colonel W.H. Jackson, Deputy Adjutant-General,
principal supply, pay and transport officer to the
North-West forces and chairman of War Claims Commission,
on matters in connection with the suppression of the
rebellion in the North-West Territories, in 1885.
Presented to Parliament. Ottawa: Maclean, Roger.
44pp. *SSA/X21 SSUS/Shortt Peel 994.

174 ------ Report of Major General Laurie, commanding base
and lines of communication, upon matters in connection
with the suppression of the rebellion in the North-
West Territories. Ottawa: Maclean, Roger. 39pp.
*SSA/X21 Peel 995.

175 **Costigan, John.** The Riel and home rule questions;
speech at Woodstock, N.B. Mr Costigan's letter to
Lord Lorne on home rule for Ireland. Gladstone's
bill foreshadowed. Opinions of the Irish national
newspapers. Messrs Curran, Coughlin etc etc. np.
27pp. OOU QMU QQL *OOP Peel 1003.

176 **Grandin, Mgr et autres.** Le veritable Riel tel que dé-
peinte dans les lettres de sa grandeur Mgr Grandin...
Revd P. Leduc...Revd P. André...Revds Pères Touze,
Fourmond, Végreville, Moulin et Lecoq, d'une relig-
ieuse de Batoche etc etc, suivi d'extraits des mande-
ments de nos seigneurs les évêques concernant l'agitation Riel. Montréal: Imp. Générale. 63pp. ACG AEU
BVAU BVIPA MWP OKQ OTP QMBM QMBN SRL SRU *SSUS/Shortt
Peel 983.

177 **Laflèche, (L.F.R.) et Alexandre Taché.** La question Riel.
Opinion de leurs grandeurs Mgr Taché et Mgr Laflèche.
(Deux lettres). Trois Rivières. 2pp. BVIPA SSU
*OTPB/1887/Riel

178 **McDougall, J.L.** The use and abuse of 'the electoral
franchise'. (?Mabou): (author). 17pp. *NSHDS/J6
'So great indeed, was the reduction made by the Act
of Union, in the legislative sphere of the provinces,
that the division of any of our local legislatures on
political party grounds, is now a thing of doubtful
propriety...All unnecessary friction between the provincial and federal powers should be avoided...An undue
assertion of individuality often results in mischief'.

179 **McMillan, Donald.** Letters and extracts on 'The Riel question', with notes. Alexandria (Ont): The Glengarrian. 27pp   ACU *OOAL OOP   Peel 1014.

180 **Mousseau, J.O.** Une page d'histoire. Montréal: W.F. Daniel. 98pp.   BVAU NSHP QMU QQL SSUS *OONL   Peel 951.

181 **One of the bunglers.** Reminiscences of a bungle. Toronto: Grip. 66pp.   ACG BVAU BVIPA MWP OKQ OOA OTP OTU *SSUS/Shortt   Peel 1019.   Variously attributed to Lewis B. Ord or T. Russell.

182 **Paine, Thomas.** The age of reason. Toronto: W.B. Cooke and W.M. Scott. 163pp.   *OONL

183 **The Riel rebellion:** how it began - how it was carried on - and its consequences. Succinct narrative of the facts. Half-breed grievances. (?Ottawa): np. (c1887) 31pp.   ACG BVAU MWP QMBM QMBN QMU SSU *ACGL   Peel 868.

184 **Thompson, Phillips.** The politics of labor. New York and Chicago: Belford, Clarke. 212pp.   MWU OOL OOP OPET OTMCL OTP *OONL

185 **White, Thomas.** Facts for the people. The North-West rebellion. The question of the half-breeds and the government's treatment of them. (Ottawa). 32pp.   OKQ *OTAR/1887/17   Peel 855.   Almost certainly identical to No. 172 above, but comparison of texts has not been possible.

1888

186 British Columbia, Commission on condition of Indians of the North-West coast. Papers relating to the commission appointed to enquire into the condition of the Indians of the North-West coast. Victoria: R. Wolfenden. 60pp.   *OONL

187 Canada, Select Committee. Report of the Select Committee appointed to enquire into the fraudulent practices perpetrated upon the farmers of the Dominion. Ottawa: Brown Chamberlin. 59pp.   *OTAR/1888/16

188 Canada, Royal Commission on rebellion losses; report. List of claims and awards with additional awards made by Committees of the Privy Council 1887-1888. Ottawa: Ministry of the Interior. 19pp plus 12pp.   *MWPA/RCR

189 **Gilpin, E.** Coal mining in Nova Scotia. Montreal: John Lovell. 53pp.   'Excerpt minutes of the transactions of the society, volume II part II section 1888' - but which society is not stated.   *NSHDS/T.1 Contains information on unemployment, wages etc.

190 **Iron Moulders Union,** District of Ontario. Supplement to the by-laws. Hamilton. (4pp).   OPET/Gainey/10 Includes list of officers.

191 Knights of Labor. Report of the Canadian Legislative
Committee, Order of the Knights of Labor. Toronto:
Miller and Soole. 16pp. QMSS *OOAL Hann 2247.
Signed by Alfred F. Jury, Geo. Collins, J.T. Redmond.
Gives an account of the Committee's meeting with the
government and prime minister and with other members
of parliament.

192 **Lancefield, Richard T.** Why I joined the new crusade:
a plea for the placing of taxes on land values only.
Toronto: Grip. 40pp. *OOAL Hann 2245. An address
to the Anti-Poverty Society of Toronto.

193 **Londonderry Co-operative Society.** General rules adopted 1888. Halifax: Morning Herald. 36pp. *NSHDS/
F6.2 Hann 2242.

194 (Murray, Norman). The trial of Sandy Wright, farmer,
for treason. Montreal: Norman Murray. 15pp. QMML
*OOAL Hann 2253. A satirical attack on nationalism
and the process of law and in favour of equal rights.

1889

(195) Brochu, M.D. Mémoire sur la nécessité d'une inspection
hygénique médicale des ateliers et des manufactures.
Québec: Dussault. 17pp. QMBN QTU.

196a Canada, Royal Commission. Report of the Royal Commission on the relations of capital and labor in Canada: evidence - Ontario. Ottawa: A. Senecal. 1351pp
comprising 1195pp evidence; topical index 1289-1351.
*OTURS/RSK Hann 2955. The evidence comes principally
from Toronto, Hamilton, Kingston, Ottawa, and Cornwall,
with some from Chatham, St Thomas, Windsor, Petrolia
and a few other centres.

196b Canada, Commission royale. Commission royale d'enquête
sur les relations entre le capital et le travail.
2 vols.

197 **Knights of Labor.** Report of the Canadian Legislative
Committee. Toronto. 20pp. *OOAL Signed by Robert
R. Elliott, W.R. James and O.D. Benoit. An account
of a meeting with the government.

198 **Montigny, B.A.T. de.** La vérité sur la question Métisse
au Nord-Ouest: biographie et récit de Gabriel Dumont
sur les événements de 1885. Montréal: np. 400pp,
illus. *SSUS/Shortt Peel 1123.

199 **Prison Reform Conference.** Report of proceedings of
a meeting held in the Education buildings, Toronto,
Tuesday, November 26th, 1889. Toronto. 15pp
*OHMA/3076

200 **Ritchie, Thomas.** The unequal distribution of wealth:
a lecture delivered before 'The Knights of Labour' in

the Opera house, Belleville. Belleville: Daily Intel-
ligencer. 48pp. OKQ OTP OTURS *SSUS/CanEcon Hann
2263.

(201) **Thorold Mechanics Institute.** Catalogue of books.
Hann 2267.

202 **United States, Senate.** Message from the President of
the United States transmitting a report upon the case
of Louis Riel. Washington: Senate. 12pp. NSHPL OKQ
*SSUS/Shortt Peel 1131. Includes Riel's petition to
President Cleveland.

1890

203 **Armour, Edward Douglas and William Bell.** Equal rights!
To the electors of the City of Toronto. Toronto: np.
(1p) broadside. *OTAR Includes platform on labour
disputes and mechanics' pay.

204 **Blake, E.** Speeches on Grand Trunk bill and Foreign
Contract Labour bill, Wednesday 19th March, 1890.
Ottawa: Brown Chamberlain. 3pp. *OOAL

205 ------ Speeches on second homesteads in the North
West Territories and Alien Labour bill. Monday,
14th April 1890. Ottawa: Brown Chamberlain. (1p).
*OOAL The speech on alien labour is one rather
meaningless paragraph.

206 ------ Speeches on the Seamen's act. Friday May 2,
1890. Ottawa: Brown Chamberlain. 3pp. *OOAL

207 **Bryce, (George).** Two provisional governments in Man-
itoba. Containing an interesting discussion of the
Riel rebellion, with an appendix embodying the four
Bills of Rights, verbatim. Winnipeg: Historical and
Scientific Society of Manitoba. 11pp. *OOA/1890/21
Peel 1152. Society transactions no. 38.

208 **Canada.** Report of the Select Committee to whom was
referred Bill No. 8 to prohibit the importation and
immigration of foreigners and aliens under contract
or agreement to perform labor in Canada, with minutes
of evidence attached. Ottawa: Brown Chamberlain.
47pp. *OOAL Hann 2956. Primarily refers to American
labor. Contains evidence of R.R. Elliott, Chairman
of the Legislative Committee of the Knights of Labor,
pp.1-8; J.T. Carey, Dominion Trades and Labor Congress
pp.8-15; and other material on the Knights.

209 **Hurrell, Charles T.** The statement of a permanently
disabled volunteer: the Minister of Militia's treatment. np. 14pp. *OOAL Peel 1181.

210 **(Iron Moulders.)** To the Canadian public. Whatsoever
ye would that men should do to you, do ye even so to
them. Toronto: (Iron Moulders Union). (4pp). *OPET/
Gainey/10. On a lockout and strike at E.& C. Gurney.

(211) (Kidner, Frank.) 'Pi', a compilation of odds and ends
relating to workers in sanctum and newsroom, culled
from the scrap-book of a compositor, by 'Red Ink'.
Hamilton: Griffin and Kidner. (ii), 216pp. BVA OH
OKQ QMU

212 Powderly, Terence V. Thirty years of labor, 1859 to
1889... Phildelphia: Exelsior. iii, 4-693pp. BVIV
BVIP Revised and corrected edition issued same year
AEU OHM. Knights of Labor: some Canadian material.

213 Reid, A.P. Stirpiculture; or, the ascent of man.
Read before the Nova Scotia Institute of Natural Science, Monday 13th January, 1890. Halifax: T.C. Allen.
12pp. *NSHPL

214 Toronto Single Tax Association. Social ethics. Toronto. (c1890). 4pp. *OTURS

215 Watt, D. A. Moral legislation: a statement prepared
for the information of the Senate. Montreal: Gazette.
47pp. QMBM *OPAL Deals with abduction, procuration
etc and complains about the inadequacy of Canadian law.

216 Watts, Charles. 'Secular Thought' sustaining fund:
to the friends of 'Secular Thought': an urgent appeal.
Toronto: Secular Thought. (4pp). *OTPB/1890/Secular.
One page of text, one page subscription form.

1891

217 Carleton Place Mechanics Institute. Catalogue of books
in the library. Carleton Place. 52pp. *OKQS. Includes by-laws.

218 Griffin, Watson. Negro competition: an objection to
unrestricted reciprocity. Montreal: (author). 4pp.
*NSHDS/D.1 Hann 2285. 'The blacks will not come
north to the factories, but the factories may go south
to the blacks'.

219 McKnight, H.A. The great colliery explosion at Springhill, Nova Scotia, February 21, 1891. Full particulars
of the greatest mining disaster in Canada, with a brief
description and historical sketch of the Springhill
collieries. Springhill: H.A. Knight. 28pp. OTP
*NSWA OPAL Hann 2284.

220 Morrow, R.A.H. Story of the Springhill disaster: comprising a full and authentic account of the great coal
mining explosion at Springhill Mines, Nova Scotia, February 21st, 1891, including a history of Springhill and
its collieries; also a description of the underground
workings...review of other great coal mining disasters.
St John (NB): author. 311pp, illus. *OOP Hann 2288.

221 Patrons of Industry. Constitution and by-laws adopted
by the Grand Association held at Sarnia, Ontario.

Point Edward (Ont). 16pp. ACG *OTPB

222 **Patrons of Industry.** Patron platform as adopted at
London September 22nd 1891 by the Grand Association
for Ontario and as subsequently adopted by the Grand
Association for Quebec and, as far as relates to federal matters, by the Grand Association for Manitoba.
(London, Ont). 43pp, errata slip. OOP *OOAL OTPB
Hann 2289. Includes rigid economy in every department
of public service; abolition of the Senate; protection
of labour etc.

223 ------ Platform of the Grand Association for Ontario
adopted at London, September 22nd, 1891. np. (1p)
broadside. *OTP

224 **Reid, A.P.** Poverty superseded: a new political econ-
omy. A paper on economic science read before the Nova
Scotia Institute of Science, January 19th, 1891.
Halifax: Gladwin. 16pp. NSHP *NSHDS/H.1 NSWA/Dennis
Hann 2290. Essentially a proposal for unemployment
insurance, welfare, government pension plans etc.

225 **Titus, F.E.** The initiative and referendum: needed
reforms in representative government. Toronto:
(?Referendum Committee). 4pp. *OTURS

226 **The true inwardness** of the Canadian Northwest rebellion of 1885 exposed; or, who is to blame? np. 16pp.
(c1891). BVIPA MWP *OTP Peel 869. Marked 'Second
edn' but no first edition seems to exist.

1892

227 **Campbell, A.C.** The problem of poverty and riches.
Toronto: Single Tax Association. (1p). *OTURS Hann
2297. Circular letter regarding a conference.

228 **Canada, Parliament.** Tenant-farmer delegates' visit
to Canada in 1890 and their reports upon the agricultural resources of the provinces of Prince Edward
Island, Nova Scotia, New Brunswick, Quebec, Ontario,
Manitoba, North West Territories and British Columbia.
Ottawa: S.E. Dawson. 230pp. *NSHDS/HN Contains
some information on labour.

229 **Carleton Place Mechanics Institute.** Catalogue of books
in the library. Carleton Place. 61pp. *OKQS

230 **Federated Association of Letter Carriers.** Assessment
system. Constitution and by-laws adopted September
28 and 29, 1892. Toronto: W.S. Johnson. 22pp. *OOAL

231 **Iron Moulders Union.** Labor struggle against capital.
(Appeal for funds). Hamilton. (1p). *OPET/Gainey/10.
On the Hamilton strike of December 1891. 'We have just
about got through with them (scabs), but we have
another dangerous element to contend with, viz: The

French Canadians from Montreal. They are the meanest men we have so far had to fight against...and if once they get their families here it will be all up with us, Satan himself could not remove them'.

232 Lefebvre, Moise. Wages ready-reckoner based on 54 hours per week. Ottawa: Government Printing Bureau. 20pp. *OOAL Hann 2294. $1.50 to $18.00 plus night shift and overtime rates.

233 **Patrons (of Industry?).** The Patrons platform. np. (c1892) (1p). *OKQS Possibly the same as No. 223 above; texts not compared.

234 **Patrons of Industry.** Constitution and rules of order of the Patrons of Industry of North America: adopted by the Grand Associations of the province of Ontario, held at Toronto, February 24th, 1892. Strathroy (Ont): 24pp. *OOAL Same item printed in Toronto in OKQS.

235 **Prison Reform Conference.** Report of the Prison Reform Conference held in Toronto, November 27th, 1891; also the seventeenth annual report of the Prisoners Aid Association of Canada for the year 1891, with list of subscribers. (Toronto). 32pp. *OOAL/1892/31 Hann 2299.

236 **Scott, Jean Thompson.** The conditions of female labour in Ontario. Toronto: Warwick. 31pp. AEU BVIP OHM OTP OTU SSU *OOL Toronto University studies in political science, first series no. III.

237 **Thompson, Phillips.** The labor reform songster. Philadelphia: Journal of the Knights of Labor. 35pp. *OOAL Hann 2303. Contains 29 songs.

1893

238 **Desjardins, L.G.** A true and sound policy of equal rights for all. Open letters to Dalton McCarthy Esq. Q.C., M.P. Quebec: Morning Chronicle. 57pp. *SSUS/ Shortt Peel 1310. 'But, Sir, if it is perfectly true that the French-Canadians do not aspire to rule Canada, they do not relish the prospect of being crushed, destroyed, annihilated, denationalized as you seem determined to try to do'.

239 **Howell, Geo. A.** The Social Problems Association of Toronto. Toronto. (c1893). (1p) broadside. *OTURS On the formation of the association.

240 **Kains, John Alexander.** 'How say you?' A review of the movement for abolishing the grand jury system in Canada. St Thomas: The Journal. 101pp. *OTP 'Mr Justice Burton...(said) scarcely any greater contempt could be offered to a court of justice than tampering with a jury. He was thereupon assured by one of the learned counsel before him, that scarcely any-

thing was more common.'

241 **Mowat, Oliver.** The Patrons of Industry from speech
   (sic) delivered in North Bruce, 23rd November 1893.
   np. 10pp. OKQ OTP *OOAL Hann 2310.

242 **Patrons of Industry.** Minutes of the 2nd annual meeting
   of the Grand Association of Ontario held in St Lawrence
   hall, Toronto, Ont., on Tuesday, Wedensday, Thursday,
   Friday, Saturday and Monday February 28, March 1, 2, 3,
   4 and 6, 1893. Strathroy. 24pp. *OTP

243 **Prison Reform Conference.** Report of the Prison Reform
   Conference held in Toronto December 13th, 1892, also
   the eighteenth annual report of the Prisoners Aid Association of Canada for the year 1892, with list of subscribers. (Toronto). 43pp. *OOAL/1893/33

1894

244 **Falconer, R.H.** The church in politics in Ontario: an
   address...before the annual convention of the Canadian
   Secular Union, September 9, 1894. Toronto: C.M. Ellis.
   8pp. *OTAR/1894/27 'The church should be sternly
   driven from politics...'

245 **Local Council of Women of Halifax.** Inaugural meeting:
   address by Her Excellency the Countess of Aberdeen,
   August 24th, 1894. Halifax: Morning Herald. 19pp.
   *NSHDS/F6.1

246 **(Mowat).** The progressive labor legislation of the
   Mowat government. Toronto: Alexander Smith. 4pp.
   *OKQS No. 3 Ontario general elections; synopsis of
   measures.

247 **National Council of Women of Canada.** Women workers of
   Canada: being a report of the proceedings of the first
   annual meeting of the conference, Ottawa, April 1894.
   Ottawa. viii, 243pp. *OONL. For subsequent reports
   see serials section.

248 **The Patrons:** an answer to the annexationist campaign
   writer in the *Canada Farmer's Sun*. (Toronto): np. 16pp.
   OOAL *OTAR/1894/7 Hann 2327. Reprints the Patron
   platform of 1891.

249 **Patrons of Industry.** Minutes of the third annual meeting of the Grand Association of Ontario held in Richmond Hill, Toronto, Ont., Tuesday, Wednesday, Thursday,
   Friday, Saturday and Monday February 27, 28, March 1,
   2, 3 and 5, 1894. Strathroy. 31pp. *OTP

250 **Pringle, Allen and others.** True religion versus creeds
   and dogmas. A discussion between two clergymen, a lay-
   man and Allen Pringle. Toronto: Canadian Secular Union.
   63pp. *OHMA2814. The two clergymen are Arthur Jarvis
   of Napanee, Stearne Tighe of Amherst Island and the lay-
   man is James A. Ducentre.

251 **The** ruling families of Ontario. How the people are
bled to feed their high and mighty masters. (?Toronto):
np. (c1894). 8pp. OTURS *OTP Hann 2270. On nepotism
in the Mowat government: 'The greediness and voracious-
ness of the Ontario cabinet is unequalled in the history
of the British nation...The office hog (illustration
of a pig) fattened on fees.'

1895

252 **Baillairgé, C.** Bribery and boodling, fraud, hypocrisy
and humbug, professional charges and pecuniary ethics.
An address to the Province of Quebec Association of
Architects on the occasion (October 2 1895) of his
vacating the presidency of the Society. (Quebec) np.
74pp. *OOAL The title is an accurate description of
the contents.

253 **Douglas, W.A.** The church and social relations. Toronto: Single Tax Association. (c1895). (4pp). *OTURS

(254)**Harmony Industrial Association.** Prospectus. Birtle
(Man). 19pp. Peel 1409.

255 Hughes, James L. Equal suffrage. Toronto: William
Briggs. 53pp. NSHPL OKQ OTP OTURS *OTAR/1895/42
Hughes was president of the Toronto Womens Enfranchise-
ment Association. Hann 2338.

256 **Nova Scotia,** Commissioner of Public Works and Mines.
Regulation of mines in Nova Scotia. Halifax: Queens
printer. 38pp. *NSHDS/T.1 Employment, wages etc.

257 **Patrons of Industry.** Minutes of the fourth annual
meeting of the Grand Association of Ontario held in
Temperance Hall, Toronto, Ont., on Monday, Tuesday,
Wednesday, Thursday and Friday March 11, 12, 13, 14
and 15th, 1895. Strathroy. 32pp. *OTP

258 ------ The political position of the Patrons. Brandon.
(4pp) *SSA/G235.2 Peel 1421. Protection from monopoly, abolition of the Senate, franchise for women
etc.

259 **Pringle, Allen.** Bibles and religions: out versus in
in the public schools. (Toronto): (Canadian Secular
Union). (c1895). 24pp. AEU *OHMA

260 **Simpson, Caleb Platt.** The problem solved. A social
statute to mitigate the evils of poverty. A code of
practicable legislation to promote true Christian
brotherhood. London (Ont): Heal and Fleming. 31pp.
*OOP Hann 2341. The act is to be called 'The Supp-
lementary Municipal Institutions Act' to provide councils with equal female representation, social councils,
houses of trade and industry, social funds, compensation etc.

261 **(Single Tax Association.)** The land question illustrated: with quotations and opinions of leading thinkers. Toronto: Geo. J. Bryan. 16pp. *OTP

262 **(Stratford.)** Rules of the City of Stratford Co-operative Society...incorporated May 2nd, 1895. Stratford.
15pp. *OTAR/1895/41

1896

263 Bengough, J.W. The up-to-date primer: a first book of
lessons for little political economists: in words of
one syllable with pictures. New York: Funk and Wag-
nalls. 75pp. *OTURS Hann 2344. 'Here is a man who
Begs. Why does he not Work? He would, but he Can not
get a Job. Can he not Go on the Land? No; for a Fat
Man Owns it, and this is the Hat he holds out for Rent.
It is a great Scheme...'

264 **The Canadian Republican Committee.** Manifesto of the
Canadian Republican Committee to the people of Canada.
Toronto. (1p). *OTPB/1896/Cndn Republic

265 **Patrons of Industry.** The campaign. Moosomin: Headquarters Douglas Central Election Committee. (4pp).
*SSA/g235.1 James M. Douglas, candidate.

266 **Saturday Night.** Departmental stores. The modern
curse to labor and capital. They ruin cities, towns,
villages and the farming community. Toronto: Dudgeon
and Thornton. (c1896). (4pp). *OTURS Hann 2268.

267 **Single Tax Association,** Trades and Labor Council and
others. Address to the churches. Toronto. (c1896).
4pp. *OTURS Hann 2282. 'Could there be anything
more contrary to the spirit of true religion than this
method by which, as fast as one party does the enrich-
ing, another party appropriates the riches?'

(268) **Toronto Trades** and Labor Council. Official directory
and label handbook. Toronto. Hann 2350. (OTMCL but
missing).

269 Winnipeg Trades and Labor Council. The Tribune lockout; statement of the case. Winnipeg. (4pp). *MWPA/
Russell/2

270a **Wright, Alexander Whyte.** Report upon the sweating
system in Canada: (with) Supplementary report as an
appendix. Ottawa: S.E. Dawson. 51pp. *OOAL/1896/65
OTAR/1896/25 Hann 2960. The supplementary report
(pp 20-51) is evidence taken in Toronto in response
to a petition of the Toronto garment workers supported
by the Dominion Trades and Labour Congress.

270b ------ Rapport sur le système de pressuration de
l'ouvrier au Canada. Ottawa: S.E. Dawson. 55pp *OOAL

1897

271 Ashplant, Henry B. Heterodox economics vs. orthodox profits: a preliminary pamphlet. London (Ont). 66pp. *OOP

272 **Bell, F.H.** Taxation in Halifax. Halifax: Halifax Printing. 37pp. NSHPL OTP SSU *OOA Reprinted from *The Maritime Merchant*. For tax reform - civic taxation to be based on benefits received from the city and the value of real estate occupied.

273 **Canada, Secretary of State.** List of newspapers authorised to receive government patronage revised to 1st June, 1897. Ottawa: Government printing bureau. 19pp. *OOAL/1897/39 Marked 'Confidential document' but apparently widely circulated.

274 **King, W.L.M.** The international typographical union. Unpublished MA thesis. University of Toronto. (i), 43, (ii)pp. *OTUAR

275 **Pater Patronucus.** The coming struggle in the United States and Canada and its origin. Toronto: J. Johnston. 16pp. OTP *OTAR Hann 2360. The struggle is between capital and labour: 'my fight is with those who dishonestly and improperly acquire wealth...by winks, connivings, or understandings with politicians, or officials, (and) rob the public.'

276 Reid, Helen R.Y. The problem of the unemployed. A paper read before the Montreal Local Council, received by the National Executive and ordered to be printed. Montreal: np. (c1897). 20pp. OONL *OTPB/331.137R24 Thanks J.A. Hobson, quotes William Morris, cites Marx and Aveling, Beatrice Potter etc etc, but what the local council or national executive are of remains a mystery. Hann 2330.

277 **Spence, J.M.** Why are people poor? Labor day sermon. London (Ont): (Canadian Searchlight). (2pp) broadside. *OTURS

278 Takahashi, K.T. The anti-Japanese petition: appeal in protest against a threatened persecution. Montreal: Gazette. 16pp. QMBM QMBN *BVIP

279 **Toronto Trades and Labor Council.** Constitution. Toronto. 22pp. *E

1898

280 **Allied Trades and Labor Association.** Labor-day souvenir. Ottawa. 80pp, illus (many photos of union leaders). OOP OWA *OOAL Includes: The future of labor by John Coates; The eight hour day by P.D. Ross; The

workers and the thinkers by A.C. Campbell; Agitation, organization, education by D.J. O'Donoghue; The value of organization by John Appleton; Organized labor by R.G. Hay; The Social Science club of Ottawa by Elfric Drew Ingall; Co-operation by J.H. Brown; notes on unions and on individuals.

281 **Bengough, J.W.** The gin mill primer; a book of easy reading for children of all ages, especially for boys who have votes. Toronto: W. Briggs. 78pp. MWU *BVAU

(282) **Brotherhood of Locomotive Firemen and Engineers.** A memento. Hann 2368. OTU not found.

283 **Central Trades and Labor Council.** Labor day souvenir: official programme. Montreal. 32pp, illus. *OOAL Includes: Preamble and declaration of principles, biographies and a short history of the Knights of Labor by B. Feeny.

284 **Coleman, J.C.** The Jim Crow car; or, a denouncement of injustice meted out to the black race. Toronto: Hill. 128pp. *OTP

285 **International Brotherhood of Bookbinders of America.** Souvenir in honor of the sixth convention held at Toronto...May 3rd to 7th, 1898. Toronto. 56pp, illus. *OTURS/RSK Includes articles on the shorter work day philosophy, Toronto Trades and Labor Council etc.

286 **McArthur, Emily.** A history of the children of peace. Newmarket: Express-Herald. (10pp) *OTP. The children formed the community at Sharon, Ont.

287 **Maxwell, George R.,** Chung Chuck and Goon Sun. To the Dominion House of Commons: an answer to Mr Maxwell's statements on the Chinese question. (?Vancouver): np. 44pp plus 10pp in Chinese. *OOAL, defective copy lacking pp 17-32. Hann 2366. Contains speech of G.R. Maxwell in the House of Commons, Sept 1896; article of Maxwell's reprinted from the Presbyterian College Journal and replies by the Chinese community.

288 **(Ontario).** The laws relating to labor. (Toronto): np. 28pp. *OOAL

289 **Reid, J.T.** The physical sufferings of the poor viewed from a sanitary and sociological standpoint. Montreal: William Drysdale. 35pp. QMSS *AEUS/Rutherford.

290 **Scott, Duncan Campbell.** Labor and the angel. Boston: Copeland and Day. 59pp. ACU AEU BVAU NBSAM OHM OKQ OPET OTMCL *OONL. Poetry - some 'labor'.

291 **Siebert, Wilbur H.** The underground railroad from slavery to freedom. New York: Macmillan. xxv, 478pp, illus, maps, bibliography, directory of operators. ACU NSHPL OOAL OTP SSU *OOP. Much on Canada including a chapter on the life of the colored refugees in Canada.

292 **Yukon Miners.** Appeal of Yukon miners to the Dominion of Canada...and incidentally some account of the mines and mining of Alaska and the provisional district of

the Yukon. Ottawa: Mortimer. 128pp. *OOAL Asking
for direct representation, measure of home rule, transportation, postal service 'instead of the wretched
thing Canada and the United States are dignifying by
that name', relief from taxation etc.

1899

293 **Elkington, Joseph S.** and others. Arrival of Dukhobors
in Canada from Cyprus. London: Committee for assist-
ing the emigration of the Dukhobortsi. 8pp, illus.
*OTURS/Mavor 37. Includes an anonymous report from
Yorkton, Assiniboia.

294 **(Fitzgibbon, Mary Agnes.)** The Canadian Doukhobor sett-
lements: a series of letters by Lally Bernard. Toronto: William Briggs. 69pp. *OTP Peel 1575.

295 **Guerin, M.** 'Rerum novarum'. How to abolish poverty.
How poverty was abolished. Montreal: Alph. Pelletier.
viii, 77pp. NSHPL OTP QMBM QMBN *OOP. A handsome
piece of printing.

296 **Spence, F.S.** Shorter hours: an important public question. Toronto. (4pp). *OTURS Hann 2387. Written
in the form of a letter on the 9-hour day.

297 **Vigouroux, Louis.** La concentration des forces ouvrières dans l'Amerique du Nord. Paris: Armand Colin.
xxvi, 362pp. QQL *OKQ. Almost exclusively USA.

298 **Western Federation of Miners.** Convention of unions
of the Western Federation of Miners District No. 6
held at Rossland, B.C., December 18th, 1899. Rossland. (12pp). *BVAUS/Mac.33f4 (xerox copy).

1900

299 **Are the workingmen satisfied?** Canadian artizans have
not a fair share of the good times. np. (4pp).
*OTPB/1900/Conservative.

300 **Un chef ouvrier.** Ou sont nos amis? Appel d'un chef
ouvrier, ancien membre du Congrès des Métiers et du
Travail; et d'un ex-secrétaire du Conseil Centrale
des Métiers et du Travail de Québec, ex-secrétaire
de l'Assemblée Feuille d'Erable No. 1160 et ex-secrétaire du District No. 20 des Chevaliers du Travail.
(?Montreal): np. 32pp. *OKQS. In favour of Laurier
and the Liberals. 'Grâce aux mesures libérales de M.
Laurier...Justice égale pour tous, quelle que soit la
nationalité ou la croyance, c'est la noble devise de
M. Laurier...La gouvernement Laurier protège le travailleur etc etc.

301 **Hatheway, W. Frank.** Poorhouse and palace. A plea for
a more equitable distribution of wealth. Saint John.
46pp. *NBSAM Hann 2410.

302 **Hume, James Gibson.** Socialism: an address delivered
before the Knox College Alumni Association at their
post-graduate session. Toronto: Knox College. (c1900)
29pp. *OTURS/RSK. Reprinted from Knox College Monthly.

303 **McLachlan, Alexander.** The poetical works, selected and
edited with introduction, biographical sketch, notes
and a glossary. Toronto: William Briggs. (iv), 424pp,
frontispiece, index. *SSUS/Shortt. Introductory essay by Rev. E.H. Dewart. He 'aimed to be an exponent
of the minds of the working men of Canada' (Editor of
Grip).

304 **National Council of Women of Canada.** Women of Canada,
their life and work...for distribution at the Paris
International Exhibition, 1900. np. xxi, 442pp, illus.
*OONL OTAR/1900/61.

305 **The shame of Canada.** Montreal: np. (1p) broadside.
*OTPB/1900/South African war. On the Boer war and
brutality shown by Canadian soldiers. Concludes:
'Fellow countrymen! Stop the war and arrest the murderers!'

306 **Vancouver Trades and Labor Council.** Official program
for Labor day, September 3rd, 1900. Vancouver. (18pp)
*BVAA. Comprises almost all advertisements.

1901

307 **Fitzpatrick, Alfred.** Library extension in Ontario:
travelling libraries and reading camps. (?Toronto):
Library extension. 37pp, illus. *OTAR

308 **Hamilton, John and others.** A Christian home for men:
the working men's home, 59 Frederick St., Toronto.
Toronto. (4pp). *OTURS

309 **Rossland Miners' Union No. 38, W.F.M.** Constitution
and by-laws adopted October 22, 1896, November 23,
1898 and May 29, 1901. Rossland. 19pp. BVIPA *BVAUS/
Mac.33f8 (photo copy).

310 **Rossland Miners Union.** A plain statement. Rossland.
(1p). *BVAUS/Mac.33f8 (photo copy). On the strike.

311 **Smith, Goldwin.** Charitable work in Toronto: on the
defects of our system of out-door relief, and suggestions for its improvement. Toronto. (4pp). *OTURS
Hann 2416.

312 **Socialist Labor Party of Canada.** Platform and constitution: amended September 2, 1901. np. 15pp. *BVAUS/
Mac.31Af.18.

313 Socialist Party of British Columbia. Statement of
principles adopted at Vancouver October 3rd 1901.
Vancouver. (4pp). *BVAUS/Steeves 5-7. Includes
platform (general and provincial demands) and constitution. Text is exactly the same as that of the Socialist Party (of America) adopted at Indianapolis,
July 31, 1901.

314 **Sutherland, James.** Speech on the department of Labour
delivered in the House of Commons 25th April 1901.
Ottawa: Kings Printer. 4pp. *OOL. Sutherland was
the acting Minister of Labour.

315 **Yukon Labor Protective and Improvement Union.** Appeal
to outside miners! Dawson: (Daily News). (1p) broadside. *OOL. Signed by R.W. Bracken, Joseph A. Clarke
and D.H. Dick. Issued with the Dawson Daily News, 10
June 1901.

1902

316 **Allied Trades and Labor Association.** Progressive Ottawa. Ottawa. 90pp. *OOL Hann 243. Includes:
Labor's onward movement by D.J. O'Donoghue; The department of labour by W.L. Mackenzie King; sketches of
some unions.

317 **Cromwell, O.** (pseud). Politicalized Canada: or Canada,
its people, politics, and some of its politicians for
the last fifty years. Toronto: J. Johnston. (c1902).
96pp. *OTPB

318 **Fitzpatrick, A.** Library extension in Ontario...reading
camps and club houses: with the second annual report
of the Canadian reading camp movement, 1901-02.
(?Toronto), Library extension. 58pp, illus. *OTAR

319 Ontario Liberal Association. Laws relating to labor:
record of the Liberal government on labor legislation:
a progressive policy in which Ontario leads. Toronto.
32pp. *OTAR OOAL Hann 2418. Gives a chronology of
Ontario labor laws and discusses the Mechanics Lien
act, master and servant, industrial disputes, factories,
employer's liability etc.

320 **Ontario Socialist League.** Socialist candidates for
the Ontario legislature. Toronto. (2pp). *OOAL
Hann 2421. Includes Ontario socialist platform.

321 **A partial history** of the corruption and electoral frauds
of the Tory party in Canada. np. 43pp. *OOAL Bound
in a volume of 1902 election pamphlets.? by the Liberal
party.

322 **Political Reform Union.** Constitution and by-laws,
adopted at a convention held in Winnipeg in July 1901
and revised at the annual convention held 20th February 1902. Winnipeg. 12pp. *MWPA/Puttee.

Includes names of officers and vice-presidents for
federal constituencies (Manitoba). Principles are
direct legislation, public ownership of utilities and
resources, abolition of the spoils system.

323 **Provincial Progressive Party.** Provincial labor convention, Kamloops, B.C. 1902. Proceedings of Tuesday
and Wednesday, April 15th and 16th. (?Vancouver).
(1p). *BVAUS/Mac.31f.14. Platform.

324 **(Robins, William.)** Whiskey sold 'privately' by the
Ladies Aid Society of the Methodist church, in aid
of the organ fund. (?Toronto): Hiram Walker and Sons.
(4pp). *OOAL. Relates to the forthcoming referendum
on prohibition; 'names of writers omitted to avoid
unnecessarily wounding feelings of individuals.'

325 **Socialist Party of British Columbia.** To members:
provincial platform. Ferguson (BC): Lardeau Eagle.
(1p). *BVAUS/Mac.30Af.2a.

326 **Territorial Grain Growers Association.** Report of the
proceedings of the annual meeting held at Indian Head,
Assa., on Thursday and Friday, December 4th and 5th.
Regina: The West. (30pp). *OOAL. Supplement to the
newspaper.

327 **(Toronto Federation for Majority Rule.)** People's veto
and direct initiative. How to get it at the next general election. Toronto. (2pp) broadside. *OOA/Good
18.

328 **Toronto Trades and Labor Council.** Directory of trades
unions and Knights of Labor assemblies with time, place
of meetings and name and address of secretaries. Toronto. 64pp. *OOAL. Cover title: Official Labor Directory 14th year. Includes trades and labor councils
across Canada.

329 **Wilshire, H. Gaylord.** The significance of the trust.
Toronto: Wilshire's Magazine. 28pp. *HI Uncat. C400.
'We demand the nationalization of industry.'

330 **Withrow, W.H.** The underground railway. (Toronto):
Royal Society of Canada. pp 49-77. *OTAR/1902/9
Reprinted from the transactions of the Royal Society.

1903

331 **A.L.O.C.** The story of a dark plot; or tyranny on the
frontier. Boston: Warren. 198pp. *OONL Hann 2365.
The dismissal of W.W. Smith of Sutton, Quebec, by the
Canadian Pacific Railway for temperance activities.

332 **Bellamy, Edward.** Looking backward (2000-1887). London (Ont): The Educationist. (c1903). 72pp. AEU
*BVAUS/Mac.41f.9A. Earliest identified Canadian
printing (of many).

333 **Canada, Dept of Labour.** Report of the Royal Commiss-
ion on industrial disputes in the province of British
Columbia. Ottawa: Government Printing Bureau. x,
77pp. *OTAR/1903/18 Hann 2976. Commissioners: Hon.
Gordon Hunter, Rev. Elliott S. Rowe; Secretary W.L.
Mackenzie King.

334 **The Farmers' Association.** The Farmers' Association:
grounds on which it seeks the co-operation of all
farmers: its purpose is to secure united effort with
a view of shaping legislation more in the interests
of the farm than has been the case in the past. Toronto. 9pp. *OOAL. 'The granting of public money to
private and corporate interests in the form of bonuses
and bounties is unjust to the masses of the people.'

335 **Flynn, E-J.** La mauvaise politique qui dépouille nos
forêts sans profit pour le travail Canadien. Discours
en réponse à l'honorable M. Parent, sur la question
forestière, prononcé à l'Assemblée législative, le 25
avril, 1903. Québec: S-A. Demers. 23pp. QMBN QQL
*OOAL

336 **Liberal** Party. Labour legislation by the Liberal
government at Ottawa. Ottawa. 14pp. *OOAL

337 **Marshall, J.R.** The growth of labour legislation in
Ontario. Unpublished MA thesis. University of Toronto. 47pp. *OTUAR

338 **Toronto Federation for Majority Rule.** Report of progress. Toronto. (1p) broadside. *OOA/Good 18.
Signed by James Simpson. 'Organized to secure the
adoption of the people's veto and the direct initiative in the city government.'

339 **Western Federation of Miners.** Proceedings of the
fifth annual convention of the Canadian district
association No. 6, held in the city of Nelson, B.C.
April 7th to 11th, 1903. (?Vancouver). 32pp. *BVAUS/
Mac.34f.23 (photo copy).

1904

340 **Canadian Labour Bureau.** (Vacancies in various trades).
London (Eng): (c1904). (4pp). *OOAL. Lists various
vacancies in detail, numbers required and average
wages paid in iron and steel, woodworking and furniture, jewellers etc.

341 **Kelso, J.J.** Thoughts for workers. Toronto: (Social
service). 19pp. *OTP

342 **Keys, William (ed).** Capital and labor: containing
the views of eminent men of the United States and
Canada on the labour question, social reform and other
economic subjects. Montreal: Dominion Assembly,
Knights of Labor. 243pp, illus. OKQ OOL OOP QMBN

QQL *OOAL OONL. Includes Rate of pay for work by Louis
F. Post; Strikes, the right and the wrong by F.D. Hunt-
ington; Industrial arbitration by A.W. Flux; Fair play
for the toiler by James Harper; The state and the working man by Michael Guerin etc.

343 **Mallory, C.A. and R.J. Vair.** From a farmer's standpoint. np. (1p) broadside. *OTAR Hann 2431.
Largely a letter by Mallory in reply to Vair as to the
course independents should follow during the election.
Mallory had been president of the Patrons of Industry.

344 **Puttee, Arthur W.** Address to the electors of Winnipeg:
platform - government ownership of public utilities,
abolition of the Senate (etc). Winnipeg. (4pp),
portrait. *G329.14(71). Independent Labor candidate.

345 **Scott, S.D.** William Cobbett on New Brunswick. A paper
read before the New Brunswick Historical Society in
1904. (?Moncton): NB Historical Society. 34pp. *OOAL
Includes extensive extracts from Cobbett.

346 **Socialist Party of Canada.** Platform. (Vancouver).
(1p) broadside. *OOA/CCF/184. 'Note - the national
secretary of the Socialist Party of Canada is D.G.Mc-
Kenzie, Box 831, Vancouver, B.C.' Added pencil note:
'Reprinted by H.H. Stuart 1908.'

347 **Stands by the working man.** The Laurier government has
always been friendly to him. Placed laws on the statute book to better his condition. Always willing to
hear and redress grievances. Status of the artizan
greatly improved since the present government came into
office. Wages have also increased in every branch of
industry. (Ottawa): (?Liberal Party). (4pp). *OOAL

348 **Trades Union guide and mercantile directory:** containing a complete list of the Toronto labor organizations
and friendly merchants, together with essays on departmental stores and articles referring to the labor question. Toronto: Trades Council. 56pp. *OTARS/1904/67.
Hann 2433.

349 **Western Federation of Miners District Association No.6.**
Proceedings of sixth annual convention held at Nelson,
B.C. March 8-11th 1904. (Nelson). 20pp. *OTURS/RSK.
Includes, as part of the text of a resolution, the
platform of the Socialist Party of B.C. as endorsed
at their 10th and 11th conventions.

1905

350 **Canada.** Report of the Royal Commission on employment
of aliens on the Grand Trunk Pacific Railway. Ottawa:
Kings Printer. 565pp. *OONL Hann 2981.

351 **Canada.** The Royal Commission in re the alleged employment of aliens by the Père Marquette Railway Company

of Canada: report of Commissioner (John Winchester).
Ottawa: S.E. Dawson. 36pp. *OOAL Hann 2983. The
aliens were from the United States brought in to supp-
lant Canadians, mainly in management.

352 **International Typographical Union.** Souvenir for 1905.
Fifty-first annual convention held in Toronto August
14 to 19, 1905. Toronto. (73pp), illus plus many
adverts. *OTURS/RSK. Includes: Toronto, its past
and present by Phillips Thompson; After a quarter
century by James M. Lynch; The futility of anti-union
crusades by W.B. Prescott; The Trades and Labor Congress of Canada by P.M. Draper; Sketch of the early
history of No. 91 (Typographical union, Toronto) by
John Armstrong; Labor laws of Canada by D.J. O'Donoghue; Toronto Labor Temple by James Simpson etc.

353 **Patrick, T.A.** The five province heresy: a menace to
national unity. (?Yorkton): (c1905). 7pp. AEU SRL
*MWPL

354 **Sandon Miners Union.** By-laws and sketch of Sandon
Miners Union hospital instituted March 1st, 1899.
Sandon. 22pp. *BVAUS/Mac.33f.9.

355 **Simpson, James.** To the electors of East Toronto.
Toronto: Canadian Socialist League. (c1905). (4pp).
*OTPB/1902/Electors.

356 **Socialist Party.** Manifesto of local Toronto municipal
elections, 1905. Toronto. (4pp). *E

357 **Socialist Party.** Ontario election campaign January
25th 1905: the class struggle. Toronto. (4pp).
Includes platform. *E

358 **Toronto District Labor Council.** Labor day and Trades
and Labor Congress souvenir. Toronto. 92pp, illus.
*OOAL. In honour of 21st annual convention of the
TLCC 18-23 September, 1905. Includes: The future weapon of organized labor by Robert Glockling; The Trades
and Labor Congress of Canada by D.J. O'Donoghue; Toronto District Labor Council by D.W. Kennedy (includes
preamble and declaration of principles and list of
officers).

1906

359 Brotherhood of Locomotive Firemen. Souvenir: Canadian
union meeting, June 19th, 20th, 21st and 22nd, City
of Ottawa. Ottawa. (94pp), illus. OTMCL *OOAL
Includes a brief sketch of the union.

360 **Bryce, Peter H.** Organized sanitary work in dealing
with overcrowding and pauperism, due to immigration.
np. 16pp. *OOAL Hann 2441. Reprinted from Papers
and reports of the American Public Health Association,
vol. XXXII, part 1. Recommends broad policy and the

forced 'distribution' of immigrants.

361 **Canadian Pacific Railway.** Women's work in western
Canada. A sequel to *Words from the women of western Canada.*
(?Winnipeg). 68pp. BVIPA OTAR *ACGL OOAL (photocopy).

362 **Fitzpatrick, Alfred.** The frontier laborer with the
sixth annual report of the Reading Camp Association,
1905-6. New Liskeard: Reading Camp Association.
24pp, illus. *OTAR Hann 2443.

363 **Great Britain.** Correspondence relating to the complaint of certain printers who were induced to emigrate
to Canada by false representations. London (Eng):
Darling. 27pp. (Cd.2980). *OOAL Peel 1876. Complains they were induced to Winnipeg to take the place
of printers on strike there by false representation.

364 **Hatheway, W. Frank.** Canadian nationality: the cry of
labor, and other essays. Toronto: William Briggs.
x, 11-230pp. *OONL.

365 **Smith, Goldwin.** Progress or evolution? A letter to
a labour friend. Toronto: William Tyrrell. 30pp.
AEU OKQ OTP QQL *SSUS/Shortt Hann 2449. Basically
anti-socialist while acknowledging 'rapacious and
unjust...heartless and cruel' capitalism.

366 **Socialist Party of Canada.** Constitution. New Westminster. (c1906). (4pp). *BVAUS/Mac.30Af.2a OTURS/
RSK.

367 **Socialist Party.** Toronto municipal elections 1906.
Manifesto. Toronto. (2pp) broadside. *E The candidates for the Board of Education are Phillips Thompson, Fred Peel and W.H. Rawbone.

368 **United Mineworkers of America.** Constitution adopted
by the fourth annual convention district 18 held at
Fernie, B.C. December 20, 21, 22 and 23, 1905. Fernie.
21pp. BVIPA *BVAA.

1907

369 **Allied Trades and Labor Association.** Labor day souvenir. Ottawa. (55pp). *OOL Hann 243.

370 **Borden's Halifax platform:** promises with strings attached. Pledges qualified by impossible conditions.
Reservations. Ifs and buts. Bribe for the new provinces...Government by commission. np. 15pp. *OTP
? published by the Liberal party.

371 **Bricklayers and Masons** International Union No. 17.
Constitution, by-laws and rules of order. Peterborough. 32pp. *OPET/Gainey 20.

372 ------ Delinquent list, revised to December 1, 1906.
Indianapolis. 145pp. *OPET/Gainey 2. Includes list

of Canadians (by province) for violations and scabbing.

373 Canada, **Minister of the Interior.** Canada wants domestic servants. High wages, good homes, healthy climate. Ottawa: Dept of the Interior. 8pp, illus. *OOAL

374 ------ Papers relating to the holding of homestead entries by members of the Doukhobor community; being part of a return...(to)...the House of Commons...: with the final report of the commission... Ottawa: Government Printing Bureau. 29pp. *OOAL Peel 1914. The papers are: Report of interview between the Minister of the Interior (Frank Oliver) and Peter Verigin; Memorandum of the Minister regarding homestead entries; Circular addressed to the elders and people of 61 Doukhobor villages; Petition...from the Christian community of the universal brotherhood of Doukhobors; Report of an interview between the Minister and representatives of the Doukhobors; Petition for reserve for Prince Albert villages near Verigin; Petition for reserve for Devil's Lake villages near Verigin; Interview between the Minister and representatives regarding the petitions; two letters from the Minister and the final report of the Commissioner.

375 Canada. Reports and maps relating to lands held under homestead entry by Doukhobors and the disposition of same. Ottawa: Government Printing Bureau. 11pp and 5pp of photographs and 2 maps. *OOAL

376 **Canadian Bureau for the Employment of Women.** Aim. Montreal. (c1907). (4pp). *OOAL

377 **Cyr, Ernest.** Les classes ouvrières au Canada. Conférence prononcée devant le club Belcourt d'Ottawa, le 21 janvier, 1907. np. 10pp. *OKQS

378 **Hanna, W.J.** The prison labor question: history of the contract system in the Toronto central prison - - - a record of continuous failures - - - the outlook for the future; speech delivered in the Ontario legislature on February 26, 1907. Toronto: L.K. Cameron. 15pp. *OTAR OONL Hann 2452.

379 **Harris, W.S.** Capital and labor. Brantford: Bradley-Garrison. 331pp. *OKQS

380 **Interprovincial Council of Farmers Associations.** Reply to the premiers as to government ownership of elevators. np. (c1907). (4pp). *MWPA/UFM.22 and CCA.3

381 **King, W.L. Mackenzie.** Report into the methods by which oriental labourers have been induced to come to Canada. (Ottawa): np. 55pp. *OOAL Hann 2987.

382 **Métin, Albert and others.** Délégation ouvrière française aux Etats-Unis et au Canada. Rapports des délégués Louis Benoist, Henri Dugué, Claude Gignoux, Etienne Hyolet, Alfred Jacquet, Jean Leblanc, Jules Malbranque, Emile Martin. Recueillis conformément aux instructions de M. le Ministre du Commerce, pub-

liés et compétés par deux études sur le travail aux
Etats-Unis et le travail au Canada par Albert Métin.
Paris: Edouard Cornély. xvi, 301pp. *OKQ. Rapport
sur Canada pp33-63. Includes declaration of principles
of the Brotherhood of Carmen, Toronto, 1890 and program
of the Socialist Party of BC.

(383)**Ontario.** Report of the Committee on Child Labor. Toronto. 13pp. Hann 3214.

384 **Reading Camp Association.** Camp education: the education of the frontier laborer: seventh annual report
1906-7. (Toronto). 76pp. *OOAL Hann 2451. Includes: The education of the frontier laborer by Alfred
Fitzpatrick; Night schools for frontier camps by
E.W. Bradwin; Camp schools in new Ontario by Dan
Keeley, etc.

385 **Saskatchewan Grain Growers Association.** Constitution.
np. (8pp). *SSA/G34.1

386 **Socialist Party of Canada.** Manifesto, Toronto municipal elections 1907. Toronto. (2pp), broadside. *E

1908

387 **Ames, Herbert B.** Our western heritage and how it is
being squandered by the Laurier government. Montreal:
np. 24pp. BVAU OOP OTP QMBM SRU *OOAL Peel 1960.
Deals with timber and agricultural lands, grazing
rights, irrigation, coal and inland fisheries. Quotes
on back cover a resolution of the Farmers Political
Association convention, Estevan, 27 March 1908 - 'The
repossession by and restitution to the people of Canada of great tracts of public lands, coal and mineral
lands and timber lands now held by corporations, political and other exploiters, and the retaining for the
people of all natural resources.'

388 **Borden, R.L.** The question of oriental immigration.
Speeches (in part) delivered in 1907 and 1908.
(Ottawa): np. 31pp. *OOAL

389a **Canada, Dept of Labour.** Report by W.L. Mackenzie King,
appointed to investigate into the losses sustained by
the Chinese population of Vancouver, B.C. on the occasion of the riots in that city in September, 1907.
Ottawa: S.E. Dawson. 18pp. Hann 2990. *OTAR/1908/43.

389b ------ Report by...Commissioner appointed to investigate into the losses sustained by the Japanese population of Vancouver, B.C. on the occasion of the riots
in that city in September 1907. Ottawa: S.E. Dawson.
22pp. OKQ *OOAL OTAR/1908/44 Hann 2986.

390 **Canada, Minister of the Interior.** Canada: farm labourers and domestic servants wanted in Ontario. Earn
capital and experience in Eastern Canada with which

to work free land in western Canada. Only workers
wanted. No room for loafers. Ottawa. 32pp, map,
letters pp 9-28. *OOAL

391 **Canada.** The east Indians in British Columbia. A rep-
ort regarding the proposal to provide work in British
Honduras for the indigent unemployed among them.
(Ottawa). 39pp. *OOAL

392 **(Dominion Cooperative Association Limited.)** Co-operative society for Canada. Toronto. (1p) broadside.
*OTURS Hann 2464.

393 ------ What is the Dominion Co-operative Association?
Toronto.)c1908). (4pp). *OTURS.

394 **Edgar, William Wilkie.** The settlement of industrial
disputes in Canada. Chicago: University of Chicago
press. pp 89-93. *OOL Reprinted from *The Journal
of Political Economy* Vol XVI, No. 2, February 1908.

395 **Edwards, Henrietta Muir.** Legal status of Canadian
women: as shown by extracts from Dominion and provincial laws relating to marriage, property, dower,
divorce, descent of land, franchise, crime and other
subjects. Calgary: National Council of Women of Canada. 61pp. ACG AEU BVIP OOP *OHMA 2952 OONL.

396 **Grainger, M. Allerdale.** Woodsmen of the west. London (Eng): Edward Arnold. x, 206pp, illus plus advts.
*T Novel about the BC loggers.

397 **Grayson, Victor.** God's country: the emigration humbug. Stockport: The Socialist Press. 16pp. *T

398 **Hodgins, Thomas.** The prerogative rights of revoking
treaty privileges to alien subjects. Toronto: Carswell and Wm. Briggs. 27pp. BVAS BVIP BVIV OKQ QMML
*OOAL Concerned mainly with United States fishermen
in Newfoundland waters.

399 Kennedy, H.A. The unemployed in Canada: causes of
the trouble. (?Toronto): np. 16pp. *OOAL Hann 2465
Naive - written by an Englishman.

400 **King, W.L. Mackenzie.** Report...on mission to England
to confer with the British authorities on the subject
of immigration to Canada from the Orient and immigration from India in particular. Ottawa: S.E. Dawson.
10pp. *OOAL

401 **Lemieux, Rodolphe.** Report by the Minister of Labour,
of his mission to Japan on the subject of the influx
of Oriental labourers into the province of British
Columbia. Ottawa: np. 32pp. *OOAL

402 **Liberal Party.** What the Laurier government has done
for labour. (Brantford). 38pp. *OTAR/1908/14 Hann
2408. Note: issues with the same or very similar
title were issued at each election. These have not
all been listed.

403 Ontario. Report of the Special Committee on prison
labour. Toronto: Kings Printer. 44pp. *OTL

404 **Socialist Party** of Canada. Ontario provincial elections June 8th, 1908. Manifesto of Toronto local.
Toronto. (2pp), broadside. *E

405 **(Stuart, Henry Harvey.)** Declaration of principles
(of the Canadian Socialist League No. 67 of Fredericton, N.B.). (Fredericton). (1p), broadside.
*OOA/CCF/184. Identical to that of the Ontario Soc-
ialist League.

406 ------ The Socialist Party: a political labor organization claiming the allegiance of 16,000,000 men.
(Newcastle, N.B.). (2pp), broadside. *OOA/CCF/184

407 **Woodsworth, J.S.** All Peoples Mission, Winnipeg.
Report 1907-1908. (Winnipeg). 8pp, illus. *OOA/
Woodsworth/37.

1909

408 Binder twine. np. 4pp. *OOAL. This and the next
item relate to binder twine being made by prison
labour.

409 **The binder twine steal.** np. 4pp. *OOAL Peel 1591.

410 B. & M.I.U. (ie. Bricklayers and Masons International
Union). Ontario provincial conference (fifth - report). Toronto. (4pp). OPET/Gainey 18.

411 **Canadian Railroad Employees.** Progress and tolerance.
Ottawa. (c1909). (3pp). *OTURS/RSK

412 **Federated Association of Letter Carriers.** Illustrated souvenir: a series of illustrations in photo-
gravure of Toronto's principal public buildings, together with the business announcements of a few of
the financial and mercantile institutions. Toronto:
Branch No. 1. 55pp, illus. *OTMCL

413 **Hope, A.T.** Canada and the unemployed problem: some
suggestions for its solution. London (Eng): Simpkin,
Marshall, Hamilton, Kent. 78pp. *OOL Hann 2472.

414 **International United Brotherhood of Leather Workers
and Horse Goods.** (A circular letter referring to
a strike in Ottawa). Ottawa. (1p). *OPET/Gainey/6.

415 **Interprovincial Council of Farmers' Associations.**
A provincial elevator system: to be operated by an
independent commission. An outline of the subject...
np. 16pp. *OKQS

416 **The introduction of Yankee political methods** into
Ontario: the Buffalo gang of pluggers and the new
nest of traitors. np. 4pp. *OOAL

417 **Kelso, J.J.** Can slums be abolished or must we continue to pay the penalty? Toronto. (c1909). 20pp.
*OTP Hann 2454.

418 **London, Jack.** Revolution. Vancouver: Socialist
Labor Party. (c1909). 16pp. *BVAUS/Mac.30Af.2a.
Hann 2485. More dramatic in title than content.

419 **Macdonald, C. Ochiltree.** The coal and iron industries
of Nova Scotia. Halifax: Chronicle Publishing. viii,
267pp. *NSHP. Includes relations between capital
and labour, wages etc.

420 **Manitoba Grain Growers Association.** (regarding a
petition for publicly owned grain elevators).
(Winnipeg). (4pp). *MWPA/UFM/22.

421 **Socialist** Party of Canada. Manifesto, Toronto municipal elections, January 1, 1909. Toronto. (2pp).
*E.

422 **Stephenson, F.C.** (comp.) What is said about 'Stran-
gers within our gates.' Canada's national problem...
Toronto: Methodist Missionary Sociaty. 16pp. *OOA/
Woodsworth/37.

423 **The story of oil.** A Canadian industry under foreign
control - two millions a year taken out of Canadians
and given to the Rockefellers. np. 4pp. *OOAL

424 **Toronto Finnish Socialist Branch.** The Canadian Socialist Party and socialdemocratism. Port Arthur:
Finnish Publishing. 31pp. *BVAUS/Steeves/5-7.

425 **Trotter, W.R.** Second report on misrepresentation to
undesirable intending immigrants from the British
Isles to Canada to the Trades and Labour Congress of
Canada, City of Quebec, 1909. Ottawa. 48pp. *OOL
OTURS/RSK. Peel 2087A.

426 **United Farmers Association.** Constitution and by-laws
adopted by the convention January 14th, 1909. (Edmonton). 16pp. *AEPAA/Inf.file.Alta.PolII. Peel 2087B.

427 **Warner, D.V.** The church and modern socialism: an
essay. Truro: News Publishing. 47pp. *OOAL

428 **Woodsworth, J.S.** All Peoples Mission, Winnipeg.
Report 1908-1909. Winnipeg. 24pp, illus. *OOA/
Woodsworth/37.

429 ------ Strangers within our gates: or, coming Canadians. Toronto: Missionary Society of the Methodist
church, Young Peoples Forward Movement department.
331pp, appendices. *MWP Peel 2091. Also published
by F.C. Stephenson in Toronto, 1911. *OKQS. First
published in the *Methodist Magazine and Review* Vol LXII,
July 1905. *OKQS

1910

430 **Blake, F.** The proletarian in politics - the socialist
position - as defined by C.M. O'Brien in the Alberta
legislature. Vancouver: Socialist Party of Canada.

*BVAUS/Mac.30Af.2a.   Hann 2486.   Largely a speech by
O'Brien.

431 **B.& M.I.U.** (ie. Bricklayers and Masons International
Union.) Constitution and by-laws of the Ontario provincial conference. (?Toronto). 27pp. *OPET/Gainey/
20. Reprinted in 1911 and 1912, 23pp and 26pp.

432 **Canada, Dept of Trade and Commerce.** Chinese immigration act as amended to date with regulations authorized by orders in council based thereon, corrected
to June 1st, 1910. Ottawa: Government Printing Bureau. 22pp. *OOAL. Reissued corrected to August 1,
1920 and again in 1922. Mainly Capitation tax ($500)
and a quota - one for every 50 tons of freight.

433 **Dixon, F.J.** Manifesto to the electors of Winnipeg
Centre. Winnipeg. (1p), broadside. *MWPA/Dixon/1.

434 **Dominion Grange.** Farmers' delegation to Ottawa.
Alliance. (1p). *OKQS.

435 **Fort William Trades and Labor Council.** Constitution
and rules of order. Fort William. 15pp. *OTAR/1910/
72.

436 **Hazell, A.P.** Summary of Marx' Capital. Vancouver:
Socialist Party of Canada. (c1910). 32pp. *BVAUS/
Mac. 30Af.2a. Hann 2484.

437 **Kelso, J.J.** Directory of the charities of Toronto
including benevolent and social reform agencies.
Toronto: Government of Ontario. 49pp. *OTP Hann
2493.

438 **Lewis, J. Walter.** Prosperous Canada. The report of
a personal inquiry into wages, prices, cost of living
and preferential policy. London (Eng): Tariff Reform
League. 54pp. *OTAR Hann 2495.

439 **Massachusetts Association in Favor of a Law for the
Investigation of Industrial Disputes.** Canadian views
of the Industrial Disputes Investigation Act: a law
for the maintenance of industrial peace. Boston.
(c1910). 15pp. *OOL Mostly the employers views.

440 **Socialist Party of Canada.** Constitution and by-laws.
Vancouver. (c1910). 17pp. *BVAUS/Mac.30Af.2a.

441 **Socialist Party of North America.** Membership card.
Toronto. (c1910). (8pp). *OTURS/RSK. Inside covers
allow for 2 years monthly membership record; contains
declaration of principles, rules and constitution.

442 **Stevens, H.H.** The oriental problem: dealing with
Canada as affected by the immigration of Japanese,
Hindu and Chinese. (Vancouver). (c1910). 20pp.
*OOAL. Against oriental labour.

443 **Stowe-Gullen, Augusta.** A letter addressed to the
members of the legislative assembly of Ontario, February 7th, 1910. Toronto: Canadian Suffrage Association. (4pp). *OTURS.

444 **Trades** and **Labor Congress of Canada.** Album of labor
leaders of Canada and the United States with biograph-
ies. Toronto: W.S. Johnson. 123pp, illus. *OOL
Includes Alphonse Verville, P.M. Draper, W.R. Trotter,
A.W. Wright, Geo. W. Murray, J.G. O'Donoghue, Wm.
Glockling, Henry R. Barton, Otto H. Zimmer and others.

445 **Wermelin, Atterdag.** Will frugality save the working
class? An address delivered in Stockholm, Sweden in
the eighties. Translated by C.H. Seaholm. Toronto:
Socialist Party of North America. (c1910). 26pp.
*OTURS/RSK. Reprinted from *The Weekly People*, NY.

446 **Woodsworth, J.S.** The Methodist social service in
Winnipeg: report 1909-1910. Winnipeg. 8pp, illus.
*OOA/Woodsworth 37.

1911

447 **Biggar, E.B.** Canada's crisis: political, commercial
and industrial relations with the United States and
with other countries: our transportation problems
and the railway rule of Canada: the naval aberration
and what it is leading to: the light of history on
Canadian nationality. Toronto: Biggar-Wilson. 42pp.
OTP OWA QMBM QMBN *OOAL. In America as Nineveh 'the
wealth and productions of the world were poured into
her, and became one fruitful source of her luxury,
her pride and her ruin.'

448 **Canadian Home Market Association.** Canada's most bon-
used industry: over $3,000,000 voted annually to aid
farmers - why imperil the good done with this money?
Toronto. 4pp. *OOAL

449 **Canadian Socialist Federation.** Constitution. Berlin
(Ont) (ie. Kitchener). 11pp. *OTURS/RSK. Includes
platform, also published separately. Adopted at
Toronto 15-16 April 1911, endorsed by party referendum
30 May 1911.

450 **Dixon, F.J.** Direct legislation: address before the
Presbyterian synod on November 15th 1911. Winnipeg:
Direct Legislation League of Manitoba. (8pp). SRL
*OTURS.

451 **Farmer, Seymour J.** The reign of the people: a brief
summary of the case for direct legislation. Winnipeg:
Direct Legislation League. 20pp. *SSA/G25.2

452 **Federated Association of Letter Carriers.** Convention
book of the Vancouver branch no. 12, published in
connection with the sixteenth biennial convention.
Vancouver. 76pp. *BVIPA.

453 **Grain Growers Grain Company.** What is the Grain Growers Grain Company and what does it stand for? Five
years of progress of the farmers' company. Winnipeg.

15pp. *OKQS.

454 **Hutcheon, R.J.** Is the growing independence of women
a good thing? Toronto: Canadian Suffrage Association.
(c1911). 15pp.   *OTURS

455 ------ Man's world. Toronto: Canadian Suffrage Association. 16pp. *SSA/McNaughton H34.

456 **Keen, George.** The co-operative movement: its principles, policy and progress. An address to the annual
convention of the Ontario Bee-Keepers Association,
Toronto, November 15, 16 and 17, 1911. Brantford:
Cooperative Union of Canada. 27pp. *SSUS/Coops.

457 **Kelso, J.J.** Early history of the humane and children's
aid movement in Ontario 1886-1893. Toronto: L.K.
Cameron. 85pp. *OTP Hann 2502.

458 **King, W.L.M.** The Grand Trunk strike: the position of
the government with reference to the big industrial
dispute. Speech delivered in the House of Commons,
March 21, 1911. (Ottawa): (Kings Printer). 23pp.
*OPAL Hann 2503.

459 Manitoba **Grain Growers Association.** Review of negotiations that led to government ownership of elevators
in Manitoba and cause of failure. Winnipeg. (c1911)
38pp. *MWPA/UFM 22.

(460)Musgrave, Fanny Wood.   The dark and bright side of
womans franchise. Hann 2506. Not found. (NSWA).

461 **Ontario, Dept of Education.** Industrial schools: recommendations and regulations for evening industrial
schools, recommendations for the establishment and
organization of general, special and co-operative
industrial schools. Toronto: Kings Printer. 10pp.
*OOL Hann 3124 (?).

462 **Ontario Tax Reform League.** Tax reform: to labour organizations. Toronto. 6pp. *OPET/Gainey 18. Hann
2509. Seeking support for a bill to allow municipalities to tax improvements at a lower rate than land
values. With list of labour organizations supporting
the proposal.

463 **Porritt, Edward.** The revolt in Canada against the new
feudalism: tariff history from the revision of 1907 to
the uprising of the west in 1910. London(Eng): Cassell.
x, 235pp, index. *OONL. Mainly on free trade and protection, but contains a chapter on farmers organizations
and the Granges.

464 **Scott, Robert L.** Direct legislation or the initiative
and referendum: what it is and why we need it. Winnipeg: Grain Growers Guide. 31pp. MWP OTP SRL *SSA/
G25.1.

(465)Seath, John. Education for industrial purposes: a
report. Toronto: L.K. Cameron. v, 390pp, illus.
Vancouver Public Library, not found.

466 (Townley, C.R.) Points in the laws of British Columbia regarding the legal status of women. Vancouver:
Political Equality League. 20pp. *BVAA. Includes
report of the first suffrage convention held in Vancouver. The pamphlet is anonymous but the author's
name has been written into the BVAA copy by her sister.

467 **Trades and Labor Congress of Canada.** Brief on workmen's compensation presented to the Ontario commissioner Sir William Meredith. (Toronto). 12pp. *MWPA/
Dixon 2.

468 **Wade, F.C.** Industrial peace: address to the Canadian
Industrial Peace Association. Vancouver: Canadian
Industrial Peace Association. 8pp. *SSUS/Labour.
Reprinted from *The BC Saturday Sunset* 7 October 1911 for
Board of Conciliation.

469 **What do our neighbours mean?** President Taft and others
say they need Canada; some say they want Canada. np.
4pp. *OOAL

470 **What we have we should hold:** the bulk of Canada's natural products consumed at home - why sacrifice a
reality for an uncertainty? Toronto: The News. (4pp).
*OTURS/RSK

471 **Woodsworth, J.S.** My neighbour: a study of city con-
ditions; a plea for social service. Toronto: The
Missionary Society of the Methodist church; The Young
People's Forward Movement department. 341pp. *OKQS.

1912

472 **Beaches Progressive Club.** A Toronto fable. Toronto.
(c1912). (4pp). *SSA/McNaughton H34. On womens
suffrage and for the Mens Equal Franchise League.

473 **Bricklayers and Masons International Union No. 17.**
Constitution and by-laws and rules of order. Peterborough. (c1912). 40pp. *OPET/Gainey 20. With
separate inserted amendments made at conferences in
Brantford, December 1914 and Windsor, September 1915.

474 **Canada, Minister of the Interior.** Canada: the opportunities offered in the Dominion for domestic servants.
How situations are procured. What servants must do.
The rates of wages. Ottawa. 16pp, map. Contains
contented letters pp 7-13. *OOAL

475 **Canada, Committee on old age pensions systems.** Old
age pensions systems for Canada: memorandum, October
1912. Ottawa: Government Printing Bureau. 144pp.
*NSHD/J4. Gives synopses of opinions submitted by
Trades and labour Councils etc.

476 **Davenport, Wm.** Why not enjoy what you produce? (and)
The fallacy of reform. Vancouver: Socialist Party of

Canada. (4pp). *T   Leaflet no. 13.

477 **Dixon, F.J.** The caterpillar of privilege. Winnipeg:
Direct Legislation League of Manitoba. (4pp). *OTURS.

478 **Dominion Grange.** Circular to subordinate granges.
Arthur. (4pp). *OKQS. Signed J.J. Morrison.

479 Granite Cutters' International Association of America.
By-laws of Victoria, B.C. branch, approved by our
International Executive Council, Oct. 31, 1912.
Boston. (4pp). *BVIPA

480 **Hatheway, W. Frank.** Speech in support of the more
complete education for mechanic and farmer. Given in
the House of the Assembly, Fredericton, N.B. March 19,
1912. Fredericton: np. 10pp. *NBSM Hann 2517.

481 **Hutchison, J.N.** Direct legislation: open letter to
Premier Roblin from the President of the League.
Winnipeg: Direct Legislation League of Manitoba. (4pp).
*OTURS.

482 **Keen, George.** Co-operation in agriculture: higher
associative intelligence the basic need: an address
delivered to the 37th annual convention of the Dominion Grange of Canada, held at Toronto January 24th
and 25th, 1912. Brantford: Dominion Grange and Cooperative Union of Canada. 31pp. *OOAL

483 **King, W.L. Mackenzie.** The Canadian method of preventing strikes and lockouts. Address delivered at the
annual dinner of the Railway Business Association:
together with an abstract of the Canadian Industrial
Disputes Investigation Act. New York: Railway Business
Association. 20pp. OTP *OHMA2954 OOL

(484)**McIvor, William John.** Revolutionary socialism. Unpublished MA thesis. University of Manitoba.

485 **Marx, Karl.** Value, price and profit addressed to work-
ing men. Edited by his daughter Eleanor Marx Aveling.
Cowansville (Que): Cotton's Cooperative. 75pp. *OTURS/
RSK BVAUS/HB201M33.1919.   (c1912). Cottons Weekly
was established in 1908 and changed its name in 1914.
It became the official organ of the Canadian Social
Democrat party in 1911.

(486)**Ontario.** Interim, second interim and final reports on
laws relating to the liability of employers to make
compensation to their employees for injuries received
in the course of their employment. Toronto: Kings
Printer. 3 vols 1912-13.

487 **Rowell, N.W.** Address to the working men of Woodstock
on workmen's compensation. Toronto: General Reform
Association. 23pp. *OTAR/1912/33. Hann 2521.

488 **Social-Democratic Party of Canada.** Constitution: adopted in unity convention at Port Arthur, Ont. Dec. 30
and 31, 1911; endorsed by party referendum March 31,
1912; amended by party referendum May 31, 1912.
Berlin (Ont): Dominion Executive Committee. 12pp.

*BVAUS/Mac.31Af.17. Includes by-laws and platform.

489 **Social Democratic Party of Canada.** Platform. Galt: (c1912). (1p) broadside. *OTURS.

490 **Socialist Party of Canada.** The evolution of human society. Vancouver. (c1912). (4pp). Leaflet 8. *BVAUS/Mac.30Af.2a.

491 ------ Religion thy name is superstition. Vancouver. (c1912). (4pp). Leaflet 10. *BVAUS/Mac.30Af.2a.

492 ------ Wage-earner and farmer. Vancouver. (c1912). (4pp). Leaflet 11. *BVAUS/Mac.30Af.2a.

493 ------ Workingmen get wise. Winnipeg: Provincial Executive Committee. (c1912). 4pp. Leaflet 6. *BVAUS/Steeves 5-7 OTURS/RSK. Includes platform.

494 **Toronto District** Labor Council. Constitution. 32pp. *OTURS/RSK. Revised, adopted November 1912.

495 **Trades and Labor Congress of Canada.** Stenographic report of a deputation upon the Dominion cabinet held in Ottawa, January 8th, 1912. Ottawa. 38pp. *OPET/Gainey 1.

496 ------ Workmen's compensation: a plain statement dealing with the proposed legislation recommended by the Commissioner of the Ontario government. An analysis of some of the evidence given before the commission. (Toronto). 15pp. *MWPA/Dixon 2.

497 **Twin-City Trades and Labor Council.** Constitution adopted March 1st 1912. Guelph. 12pp. *OOA/KWLC. (The twin cities are Kitchener-Waterloo).

498 **Victoria Trades and Labor Council.** Official labor review and book of reference: containing a history of the Victoria Trades and Labor Council, its aims and purposes; engravings of its officers; of the Labor Temple and what it means to the laboring man; the provincial labor laws; the aims and objects of trade unionism; a directory of the Victoria unions. Victoria. 63pp. *BVIPA.

499 **Wade, F.C.** The single tax humbug in Vancouver. Vancouver. 8pp. OOP QMBN SSUS *OOAL. Protesting that the single tax as instituted in Vancouver has nothing to do with the Henry George system.

500 **Woodsworth, J.S.,** Nellie McClung and others. Organized helpfulness; All Peoples' Mission 1911-1912. Winnipeg: All Peoples Mission. 28pp. *OOA/Woodsworth 37. Woodsworth: A social survey pp 9-11; McClung: Through the eyes of a visitor pp 3-8.

1913

501 **Blewett, Jean.** Canadian woman and her work. Toronto:

Canadian Suffrage Association. (c1913). (4pp).
*OTU SSU/McNaughton H34.   Hann 2338.

(502)**British Columbia.** Report of the Royal Commission on matters relating to the sect of the Doukhobors, 1912. Victoria: William H. Cullin. 66pp.

503 **Broad, Isabella Ross.** An appeal for fair play for the Sikhs in Canada. (Victoria): np. 16pp. BVAU BVIP BVIPA OTP QQL SSU *OOAL. Hann 2526. Includes text of a petition to Ottawa. Mainly on racial discrimination preventing wives and families from joining husbands.

504 **Buchanan, D.W.** Toward democracy: or the revival of an old idea. Direct legislation the next step in democracy. Winnipeg: Grain Growers Guide. 68pp. *MWPA/UFM 22   SSA/G25.3

(505)**Canada, Royal Commission.** Report of the Royal Commission on industrial training and technical education. Ottawa: Kings Printer. 2 vols. Hann 3004.

506 **Canada, Royal Commission on coal mining disputes** on Vancouver island. Report by Samuel Price. Ottawa: Government Printing Bureau. 43pp. *BVAA OTU   Hann 3002.

507 **Canada, Minister of the Interior.** Woman's work in Canada. Duties, wages, conditions and opportunities for domestics in the Dominion. Ottawa. 32pp. *OOAL Reissued in 1915. Largely the same as previous issues of 'Opportunities'.

508 **Canadian Council for Agriculture.** Organized farmers' case: resolutions presented to the Dominion government on December 16th, 1913, in Premier Borden's office, Ottawa, and memorandum in support of tariff resolutions. (Winnipeg). 24pp. *OKQS OTURS.

509 **Canadian Welfare League.** Purpose; programme; origin. Winnipeg. 8pp. *OOA/Woodsworth 37. Secretary J.S. Woodsworth.

510 **Cotton, W.U.** Cotton's compendium of facts. Cowansville: Cotton's Cooperative. 128pp, index. 3rd edn. *OTURS   Hann 2527. 'A handbook for socialists to refer to when agitating for the revolution.' Includes: Definitions of socialism by H. Martin (National sec. Social-Democratic Party): World statistics; Prussian millionaires; World wide statistics; United States statistics; Constitution of Canada ('Every agitator should know something of the constitution'); The Social Democratic Party of Canada by H. Martin; How to organize a local of the Social Democratic Party of Canada, with by-laws; Canadian statistics; Twenty-three men control Canada; Annual statement of Cottons Weekly for 1912; Where Cottons goes; The machine and the worker; Excerpts for speakers (Kautsky, Ely, Mazzini, Greeley, Engels, Marx, Debs); index.

511 Crawford, Mary E. (comp). Legal status of women in

Manitoba as shown by extracts from Dominion and provincial laws. Winnipeg: Political Equality League of Manitoba. 48pp. OTV *MWPA/PEL SSUS/Shortt. Peel 2384.

512 **Dominion Grange.** Circular letter to secretaries of farmers' clubs and other farmers' associations. Arthur. (4pp). *OKQS. Announcing a cooperative conference.

513 **Hedley, John.** The labor trouble in Nanaimo district: an address given before the Brotherhood of Haliburton street Methodist church. Nanaimo: (author). 19pp. BVIP BVIV OOL *BVAUS/Mac.34f.9 OTURS/RSK. Hann 2528.

514 **International Association of Machinists.** Proceedings of the first annual convention of District Lodge No.2, Montreal, September 29 to October 4, 1913. Montreal. 45pp. *MWPA/RvIvens 1

515 **Laut, Agnes C.** Am I my brother's keeper? A study of British Columbia's labor and oriental problems. Toronto: Saturday Night. 48pp, illus. *OHMA OTP. Articles reprinted from Saturday Night.

516 **MacDougall, John.** Rural life in Canada: its trend and tasks. Toronto: Westminster. 248pp, biblio. *OONL. Written for the Board of Social Service and Evangelism, Presbyterian church in Canada.

517 **MacGill, Helen Gregory.** Daughters, wives and mothers in British Columbia: some laws regarding them. Vancouver: Moore. 65pp plus supplement (82pp total). *BVAA. Marked as 2nd edition.

518 **Methodist and Presbyterian Churches.** The city of London, Ontario. Report on a limited survey of educational, social and industrial life. (?Toronto): Presbyterian Committee on Religious Education; Methodist Department of Temperance and Moral Reform and Presbyterian Board of Social Services and Evangelism. 99pp, illus, reading list. *OTV. Cover title: The London survey.

519 ------ Report of a preliminary and general social survey of Fort William, March 1913. Toronto: (publisher as no. 518). 36pp, maps and list of books on social problems in Fort William public library - includes Woodsworth, Riis, Beveridge, Ely, Hasbach, Howells, Nicholson, Dawson, Shaw, Webb, Wells. *OTV Hann 2533.

520 ------ Report of a preliminary and general social survey of Hamilton, April 1913. (Toronto): as 518. 49pp, illus. *OTV Hann 2534.

521 ------ Report of a preliminary and general social survey of Port Arthur, March 1913. (Toronto) as 518. 27pp, illus. *OTV Hann 2535.

522 ------ Report of a preliminary and general social survey of Regina, September, 1913. (Toronto): as 518. 48pp. *OTV Hann 2536.

523 ------ Vancouver, British Columbia. The report of a brief investigation of social conditions in the city which indicate the need of an intensive social survey,

the lines of which are herein suggested. (Toronto):
as 518. 32pp, illus. *OTV. Cover title: Vancouver,
B.C. A preliminary and general social survey.

524 **No-Party League of Western Canada.** Manifesto. np.
(c1913). 26pp. *SSA/G30.1. Prepared by E.A. Partridge, revised and endorsed by a committee. Peel 2420.

525 **Ontario.** Report re limitation of the hours of labor
of underground workmen in the mines of Ontario by S.
Price. Toronto: L.K. Cameron. 11pp. *OTAR/1913/33.

526 **Osborne, J.B.** The way to power. (?Vancouver): Dominion Executive, Socialist Party of Canada. 16pp.
*OTURS/RSK. 'My only endeavour here is to assist the
working class to discover their plane of power...'

527 **Scott, C.T.** The ethics of money. Toronto: Department of Temperance and Moral Reform of the Methodist
church. (c1913). 12pp. *SSUS/CanEcon.

528 **Socialist Party of Canada.** The socialist and the
sword. Vancouver. (c1913). (4pp). *BVAUS/Mac.30Af.2a
Leaflet no. 12.

529 **Toronto District Labor Council.** (Circular letter reg-
arding carpenters strike and reaction of the province).
Toronto. (1p). Signed Thomas A. Stevenson. *OPET/
Gainey 1.

530 **Toronto Suffrage Association.** Opinions of Toronto
clergymen on woman suffrage. Toronto. (c1913). 16pp.
*SSA/McNaughton H34.

531 **Trades and Labor Congress of Canada.** Constitution
and by-laws governing provincial federations of labor,
trades and labor councils and federal labor unions:
amended...Montreal. 16pp. *OPET/Gainey 1.

532 **Voaden, Thomas.** Christianity and socialism: a lecture.
Toronto: William Briggs. 75pp. NBFU OH OKQ OOP QMM
*OTURS/RSK. Prepared for the Theological Union of
the Hamilton conference, June 1913. Pro-socialism.

1914

(533) **British Columbia.** Report of the Royal Commission on
labour appointed on the 4th day of December, 1912
under the Public Inquiries act. Victoria: William H.
Cullin. v, 28pp. Hann 3294.

534 **Brotherhood of Locomotive Firemen.** Canadian union
meeting souvenir, city of Calgary, Alberta, Canada.
Calgary. 79pp. *ACGL

535 **Bryce, P.H.** The problem of housing our working people.
Ottawa: (Carnegie Literary and Scientific Association).
19pp. *OOA Hann 2541. Discusses rise in land values,
congestion, slum landlords etc.

536 **Bureau of Municipal Research.** A tentative scheme for central control of labour supply, unemployment and immigration. Toronto. (6pp). *OOL Bulletin 28.

537 **Canada, Senate.** Evidence given before the Senate Committee on immigration and labour, 6th May 1914. Ottawa: J. de L. Taché. 27pp. *OOAL. Includes evidence of J.C. Watters, President TLCC.

538 **Copeland, Winifred L.** (convenor). The work of women and girls in the department stores of Winnipeg. Winnipeg: Civic Committee of the University Women's Club. 21pp. *OTAR/1914/46. Hann 2555.

539 **Dingman, H.J.** The unemployed: a world problem. Toronto: np. 10pp. *OOL Hann 2544.

540 **Dixon, F.J.** The progress of land value taxation in Canada. Winnipeg: Manitoba League for Taxation of Land Values. 8pp. *MWPA/Brigden 7.

541 ------ The progress of land value taxation in western Canada: a paper read to the National Taxation League, Denver, September 14th, 1914. Winnipeg: Land Values League. (4pp). *MWPA/Brigden 7.

(542) **Federated Association of Letter Carriers.** Convention book of Vancouver branch No. 12. Vancouver: News Advertiser. 71pp, illus. BVIP BVIPA.

543 **Hanna, W.J.** 'Social problems' and what the Whitney government is doing to solve them; speech in reply to Mr Rowell's amendment to the effect that present conditions call for the creation of a department to deal with social problems, including labour matters, delivered in the Legislative Assembly on 19th February, 1914. Toronto: Kings Printer. 23pp. *OTAR

544 **Hardenburg, W.E.** What is socialism? A short study of its aims and claims. Vancouver: Socialist Party of Canada. 32pp. *BVAUS/Mac30Af.2a. Hann 2483. Includes platform.

545 **Joint Committee of Socialist and Labor organizations** of Toronto. The significance of May Day: what it should mean to the working class. Toronto. (4pp). *OTURS Hann 2551.

546 **Kavanagh, J.** The Vancouver Island strike. Vancouver: B.C.Miners' Liberation League. 16pp. BVIP OOL *BVAUS/Pam. OTU. Hann 2529 and 2548. Includes summary of events.

547 **McClung, Nellie L.** The new citizenship. Winnipeg: Political Equality League of Manitoba. (c1914). (7pp). *SSA/G294.1

548 **Methodist and Presbyterian churches.** County of Huron, Ontario. Report on a rural survey of the agricultural, educational, social and religious life. Toronto: as no 518. 56pp. *OTV. Cover title Rural survey, County of Huron, Ontario.

549 **Methodist and Presbyterian churches.** Swan river valley Manitoba including the municipalities of Swan River
and Minitonas. Report on a rural survey of the agricultural, educational, social and religious life.
(Winnipeg). 73pp, illus., map. *OHMA2106 OTV Hann
2552. Includes co-ops, labor and wages etc.

550 ------ Sydney, Nova Scotia. The report of a brief
investigation of social conditions in the city which
indicate the need of an intensive social survey, the
lines of which are herein suggested. (Toronto): as
no.518. 29pp, illus. *OTV Hann 2537. Cover title:
Sydney: a preliminary and general social survey.

551 ------ Turtle mountain district, Manitoba, including
the municipalities of Whitewater, Morton and Winchester. Report of a rural survey of the agricultural,
educational, social and religious life. (Toronto)
as no. 518. 78pp, illus, map. *OHMA792 OTV Hann
2554. Cover title: Rural survey, Turtle mountain
district, Manitoba.

552 **Michell,** H. The Grange in Canada. Kingston: Queens
University. 20pp. *OOAL Bulletin no.13 of the
departments of history and political science.

553 **Myers, Gustavus.** A history of Canadian wealth, volume 1 (all published). Chicago: Charles Kerr. vi,
337pp. *OONL. Reprinted in 1972 with an introduction
by Stanley Ryerson, pp vii-xxx, biographical details
and references.

554 **Pilkington,** J. Wage worker and farmer. Vancouver:
Socialist Party of Canada. 16pp plus 1p 'How to org-
anize'. *BVAUS/Mac30Af.2b OTURS/RSK Hann 2488.
Includes platform.

555 **Political Equality** League. Constitution 1914. Winnipeg. 8pp. *MWPA/PEL.

556 **Rutherford,** W.H. The industrial worker in Ontario.
Toronto: np. 123pp. AEU OKQ OTU QMM *OTPB. Originally a thesis at the University of Toronto.

557 **Simpson, James.** James Simpson's years of public service assure fitness as controller. Toronto. (2pp),
broadside. *OTPB/1913/Simpson. Summary of career.

558 **Social Service** Council of Canada, Indian affairs commitee. The British Columbia Indian land question from
a Canadian point of view: an appeal to the people of
Canada. 'We want justice to be done to us' (?Vancou-
ver): Conference of Friends of the Indians of British
Columbia. 16pp. *OOAL

559 **Social Service** Council of Canada. Social service congress, Ottawa. Report of addresses and proceedings.
Toronto. viii, 358pp. *OTP. Includes: Capturing
the labor movement and Radical tendencies among workmen by Charles Stelze; The extension of social justice
by James Simpson; The church and labor in British Columbia by G.C. Pidgeon; The labor problem by T.W. Croth-
ers; Co-operation among farmers by Alphonse Desjardins

Cutting down an evil tree by A.E. Smith (commercial-
ized vice); Political corruption and its cure by W.
W. Andrews; The relation of political institutions to
political purity by W.C. Good etc.

560 **Socialist and Labor organizations of Toronto.** A grand
concert to celebrate May Day, the international working
class holiday, the holiday of the awakened and intelligent section of the working class. Toronto. (4pp).
*E. Contains inside: The significance of May Day.

561 **Socialist Party** of **Canada.** Manifesto: to the workers
of Canada. Vancouver. (1p). *BVAUS/Mac.30Af.2a &
Steeves 5-7.

562 ------ Socialism and unionism. Vancouver. 13pp.
*BVAUS/Mac.30Af.2b OTURS/RSK.

(563) ------ Socialism, revolution and internationalism.
Advertised 1914. Not found.

564 ------ Why not enjoy what you produce? Vancouver.
(c1914). (4pp). Leaflet 13. *BVAUS/Mac.30Af.2a

565 ------ The working class and master class. Vancouver.
(c1914). (4pp). *BVAUS/Mac.30Af.2a. Apparently a
reprint of leaflet 5 first printed in 1910.

566 **Stuart, Henry Harvey.** Socialism: its principles and
progress. Synopsis of an address delivered in St
James Hall, Newcastle, N.B. February 2nd, 1914. np.
(4pp). *OOA/CCF184.

567 **Thomas, Lillian** Beynon. The homeless and childless
women of Manitoba: laws relating to the ownership of
property and the guardianship of children. Winnipeg:
Political Equality League. (c1914). (2pp), broadside. *SSA/McNaughton H34.

568 **Wade, F.C.** Experiments with the single tax in western Canada. Paper read before the eighth annual conference on taxation, Denver, Colorado, September 11,
1914. Vancouver: Sunset. 20pp. AEU BVIPA MWU OOP
OTP SRL *SSUS/Shortt Hann 2556 Peel 2487.

569 ------ The single tax failure in Vancouver. Vancouver. 15pp. BVIPA OKQ OOP *SSUS/Shortt. Hann 2557.

570 **Welland Co-operative Society Ltd.** Prospectus. Well-
and. 8pp. *OOA/CUC223

571 **Woodsworth, J.S.** Canadian Welfare League: secretary's
report of first year's work (Sept. 1913 - Sept. 1914).
Winnipeg: Canadian Welfare League. 10pp. *OOA/Woods-
worth37.

572 ------ and others. Studies in rural citizenship designed for the use of grain growers associations, wom-
en's institutes, community clubs, young people's societies and similar organizations and groups desirous
of obtaining an intelligent view of rural life in Canada, with its various needs and possibilities. Winnipeg: Canadian Council of Agriculture. (c1914). 87pp.

AEU MWU OTP SSU *MWPA/CCA 3   Peel 2490.   Others include R. McKenzie, S.G. Bland, Lillian Beynon Thomas,
Nellie McClung.

1915

573 **Bryce, Peter H.** The illumination of Joseph Keeler,
Esq., or On, to the land! (A story of high prices.)
Boston: American Journal of Public Health. 97pp.
*OOA An allegory concerned with urban growth in Can-
ada and the remedies.

574 **Canada India Committee.** A call for Canadian justice.
Toronto. (4pp). *OOAL. Leaflet 2 on allowing Sikhs
to bring their families to Canada.

575 ------ The Hindu case. Toronto. 11pp. *OOAL

576 **Fitzpatrick, Alfred.** Settlement camps: a cure for
slum conditions. Toronto: The Reading Camp Association.
28pp. *OOA/Frontier 179.

577 Hatheway, W. Frank. Why France lost Canada and other
essays and poems. Toronto: William Briggs. 210pp.
*OONL. Includes The people and their leaders etc.

578 **Liberal Party.** Stuffing the pay lists: the patronage
evil in the civil service. Ottawa. (4pp). *OOP.

579 **Manitoba.** Report of the Royal Commission appointed
to inquire into certain matters relating to the new
Parliament buildings. Winnipeg: Jas. Hooper. 82pp.
*MWPA/Manning 2. Finding fraudulent conspiracy to
obtain an election fund on the part of the Premier
(Sir Rodmond Roblin)and others.

580 **Methodist and Presbyterian churches.** The Pictou district Nova Scotia including adjoining sections of Pictou
and Colchester counties. Report on a limited survey
of both rural and urban conditions. (Toronto) as no.
518. 59pp, illus. *OTV Hann 2564. Cover title:
The Pictou survey; parts of Pictou and Colchester
counties, Nova Scotia.

581 ------ The St Catharines district, Ontario. Report
on a limited survey of religious, moral, industrial
and housing conditions. (Toronto) as 518. 35pp, illus.
*OTV Hann 2565. Cover title: The St Catharines survey
including the towns of St Catharines, Port Dalhousie,
Merritton and Thorold.

582 **Ontario.** Ontario commission on unemployment: interim
report, July 20th, 1915. Toronto: Kings Printer.
11pp. *OOL OTAR Hann 3216.

583 **Social Democratic League.** May Day, 1915. Manifesto
to the toilers of Canada: this day is the emblem of
hope to the international visioned workers the world
over. Toronto: Forward. (4pp). *E

584 **Social Survey Commission.** Report of Toronto presented to the City Council October 4th, 1915. Toronto: Carswell. 72pp. *OTV

585 **Socialist Party of Canada.** 'Blood and iron.' Our immediate demand is: 'the abolition of the wage system'. Winnipeg: Manitoba Provincial Executive Committee. 5pp. *BVAUS/Steeves 5-7 OTURS/RSK.

586 ------ Manifesto of the Socialist Party of Canada. Vancouver. (c1915). 32pp. *AEUS. Includes platform. 3rd edn. 4th edn 47pp (c1916) *MWPA/Russell 1 5th edn 43pp 1920 *MWPA/Russell 1.

587 ------ 'Who are the dreamers?' Winnipeg: Manitoba Provincial Executive Committee. (c1915). 4pp. *BVAUS/Mac.30Af.2a. OTURS/RSK.

588 **United Mineworkers District 18.** Report of the twelfth annual convention held at Lethbridge, Alberta, February 15th to 23rd, 1915 inclusive. Fernie: District Ledger. 82pp. *AEPAA/Farmilo 4.

589 **Winnipeg Trades and Labor Council.** (Circular letter regarding dissatisfaction in factories producing war materials) signed R.A. Rigg. Winnipeg. (1p). *OPET/ Gainey 1.

1916

590 **Ager, Clarus.** The farmer and the interests: a study in economic parasitism. Toronto: Macmillan. 162pp. AEP MWP MWU OKQ OOP OTP *OOAL Attacking the privileged classes engaged in secondary interests - banking, transportation, commercial etc.

591 **Bureau of Social Research.** Community organization. Winnipeg. (4pp). *OOA/Woodsworth 37. (J.S. Woodsworth.)

592 **Conner, James McArthur.** Why send Canadian nickel to kill Canadian soldiers? Toronto: Banner. (c1916). (1p). *E. (Social Democratic Party).

593 **Edmonton Board of Public Welfare.** Mothers' pensions or charitable relief. Which? Edmonton. 32pp. *AEUS/Rutherford.

594 **Grain Growers Grain Company.** Farmers in business for ten succesful years 1906-1916: the story of the Grain Growers Grain Company. 31pp. MWP OTU *OKQS

595 **Kingsley, E.T. and R. Parm Pettipiece.** (compilers). The genesis and evolution of slavery. Showing how chattel slaves of pagan times have been transformed into the capitalist property of today. Vancouver: B.C. Federationist. 62pp. BVIPA *BVAUS/Mac.42f.29a. Hann 2572.

596 **Lindsay Local** (compilers). Gems of socialism. Lindsay:

24pp. *OTURS Hann 2570. 'Capitalism is economic cannibalism.'

597 **May Day Conference Committee.** May Day conference, May 1st, 1916. Toronto. (4pp). *E

598 **Michell, H.** The cooperative store in Canada. Kingston: Queens University. 22pp. BVAU BVIP MWU OH OKQ OOL OOP QQL SSU *OOAL Hann 2573. Bulletin 18 of the Dept of history and political science.

599 **Musselman, J.B.** Romance of the grain growers of Saskatchewan: history, aims, objects. Regina: Saskatchewan Grain Growers Association. 8pp. *SSA/G34.54.

600 ------ and S.G. Bland. True ideal of the Saskatchewan Grain Growers Association: plea for unity and co-operation (and) No organisation has a clearer right to live. (Regina): Saskatchewan Grain Growers Assn. (c1916). (8pp). *SSA/G34.72.

601 **Ontario.** Report of the Ontario commission on unemployment. Toronto: Kings Printer. viii, 334pp. *OTL Hann 3216. Chairman, Sir John Williams.

602 **Provincial Equal Franchise Board of Saskatchewan.** Constitution and by-laws. (Saskatoon). 12pp. *SSA/ G97.1.

603 **Richardson, Gertrude.** The women's crusade (International). Swan River. (c1916). (1p), broadside. *SSA/McNaughton H23. 'We desire social and political purity, the world for the workers to whom it belongs.'

604 **Simpson, James.** International socialism and its policy regarding war: an address before the International Polity Club of the University of Toronto. Toronto: Social Democratic Party of Canada. (c1916). 20pp. *OTCPA

605 ------ To soldiers, citizens, ratepayers, teachers, all voters interested in safe, sane, progressive civic government! Simpson should be elected a controller. Toronto: Banner. (c1916). 4pp. *E (Social Democratic Party).

606 **Stelzle, Charles.** A temperance society composed of labor leaders. Vancouver: Peoples Prohibition Movement. (c1916). (4pp). *BVIPA.

607 **Troman, R.** Struggles of the working class: a historical review of the growth and development of the modern proletariat since the year 1750. Toronto. (c1916). 32pp. *OTCPA OTURS/RSK.

608 **Vancouver Trades and Labor Council.** Our first appeal. Vancouver. (10pp). *OPET/Gainey 1. On the impending foreclosure of the Vancouver Labor Temple.

(609)**Wileman, E. St.John.** Government labor bureaus: their scope and aim. BVIP Hann 2575. Not found.

610 **Woodsworth, J.S. and R.C. Henders.** Bureau of Social Research, governments of Manitoba, Saskatchewan and

Alberta. np: Bureau of Social Research. (4pp).
*SSA/G326.3. A letter to all districts outlining the
new bureau and enclosing a questionnaire.

1917

611 **Anti-Conscription League.** Against conscription: the
trades union position. Winnipeg. (4pp). *E

612 **Biggar, E.B.** The Canadian railway problem. Toronto:
Macmillan. viii, 258pp, index. *SSUS/Shortt. For
full public ownership and against 'the wicked and un-
patriotic party-patronage system of making civil service appointments.'

613 **Bourassa, Henri and others.** The case against conscription. Montreal: Le Devoir. 6 separately paged pamphlets as follows: 1. Win the war and lose Canada by
Henri Bourassa. 2. Canada's economic destruction by
Edouard Montpetit. 3. The free American and the Canadian flunkey by Paul-Emile Lamarche. 4. Conscription
and agriculture by J-E. Caron. 5. The economics of
war by Adélard Fortier (and) Canadian labor and conscription by Joseph Ainey. 6. Conscription and true
liberalism by Sydney Fisher. QMBM QQL *OOAL.

614 ------ Conscription. Montreal: Le Devoir. 46pp.
*OONL OTURS/RSK.

615 **'Brockway's defence.'** (Toronto): (Canadian Forward).
(2pp). *OOA/Censor 604. Text of a statement made by
Fenner Brockway in England. Isaac Bainbridge found
guilty of publishing this seditious libel. 5000 copies
printed; banned 23 May 1917.

616 **Bryce, P.H.** The medical officer a cooperative social
force in rural districts. np: (Canadian Medical Assn).
10pp. QMBM *OOAL

617 **Buchanan, D.W.** To the delegates of the western Liberal
convention. Winnipeg, August 1917. Winnipeg: Single
Tax Association. (4pp). *OTURS Hann 2583.

618 **Campbell, T.A.S.** A call to independence! by an Independent candidate. (Saskatoon). (4pp). *SSA/G93.1.
Supporting the farmers platform etc.

619 **Canada.** Report of the Standing Committee on Neighbourhood work: Canadian conference of charities and correction, September 23-25, 1917. Ottawa: J. de La Broq-
uerie Taché. 16pp. *OTP.

620 **Canadian Council of Agriculture.** The farmers' plat-
form; drafted by the Canadian Council of Agriculture,
and adopted by the United Farmers of Alberta, the
Saskatchewan Grain Growers Association, the Manitoba
Grain Growers Association and the United Farmers of
Ontario. Winnipeg. 54pp. ACU AEU BVIP MWU SSU
*ACGL MWPA/CCA 3 OOAL OKQS

621 **Canadian Freedom League.** (Platform). Victoria.
(c1917). (1p). *E Also published in Toronto, and
signed there by J. McArthur Conner.

622 **Canadian League for Taxation of Land Values.** (Our
purpose, our method, our explanation, our desire, our
ambition, the goal). Ottawa. (c1917). (4pp). OKQ
*OTMCL OTURS. Probably Hann 2389. Signed by T.A.
Crerar, W.C. Good, J.W. Bengough, Nellie McClung,
H.W. Wood, F.J. Dixon, S.J. Farmer, H.H. Stuart etc.
(Single tax proposals).

623 **Canadian Liberal Party.** Who shall rule? The people
or the big interests: democracy and a free people or
autocracy and organized privilege: on which side are
you on? Ottawa. 251pp. BVIP OOP OTP QQL SRU SSU
*OOAL OTURS/RSK. A record of war scandals of the
Borden government and various Liberal measures.

624 **Central Liberal Information Office.** Shell and fuse
scandals: a million dollar rake-off, taken from government records. Ottawa. 12pp. *OOAL. Refers to
contracts given by members of the Conservative government Shell Committee to themselves.

625 **Conner, J. McArthur.** Jas. Keir Hardie's life story:
from pit trapper to parliament. Toronto: Banner.
30pp. OTP *OKQS OTURS/RSK.

626 **Ewart, John S.** The disruption of Canada. Ottawa.
30pp. ACU BVAU MWP OTP QMBN *OOA/Underhill 63.

627 **Industrial Workers of the World.** (Poems). Dan McGann
by Dublin Dan; Union poem by J.P. Thompson; Labor
speaks by an unknown worker. Vancouver: Vancouver
branch IWW. (c1917). (2pp) broadside. *BVAUS/IWW.

628 ------ Isn't it time for decent people to act? IWW
song. Cleveland. (1p). Stamped for publication in
Canada. *OOA/Censor 586. Song begins 'Onward Christian soldiers! Duty's way is plain: Slay your Christian neighbours, or by them be slain..'

629 **ILA** (ie. International Longshoreman's Association).
Constitution, by-laws and rules of order, amended
February 2nd, 1917. Vancouver. 19pp. *BVAUS/Mac.
33f.8.

630 **Laidley, Frederick W.** The why of the Non-Partisan
League. Swift Current: Non-Partisan League. 24pp.
ACG *SSA/G28.7 Peel 2591.

631 **Law Society of Manitoba.** re: 'The initiative and referendum act'. Winnipeg. 45pp. *MWPA/Pitblado 3.
Judgements of the Manitoba Court of Appeal disallowing
the initiative and referendum act passed by the legislature which would have permitted not less than 8% of
the total votes polled at a general election to submit
a new law to the legislature and, if not passed by it,
directly to the electors at the next election.

632 **May Day.** Manifesto, May 1, 1917. Toronto: (?Social

Democratic Party). (2pp). *E

633 **Metal Trades Council of Vancouver Island.** By-laws in
effect after January 1, 1918. Victoria. 15pp. *BVIPA.

634 **Rigg, R.A.** Verbatim report of speech 'National Serv-
ice' in the Manitoba legislature 22 January 1917.
Winnipeg: Social Democratic Party of Canada. 16pp.
OTP *MWPA/RvIvens 1 SSA/McNaughton H24.

635 **Selekman, Ben M.** Industrial disputes and the Canadian
act: facts about nine years' experience with compulsory
investigation in Canada. New York: Russell Sage Foundation. 42pp. AEU NSHPL OH OKQ OOL OTP *SSUS/Labour.

636 **Simpson, James.** Mr Voter! a moment please. Toronto.
(4pp). *E.

637 **Single Tax Association.** Social ethics. Toronto.
(c1917). (4pp). *OTURS.

638 **Single Tax League.** To the delegates of the western
Liberal convention, Winnipeg, August, 1917. Winnipeg.
(4pp). *OTURS Hann 2583.

639 **Social Democratic Party of Canada.** Manifesto re conscription. Toronto: Dominion Executive Committee.
(1p). *E. Signed by Isaac Bainbridge.

640 **Socialist Party of Canada.** The mission of capitalism.
Vancouver. (c1917). (4pp). *T Leaflet 4.

641 ------ The modern juggernaut. Vancouver. (c1917).
(4pp). *T Leaflet 3.

642 ------ No conscription. To the workers of Canada.
Vancouver. (1p), broadside. *OOA/Censor 604.

643 ------ No conscription. To the workers of Canada.
Vancouver. (4pp). *OOA/Censor 604 Hann 2584. Not
the same text as 642 above.

644 ------ No conscription! Uncompromising opposition
to military despotism. Edmonton. (1p), broadside.
*OOA/Censor 604. Signed John F. Maguire. Not the
same text as 642 above.

645 **Trades and Labor Congress of Canada.** Pronouncement
of organized labor in Canada on war problems. Ottawa.
(4pp). *OOA/Bengough 4. Report of a special conference held in Ottawa 1-4 June 1917, particularly with
regard to the Imperial Munitions Board.

646 **Tucker, Irwin St. John.** The price we pay. Toronto:
(Canadian Forward). (4pp). *OOA/Censor 604 OTURS.

647 **Unity Brotherhood.** Jean-Baptiste to his anglo-Canad-
ian brother: an open letter as a contribution to the
national unity movement. Quebec: Telegraph. 26pp.
AEU NSWA OH OPAL OTP QMBM QQL *OOAL.

648 **UFA** (ie United Farmers Association). The UFA: what
it is, what it has done, what it aims to do. Calgary.
6pp. *SSA/G291.20 Later edn (c1922) *ACGA/Smith 15.

649 **Unity Publicity Bureau.** Beware of mischief makers!
Quebec. 31pp. NFSM OKQ OPAL *OHMA205 OTAR/1917/122.
On the relations between Quebec and Ontario and for
Canadian unity.

650 **Woodsworth, J.S.** Nation building. (Toronto): The
University Magazine. 15pp. *MWPA/Brigden 7. Reprinted from February 1917 issue.

1918*

651 **Billiarde, F.J.** Canada's greatest asset – are we
safeguarding it? – a vital question for all Canadians.
A plea for the establishment of a Canadian childrens
welfare bureau. Winnipeg: np. 12pp, illus. *AEUS.

652 **Boyd, John and La Presse.** What Quebec wants: reply
of La Presse to a question from Ontario for the English speaking people of the Dominion. Montreal:
Beauchemin. 26pp. *OHMA2223 OOAL. Proper recognition of language, especially in Ontario; that
French ideals and aspirations should not be despised;
that it shall cease to be believed that national unity
can only be acquired at the price of unity of language.

653 **Brant Farmers' Co-operative Society** Limited. By-laws.
Brantford. 12pp. *OOA/Good 14. W.C. Good, President,
George Keen, Secretary.

654 **Bryce, P.H.** Conservation of man-power in Canada: a
national need. Ottawa: Committee of Conservation,
Committee on Public Health. 23pp. AEP OOP *SSUS/
Shortt.

655 **Budden, Alf.** The slave of the farm: being letters
from Alf Budden to a fellow farm slave and comrade
in revolt. Vancouver: Socialist Party of Canada.
63pp. *BVAUS/Mac.42f.29a MWPA/RvIvens 6 and Russell 1
OHMA2534 OTURS/RSK SSA/G173.3. Errata slip tipped
in. Written in August 1914, but publication delayed
until January 1918 with an amended note.

656 **Bureau of Municipal Research.** What is 'The Ward'
going to do with Toronto? A report on undesirable
living conditions in one section of the city of Toronto – 'The Ward' – conditions which are spreading
rapidly to other districts. Toronto. 75pp, illus.
*OTAR

657 **Cahan, C.H.** Socialistic propaganda in Canada; its
purposes, results and remedies. (?Montreal): (St.
James Literary Society). 38pp. *OOAL Hann 2588.
Anti-socialist, but included because it quotes extensively from the platform and manifesto of the Social
Democratic Party of Canada, IWW preamble, and translations from Finnish, Ruthenian and Russian pamphlets.

658 **Canada, Dept of the Interior.** Farm labourer, 1918.

---

*See also entry 4755 erroneously dated 1968.

Ottawa. 4pp. *OOAL Summary of regulations made on 7 March 1918.

659 **Canadian Council of Agriculture.** The farmers' platform: a new national policy for Canada adopted at Winnipeg on November 29, 1918. Winnipeg. 8pp. AEU OKQ *ACGA/Spencer 2 ACGL/PDg.CCA AEPAA/Inf.file Alta.Pol.III MWPA/CCA 3 and Salton OOA/Spencer OOAL. Peel 2623. Not the same text as 1917 edition. Extension of cooperatives, public ownership of railway, water, air, telephone, telegraph, natural power, coal mining; reform of the Senate etc. Translated into German: Die neue nationale Politik *MWPA/CCA 3.

660 ------ The new national policy as adopted by the organized farmers of Canada...drafted and issued at Winnipeg November 29, 1918. Winnipeg. 16pp. *MWPA/ CCA 3. Much expanded version of 659 above.

661 **Co-operative Union of Canada.** The Co-operative Union of Canada and its objects. Brantford. 11pp. *OTAR/ 1918/45. Possibly Hann 2593. Includes rules.

662 **Debs, Eugene V.** Eugene V. Debs and Jesus of Nazareth. Winnipeg: Winnipeg Labor Church. 13pp. *MWPA/Ivens 6 and CCF 39 SSA/McNaughton H23. Hann 2596. Contains Debs speech to the court 14 September 1918 and his pamphlet *Jesus, the supreme leader*.

663 **Dixon, F.J.** The power of ideals: address to the 'Labor Church' Sunday July 14th, 1918. Winnipeg: Western Labor News. (8pp). *SSA/G183.1.

(664) **Federated Association of Letter Carriers.** Convention souvenir. Hamilton: Griffin and Richmond. OH, not found.

665 **Gompers, Samuel.** Speeches delivered in the Canadian House of Commons April 26th, 1918 and before the Canadian Club, Ottawa, April 27, 1918. Ottawa: J. de Labroquerie Taché. 11pp. OKQ *OOAL Hann 2597.

666 **Grain Growers Guide.** History of the Grain Growers. (Winnipeg). 16pp. *ACGL Peel 2624B.

667 **Gribble, Wilfred and George F. Stirling.** What we want (and) Prosperity. Winnipeg: Socialist Party of Manitoba. (4pp). *BVAUS/Mac.30Af.2a MWPA/RvIvens 5.

668 **Ivens, Wm.** War and its problems. Winnipeg. 8pp. *SSA/McNaughton H23

669 **Joint Committee of Commerce and Agriculture.** Minutes of a conference held at Regina, March 13th and 14th, 1918. (Winnipeg): (Canadian Council of Agriculture). 35pp. *MWPA/CCA 3.

670 **Keen, George.** Co-operative societies: the responsibilities and opportunities of members. Brantford: Cooperative Union of Canada. 7pp. *OTAR/1918/69 Hann 2599. Refers to the 'Cooperative Commonwealth'.

671 **Khaki Labor Union.** What is the Khaki Labor Union?

(Vancouver). (1p), broadside. *OOL/microfiche 138/3

672 **King, W.L.M.** Industry and humanity: a study in the principles underlying industrial reconstruction. Toronto: T. Allen. xxi, 567pp, biblio, footnotes. *OONL.

673 ------ Industry and humanity: a study in the principles underlying industrial reconstruction. Letter of transmittal to the Trustees of the Rockefeller Foundation. Ottawa. 7pp. *OOAL

674 **Leake, Albert H.** The vocational education of girls and women. Toronto: Macmillan. xix, 430pp, biblio. OH SSU *OONL

675 **Lenine, Nikolai.** Ideas of Russia's revolution. Winnipeg: Socialist Party of Canada. 6pp. *MWPA/RvIvens 4 OTURS/RSK. Translated by Robert Crozier Long and reprinted from *Chicago Eye Opener* February 1918. Note on MWPA copy '5,000 printed March 11/1918.'

676 **Manitoba Grain Growers Association.** Manitobans on the job. Winnipeg. (6pp). MWPA/UFM 22.

677 ------ A social and educational organization. Winnipeg. (6pp). *MWPA/UFM 22

678 **Moorhouse, Hopkins,** (ie. Arthur Herbert Joseph). Deep furrows: which tells of pioneer trails along which the farmers of western Canada fought their way to great achievements in co-operation. Toronto and Winnipeg: George S. McLeod. 303pp. *SSUS/Shortt Peel 2010. Appendix lists officers and committees of farmers movements.

(679)**Ontario.** Standards for industrial houses recommended for Ontario by the Ontario housing committee under the proposals contained in the Premier's letter of July 1918. (4pp).

(680)**Peirce, W.E.** A protest: free speech in Canada. OOA/Censor, not found. Hann 2602.

681 **Peltier, L.L.** Industrial bonds: text of an address before the Trades and Labor Council, Fort William, June 27th, 1918. Fort William: Trades and Labor Council. (4pp). *OTAR/1918/103.

682 **Provisional Council of Soldiers and Workers Deputies** of Canada. Comrade soldiers and workers: second manifesto. (4pp). *OTURS/RSK. A first manifesto has not been located.

683 **Rowe, Florence** and others. Hymns and songs of Winnipeg Labor Church. Winnipeg. (2pp). *OOA/CCF309.

684 **Simpson, James.** Labour and prohibition: Jimmy Simpson's appeal to the workers. (Toronto). (1p), broadside with photo. *OTPB/1918 Labour.

685 **(Social Democratic Party of Canada.)** Peace and the workers. (Toronto): (Canadian Forward). (4pp). *OOA/Censor 605. Authorship assumed as this is typographically identical with other Bainbridge pamphlets.

686 **Socialist Party of Canada.** All I possess. (Vancouver): (c1918). (4pp). *BVIP

687 ------ Causes of the irreligion of the proletariat. Vancouver. 4pp. *OOA/Censor 602 Hann 2606.

688 ------ Circular letter dated 1st November advising subscribers that the *Western Clarion* has been suppressed and containing an advertisement for literature. Vancouver. (4pp, 2 blank). *OOA/Censor 602.

689 ------ The Marxian theory of value. Vancouver. (4pp). *OOA/Censor 602.

690 ------ Plain talk to workingmen. Vancouver. (4pp). (c1918). *T

691 ------ Religion, thy name is superstition. Winnipeg. 6pp. *MWPA/RvIvens 4. Leaflet 6. Note on MWPA copy '5,000 printed April 1918'.

692 **Stevenson, Jean C.** Homesteads for women. Calgary: United Farm Women of Alberta. (1p), mimeo. *SSA/G311.12.

693 **United Farm Women of Ontario.** Organization of a United Farm Womens organization. Toronto. (1p) mimeo. *SSA/G310.7 Reprinted as circular no. 2, 1919 *SSA/G310.4.

694 ------ Rules and suggestions for United Farm Womens organizations. Toronto. (1p), mimeo. *SSA/G310.7 Reprinted as circular no.3, 1919 *SSA/G310.5.

695 **Victoria District Metal Trades Council.** The truth about the shipyard situation. (Victoria). (2pp). *OOA/Bengough 4 (scrapbook).

696 **(Western Clarion).** The Bolshevist declaration of rights. (Vancouver). (4pp). *OOA/Censor 589 OOA/Woodsworth 6. Banned October 1918. No place or publisher, but advertises *Western Clarion* as the source. Reprinted from September issue of *Current History* translated from the German. Published in Moscow in the summer of 1918. Includes also 'Genuineness of Bolshevik documents' and editorial reprinted from the *New York Evening Post* 16 September 1918.

1919

697 **Alberta.** Report of the coal mining industry Commission. Edmonton: J.W. Jeffery. 13pp. *OOA/Woodsworth/11 OOL.

698 **Alien labor.** np. (2pp). *MWPA/Ivens 7 OTURS/RSK. A socialist reply to questions asked by members of the G.W.V.A (?Great War Veterans Association). Printing quite unlike those of the SPC, OBU etc. 'The writer has been asked...what is the attitude of socialism on the alien labor question...Join a socialist political party supporting industrial unionism.'

699 **Allied Tribes of British Columbia.** Statement for the government of British Columbia. Vancouver. 16pp. *OOAL. On tribal rights to lands.

700 **(Ashall, William.)** Unemployment and the way out by Cannon Fodder. (Winnipeg): Tank. (c1919). 125pp. ACU *OONL Peel 2650A.

701 **Ashplant, Henry B.** Karl Marx's theory of exchange: a criticism in political economy. London (Ont). 4pp. *OTURS/RSK.

702 ------ Royal Commission on industrial relations in Canada, abstract of evidence re moral delinquency of lay-churchmen, counterfeit money-currency, absence of social enterprise in industry. (London). 10pp. *OOAL Hann 2609. Ashplant, an accountant, represented the Independent Labor Party.

703 **Blair, E. Clay.** The challenge. Stewiacke (N.S.). 13pp. *OOA/Censor 597. 'I am the Bolsheviki...I am an individual anarchist.' Violently anti-Christian.

704 **Blunt, Bill.** (?pseudonym). The rubaiyat of a rebel. Leicester (Eng): Blackfriars. (c1919). 15pp. *BVAUS/ Young. Dedicated to the memory of Jack London and 'Ginger' Goodwin; distributed in B.C.

705 **Bonger, William Adrian.** The present economic system. Vancouver: Political Economy Club. (c1919). 29pp. BVIP BVIPA MWU *BVAUS/Mac.39f.27 MWPA/RvIvens 4 OTURS/RSK. Reprinted from his *Criminality and economic conditions* and based on Marx and Kautsky.

706 **Bourassa, Henri.** Syndicats nationaux ou internationaux? Montréal: Le Devoir. 48pp. *OONL. Reproduction d'articles parus dans le Devoir du 15 avril au 7 mai 1919.

707 **Boyd, John.** Tracts for the times. Montreal: People's Council of Canada. 4pp. *SSA/G368.1. 'Democratic and progressive.'

708 ------ Tracts for the times, No.1. The issues. Montreal: People's Council of Canada. 4pp. *OHMA2841. 'The dangerous element of the community, the worst enemy of Canada, is not the workingman...but the profiteers.

709 **BC Federation of Labor.** Report of proceedings of the ninth annual convention. Vancouver. 105pp, illus. *OTURS/RSK. This conference immediately preceded the Calgary conference of western labour (see no. 803) and discussed many of the same issues, including the proposal to sever connections with the international unions.

710 **Canada, Royal Commission.** Report of Commission...to enquire into industrial relations with a minority report and a supplementary report. Ottawa: Kings Printer. 28pp. *OTU Hann 3027. Printed as a supplement to the *Labour Gazette* July 1919.

711 **(Canadian Council of Agriculture.)** The farmers' platform: official text. (?Winnipeg). (c1919). 8pp.

*MWPA/UFM 22.

712 **Canadian Council of Agriculture.** A new national policy: memorandum on the farmers' platform presented before the national Liberal convention in Ottawa on August 5. Winnipeg. (4pp). ACGL/PDg.CCA AEPAA/Inf. file Alta.Pol.II.

713 **Canadian National Union of Ex-Servicemen.** Constitution. (?Toronto). (c1919). 8pp. *OOL

714 **Canadian Workers Federation of Returned Soldiers** and Sailors. Constitution, by-laws, rules and regulations, July 1919. 16pp. *OOL

715 **Communist Party of Canada.** Programme (and) May Day. (Toronto). (1p), broadside. Distributed April 1919, perhaps through Canada Forward or the SDPC.

716 **Conner, James McArthur.** Public ownership. Toronto: Independent Labor Party. 10pp. *OKQS OTURS/RSK. Demand for public ownership of railroads, steamships, mines, forests, fisheries, factories, telegraph and telephone, water and lighting, cold storage.

717 **Cooke, A.E.** The high cost of living: its causes and its cure. A sermon. Vancouver: First Congregational church. 12pp. *BVAUS/Mac.39Bf.27.

718 **Defense Committee.** The Winnipeg general sympathetic strike May-June 1919: trial by jury destroyed by stampede forty-five minute legislation - workers arrested and rushed to penitentiary to smash strike - leading lawyers, members of employers' committee of 1000 - engaged by federal government to prosecute workers. Strike - arrest - trials - penitentiary. Winnipeg. 276pp. *MWPA/Russell 2 OHMA1800 NSWA OTURS/RSK Hann 2686 Peel 2688.

(719) **Definitions of collective bargaining:** statement by certain unions relating to the Winnipeg general strike. OTV, not found. Hann 2616.

720 **Dominion Labor Party.** The new political party. Brandon. (6pp). *OTURS/RSK. Following the proposal of the Winnipeg farmers' convention for a new political party.

721 ------ Reconstruction program for Canada. Winnipeg. (4pp). *MWPA/RvIvens 1 OOA/Woodsworth 14 SSA/G26.1.

722 **Drummond, Lawrence.** The sheet anchor: national labor unions in Canada. Montreal: L'Oeuvre des Tracts. 16pp. *OHMA2149 OOL OTURS/RSK. 'Quebec will yet prove to be the sheet anchor of civilization' (Lord Shaughnessy, 1919). Strongly against international unions, but pro-church.

723 **Fraser, Dawn.** Songs of Siberia and rhymes of the road. Halifax: Eastern. 83pp. NSHPL OTP *T. Not, however, the swimming champion, as the National Library seems to think.

724 **Gallacher, Wm. and J.R. Campbell.** Direct action.
Winnipeg: One Big Union. (c1919). 7pp. *MWPA/Russ-
ell 2 OTURS/RSK.

725 **Good, W.C.** Production and taxation in Canada from
the farmers standpoint. Toronto: J.M. Dent. xviii,
133pp. *MWP Hann 2623.

726 **Hall, R.P.** The only way out: extinguishable legal
tender and banking reform. If the burden of interest
charges are removed wages will be doubled. What we
have lost by borrowing in other countries. Toronto:
R.A. Craig. 80pp. *OOAL Hann 2624. Includes chapters on labor's burden, how wages may may be increased
etc. 'If I could influence organized labor...I would
advise political action.'

727 **Hallam, Mrs W.T.** (ie.Lilian Gertrude). Slave days in
Canada. (Toronto): Canadian Churchman. 15pp. AEU
OHM QMBM SRL *OTP.

728 **Hamilton Trades and Labor Council.** Hamilton labor
directory, 1919. Hamilton. 76pp. *OOAL Hann 2625.
Directory of unions and secretaries, of all trades and
labor councils in Canada with names and addresses of
secretaries, Ontario provincial conference boards,
international union organizers in Canada, Hamilton
Independent Labor Party organized 15th June 1907;
Independent Labor Party of Ontario.

729 **Hatheway, W. Frank.** Labor's just and reasonable demands; a lower tariff to reduce living cost and regulation of cold storage. Prompt decrease in high profits. Should not their demands be granted? A review
of what Australia and other countries have done and
what Canada must do. St John. 13pp. *NBPL Hann 2628.

730 **Hunt, J.D.** Present electoral system condemned. (Edmonton): United Farmers of Alberta. (c1919). (4pp).
*MWPA/UFM 22.

731 **Independent Labor Party of Toronto.** Constitution.
Toronto. (c1919). (4pp). *OKQS.

732 **International Association of Machinists.** Printed let-
ter signed by P. Bengough revoking the charter of
Lodge 777 because of its adherence to the One Big
Union. Vancouver. (1p). *OOA/Bengough 4.

733 **International Union of Steam and Operating Engineers**
(AFL) Local 690. (By-laws) approved as amended 1 May
1919. Peterborough. (4pp). *OPET/Gainey 5.

734 **Julian, T.E.** Aims of the strike leaders as set forth
in the report of proceedings of the western Canada
labor conference held at Calgary, Alberta, March 13,
14, 15, 1919. Vancouver. 15pp. BVIP *OOAL. Almost
entirely excerpts from the report with a brief linking
commentary and a few antipathetical notes at the end.

735 **King, W.L. Mackenzie.** The four parties to industry.
Address before the Empire Club of Canada at the King
Edward hotel, Toronto, March 13th, 1919. (Toronto):

(Empire Club). 32pp. *OHMA2965 Hann 2629.

736 **Labor Church.** Labor church Sunday school: lesson outlines. (Winnipeg). (4pp). *OOA/Woodsworth 14.

737 **(Labor Party.)** Public ownership of government. Winnipeg: (Labor Party). (1p), broadside. *MWPA/Manning 1
Actually public ownership of utilities.

738 **Labor Party of Canada.** Constitution and by-laws,
section of the province of Quebec, adopted by the
convention held in Montreal, November 3rd, 1917:
amended...1918. Montreal. 14pp plus 15pp French
text. *HI Uncat. Box C150.

739 **Labor Representation Political Association.** Manifesto:
to the workers and citizens of Canada. Toronto.
(c1919). (4pp). *E

740 **Lear, Walter Edwin.** Labour laws; or the rights of
employer and employed. Toronto: Law Books. 32pp.
*OTURS Hann 2630.

741 **Lenin, Trotzky, Platten, Zinoviev and Rakovsky.** The
manifesto of the Moscow international. Montreal:
Educational Press. 12pp. *BVAUS/WB39f.16 OTURS/RSK
Pamphlet no. 2; pamphlet no. 1 not traced.

742 **Lenin, Nicolai.** The Soviets at work. A discussion
of the problems faced by the Soviet government of
Russia after the revolution...Program address before
the Soviets, April 1918. Published in this form with
forward *(sic)* and paragraph headings added by Anna
Louise Strong by the Seattle Union Record Publishing
Co. Vancouver: Vancouver Trades and Labor Council.
39pp. OTP *MWPA/RvIvens 4 and 5 (4 copies) OOA/
Woodsworth 6.

743 **Lumberworkers Industrial Union of the One Big Union.**
Constitution and by-laws adopted January 1919, amended
July 1919. Vancouver. 33pp. *BVAUS/Mac.33f.7.

744 **McKinney, Mrs.** The farmers' opportunity: speech at
the UFA convention, Edmonton, January 22nd, 1919.
Calgary: Non-Partisan League. 24pp. *MWPA/Salton.

745 **Maclean, J.S.** Condemned from the dock: a burning indictment of capitalism. Winnipeg: Western Labor News.
24pp. *BVAUS/WB43f.11a MWPA/RvIvens 4 OTURS/RSK.
Account of trial, sentence and verbatim report of the
final speech by John Maclean at Edinburgh, 1918.

746 **Manitoba Grain Growers Association.** Constitution as
revised January 1919. Winnipeg. 24pp. *MWPA/UFM 22.

747 ------ Taxed to death: something that is with a returned soldier on his homestead from dawn till night
every day. Winnipeg. (c1919). (2pp), broadside.
*MWPA/UFM 22.

748 **Marx, Karl.** Capital: a critique of political economy:
the process of capitalist production edited by Frederick Engels. Vancouver: Political Economy Club.
192pp. BVIP BVIPA OTU *BVAUS/Mac.38f.15 MWPA/RvIvens

2 and 3 (4 copies) OHMA1854 OTAR Hann 2634. Comprises mainly the first nine chapters of vol.1 of *Capital* plus the 32nd chapter, together with an extract from *A contribution to the critique of political economy*.

749 **Marx, Karl and Frederick Engels.** Manifesto of the Communist Party. Authorized English translation edited and annotated by Frederick Engels. Vancouver: Whitehead Estate. 59pp. BVIP *BVAUS/Mac.31f.6 and 38f.15 MWPA/Brigden 7 and RvIvens 4 OTURS/RSK. Whitehead Library no.1.

750 **Marx, Karl.** Value, price and profit addressed to working men. Vancouver: Whitehead Estate (c1919). 78pp. BVAU BVIP *MWPA/Russell 1 Hann 2635. Whitehead Library no. 5.

751 ------ Wage-labor and capital: with an appendix by Frederick Engels, translated by J.L. Joynes. Vancouver: Whitehead Estate. (c1919). 60pp. MWU *BVAUS/ Sp.HB301 M39.1919 OTURS/RSK.

752a **Mathieu, O.E.** La question sociale. Prince Albert: Patriote de l'Ouest. 31pp. *OOAL SSUS Peel 2676. Includes: L'église amie de l'ouvrier; L'église a fondé les premières associations ouvrières; Les devoirs de l'état envers les ouvriers etc.

752b ------ The social question. Prince Albert: Patriote de l'Ouest. 26pp. ACU OKQ QQL.

753 **Mavor, James.** Open letter to Sir Thomas White, acting prime minister of Canada. Toronto. (4pp). *BVIP OTURS/Mavor 37. Regarding the proposed forced sale of Doukhobor lands to provide land grants to returning soldiers.

754 **Methodist Church in Canada.** Christian churches and industrial conditions: a summary of the findings of leading churches in Canada, Great Britain and the United States on present day industrial conditions; together with the report of the Canadian Royal Commission on Industrial Relations. Toronto: Dept of Evangelism and Social Service. 12pp. *OOL

755 **Moncton Amalgamated Central Labour Union.** Moncton's Labor Day celebrations, September 1, 1919: souvenir programme. Moncton. 33pp. *OOL

756 **National Liberal Convention.** The double game as played by the big interests: religious prejudice a favorite pastime. 'Divide your opponents into groups and thus you conquer them' is the rallying cry of special privilege. Ottawa. 20pp. *OOAL.

757 **Neighbourhood Workers Association.** From war to peace: annual report, 1919. Toronto. 23pp. *OKQS.

758 **O'Boyle, Wm. P.** Christ or Bar Abbas? A series of lectures on social reconstruction. (Vancouver): Knights of Columbus. BVIV *BVAUS/Mac.31Af.32. 'The keynote of the program outlined is the substitution of an aristocracy of service...in lieu of aristocracy of

money or politics.'

759 **One Big Union.** Constitution and laws of the One Big Union. Vancouver. (4pp). *AEPAA/Farmilo 4 BVAUS/ Mac.33f.7 MWPA/RvIvens 7 OOA/Bengough 4. Signed by V.R. Midgley, Secretary.

760 ------ Industrial organization of labor in Great Britain. Vancouver. (4pp). *MWPA/Salton and RvIvens 7 OOA/Bengough 4. Inside title: The temper of British labor by Leland Olds. Bulletin no. 5.

761 ------ Manifesto of the One Big Union. Vancouver. 2pp, mimeo. *MWPA/RvIvens 7.

762 ------ One Big Union: Bulletin No. 1. Vancouver. (4pp). *MWPA/RvIvens 7 OOA/Bengough 4 and Censor 605. Hann 2785. These bulletins issued immediately after the Calgary conference.

763 ------ One Big Union or ---? Vancouver. (1p). *MWPA/RvIvens 7 OOA/Bengough 4. Bulletin no.4.

764 ------ The origin of the One Big Union: a verbatim report of the Calgary conference, 1919. Winnipeg. 87pp. *MWPA/Russell 2 OHMA1922 OTURS/RSK Hann 2750.

765 ------ The question of the six-hour day. Vancouver. *MWPA/RvIvens 6 and 7 OOA/Bengough 4 and Censor 605. Hann 2786. Bulletin no. 2.

(766) ------ Revolutionary industrial unionism. MWPA Hann 2487. Not found. Perhaps a US edition.

767 ------ Tentative outline of industrial organization. Vancouver. (1p). *MWPA/RvIvens 6 and 7 OOA/Bengough 4 Censor 605. Bulletin 3.

768 ------ Workers take notice: government recognises One Big Union. Toronto. (1p). *OOL microfiche 138/10.

769 **Ontario.** The labour legislation of Ontario, a survey. Toronto: Kings Printer. ii, 20pp. *OTP.

770 **Ontario Labor Party.** Manifesto for the provincial elections October 20th, 1919. Toronto. (1p), broadside. *OTPB/Buckley.

771 **The People's Anti-Graft League of Canada.** (Winnipeg). *OOA/Censor 637. Referred to as being sent to the Censor 18 September 1919, having been apparently distributed at a meeting of the Ex-Soldiers and Sailors Labor Party of Canada, Winnipeg Branch, 1 September. Not now in file.

772 **Peoples Church.** The Peoples' Church, Brandon, Manitoba. A.E. Smith, Minister. Brandon. (8pp). *OTURS/ RSK. Sets forth the need for an agency to be called The Peoples' Church 'or some other suitable name'.

773 **Price, E.M.** Industrial occupation of women. Unpublished MA thesis, McGill University. 86pp.

774 **Provisional Council of Soldiers' and Workers' Deputies of Canada.** Comrade soldiers and workers: - (?St Cath-

arines). (2pp), broadside. *OOA/Censor 605. Distributed in St Catharines. Begins 'This is the third manifesto..' (see no. 682).

775 **Reed, John and A.R. Williams.** Shall socialism triumph in Russia. Edmonton: Socialist Party of Canada. 15pp. *OTURS/RSK. Contains: On intervention in Russia by Reed and The red funeral of Vladivostock by Williams. Back cover has Platform of the SPC.

776 **Rossett, Joshua and William Hard.** Kolchak, autocrat and tyrant. The actual story of Kolchak and his methods, told by an American official recently returned from Siberia. (with) Anti-Bolsheviks and Mr Spargo. Vancouver: Socialist Party of Canada. 22pp. *BVAUS/ Mac.30Af.2a. OTURS/RSK Hann 2627.

(777) **Smith, A.E.** Industrial and economic reorganization from the Christian viewpoint. OTV, not found. Hann 2645.

778 **Smith Jones** (presumably pseudonym). The panacea for the crisis: a rally call to unite. Much in little tell you how *(sic)*. np. 29pp. *SSA/McNaughton H9. Perhaps a US publication.

779 **Social Democratic Party of Canada.** The Russian constitution. (?Toronto). 20pp. *OTURS/RSK.

780 ------ Victims of capitalism. Toronto. (2pp), broadside. *OTURS/RSK. Mainly on the famine in India.

781 **Social Service Council of Canada.** The community survey, a basis for social action: A. The urban and industrial community: B. The rural and agricultural community. Toronto. 19pp. *OTP.

782 **Socialist Labor Party.** The Russian Soviet Republic of Workers and Peasants. Who and what are the Bolsheviki? np. (4pp). *OOA/Censor 605 Hann 2646. Distributed extensively in London, Ont, but ? a US publication.

783 **Socialist Party of Canada.** Causes of industrial unrest. Winnipeg. (4pp). *MWPA/RvIvens 5.

784 ------ On the job: being a statement of the socialist position on the industrial question. Winnipeg. (4pp). *OOA/Censor 602 Hann 2792. Leaflet no. 7.

785 ------ A reply to the press lies concerning the Russian situation. Edmonton. *OTURS/RSK has cover only.

786 ------ The shame of being a scab. The following is a 'sample' of the 'Bolshevik' propaganda at the Archangel front. (Vancouver). (2pp), broadside. *OOA/ Censor 602. Described as being circulated under cover of *The Red Flag* May 1919 in North Battleford.

787 ------ Trades unionism. Winnipeg. (4pp). *OHMA Leaflet no. 8. Described in OOA/Censor 602 as being written by J. Harrington. A police report also says '10,000 printed'. (Not present in OOA/Censor).

788 **Somerville, Jas.** International Association of Machinists: circular letter addressed to Canadian members generally. Moose Jaw: International Association of Machinists. (4pp). *AEPAA/Farmilo 5 OOA/Bengough 4. Two articles reprinted from the district bulletin and a third designed to be published 'but on account of the general tie-up in Winnipeg, same could not be printed.' Critical of the OBU.

789 **Southam, W.M.** Industrial unrest. Read before the Commission on Industrial Relations sitting at Ottawa June 13th, 1919. Ottawa: Citizen. 15pp. BVIP OTP *OOAL. Espousing land value taxation as recommended by Louis F. Post in the USA.

790 **Stevenson, J.A.** Protection does not help new countries. (Winnipeg): Canadian Council of Agriculture. (4pp). ACGL/PDg.CCA AEPAA/Inf.file Alta.Pol.II.

791 **Tchicherin, W.W.** (printed Tschitscherin). Russia's answer to charge of terrorism. (?Winnipeg): (?Socialist Party of Canada). (4pp). *MWPA/RvIvens 5.

792a ------ Soviet Russia to President Wilson. A letter reproduced in the Toronto *Daily Star* January 25, 1919. (Toronto): np. (4pp). *OTURS/RSK.

792b ------ The Russian Soviet republic speaks to President Wilson. (?Winnipeg): (?Western Labor News). 4pp. *MWPA/RvIvens 5.

793 **Thompson, Bram.** Canada's suzerainty over the west: an indictment of the Dominion and Parliament in Canada for the national crime of usurping public lands of Manitoba, Saskatchewan and Alberta. Toronto: Carswell. 42pp. ACU BVAU OKQ *SSA/G104.2 Peel 2682.

794 **United Brotherhood of Carpenters and Joiners of America.** Trade rules and by-laws, Local 1779, Calgary, Alberta. Calgary. 14pp. *T.

795 **United Farmers of Alberta.** How to organize and carry on a local of the UFA. Calgary. (c1919). 48pp. *SSA/G291.16 Peel 2683.

796 ------ Objects. (Calgary). (c1919). (1p), mimeo. *SSA/G291.31.

797 ------ Resolution re political action passed by UFA annual convention, January 1919. (Calgary). 2pp, mimeo. *SSA/G291.26.

798 **United Farm Women of Alberta.** re: young people's work through junior branches. Calgary. (2pp), mimeo. *SSA/G311.6. Bulletin no. 1.

799 **United Farm Women of Ontario.** Equal opportunity for all – special privilege for none. Oakwood (Ont). (1p) mimeo. *SSA/G310.3.

800 **Wallace, W.B.** The housing problem in Nova Scotia; an evil, its growth and its remedy. Halifax. 19pp. *NSHDS/F4.

801 **Western Labor News.** The Russian constitution: Constitution (Fundamental law) The Russian Socialist Federated Soviet Republic. Winnipeg. 8pp. *MWPA/Rv
Ivens 5.

802 ------ Western convention report: western Canada labor
conference held at Calgary, Alberta, March 13, 14, 15,
1919. Winnipeg. 6pp. *AEPAA/Farmilo 2 OOA/Bengough
4. (see also no. 764).

803 **Williams, Albert Rhys.** 76 questions and answers on
the Bolsheviks and the Soviets. Vancouver: Trades
and Labor Council. (c1919). 48pp. *MWPA/Russell 1
and RvIvens 2 and 5 SSA/McNaughton H9 OTURS/RSK.
Second title: The Bolsheviks and the Soviets.

804 **Williams, Francis Fenwick.** The Winnipeg general strike
New York: Peoples Print. (2pp), broadside. *T.
Reprinted from *The Liberator*, July 1919.

805 **Winnipeg Defence Committee.** News letter: Defence
claims Crown offered witness $500.00 to give false
testimony. Winnipeg. 5pp, mimeo. *OOA/Woodsworth 14.
Dated 17 December 1919.

806 **Winnipeg General Strike.** Rex v. Ivens, Johns, Russell
et al charged with seditious conspiracy. Typescript
of evidence in 4 volumes, 1,496pp plus (19pp) index
in *OTURS/Woodsworth 48-51.

807 **Wood, H.W.** Political action in Alberta. Winnipeg:
Grain Growers Guide. (1p), broadside. *OTURS.

808 **Woodsworth, J.S.** Re-construction from the viewpoint
of labor. Winnipeg: Dominion Labor Party. 15pp.
AEU BVIP *OHMA2397 OTURS/RSK. Peel 2689. Reprinted
from *The Western Labor News*.

809 **Workers Educational Association of Toronto** and District.
WEA Session 1919-20. Prof. R.M. MacIver, Prof. Pelham
Edgar, Principal W.L. Grant, Prof. W.S. Milner, Mr A.J.
Glazebrook, Mr E.J. Pratt. Toronto. (6pp). *OOL

1920

(810) Anderson, Harley C.E. A brief outline of the principles and purpose of 'socialism'. Vancouver: np.
BVIP, not seen. Perhaps an anti-socialist tract.

811 **Anstey, Frank.** Red Europe. Vancouver: Industrial
History Club. 160pp. BVIP BVIV MWU *BVAUS/WB39f.16
MWPA/Russell 1 OTURS/RSK Hann 2657. Anstey was an
Australian and this was written in Melbourne.

812 **Ashplant, Henry B.** Counterfeit money and the pursuit
of righteousness. One of a series of short studies
in currency, and industrial unrest in the body politic.
London (Ont). 8pp. *OTURS/RSK.

813 **Ashplant, Henry B.** The gold standard challenged.
(London). (c1920). (4pp). *OTURS/RSK. Selections
from his 'Orthodox profits.'

814 **Bax, Ernest Belfort.** The criminal court judge and
the odd trick. Vancouver: Socialist Party of Canada.
BVIP *BVAUS/Mac30Af.2a. Hann 2658. Two articles:
the odd trick relates to the moral basis of socialism.

815 **Bland, Salem Goldworth.** The new Christianity or the
religion of the new age. Toronto: McClelland and
Stewart. 168pp. *OTMCL.

816 **Bölsche, Wilhelm.** The evolution of man. Vancouver:
Whitehead Estate. (c1920). 102pp. MWU OHM *BVAUS/
WB40f.3a, lacking title page.

817 **Boomer, Mrs H.A.** Something about the National Council
of Women of Canada. London (Ont): National Council of
Women of Canada. 12pp. *SSA/McNaughton H19.

(818)**British Columbia, Dept of Agriculture.** The co-operative farmers' institutes of British Columbia. Victoria: W.H. Cullin. 12pp. Revd edn. Not seen.

819 **Bucharin, N.** Communism and capitalism: a review of
capitalism and the cause of its collapse. The advent
of communism, its claim of the people's right to self-
determination and the emancipation of the workers
through a proletarian dictatorship. Victoria: Victoria
Printing and Publishing. (c1920). 7pp. BVIP *OTURS/
RSK.

820 **Canada, Dept of Labour.** Information respecting the
Russian Soviet system and its propaganda in North Am-
erica. Ottawa. 18pp. *BVAUS/WB42f.25a OOAL OTAR/
1920/73. See no. 853 for reply. Lists as socialist
organizations the following: Socialist Party of Canada,
International Bible Students, One Big Union, Labour
Church, Russian Socialist Group, Ukrainian Socialist
Group, Finnish Socialist Group, Ukrainian Dramatic
Society, Ex-Soldiers and Sailors Labour Party, Union
of Russian workers, Zluka (Ukrainian), Spujna (Polish)
Bulgarian Bolshevists, Jewish Bolsheviki Party, Socialist Revolutionary Group, Anarchist Communists and
Communist Labour Party. Considering the ommissions
their information would seem to be not too reliable.

821 **Canadian Council of Agriculture.** How to reduce the
cost of living. Lower customs duties in Canada would
mean lower prices for food and clothing - revenues
raised by direct taxation would mean justice for common people. (Winnipeg). (4pp). *ACGL/PDg.CCA AEPAA/
Inf.file Alta.pol II MWPA/Salton

822 ------ Making money for the shareholders. Profits,
wages and protection involved in the Canadian textile
industry - a mill which was not built for the glory
of God. Winnipeg. (4pp). *ACGL/PDg.CCA AEPAA/Inf.
file Alta.pol II MWPA/CCA 3.

823 ------ Where ought the revenue to come from? An

answer to the Canadian manufacturer's false cry:
'Where will the revenue come from?' (Winnipeg).
(4pp). *ACGL/Pdg.CCA AEPAA/Inf.file Alta.pol II
MWPA/Salton.

824 **Canadian 'Hands Off Russia' Committee.** Fellow-workers:
Toronto. (1p), broadside letter. *OTURS/RSK. On the
allied intervention in Russia.

825 ------ Hands off Russia! Toronto. (2pp). *OTURS/
RSK.

826 **Charpentier, Alfred.** Dans les serres de l'aigle:
historique de l'emprise du trade-unionisme américain
sur le mouvement ouvrier au Canada. Montréal: Action
française. (c1920). 32pp. OOU OTY QMBM *OKQ.

827 **Coaker, W.F.** (compiler and editor). The history of
the Fishermen's Protective Union of Newfoundland; containing the records of the Supreme Council since the
union's inception, and other matter of interest to
members of this great organization. NFSM *OONL Hann
2660.

828 **Crerar, T.A.** Mr Crerar replies to all charges against
United Grain Growers: speaking to his own constituents
at Basswood he scathingly denounces the campaign of
misrepresentation and cowardly insinuations carried
on by a discredited government. Winnipeg: United
Grain Growers. 12pp. *OOA/Spencer.

829 ------ On new national policy: viewpoint of former
Minister of Agriculture on some of the outstanding
national problems. (?Calgary): Canadian Council of
Agriculture. 8pp. *AEPAA/Inf.file Alta.pol II MWPA/
CCA 3.

830 **Deachman, R.J.** Deachman before the Tariff Commission:
a destructive criticism of the fallacies of protection.
Calgary: The Westerner. 30pp. OTP *ACGA/Coote 10.

831 **Desmond, Gerald.** The struggle for existence. Vancouver: Socialist Party of Canada. (c1920). 16pp.
*BVAUS/Mac.30Af.2a MWPA/Russell 1.

832a **Dixon, F.J.** Dixon's address to the jury in defence
of freedom of speech and Judge Galt's charge to the
jury in Rex v. Dixon. Winnipeg: Defence Committee.
126pp. ACG BVIP MWU OKQ OOL OONL OOP *MWPA/Russell
1 and 2 and Brigden 7 OHMA1801 OTURS/RSK. Peel 2703
Hann 2661.

832b as above but printed for the Dominion Labor Party.
96pp. MWU SRL *T.

833 **Dobbs, James E.** Equality of opportunity. Toronto:
Indepndent Labor Party of Toronto. 9pp. *OKQS

834 **Dominion Labor Party.** Manitoba provincial platform
adopted April 10th, 1920. Winnipeg. (1p), broadside. *OTURS/RSK.

835 **The Emporium Co'y Limited.** Food department: the co-
operative store. Vancouver. (c1920). (8pp). *T

836 Engels, **Frederick.** Socialism utopian and scientific.
Vancouver: Whitehead Estate. (c1920). 95pp.
BVIP MWU *BVAUS/Mac38f.15 and Young MWPA/Russell 1
and RvIvens 4 OTAR/CPC27 OTURS/RSK.

837 **Federated Labor Party.** Manifesto in connection with
British Columbia provincial election to be held December 1st, 1920. Federated Labor Party platform.
Vancouver. (4pp). *OOA/Woodsworth 10 and 37. Signed
by Thos. Richardson, W.R. Trotter and J.S. Woodsworth.

838 **Geeson, John R.** The development in the relations be-
tween government and the labor movement during the war.
Unpublished BD thesis, University of Alberta. Undated.
*AEUS/Undated BD2.

839 Healy, W.J. How much does the west pay? The question
of the tariff taxation levied upon the prairie provinces and how it was once dealt with. (Winnipeg):
Canadian Council of Agriculture. 4pp. *ACGL/PDg.CCA
AEPAA/Inf.file Alta.pol II.

840 **Hogue, Georges.** Appel aux ouvriers par un ouvrier;
les avantages des syndicats catholiques, une confédération internationale, constitution et règlements.
Montréal: L'Oeuvre des Tracts. 16pp. *OOAL.

841 **Independent Labor Party of Manitoba.** Constitution
and platform. Winnipeg. (4pp). *MWPA/Dixon 1.
Adopted 23 December 1920.

842 **Independent Labor Party of Ontario.** Constitution and
by-laws. Toronto. (4pp). *OTURS.

843 ------ Declaration of principles, constitution and
by-laws: as adopted in Hamilton, July 2nd, 1917 and
amended in London, April 3rd, 1920. Toronto. 16pp.
*OKQS. Loosely inserted page of amendments from
Welland convention, 1921.

844 **Independent Labor Party of Toronto.** Constitution.
Toronto. (c1920). (4pp). *OTURS.

845 **Industrial Workers of the World.** Comparisons are
odious to labor skates and grafters (and) The contrast.
Vancouver. (c1920). (2pp), broadside. *BVAUS/IWW.
Printed in the USA and additionally printed in Canada
'adopted by the membership of the Vancouver branch' etc.

846 **Irvine, William.** The farmers in politics. Toronto:
McClelland and Stewart. 253pp. *ACGL MWP Peel 2715.
Foreword by Salem Bland.

847 **Labor Church.** Hymns and songs. Edmonton. (c1920).
(4pp). *AEPAA/Brown 6 OTURS/RSK. Twelve hymns and
songs including A call to arms; These things shall be;
The red flag; The people's banner etc.

848 **Labor Educational Association of Ontario.** A great
voluntary organization. Toronto. (2pp). *OPET/
Gainey 1.

849 **Leckie, Peter T.** Economic causes of war. Vancouver:

Socialist Party of Canada. 132pp. *AEPAA/Inf.file
Alta.pol II BVAUS/Mac30Af.2b and Young OKQS OTURS/
RSK SSA/G173.2. Hann 2667. Reprinted from the *West-
ern Clarion* March-November, 1920.

850 **Lenin.** The idea behind the Russian social revolution.
Lenin interviewed by Colonel Robins. Toronto: Workers
Educational League. (c1920). (1p), broadside. *OTURS/
RSK.

851 **Lumber and Camp Worker's Industrial Union** of the One
Big Union. Constitution and by-laws adopted January
1919, amended January 1920. Vancouver. 40pp. *BVAUS/
Mac33f.7.

852 **Manitoba Labor Party.** Platform. Winnipeg. (c1920).
(1p), broadside. *MWPA/Dixon 1.

853 **Martens, L.** Information respecting the Russian Soviet
system and its *alleged* propaganda in North America.
Montreal: Educational Press. 15pp. OKQ *OTURS/RSK.
Issued in reply to no. 820 above. Martens was the
USSR representative in its New York bureau.

854 **Massey, Alice Vincent.** Occupations for trained women
in Canada. London and Toronto: J.M. Dent. 94pp.
BVAU NSHPL OH OHM OKQ OTMCL *OOP Hann 2672.

855 **Musselman, J.B.** How to form incorporated co-operative
locals. Regina: Saskatchewan Grain Growers Association.
12pp. *SSA/G34.38. Pamphlet no. 14.

856 ------ New provincial political platform. (Regina):
Saskatchewan Grain Growers Association. 4pp. *SSA/
G34.46. (2,000 printed).

857 **Non Partisan League.** Grain growers and the Nonpartisan League. Saskatoon: (c1920). (4pp). *SSA/G28.5.

858 **Nova Scotia Teachers' Union.** Constitution. (Halifax):
(c1920). (2pp). *OOL.

859 **O'Donoghue, J.G.** Legal opinion on certain stated
questions submitted by the Executive Council of the
Trades and Labor Congress of Canada. Toronto: Trades
and Labor Congress of Canada. 11pp. *OOL Hann 2674.
The questions are of sedition, seditious conspiracy,
picketing and strikes.

860 **One Big Union.** Constitution and laws as amended at
the Port Arthur convention, September 1920. (Vancouver). (4pp). *BVAUS/Mac33f.7 OOA/Woodsworth 10.
Amended August 1923, 16pp *MWPA/Russell 2 and December
1930, 21pp. *MWPA/OBU.

(861) ------ A historical sketch. BVAUS, not found. Hann
2654.

862 ------ Report of proceedings, first semi-annual convention of the One Big Union. (Winnipeg). 27pp,
mimeo. *OTURS/RSK. Held in Winnipeg 26-29 January.

863 ------ What is the OBU? Vancouver. (4pp). *BVAUS/
Mac33f.7 MWPA/Russell 1. Mainly constitution.

864 **Ontario Labor College.** To the workers of Ontario.
Toronto. (1p). *E. The objects of the college.

865 **Pritchard, W.A.** W.A. Pritchard's address to the jury
in the Crown vs. Armstrong, Heaps, Bray, Ivens, Johns,
Pritchard and Queen (R.B. Russell was tried previously)
indicted for seditious conspiracy and common nuisance,
fall assizes, Winnipeg, Manitoba, Canada 1919-1920.
Winnipeg: Defense Committee. 219pp. ACG BVIPA MWU
OKQ OPAL SSU *BVAUS/Mac34f.15 MWPA/Russell 1 and 2
and Brigden 7 OTURS/RSK Peel 2736 Hann 2675.

866 **Ridley, Hilda.** A synopsis of woman suffrage in Canada.
np. (c1920). 21pp. MWP OH *OTP.

867 **Ryder, W.S.** Canada's industrial crisis of 1919. Unpublished MA thesis. University of British Columbia.
i, 55pp.

(868) **Saint-Martin, Albert.** T'as menti. Montréal: Parti
socialiste. 40pp. OPAL QMBN.

869 **Saskatchewan Grain Growers Association.** Report of
managers of agricultural co-operative associations
held at Regina 16-17 March, 1920. Regina. 29pp.
*SSA/G34.53.

870 **Smith, Alexander.** Effect of third parties on public
opinion after class idea subsides. United Farmers or
Patrons of Industry in Canada from 1890-1896-1900.
The equal rights movement in 1891. Ottawa: Modern.
8pp. *OOAL.

871 **Smith, A.E.** Group government. (Brandon): np. (8pp).
*OTURS/RSK. On a farmers and labor party.

872 **Socialist Party of Canada.** Declaration of principles.
Vancouver. (c1920). (1p), broadside. *BVAUS/Steeves
5-7.

873 ------ Manifesto. Vancouver. 43pp. *BVAUS/Mac30A
f.2b OTURS/RSK SSUS Hann 2681. Fifth edition (the
1st published in 1909) containing also the preface
to the fourth edition.

874 ------ Platform and constitution with a brief sketch
of the evolution of society. Vancouver. 48pp. *SSUS

875 **Stevenson, J.A.** Profiteering: protection two in one.
Examples from evidence before the cost of living commission reveal close relation between tariffs and profits. (Winnipeg): Canadian Council of Agriculture.
(4pp). *ACGL/PDg.CCA AEPAA/Inf.file Alta.pol II.

876 **J.A.S.** (ie. J.A. Stevenson). Proportional representation. A truly democratic form of voting for government - just what it means and how it works. (Winnipeg): Canadian Council of Agriculture. (c1920). (4pp).
*ACGL/PDg.CCA AEPAA/Inf.file Alta.pol II.

877 **Stevenson, J.A.** Where the farmer touches city labor.
(Winnipeg): Canadian Council of Agriculture. (4pp).
*ACGL/PDc.CCA MWPA/Salton 8.

878 **Telford, S. and Andrew Green.** The need for a labor
party: the common people want a new world. (Toronto):
Ward 5 Independent Labor Party. (4pp). *OKQS.

879 **Trades and Labor Congress of Canada.** Annual interview
with the federal cabinet. Ottawa. 8pp. *OOA/CUC223.
Immigration, right to organize, 8 hour day etc.

880 **Trueman, W.H.** Russell trial and labor's rights: opin-
ion. Examination and statement of law and review of
Mr Justice Metcalfe's charge to the jury, in trial of
R.B. Russell, Winnipeg, December, 1919. Winnipeg: np.
31pp. OOP *BVAUS/Mac34f.15 MWPA/Russell 1 OOL OTURS/
RSK Hann 2683.

881 **United Farmers of Alberta.** Provincial platform and
declaration of principles. Calgary. (c1920). (2pp).
*ACGL/PDf.1 ACGA/Smith 5 SSA/G291.36.

882 **United Farmers of Manitoba.** Let us get together!
(Winnipeg). (c1920). (4pp). *MWPA/Salton.

883 **United Farm Women of Alberta.** Working hints for local
unions. Calgary. (c1920). 16pp. *SSA/G311.4.
Includes history and plan of work etc.

884 **United Farm Women of Manitoba.** Doors of opportunity
open to Canadian women. Winnipeg. (c1920). (1p).
*SSA/G312.14.

885 **Veblen, Thorstein.** On the nature and uses of sabotage.
Vancouver: Socialist Party of Canada. 26pp. *BVAUS/
Mac30Af.2a. Not a handbook but a history. Includes
SPC platform.

886 **Winnipeg Labor Defense Committee.** A comparison:
Judge's charge to jury. Metcalfe in The King vs R.B.
Russell, seditious conspiracy, Winnipeg, December,
1919. Cave in The King vs. Burns, 1886, Central Crim-
inal Court, London, England. Winnipeg. 16pp. *BVAUS/
Mac34f.15 OOA/Woodsworth 20 OTURS/RSK.

887 **Woodsworth, J.S.** The first story of the Labor Church
and some things for which it stands. An address in
the Strand Theatre, Winnipeg, April 5th, 1920. Winnipeg: Labor Church. 16pp. BVAU MWU *MWP OHMA1824
OKQS OOA/CCF326 SSA/G171.3. Address given after the
funeral of Wm. Iven's son.

888 (------) The King vs. J.S. Woodsworth: indictment for
publishing seditious libels, six counts, and speaking
seditious words. Winnipeg: The Defense Committee.
14pp. OPAL *OHMA2882 OKQS OTURS/RSK SSA/McNaughton
H31. Peel 2755. When the words complained of included those of the prophet Isaiah.

889 ------ War. Clippings from a war-time scrap-book.
Winnipeg: Labor Church. (c1920). 16pp. BVIP *BVAUS/
Mac43f.17 MWPA/CCF39 OHMA1823 SSA/G171.10.

890 ------ Where the baby came from: for the girls and
boys. Winnipeg: Winnipeg Labor Church. (c1920).
(4pp). *OOA/Woodsworth 37.

891 **Zinovieff, G.** N. Lenin: his life and work. Toronto: OBU General workers unit. (c1920). 48pp. *BVAUS/ WB38f.14a.

1921

(892) Ashplant, Henry B. The market price of gold. Not found. Advertised 1921 as 'now available'.

893 **Brotherhood of Railway Carmen of America.** Proceedings of the fourteenth convention, Massey Music Hall, Toronto, August 8th, 1921. Toronto. 7pp. *OTPB/Buckley. For first day only. Contains speeches by J.W. Buckley, James Simpson etc.

894 **Canadian Council of Agriculture.** Canada compared with Great Britain: in proportion to population and accumulated wealth Canadians bear heavier financial burdens than the motherland. Winnipeg. (4pp). *MWPA/CCA3.

895 ------ Co-operative wheat pool: wheat marketing agreement. Winnipeg. (4pp). *ACGL/PDg.CCA MWPA/CCA3

896 ------ Hits tax-payer in two ways. Winnipeg. (4pp). *ACGL/PDg.CCA.

897 ------ The 1921 budget. Finance minister has ingenious way of increasing tariff...rate of exchange not sympathetic to trade balance. Winnipeg. (4pp). *ACGL/PDg.CCA.

898 ------ Painted ships on painted ocean. Government shipbuilding fiasco already has cost Canadian people over seventy million dollars...End is not yet. Winnipeg. 4pp. *MWPA/CCA3 OOA/Woodsworth 12.

899 ------ Premier Meighen's London speech: comparison of Prime Minister's statements with facts reveals fallacy and inadequacy of old-time tactics. Winnipeg. (4pp). *ACGL/PDg.CCA.

900 ------ Railway burden means taxation. Winnipeg. (4pp) *MWPA/CCA3.

901 ------ Sales tax hits the poor man. An examination of the principal feature of the federal government's budget for 1921-22. Winnipeg. 4pp. *OOA/Woodsworth 12.

902 ------ Speakers handbook. Winnipeg. 36pp. *ACGL/ PDg,CCA MWPA/CCA3.

903 ------ Try-outs in taxation. Government tries income taxes, business profits, luxury and now sales taxes... Income tax has come to stay and must be chief source of revenue. Winnipeg. 4pp. *ACGL/PDg.CCA OOA/ woodsworth 12.

904 **(Canadian) Labor Party.** Labor Party platform. (Brandon). (4pp). *OTURS/RSK.

905 **Canadian Labor Party.** Minutes of convention to organize Canadian Labor Party, Winnipeg, week of August
22nd. Toronto. (1p),broadside. *OOA/CLP photocopy.
Called by James Simpson: opening session 24 August
includes platform.

906 ------ Ontario section: programme and standing orders
as amended July 1st, 1921. Toronto. 11pp. *OKQS.

907 ------ Programme and standing orders. Toronto. (4pp)
Includes convention. *E.

908 **Communist Party of Canada.** Manifesto of the Communist
Party of Canada regarding the federal election. To
the workers of North Winnipeg. Winnipeg. (1p), broadside. *OOA/Woodsworth 10.

909 ------ The 21 points: submitted to the Socialist
Party of Canada by the Communist Party as a basis for
union and admission of the Socialist Party of Canada
to the Third International. (?Toronto). 3pp.
*BVAUS/Smith CP. Apparently distributed to all members
of the Socialist Party, but this copy a typescript.

910 **Cook, D'Arcy George.** Western radicalism and the Winnipeg strike. Upublished MA thesis, Brandon. 67pp.
Note on sources p.1. *OHMA.

911 **Crone, Kennedy.** A primary *(sic)* on labor organization
in Canada. Montreal: Fifth Sunday Meeting Association
of Canada. 8pp. *OOL.

912 **Dennison, L.E.** Facts and figures. A reply by Typographical Union no. 91 to advertisements published
by the Toronto Typothetae, appearing in the public
press of Toronto during May and June 1921. Toronto:
Typographical Union. 22pp. *OOL OTURS/RSK Hann 2688.
On the printers strike.

913 **Edwards, Henrietta Muir** (comp). Legal status of women
in Alberta as shown by extracts from Dominion and provincial laws. (Edmonton): Government of Alberta.
80pp ? not complete. *New York Public Library. Marked
'2nd edn'. The first edition was of 2,000 copies in
1917; not found, but see 395 above.

914 **Gordon, C.W.** To him that hath: a novel of the west
today by Ralph Connor. New York: George H. Doran:
Toronto: McClelland and Stewart. 291pp. *OTP. Based
on the Winnipeg general strike.

915 **Griffin, Watson.** Workmen and farmers. np. 63pp.
*SSUS/Shortt. Largely on protection and free trade.

916 **Independent Labor Party.** Declaration of principles
of the Edmonton branch. Edmonton. (4pp). *AEPAA/
Brown 6. Note on this copy: 'Mostly E.B.'s compiling
about 1921.'

917 ------ Independent Labor Party's appeal to all labor
for support. Edmonton. (1p), broadside. *AEPAA/
Brown 6.

918 **Independent Labor Party of Ontario.** Official call to

the fourth annual convention which meets in Welland
on Friday and Saturday, March 25th and 26th, 1921.
Toronto. (1p),broadside. *OTPB/Buckley. Signed by
Buckley and Jos. T. Marks.

919 **Independent Political Action (Association).** Tentative
platform: convention to be held in Rosetown, Thursday
May 26th, 1921. (?Saskatoon). (4pp). *SSA/G93.4.

920 **International Stereotypers and Electrotypers Union** of
North America. The maple leaf souvenir: twentieth
annual convention 18-23 July 1921, Toronto. Toronto.
72pp. *OOL. Includes Labor legislation in Canada by
Tom Moore; The 8-hour day and the 40-hour week by P.M.
Draper etc.

921 **Labor Representation Committee.** Manifesto, federal
elections, December 6, 1921. Toronto. (4pp). *OTURS

922 ------ Workers, why unemployment? Toronto. (c1921).
(4pp). *OTURS

923 **Lefeaux, W.W.** Winnipeg-London-Moscow: a study of Bolshevism. Winnipeg: Canadian Workers Defense League.
77pp. ACG AEU BVIP OKQ OONL SRL *BVAUS/Mac34f.15
OHMA1778 OTAR/CPC 26 OTURS/RSK Peel 2780 Hann 2693.
Lefeaux was assistant to defence counsel in the Winnipeg trials and as a result of the evidence determined
to visit the Soviet Union on his own to try and answer
the question 'What is Bolshevism: What are Russian conditions?'

924 **Liberal Party.** Speakers handbook: economy, entrench-
ment, reform. Ottawa. 23 pamphlets bound together.
Includes the Farmers Party platform proposed by the
Canadian Council of Agriculture. *OHMA992.

925 **Macdonald, A.R.** An open letter to the workingmen and
women of West Peterboro. Ex Vice-president of the
Dominion Trades Congress speaks out: reasons why Mr
Gordon is entitled to the support of labor. Ottawa.
(?Liberal Party). (4pp). *OOAL

926 **Master Printers Association of Ottawa.** Five facts:
facts about the so-called forty-four hours week.
Ottawa. 12pp. *OOL. See also 912 above.

927 **Mills, Margery.** Women's part in the organization.
(?Toronto): (United Farm Women of Ontario). (c1921).
(4pp), mimeo. *SSA/G310.13.

928 **One Big Union.** Learning our lesson. Winnipeg. (4pp).
*MWPA/Russell 2. Bulletin 3, reprinted from an edit-
orial in the bulletin, 8 October 1921.

929 **Parlby, Irene.** Progress or reaction? Ottawa government's attitude towards needs of Canadian people con-
trasted with the aims and aspirations of the farmers'
movement. Calgary: United Farmers of Alberta. (4pp).
*ACGA/Coote 17 and Smith 15 OTURS SSA/G291.17.

930 **Partridge, E.A.** National wheat marketing. (?Sintaluta)
(c1921). (3pp). *SSA/G174.6

931 **Partridge, E.A.** The present crisis in Parliament.
(?Sintaluta). (c1921). (1p), broadside. *SSA/G174.4

932 **Raymond, A. Pauline.** Gathered sheaves from the National Council of Women. Calgary: National Council of
Women. 134pp. AEU BVIPA NSHPL OH OOP *ACGL Peel 2790.

933 **Social Service Council of Canada.** Co-management experiments in Canadian industry. Toronto. 24pp. *OOL
Hann 2694.

934 **Socialist Party of Canada.** Federal election 1921:
Manifesto no.1. Vancouver. (4pp). *BVAUS/Steeves 5.

935 ------ What's the matter with Canada? Vancouver.
(c1921). 4pp. *BVAUS/Steeves 5-7

936 **Staples, Melville H.** (ed). The challenge of agriculture: the story of the United Farmers of Ontario.
Toronto: Morang. 197pp. *OONL. Includes lists of
officers of the Dominion Grange, Farmers Association
and United Farmers.

937 **Stephenson, C. and Gabriel Deville.** Two essays on
history. Vancouver: Socialist Party of Canada. 16pp.
*BVAUS/Mac.30Af.2a and Young.

938 **Toronto Labour Party.** May day manifesto. Toronto.
(4pp). *E.

939 **Toronto Typographical Union.** Agreement between Toronto Typographical Union no. 91 and the Master Printers' and Publishers Association of Toronto to take
effect June 1st, 1921. Toronto. 4pp. *OTPB/1921
Agreement. See 912 above.

940 **United Farmers of Alberta.** Alberta plan of co-operation between groups spreading. Calgary. (4pp).
*ACGA/Coote 17 ACGL/PDf.1.

941 ------ Co-operation between organized democratic
groups. Calgary. (2pp). *ACGA/Coote 17.

942 ------ Group organization a dominating issue in federal elections. Calgary. 4pp. *ACGA/Coote 17 ACGL/
Pdf.1.

943 ------ Group organization and co-operation between
groups. Calgary. 7pp. *ACGA/Coote 17 and Smith 5
*SSA/G291.40.

944 ------ How groups function in Manitoba legislature.
(Edmonton). (c1921). (2pp). *ACGL/PDf.1

945 ------ Party system failure as business proposition.
Calgary. (4pp). *ACGA/Coote 17.

946 ------ Political awakening of the Canadian people
feared by reactionaries of both parties. Calgary.
(4pp). *ACGL/PDf.1 SSA/G291.41.

947 ------ Present electoral system condemned. (Calgary).
(c1921). (4pp). *ACGA/Smith 5 ACGL/PDf.1.

948 ------ The UFA and the provincial government. Calgary. 6pp. *ACGA/Spencer 2.

949 United Farmers of Manitoba. Draft platform. (Winnipeg). 7pp. *SSA/G314.7.

950 ------ Handbook of practical work. Winnipeg. 51pp. *MWPA/UFM 22.

951 ------ The nine of power: a word to the members of the key group of every United Farmers' local in Manitoba. (Winnipeg). 4pp. *SSA/G314.9.

952 ------ Provincial platform accepted in their annual convention in Winnipeg, January 11-13, 1921. (Winnipeg). 7pp. *MWPA/UFM 22 OOA/Coldwell 59.

953 **United Farmers of Ontario.** By-laws. Toronto. 19pp. *SSA/G292.1.

954 **United Farm Women of Alberta.** Calgary rest centre. Calgary. (1p), mimeo. *SSA/G311.20. Crèche and rest rooms for farm women.

955 **Wilson, R.N.** Our betrayed wards; a story of 'chicanery, infidelity and the prostitution of trust'. Ottawa. 40pp. *AEU BVIPA. The North American indians and their relations with the government.

956 **Workers Party of Canada.** (Manifesto): to the workers of Canada. Toronto. (4pp). *OTURS/RSK. The first national manifesto of the Communist Party.

1922

957 **Ashplant, Henry B.** The market price of wheat. First in a series of short studies: currency, inflation and deflation. London(Ont). (c1922). (3pp). *OKQ OTURS/ RSK.

958 ------ The revolt of the silversmiths of Ephesus: a short study in history - ancient and modern - related to the United Farmers of Ontario and Independent Labor Party movement in Ontario. London. (c1922). 7pp. *OTURS/RSK Hann 2777.

959 **Brandon Teachers Association.** To the citizens of Brandon. (Brandon). (4pp). *OTURS/RSK. Regarding a proposal to cut the teachers pay by 25%.

960 ------ To the teachers of Manitoba. (Brandon). (4pp). *OTURS/RSK.

961 **Bryce, P.H.** The story of a national crime: being an appeal for justice to the Indians of Canada. Ottawa: J.Hope. 18pp. OTU *OOAL.

962 **Cascaden, Gordon.** Shall unionism die? Report on the 'Red' unions international congress held in Moscow, Russia: plans - division of workers of Canada and United States: and destruction of world-wide labor movement. Windsor: Industrial Union League of Canada. 96pp. AEU *MWPA/Russell 1 OTURS/RSK. Cascaden was

one of two Canadian delegates. He was later found
in the river with his feet roped together, rocks tied
round his ankles and a bullet in his head. The verdict was suicide.

963 **Confédération des Travailleurs Catholiques du Canada.**
Programme-Souvenir du premier congrès tenu à Montréal,
du 12 au 17 août 1922. Montréal: Imp. Populaire.
80pp. *OHMA2893 OOL. Contains: Le syndicalisme catholique et national par Edmour Hebert; Le cercle Léon
XIII par Edmond Lacroix; Historique du mouvement syndical catholique et national à Montréal par Gérard
Tremblay; Le syndicalisme catholique à Québec par X;
Notes historiques sur les syndicats catholiques et
nationaux de Hull, Chicoutimi, Trois-Rivières, Cantons
de l'Est, Lachine, Hawkesbury etc.

964 **Consulate-General of Japan.** Facts about Japanese in
Canada and other miscellaneous information. Ottawa.
50pp. *OTAR/1922/63. Hann 2700. Statistics on Japanese labour and immigration etc.

965 **Derry, Kathleen and Paul H. Douglas.** The minimum wage
in Canada. Chicago: Journal of Political Economy.
pp 155-188 and chart. *SSA/Dunning 34. A reprint
from Vol.XXX no. 2, April 1922.

966 **Honorary Advisory Council for Scientific and Industrial
Research.** Research and the problems of unemployment,
business depression and national finance in Canada.
Ottawa. 20pp. *OTAR. Pressing for the establishment of a National Research Council: 'Monopolies of
knowledge constitute one of the most powerful weapons
of trade today.'

967 **Ivens, W.** Labor the world over. Winnipeg: np. (4pp).
*MWPA/Salton. Reprint from *The North Star* of an address in the Labor Church, Winnipeg, 3 September 1922.

968 **Legere, Ben.** Canadian autonomy: another foolish slogan of the Workers Party. Winnipeg: One Big Union.
(c1922). 4pp. *BVAUS/Mac.33f.7 OTURS/RSK

969 **Maharg, J.A.** Manifesto on provincial political action.
Regina: Saskatchewan Grain Growers Association. (4pp).
*SSA/G34.43.

970 **No More War Committee.** For the people: to read, adopt
and distribute. Vancouver. (1p), broadside. *SSA/
McNaughton H23. Mostly quotations.

971 **One Big Union.** Crawling in at the back door. (Winnipeg). (4pp). *MWPA/Russell 2. Leaflet 4. An attack
on the Workers Party.

972 ------ The Knights of Labor, the A.F. of L. and the
One Big Union. Winnipeg. (c1922). (4pp). *BVAUS/
Mac.33f.7 Leaflet 2.

973 ------ Leaving the sinking ship. Winnipeg. (4pp).
*MWPA/Russell 2 Leaflet 3.

974 ------ The One Big Union: a historical sketch. Winnipeg. (c1922). *BVAUS/Mac.33f.7 Hann 2654. Leaflet 7

975 **One Big Union.** Will industrial unions suffice?
Winnipeg. (8pp). *OHMA1924 OTURS/RSK. Also issued
as 'Will industrial unionism suffice?' in MWPA/
Russell 2.

976 ------ The Workers Party and the One Big Union.
Winnipeg. 16pp. *BVAUS/Mac.33f.7 MWPA/Russell 1 and
2 OTURS/RSK. Hann 2706. The OBU view of the dispute.

977 **Ontario, Dept of Labour.** The Ontario advisory committee on unemployment. A job for every man, prosperity
for all. Toronto. 19pp. *OOAL OOL. An advertising
scheme reproducing posters, tables etc.

978 **Paynter, W.C.** Canadian money and progress. Tantallon
(Sask). 12pp. ACG *OOA/MacPhail 3 SSA/G150.1. Peel
2788. Proposing a Bank of Canada.

979 **School Reform League.** Rebuke gross injustice done
faithful public servants. Send former school board
members and those supporting them to deep oblivion...
vote for School Reform League candidates. Brandon.
6pp. *OTURS/RSK. See 959, 960 above.

980 **Social Service Council** of Canada. Industrial life
and immigration report. (Toronto). 28pp. *BVIP.

981 ------ The national guilds; syndicalism; the Soviet.
An impartial study of their politics and aims. Toronto. 27pp. *OOL Hann 2711.

982 **Street Railway Employees Unit of the OBU.** Constitution and by-laws as amended July 1922. Winnipeg.
27pp. *MWPA/Russell 1.

983 **Sue, Eugene.** The gold sickle, or Hena, the virgin of
the isle of Sen, a tale of Druid Gaul translated from
the original French by Daniel de Leon; (and) The brass
bell, or The chariot of death, a tale of Caesar's
Gallic invasion translated from the original French
by Solon de Leon. Winnipeg: One Big Union Bulletin.
xiv, 146pp. ACG OONL *T

(984)**Troop, G.R.F.** Socialism in Canada. Unpublished MA
thesis, McGill University. 121pp.

985 **United Farmers of Alberta.** Method of organization
for political purposes. (Calgary). (3pp), mimeo.
*SSA/G291.33.

986 **United Farmers of Manitoba.** Plan for provincial political campaign. Winnipeg. 8pp. *MWPA/UFM 22.

987 ------ The UFM outlook, August 1922. (Winnipeg).
4pp. *MWPA/UFM 22.

988 ------ Why the electors of Manitoba should support
the progressives. Winnipeg. (4pp). *MWPA/UFM 22.

989 **United Farmers of Ontario.** Their aims, their organization, their operation. Toronto. 8pp. *SSA/G292.9.

990 **United Farm Women of Ontario.** Origins and growth of
the UFWO. (?Toronto). (1p), mimeo. *SSA/G310.6

991 **Workers International Educational League.** An open letter to the striking printers and bookbinders: the open shop versus workers control of industry. Toronto. (c1922). (2pp), broadside. *OTURS/RSK.

992 **Workers Party of Canada.** Constitution of the Workers Party of Canada. Toronto. (c1922). 8pp. *OTAR/CPC 9.

993 ------ May day manifesto. Toronto. 4pp. *OTAR/CPC 21.

994 ------ Unemployed workers! Organized workers! Unite for your defence against capital! Winnipeg. (2pp), broadside. *OTAR/CPC 21.

995 ------ A united front of labor against the onslaught of capital. Winnipeg. 4pp. *OTAR/CPC 1.

1923

996 **Bennett, A.S.** Is the West worth while? A candid review of the economic problems of western Canada, and the urgent need for co-operative actions by the east and the west in the interests of national progress. (?Swift Current). 47pp. *ACGL Peel 2834.

997 **Bergen, N.J.L.** The Farmers Union of Canada: its origin, basis, structure, principles, methods, obligations and aims. Wetaskiwin (Alta). (10pp). *MWPA/Ivens 6.

998 **Canada, Dept of Labour.** Proposed amendments of Industrial Disputes Investigation act: disagreement between Senate and the House of Commons. Ottawa. 7pp. *OOAL.

999 **Canadian Labor Party.** Shall the bankers or the citizens rule the city of Edmonton? Edmonton. (4pp). *OOA/Farmilo 5. Bulletin 1.

1000 **Cooper, William.** Winnipeg Labor church university class. Synopsis of short studies in current social and economic evolution. Winnipeg: Labor Church. (8pp). *MWPA/CCF 39.

1001 **Dingle, Lloyd C.** The principle of conscientious objection. Unpublished (MA) thesis, McMaster University. (ii), 61pp. no biblio. *OHMA.

1002 **Doherty, Manning.** Address on the Sinclair (South Ontario) motion re industry of agriculture, Ontario legislature, Wednesday, February 28th, 1923. (Toronto): (?United Farmers of Ontario). 32pp. *OOP.

1003 **Dominion Labor Party.** Constitution, Brandon and District branch. (Brandon). (c1923). 12pp. *MWPA/Salton OTURS/RSK.

1004 **Ewart, John S.** Canada and British wars. Ottawa.

88pp. *BVAUS/Mac.43f.17 OOA/Underhill 63. Strongly
opposed to any Canadian involvement.

1005 **Fitzpatrick, Alfred.** The university in overalls: a
plea for part-time study. Toronto: Frontier College.
xvi, 184pp, illus. *OOA/Frontier 180 SSUS/Shortt
Hann 2663.

1006 **Independent Labor Party (Ontario).** Report of the 6th
annual convention, Brantford, March 30, 1923. Toronto.
4pp. *OOL

1007 **Kennedy, W.P.M.** (ed). Social and economic conditions
in the Dominion of Canada. Philadelphia: American
Academy of Political and Social Science. viii, 319pp.
*OTP. Includes: Canada's rural problem by W.C. Good;
Agricultural cooperation in the Canadian west by C.R.
Fay; The agrarian movement by M.H. Staples; Protect-
ion of workers in industry by Marion Findlay; The
labour movement in Canada by R.H. Coats; Unemployment
and organization of the labour market by Bryce M.
Stewart; Arbitration and conciliation in Canada by
R.M. MacIver; Political devleopments within the labor
movement in Canada by J.S. Woodsworth; select biblio.

1008 **(King, W.L. Mackenzie).** Catalogue of pamphlets, rep-
orts and journals in the library of the Rt. Hon. W.L.
Mackenzie King, Prime Minister of Canada: Laurier
House. Ottawa: Mortimer. 72pp. OONL *OOAL.

1009 **Labor Representation Political Association.** Workers
and citizens of Toronto. (Toronto). (1p), broadside.
*OTURS/RSK. Provincial election manifesto.

1010 **Lenin, Nikolai.** 'Left wing' communism: an infantile
sorder. Vancouver: BC Federationist. (c1923).
65pp. BVIP *BVAUS/Young OTAR/CPC. Hann 2600 and
2668.

1011 **Lumber Workers Industrial Union of Ontario of the** OBU.
Constitution and laws as amended January and December
1922. Sudbury. 21pp. *MWPA/Russell 1.

1012 **McPhail, Agnes.** Address to convention. (Toronto):
United Farm Women of Ontario. (c1923). 2pp mimeo
plus 1p covering note. *SSA/G310.15. Abbreviated.

1013 **Marx, Karl.** Two speeches by Karl Marx: Address to
the Communist League, 1850 and The inaugural address
of the International Workingmen's Association. Vancouver: Historical Research Bureau. 15pp. BVIP
*BVAUS/Sp.HX276, M2773A5 OTURS/RSK.

1014 **Marxian Educational League.** Socialism: food for manufacturing thoughts. Education a guide to working
class action. Toronto. (3pp), mimeo. *OTURS.
Course outline by W. Moriarty, T.J.Simons, W. Shainak.

1015 **Nova Scotia, Commissioner of Public Works and Mines.**
Report of commission on the hours of labour, wages
and working conditions of women employed in industrial
occupation. Halifax: Kings Printer. 28pp. *NSHP
Hann 3095.

1016 **One Big Union.** Why you should join the One Big Union. Winnipeg. (1p), broadside. *OOL. Leaflet 5.

1017 **Ontario.** Report of the accomplishments of the Dept of Labour and Health and outline of legislation to advance the rights of wage earners and to protect the interests of women and children enacted under the UFO-Labour government for the years 1920, 1921, 1922, 1923. Toronto: (Kings Printer). 36pp. *OTAR/1923/31.

1018 **People's Church.** The People's Church, Toronto, Ontario. Toronto. (6pp). *OKQS OTURS/RSK. Statement of intent to establish the church.

1019 **Reid, Mary William.** Works councils: do they offer a solution for the present day industrial problem? Unpublished MA thesis, University of British Columbia. ii, 107pp. biblio 103-107. *BVAUS.

1020 **Robson, J.W.** Our monetary system. Saskatoon: Farmers Union of Canada. (c1923). 31pp. SRL *ACGA/Spencer 1 SSA/G36.9.

1021 **Saskatchewan Grain Growers Association.** The Saskatchewan Grain Growers Association: it's origin and growth. Regina. 16pp. *SSA/G34.9.

1022 **Sheriff, Annie Bell.** Agricultural cooperation in Saskatchewan. Unpublished MA thesis, University of Saskatchewan. (iii), 130pp. *SSU.

1023 **Smith, A.E.** The People's Church, Brandon, Manitoba. A personal letter on divine healing. Brandon. (6pp). *OTURS/RSK.

1024 **Student Christian Movement of Canada.** Some Canadian questions: studies in preparation for the first Canadian national student conference, December 28-January 2nd, 1923. Toronto. 42pp. *OTP. Includes studies on farmers movements, industrial discord etc.

1025 **United Farmers of Ontario.** By-laws, 1923. Toronto. 20pp. *MWPA/UFM 22.

1026 ------ Direct legislation by means of the initiative, referendum and recall. Toronto. 4pp. *MWPA/UFM 22 SSA/G292.22.

1027 ------ Election campaign funds. Toronto. 4pp. *MWPA/UFM 22.

1028 ------ Keep the farmer representation intact. Toronto. 4pp. *MWPA/UFM 22 SSA/G292.23.

1029 ------ Political parties and government. Toronto. 4pp. *MWPA/UFM 22.

1030 ------ Proportional representation and the transferable vote in single member constituencies. Toronto. 4pp. *MWPA/UFM 22 SSA/G292.4.

1031 ------ Public schools in French speaking districts of Ontario. (Toronto). (c1923). (4pp). *OOA/Woodsworth 12.

1032 **Wood, H.W., Marion Sears and H. Higginbotham.** United
Farmers of Alberta President's address; United Farm
Women of Alberta President's address; Secretary's
report for the year 1922. (Edmonton): United Farmers
of Alberta. 16pp. *ACGA/Coote 7.

1033 **Workers Party of Canada.** Educational program. Toronto. (14pp), mimeo. *OTURS/RSK. Includes: The
class struggle; Trade unions as organs of struggle;
The process of awakening etc.

1034 ------ Manifesto of the Workers Party of Canada on
the immediate problems of Canadian labor. Toronto.
(4pp). *OTURS/RSK.

1035 ------ The press - agent or critic? Toronto: The
Worker. (4pp). *OTURS/RSK.

1036 ------ Program, constitution and resolutions. Toronto. (c1923). 19pp. *OOL OTURS/RSK.

1037 ------ Recommendations of the Constitution committee.
Toronto. 3pp, mimeo. *OTURS/RSK. Comprises amendments to the proposed constitution.

1038 ------ Report of the executive secretary presented
to the 2nd annual convention. Toronto. 7pp, mimeo.
*OTURS/RSK. Mainly a financial statement, but gives
details of travel of various members of the executive.
The last (unnumbered) page is on the party press.

1039 ------ Workers of Canada! Toronto. 4pp. *OTAR/
CPC 2. Refers to the eve of the Dominion trades and
labor congress and attacks by the Canadian Congress
journal on the WPC.

1040 **Young Communist League.** Program, constitution and
resolutions. Toronto. 20pp. *OTURS/RSK.

1924

1041 **Allied Trades and Labor Association.** Labor day annual, 1924. Ottawa. incomplete, 14pp only. *OOL
Hann 243.

1042 **Bolton, A.E.** The dawn of freedom for farm slaves.
(Saskatoon): Farmers Union of Canada. (c1924).
21pp, plus poem inside back cover. *SSA/G36.4.
Pamphlet 1: demand for a national banking system.

1043 **Bricklayers and Masons International Union.** Delinquent list, revised to December 1, 1923. Indianapolis. 142pp. *OPET/Gainey 2. Includes Canadians.

1044 **Canada, Privy Council.** Fair wages policy of the gov-
ernment of Canada as set forth in a report of the
Committee of the Privy Council, approved by H. E. the
Governor General, on the 7th June, 1922, amended 1924.
Ottawa. 8pp. *OOAL

1045 **Canada.** An old age pension system for Canada. Proceedings of a special committee appointed to make an inquiry into an old age pension system for Canada. Comprising the order of reference, the final report and the evidence given before the committee with certain papers relating thereto. Ottawa: F.A. Acland. 99pp, biblio. *OOAL. Includes memorandum from Tom Moore, Trades and Labor Congress; Railway Transportation Brotherhood and others.

1046 **Canada.** Report of a commission to inquire into the industrial unrest among the steel workers of Sydney, N.S., creating conditions which have occasioned the calling out of the active militia in aid of the civil power and their retention for a considerable period of time in the areas affected. Ottawa: Government Printing Bureau. 24pp. *MWPA/Russell 1 OOA/Forsey 8 Hann 3034.

1047 **Canada.** Report of proceedings at interview held in the office of the Postmaster General, Ottawa, on Thursday, September 11, 1924, between representatives of the Canadian Federation of Postal Employees, officials of the Post Office department and the Civil Service Commission: together with the reply of Hon. Charles Murphy, Postmaster General, to the requests made by the representatives of the Postal Federation. Ottawa: F.A. Acland. 35pp. *OOAL. Regarding the reinstatement of workers following the strike.

1048 **Canadian Council of Agriculture.** Debate on the Senate. Resolved that the Senate of Canada, being a non-elective, irresponsible chamber, tends to become reactionary and autocratic and ought to be abolished. Winnipeg. 7pp, mimeo. *Ottawa, Dept of Agriculture.

1049 **Canadian Labor Party.** The Forum book of song. Toronto: Forum Committee. 32pp. *OTURS/RSK. Includes: Precepts of the new social order and a note on the Forum movement in Canada.

1050 ------ Manifesto in connection with the British Columbia provincial election to be held June 20, 1924. Canadian Labor Party platform. Vancouver. (4pp), illus with portraits. *G 329.14 (71).

1051 ------ Minutes of the fifth annual convention held in the Labor Temple, Hamilton, March 22nd, 1924. (Toronto). (4pp). *OOA/Woodsworth 10. Vice-President - John MacDonald; Sec-Treas. James Simpson; Socialist and Fabian society - Wm. Moriarty; Labor party - A.E. Smith; TLC - J.W. Buckley etc.

1052 ------ Platform, Vancouver civic elections, December 10, 1924: Shall Vancouver citizens control their own city? Vancouver. (4pp). *BVAUS/Smith CCF and LP.

1053 **Communist Party of Canada.** Against imperialist war! - class war! 1914-1924. Toronto. (2pp), broadside. *OTURS/RSK.

1054 **Communist Party of Canada.** Draft constitution.
(Toronto). 24pp. *OTCPA. Two page introduction on
the First and Second Internationals omitted later.

1055 ------ For a farmer-labor party: for a workers and
farmers government: to the working farmers of Canada.
Toronto. (4pp). *OTURS/RSK. Farmer-labor leaflet 1.

1056 **Darby, A.E.** Some observations on farmers indebted-
ness and rural credits. Winnipeg: Canadian Council
of Agriculture. 19pp. OTV *ACGL/PDg.CCA MWPA/
Salton and CCA 3.

1057 **Dominion Coal Workers Relief Association.** Fifth
annual report, Glace Bay, N.S. for the year ending
February 29th, 1924. (Glace Bay). 72pp. *OOA/
Forsey 8.

1058 **Ephron, Harmon Saul.** A study of the internal workings
of the International Typographical Union during the
forty-four-hour strike. Unpublished MA thesis, University of Toronto. (i-vi), iv, 175pp. *OTUAR.
Reprints Toronto Progressive Club leaflet of 21 May
1923 'Thirty-two Judases in our midst' not otherwise
located.

1059 **Henderson, Rose.** Woman and war. Vancouver: Federated Labor Party. 23pp. *OTURS/RSK. Also published
in Winnipeg in 16pp, also OTURS/RSK.

1060 **Independent Labor Party** (Ontario). Report of the
7th annual convention, Toronto April 18, 1924.
Toronto. 4pp. *OOL.

1061 **International Typographical Union.** Souvenir, 69th
annual convention, Toronto, August 11-16, 1924.
Toronto. (38pp) plus many adverts., illus. *OTURS/
RSK. Includes: The early printers unions of Canada
by J. McArthur Conner; The modern Samson by W.R.
Trotter and others.

1062 **Kolarow, W.** Letter from the Executive Committee of
the Communist International to the Workers Party of
Canada. np. 2pp, mimeo. *OTURS/RSK. On WPC membership in the Canadian Labor Party, the Nova Scotia
strike etc. See also 1066 below.

1063 **Labour Party of Canada/Parti Ouvrier du Canada.**
Constitution and by-laws (Section of the province of
Quebec (bilingual). Montreal. 20pp plus 20pp.
*OOA/CCF 39 and Woodsworth 10. Contains the federal
programme, 1924.

1064 **Laidler, Harry W.** Canada shows how to manage electrical power. New York: League for Industrial Democracy. 12pp. *OOAL. Leaflet 1.

1065 **McCurdy, F.B.** Nova Scotia's right to live. (Halifax)
(?Halifax Herald). 16pp. *NSHD/J6.

1066 **MacDonald, J.** To the national convention of the
Workers Party of Canada; secretary's report. Toronto:
Workers Party of Canada. (6pp), mimeo. *OTURS/RSK

Deals with the Nova Scotia steel strike, Canadian Labor Party etc and refers to letter from Communist International (presumably 1062 above) and to reports from Bruce, Buck, Moriarty etc but the latter may have been given verbally.

1067 **Mackintosh, Margaret.** Government intervention in labour disputes in Canada. Kingston: Queens University. 30pp. *NSHDL/J4 OOL OTAR/1924/7. Hann 2724. Bulletin 47.

1068 ------ The social significance of child labour in agriculture and industry. Ottawa: Canadian Council on Child Welfare. 12pp. *OONL.

1069 **Mackintosh, W.A.** Agricultural cooperation in western Canada. Kingston: Queens University and Toronto: Ryerson. x, 173pp. *OONL Peel 2897.

1070 **One Big Union.** An appeal to the workers in the metalliferous industry. Winnipeg. (2pp), broadside. *OOL Hann 2725.

1071 ------ History of American trade unionism. Winnipeg. (c1924). 8pp. *OHMA1923.

1072 **Owens, R.C.** The peoples financial catechism. Edmonton: (Alberta Monetary Educational League). 48pp. *OTURS/RSK. In favour of the United Farmers of Alta.

1073 **Partridge, E.A.** Let us, the people of the west, build, own and operate a Hudsons Bay railway. Winnipeg: Grain Growers Guide. (c1924). 11pp. *SSA/G174.5, photocopy.

1074 ------ A people's road to Hudsons Bay: operation in the public interest or nothing. Winnipeg: Grain Growers Guide. (c1924). 8pp. *SSA/G174.2, photo.

1075 ------ The proposed people's Hudsons Bay railway company. Winnipeg: Grain Growers Guide. (c1924). 10pp. *SSA/G174.3, photocopy.

1076 **Patrick, T.A.** Our Senate problem and its solution. Yorkton. 19pp. BVIP MWU SSU *OOA/Woodsworth 13.

1077 **Peoples Church.** The Peoples Church, Toronto, Ontario. Declaration and precepts. Mr A.E. Smith, General Secretary. Toronto. (c1924). (4pp). *OTURS/RSK.

1078 **Pierce, H.C.** Our money system and what it is doing to us. (It sure is doing plenty). The remedy and how to apply it (inject gently to prevent shock). Dahlton (Sask). (c1924). 27pp. *SSA/G136.1 SSUS/CCF. Peel 2950.

1079 **Robson, J.W.** An economic remedy. Saskatoon: Farmers Union of Canada. (c1924). 8pp. *SSA/G36.5. Pamphlet 1: banking and deflation.

1080 ------ The economic travesty. Saskatoon: Farmers Union of Canada. (7pp). *OOAL SSA/G36.6.

1081 **Saskatchewan Grain Growers Association.** Some ways
in which the Saskatchewan Grain Growers Association
has helped the farmer: a partial record of its activities from 1901 to the present time. Regina.
26pp. *SSA/G34.11.

1082 **Schmidt, Emerson Peter.** The organization of labour
in Canada. Unpublished MA thesis, University of
Toronto. vii, 181 (182-192)pp. No biblio. *OTUAR.

1083 **Sinclair, Bertrand W.** The inverted pyramid. Boston:
Little, Brown. (viii), 339 pp. *T. Socialist novel
about lumber in BC.

1084 **Smith, A.E.** Education of the working class, by the
working class, for the working class. Toronto: Forum
Committee, Labor Temple. 8pp. *OTURS Hann 2727.

1085 **Trades and Labor Congress of Canada.** Memorandum on
immigration. Montreal. 8pp. *HI/Uncat. C300.

1086 **Waltherr, Joseph, Coy Nelder and William Bunting.**
Liberty, equality, fraternity. Three addresses delivered by employees of the Spanish River Pulp and
Paper Mills Ltd at the 8th annual President's Banquet. Sault Ste Marie: Spanish River Mills. 16pp.
*OTAR Hann 2723. Interesting solely for the qual-
ity of printing and design and as an example of
sycophancy.

1087 **Ward, John W.** The Canadian banking system. A simple
explanation of the banking and currency systems of
Canada. Winnipeg: Canadian Council of Agriculture.
16pp. *ACGL/PDg.CCA MWPA/CCA 3.

1088 **Whitton, Charlotte.** The immigration problem for
Canada. Kingston: Queens University. 33pp. *NSHD/
J4. Bulletin 48.

1089 **Wood, Louis Aubrey.** A history of farmers' movements
in Canada. Toronto: Ryerson. 372pp, index. *OONL

1090 **Woodsworth, J.S.** Speech on the address in reply to
the Governor General's speech, delivered in the House
of Commons on Tuesday, March 4, 1924. Ottawa: (Kings
Printer). 7pp. *SSA/G171.1.

1091 ------ Speech on the budget, delivered in the House
of Commons on Thursday, April 24, 1924. Ottawa:
(Kings Printer). 8pp. *SSA/G171.2.

1092 **Young Communist League.** Resolutions adopted at the
second national convention. Toronto. 36pp. *OTURS/
RSK.

1925

1093 **Allied Trades and Labor Association.** Souvenir program, Labor day 1925. Ottawa. 64pp, illus. *OOAL
Hann 243. Includes: The need for unification of

labor legislation in Canada by Tom Moore; The 8-hour day and 44-hour week by P.M. Draper; Unemployment by Wm. J. McDowell etc.

1094 **Associated Boards of Trade** of the island of Cape Breton. Memorandum with regard to the conditions presently existing in the coal and steel industries of the province of Nova Scotia, and suggestions for the relief of these conditions and the permanent betterment of these industries, submitted to the federal government on 2nd December, 1924, by a delegation from that province. (Halifax). 30pp. *OOA/Woodsworth 10 OOAL. Mainly on duties and imports, Canadian National purchases etc.

1095 **Buck, Tim.** Steps to power: a program of action for the trade union minority of Canada. Toronto: Trade Union Educational League. (ii), 62pp. BVAU BVIP OOAL OTP *AEPAA/Brown 6 OHMA2719 OTURS/RSK SSA/ G539.1. Hann 2721.

1096 **Canadian Labor Party.** Constitution of the Greater Vancouver Central Council of the Canadian Labor Party. Vancouver. (c1925). (1p), long broadside. *OOA/ Woodsworth 10.

1097 **Canadian Labor Party (Ontario section).** Minutes of the sixth annual convention held in the Labor Temple Toronto April 10 and 11, 1925. Toronto. 4pp. *E.

1097 **Communist Party of Canada.** Constitution. Toronto. (c1925). 19pp. *OKQS OTURS/RSK.

1098 ------ Draft constitution. (Toronto). (c1925). 9pp, mimeo. *OTAR/CPC 9f.9. Two copies, one of which has hand corrections.

1099 **Coote, G.G.** Speech on customs tariff on automobiles and motor trucks delivered in the House of Commons 16th March, 1925. Ottawa: F.A. Acland. 8pp. *ACGA/ Coote 14.

1100 **Coughlin, T.J.** Questions and answers on labor compensation for accidents in Canada. (?Ottawa): np. 36pp. BVIP *OOL Hann 2730.

1101 **Darby, A.E.** Currency and prices. Winnipeg: Canadian Council of Agriculture. 8pp. *SSUS/Can.Econ.

1102 **Dominion Grange Patrons of Husbandry.** Synopsis of proceedings, fifty-first annual meeting, Carls Rite hotel, Toronto, December 7th, 1925. (?Toronto). 8pp. *OTAR.

1103 **Farmers Union of Canada.** Constitution and by-laws. Saskatoon. 16pp. *SSA/G36.1.

1104 **Fay, C.R.** Agricultural co-operation in the Canadian west. London: P.S. King. (iv), 439-470pp. *OTP. Reprinted from *Co-operation at home and abroad*.

1105 **Fraser, Dawn.** Songs of Siberia and rhymes of the road. Glace Bay: Eastern. 229pp. *OTP. New and enlarged edition (see 723 above).

1106 **Good, W.C.** The death of the Progressive Party. (Ottawa). 4pp, mimeo. *OOA/Good 18. The Farmers Progressive Party, not the Conservative.

1107 ------ What's wrong with Parliament? (Ottawa). 5pp, mimeo. *OOA/Good 18.

1108 **Harding, Cyril and H.M. Bartholomew.** The grain commission exposed. Saskatoon: The Furrow. (c1925). 15pp. *OTURS/RSK.

1109 **Henderson, Rose.** Russia today: old Russia - the causes of the revolution; the significance of the Russian revolution; women and children under Soviet rule. Vancouver: Federated Labor Party. (c1925). 14pp. BVIP *SSA/McNaughton H9.

1110 **Irvine, William.** Efficiency and permanence of economic organization. (Toronto): United Farmers of Ontario. 10pp. *ACGA/Spencer 1.

1111 ------ Purchasing power and the world problem: Pamphlet no. 1: Capitalism, communism and credit. Calgary: Dominion Labor Party. 8pp. *SSUS/JL197.

1112 ------ Purchasing power and the world problem: Pamphlet no. 2: Social control of credit. Calgary: Dominion Labor Party. 16pp. *ACGL OOA/CCF310 and 539 SSA/G26.2 SSUS/JL197.

1113 **Keen, George.** Consumers cooperation: the way to success. Brantford: Cooperative Union of Canada. (4pp). *OOA/CUC223.

1114 **Mackintosh, W.A.** The Canadian wheat pools. Kingston: Queens University. 28pp. *NSHD/H2 Peel 2941. Bulletin 51.

1115 **One Big Union.** Let's pull together, fellow workers: the OBU behind the railroad shopmen. Winnipeg. (c1925). (4pp). *MWPA/Russell 2.

1116 ------ A solution to our problem. Winnipeg. (c1925). (4pp). *MWPA/Russell 2. Leaflet 6. Widely translated as Une solution de nos problèmes: La soluzione del nostro problema; Rešenje naših problema (Yugoslav): and En lösning av våra problem (Swedish).

1117 Ontario and Quebec **Conference of Typographical** Unions. Fourteenth annual meeting, Windsor, Ontario, June 25, 26, 27, 1925. (Hamilton). 20pp. *OOL. Dissolved in 1938.

1118 **Partridge, E.A.** The book a war on poverty - with which, to form this volume, is bound in, besides a preface, the contents of a previously published pamphlet entitled *A call to a politico-socio-economic conference,* re-appearing here under the caption - a call to conference. Sintaluta (Sask). (vi), xii, 225pp plus (226-240) left blank for notes. Frontispiece portrait tipped in. ACG AEU BVAU BVIP OKQ OONL OOP OOU OPET *MWP.

1119 ------ A call to a politico-socio-economic conference.

Sintaluta (Sask). 11pp. *SSA/G174.1.

1120 **Pierce, H.C.** A strong back and a weak mind. (Saskatoon): Farmers Union of Canada. 11pp. *SSA/G36.10.

1121 **Saskatchewan Grain Growers Association.** Does it pay to join the SGGA? Regina. (c1925). (5pp). *SSA/ G34.29.

(1122) **Sealey, W.O.** Make Canada prosperous: stop foreign capitalists. Not found.

1123 **Unemployed Association of Alberta.** Report of conference between the Unemployed Association of Alberta and the provincial government. Calgary. 8pp. *ACGL/ PDh2.

1124 **United Farmers of Alberta.** Declaration of principles unanimously adopted by the annual convention January 23rd, 1925. (Edmonton). (2pp), mimeo. *OOA/Spencer SSA/G291.37.

1125 ------ A few facts about the present administration of the province of Alberta and what it has accomplished. (Edmonton): (United Farmers of Alberta). (c1925). 8pp. *ACGA/Spencer 2.

1126 ------ The tariff issue and East Calgary: why the UFA is in politics. Calgary. 8pp. *ACGL/PDf1. Mainly on William Irvine's record.

1127 **V.U.W.A.** (?Vancouver United Workers Association). Inflation: what is it? (Vancouver). (c1925). 15pp, mimeo. *BVAUS/WB39f.27.

1128 **Williams, G.H., B. George and W.G.A. Gourlay.** Debt adjustment plan. Saskatoon: United Farmers of Canada (4pp). *OOA/Underhill 58.

1129 **Wood, H.W.** United Farmers of Alberta President's address, January 1925. Calgary. 8pp. *ACGA/Smith 15.

1130 **Woodsworth, J.S.** On the waterfront. With the workers on the docks at Vancouver - some observations and experiences. Ottawa: Mutual. 31pp. *BVAUS/Mac. 43f.20 MWP MWPA/Brigden 7 OHMA2398 OOA/CCF309 OTURS/RSK SSA/G171.7 SSUS/JL197. Includes inside back cover: Manifesto of the Independent Labor Party of Manitoba, federal elections, 1925.

1131 ------ Speech on national defence delivered in the House of Commons on Monday, May 18, 1925. Ottawa: F.A. Acland. 8pp. *SSA/G171.6.

1926

(1132) **Bennett, Annie D.** The local council of women of Regina. 64pp. Peel 2956. OTU not found.

1133 **Booth, Noel.** Dominion election 1926: the Labor Party does not want to take away your farm; it seeks to take the mortgage off. New Westminster: Labor Party. (4pp). *BVAUS/Smith CCF and LP.

1134 **Brownlee, J.E.** Five years of progress. Calgary: United Farmers of Alberta. 11pp. *ACGA/Smith 15.

1135 **Canadian Council of Agriculture.** National policies of the CCA as presented to the Dominion government April 21, 1926. Winnipeg. 11pp. *MWPA/CCA 3.

1136 **Canadian Labor Party.** Manifesto, general election, September 14th, 1926. Toronto. (4pp). *OKQS OOL OTAR/CPC21. Signed A.E. Smith & James Simpson.

1137 ------ Canadian Labor Party - Unity - Progress: minutes of the seventh annual convention (Ontario section) held in the Ritz hall, London, 2-3 April 1926. 14pp (in triple columns). *OOL OTURS/RSK. Executive included: A.E. Smith, President; Florence Custance, J.W. Ahlquist, John Macdonald, Morris *(sic)* Spector, James Simpson etc.

1138 ------ Municipal election 1927: Manifesto. Toronto. 4pp. *OTURS/RSK. (Dated 1926).

1139 ------ Over the top! Edmonton. (1p), broadside. *AEPAA/Farmilo 5. Bulletin 7. Other bulletins not found.

1140 **Carmichael, C.F.** and others. Canada: a call to work. (?Ottawa): National Council of Women of Canada. (c1926). 46pp. *OONL.

1141 **Carpendale, Maxwell.** Philosophy from a worker. Vancouver: np. 64pp. *BVAUS/Young. Pro-communist.

1142 **Cheng Tien-Fang.** Oriental immigration in Canada. PhD thesis, University of Toronto *OTUAR published under the same title: Shanghai: Shanghai Commercial Press, 1931. x, 306pp. ACU BVAU BVIP OKQ OOP QMG.

1143 **(Clarke, Joe).** Something to think over! When the 1920 increases were given Joe Clarke was not an officially nominated labor mayor - just a human being. Vote for Joe Clarke - the square dealer. Edmonton: Members of organized labor. (1p), broadside. *AEPAA/Farmilo 5. 'Perhaps you do not favor Joe Clarke personally but his fair wage record must count when you cast your ballot.' Marginal but irresistible.

1144 **Communist Party of Canada.** Election manifesto. 4pp. *OTAR/CPC21. Federal election.

1145 ------ Federal election and constitutional issue. Toronto. 4pp. *OOA/Woodsworth 10 OTAR/CPC21.

1146 **Coote, G.G.** The issues in the coming election. Calgary: (United Farmers of Alberta). 15pp. *ACGA/ Coote 4. Address at constituency convention 2 August.

1147 ------ Speech on proposed tariff reductions on automobiles and motor trucks delivered in the House of Commons 29 March 1926. Ottawa: F.A. Acland. 9pp. *ACGA/Coote 14.

1148 **Drummond, Robert.** Recollections and reflections of a former trades union leader. (c1926). *OOL, lacks title page, not found elsewhere. c312pp.

1149 **Fitzgerald, Maurice C.** The status of farm labour in Saskatchewan. Unpublished MA thesis, McMaster University. (iv), 105, 1-25 pp. No biblio. *OHMA.

1150 **Forsey, Eugene.** Economic and social aspects of the Nova Scotia coal industry. Toronto: Macmillan. 126pp. *OOA/Forsey 8.

1151 **Glace Bay Board of Trade.** Coal, steel and the Maritimes: an illustration of the disabilities under which the Maritime provinces labour: presented to the Dominion Board of Trade at the annual convention at St Johns, N.B. October 19th, 1926. Glace Bay. 15pp. *OOAL. Mainly on competition and transportation, but also gives 'A picture of Glace Bay without winter work.'

(1152)**Grant, Henry Clark.** The function of government in the cooperative marketing of farm products. Unpublished MA thesis, University of Manitoba. 91pp.

1153 **Heenan, Peter.** Speech on the Winnipeg strike of 1919 delivered in the House of Commons, Wednesday, June 2, 1926. Ottawa: F.A. Acland. 6pp. *MWPA/Russell 1.

1154 **Independent Labor Party.** Platform and manifesto. Vancouver. (c1926). (4pp). *BVAUS/Smith CCF & LP.

1155 **Labor News Stand.** Price list of working class literature. Edmonton. (4pp). *AEPAA/Inf.file Alta. pol.II. Lists magazines, papers, foreign language papers and books.

1156 **Labor Representation Political Association.** The declaration of labor, municipal elections 1926. Toronto. 4pp. *OTAR/CPC21. Candidates include John Macdonald, Tim Buck, A.E. Smith, Florence Custance and others.

1157 ------ Manifesto to the workers and citizens of north-west Toronto. Toronto. (2pp), broadside. *OTAR/CPC21.

1158 **Lawson, Margaret Ruth.** Some economic phases of minimum wage legislation in Ontario. Unpublished MA thesis, University of Toronto. 141, 1-3 pp. Biblio pp 1-3 at end. *OTUAR.

1159 **McCabe, Joseph.** Short talks on evolution and other lectures. Winnipeg: One Big Union. (c1926). 62pp. *BVAUS/Young (3 copies) MWPA/Russell 2 OTURS/RSK. Introduction (signed T.E.M.) records that the Winnipeg OBU Committee invited McCabe to lecture. The lectures were printed in the OBU Bulletin and are now reprinted in book form with three extra articles of special interest to labor.

1160 **MacGill, Helen Gregory.** The child in industry. (?Vancouver): Hospital Social Service. pp349-367. *BVAA. Reprinted from Vol XIII, 1926.

1161 **Nova Scotia.** Report of the Royal Commission respecting the coal mines of the province of Nova Scotia,
1925. Halifax: Kings Printer. 64pp. *OOA/Woodsworth
11 Forsey 8. Hann 3096. Known as the Duncan report.

1162 **One Big Union.** A call to action: to all workers on
the railroads of Canada. Winnipeg. (c1926). (4pp).
*MWPA/Russell 2.

1163 ------ How McLeod tried to sell out the Inverness
miners. (Winnipeg): (?OBU). (4pp). *MWPA/Russell 2.

1164 ------ The new conspiracy: Besco and district no.26,
UMW of A, believed to have entered into a pact to
provide scab coal and fire OBU miners. (Winnipeg).
(c1926). (2pp), broadside. *MWPA/Russell 2.

1165 ------ The truth about the coal miners strike: great
possibility of a coal famine this winter: autocratic
policy of the government creates serious situation.
Winnipeg. (2pp), broadside. *MWPA/Russell 2.

1166 **Owens, R.C.** The bridge to liberty: a plan to evolve
from the capitalist system to a co-operative system.
Edmonton. 38pp. *ACGL OTURS. Peel 2975.

1167 **Saskatchewan Grain Growers Association.** A quarter
century of progress: a partial record of the activities
of the SGGA from 1901 to the present time. Regina.
47pp. *SSA/G34.51 SSUS/Shortt. Peel 2986.

1168 **Simpson, James.** Canada's experiments in public ownership. London (Eng): The Labour Party. 23pp.
AEU SSU *OTURS/RSK. Hann 2742.

1169 **Smith, A.E.** Cold feet! Frozen! Bottled up! A
statement by A.E. Smith. (Fort Frances). (2pp).
*OTURS/RSK. Regarding the election in Fort Frances.

1170 **Stewart, Bryce M.** Canadian labor laws and the treaty.
New York: Columbia University Press. 501pp, biblio,
cases, index. *OONL. Labor section of the Treaty
of Versailles.

1171 **Stirling, Geo. F.** Mind your own business. (Saskatoon)
Farmers Union of Canada. 12pp. *SSA/G36.8 SSUS/
UFC. For cooperative marketing.

1172 **Thompson, Bram.** Constitutional issues of the election.
Regina. 15pp. *SSA/G104.3.

1173 **Veterans Publicity Bureau.** The disabled veterans red
book: dealing with facts the public ought to know; the
poppy tag day fund scandal. Local ex-soldiers suffer -
a tale of sordid graft and wasted funds; startling dis-
closures; told by unemployed disabled ex-soldiers.
Toronto. 11pp. *OTURS/RSK. 'The next issue will
expose the canteen fund fraud' - not located.

1174 **Wood, H.W.** UFA President's address, January 1926.
Calgary: United Farmers of Alberta. 8pp. *ACGA/
Smith 15.

1175 **Woodsworth, J.S.** Following the gleam. A modern pil-

grim's progress - to date! (Ottawa): np. 20pp.
BVIP MWU OTU *AEUS/CCF XIII-14 MWPA OOA/CCF198
and Woodsworth 37 SSA/G171.4 SSUS/JL197. Peel 2996.
Includes manifesto of the Independent Labor Party,
Manitoba elections, 1925.

1176 Woodsworth, J.S. The structure of society. np.
(c1926). (2pp), broadside. *SRA/CCF misc.

1927

1177 **Alberta Co-operative Wheat Producers.** The wheat
pool. (?Calgary). (8pp). *OOA/CUC223.

(1178) **Ashplant, Henry B.** Freedom and truth: an essay.
c1927. Advertised, but not found.

(1179) **Bailey, Arthur.** Co-operation in marketing with
special reference to the Canadian wheat pools.
Unpublished MA thesis, University of Manitoba. 38pp.

1180 **(Canadian) Farmers Educational League.** Manifesto.
(?Saskatoon). (4pp). *SSA/G198.2 Peel 3020.
Announces also a left-wing general convention to be
held in Saskatoon, July 12-14, 1927. G.H. Williams,
Secretary.

1181 **Canadian Labor Defence League.** Constitution, 1927.
Toronto. 6pp. *OTAR/CPC 11f.29. Amended 1932,
4pp. *OTURS/RSK. The League called itself Labor/
Labour and Defence/Defense in various combinations.

1182 **Canadian Labor Party.** Canadian Labor Party candidates
for South Vancouver municipal elections: to the electors of South Vancouver: municipal program. Vancouver. (4pp). *BVAUS/Smith CCF & LP.

1183 **Cohen, J.L.** Mothers allowance legislation in Canada:
a legislative review and analysis with a proposed
'standard' act. Toronto: Macmillan. (vi), 134pp,
biblio. *OOP.

1184 **Communist Party of Canada.** It is 13 years since war
was declared! Toronto. (1p), broadside. *OTAR/CPC
21. Calls for preparation for a general strike.

1185 ------ Lessons of British general strike. (Toronto).
(c1927). (4pp). *OTURS/RSK.

1186 ------ Manifesto against King's destroyers! Toronto.
(2pp), broadside, triple columns. *OTAR/CPC21.

1187 ------ Organize against war! Toronto. 4pp. *OTAR/
CPC21.

1188 ------ Wanted - recruits for the Communist Party!
Toronto. (2pp), Broadside. *OTAR/CPC21.

1189 **Davisson, Walter P.** Pooling wheat in Canada. Ottawa:
Graphic. 275pp, illus, tables. *OONL Peel 3015.

1190 **Fag** *(sic)*. Cogent facts: economic analysis of Great Britain, United States and Canada. Toronto: Canada Forward Research. 16pp. *E.

(1191)**Janes, Henry.** Industrial and craft unionism in Canada. Unpublished MA thesis, McGill University. ii,106pp.

(1192)**Latham, Allan Brockway.** The Catholic and national labour unions of Canada. Unpublished MA thesis, McGill University. 147pp.

1193 **MacPhail, Agnes.** Education for the new social order. An address delivered before the annual convention of the United Farmers of Alberta on January 20thm 1927. (Edmonton): United Farmers of Alberta. 6pp. *OOA/ MacPhail 4 SSA/G291.14.

1194 **Mine Workers Union of Canada.** Constitution, district no. 1. Calgary. 21pp. amended in 1927 *BVIPA.

1195 **Neighbourhood Workers Association.** Social services directory of Toronto. Toronto. 72pp. *OKQS.

1196 **Northwest Grain Dealers Association.** Serious charges made by pool director. Winnipeg. 7pp. *OKQS. The charges were of corrupt grading. (The NGDA was opposed to the pools.)

1197 **One Big Union.** Action front: miners rally their forces to fight Besco and the UMWA. (Winnipeg). (1p), broadside. *MWPA/Russell 2. See also 1164 above.

1198 ------ The A.F. of L. or the O.B.U.: which? Winnipeg: (c1927). (4pp). *MWPA/Russell 2. Leaflet 8.

1199 ------ Avis aux forestiers. Winnipeg. (c1927). (2pp), broadside. *MWPA/Russell 2.

1200 ------ Beware of the trap! An appeal to CNR machinists. (Winnipeg). (2pp), broadside. *MWPA/ Russell 2.

1201 ------ Moving forward backwards: craft unions sabotage the shorter-work week. Winnipeg. (4pp). *MWPA/ Russell 2.

1202 ------ Stop! Look! Listen! An appeal to Canadian workers. Winnipeg. (c1927). (4pp). *MWPA/Russell 2.

1203 ------ The U.M.W. red herring: keeping the miners contented with starvation wages. (Winnipeg). (2pp) broadside. *MWPA/Russell 2.

1204 ------ Why you should join the One Big Union. Winnipeg. (c1927). (4pp). *MWPA/Russell 2. Leaflet 5. Translated into French (Pourquoi vous devez vous joindre à la Grande Union); Finnish (Miksi teidän on liittyttävä One Big Union); Jugoslav (Zašto moraš priči velikoj zajedničkoj juniji?); and Swedish (Varför ni bör ingä i One Big Union).

1205 **Roper, Elmer E.** Personal stuff and Christmas greetings. Edmonton. 15pp. *ACGA/Smith 16.

1206 **Selekman, Ben M.** Postponing strikes: a study of the

industrial disputes investigation act of Canada.
New York: Russell Sage Foundation. 405pp, index.
*OONL.

1207 **Smallwood, J.R.** Coaker of Newfoundland; the man
who led the deep-sea fishermen to political power.
London (Eng): Labour Publishing. 96pp. NFSM *OONL.

1208 **Social Service Council of Canada.** The man out of
work: a report on and study of five hundred unemployed
men, submitted by the industrial life committee.
Toronto: Kings Printer. 31pp. *BVIP Hann 2754.

1209 **Socialist Party of Ontario.** Statement of principles.
Toronto. 3pp, mimeo. *OTURS.

1210 **Sun Yat Sen.** Program for the reconstruction of China.
Calgary: Kuo Min Tang (Chinese National League).
21pp. BVIPA *OTURS/RSK.

1211 **Toronto District Labor Council.** The official labor
day souvenir programme, confederation year 1927.
Toronto. 88pp, illus. *OTURS/RSK. Includes: The
shorter hour movement by James McArthur Conner;
Early trade unions and the law by J.L. Cohen; Labor's
banking and investment enterprises by Herbert A.
Spence etc.

1212 **Typographical Union and others.** Tentative program
for the stabilization of the printing industry in
Toronto. Toronto. (c1927). (1p). *OTAR/CPC21.
A nine-point program by three unions.

1213 **United Farmers of Alberta.** You see more of the game
from the bleachers than from the diamond: achievement
of the UFA in putting over the wheat pool and what
the success of the pool means to the business of
western Canada. (Calgary). 8pp. *AEPAA/Inf.file
Alta.pol II.

1214 **United Farmers of Canada.** Agricultural land policy.
Saskatoon. (c1927). (4pp). *BVAUS/Steeves 4-6.
SSA/G37.5.

1215 ------ Applications for reductions in the tariff to
be presented to the federal government and to the
Tariff Advisory Board. (Saskatoon). 8pp. *SSA/
G37.7 SSUS/UFC.

1216 **United Farmers of Manitoba.** Useful facts for many.
Winnipeg. 8pp. *ACGA/Smith 15 MWPA/UFM22.

1217 **Womens International League for Peace and Freedom.**
Aims: Canada and arbitration. Vancouver. (4pp).
*SSA/McNaughton H32.

1218 ------ Military training in Canadian schools and
colleges. Toronto. (4pp). *SSA/McNaughton H32.

1219 ------ War toys: a crime against children. Toronto.
(c1927). (1p), broadside. *SSA/McNaughton H32.

1220 ------ What can I do for peace? An appeal to teachers. Vancouver. (c1927). (4pp). *SSA/McNaughton
H32.

1221 **Womens International League for Peace and Freedom.**
World federation takes a stand on military training.
Vancouver. (c1927). (1p), broadside. *SSA/McNaugh-
ton H32. The world federation is of educational
associations.

1222 **(Wood, H.W.).** Annual Presidential address, 1927.
(Calgary): United Farmers of Alberta. 6pp. *ACGA/
Smith 15.

1928

1223 **Alberta Cooperative Wheat Producers Ltd.** Pooling
Alberta's wheat. Calgary. 64pp, illus. ACG AEP
OLU OOP OTU *SSUS/Shortt Peel 3049.

1224 **Alberta Federation** of Labor. Constitution and by-
laws. Edmonton. 20pp. *AEPAA/Farmilo 4.

1225 **Booth, J.F.** Cooperative marketing of grain in the
United States and Canada. Journal of Farm Economics.
Pp331-356. *SSUS/Coops. Reprinted from Vol.·X, no.2
July 1928.

1226 **Bradwin, Edmund W.** The bunkhouse man: a study of
work and pay in the camps of Canada, 1903-1914. New
York: Columbia University Press. 306pp, index.
*OONL.

1227 **Bryce, Peter H.** The value to Canada of the continental immigrants. (Ottawa): np. 56pp. *OOAL Hann
2755. Discusses emigrants, including Doukhobors,
but from economic and social view only.

(1228)**Burton, J.** Berry growers co-operative union of British Columbia. Unpublished MA thesis, University of
Alberta. i, 295pp.

1229 **Canadian Labor Party.** Fifth convention, Alberta section. Minutes. (Edmonton). 13pp, mimeo. *ACGA/
UMWA 4.

1230 **Communist Party of Canada.** Organizational and inner-
party problems. (Toronto). (c1928). 9pp, mimeo.
*OTAR/CPC9f.8.

1231 ------ Revolutionary greetings! (Toronto). (c1928).
7pp. *OTAR/CPC27. Given to new party members - has
what to read etc.

1232 ------ Thesis on cooperatives. (Toronto). (c1928).
5pp, mimeo. *OTAR/CPC9f.9.

1233 ------ Trade union thesis. (Toronto). 18pp, mimeo.
*OTAR/CPC9f.9.

1234 **Dysart, A.K.** Judge Dysart's decision in the Young
case. (?Winnipeg): (?OBU). (7pp). *MWPA/Russell 1
OOA/Woodsworth 10. Concerning wage rates under a
wage agreement not expressly included in a hiring
agreement.

1235 **Hull, J.T.** Co-operative education: a paper read at the international pool conference, Regina, June 1928 (and) What to read on co-operation. Winnipeg: Manitoba Wheat Pool. 24pp. *MWPA/Brigden 7 SSUS/Shortt.

1236 **Independent Labor Party.** Manifesto and platform, British Columbia provincial election, 1928. Vancouver. (4pp). *BVAUS/Smith/CCF & LP.

1237 **Labor Party of Toronto.** Manifesto, municipal elections, 1928. Toronto. 4pp. *OTAR/CPC21.

1238 **Logan, Harold A.** The history of trade-union organization in Canada. Chicago: University of Chicago Press. xiv, 427pp, biblio, index. *OONL.

1239 **Murchie, R.W., W.H. Carter and F.J. Dixon.** Seasonal unemployment in Manitoba. A report. Winnipeg: Legislative Assembly. 80pp. BVAU OOL OOP *MWPA/Brigden 7.

1240 **National Council of Women** (of Canada). Women of Canada. (Kingston). 8pp. *SSA/McNaughton H19.

1241 **One Big Union.** What is the OBU? Winnipeg. (8pp). *MWPA/Russell 2 Hann 2761. Not the same as 863.

1242 **Ontario, Dept of Agriculture.** Ontario farm service force: women's work on the land. Toronto. (c1928). (6pp). *OOL.

1243 **Patton, Harald S.** Grain growers cooperation in western Canada. Cambridge: Harvard University Press. xx, 471pp. *OTP Peel 3092. Harvard Economic Studies XXXII.

1244 **Roten Gewerkschafts-Internationale.** Protokoll über den 4. Kongress, abgehalten in Moskau vom 17. März bis 3. April 1928. Berlin: Führer-Verlag. *OTARS/CPC25. Contains pp 174-178 report by Comrade Buhay on Canada.

1245 **Saskatchewan Co-operative Wheat Producers.** Its aims, origin, operations and progress, June 1924 - January 1928. (Regina). 72pp. *SSA/G39. Pamphlet 1.

1246 **Smith, W.L. and others.** A series of articles reprinted from *The Farmers' Sun* on subjects to be discussed at the annual convention of the United Farmers of Ontario in Hygeia Hall, Toronto, December 4th-5th, 1928. (Toronto): (?United Farmers of Ontario). (16pp). *OTURS.

1247 **Society of Named Doukhobors.** Report: minutes of a meeting of sixty duly authorized delegates residing in the province of Saskatchewan, Canada, held in the vicinity of Kamsock, on the farm of Wasil (K)opoff, a Doukhobor, on the 27th June, 1928 with Michael Petrovitch Diakoff, in the chair and Evan Evanovitch Mahonin acting as secretary of the meeting. (Saskatoon). 5pp, mimeo. *OOA/Woodsworth 7. Regarding conscription, schooling, taxes etc.

1248 **Thompson, Bram.** Canada's national status: Canada's constitution 1867: subversive enactments of Parliament of Canada: Canada's constitution now a hotchpotch. Regina. 20pp. BVAU OTP *SSA/G104.1.

1249 **Toronto District Labor Council.** Official Labor day souvenir programme. Diamond jubilee year, 1928. Toronto. 108pp, illus. *OTURS. Includes: National and international activities of labor by Tom Moore; Triumph of British co-operators by James Simpson; Women's progress by Mary McNab; Lawyers and printers strikes by James McArthur Conner etc.

1250 **United Farmers of Canada.** Mainly for women. (Regina). 12pp. *OOAL SSA/G37.47.

1251 ------ Your money's worth. Saskatoon. (c1928). 19pp. *SSA/G37.105 SSUS/UFC.

1252 **(Wood, H.W.) and Margaret Gunn.** Annual presidential address 1928 (and) UFWA President's address. (Calgary): United Farmers of Alberta. 8pp. *ACGA/Smith 15.

1929

1253 **Auto Workers Industrial Union of Canada.** Manifesto: to the automobile workers of Canada. Toronto. (1p). *OTAR/CPC21. Signed H. (Harvey) Murphy.

1254 **Brotherhood of Locomotive Engineers.** Souvenir booklet Canadian union meeting, Moncton, New Brunswick - August 6,7,8,9, 1929. Moncton. 112pp, illus. *NSHP/HD6528.R32. Many portraits, text mostly about Moncton, plus adverts.

1255 **Canadian Labor Defense League.** What is the CLDL? Why there should be a defense league in Canada and why you should join it. Toronto. (4pp). *OOA/ Underhill 52 OTURS/RSK.

(1256) **Communist International.** Closed letter to the Central Committee, Communist Party of Canada. OTU Hann 2766. Not found.

1257 **Communist Party of Canada.** Communism: an educational course. Toronto. (c1929). 62pp, mimeo. *OTAR/CPC 9f.14. Thirteen lessons, signed by W. Moriarty.

1258 ------ Draft thesis on the Canadian perspectives adopted by the enlarged executive. (Toronto). (c1929) 7pp, mimeo. *OTAR/CPC9f.9.

1259 ------ Political thesis. Toronto. 4pp plus 10pp. *OTAR/CPC9f.9. Pencil note: 'Adopted July 12 1929'.

1260 ------ Statement of the Central Executive Committee on Trotskyism and the expulsion of Maurice Spector from the party. (Toronto). (4pp) double column. *OTCPA.

1261 **Communist Party of Canada.** Strengthen the struggle
against the right danger! Statement of the Political
Committee. (Toronto). 24pp, mimeo. *OTCPA.

1262 **Crew, F.A.E.** Our changing civilization: whither and
how? (Regina): Saskatchewan Co-operative Wheat Producers Ltd. 8pp. *SSA/639. Pamphlet 5.

(1263)**Epstein, Elsie.** The minimum wage for women and its
application in Canada. Unpublished MA thesis, McGill
University. 151pp.

(1264)**Gruchy, Allan Garfield.** Collective bargaining in the
building, coal mining and transportation industries
of Canada 1900-1927. Unpublished MA thesis, McGill
University. 162pp.

1265 **Hamilton strike:** Group of broadsides and leaflets
as follows:
Build the industrial union of steel car workers
(National Car Workers Industrial Union).
Don't be a scab! Join the union! (?)
Fellow workers! Don't allow yourselves to be used by
the company to take away the bread from our wives
and children! (Strike Committee).
Organize to fight! Build a strong industrial union!
(Trade Union Educational League).
Stand together with us against starvation wages!
(Strike Committee).
Two monster mass-meetings (Strike Committee).
*OTAR/CPC10f.24. The strike was from 4 September to
18th October.

1266 **Hull, John T.** The history of co-operation. (Sask-
atoon): (University of Saskatchewan). 20pp. *MWPA/
UFM22 SSA/G37.39. revised edition, 1937 in MWPA/
CCF33 OHMA2871.

1267 ------- Reform movements and ideas. (Saskatoon): (United Farmers of Canada). 22pp. *BVAUS/
Young SSA/G37.71 SSUS/Coops.

1268 ------- What to read on co-operation. (Saskatoon)
(United Farmers of Canada). 10pp. SSA/G37.101
SSUS/Coops. Pamphlet 7.

1269 **Industrial Union of Needle Trades** Workers of Canada.
Call to all needle trades workers of Canada.
Montreal. 4pp (2 English, 2 French). *OTAR/CPC21.
Calling for a first national convention to be held
in Montreal in May 1929.

1270 ------ Convention souvenir issued on the occasion
of the first national convention held in Montreal
May 10thm 11th and 12th, 1929. Montreal. 28pp.
*OTAR/CPC10f.19. Contains articles by J.B. Salsberg,
A.R. Mosher and others, and reports from locals.

1271 **Irvine, William.** Co-operative government. Ottawa:
Special United Farmers edition. 246pp. *ACGL MWP.

1272 **Jamieson, Laura.** Co-operation and world peace.
(Saskatoon): (United Farmers of Canada). 8pp. *SSA/

G37.11 SSUS/Coop. Pamphlet 5.

1273 **Johnston, Pearl.** Education for peace. (Saskatoon):
United Farmers of Canada. (4pp). *SSA/G37.25.

1274 **Labor Party of Ontario.** Election appeal. Toronto.
4pp. *OKQS OTURS/RSK.

1275 **Lattimer, J.E.** Production per man: a bulletin tracing
the relation of man power to production and the alloc-
ation of man power to various industries. (?Montreal):
(?Macdonald College). 20pp. *OOP.

1276 **Lebel, Leon.** Family allowances as a means of preventing emigration: a plea for the family of the worker
so that it may share in the general prosperity of the
nation. Montreal: np. 64pp. BVIP NBSAM OOL QMBM
QMBN QQL *MWPA/Russell 1.

1277 **Lloydminster Farmers Economic Group.** Manifesto.
Lloydminster. (2pp), broadside. *SSA/G93.5.

1278 **Lumber and Agricultural Workers Industrial Union** of
Canada. Constitution and laws. Fort William. (c1929).
14pp. *OTAR/CPC10f.20.

1279 **MacPhail, A.J.** Not unto himself alone: an address at
the co-operative rally, Carlyle lake, Saskatchewan,
July 3, 1929, on the occasion of the inception of the
George Talbot memorial foundation. (Regina): Sask-
atcchewan Co-op Wheat Producers. 4pp. *OOAL SSA/
G39. Pamphlet 4.

1280 **Maurer, James H.** Unemployment and the mechanical man.
Chicago: Socialist Party of America. (c1929). (4pp).
*OOA/CCF184. Overstamped 'Young Peoples Labour League,
Montreal.'

1281 **Ontario.** Survey of industrial welfare in Ontario.
Toronto: Kings Printer. 39pp. *OTP Hann 2156.

1282 **Osterhout, S.S.** Orientals in Canada: the story of the
work of the United Church of Canada with asiatics in
Canada. Toronto: Board of Home Missions. xiv, 222pp,
index. *OONL.

(1283)Patton, Harald S. Cooperative achievements of Canadian grain growers. Winnipeg: Canadian Wheat Pool.
19pp. BVIV.

1284 Roberge, **Hector L.** (comp). Some views expressed on
the political party system. North Battleford. (4pp).
*OOA/Underhill 57 SSA/G176.2. Comprises extracts
from many speakers designed to demonstrate the failure
of the party system.

1285 **Robertson, George W.** The romance of co-operative
achievement. (Saskatoon): (United Farmers of Canada).
8pp. SRU *SSA/G37.81 SSUS/Coops. Pamphlet 6.

1286 Saskatchewan **Co-op Wheat Producers.** Open market
crashes under pressure --- pools unaffected by dem-
oralization. (Regina). 8pp. *SSA/G39. Pamphlet 3.

1287 **Sharrard, James A.** Co-operation in nature. (Saskatoon): (United Farmers of Canada). 8pp. *SSA/G37.13
Pamphlet 4.

1288 **Swanson, W.W.** Our economic system. (Saskatoon):
(United Farmers of Canada). 8pp. *SSA/G37.61.
Pamphlet 1.

1289 **Toronto District Labor Council.** Official Labor day
souvenir programme, 1929. Toronto. 136pp, illus.
*OTURS. Includes: Recent labor legislation throughout
Canada by Tom Moore; Have we freedom in Ontario? by
James McArthut Conner; Canada needs a labor party by
Mary McNab etc.

1290 **United Farmers of Canada.** The proposed gas franchise.
Saskatoon. (c1929). 4pp. *K.

1291 ------ Summary of resolutions which were passed by
the various district conventions, 1929. Saskatoon.
26pp. *SSUS/UFC.

1292 **United Farmers of Ontario.** Programme and material
for eight club meetings. Flesherton: S-E. Grey executive. 22pp. *OOA/MacPhail 5.

1293 **Womens International League for Peace and Freedom.**
What is the Women's International League? Plan of
work for Canadian section of W.I.L. Vancouver.
(4pp). *SSA/McNaughton H32.

1294 **Woodsworth, J.S.** Hours that stand apart. Ottawa:
Mutual. 40pp. *MWP MWPA/Brigden 7 OKQS OOA/Woods-
worth 37 OTURS/RSK SSA/G171.5 SSUS/JL197.

1295 ------ Labor's case in Parliament. A summary and
compilation of speeches in the Canadian House of
Commons 1921-1928. Ottawa: Canadian Brotherhood of
Railroad Employees. 92pp. AEP AEU BVIP NSHPL OPET
OTU *AEPAA/Farmilo 5 BVAUS/Mac.43f.20 MWP MWPA/
Russell 1 OHMA2883 OOA/CCF326 and Underhill 44 and
Woodsworth 37 SSUS/JL197. Hann 2772. Compiled by
J.L. Cohen.

1296 ------ and A.A. Heaps. Speeches on the budget delivered in the House of Commons on March 14 and April
5, 1929. Ottawa: F.A. Acland. 12pp. *OHMA1562.

1297 **Workers Benevolent Association of Canada.** Constitution and by-laws adopted by constituent meeting of
September 30th 1922, amended 1925, 27, 28, 29.
Winnipeg. 122pp. *OTAR/CPC26 ?Hann 2712. In Ukrainian and English (Statut robitnichovo etc).

1298 **Young Communist League.** 10 years: long live the YCI!
Fight against imperialist war! Fight against speed-
up and wage cuts. Toronto. 6pp, mimeo. *OTAR/CPC11.
Ten years of the Young Communist International, not
the Canadian League.

1299 ------ Young workers! Demonstrate on August 1st
Red day! Toronto. (1p), broadside. *OTAR/CPC21.

1930

1300 **Adshead, H.B.** Facing both ways: Conservative immigration policy. Calgary: Dominion Labor Party. (4pp).
*OOP.

1301 **Armstrong, Rinaldo William.** The salt of the earth.
A study in rural life and social progress. Ottawa:
Graphic. 233pp. *OHMA1658 OONL OTURS. Studies
designed to draw attention to the psychological forces
shaping and stimulating social movements in the country.

1302 **Beames, John.** An army without banners. Toronto:
McClelland and Stewart. (viii), 301pp. BVIV NBSAM
OHM OKQ SRU SSU *OONL Peel 3163. A novel of prairie
hardships.

1303 **Bricklayers, Masons and Plasterers International**
Union of America. Proceedings of the twelfth biennial
and fifty-second convention held at Mount Royal hotel,
Montreal, Quebec, Canada, beginning Monday, September
8, 1930. Washington. 170pp. *OPET/Gainey 2. Held
in Toronto in 1891 and 1916.

1304 **Canadian Farmers Economic League.** A call to action:
to all oppressed farmers in the prairie provinces.
Saskatoon. (1p), broadside. *SSA/G198.3.

1305 **Canadian Labor Defense League.** Eastern Canada emergency defense conference: report. (Hamilton). 22pp,
mimeo (not continuously paged). *OOA/Woodsworth 10
OTURS/RSK.

1306 ------ Official statement re the case of T. Ewen
and O. Ryan. Toronto. 3pp, mimeo. *OOA/Underhill
52.

1307 ------ Smash the fascist police terror that is
spreading throughout Canada. Sudbury. (1p), broadside; French on verso. *OTAR/CPC21.

1308 ------ The tyrant. The Italy of Mussolini. Toronto.
16pp. *OTCPA.

1309 **Canadian Republic League.** Canada must become a republic. Montreal. (1p), broadside. *OTAR/CPC21.
Note says 20,000 printed.

1310 **Committee of the Executive of the Twentieth Century**
Fund (eds). Historic sketches of the pioneer work
and the missionary, educational and benevolent agencies of the Presbyterian church in Canada. Toronto:
Murray. 127pp. *NSHPL.

1311 **Communist Party of Canada.** Agrarian programme. Toronto. (c1930). (7pp), mimeo. *OTAR/CPC9f.8.

1312 ------ The lessons of the sixth convention. Toronto.
13pp, mimeo. *OTAR/CPC9f.8.

1313 ------ Manifesto: to the workers and poor farmers

of Alberta. Edmonton. (c1930). (2pp), broadside. *ACGL/PE.Communist.

1314 **Communist Party of Canada.** The platform of the capitalist parties is an attack on the living standards
of the workers! Toronto. 4pp. *OTAR/CPC21. Election manifesto for the federal general election 1930.

1315 ------ Special bulletin: Special instructions for
party membership campaign: Outline for agitation
and propaganda for May 1st. (Toronto). 7pp plus
5pp, mimeo. *OTAR/CPC9f.11.

1316 ------ The triumph of socialism in the Soviet Union.
Toronto. 16pp. *BVAUS/WB31f.2b OTURS/RSK. 'An
unanswerable refutation of the lies and calumny prop-
agated against the Soviet Union by the capitalist
press and the lickspittles of the bosses...'

1317 ------ Why every worker should join the Communist
Party. Toronto: Workers Publishing. 14pp. *BVAUS/
Smith and WB/31f.2d OTAR/CPC OTURS/RSK. Canadian
workers pamphlet series 3.

1318 **Coote, G.G.** Speech on tariff on motor trucks delivered in the House of Commons, 3 March 1930. Ottawa:
F.A. Acland. 6pp. *ACGA/Coote 14.

1319 **Darby, A.E.** The Canadian Council of Agriculture. A
review of the history and work 1925 to 1930. Winnipeg. 14pp. *MWPA/CCA 3.

1320 **Edwards, George F.** Report of the investigation into
the milling industry. (Saskatoon): United Farmers
of Canada. 11pp. *SSA/G37.74.

1321 **Eisendrath, M.** Unemployment; what can we do? Toronto: np. (c1930). (14pp). *AEU.

1322 **Fraser, Dawn.** At last! The truth about Canada's
miners and mining communities. If we saw ourselves
as others see us; an answer to our critics. Glace
Bay: Eastern. (c1930). 22pp. *NSHPL.

1323 **Gorki, Maxim.** In the clutches of the Cheka: the
story of Maxim Gorki's visit to the commune prison.
Toronto: Canadian Labor Defense League. (c1930).
8pp. *OTURS/RSK.

1324 **Hannam, H.H.** The farmer pays...inflated debts...
with deflated prices. Toronto: United Farmers of
Ontario. (c1930). (4pp). *SSA/G292.24.

1325 **Hull, John T.** History of cooperation in western Can-
ada. A lecture delivered at the Manitoba Institute of
Co-operators June 16-21, 1930. Winnipeg: Cooperative
Marketing Board. 16pp. *BVAUS/Young OHMA2873 MWPA/
CCF 33.

1326 **Independent Labor Party.** Platform and manifesto.
Vancouver. (4pp). *BVAUS/Mac.30Af.1.

1327 **International Labour Office.** Studies and report
series A, No. 32: Freedom of association - Canada.

Geneva. pp 121-149. OTU *OOAL.

1328 **Kinley, James.** The dawn of a new era: suggested social and economic changes, of vital interest to the
farmers and laboring classes. North Vancouver:
Burrard Review. (viii), 127pp. ACG BVAU BVIP SSU
*T.

1329 Legge, Katherine Boole. Labour legislation in Canada
affecting women and children. Unpublished MA thesis,
McGill University. 167pp, biblio 166-167. *QMM

1330 **Magnusson, Leifur.** Unemployment: an international
nemesis. Toronto: National Council Young Womens
Christian Association. 6pp, mimeo. *OTURS.

1331 **Mine Workers Union of Canada.** Fifth annual convention,
District no.1. (Calgary). 32pp, mimeo. *OTAR/CPC10.

1332 **Neighbourhood Workers Association.** Annual report.
Toronto. (8pp). *OKQS.

1333 ------ The working policy. Toronto. (4pp). *OKQS.

1334 **Organization of 900 Unemployed Workers of Edmonton.**
Manifesto of the unemployed workers of Canada re the
press and immigration. (Edmonton). (c1930). (1p),
broadside. *AEPAA/Brown 6.

1335 **Peoples Emancipation Party of British Columbia.** Declaration of principles. Vancouver. (c1930). (4pp).
*BVAUS/Mac.31f.12. Includes charter of liberty.

1336 **Regina and Saskatoon Labour Councils.** The Saskatchewan all-Canadian labour annual, 1930. First year.
(Saskatoon). 52pp. *SSUS/Labour. Includes: A living
wage for capital by M.M. Maclean; The cause of unemployment by Walter Fyfe; The unemployment problem by
E.J. Garland.

1337 **Sapiro, Aaron.** 100% control by legislation. (Saskatoon): United Farmers of Canada. 24pp. *SSA/G37.57.
Peel 3155. Control of the wheat pools.

1338 **Saskatchewan Farmers Political Association.** Constitution. Regina. (4pp). *SSA/G92.1.

1339 ------ Convention, City hall, Regina, April 2-3, 1930.
(Regina). 16pp. *SSA/G92.4. SSA copy includes draft
constitution heavily marked by William Irvine.

1340 ------ Provisional platform. (Regina). (1p), broadside. *SSA/G92.3.

(1341) Scott, F.R. The Privy Council and minority rights.
Kingston: Queens Quarterly. pp 668-678. Offprint or
excerpt from vol. 37. York University law library.

1342 **Smith, Stewart.** Fight or starve. Toronto: Communist
Party of Canada. 22pp. *OTURS/RSK. Canadian workers
pamphlet series 2.

1343 **Social Service Council of Canada.** A survey of the
steel industry in Canada, submitted by the Committee
on Industrial Life. Toronto. (ii), 26pp. *BVAV.

1344 **Socialist Party** (of America). The most frequent objections to socialism answered. Chicago. (c1930).
(4pp). Overstamped 'Young Peoples Labour League...
Montreal. *OOA/CCF184.

1345 ------ What is socialism? Chicago. (c1930). (6pp).
*OOA/CCF184 SSA/G165.7. Overprinted as 1345 above.

1346 **Socialist Party of Canada.** Unemployment! Winnipeg:
Local no.3. (c1930). (1p), broadside. *OHMA

1347 **United Farmers of Alberta.** Nine years of achievement:
the best promise of good government. Calgary. 8pp.
*ACGA/Smith 15.

1348 **United Farmers of Canada.** A matter of life and death.
(Saskatoon). 15pp. *SSA/G37.48 SSUS/UFC. On medical insurance.

1349 ------ Memorandum to Mr Bennett. (Saskatoon). (4pp).
*SSA/G37.50.

1350 ------ The municipal doctor. Saskatoon. 7pp.
*SSUS/UFC.

1351 ------ Nationality and naturalization of women.
(Saskatoon). (c1930). (1p), broadside. *SSUS/UFC.

1352 ------ On immigration. Saskatoon. 10pp. *SSA/
G37.56. Peel 3234.

1353 ------ Starting a co-operative store. Saskatoon.
11pp. *OOAL SSA/G37.86.

1354 ------ and Independent Labor Party. Organized far-
mer and labor programme: ultimate objective of the
United Farmers of Canada: ultimate objective of the
Independent Labor Party. (?Regina). (c1930). (4pp).
*SSA/G18.Ind.4 SSUS/CCF.

1355 **United Farmers of Ontario.** The new trail. Flesherton: S-E. Grey. (4pp). *OOA/Heaps 2. For the
election of Agnes MacPhail.

1356 **Westbury, G.H.** Misadventures of a working hobo in
Canada. London (Eng): George Routledge: Toronto:
Musson. viii, 172pp. *OKQ.

1357 **Winnipeg May Day Conference.** The May day bulletin.
Winnipeg. 4pp. *OOA/Heaps 2. Issued by the Communist Party of Canada. Back page has demonstration
notice in Ukrainian, Yiddish, German, Polish. Includes manifesto, significance of May day etc.

1358 **Womens Citizenship Association.** Apron strings?
Saskatoon. (c1930). (2pp). *OOA/Lucas 3.

1359 **Womens Labour Leagues.** Workers, mothers, domestic
servants! Organize! (Kirkland Lake. (1p), broadside, double columns. *OTAR/CPC21, marked 'Distributed July 13-1930.'

1360 **Workers Educational League.** The materialist conception of history. Vancouver. (c1930). 6pp, mimeo.
*BVAUS/Young, marked '4th reprint, 3rd edn revised'.

1361 **Workers Educational League.** Unemployment--wage red-
uctions-- the open shop. Toronto. (c1930). (2pp)
broadside. *OTURS/RSK.

1362 **Workers Unity League.** Draft constitution governing
all sections until first national convention. Toronto. 3pp, mimeo. *OTAR/CPC10f.17. See 1488 above.

1363 Not used. Original entry transferred to later date
on basis of new evidence.

1364 **(Young, William).** In the Privy Council: an appeal
from the Court of Appeal for the province of Manitoba
between William Young (plaintiff) appellant and Canadian Northern Railway company (defendant) respondent:
record of proceedings. (Winnipeg). xxxiii, 1113pp.
*MWPA/Russell 1. Includes case and judgement in
Kings Bench (see 1234 above) and judgement of the
Court of Appeal.

1365 **(Young, William).** In the Privy Council: an appeal
from the Court of Appeal for the province of Manitoba
between William Young...and the Canadian Northern
Railway. Appellant's case. (Winnipeg). 14pp.
*MWPA/Russell 1.

1366 **Young Communist League.** Draft resolution on the situation and tasks of the Young Communist League of Canada. Toronto. (c1930). 8pp, mimeo. *OTAR/CPC11f.27.

1367 ------ The program of the Young Communist International. (c1930). 25pp. *OTAR/CPC11f.27.

1368 ------ Young workers! September 8 is our day! Demonstrate on the 16th International Youth Day! (Kirkland Lake). (2pp), broadside. *OTAR/CPC21.

1369 **Young Peoples Socialist League.** The young vs. the
old world. Chicago. (c1930). (4pp). *OOA/CCF184.
Overstamped as 1344 above.

1931

1370 **Alberta Wheat Pool.** A defence of Canada's wheat pool.
A reply to Gampell. Calgary. 48pp. AEU BVIP BVIV
*ACGL. See Peel 3177 for Gampell.

(1371) **Ashplant, Henry B.** Jesus of Nazareth on unemployment.
c1931. Advertised. Not found.

1372 **Ballam, John J.** Soviet 'dumping' and 'forced labor'.
Toronto: Friends of the Soviet Union. 30pp. *OTAR.
FSU series 1.

1373 **Bergen, N.J.L.** Songs for the times: dedicated to
the united farmers. Dodsland (Sask): Prairie Times.
(c1931). 63pp. *AEUS SSUS.

1374 **Campbell, Allan.** The frame-up. The story of the

unemployed of Vancouver and their fight against the police terror. Toronto: Canadian Labor Defence League. 16pp. *BVAUS/Mac.43Af.12 and WB.31f.27. Campbell was convicted in Vancouver in March 1931 and deported to Scotland.

1375 **Canadian Council of Agriculture.** Manifesto on agricultural conditions and national policies. (Winnipeg). (4pp). *ACGA/Smith 14 ACGL/PDg.CCA MWPA/CCA3.

1376 **Canadian Labor Defence League.** (First) plenum, minutes and reports, July 11-12, 1931. (Toronto). 36pp, mimeo. *OTAR/CPC11f.29 OTURS/RSK. Speech of J.L. Engdahl, resolution on situation and tasks, letter from International Red Aid, resolution on organization and others.

1377 ------ Important bulletin and instructions. Toronto. (3pp), mimeo. *OTURS/RSK. Sent 4 days after the arrest of the Communist leaders to which it refers.

1378 ------ Long live the memory of the Paris commune! Defend the commune of to-day --- Soviet Union! Sudbury. (1p), broadside. *OTAR/CPC21.

1379 ------ Manifesto on unemployment prepared by the League against imperialism and issued by the CLDL. (Toronto). 2pp, mimeo. *OTAR/CPC11f.31.

1380 ------ Monster demonstration Wednesday, September 30th, 1931 at 7.00 pm. Workers of Toronto, come in thousands to this demonstration and protest against the attack upon your rights. Toronto. (1p), broadside. *OPTB/1931. Can.Labour.

1381 ------ Not guilty! The verdict of the workers' jury on the trial and conviction of the eight Communist leaders. Preface by Tim Buck: introduction by Oscar Ryan. Toronto. 27pp, mimeo. *BVAUS/WB31f.27 OTURS/ RSK SSUS. Contains also an article by F.R. Scott from the *Canadian Forum* and a letter from Ben Lennard on Sgt. Leopold.

1382 ------ Protest against brutal murder of miners in Estevan! Demand immediate withdrawal of armed government forces from strike area and punishment of murderers! Help the strikers in their hard struggle! Toronto. (1p), broadside. *SRA/Riot.

1383 ------ Sedition: the bosses weapon to stifle protest against hunger, exploitation and war! Toronto. (20pp). *BVAUS/WB31f.27 OTURS/RSK.

1384 ------ To all who value freedom! We are sounding the alarm today! (Winnipeg). (1p), broadside. *MWPA/AG4.

1385 **Cessna, P.W.** The co-operative commonwealth: the proposed system at work. Kimistino: Melfort Journal. 46pp. ACG *BVAUS/Mac.30Af.46 SSA/G234.1.

1386 **Colquette, R.D.** The farmer comes to town. Brantford: Cooperative Union of Canada. 8pp. *OKQS OOAL.

1387 **Communist Party of Canada.** Bennett's starvation budget. Toronto. 15pp. *BVAUS/WB31f.2d OOAL OTURS/RSK. Workers pamphlet series 4.

1388 ------ Celebrate the November anniversary. Calgary. (1p). *ACGA/Smith 12. The anniversary of the Russian revolution.

1389 ------ Communism on trial! Toronto. 28pp. *BVAUS/ WB31f.1c OHMA2477 OTURS/RSK. Also workers pamphlet series 4 (see 1387 above).

1390 ------ Face to the shops. Toronto. 14pp plus 1p. letter bound in, mimeo. *OTAR/CPC9f.11.

1391 ------ The past year. Toronto. (2pp). *BVAUS/WB 31f.2d. Refers to a previous issue of same title published a year ago; not traced.

1392 ------ The program of the Communist International. (Toronto). 96pp, mimeo. *OTURS/RSK.

1393 ------ Resolutions of enlarged plenum, February 1931. (Toronto). 63pp. *BVAUS/WB31f.2a OHMA2481 OTURS/RSK. Refers to various tasks in the unions, YCL, womens and language areas and to the expulsions of Macdonald, M. Buhay and Margolese.

1394 **Drew, George A.** Salesmen of death: the truth about war makers. A plain spoken denunciation of an armaments industry which makes wars to make money. Toronto: Womens League of Nations Association. 23pp. *OTUR. 3rd edition published 1933.

1395 **Farmers Unity League of Canada.** Membership card: organize and fight! Saskatoon. 8pp. *SSA/G309.1. Contains preamble and structure.

1396 **Hollis, Annie L.** Grain marketing act no. 11. Mainly for women. Regina: Saskatchewan Cooperative Wheat Producers. 8pp. *SSA/G39.

1397 **King, Tom.** The black ox; or, 'Of the fruits of the earth you shall live'. Moose Jaw. 76pp. AEU *SSU Peel 3263. A farmer and his involvements with politics in western Canada.

1398 **Lumber and Agricultural Workers Industrial Union** of Canada. General report and plan for future activities. (?Fort William). 13pp, mimeo. *OTAR/CPC/10f.20. Includes minutes of convention held 24 December 1930 in Port Arthur.

1399 **Moore, H. Napier.** Britain's consumers keep shop. Brantford: Cooperative Union of Canada. 10pp. *BVAUS/ Mac.39Af.17.

1400 **Paynter, W.C.** The trumpet call of Canadian money and progress: an ideal handbook of monetary reform. Vancouver: Canadian Currency and Banking Reform League. 59pp. BVIP OTU *SSA/G98.3 SSUS Peel 3272A.

1401 **Robert Owen Foundation.** The co-operative programme for social reconstruction and the objects of the...

Foundation. Toronto. 6pp plus membership form.
*ACGA/Coote 17.

1402 **Ross, Margaret.** Amor de Cosmos, a British Columbia
reformer. Unpublished MA thesis, University of British Columbia. 191, ii, vii pp. biblio. *BVAUS.

1403 **(Ryan, Oscar.)** The story of the trial of the eight
Communist leaders: November 2nd to November 13th,
1931 by J.S. Toronto: Canadian Labor Defence League.
29pp. *BVAUS/WB43f.11a OTURS/RSK SSUS.

1404 **Stirling, G.F.** Speculation or business? (Saskatoon):
United Farmers of Canada. 7pp. *SSA/G37.85 SSUS/UFC.
For 100% control of the wheat pool.

1405 **Stowe-Gullen, Augusta.** History of the formation of
National Council of Women of Canada. (Toronto): National Council of Women of Canada. 16pp. *OTAR/1931/
59.

1406 **Toronto (City of).** Civic unemployment relief committee: report and recommendations. Toronto. 63pp.
*OTAR/1931/49.

1407 **Toronto District Labor Council.** Official souvenir
programme, Labor day, 1931. Toronto. 84pp, illus.
*OTURS. Includes: Unemployment insurance for Canada
by H.M. Cassidy; Labor day 1931 by P.M. Draper; The
conflict in political thought by J. McArthur Conner;
Our way of thinking by J.W. Buckley; the ILO by James
Simpson etc.

1408 **Trades and Labor Congress of Canada.** Policies on
employment, unemployment and underemployment, 1883-
1930. Submitted by the Executive Council to the 47th
annual convention, Vancouver, September 1931. Ottawa. 24pp. *OOL. Includes convention decisions.

1409 **United Farmers of Alberta.** Federal affairs in review.
A summary of the legislative work done, and the rec-
ommendation made by the UFA members at the House of
Commons, Ottawa, in co-operation with other independ-
ent groups during the years 1922 to 1930 inclusive.
Ottawa. (6pp). *ACGA/Coote 7 and Smith 14 and
Spencer 2 ACGL/PDf.1 OOA/Spencer.

1410 ------ Memorandum to the annual convention, January
1931. (Calgary). (4pp). *ACGA/Coote 17. Regarding
repression and measures needed.

1411 **Ward, John W.** Co-operative oil stations in Manitoba.
Winnipeg: Co-operative Marketing Board. 11pp. *MWPA/
CCF33 OOA/CCF174.

1412 **Williams, G.H.** The land of the soviets: a western
farmer sees the Russian bear change his coat. (Saskatoon): United Farmers of Canada. 86pp. OOP OTP SRL
*BVAUS/Mac.38f.18K OHMA1803 OTURS/RSK SSA/G37.45
SSUS/Comm.

1413 **Workers Co-operative of New Ontario.** Appeal to the
workers and toiling farmers of New Ontario. (Kirk-

land Lake). 4pp. *OTAR/CPC21. 'Organized under the leadership of the Communist Party...affiliated to the Canadian Labor Defence League.'

1414 **Workers Sport Association of Canada.** Carry out the plan of action and Spartakiade campaign. Toronto. 4pp, mimeo. *OTAR/CPC11.

1415 **Workers Unity League.** Open letter to the miners of the Sask. coalfields. (?Saskatoon): Saskatchewan-Manitoba District Council. (1p), broadside. *SRA/Riot. On the Bienfait-Estevan strike.

1416 ------ Programme and policy in the Canadian mining industry. Toronto. 8pp, mimeo. *OTAR/CPC10f.22.

1417 ------ To the unemployed workers, to all workers! (Kirkland Lake). 4pp. *OTAR/CPC21.

1932

1418 **Adams, Frank Dawson.** The day shelter for unemployed men Montreal: a social experiment. Montreal: (?McGill University). 23pp. BVAU *OONL.

1419 **Anti-War Conference.** Another war coming: a call to the workers and all elements opposed to war. Toronto. 6pp. *OTURS/RSK.

1420 **Bowles, R.P.** Some reflections on the present attitude of the church toward the social economic order. Toronto: United Church. 16pp. *OOL

1421 **British Columbia.** Report of the Select Committee of the Legislative Assembly on unemployment, 1932. Vancouver. 16pp. *BVAA.

1422 **Brown, Gordon W.** Unemployment in the city of Brandon: a statistical study based on the unemployment registration of September 1931. Unpublished MA thesis, McMaster University. 63, (70)pp. *OHMA.

1423 **Buck, Tim.** An indictment of capitalism: the speech of Tim Buck address to the jury on November 12th, 1931 at the trial of the eight leaders of the Communist Party of Canada with an explanatory introduction by Tim Buck and a preface by A.E. Smith. Toronto: Canadian Labor Defense League. 80pp. BVAS BVIP QQL *BVAUS/WB39f.7 OHMA2720 OTURS/RSK SSUS.

1424 **Campbell, J.G.** Concealed weapons: the racketeers banquet. Saskatoon. 200pp. *BVAUS/Mac.41f.7. The racketeers are in life insurance.

1425 **Canadian Currency and Banking Reform League.** Bank of Canada - why not? Vancouver. 45pp. *OOA/Bengough 3. Includes letter of endorsement from Percy Bengough.

1426 **Canadian Labour Defence League.** Constitution. Toronto. 4pp, mimeo. *OTURS/RSK.

1427 **Canadian Labor Defense League.** Eastern Canada conference for the repeal of section 98 of the Criminal
Code: resolutions, Ottawa deputation, reports, proceedings. (Toronto). (26pp), mimeo. *OKQS OTURS/
RSK. For details of section 98 see appendix.

1428 ------ Eight prisoners in the Kingston cells: what
they stand for - who are the eight? Toronto. 11pp.
*OTURS/RSK.

1429 ------ Report of conference proceedings: minutes of
constituency repeal conference, Trades and Labour
Hall, Sept. 11 - 1932. (Port Arthur). (4pp), mimeo.
*OTURS/RSK.

1430 ------ Section 98 of the Criminal Code - passed in
40 minutes in 1919 - used to smash the fighting working class movement today. Toronto. (3pp), mimeo.
*OOA/Underhill 52.

1431 **Cassidy, H.M.** Unemployment and relief in Ontario
1929-1932. A survey and report. Toronto: Dent.
290, xiv pp, appendix. *OONL.

1432 **Cessna, P.W.** The co-operative commonwealth: a con-
cise analysis of the world depression, its cause and
remedy. Mimistina: Melfort Journal. 45pp. *SSA/
G234.2. Marked 'Vol. III' - see 1385 above.

1433 **Coldwell, M.J.** Radio addresses, prepared and delivered over station CHWC. Saskatoon: Independent
Labor Party. (1p). *SSUS/JL197.

1434 **Communist Party of Canada.** Down with imperialis(t)
war! Manifesto of the central committee. (Toronto).
(4pp). *MWPA/AG4. On the Japanese invasion of Man-
churia and attack on China.

1435 ------ Rules for underground party work. (Toronto).
(c1932). (4pp). *OTURS/RSK.

1436 **CCF.** A call to the people of Canada: the Co-operative Commonwealth Federation, (Farmer - Labor -
Socialist). A description of the inception, objects
and plans of the new Canadian political movement
launched at Calgary, Alberta, August 1st 1932.
(Calgary). (4pp). *ACGA/Smith 15 ACGL/PDbl AEUS/
CCF.XIII.54 BVAUS/Steeves 4-6 OOA/CCF10 and Spencer
SSA/G21932.3 and G3 Alta.3. Text mainly by the editor
of the United Farmers of Alberta official organ; final
page signed J.S. Woodsworth and Norman F. Priestley.
The Dominion day manifesto of the UFA (July 1932)
offered co-operation with other social units 'to
secure the foundations of the co-operative state -
the day approaching when constructive forces must
make a bid for power.'

1437 ------ An outline of its origins, organization and
objectives together with a statement of principles
and news of its development. Calgary. 16pp. *ACGL/
PDbl BVAUS/Steeves 4-6 OHMA1536 OTURS SSA/G2.
1932.1 SSUS/CCF. First draft of the Regina mani-

festo published between the Calgary conference of
August 1st and the first convention in Regina, 1933.
Text differs from the Manifesto.

1438 **Drummond, W.M.** The Canadian farmer and the machine
age. Toronto: Social Service Council of Canada.
16pp. *MWPA/Brigden 7 OTAR/1932/6 OTURS/RSK.
Machine age series 2.

1439 **Fairchild, Henry Pratt.** The fallacy of profits.
Regina: Cooperative Union of Canada. 20pp. *SSA/
G49.4.

1440 **Gardiner, Robert** and others. Speeches on the add-
ress in reply to the speech from the throne. Ottawa:
F.A. Acland. 34pp. *BVAUS/Mac.27f.44. Others are
J.S. Woodsworth, William Irvine, G.G. Coote, Angus
MacInnis, and Agnes MacPhail.

(1441)**Goodman, S.J.** Planned economy in the capitalist
state. Unpublished MA thesis, McGill University.
158pp.

1442 **Hauck, Arthur A.** Some educational factors affecting
the relations between Canada and the United States.
Easton (Penn.): np. 100pp. *OOP. Study of text
books and student ideas.

1443 **Howard, Clifford H.** The crusade for peace. Unpublished MA thesis, McMaster University. (v), 56pp,
biblio. *OHMA.

1444 **Independent Labor Party of Manitoba.** Vote Labor if
you are not satisfied with things as they are. Manitoba provincial election, June 16th 1932. Winnipeg.
(4pp). *OOA/Heaps 1.

1445 **Independent Labor Party (Socialist).** Platform and
manifesto. Vancouver. (2pp). *BVAUS/Mac.30Af.1
and Steeves 4-6. The qualifier 'Socialist' was adopted in December 1931. This manifesto is identical
to the one of 1930 but omits the clause 'Collective
ownership of the means of production, social appropriation of that which is socially produced, is the
only means to end exploitation.'

1446 **King, W.L.M.** Unemployment in Canada. A contrast in
Liberal and Conservative methods. Complete failure
of Bennett government to redeem pledges made at general elections, 1930. Speech in the House of Commons
1 March 1932. Ottawa: F.A. Acland. 17pp. *OOAL.

1447 **Kwauk, S. and W.H. Fong** (eds). The Sino-Japanese
conflict. Montreal: Montreal Chinese Students Assn.
52pp. OKQ OOP *MWPA/Russell 1.

1448 **League for Social Reconstruction.** Constitution.
(Toronto). (c1932). 2pp, mimeo. *OOA/CCF168.

1449 ------ A programme for the new social order in Canada to end the existence of poverty in the midst of
plenty. Vancouver. 8pp. *ACGL/PDb.LSR OOAL.

1450 ------ What to read: a guide to books and articles

on current social and economic questions. (Toronto).
16pp. *ACGL/PDb.LSR OTURS/RSK.

1451 **Logie, J.** A socialist manifesto/(revised) Believe it
or not! New Westminster: Socialist Party of Canada.
(c1932). (2pp), broadside. *BVAUS/Mac30Af.1 and
Steeves 4-6 OHMA. Published originally by the Independent Labor Party (Socialist) but crossed out and
overstamped Socialist Party.

1452 **McCawley, Stuart.** The soreness of the soul of Cape
Breton. (?Glace Bay). (c1932). 30pp. OOP *NSHD/
Tl OOAL Hann 2733. Has cover title: 'Standing the
gaff! The Cape Breton mines and miners.'

1453 **MacInnis, Angus.** Speech on the budget delivered in
the House of Commons, Monday, April 25, 1932. Ottawa:
F.A. Acland. 6pp. *BVAUS/Mac.27f.44.

1454 ------ Speech on imperial economic conference trade
agreements delivered in the House of Commons on Friday, October 28, 1932. Ottawa: F.A. Acland. 6pp.
*BVAUS/Mac.27f.44.

1455 MacInnis, **Angus.** Speeches on co-operative commonwealth and unemployment relief delivered in the House
of Commons on Wednesday March 2 and Thursday March 10,
1932. Ottawa: F.A. Acland. 10pp. *BVAUS/Mac.27f.44.

1456 **National Railway Labour Unions of Canada.** Memorandum
with respect to Bill A introduced in the Senate of
Canada by the Rt Hon. Senator Meighen. (Ottawa).
(3pp). *OOA/CCF179. Presented by A.R. Mosher, Pres.
of the ACCL and CBRE. Bill A dealt primarily with
the voluntary and enforced cooperation of the CN and
CP railways.

1457 **National Unemployed Workers Association.** To all members of the Manitoba provincial legislature. Winnipeg. (2pp), mimeo and broadside 'Join the national
demonstration against needless starvation!' *MWPA/
AG4. Lists unemployed workers demands.

1458 **Nationalist League of Canada.** Manifesto: All for all!
To the masses of all classes! Vancouver. 8pp. *OOA/
Woodsworth 12. For the nationalization of banks, in-
surance companies, railways and all natural resources.
Will support the People's Party of British Columbia.
The League seems to be excessively right-wing - or
perhaps merely confused - it also supports Mussolini.

1459 ------ Hard times no more. Nationalist plan: direct
and immediate relief for all unemployed men at good
wages! Vancouver. (1p), broadside. *OOA/Woodsworth
12.

1460 **Nationalist Party.** To all nationalists: free Canada
from the ruthless and unjust rule of the chartered
banks. (Vancouver): Nationalist League of Canada.
2pp, mimeo. *OOA/Woodsworth 12.

1461 **Ontario.** Report of the commissioner in the matter
of the Workmen's Compensation act. Toronto: Kings

Printer. 17pp. *OTL.

1462 **Ontario.** Report on provincial policy on administrative methods in the matter of direct relief in Ontario. Toronto: Kings Printer. 24pp. *OTP.

1463 ------ The King vs. Buck and others: the judgement
of the Court of Appeal of Ontario concerning the
Communist Party in Canada. (Toronto): np. *OTURS/
RSK. 'Published by direction of W.H. Price, Attorney
General for Ontario'.

1464 **Roddan, Andrew** (ed). Canada's untouchables: the story
of the man without a home. Vancouver: Clarke and
Stuart. 111pp. ACG BVAUS BVIPA BVIV OHM OTP *T
Also published in parts as *God in the jungles.* 64pp.

1465 **Rosenberg, Louis.** The land policy of the farmer-
labour group, Saskatchewan. Regina: np. 10pp.
*ACGL Peel 3312A.

1466 **Ryan, Oscar.** Deported! The struggle against deport-
ations and for the defense of the foreign-born workers: the case of the ten prisoners in Halifax; of the
thousands who face deportation. Toronto: Canadian
Labor Defence League. 12pp. *ACGL/PE.Communist
BVAUS/WB39f.11 OHMA3138 OTURS/RSK.

1467 **(Saint-Martin, A.)** Sandwiches 'à la shouashe': cit-
ations du journal Spartakus: preuve de plus monstreux
meutre commis dans l'Amerique du Nord. Montreal:
Spartakus. 24pp. QMBM *OKQS.

1468 **Saskatchewan Farmer-Labor Group.** Agricultural land
policy. Saskatoon. (4pp). *ACGL/PDb.Labor SSA/
G18.1932.1. Issued in various editions.

1469 ------ Economic policy. As formulated by the delegates assembled in annual convention, Saskatoon, July
27th, 1932. Saskatoon. (4pp). *OOA/Woodsworth 12
SSA/G18.1932.2. Issued in various editions.

1470 **Scudamore, T.V.** Aid to the civil power. Ottawa:
Canadian Defense Quarterly. pp 253-260. *BVAA .
Offprint from vol 9 no. 2, January 1932.

1471 **Socialist Party of Canada.** Constitution: the Socialist Party of Canada is formed for the purpose of creating a working class consciousness with a view of
securing the collective ownership and the democratic
control of the means of wealth production. New Westminster. (c1932). (4pp). *OTURS/Woodsworth 8.

1472 ------ Manifesto and declaration of principles, municipal campaign, 1932. Vancouver. (4pp). *BVAUS/
Smith CCF and LP.

1473 **Spector, Maurice.** Selected readings in Marxism.
Toronto: np. 99pp, mimeo. *E.

1474 **Thompson, Bram.** Exhortation to the farmers for unity.
(?Regina). (4pp). *SSA/G104.4.

1475 **Underhill, Frank H.** The party system. A paper read

at the meeting of the Canadian Political Science
Association, Toronto, 25th May 1932. Toronto: League
for Social Reconstruction. 6pp, mimeo. *ACGA/Smith
13 BVAUS/Mac.31Af.32 OOA/Good 18.

1476 **United Farmers of Alberta.** Declaration of ultimate
objectives. (Calgary). (4pp). *ACGA/Smith 15.
'Resolved that we reaffirm our definition of a co-operative commonwealth and declare it to be our ultimate
objective.' Quotes from 1477 below.

1477 ------ Declaration of ultimate objectives: definition
of co-operative commonwealth passed by UFA convention
January 1932. (Edmonton). (4pp). *OOA/Spencer.

1478 ------ Provincial platform: declaration of principles.
(Edmonton). (c1932). (2pp). *OOA/Spencer OTURS

1479 ------ UFA Government's record: a reply to government
critics on the financial record of the UFA administration. Taken from the budget speech of a UFA back
bencher in the Alberta legislature. (Edmonton).
12pp. *ACGL/PDf1 AEPAA/Inf.file Alta.pol II.

1480 **United Farmers** of Canada. Economic policy and convention resolutions: Farmer-labor economic policy
ultimate objective. Seventh annual convention July
25-27 1932. (Saskatoon). (4pp). *SSA/G37.23 SSUS/
UFC.

1481 ------ Economic policy (Saskatchewan) as formulated
by the delegates assembled in annual convention, February 23-26, 1932. Saskatoon. (4pp). *BVAUS/Steeves
4-6.

1482 ------ UFC agricultural policy. Saskatoon. (4pp).
*OOA/Underhill.

1483 **Winnipeg Trades and Labor Council.** Annual Labor day
supplement and weekly news. Winnipeg. 48pp, illus.
*G 329.14 (71). Includes: Social legislation in Man-
itoba by H. Kempster; Co-operation and labor by J.T.
Hull; The march on Ottawa by J.S. Woodsworth; Organize for action by S.J. Farmer; Labor day message by
Tom Moore etc.

1484 **Wolfenden, Hugh H.** The real meaning of social insurance; its present status and tendencies. Toronto:
Macmillan. xvi, 227pp. *OONL. A statistical study.

1485 **Woodsworth, J.S.** Socialism in the House of Commons,
1932. Extracts from revised Hansard. Compiled by
J.S. Woodsworth. Ottawa: np. 16pp. BVIP NBSAM
*ACGL/PDbl BVAUS/Mac.43f.20 MWPA/Brigden 7 and CCF
39 and Ivens 6 OHMA1825 OKQS OOA/Underhill 57
OTURS/RSK SSA/G171.9 and G2.1932.2.

1486 ------ Speeches on the address - planned economy -
co-operative commonwealth and criminal code delivered
in the House of Commons on February 9, 11, 22 and
March 2, 1932. Ottawa: F.A. Acland. 23pp. *OOA/
Underhill 44.

1487 **Workers Unity League.** Charter of affiliation (for
the British Columbia Relief Camp Workers Union).
(Vancouver). (1p) for framing. *SRA/Riot f.1.
Signed by J.B. McLachlan, Sam Scarlett, Nick Thachuk,
Thos. A. Ewen (stamped), T.C. Sims and others.

1488 ------ Constitution adopted at the first national
congress, Montreal August 5,6, 7th. (Toronto).
20pp. *OTCPA.

1489 ------ Report of first national congress, August 5-
6-7, 1932. Montreal. (?Toronto). (45pp), all sections separately paged. *OHMA. Includes reports
(by J. Litterick etc), programs and resolutions.

1933

1490 **Anti-War Youth Conference.** War against war. Toronto.
(14pp). *BVAUS/WB43f.22 OTURS/RSK. To 'expose the
war preparations of the Canadian government, and the
militarization of the youth in Canada'.

1491 **Buhay, Becky and A.E. Smith.** 14,000,000 fighters
against terror: the World Defense Congress - its
lessons for Canadian workers and farmers. Toronto:
Canadian Labor Defense League. 16pp. *OTURS/RSK.

1492 **Campbell, Annie.** The social services. Calgary: CCF
4pp, mimeo. *OOA/CCF76. Radio address, 24th April.

1493 **Canadian Council on Child and Family Welfare.** Problems in the social administration of general and unemployed relief, Canada, 1933. Ottawa. (ii), 53pp.
*OOL. Discussions and findings of a conference, 1-4
May, 1932.

1494 **Canadian Labor Defense League.** The Alberta hunger-
march and the trial of the victims of Brownlee's
police terror. A document to all workers and farmers
to remember the events of 20th December 1932. Edmonton. 38pp. *BVAUS/WB31f.27 OTURS/RSK.

1495 ------ The Bennett-jailers blame Tim Buck for the
Kingston disturbances of last October - this is a
frame-up! Mobilize for his defence! Toronto. (4pp).
*OTURS/RSK.

1496 ------ Call for western congress against section 98.
Calgary. 2pp, mimeo. *OOA/CCF394.

1497 ------ A call to the rank and file of the CCF! For
united action against section 98 and for release of
class war prisoners. Toronto. (4pp). *BVAUS/WB31f.
27 OTURS/RSK.

1498 ------ Government charged with responsibility for
attempted murder of Tim Buck. Toronto. 9pp, mimeo,
not continuously paged. *OTURS/RSK. Includees memorandum and demands for class war prisoners.

1499 **Canadian Labor Defense League.** Protest resolution:
against cruel treatment of eight workers' leaders
in Kingston penitentiary. Toronto. (1p), broadside
mimeo. *OKQS OTURS/RSK.

1500 ------ Repeal Section 98! Release all class war
prisoners! Resolution. Toronto. (1p), broadside.
*OOA/CCF394.

1501 ------ Report: first representative national convention, Toronto 14-17 July 1933. (Toronto). 31pp,
mimeo, not continuously paged. *OTURS/RSK. Includes
reports and resolutions.

1502 ------ Section 98: its application to the Evans
case. Vancouver. 23pp. BVIP *BVAUS/WB31f.27 OTURS/
RSK. Evans was arrested in connection with the Prince-
ton miners strike in BC.

1503 ------- Smash the frame-up on Tim Buck! Defend the
eight in Kingston from this new savage attack! Down
with the Bennett terror and frame-up government!
Toronto. (2pp), mimeo. *OTURS/RSK.

1504 ------ Take up the challenge of the iron heel! Declaration of national Executive Committee. (Toronto).
(1p), broadside. *OTURS/RSK.

1505 ------ Unity of all workers - native and foreign-
born - against deportation! Statement of national
committee. (Toronto). (2pp), mimeo. *OTURS/RSK.

1506 ------ Workers solidarity against fascism: stop
Hitler's horrors! Toronto. 16pp. *BVAUS/WB40f.8a
OTURS/RSK.

1507 **Canadian Labor Party.** Report of Executive Committee.
Edmonton. 4pp. *OOA/Woodsworth 10 OOL.

1508 **Communist Party of Canada.** Honor the memory of our
working class leaders Lenin, Liebknecht, Luxemburg.
(Toronto). (1p), broadside. *OTURS/RSK. Also relates to section 98.

1509 **CCF.** Canada's Charter of Freedom: CCF national manifesto. Control Canada's Future. Vancouver. 7pp.
*ACGA/Hutchison.

1510 ------ A catholic can join the CCF. (?Ottawa).
(4pp). *ACGA/Smith 11 SSA/G2.1933.7.

1511 ------ Constitution: adopted Regina 1933. Amended
Toronto 1936, Winnipeg 1937, Edmonton 1938, Winnipeg
1940, 1942 etc. *OOA/CCF various. Early issues mimeo.

1512 ------ Handbook for speakers compiled from reports
of conferences held in Saskatoon and Regina January
7 and February 11 respectively, 1933. Saskatoon.
24pp. *ACGL/PDb.Labor OHMA2944 OOA/CCF321 SSA/
G18.1933.4. SSUS/JL197. Folding 'Economic programme'
stapled in; includes Farmer-labor group economic policy - federal.

1513 ------ The independent CCF: BC provincial platform.

Vancouver. 12pp. *OTURS/RSK.

1514 **CCF.** Letter to all CCF clubs in Ontario: headed Toronto Regional Labor Council of the CCF. Toronto.
(1p). *OTURS/RSK. The letter declares 'unalterable
opposition' to the provincial council recommendation
barring former members of the Communist Party from
membership or office in the CCF and asks for the
support of all CCF clubs in their opposition.

1515a------ Programme adopted at first national convention
held at Regina, Sask., July 1933. Ottawa. 8pp.
*AEUS/CCF XIII-19 OOA/CCF109 SSA/G2.1933.1.

1515b------ Manifesto and program as adopted by the first
annual convention of the federation at Regina, July
19th to 21st, 1933. Calgary. (2p) cover plus (3)
fold out pages. *ACGA/Coote 4 SSA/G2.1933.4 SSUS/
CCF. Has cover title: You are invited to become a
member of the one movement in Canada which offers to
the Canadian people a way out of the present morass
of poverty, suffering and injustice..Join in the war
against poverty!

1515c------ Regina manifesto adopted at first national
convention held at Regina, Sask, July, 1933. Ottawa.
8pp. BVIP NSHPL OKQS OOP OTURS *ACGA/CCF29 BVAUS/
Mac.30f.8 OHMA1557 OOA/CCF310 SSA/G2.1933.6.

1515d------ Manifesto: programme. Toronto: Ontario section. 11pp. *ACGL/PDb; BVAUS/Mac30f.8 OOA/CCF310
SSA/G3.Ont5.

1515e------ Regina manifesto. Toronto. 4pp. *OOA/CCF109.
It is probable that 1515a or b are the true first
editions of the Regina manifesto. Ottawa was the
federal centre, while Calgary had the office of the
national secretary (Norman Priestley). The other
three issues, although all published in 1933, seem
to be later printings.

1516 ------ Proceedings of organization meeting New Brunswick section. Moncton. 6pp, mimeo. *OOA/CCF318
OTURS lacking last page. Proceedings of the 2nd, 3rd
and 4th convention exist in typescript only; no trace
of later conventions.

1517 ------ A reply to mudslingers: William Arthur Pritchard. Vancouver. (c1933). (1p). *BVAUS/Steeves
3-11.

1518 **Davies, Stanley J.** Socialization of the credit and
banking system of Canada. Calgary: CCF. 4pp, mimeo.
*OOA/CCF76. Radio address, 6th March.

1519 **Dawson, Robert MacGregor** (ed). Constitutional issues
in Canada. xvi, 482pp. "OONL. Contains material on
election frauds, farmers movement, Senate reform, farmer-labor platforms etc.

1520 **Farmer-Labor Group.** Liberal 'beliefs' and 'willing-
ness'. Saskatoon. (c1933). (1p), broadside. SSUS/
JL197.

1521 **Farmer-Labor Group (CCF).** The Liberals say...
Prince Albert. (4pp). *SSA/G18.1933.8.

1522 **Friends of the Soviet Union.** Constitution. (Toronto).
(c1933). 2pp, mimeo. *OTAR/CPC/11f.33.

1523 ------ November seventh 1933. Sixteen years of socialism in the Soviet Union. Toronto. (4pp). OHMA.

1524 ------ Who are the friends of the Soviet Union?
Toronto. 16pp. *BVAUS/WB31f.41. OTURS/RSK.

1525 **Glen, Andrew.** Lessons from Russia. (Toronto): (?CCF)
28pp. *OHMA1610, photocopy.

1526 **Good, W.C.** Is democracy doomed? Toronto: Ryerson.
31pp. OKQ *OHMA1609 OOA/Woodsworth 12 SSUS/JL197.

1527 **Graham, Jean.** Parent education with particular ref-
erence to the working classes. Unpublished MA thesis
University of Toronto. (ii), 87, ii pp. biblio.
*OTUAR.

1528 Howard, **Roy and Joseph Stalin.** Russia and Japan.
Will war come? Full text of interview. Vancouver:
Commonwealth. 15pp. BVIP *BVAUS/Mac42f.25a.

1529 Hugli, **Edwin E.H.** The new Canada: an engineer's plans
and specifications for a new economic structure for
Canada and policies relating thereto. Toronto. 53pp.
AEU NSHPL OH OTP SRU *OOP. Author acknowledges being
a member of the CCF and Socialist parties, the League
for Social Reconstruction, the movement for a Christian
social order and the Canadian commonwealth movement.

1530 **Irvine, William.** Political servants of capitalism:
answering Lawson and Mackenzie King. Ottawa: Labour
publications. 112pp. AEU OTU *ACGL BVAUS/Mac30f.4
and Young OHMA2723 OKQS OOA/CCF310 and 538 SSUS/
JL 197.

(1531)Ison, Francis James. The functions of organized labour. Unpublished MA thesis, University of Manitoba.
190, (1)pp. biblio.

1532 **Keen, George.** Essentials of co-operative success.
Brantford: Cooperative Union of Canada. (4pp).
*BVAUS/Mac39Af.17.

1533 League for Social Reconstruction. Canada and socialism. Toronto. (4pp). *AEUS/CCF XIII-27 BVAUS/Mac
31Af.32 OOA/CCF168 OOAL.

1534 ------ Handbook : - manifesto, constitution, reports
pf national conventions, activities of branches. Toronto. 16pp. *ACGL/PDb.LSR BVAUS/Mac31Af.32 OOA/
Underhill 56 SSUS/Comm.

1535 ------ How can we begin? Montreal. (c1933). (1p)
broadside. *SSA/G105.1. Leaflet 3.

1536 ------ We want member groups! Montreal. (c1933).
(1p), broadside. *SSA/G105.4. Leaflet 1.

1537 ------ Why social reconstruction? Montreal. (c1933).
(4pp). *SSA/G105.5. Leaflet 2.

1538 **Lealess, Bob.** Supressed radio speech. Vancouver: United Front. (4pp). *BVAUS/Mac31Af.19 and Smith/CP. Attacking all other parties, BC provincial election.

1539 **Leisemer, Aylmer.** The need of today. Calgary: CCF. 4pp, mimeo. *OOA/CCF76. Radio address, February 20.

1540 **Losovsky, A.** The workers economic struggles and the fight for workers rule: some challenging international lessons. Montreal: Contemporary. 32pp. *BVAUS/WB 48f.18b. OHMA3106 OTURS/RSK. 'Of invaluable assistance to all revolutionary workers in Canada' (intro).

1541 **Lyon, H. Edward,** (interpreter)*(sic)*. The independent CCF, BC provincial platform. More action! Less talk! Vancouver: Independent CCF. 14pp. *BVAUS/Webster 3-7.

1542a **(McFarlane, A.T.)** Monkey sense: a picture story with a moral for grown-up people by Mack Cryland. Ottawa: Peoples Publishing. 28pp, illus. *OOA/CCF310.

1542b ------ as above, reissued under McFarlane's name, new illus. Toronto: Canadian Forum Book Service, 1945. 32pp. *OOA/CCF537.

1543 **MacGibbon, Inez Kilburn.** Unemployment, its causes and remedies. Unpublished (?MA) thesis, Acadia University. (vi), 103pp. ms only. biblio. *NSWA.

1544 **MacGregor, D.C.** The Canadian wage earner in the machine age. Toronto: Social Service Council of Canada. 16pp. *OTAR/1933/8. Machine age series 3.

1545 **McGuigan, D.F.** After capitalism - what? Why not? A new and definite plan. Toronto. 52pp. *OTURS/RSK. A socialist proposal.

1546 **MacInnis, Angus.** Speech on the budget delivered in the House of Commons on Tuesday, April 11, 1933. Ottawa: J.O. Patenaude. 6pp. *BVAUS/Mac27f.44.

1547 **MacPhail, Agnes.** The economic crisis and the CCF; an address to the annual convention of the United Farmers of Alberta on January 18th, 1933. Calgary: (UFA). 10pp. *ACGL Peel 3347.

(1548) **Marsh, L.C.** The problem of seasonal unemployment: a quantitative and comparative survey of seasonal fluctuations in Canadian employment. Unpublished MA thesis, McGill University. 196pp.

1549 **National Committee of Unemployed Councils.** Building a new unemployed movement. Toronto. 32pp. *BVAUS/ Mac43f.12 OTURS/RSK. For non-contributory unemployment insurance, adequate relief, no evictions, free medical services etc.

1550 **Ontario, Dept of Labour.** Report on wages, hours and working conditions in the automotive transport industry. Toronto: Kings Printer. 10 plus (24)pp, mimeo. *OOL.

1551 **Ontario Provincial Council of Carpenters.** Proceedings held in city of Brantford, July 22nd, 1933. (?Toronto). 24pp, mimeo. *OPET/Gainey 4. 22nd Convention.

1552 **Ormond, D.M.** Report of the superintendent of penitentiaries re Kingston penitentiary disturbances, 1932.
Ottawa:F.A. Acland. 29pp. *OOA/MacPhail 3. Convict
J has been identified as Tim Buck: his evidence appears on pp 21-22.

1553 **(Piroshko, M.)** Holy Russia and underground Russia.
Vancouver. (c1933). 30pp. BVAU BVIP *MWPA/Russell
1 OHMA1928 OTURS/RSK. The pamphlet is anonymous,
the introduction signed M.P. A typewritten note inserted into one copy gives Piroshko's name and address. He was a longshoreman and a political refugee
from the 1905 revolution in Russia; this pamphlet
records the first 25 years of his life under the Czars.

1554 **Price, Harvey S.** The menace of a dictatorship. Calgary: CCF. 4pp, mimeo. *OOA/CCF76. Radio address,
13th February (first of the series).

1555 **Priestley, Norman F.** Unity. Calgary: CCF. 4pp,
mimeo. *OOA/CCF76 Radio address, 1st May.

1556 ------ What the CCF means to agriculture. Calgary:
CCF. 4pp, mimeo. *OOA/CCF76. Radio address 13 March.

1557 **Roebuck, Arthur W.** Roebuck exposes forest fiasco:
mal-administration of our forest resources, monstrous
pulpwood monopoly created...Toronto: Ontario Liberal
Association. 16pp. *OTURS/RSK.

1558 **Royall, W.H.** Real wages in Canada 1919-1932 with a
special analysis of earnings in 1931. Unpublished
MA thesis, McMaster University. (ii), 50pp. *OHMA.
'We may expect wages to rise very rapidly in 1934-35.'

1559 **Ryan, Oscar.** The 'sedition' of A.E. Smith. Toronto:
Canadian Labor Defence League. 19pp. *OTURS/RSK.

1560 **Saskatchewan Farmer-Labor Group (CCF).** Economic policy. As formulated by the delegates assembled in
annual convention July 1933. (Saskatoon). (4pp).
*ACGL/PDb.Labor BVAUS/Steeves 4-6 SSA/G18.1933.2.
Not same text as 1469 above. Various editions.

(1561) **Scott, F.R.** Freedom of speech in Canada. (Toronto):
Canadian Political Science Association. (20pp).
QMM QMU. ?Offprint from Papers and proceedings vol 5.

1562 **Skey, B.P.** Co-operative marketing of agricultural
products in Ontario. Unpublished PhD thesis, University of Toronto. (vi), 272pp. no biblio. *OTUAR.

1563 **Smith, A.E.** Is Tim Buck a political prisoner or a
criminal? Toronto: Canadian Labor Defence League.
(1p), broadside. *OTURS/RSK. A letter to Attorney-
General Price, challenging him to a debate.

1564 **(Smith, Stewart.)** Comments on the CCF program by G.
Pierce. Toronto: The Worker. 8pp, mimeo. *BVAUS/
WB/30Af.8a. Reprinted from The Worker, July 29, 1933.

1565 **Smith, W. Norman.** Co-operation between social units.
Calgary: CCF. 4pp, mimeo. *OOA/CCF76. Radio address
3rd April.

1566 **Stephen, A.M.** Marxism: the basis for a new social order. Vancouver: B.C. Clarion. 16pp. BVIP *BVAUS/ Mac41f.11 and Steeves 5-7 OHMA OTURS/RSK.

(1567) ------ The materialist conception of history. Vancouver: np. (c1933). 9pp. BVIP.

(1568)**Stone, Fred Victor.** Unemployment and unemployment relief in western Canada. Unpublished MA thesis, McGill University.

1569 **Taylor, K.W.** and others. The Church's attitude towards society: a series of five papers indicating the Church's approach to certain social and economic problems of the day. Toronto: Baptist Social Service Boards. (c1933). 30pp. *OTURS/RSK. Includes: The church and capitalism by K.W. Taylor; The church and wealth by M.C. Maclean; The church and unemployment by Alexander Stark; The church and state by Carl V. Farmer.

1570 **Turner, Amelia.** The CCF - development and purpose. Calgary: CCF. 4pp, mimeo. *OOA/CCF76. Radio address 27th February.

1571 **Underhill, Frank H.** The political ideas of John S. Ewart. Ottawa: Progressive. 10pp. *OAA/Underhill 63.

1572 **United Farmers of Canada.** The evolution of a policy. (Saskatoon). (8pp). *SSA/G37.28.

1573 ------ Report and copy of memorandum presented to the Royal Commission on Banking as it appeared in the August 31st, 1933 issue of the *Western Producer*. (Saskatoon). 5pp, mimeo. *SSA/G37.72.

1574 **United May Day Conference.** Manifesto to the workers of Toronto. Toronto. (4pp). *OHMA. Cover title advertises May day meetings. The conference represents '75 trade unions, labor and socialist organizations.'

1575 **Vogel, C.H.** Facts and fallacies in economics. Calgary. 11pp. *OOA/CCF296. Partially a social credit approach.

1576 **White, F.J.** What the CCF means to labor. Calgary: CCF. 4pp, mimeo. *OOA/CCF76. Radio address March.

1577 **Wiggins, W.E.** The Canadian farmers' next step. Saskatoon: Farmers Unity League. (c1933). 40pp. BVIP *OTURS/RSK. Includes Aims of the FUL.

1578 **Womens International League for Peace and Freedom.** Shall civilization perish? To parents, teachers, clergymen and you. Toronto. (c1933). (4pp). *SSA/McNaughton H32.

1579 **Woodsworth, J.S.** Canada's parliamentary machine. Prince Albert: North Star. (c1933). (4pp). *SSA/ G157.1 SSUS/CCF.

1580 ------ and others. Speeches on the cooperative commonwealth delivered Wednesday and Thursday, Feb-

ruary 1 and 2, 1933. Ottawa: F.A. Acland. 45pp.
QMMS OHMA1563 OOA/Spencer SSUS/JL197. The others
are Agnes MacPhail, G.G. Coote, A.A. Heaps, E.J. Garland, Angus MacInnis, William Irvine and Henry E.
Spencer.

1581 **Workers and Farmers United Front.** A call for unity!
Vancouver. (1p), broadside. *OOA/Woodsworth 6.
Signed by Arthur Evans and J.A. Bowles: attacking
the CCF.

1582 **Workers Publishing** Association. Workers calendar,
1934. Toronto. (12pp). *OHMA. Contains photos
of Communist leaders, Estevan strike etc.

1583 **Workers Unity League.** For the building and streng-
thening of the united front of the working class!
An open letter to the trade union movement of Canada
from the National Executive Board, May day 1933.
(Toronto): 3pp, mimeo. *OHMA.

1584 ------ Manifesto: To working men and women! To the
working class youth! Winnipeg. 4pp. *OTAR/CPC21.

1585 ------ The tasks of the revolutionary trade organizations in the work at the factories. Resolution of
the 8th session of the Central Council of the Red
International Labor Unions. (Toronto). (c1933).
7pp, mimeo. OHMA.

1586 ------ Policy, tactics, structure, demands. Toronto:
48pp. *BVAUS/WB33f.22 OTURS/RSK. Unemployment insurance, united front, strike, political affiliations.

1587 **Young Communist League of Canada.** Section 98: 20
years for fighting hunger. Toronto. (12pp). *BVAUS/
WB31f.2c OHMA3140 OTURS/RSK. On the arrest of Joe
Derry: written in the form of a trial (which had not
taken place at that time). Pamphlet 2.

1588 ------ What lies ahead for the working-class youth?
An answer! Toronto. 32pp. *BVAUS/WB31f.1a OHMA
3137 OTURS/RSK.

1589 **Young Socialist League.** Constitution as endorsed by
the first annual convention January 29, 1933. (?Van-
couver). (1p). *BVAUS/Mac30Af.2a.

1934

1590 **Alexander, W.H.** Taking the fortress - and after.
An address on the CCF delivered at the annual con-
vention of the United Farmers of Alberta, Edmonton,
January 16th, 1934. Calgary: (UFA). 8pp. *ACGL/
PDbl. OOA/Underhill 44.

1591 **Barritt, Mrs R.W.** History of the United Farm Women.
(Calgary): (UFW). 8pp. *ACGL Peel 3369.

1592 **Bellamy, Edward.** Looking backward, 2000-1887. Vancouver: Totem. 263pp. BVIP BVIPA *BVAU. Introduction by W.A. Pritchard.

1593a **Bourassa, Henri.** Discours sur les réformes économiques et sociales, prononcé à la Chambre des Communes le 20 mars 1934. Ottawa: J.O. Patenaude. 18pp. QMM

1593b ------ Speech on economic and social reform delivered in the House of Commons, Tuesday March 20, 1934. Ottawa: J.O. Patenaude. 18pp. *OOAL. 'Socialism is sounder - I am not afraid to say this - than either democracy or liberalism.'

1594 **British Columbia Workers and Farmers United Front** Election Campaign Committee. For bread, jobs and freedom. Vancouver. (c1934). 16pp. *OTURS/RSK. Manifesto and program of demands: with a list of provincial candidates in BC.

1595 **Bronson, Harold E.** Power lines should be installed free! Edmonton: CCF. (6pp). *ACGA/CCF25.

1596 **Bureau of Municipal Research.** Unemployment relief in a metropolitan community. Toronto. (4pp). *OOL

1597 **Bureau of Social Research.** Money power in Canada - capitalism. Regina: CCF (1p). *SSA/G2.1934.2.

1598 **Canadian Labor Defense League.** Defense educational courses. (Toronto). 16pp, mimeo. *OTURS/RSK.

1599 ------ For a public investigation into the attempt on Tim Buck's life! Manifesto of the National Executive Committee. Toronto. (1p), broadside. *OTURS/RSK.

1600 ------ Mass unity wins! The story of the A.E. Smith trial. Toronto. 23pp. *OHMA3139 OTURS/RSK.

1601 ------ Problems in building a mass defense movement: against the arrest and imprisonment of workers engaged in labor activities! For the right to strike and picket! Against section 98 and all anti-labor news! Toronto. 24pp. *OTURS/RSK. Sub-title inside: Documents on tasks and role of the CLDL - national gathering September 29 and 30 1934, Toronto.

1602 ------ Workers self-defense in the courts. Toronto. (c1934). 34pp. *BVAUS/WB31f.27 OHMA3146 OTURS/RSK. What to do if arrested. Includes (pp19-34) Annie Buller's self-defence (final speech) in Estevan.

1603 **Canadian Labor Party.** Labor candidates merit your support. Why? Calgary. (4pp). *ACGA/Smith 5. Contains policy statements.

1604 **Canadian League Against War and Fascism.** Report: first Canadian congress against war and fascism, 6 and 7 October, 1934. Toronto. 25pp. BVIP *BVAUS/WB43f.17(i) OTURS/RSK.

1605 **Chemodanov, (V).** Unite the youth! (Toronto): Young Worker. 16pp. *OTURS/RSK. Chemodanov was secretary to the Young Communist International.

1606 **Citizens Research** Bureau of Canada. A cross section
of certain features of direct unemployment relief.
Toronto. (4pp), and fold out chart. *OOL.

1607 **Communist Party of Canada.** Ce que veut le Parti
Communiste. Montréal: Association des Editions
Contemporaines. 88pp. *OHMA.

1608 ------ Constitution: as amended by the sixth convention 1929 and the seventh convention July 1934.
(Toronto). 18pp, mimeo. *OKQS OTURS/RSK. Issued
in plain wrappers; first publication traced since
1925. From now various editions, almost annually.

1609 ------ Educational course. (Toronto). (c1934).
59pp, mimeo. *BVAUS/WB31f.1c. OTURS/RSK. Plain
wrappers: gives history of CPC up to resignation
of Macdonald after the sixth convention.

1610 ------ Manifesto: unite and fight the pacifist-
screened war plans of the Bennett government! Fight
for higher wages and relief to meet the increasing
inflation prices. (Vancouver). 8pp, mimeo. *BVAUS/
WB31f.4.

1611 ------ Message from the Communist Party of Canada
southern Ontario district: Commemorate the tenth
anniversary of the death of Vladimir Ilyich Lenin,
leader of the toilers of the world. Toronto. (1p)
broadside. *OTURS/RSK.

1612a------ What the Communist Party stands for: plain
talks on vital problems. Montreal: Contemporary.
93pp. *OHMA2379 OKQS OTURS/RSK SSUS/Comm. Based
on *Why communism?* by M.J. Olgin.

1612b------ the same, 3rd revised edition 1936. 119pp.
Enlarged with considerable Canadian material. *BVAUS/
WB31f.1a OTURS/RSK OOA/Woodsworth 54.

1613 ------ Workers leaflet manual. (Toronto). 21pp.
*OTURS/RSK. On organizing, issuing and distributing
leaflets.

1614 ------ Workers school: trade union strategy and
tactics. (Outline) by P.T. (Toronto): Workers School.
15pp, mimeo. *OTURS/Salsberg T.10.24.

1615 **Contemporary Publishers.** Tim Buck - dauntless leader
of the Canadian working-class. A brief sketch of his
manifold activities in the interests of the Canadian
toilers. Montreal: Contemporary. (c1934). 16pp.
*BVAUS/WB39f.2a(ii) OTURS/RSK.

1616 **CCF.** Conservative and liberal objections answered.
Ottawa: Peoples. (4pp). *ACGA/Smith 15 MWPA/Ivens
6 OHMA1555 SSA/Glnd9 and G2nd5.

1617 ------ The CCF goal. Regina. (4pp). *OOA/CCF126
SRA/CCF.Miscl3. SSA/Glnd4 and G2.1934.3 SSUS/CCF.

1618a------ National manifesto and immediate program.
Regina. (2pp) plus 3 inside foldout pp. *SSA/G2.
1933.3 and G1.1934.2 SSUS/CCF.

also published in Vancouver, same title, (4pp).
*ACGA/Hutchison.

1618b **CCF.** Federal manifesto: immediate federal programme
adopted by the Winnipeg convention, July 17-19th, 1934.
Toronto. (8pp). *OOA/CCF316 OTURS/RSK.

1618c------ Immediate program, Winnipeg convention July 17-
19th, 1934. (Winnipeg). 2pp, mimeo. *OOA/CCF10.
These issues all contain essentially the same text
with minor additions. This program includes for the
first time the celebrated clause that the CCF 'is un-
alterably opposed to war'.

1619 ------ The most frequent objections to socialism
answered. Regina. (4pp). *OOA/CCF126 SSA/Glndl9
SSUS/CCF.

1620 ------ Pamphlet list. (Toronto). (4pp). (c1934).
*OTURS/RSK. 26 titles and CCF manifestos.

1621 ------ What is the C.C.F? Ottawa: Peoples Publishing.
4pp. *OOA/CCF299. There are other editions with this
title but with varying texts, listed under appropriate
years.

1622 ------ The CCF: what it is and what it stands for.
Edmonton: Alberta Labor News. (c1934). (4pp).
*ACGL/PDbl.

1623 **Coote, G.G.** and others. Speeches on the revision of
the Bank Act and on the act to incorporate the Bank
of Canada delivered in the House of Commons on Thursday March 1 and Thursday March 8, 1934. Ottawa: J.O.
Patenaude. 31pp. *SSA/G2.1934.1. The others are
H.E. Spencer, J.S. Woodsworth, E.J. Garland and W.
Irvine.

1624 **Economic Safety League.** Statement of reasons for
opposing social credit. Calgary. (c1934). (4pp).
*OTURS.

1625 **Evans, John.** A reply to Motherwell. (Saskatoon): np.
(4pp). *K. An attack on Motherwell's review of the
CCF Farmer-Labor program.

1626 **Farmer-Labor Group.** Declaration of policy: official
manifesto. Regina. 4pp. *SSA/G18.1934.2.

1627 **Farmer-Labor Political Group.** A summarised report
of the conferences held in Regina, December 27th and
Saskatoon, December 29, 1933. Prince Albert. 17pp.
*ACGL/PDbl SSA/G18.1933.10.

1628 **Forsey, E.A.** Dividends and the depression. Toronto:
Thomas Nelson. 35pp. BVIP OH OPET *BVAUS/Mac31Af.32
MWP. LSR pamphlet 1. Includes LSR programme.

1629 **Friends of the Soviet Union.** For the resumption of
full diplomatic and trade relations between Canada
and the Soviet Union come to the mass meeting at
Hygeia Hall, January 30, 1934. Toronto. (4pp).
*OHMA.

1630 **Gardiner, Robert.** Annual UFA presidential address, UFA convention January 16th, 1934. Edmonton: United Farmers of Alberta. 8pp. *OOA/Underhill 44.

1631a**Gauthier, Georges.** La doctrine sociale de l'église et la C.C.F.: lettre pastorale. Montréal: L'école sociale populaire. 31pp. *OKQS.

1631b------ La CCF et les catholiques. Québec: L'action catholique. 40pp. *OKQS. Same texts.

1632 **Graham, Thomas.** Report of the engineer respecting the wage dispute between the liquidators of the Acadia Coal Company and their employees represented by the United Mine Workers of America. (?Halifax): np. 21pp. *NSHP OOL.

1633 **Harris, Eric.** The new deal in Canada. Toronto: Ryerson. 139pp. MWP OKQ QMBN QQLA *OTURS.

1634 **Heaps, A.A.** and others. Speeches on unemployment relief, financing public works, national insurance, federal health policy etc. Ottawa: J.O. Patenaude. 31pp. *ACGL/PDfl. MWPA/Ivens 6 OOA/Spencer. The others are G.G. Coote, W. Irvine, H.E. Spencer and J.S. Woodsworth.

1635 **Henderson, Fred.** The social credit illusion. Vancouver: Commonwealth. 20pp. BVIP OOP *BVAUS/Mac31 f.20 and Young OOA/CCF541. Report of a speech.

1636 **(Independent Labor Party).** Labor manifesto. (Toronto). (4pp). *OTPB/Buckley. Cover has slogan: 'Electors of West York: J.W. Buckley, official labor candidate' with photograph.

1637 **Industrial Workers of the World.** Minutes of the 21st constitutional general convention of the IWW, November 12-18, 1934. Chicago. *BVAUS/IWW. Contains report from Canadian administration pp 4-6, signed Wm. McPhee and Jalmar Salmi. Note that most minutes of IWW conventions in the United States have some references to Canadian affairs, but these (the references) are largely miniscule.

1638 **Irvine, Wm.** Co-operation or catastrophe. An interpretation of the CCF and its policy. Ottawa. 48pp. *ACGL BVAUS/Mac30f.4 and Young OOA/CCF310 and 536 OTURS/RSK SSA/G501.2 SSUS/JL197. Second edition published c.1940 with slight change in wording on the last page.

1639 ------ The forces of reconstruction. Ottawa: Labour Publishing. 40pp. BVIP NBSAM OH OTP OTU *ACGL MWPA/ CCF39 OOA/CCF310 SSA/G501.3. Peel 3385.

1640 **Keen, George.** Education of the public in consumers co-operation. Brantford: Co-operative Union of Canada (4pp). *BVAUS/Mac39Af.17 SSUS/Coops.

1641 **Lamberti, Carlo.** CCF anthem. Toronto: Barraud Music. 4pp. *OOA/Lucas 3. See also 1647 below.

1642 **League for Social Reconstruction.** Combines and the consumer. Toronto: Thomas Nelson. 32pp. BVIP OH OOP OPET OTU *BVAUS/Mac31Af.32 NSHD/J4. LSR pamphlet 2. Includes programme.

1643 ------ Manifesto. Toronto. (4pp). *OHMA OKQS.

1644 ------ Socialism or social credit? Toronto. (2pp) (4 columns per page). *OTURS. Attacking Aberhart.

1645 ------ Third annual report. Toronto. 10pp, mimeo. *OOA/Underhill 52.

1646 **Left-wing Organizations.** Workers of Toronto: for unity in the struggle against fascism, hunger and terror! Down with the Trotskyite renegades, the supporters of the social democracy, the disrupters of the unity of the masses! Down with the mud-slingers against the Communist International and the Soviet Union! Who paved the way to fascism in Germany? Toronto. (c1934). (2pp), mimeo broadside. *OHMA.

1647 **Loveless, George.** Tolpuddle martyr's song: proposed as an official song for the CCF. London (Ont): (Brotherhood of Railway Carmen of America). (4pp). *OOA/CCF. See also 1641 above.

1648 **Martin, John L.** The social effect of machine development: facts and figures showing the relative increase in productive capacity and the resulting social and economic changes. Vancouver: Commonwealth. 15pp. *ACGL/PDb1 BVAUS/Mac39f.1D SRA/CCFmisc 3.

1649 **Maund, C.J.** A plan for Canada. (Toronto). 23pp. *OTURS/RSK. A public works program.

1650 **Named Doukhobors of Canada.** Declaration proclaimed and accepted at the second convention of the authorized delegates held at Verigin, Saskatchewan, from 29th July to the 7th August, 1934. (Verigin). 2pp, mimeo. *SSA/McNaughton H10.

1651 **Pieck, W.** Towards soviet Germany. Montreal: Contemporary. 36pp. *BVAUS/WB39f.16 OTURS/RSK.

1652 **Price, Eleanore.** Address of the UFWA President to UFA convention: Edmonton January 16, 1934. Edmonton: United Farmers of Alberta. 6pp. *ACGA/Smith 15.

1653 **Roberge, Hector L.** Shall we have socialism, christianity and the golden rule or capitalism, christianity and the rule of gold? Battleford. 20pp. *OOA/CCF296 and Lucas/ 3 SSA/G176.1. 3,000 printed.

1654 **Ryan, Oscar, E. Cecil-Smith, H. Francis and Mildred Goldberg.** Eight men speak: a political play in six acts. Toronto: Progressive Arts Clubs of Canada. 43pp, illus. AEU OH OHM OKQ OTP SRU *BVAUS/WB41f.9a OTURS/RSK. Based on the trial of the Communist leaders and the disturbances in Kingston penitentiary.

1655 **Saskatchewan Youth Congress.** Report of the first congress. Saskatoon. (c1934). 20pp, mimeo. *SSA/G205.3. Includes constitution.

1656 **Scott, F.R.** Social reconstruction and the BNA Act. Toronto: Thomas Nelson. 38pp. AEU BVIP NBSAM OH OOP OPET *BVAUS/Mac31Af.32 OHMA2950 OOA/CCF539, photocopy. LSR Pamphlet 4. Includes program of LSR.

1657 **Simpson, James.** The International Labour Office at Geneva. Toronto: Oxford University Press. 19pp. *OTURS/RSK. An address given before the Liberal-Conservative summer school, Newmarket, Sept. 1933.

1658 **Sims, T.C.** Strike strategy and tactics. (?Toronto): Workers Unity League. 35pp. *BVAUS/WB34f.16 OTURS/RSK. Sims was secretary of the WUL and this pamphlet is taken from his report to the League in September 1934. 'It is in line with the strike strategy by Lozovsky, but based upon the experiences of the working class of Canada.' (Foreword).

1659 **(Smith, Stewart).** Socialism and the CCF by G. Pierce. Montreal: Contemporary. 218pp. OTP *BVAUS/WB30Af.4b OHMA3145 OTURS/RSK SRA/CCFmisc.54.

1660 **Socialist Labor Party of Canada.** Constitution. Toronto. (c1934). 21pp plus 3 numbered blanks. *OTURS/RSK. Amendment slip pasted in.

1661 **Socialist Party of Canada.** The industrial union: the revolutionary weapon. Toronto. (c1934). (2pp), broadside. *OHMA.

1662 ------ Leaflet no. 1. St.Vital (Man). (1p), broadside. *BVAUS/Steeves 4-6. Gives brief history of the SPC, ILP, CPC etc.

1663 **Springett, E.J.** The bible vs. Karl Marx et al. A verbatim report of an address delivered before the East York Workers Association. Toronto: Commonwealth. 30pp. *T. Slip pasted over: earlier title was 'Christ vs. Karl Marx.'

1664 **Stephen, A.M.** Fascism: the black international. Vancouver: B.C. Clarion. (c1934). 23pp. BVIP *BVAUS/Mac43f.5a OTURS/RSK.

1665 ------ Hitlerism in Canada. Vancouver: Canadian League against War and Fascism. (c1934). 31pp. BVIPA BVIV SRL *BVAUS/WB43f.5a OTURS/RSK. Includes the League's plan of action.

1666 **Stevens, H.** Stevens' booklet, as suppressed by Rt. Hon. R.B. Bennett. Toronto: New Commonwealth. (4pp). *OTURS.

1667 **Stuart, Henry Harvey.** Some world problems of major importance. An address delivered in Oddfellows Hall, Fredericton, N.B., Sunday afternoon, January 7th, 1934. (Fredericton): np. (4pp). *OOA/CCF184.

1668 **Thomas, Ernest.** Christian churches and economic conditions. (Toronto): United Church of Canada. 15pp, mimeo. *OOA/Good 19. The condemnation of capitalism as unchristian.

1669 Thomas, Ernest. The Church and the economic order.
Toronto: Thomas Nelson. 28pp. BVAS BVIP OH OOP
*BVAUS/Mac42f.27a OOA/Woodsworth 13 OOL. Contains
programme of the League for Social Reconstruction.

1670 **United Farmers of Alberta.** The Alberta government's
record and a reply to its critics. Edmonton. (c1934).
16pp. *ACGA/Spencer 2.

1671 **United Farmers of Ontario.** A message to the people
of Ontario. (Toronto). 3pp, mimeo. *OOA/CCF10 and
Good 14.

1672 ------ A programme for Canada's next parliament endorsed by the annual convention in Toronto, December
13-14, 1933. (Toronto). (4pp). *OOA/MacPhail 3.

1673 **United Mineworkers of America.** Constitution as amen-
ded and adopted by district convention at Truro, N.S.
November 19th-24th, 1934. (Halifax). 24pp. *OOA/
CCF31. District 26 of the UMA.

1674 **Vapaus.** Vapaus 1917-1934. Sudbury. 103pp plus advts
*OTURS/RSK. Commemorating 17 years of the Finnish
paper (and 17 years since the Russian revolution).
Includes articles by J.W. Ahlqvist, Jussi Latva,
Eero Haapalainen, T.C. Sims and others.

1675 **Wallace, J.S.** Class justice and mass defence. Montreal: Canadian Labor Defense League. (c1934).
8pp plus 8pp (bilingual). *OTURS/RSK. On section
98, the Feigelman case, Rouyn-Noranda and the organization of the CLDL. French title: Justice de
classe et défense de masse.

1676 **Weaver, W. Craig.** Unemployment insurance for Canada.
Unpublished MA thesis, McMaster University. (ii),
47pp; biblio. *OHMA.

1677 **Williams, Geo.** Old soldiers and the CCF. (?Regina):
CCF. (4pp). *SSA/G18.1933.9.

1678 **Winch, Harold E.** The politics of a derelict. Vancouver: B.C. Clarion. (c1934). 30pp. *BVIPA OTURS/
RSK. Printing his maiden speech. The title refers
to R.B. Bennett's remark that the government was 'not
going to wet-nurse every derelict in Canada'.

1679 **Winkel, Emil.** Gestapo: Hitler's secret service police.
Toronto: Canadian Labor Defense League. 20pp, mimeo.
*BVAUS/WB40f.8A(ii) OTCPA.

1680 **Winnipeg Trades and Labor Council.** Labor day annual,
1934. Winnipeg. 40pp. *T

1681 **Wolfenden, Hugh H.** Unemployment funds: a survey and
proposal. A study of unemployment insurance and other
types of funds for the financial assistance of the unemployed. Toronto: Macmillan. xviii, 229 pp, index.
*OONL.

1682 **Woodsworth, J.S.** The distribution of personal income
in Canada. Ottawa: Labour Publishing. (c1934). 8pp.
OTP *OOA/CCF198, 309, 326 OOP.

1683 **Woodsworth, J.S.** A plea for social justice. Extracts
from speeches in the House of Commons, 1930-1933.
Selected by Grace MacInnis. Ottawa: Labour Publishing.
80pp. ACG AEU BVIP MWU OH OOP *BVAUS/Mac43f.20 MWP
OHMA2881 OKQS OOA/CCF326 and Coldwell 62 OTURS/RSK
SSA/G171.11 SSUS/JL197. Peel 3364.

1684 ------ Speeches on the address in reply to the speech
from the throne, and the co-operative commonwealth,
delivered in the House of Commons, February 1 and 5
1934. Ottawa: J.O. Patenaude. 13pp. *ACGA/Hutchison
ACGL/PDbl. OOA/Underhill 44.

1685 ------ and others. Speeches on Natural Products
Marketing act, 1934 delivered in the House of Commons
April 19 to May 1st, 1934. Ottawa: J.O. Patenaude.
35pp. *OOA/Underhill 44 SSUS/JL197. Others include
A.A. Heaps, E.J. Garland, Angus MacInnis, Agnes Mac-
Phail.

1686 **Workers Unity League.** Rally to united struggle
against bosses and their agents! (Calgary). (c1934)
(1p). *ACGA/Smith 12.

1687 **Young Communist League.** Against hunger, war and
fascism! Young workers! Young farmers! Students.
Strike and demonstrate on May day! Toronto. (4pp).
*OHMA

1688 ------ A program for Canadian youth: resolution of
seventh national convention August 1934. Toronto.
24pp. *OTURS/RSK.

1689 **Ziegler, Olive.** Woodsworth, social pioneer (authorized sketch). Foreword by Dr Salem Bland. Toronto:
Ontario Publishing. 202pp. *OTURS/RSK.

1935

1690 **Action Committee for Relief Camp Workers.** Condemned
to starve...compelled to act! Vancouver. (1p),
broadside. *SRA/Riot 4.

1691 ------ Support the relief camp workers in their
fight against forced labor! Vancouver. (1p), broadside. *SRA/Riot 4.

1692 **Bellamy, Edward.** The parable of the water tank.
Saskatoon: CCF. 8pp. *ACGL/PDbl BVAUS/Mac39f.7
SSA/G2.1935.8. Several later editions.

1693 **Bickerton, G.** Address over CFQC, Saskatoon. Saskatoon: United Farmers of Canada. 3pp. *K.

1694 **BC Joint Defence Committee.** An appeal for justice!
Revive your support for the camp boys: it might have
been your boy! Vancouver. (4pp). *T.

1695 **Britnell, G.E.** The western farmer. Toronto: Social
Service Council of Canada. 16pp. ACG BVAS BVIP OOL

OONL OTP SSU *OTAR/1935/25 SSA/G154.7. Machine age
series 6.

1696 **Canada.** Dominion department of labour. (Regina).
(1p), broadside. *SRA/Riot 1. 'The Dominion government recognizes that many in the On to Ottawa trek
have been misled by extravagant promises.'

1697 **Canadian Labor Defense League.** Every worker a defender.
Toronto. *OTURS/RSK. Single card printed with charter
for the defense of workers rights and what to do when
arrested.

1698 ------ Free speech struggle, Toronto. The seditious
literature trial. Six workers rescued from police
terrorism. Toronto. (c1935). (4pp). *OTCPA.

1699 ------ Minutes of third national convention, Toronto
19-20 October 1935. (Toronto). 17pp plus 2pp financial statement, mimeo. *OTURS/RSK.

1700 ------ Report annual district convention, Toronto,
14-15 September 1935. (Toronto). 19pp, mimeo.
*OTURS/RSK. Prepared for presentation to the third
national convention.

1701 ------ Repprt annual district convention, Vancouver
BC, 25-26 August 1935. (Vancouver). 21pp, mimeo.
*OTURS/RSK. For presentation to the third national
convention.

1702 **Canadian League Against War and Fascism.** The people
versus war and fascism: proceedings second national
congress. Toronto. 39pp plus 1p index plus 3pp
classified list of organizations represented, mimeo.
*OTURS/RSK. Contains speech of Tim Buck pp15-20.

1703 ------ Will Canada escape fascism? Toronto. (c1935).
32pp. BVIP OHM SSU *BVAUS/Mac40f.8a NSHD/J4 OHMA
1491 OTURS/RSK.

1704 **Canadian Wheat Pools.** The Canadian wheat pools on
the air: a series of radio messages. Saskatoon. 46pp.
*ACGL OTMCL. Thirteen addresses.

1705 ------ The wheat pools in relation to rural community
life in western Canada: an account of some of the ways
in which the wheat pools have endeavoured to assist
the prairie community toward a happier and fuller manner of living. Saskatoon. 30pp. *SSUS/Short Peel
3424.

1706 **Canadian Youth Council.** Report on war. (Toronto).
(i), 9pp plus 5pp maps and charts. *OTURS/RSK. An
organizing committee for the Congress of Youth to be
held in Toronto 24-25 May.

1707 **Cassidy, H.M.** The British Columbia plan of health
insurance. (?Victoria): np. 16pp. *OOA/Bengough 3.

1708 **Cohen, J.L.** The Canadian unemployment insurance act
- its relation to social security. Toronto: T. Nelson.
167pp. *OOL.

1709 **Communist Party of Canada.** The Communist election program: a program for a better life! Toronto. 16pp. *BVAUS/Mac31f.1 and WB/31f.1a. OTURS/RSK. Also published in French.

1710 ------ Out on the streets on May first! Rally to defend the camp workers and Corbin miners! Unite your forces! Demonstrate against poverty, fascism and war! Vancouver. (1p), broadside. *BVIPA.

1711 ------ Stop the Pattullo-McGeer terror! Down with fascist citizen's league! Vancouver. (1p), broadside. *BVAUS/WB31f.2c. McGeer was mayor of Vancouver.

1712 ------ They want your votes! An exposure of capitalist parties and policies. (Toronto). 32pp. *BVAUS/WB31f.1c.

1713 ------ Toward a Canadian peoples front. Reports and speeches at the ninth plenum of the Central Committee, CPC, November 1935. (?Toronto). 216pp. *BVAUS/WB31f.1c OHMA2744 OOA/CCF542 OTURS/RSK. Contains reports by Stewart Smith, Earl Browder, Tim Buck, Bill Kashton *(sic)*, Jim Warner and others.

1714 ------ Unite and fight the pacifist-screened war plans of the Bennett government! Fight for higher wages and relief to meet the increased inflation prices! (Toronto). (4pp). *OHMA. See 1610 above for original. Apparently some changes in text.

1715 ------ The way to socialism: the program of the working people in the struggle against hunger, fascism and war. Montreal: Contemporary. 72pp. *OHMA2745 OTURS/RSK. Manifesto and principal resolutions adopted by the seventh national convention, July 1934.

1716 ------ Why merge? (Vancouver). (c1935). (4pp), mimeo. *BVAUS/Smith CP.

1717 ------ Workers school: trade union strategy. (Toronto): Workers School. (c1935). 9pp, mimeo. *OTURS Salsberg T-10. 24.

1718 **Conference Committee on Relief Camp Workers.** To the citizens of Vancouver district. Vancouver. (1p), broadside. *SRA/Riot 4.

1719 **Congress on Social and Unemployment Insurance.** The workers social and unemployment insurance bill adopted at the February 1935 congress: presented to the federal government 18 February 1935. Toronto. (4pp). *BVAUS/Smith CP.

1720 **Connell, Robt.** The co-operative commonwealth - what does it mean? Vancouver: (CCF). 15pp. *SSA/G3.BC.4 Text of a radio address, 9 June 1935.

1721 **CCF.** A brief autobiography and record of public service of M.J. Coldwell. Regina: CCF. (4pp). *OOA/CCF126. A biography, not an autobiography.

1722 ------ Constitution of the urban unit, CCF Saskatchewan section. (Regina). 3pp, mimeo. *OOA/CCF72.

1723 **CCF.** The CCF and religion. (Ottawa). (2pp).
*OOA/CCF126 SSA/G2.nd.2.

1724 ------ CCF election address. Regina. 4pp. *SSA/
G2.1935.2.

1725 ------ The CCF in Ontario. Toronto. (c1935). (4pp).
*D

1726 ------ Inflation and the worker. Vancouver. (c1935).
9pp, mimeo. *BVAUS/Turner 1.

1727 ------ Mr Stevens and exploitation. Vancouver.
*BVAUS/Smith. Stevens initiated the Canadian Recon-
struction Party.

1728 ------ The national election declaration of the CCF:
a new social order. Toronto. (4pp). *OOA/CCF126.

1729 ------ Program amd manifesto of the CCF: a compre-
hensive statement of the policies and ideals of the
CCF. Regina. 4pp. *OOA/CCF299 SSA/G1.1934.1.
Same text as the 1934 manifesto; also published in
French (Programme et manifest...) and German (Pro-
gramm und Aufruf...).

1730 ------ Provincial platform and manifesto (BC).
Vancouver. (4pp). *BVAUS/Smith CCF and Steeves 4-6.

1731 ------ Records of votes cast by the farmer and labor
group on the House of Commons, 1930-35. Regina.
19pp. OOA/CCF310 OTURS/Woodsworth.

1732 ------ We appeal! Vancouver. (4pp). *BVAUS/Smith
CCF and LP.

1733 ------ What is the answer of the CCF? A series of
questions and answers of the policy of the CCF.
Vancouver. (c1935). 16pp. *ACGL/PDbl BVAUS/Mac30A
f.4b OTURS/RSK SSA/G3.BC.14. Includes inside back
cover 'The CCF and war.'

1734 **Cooperative League.** How St Francis Xavier University
educates for action. The story of the remarkable
results achieved by the extension department of St
Francis Xavier University in Antigonish, Nova Scotia.
New York. 56pp. *OOA/MacPhail 3 SSUS/Coop.

1735 **Co-operative Movement.** Some still say...'It can't
be done' but...these farmers have done it. Toronto:
(c1935). (4pp). *OTURS/RSK.

1736 **Davidson, W.M.** The Aberhart plan: a survey and analysis of social credit scheme as placed before the
electors of Alberta. Calgary: Economic Safety League.
32pp. *ACGL Peel 3429.

1737 ------ The Aberhart proposals: an analysis of the
scheme offered Alberta in the name of social credit.
(Calgary): United Farmers of Alberta. 30pp. *ACGL
Peel 3430.

1738 **Davis, H.H.** Findings and report of the commissioner
re industrial dispute on the Vancouver waterfront
involving the Shipping Federation of British Columbia

Limited, and the longshore workers at that port. (Ottawa): Dept of Labour. 29pp. *BVAUS/Mac34f.16.

1739 **Employed Girls Council of Regina.** Constitution. Regina. (c1935). (4pp). *OTCPA.

1740 **Ewen, Thomas A.** Unity is the workers lifeline. Toronto: Unity. 34pp. *OTURS/RSK. Ewen was Dominion secretary of the Workers Unity League; this reprints most of his report to the 3rd Dominion convention of the WUL, 9 November 1935.

1741 **Farmer-Labor Party.** Know the facts. Wynyard (Sask). (7pp). *SSA/G18.nd.8.

1742 **Farmers National Committee for Action.** The farmers struggle. Regina. 31pp. *OTURS/RSK. A popular explanation of the farm emergency bill drafted by the first national conference of toiling farmers, Regina July 1934. This committee was formed at that time and intended to present the bill at the next session of the federal parliament.

1743 **Forsey, E.A.** Unemployment in the machine age: its causes. Toronto: Social Service Council of Canada. 16pp. AEU BVAS OKQ OOL OTP OTU SRU *OTAR/1935/24. SSUS/Labour. Machine age series 5.

1744 **Fournier, Leslie T.** Railway nationalization in Canada: the problem of the Canadian national railways. Toronto: Macmillan. xiv, 358pp. *OONL.

1745 **Francis, Edmund D.** (ed). Why? The diary of a camp striker. Vancouver: Commonwealth. 24pp. *BVAUS/ Mac34f.12. Inserted illus.

1746 **Gilman, C.P.** and **Huntly M. Sinclair.** Unemployment: Canada's problem. Ottawa: Army and Navy Veterans. xii, 119pp. *OONL.

1747 **Gordon, C.W.** (Ralph Connor). The trekkers: a statement, a protest, an appeal. Regina: Winnipeg Citizens Defence Committee. (1p), broadside: also issued in Vancouver. *OOA/Lucas 3 and OTURS/RSK.

1748 **Gordon, J. King.** A word to you! Victoria: CCF. (4pp). *SSA/G3.BC10. Cover title: Dominion elections October 14th 1935.

1749 **Halifax Trades and Labor Council.** Labor journal: history of the labor movement. Halifax. 80pp, illus. *NSHP. Published on the occasion of the TLCC meeting. Many portraits. Includes: Halifax Longshoremens Association by A.M. Sullivan; Plumbers and pipefitters by F.C. Craig; Bricklayers, masons and plasterers; typographers etc etc and Review of labor conditions by P.M. Draper.

1750 **Hughes, George B.** Profit sharing in Canada. Unpublished BA thesis, McMaster University. 62pp. *OHMA.

1751 **Humble, Harry.** Social credit democracy vs. dictatorship. Edmonton: W.D. Stovel. 22pp. *ACGL Peel 3443.

1752 Humble, Harry. Social credit for Alberta? Calgary:
W.D. Stovel. 18pp. *ACGL.

1753 **Hunter, Peter.** Forward to youth congress against
war and fascism! A call to action! To the youth of
Canada! Toronto: All Canadian Youth Congress against
War and Fascism. (4pp). *OHMA OTURS/RSK.

1754 **Industrial Workers of the World.** The IWW program:
education, organization, emancipation: labor's three
stars. Port Arthur. (c1935). (4pp). *BVAUS/IWW.

1755 ------ Minutes of the 3rd annual convention of the
Canadian administration of the IWW, October 21-25,
1935. (?Toronto). 12pp, mimeo. *BVAUS/IWW.

1756 **Irvine, William.** The brains we trust. Toronto:
Thomas Nelson. 48pp. AEU BVIP OH OTU OTP SSU *SSA/
G501.1 SSUS/JL197. A play.

1757 ------ Can a Christian vote for capitalism? Ottawa:
Labour Publishing. 32pp. BVIP NBSAM OOP *ACGA/CCF29
BVAUS/Mac39f.7 OOA/CCF310 OOAL SSUS/JL197.

1758 Kirkwood, M.M. Women and the machine age. Toronto:
Social Service Council of Canada. 20pp. OOL OTP
*OTAR. Machine age series 7.

1759 **League for Social Reconstruction.** Social planning
for Canada. Toronto: Thomas Nelson. xvi, 528pp.
*OTURS/RSK. Foreword by J.S. Woodsworth. The comm-
ittee consisted of Eugene Forsey, J. King Gordon,
Leonard Marsh, J.F. Parkinson, F.R. Scott, Graham
Spry and Frank H. Underhill.

1760 **Love, J.R.** A cross examination of the Aberhart plan
of social credit. Edmonton: United Farmers of Alberta.
(7pp). *ACGA/Smith 15. Peel 3454.

1761 ------ Some achievements of the Alberta government.
(Edmonton): United Farmers of Alberta. 15pp. *ACGA/
PDfl. Presented to the 1935 annual convention.

1762 **Lucas, Frank.** In defense. Vancouver: Canadian Labor
Defense League. 25pp, mimeo. *BVAUS/WB31f.27.
Partly a history of workers defense in Canada.

1763 **McCool, R.M.** Some facts: a series of 18 leaflets -
Fact finders series. Calgary: United Farmers of
Alberta. *ACGL/Smith 15. various pagination; all
reprinted from *The United Farmer* for the August election.

1764 **MacInnis, Angus and J.S. Woodsworth.** Speeches on Dominion elections and relief camps delivered in the House
of Commons February 19, 22, 26 and March 4 and 8, 1935.
Ottawa: J.O. Patenaude. 11pp. *SSA/G2.1935.4.

1765 **MacInnis, Grace and William Irvine.** The CCF and the
Liberals: how old-age pensions came to Canada (and)
The Liberals and the banks. Vancouver: Commonwealth.
16pp. *BVAUS/Smith.

1766 ------ and Charles J. Woodsworth. Canada through
CCF glasses. Vancouver: Commonwealth. (c1935). 88pp.

148

AEU BVIP NBSAM OOA OTU SRL *BVAUS/Mac30Af.3C and Young
MWPA/Brigden 7 OKQS.

1767 **Mackintosh, Margaret.** Trade union law in Canada.
Ottawa: J.O. Patenaude. 114pp. *OOL.

1768 **Macklin, I.V.** Politics and economics from the farmers standpoint in 1935. Grande Prairie. 16pp. *ACGL
PDf.1.

1769 **Marsh, Leonard C.** Employment research: an introduction to the McGill programme of research in the social
sciences. Toronto: Oxford University Press. xx,
344pp, biblio, index, errata slip. *OONL.

1770 **Martin, John L.** The Canadian cossacks: a review of
facts concerning the RCMP. Vancouver. 20pp. *BVAUS/
Mac44f.5 MWPA/Russell 1 OTURS/RSK. On various RCMP
activities, especially as *agents provocateurs* and strike
breakers, giving costs and statistics extracted from
government documents.

1771 **(May day).** All out to Cambie grounds May 1st. Join
the labor parade to Stanley Park. Vancouver: United
May day Conference. (1p) broadside. *T.

1772 **Moore, William Henry.** Mackenzie King and the wage
earner. Ottawa: National Liberal Federation. (c1935).
(8pp). *OOP.

1773 **Muir, E. St.C.** Poems of protest. North Vancouver.
(c1935). 36pp. BVAU *T.

1774 **National Conference of Friendship with the USSR.** The
first Canadian conference of friendship with the Union
of Socialist Soviet Republics to be held at Toronto,
Ontario, Saturday and Sunday June 29th and 30th, 1935.
Toronto. (4pp). *OOA/Woodsworth 6.

1775 **New, Gordon C.** Principles and practices of minimum
wage legislation with special reference to Canada.
Unpublished BA thesis, McMaster University. (ii),
100pp. biblio. *OHMA.

1776 **North Star.** The battle. (Prince Albert). (c1935).
(1p) broadside. *SSUS/CCF. Refers to the start of
The North Star to replace *The Farmer-Labor News* and the
lack of encouragement 'opposition and sniping within
our own ranks.'

(1777)**Ontario.** Report of the meeting of foundrymen called
by the Honourable Dr J.A. Falkner, Minister of Health
for December 28th, 1934 at Parliament buildings, Toronto, Ontario to consider measures for the prevention
of silicosis in foundries. Toronto: Kings Printer.
15pp. Ontario Ministry of Health Library.

1778 **Ontario Workers Federation on Unemployment.** One year
of Hepburn 'Liberalism' June 1934 to June 1935 as a
worker sees it. Toronto. (4pp). *OTCPA.

1779 **Patton, Harald S.** The Canadian wheat pool in prosperity and depression. Saskatoon: Canadian Wheat
Pool. 18pp. BVIP NBSAM OOP SSU *OTMCL Peel 3466.

1780 Regina Citizens Defence Committee. Bulletin no.3,
November 23, 1935. Regina. (1p) mimeo. *SRA/Riot
4. Regarding a provincial judicial commission.
The defence committees were anti-union.

1781 **Relief Camp Workers Union.** Appeal to the people of
British Columbia and citizens of Vancouver. Vancouver
2pp, mimeo. *BVAUS/Mac55Af.24. Report from a conference in Kamloops.

1782 **Richards, A.E.** Farmers business organizations in
Canada 1935. Ottawa: Dept of Agriculture. 55pp.
BVIV MWP *OOA/Avison 9. Co-operatives.

1783 **(Rosenberg, Louis or Lewis).** Who owns Canada? An
examination of the facts concerning the concentration
of the ownership and control of the means of production, distribution and exchange in Canada by Watt Hugh
McCollum. Regina: CCF. 60pp. BVIP OOP OTP *ACGL/
PDbl BVAUS/Mac41f.15a MWPA/Brigden 7 OHMA1578
OKQS OOA/CCF305 OTURS/RSK. Peel 3456A.

1784 **St Francis Xavier** College. Co-operative buying clubs.
Antigonish. 15pp. *OTURS/RSK.

1785 **Saskatoon Cooperative Association.** The co-operative
movement. Saskatoon. 4pp. *K.

1786 **Scott, F.R.** The efficiency of socialism. Kingston:
Queens Quarterly. pp215-225. *BVAUS/Mac43f.2 OTURS.
Offprint.

1787 ------ and H.M. Cassidy. Labour conditions in the
mens clothing industry: a report. Toronto: Thomas
Nelson. x,106pp. *MWP OONL.

1788 **Smith, Elizabeth H.** A survey of unemployment relief
in Canada. Unpublished BA thesis, McMaster University
(vii), 114, (115-124)pp. biblio. *OHMA.

1789 (Smith, Stewart). The communists fight for working
class unity: reports to the central committee, Communist Party of Canada by G. Pierce and Jim Warren.
Montreal: Contemporary. 59pp. *OTURS/RSK. Two
reports: The lessons of the struggle for a united
working class front; and Towards a mass party.
G. Pierce was Smith's psudonym; Jim Warren is doubtless another pseudonym since he is Warren on the
title and Warner at head of the report. It is also
probable that many of the so-called 'Montreal'
printings of these years actually originate in Toronto.

1790 **Socialist Labor Party of Canada.** Manifesto: to the
working class of Canada. Toronto. (2pp). *BVAUS/
Mac31Af.18.

1791 **Socialist Party of Canada.** Final report July 1935
(and) Report to the convention of CCF affiliates
held in Vancouver July 27th and 28th, 1935 (and)
Constitution of the CCF (BC section). Vancouver:
SPC and CCF. 1,plus 3 plus 3pp, mimeo. *T.

1792 **Soper, Robert Armitage.** Industrial labour conditions in Canada. Unpublished BA thesis, McMaster University. (ii), 137pp. biblio. *OHMA.

1793 **Strachey, John.** Fascism means war! Toronto: Canadian League Against War and Fascism. (c1935). 17pp. *BVAUS/WB40f.8a(i) OTURS/RSK. Includes plan of action of the League.

1794 **Toronto District Labor Council.** Official Labor day souvenir programme; September 2nd, 1935. Toronto. 60pp. *OHMA3104. Includes: Labor day recognition by James Simpson; Review of labor conditions by P.M. Draper etc.

1795 **Trade Union Action Committee.** An appeal to all members of the A.F. of L. Vancouver. (1p) broadside. *SRA/Riot 4. Regarding relief camps.

1796 **Trotsky, Leon.** The Kirov assassination. Toronto: Workers Party. 32pp. *BVAUS/Mac38f.13 OTURS/RSK.

1797 **Underhill, Frank H.** The conception of a national interest. Toronto: Canadian Journal of Economics and Political Science. pp396-408. *OOAL. Offprint.

(1798) ------ Labour legislation in British Columbia. Unpublished PhD thesis, University of California. iv, 298pp.

1799 ------ The railway problem and the BNA act. (Toronto): (CCF). 12pp, mimeo. *OOA/Woodsworth 12.

1800 **United Farmers of Alberta.** Manifesto of the Alberta government. Progressive program sets forth immediate practical steps on way to ultimate objective of UFA movement. Edmonton. (c1935). (6pp). *ACGL/PDf1 OTURS.

1801 ------ Provincial program of the UFA as finally adopted by the annual convention held in Calgary January 15th to 18th inclusive, 1935. (Calgary). (4pp). *ACGL/PDf1. OTIRS.

1802 **United Farmers of Canada.** Land nationalization programme of the UFC. (Saskatoon). (c1935). (4pp). *SSA/G37.44 SSUS/UFC.

1803 **Ward, Burnett.** Verey lights from The Listening Post by Flare-Pitol Pete. Vancouver: Commonwealth. (c1935). 64pp, illus. *T.

1804 **Woodsworth, J.S.** Political democracy. Toronto: University of Toronto Quarterly. pp296-314. *OOA/CCF326 OTURS/RSK SSUS/JL197. Offprint.

1805 ------ Speech on co-operative commonwealth and unemployment insurance delivered in the House of Commons on February 11 and 18, 1935. Ottawa: J.O. Patenaude. 12pp. *SSA/G2.1935.3.

1806 ------ and others. Speeches on the co-operative commonwealth, a national health policy (and) the budget during the session of 1935. Ottawa: J.O.

Patenaude. 34pp. *OTURS/RSK SSUS/JL197. Others include Angus MacInnis and E.J. Garland on the CCF; Henry E. Spencer on national health; G.G. Coote and William Irvine on the budget.

1807 **Workers Alliance.** Resolution - for the creation of useful, productive work. Vancouver: (c1935). (1p) broadside. *BVAUS/Mac55Af.24.

1808 Yates, S.W. State medicine. Saskatoon: United Farmers of Canada. 16pp. *OOA/Lucas 3 SSA/G37.87.

1809 **Young Communist League.** How shall young Canada vote? Toronto. (4pp). *OHMA.

1810 ------ To the youth of British Columbia. Vancouver: (c1935). (1p) broadside. *BVIPA.

1936

1811 **Alberta Wheat Pool.** Tides in the west: a brief history of the origin, aims and objectives of the wheat pool movement in western Canada. Calgary. 45, vi.pp. *ACGL Peel 3490.

1812 **Andrews, Lilian.** Youth of the happy land. Toronto: Youth Publishers (c1936). 36pp. OONL *BVAUS/WB43 f22.

1813 **Anti-War Day Conference** Committee. Against imperialist war! Anti-war day August 1st! (Vancouver). (1p) broadside. *BVAA. Refers to a conference called on 12th July by the Communist Party of Canada with 34 workers organizations represented.

1814 **Buck, Tim.** Celebrate the repeal of section 98! A message to you. Toronto: Communist Party of Canada. (4pp). *OTURS/RSK.

1815 ------ A message to you: signalize triumph by building party of social progress! Toronto: Communist Party of Canada. (4pp). *BVAUS/WB31f.2c OTURS/RSK.

1816 ------ The road ahead: report to the eleventh session of the Central Committee, Communist Party of Canada. Toronto: New Era. 64pp. BVIP MWU *BVAUS/WB31f.2b OHMA2414 OOA/CCF542 OTURS/RSK.

1817 ------ What we propose. Toronto: Communist Party of Canada. 80pp. *BVAUS/WB31f.1a OOA/CCF542 OTURS/ RSK SSUS/Comm.

1818 Canadian Administration of Lumber Workers Industrial Union No. 120 of the IWW. By-laws as amended by referendum June 1936. Toronto. 8pp. *BVAUS/IWW.

1819 **Canadian Labor Defense League.** Fascism and reaction in all lands and the struggle against it. Toronto. 5pp, mimeo. *OTURS/RSK.

1820 (Canadian Labor Defense League). Promoting change
by unlawful means: section 98 of the Criminal Code.
(Toronto). 2pp plus (1p) 'A record of section 98',
mimeo. *ACGA/Smith 13.

1821 ------ Statement re police terror, Toronto 1928-1936.
Toronto. 7pp, mimeo. *OOA/CCF394. Addressed to the
Royal Commission appointed to investigate the actions
of the police in Toronto. A copy of the Commission's
report, which was not printed, is in the OTL.

1822 ------ Statement to advise the general public and
also our friends and supporters as to the role of
the CLDL at the present time. Toronto. 2pp, mimeo.
*OTURS/RSK.

1823 Canadian League Against War and Fascism. Spain's
democracy talks to Canada: representatives of the dem-
ocratic government of Spain interviewed by A.A. Mac-
Leod and Harry F. Ward: and other facts about the
Spanish situation. Toronto. 16pp. BVIP *OTURS/RSK.
Those interviewed include Marcelino Domingo, Dolores
Ibarruri, Antonio Lara, Luis Sarasole etc.

1824 Canadian Wheat Pools. Canadian wheat pool on the air;
second series. Saskatoon. 51pp. *OTMCL Peel 3496.
Thirteen speakers, including H.W. Wood, J.T. Hull etc.

1825 Canadian Youth Congress. Canadian youth act: submitted to all youth organizations in Canada for discussion and amendment. Toronto. 4pp, opening out to
become a broadside. *E.

1826 ------ Declaration of rights of Canadian youth accepted at Ottawa, May 1936. Toronto. 16pp, bilingual.
OTP *BVAUS/Mac43f.22 OHMA SSA/G392.2.

1827 Canadian Youth Council. Slums and re-housing. Toronto. 16pp. OOP *E.

1828 Carr, Sam. From opposition to assassination. The
story of Trotsky and the trial of his terrorist group.
Toronto: Communist Party of Canada. 48pp. AEU BVIP
MWU SSU *BVAUS/WB31f.1a OHMA2147 OKQS OTURS/RSK.

1829 Citizens Defence Movement. Help Canadian youth in
their fight for justice! Regina. 6pp. *BVAUS/Smith
CP. On the Regina riot.

1830 ------ Mottl, Stevens, Gallinger, Wedin, Forsyth,
Kyle cases reach appeal court. Severity of the sent-
ences - contradictory police evidence - basis for
appeals. Regina. 2pp. *OOA/CCF72. Ottawa trek.

1831 ------ News bulletin. Calgary. (1p), mimeo. *ACGA/
Smith 13. On the Calgary riot on Dominion day.

1832 ------ Why did the riot commission omit these facts?
Who are the guilty ones? Has justice been served?
Vancouver. 6pp. *BVAUS/Steeves 4-6.

1833 Committee of Former Employes (sic). Now it will be
told! The truth about *The Commonwealth*. Vancouver.
19pp. *BVAUS/Steeves 4-6.

1834 Committee to Aid Spanish Democracy. Cunard line
announced MacLeod on 'Queen Mary': big Toronto meeting October 11th in Massey Hall to hear Spanish leaders, A.A. MacLeod, Ald. Crang. Toronto. (5pp)mimeo.
*ACGA/Smith 13.

1835 ------ Murder! Why? Toronto. (5pp). *T. On
Norman Bethune.

1836 Communist Party of Canada. Canada and the VII world
congress of the Communist International. Outline of
study and the decisions of the 7th congress and the
9th plenum of the Central Committee of the Communist
Party of Canada. Toronto. 75pp. AEU *BVAUS/WB31f.
1c OHMA1510 OKQS.

1837 ------ Let us learn from the first of May! A statement by the southern Ontario district committee of
the Communist Party of Canada. Toronto. (4pp).
*OHMA

1838 ------ New members study course: three outlines with
recommendations for further reading and study. (Toronto). 15pp, mimeo. *OTURS/RSK and Salsberg T10.24.
Includes platform, how the party is built and how it
works etc.

1839 ------ Outline of study: Communist Party of Canada
provincial training schools, summer 1936. (Toronto).
78pp, mimeo. *OTURS/Salsberg T10.24.

1840 ------ Stevens party is a party of fascism. (Toronto): (c1936). 4pp. *BVAA.

1841 ------ What every communist must know. Vancouver.
(c1936). 28pp, mimeo. *BVAUS/WB31f.2d.

1842 CCF. The annual report of the executive committee
of the CCF (Ontario section) from April 20th 1935 to
March 31st 1936. Toronto. 7pp. *OOA/CCF49.

1843 ------ Canada's charter of freedom: national manifesto 'Let's own Canada'. Vancouver: (c1936). (8pp).
*BVAUS/Mac30Af.12.

1844 ------ Constitution (Manitoba section). New constitution as adopted by the Manitoba provincial convention of the CCF at Portage la Prairie, October 17,
1936. Winnipeg. 4pp. *OOA/CCF318. Amended Winnipeg
1942, Winnipeg 1943 etc.

1845 ------ Constitution as passed by the first annual
convention of the CCF, S.S. (ie. Saskatchewan section)
held in Regina, July 15, 1936. 8pp, mimeo. *OOA/
CCF109. Preceded by a draft in 9pp dated May 1936.
Amended at the 5th, 8th and 9th conventions in 1940,
1943 and 1944 etc.

1846 ------ Constitution of CCF units. np. 3pp, mimeo.
*OOA/CCF11.

1847 ------ Council makes statement on expulsion order.
Toronto. (2pp), broadside. *OOA/CCF394. On the
expulsion of Ben Spence, Arthur Williams, Jimmie

Connor and Mrs Laing.

1848 CCF. Is social credit in Saskatchewan a cat's-paw for the old parties? Regina. (4pp). *G/329.14(71).

1849 ------ Provincial platform as formulated by the delegates assembled in annual convention July 1936. Regina. (4pp). *OOA/CCF539 SSA/Gl.1936.14 SSUS/CCF. The same was also published in 1937 SSUS/CCF.

1850 ------ Revolution··· democratically achieved. The history of New Zealand's first labour government. Vancouver. 8pp. *G/329.14(71).

1851 ------ The way of reason. Calgary. 47pp. *ACGL/PDbl. 300 copies printed.

1852 CCF Continuing Committee. May day in Toronto. Toronto. 10pp, mimeo. *OOA/CCF394. Covering letter signed Alice Loeb and Wm. H. Temple. A statement covering expelled members (see 1847 above).

1853 Cooperative Union of Canada. Genuine and imitative co-operatives. Brantford. (4pp). *BVAUS/Mac39Af.17.

1854 Davis, Roy and William Kashtan. An eye-witness account: war in Spain. Toronto: Francis White. 14pp. *OTURS/RSK.

1855 Dimitrov, George. Rally the forces of youth for peace and freedom. Toronto: Youth Publishers. 15pp. *OKQS OTURS/RSK. A speech to the 6th congress of the Communist International.

1856 Dimitroff, G. The united front against fascism and war. (Toronto): (Communist Party of Canada). 60pp. AEU BVAUS BVIP SRU *OTURS/RSK. Abridged edition of speeches to the 7th congress of the Communist International.

1857 Economic Safety League. The dangers of Douglasism: a one night study of the craze called 'national dividends'...farmers, laborers, merchants and all producers strike a blow for the defense of Alberta... Drumheller: (c1936). 24pp. BVIP OTP OTV *BVAUS/Mackenzie MWPA/Russell 1 Peel 3558.

1858 Farmer, S.J. Social credit or social ownership. Winnipeg: Garry. 36pp. OOP *MWPA/Brigden 7 OOA/CCF541 SSA/G3Man.13. Comparing CCF and social credit.

1859 Fisher, Ernst. Rise and fall of Austro-Marxism. (Toronto): (New Era). (c1936). 25pp, mimeo. *BVAUS/WB41f.11 OTURS/RSK.

1860 Goldberg, Leo. Work for brains, hands and capital: a prospectus. Montreal. 14pp, with application for registration loosely inserted and 2pp mimeo letter headed 'Professional services requested' dated 20 Oct 1938, corrected to 1939. *OKQS. A proposal for colonies like those described by John Bellers.

1861 Henderson, Fred. The case for socialism. Winnipeg: Manitoba Commonwealth. 156pp. MWU NFSM *ACGL. Reprinted 1944 in 146pp, Toronto, CCF. *SSA/G3Ont4.

1862 Hooper, A.S. Efforts for peace: a radio broadcast. Vancouver: Friends of the Soviet Union. (15pp). *OTURS/RSK.

1863 Hull, J.T. Education for co-operation. Minneapolis: Midland Cooperation Wholesale. 14pp. *MWPA/Brigden7.

1864 Hutchison, W. Bruce. Alice in Blunderland. Vancouver: CCF(BC). (c1936). 4pp. *BVAUS/Mac30Af.14 SSA/G3. BC.1.

1865 IWW Canadian Administration. Preamble and constitution of the Industrial Workers of the World organized July 7th, 1905: Canadian administration 1936. (?Montreal). 38pp.

1866 Irvine, W. Open letters to Premier Aberhart. (Edmonton): (Peoples Weekly). 32pp. *BVAUS/Mac39f.2 and Steeves/5-3 OTURS/RSK SSA/G501.6. Letters reprinted from *The Peoples Weekly* from 25 January to 23 May 1936 'substantially' as they appeared.

1867 ------ Take profit out of war: suggestions as to how it may be done in Canada. Edmonton: Peoples Weekly. (4pp). *SSA/G501.8.

1868 ------ You can't do that: a play in three acts. Toronto: Thomas Nelson. 48pp. *ACGL SSA/G501.10.

1869 Ivens, William. The place of the industrial arts in the program of education: at the thirty-first annual convention of the Manitoba Educational Association, Winnipeg, April 1936. Winnipeg. (101pp) mimeo. *MWPA/Ivens 4. Part I only: 'a compendium of opinions of progressive educational leaders, and a factual statement'. Inside title: The contribution of industrial arts to modern education.

1870 Kuusinen, O. Youth and fascism: speech at the seventh world congress of the Communist International: and The tasks of the united front of youth: resolution adopted by the sixth world congress of the Young Communist League. Toronto: Youth Publishers. 32pp. BVIP *BVAUS/WB43f.22 OTURS/RSK.

(1871)Landry, R.J. Development of Canadian labor legislation since 1929. Unpublished MA thesis, Columbia University.

1872 League for Social Reconstruction. Report of the national convention. (Montreal). 4pp plus secretary's postscript (2pp) plus treasurer's report (1p); all mimeo. *OOA/CCF168 and Underhill 52.

(1873)McGill, J.J. The minimum wage and its proposed application to the Dominion of Canada. Unpublished M.Comm thesis, McGill University.

1874 McGoey, Francis J. Back to the land: turning an ancient slogan from a bit of counsel to a remarkable reality. (Toronto): (?author). (c1936). (13pp). *OTP. Resettlement of city families at King City.

1875 (May Day). All out to Cambie grounds, Friday May 1st.
Vancouver: May day conference. (1p) broadside. *T.

1876 Montreal Committee for Medical Aid to the Spanish
Republic. An open letter on Spain. Montreal. 4pp,
bilingual. *OTURS/RSK. Reprints the open letter
published in England by Lascelles Abercrombie, Norman
Angell and others, with a Canadian footnote.

1877 Murray, Alexander Sutherland. Die sozialen Probleme
Kanadas und Mittel und Wege für ihre Lösung. Inaug-
ural-Dissertation zur Erlangung der Doktorwürde einer
Hohen Philosophischen Fakultät der Schlesischen Frie-
dric-Wilhelms-Universität zu Breslau. Breslau:
Sparling. 46pp. OKQ *HI/Uncat.C200.

1878 Piroshko, Michael. Know your own country. Vancouver.
(c1936). 40pp. BVIPA *BVAUS/SpHX OOA/Woodsworth 20.

1879 Pouderoux, George & Viscount Cecil of Chelwood. War
is not inevitable. Toronto: Canadian League Against
War and Fascism. 16pp. *BVAUS/WB43f.17(i).

1880 Regina Citizens Defence Conference. To all organizations which value civil rights. Regina. (1p)
broadside. *SSA/G99.1. On the Regina riot.

1881 Regina Citizens Emergency Committee. The truth about
the relief camp strikers. Who uses force and violence? Regina. (4pp). *OOA/Lucas 3 SSA/G99.6.
A commission of inquiry was set up for the strikes
in BC and Saskatchewan.

1882 Rountree, G. Meredith. The railway worker: a study
of the employment and unemployment problems of the
Canadian railways. Toronto: Oxford University Press.
xx,364pp. *OONL.

1883 Scott, R.B.Y. and Gregory Vlastos (eds). Towards
the Christian revolution. Chicago: Willet, Clark.
viii, 254pp. *OONL. Contains: The economic problem
and A new economic order by Eugene Forsey. Also
published in the Left Book Club 1937.

1884 Socialist Party of Canada. Manifesto: Manitoba
provincial election, July 27, 1936. Winnipeg. (4pp).
*OOA/Heaps 1.

1885 Stalin, Josef. Stalin hails happy life...report on
the new constitution to the 8th congress of Soviets.
Toronto: New Era. 31pp. *BVAUS/WB38Ef.19 OTURS/
RSK. Foreword by Tim Buck.

1886 Steeves, Dorothy. The indictment: grave charges made
in the legislature relating to the British Columbia
public accounts. (Reference to these charges has
been studiously avoided by a muzzled press). Notes
on Mr Hart's so-called balanced budget and a pyramid-
ing public debt. General remarks. Vancouver: Tax-
payers Defence League. 8pp. *BVAUS/Steeves 4-6.

1887 Toronto District Trades and Labour Council. The
truth, the whole truth and nothing but the truth.

Toronto. 14pp. *OTURS. On the repeated attempts
to reduce wages in the civil service.

1888 Tucker, Muriel. Family relief in Canada and the
United States. Ottawa: Canadian Welfare Council.
18pp. *OOL.

1889 United Farmers of Canada. What is the UFC doing?
(Saskatoon). (c1936). (4pp). *SSA/G37.99.

1890 United Farmers of Ontario. A charter for economic
action. (Toronto). (4pp). *OOA/MacPhail.

1891 Vancouver, New Westminster and District Trades and
Labor Council. Important information to trade unionists. Vancouver. (4pp). *OOA/Bengough 3. An attack
on the united front and communists generally, taken
from the *Daily Herald* (Eng.) 16 July 1936.

1892 Vayo, Don Julio Alvarez del. The case for Spain:
speech before the assembly of the League of Nations
25 September 1936. Edmonton: Committee to Aid Spanish Democracy. 18pp. *ACGA/Smith 14.

1893 Williams, G.H. The budget debate: session 1936.
Speech delivered by the leader of the opposition in
the Legislative Assembly of Saskatchewan, Monday
March 9th, 1936. Regina: Kings Printer. 27pp. *OOP.

1894 ------ Co-operation. Radio address, Wednesday December 9th, 1936. (Regina): (CCF). (4pp). *SSA/G1.
1936.1 SSUS/CCF.

1895 ------ Work and wages: radio address, Wednesday
January 20, 1936. (Regina): (CCF). (4pp). *SSA/G1.
1936.5 SSUS/CCF.

1896 Woodsworth, J.S. and others. Budget speeches: Can-
adian national railways (and) unemployment, April-
May 1936. Ottawa: J.O. Patenaude. 39pp. *BVAUS/
Mac27f.44 and Young SSA/G2.1936.1. Others include:
Angus MacInnis, M.J. Coldwell, J.S. Taylor, T.C.
Douglas, C.G. MacNeil, A.A. Heaps.

1897 ------ Speeches on the co-operative commonwealth,
national ownership of banks, pensions at sixty, unemployment - public works, Canadian citizenship,
League of Nations, February 1936. Ottawa: J.O. Patenaude. 48pp. *BVAUS/Garrison 1-51 OHMA1563.
Others Include: M.J. Coldwell, J.S. Taylor, A.A.
Heaps, C.G. MacNeil, Angus MacInnis, T.C. Douglas.

1937

1898 Barnard, T.A. The truth about Soviet Russia. Nanaimo. 17pp. *BVAUS/Mac38f.18.

1899 Bennett, William. Builders of British Columbia.
Vancouver: np. 160pp. *BVAUS/Young MWPA/Russell 1
OTURS/RSK. Deals with the labour movement before

1900, Fraser river fishermens strikes 1900-1901 and other strikes, Indians and orientals in the labour movement, working class press, Communist and CCF parties etc.

1900 Bethune, N. The crime on the road to Malaga - Almeria. Narrative with graphic documents revealing fascist cruelty. np: Publicaciones Iberia. (28pp). *OTPB. Illustrated with photographs by Hazen Sise.

1901 ------ and others. Listen in! This is station EAQ, Madrid, Spain. Toronto: Committee to Aid Spanish Democracy. (17pp). *ACGA/Smith 12 BVAUS/WB43f.4a. Others are J.B.S. Haldane and Hazen Sise.

1902 Browder, Earl. North America and the Soviet Union: the heritage of our people. Toronto: New Era. 15pp. BVAS OKQ *BVAUS/WB42f.25a OOA/CCF542 OTURS/RSK. Address to the 8th Dominion convention of the Communist Party of Canada.

1903 Buck, Tim. The Communist Party and the maturing situation in Canada: report to the 12th session of the Central Committee of the Communist Party of Canada, June 1937. Toronto: Communist Party of Canada. 29pp, mimeo. *OTURS/RSK.

1904 ------ Help Spain make the world safe for democracy. Toronto: Communist Party of Canada. (4pp). *ACGA/ Smith 12 BVAUS/Mac43f.4a.

1905 ------ The people vs. monopoly. Toronto: New Era. 55pp. ACU BVIV *BVAUS/WB31f.2a MWP OHMA2425 OKQS OOA/CCF542 OTURS/RSK SSUS/Comm.

1906 ------ Unhitch Canada from Baldwin's war policies. Toronto: Communist Party of Canada. (c1937). (4pp) *OTURS/RSK.

1907 Canadian Broadcasting Corporation. Canadian defence: what we have to defend: by the Kelsey Club of Winnipeg. (Ottawa). 98pp. *ACGA/Smith 14. Includes: An economic security peace policy by J.S. Woodsworth.

1908 Canadian Congress for Peace and Democracy. Action for peace and democracy: program November 19th, 20th and 21st, Toronto. Toronto. 16pp, illus. *OTURS/ RSK.

1909 (Canadian League Against War and Fascism?). The fascist net-work in Canada. (?Toronto). (?1937). 8pp, mimeo. *OTURS.

1910 Canadian League for Peace and Democracy. Press release. Toronto. 3pp, mimeo. *ACGA/Smith 13. Announcing change of name from Canadian League Against War and Fascism and outlining a new program.

1911 ------ 3 peace proposals. Toronto. (8pp). *ACGA/ Smith 14.

1912 Canadian Youth Congress. Youth's peace policy. Toronto. 8pp. *OTURS/RSK. A summary of resolutions.

1913 Carr, Sam. Communists at work: speech delivered at
the 8th Dominion convention of the Communist Party
of Canada. Toronto: CPC. 46pp. *BVAUS/WB31f.2b
OKQS OOA/CCF542 OTURS/RSK.

1914 Cheshire, S.W. A brief study of the Rochdale plan
of consumer co-operation. Toronto: Canadian Co-operative Youth Movement. (c1937). (5pp). *OHMA2872
SSA/G3.Ont.1.

1915 Chicanot, E.L. (compiler and ed.) Rhymes of the miner.
Gardendale: Federal Publications. 222pp. *BVIPA.
Nothing very genuine.

1916 Citizens Defence Movement. News bulletin: for youth
and democracy: eleven charged under section 87 of the
Criminal code: two charged under section 296B, assault.
More arrests. Calgary. 2pp, mimeo. *ACGA/Smith 13.

1917 ------ Special news bulletin: events leading to
strike at union packing plant. Calgary. 2pp, mimeo.
*ACGA/Smith 13.

1918 Coats, R.H. History of the labor movement in Canada.
Toronto: Communist Party of Canada Training School.
51pp, mimeo. *OTURS/RSK.

1919 Coldwell, M.J. Speeches on the address and purchasing
power: January 18 and January 21, 1937. Ottawa: J.O.
Patenaude. 13pp. *ACGL/PDbl.

1920 ------ Speech on Canadian Wheat Board Act delivered
in the House of Commons, Wedensday March 17, 1937.
Ottawa: J.O. Patenaude. 8pp. *ACGL/PDbl.

1921 Committee to Aid Spanish Democracy. Canada to the
aid of Spanish democracy. Toronto. (1p) broadside.
*BVIP.

1922 ------ Heart of Spain: northern trip. Toronto. 3pp
mimeo. *ACGA/Smith 13. On the film Heart of Spain.

1923 ------ Overseas news: Kate Mangan reports. Toronto.
4pp, mimeo. *ACGA/Smith 13.

1924 ------ Proceedings of conference (including reports
presented) held in the King Edward hotel, Toronto,
Saturday and Sunday October 23rd and 24th, 1937.
Toronto. 40pp, mimeo. *ACGA/Smith 13

1925 ------ Spanish-Canadian bulletin: Spain calls -
Canada responds. Toronto. (4pp), illus. *ACGA/
Smith 12.

1926 Communist Party of Canada. Conference: southern Ontario district CPC, Toronto February 27-28, 1937.
27pp, mimeo, separately paged reports. *OTURS/RSK.
Contains: Report on the struggle for the united front
in Ontario by Stewart Smith; Report on the unionization drive in basic industries in southern Ontario
by J.B. Salsberg.

1927 ------ Eighth Dominion convention CPC, October 8th
to 12th, 1937. Branch study outlines. Toronto.

10pp, mimeo. *OTURS/RSK. Reissued in printed format (8pp) with an errata slip for no. 1902 above. *BVAUS/Mac31f.7 and OTURS/RSK.

1928 Communist Party of Canada. Eighth convention: reports, separately paged, as follows:
China (1p): For a happy childhood by Millie Stern (12pp); For a mighty Communist Party in Canada! Resolutions on organization 3pp. French Canada awakens by E. Dubé 13pp. The movement for civil progress (draft resolution) 5pp; The youth movement and people's unity 3pp; Financial report of the Clarion Publishing Assn by O.C. Doolan 25pp; Memorandum on education and publicity prepared by Bill Rigby 12pp plus appendix. *OTURS/RSK. Issued together. See also 1980 below.

1929 ------ History of the CPSU. Toronto. 28pp, mimeo. *OTURS/Salsberg T10.24.

1930 ------ History of labor internationals. (Toronto). (c1937). 9pp. *OTURS/RSK.

1931 ------ Labor college: a short course in trade unionism. Toronto. 34pp, mimeo. *OTURS/Salsberg T10.24.

1932 ------ The Senate and social legislation. Toronto. (c1937). (1p) broadside. *OTAR/CPC21.

1933 ------ A program for the needs of the people of British Columbia. Vancouver. 6pp. *T.

1934 ------ Souvenir program: international concert-meeting to celebrate the occasion of the fifteenth anniversary of the founding of the Communist Party of Canada. Winnipeg. 16pp. *OTURS/RSK.

1935 ------ Unity will win! To the members of the CCF. Toronto. (4pp). *OTURS/RSK. In favour of the united front; signed by Tim Buck and Norman Freed.

1936 ------ We propose: resolutions adopted at the eighth Dominion convention of the Communist Party of Canada, Toronto 8-13 October, 1937. Toronto: New Era. 76pp. BVIP OKQ SSU *BVAUS/WB31f.1c OHMA OOA/CCF542 OTURS/RSK.

1937 CCF. Constitution (as approved at the 1937 convention). (Vancouver). 6pp, mimeo. *OOA/CCF79.

1938 ------ 1937 provincial programme. Vancouver. (4pp). *BVAUS/Mac30Af.10.

1939 ------ The Saskatchewan CCF provincial platform as adopted by the annual convention July 1937. Regina. 4pp. *OOA/CCF109 SSA/G1.1937.6.

1940 ------ Why armaments? Ottawa. (8pp). AEU *ACGL/PDbl BVAUS/Mac43f.17 OHMA OOA/CCF310 SSA/G2.nd14. SSUS/CCF.

(1941)Couper, W.J. Wages and labor conditions in certain selected industries in Canada 1933-34. Unpublished PhD thesis, University of California. 247pp.

1942 Davis, Edward. Big industry in Canada: a Marxian survey. (?Toronto): League for a Revolutionary Workers Party. 62pp. OTP *OHMA2479 OTURS/RSK.

1943 Dingwall, James Malcolm. Consumers cooperation in Canada. Unpublished BA thesis, McMaster University. (iv), 70pp. biblio. *OHMA.

1944 Douglas, T.C. Speeches on foreign policy: conscription of wealth; drought area; why increase armaments delivered in the House of Commons on January 25, February 4 and 19, 1937. Ottawa: J.O. Patenaude. 18pp. *AEUS/CCFXIII-10 SSA/G2.1937.1. Neutrality in the event of war.

1945 Dubé, E. Pourquoi la loi du Cadenas? Montreal: (?Clarté). 29pp. *OTURS/RSK.

1946 Forsey, Eugene. Does Canada need immigrants? Toronto: League for Social Reconstruction. 9pp. AEU BVAS BVIP OH *OOA/CCF318 and 536 OOAL.

1947 ------ Recovery for whom? (Montreal): (League for Social Reconstruction). (10pp). *BVAS.

1948 Friends of the Mackenzie-Papineau Battalion. Hello Canada! Canada's Mackenzie-Papineau Battalion 1837-1937: 15th brigade I.B. 'Fascism shall be destroyed'. Toronto. 46pp. *BVAUS/WB43f.4a OTURS/RSK.

1949 Good, W.C. The history of cooperation in Canada. np. 7pp, mimeo. *OOA/Good 12.

1950 Grant, H.C. Developments in the concept of co-operation in western Canada. Paper presented at the annual meeting of the Canadian Political Science Association at McMaster University, Hamilton on Monday, May 24th. (Hamilton): (McMaster University). 9pp, mimeo. *OOA/Good 12.

1951 Hannam, H.H. Co-operation. The plan for tomorrow which works today. Toronto: United Farmers of Ontario. 80pp. *OKQ. Revised editions published in 1938, 1939, 1940, 1943 and 1945 in OH, OOAL, BVAS, *OOA/CCF148 and SSUS/Coop respectively.

1952 Harris, J.C. Conscription for peace. Nelson: Useful Peoples Party. 60pp. *BVAUS/Mac42f.3A.

1953 ------ The cook's strike. Nelson: Useful Peoples Party. 16pp. *OHMA1707.

1954 Heather, G.A. Unemployment and Empire settlement: a national colonization scheme. (?Kitchener). 12pp plus inserted letter to the editor. *OOAL.

1955 Henry George Society. A minimum wage of $5,000 a year! Toronto. (c1937). 7pp. *SSA/G167.2. Formerly the Single Tax Association.

1956 Hull, J.T. Why the state should intervene to help the farmers. Memorandum presented to the Royal Grain Inquiry Commission on behalf of Manitoba Co-operative Conference. Winnipeg. 14pp. *OTAR/1937/7.

(1957)Hunter, John. A survey of wage and labour conditions in the province of New Brunswick. Unpublished MA thesis, University of New Brunswick. iii, 139pp.

1958 Innis, H.A. (ed): N.J. Ware and H.A. Logan. Labor in Canadian-American relations: the history of labor interaction by Norman J. Ware and Labor costs and labor standards by H.A. Logan. Toronto: Ryerson. xl, 212pp, index. *OONL.

1959 Kashtan, Dave and Philippe Richer. For life with a purpose...Toronto: Young Communist League of Quebec. 23pp. *OTURS/RSK. Based on a report given at the provincial convention of the YCL of Quebec, Oct. 1936.

1960 Kennedy, Howard Angus. Medicine-man rule in Canada: story of a national scandal, a suppressed exposure, and a drastic prescription. Told in letters to the Prime Minister, with a sequel. Montreal. (c1937). 32pp. BVIP OTP *OOA/Underhill 63.

1961 Krehm, William. Spain: revolution and counter-revolution. Toronto: League for a Revolutionary Workers Party. 56pp. OTP *OHMA3156 OTURS/RSK.

1962 Landon, Fred. The Knights of Labor: predecessors of the C.I.O. (London, Ont.). 7pp. *OHMA1684 OTAR/ 1937/15. Reprinted from the Quarterly Review of Commerce, University of Western Ontario, Autumn 1937.

1963 League for a Revolutionary Workers Party. If Lenin were living... (Toronto). 6pp. *T.

1964 League for Social Reconstruction. LSR: Proceedings of the sixth annual convention, Toronto, March 20-21 1937. Montreal. 8pp. *BVAUS/Steeves 3-11 MWPA/ Brigden 7 OOA/Underhill 52 SSA/G105.3.

1965 Lewis, Orlo Ellis. The cooperative movement. Unpublished MA thesis, Acadia University, Wolfville. (ii) 131pp, biblio. *NSWA.

1966 Libertarian Groups in Canada. May day! Labour's day! np (?Vancouver). (4pp). *BVAUS/IWW.

1967 Litterick, J. Whither Manitoba? Toronto: New Era. 32pp. AEU BVIP OKQ OONL *BVAUS/WB31f.2a and 4 OTURS/ RSK. First communist elected to a legislative assembly in Canada: opening speech.   Peel 3567.

1968 McCready, S.B. Rural reconstruction. (?Halifax): L.A. DeWolfe. (c1937). 32pp. *NSHD/SpColl HN.

1969 ------ Rural reconstruction: education for co-operation. St Marys (Ont): Journal-Argus. 56pp. MWP OKQ OOP OTP *OOA/MacPhail 3.

1970 McDonald, J.A. The abyss (how to avoid it). Vancouver: Socialist Party of Canada (c1937). (8pp). *BVAUS/Steeves 4-6.

1971 MacDonald, R.L. Some wider aspects of co-operation. An address given at the industrial and rural conference at Antigonish, August 19, 1937. (Antigonish):

(?St Francis Xavier University). 13pp. *NSHP/HD C OTP.

1972 MacInnis, Grace and Charles J. Woodsworth. Jungle tales retold: a survey of capitalist monopoly in Canada. Ottawa: Labour Publications. 58pp. BVIP MWU OTP SSU *BVAUS/Mac39f.7 MWPA/Brigden 7 OOA/ CCF310 and 537. Deals with tobacco, meat packing, needle trades, furniture, canning, milk, farm imp- lements, milling and baking, coal, textiles, gasoline and retailing.

1973 MacLeod, A.A., Harry F. Ward and others. Spain's democracy talks to Canada: representatives of the democratic government of Spain interviewed by MacLeod and Ward. Toronto: Canadian League Against War and Fascism. 16pp. *OTURS/RSK. MacLeod and Ward were chairmen of the Canadian and American leagues respec- tively. Includes appendixes.

1974 MacNeil, C.G. and others. Wny increase armaments? Speeches by C.G. MacNeil, M.J. Coldwell, Angus Mac- Innis, T.C. Douglas, J.S. Woodsworth, A.A. Heaps. Ottawa: J.O. Patenaude. 44pp. *ACGL/PDbl BVAUS/ Mac43f.17 and 27f.4a OHMA OTURS/RSK SSA/G2.1937.20 SSUS/JL197.

1975 Marsh, Helen. Guide to LSR activities. Montreal: League for Social Reconstruction. (4pp). *OOA/ Underhill 52.

1976 May Day Committee. Celebrate May day, a day of inter- national solidarity! Unite for peace, democracy and freedom! Vancouver. (1p) broadside. *T.

1977 ------ (Songs and poems). Vancouver. (2pp) broad- side. *T. With a poem 'Madrid' by A.M. Stephen.

1978 Michell, H. The future of co-operation in Canada. Paper presented at the annual meeting of the Canadian Political Science Association to be held at McMaster University, Hamilton, May 24-25, 1937. (Hamilton): McMaster University. 7pp, mimeo. *OOA/Good 12. See also no 1950 above.

1979 Peterson, C.W. Social credit: a critical analysis. Calgary. 16pp. ACG AEU BVIP OOP SRL. *OOA/CCF541 SSA/G255.1. Marked 'new and revised edition'. '...I have always been temperamentally unable to take party politics seriously' (preface). Peel 3581.

1980 Phillips, P. Memorandum on the work of the national language organizations: 8th Dominion convention, Communist Party of Canada. Toronto: CPC. 33pp, mimeo *OKQS.

1981 Ryerson, Stanley B. 1837: the birth of Canadian dem- ocracy. Toronto: Francis White. 136pp. *OTURS/RSK.

1982 (------) Le reveil du Canada français par E. Roger. Montréal: Les editions du peuple. 48pp. *OTURS/RSK.

1983 St Francis Xavier University. With an eye to the

future. Antigonish. 14pp. *SSUS/Coops.

1984 Smith, Stewart. Hepburn's betrayal...what now?
Toronto: Communist Party of Canada. 32pp. OTP SSU
*OTURS/RSK.

(1985) Smythe. Limen T. The Lumber and Sawmill Workers
Union in British Columbia. Unpublished MA thesis,
University of Washington, Seattle. 73pp, biblio.

1986 Socialist Labor Party of Canada. Manifesto on war
and decay and corruption of international capitalism.
New York: New York Labor News Co. 30pp. *SSUS/Soc
and TU. Stamped as issued by the Canadian party.

1987 Socialist Party of Canada. British Columbia provincial election: election manifesto no 1. (Vancouver).
(1p). *BVAUS/Mac30Af.2a and Steeves 5-7. Includes
objects and declaration of principles.

1988 ------ British Columbia provincial election: election
manifesto no 3. (Vancouver). (2pp). *BVAUS/Mac30A
f.2a.

1989 ------ British Columbia provincial election - June
1st, 1937: election manifesto. Vancouver. (4pp).
*BVAUS/Mac30Af.2a. Possibly this is manifesto no 2;
not other no. 2 has been found.

1990 ------ Statement of principles. Toronto. (4pp).
*BVAUS/Steeves 5-7 OTURS/RSK. This is the Ontario
section: the SPC in Vancouver was a splinter of the
old SPC.

1991 Spanish Defence Committee. Spain. Vancouver. (4pp).
*BVAUS/WB43f.4a. Inside title: 'Madrid'.

1992 Stubbs, Lewis St. George. Human rights and social
justice: maiden address in the legislature of Manitoba. Winnipeg. 31pp. *OTURS/RSK. Sat as an independent, but he refers to two quotations from Harney
and Lenin on the title page of Strachey's *Theory and
practice of socialism* as 'summing up my political faith
and objective'.

1993 Williams, G.H. The budget debate: session 1937.
Speech delivered by the leader of the opposition in
the Legislative Assembly of Saskatchewan, March 24,
1937. Regina. 30pp. *SSA/Gl.1937.1 and G529.1.

1994 ------ Farmer-labor work and wages: radio address,
Wednesday January 20, 1937. Regina: CCF. (4pp).
*SSA/Gl.1937.3.

(1995) Wilson, Bernard. The surge of industrial unionism.
Unpublished MA thesis, University of Western Ontario.
178pp.

1938

1996 Anderson, Violet (ed). Problems in Canadian unity:

lectures given at the Canadian Institute on economics and politics, August 6 to 19. 1938. Toronto: Thomas Nelson. x, 153pp. *OKQS. Includes: Some observations upon nationalism and provincialism in Canada by Frank H. Underhill; Collective bargaining by J. Finkelman and Bora Laskin; The legal status of trade unions in Canada by Bora Laskin; Cooperation among farm people in Ontario by H.H. Hannam etc.

1997 Arnot, R. Page and Tim Buck. Fascist agents exposed in the Moscow trials: the background, the indictment; how the Soviet court works, the admission of guilt; conclusion. London: Communist Party of Great Britain. 23pp. *OTURS/RSK.

1998 Bartley, George. An outline history of Typographical Union no. 226, 1887-1938. Vancouver: Typographical Union 226. 64pp, illus. *BVIPA QQLA *OOL.

1999 Bilecki, A. Not another cent! The story behind the extra cent on milk. Winnipeg: Beaver Special. 16pp. *OTURS/RSK. No. 2 of a series.

2000 Boyd, Hugh. New breaking: an outline of co-operation among the western farmers of Canada. Toronto: J.M. Dent. 215pp, chronology, book list, index. *SSUS/ Shortt. Peel 3599.

2001 Bruce, Malcolm. War! and the Chamberlain betrayal. (Vancouver): Communist Party of Canada. 24pp. *BVAUS/ WB31f.1b.

2002 Buck, Tim. For the assistance of May day speakers: excerpts from the speech of Tim Buck delivered in Massey Hall, 19 April 1938. Toronto: Communist Party of Canada. 4pp, mimeo. *OTURS/RSK. These excerpts are from no. 2004 below which gives the full text, without, however, identifying it as a speech.

2003 ------ May day manifesto: a message from the Dominion Executive Committee of the Communist Party of Canada. Vancouver: CPC. (4pp). *T.

2004 ------ War in Europe. Toronto: New Era. 30pp. *BVAUS/WB43f.17(i) MWP OHMA2413 OKQS OTURS/RSK.

2005 Calder, R.L. 'Our vanishing civil liberties': the Padlock law. Vancouver: Canadian League for Peace and Democracy. (8pp). *BVAUS/WB39f.11. Extracts from an address: includes program.

2006 Campbell, A.C. Unite against the marauders. Saskatoon: Communist Party of Canada. (c1938). (1p) broadside. *SSA/G333.2. Leaflet 3.

2007 ------ Unity will win. Saskatoon: Communist Party of Canada. (1p) broadside. *SSA/G333.4.

2008 ------ Who suffers? Saskatoon: Communist Party of Canada. (1p) broadside. SSA/G333.1 Leaflet 1.

2009 Canada: Royal Commission. Report of the Royal Commission to investigate the penal system of Canada. Ottawa: Kings Printer. vi, 418pp, appendixes, biblio, index. *OTURS/RSK. Chapters VI and VII on riots and disturbances and the use of firearms in penitentiaries contain material relating to the shots fired into Tim Buck's cell.

2010 Canadian Broadcasting Corporation. Whither democracy: a series of forum broadcasts on economic and political problems. Ottawa. 100pp. OOP *OTURS/RSK. Includes: Sidney Smith (Chairman); Problems of rural debt structure by G.E. Britnell; Taxation by Henry Morgan and Robert McQueen; The railway problem by Edward Beatty and R.J. Deachman; Social credit by William Aberhart and Irene Parlby; Labour problems by George Drew and Tom Moore; The attitude of Quebec towards communism by T.J. Coonan and J.B. Coyne; Communism and democracy by Stewart Smith and H.N. Fieldhouse; Co-operation, the Antigonish experiment by A.B. MacDonald and J. King Gordon; The case for planning by W.D. Herridge and C.A. Curtis; Socialist planning by M.J. Coldwell and Clifford Sifton; Summary and conclusions by J.M. MacDonnell, F.R. Scott and J.T. Thorson.

2011 Canadian League for Peace and Democracy. Are you in favour of this? Vancouver. (2pp) broadside. *T. Opposing trade with Japan.

2012 ------ Bloody bargains made in Japan are being sold to well intentioned people throughout Canada. Edmonton. (c1938). (1p) broadside. *SSA/McNaughton H23. Information to consumers 1.

2013 ------ Call to action; third national congress. Toronto. (4pp) plus 1p inserted message from Phillip Noel-Baker. (Own copy).

2014 ------ Essential facts concerning the problem of the withdrawal of foreign troops from Spain. A resume of the present position as regards the work of the Non-Intervention Committee. Toronto. 9pp, mimeo. *OTURS/RSK

2015 ------ Lecture by Thomas Mann, Nobel prize winner, Massey Hall, Wednesday May 4th, 8.30pm. Toronto. (4pp). *OTPB/1938 Mann. Contains League program for 1938. The lecture is called 'The coming victory of democracy'.

2016 Canadian Section of the Bureau for the Fourth International. Who is Kerensky? (Toronto). (c1938). (1p) broadside. *OTURS/RSK. 'Throw Kerensky back into history's ashcan and Stalin after him.'

2017 Canadian Society of Technical Agriculturists. Agricultural co-operation in Canada. Ottawa. pp 345-417 *OTAR/1938/7. Reprinted from their review no. 19.

2018 Chinese Patriotic League of Toronto. Japanese aggression in China. Toronto. 32pp. BVIP *OTP.

2019 Citizens Defence Movement. Conference for the repeal of section 98 held at Calgary Public Library, April 16th and 17th, 1936. Calgary. 24pp, mimeo. *ACGA

Smith 13. Reports by J.C. Cosgrove, Norman Priestley and others.

2020 Coldwell, M.J. and T.C. Douglas. Saskatchewan conditions: addresses on the address in reply to the
speech from the throne, delivered in the House of
Commons on February 2 and 7, 1938. Ottawa: J.O. Patenaude. 14pp. *SSA/G2.1938.2.

2021 Committee to Aid Spanish Democracy. Bulletin to be
issued weekly in future. Toronto. 3pp, mimeo.
*ACGA/Smith 13. Dated 2nd May.

2022 ------ Campaign arrangements must commence immediately. Toronto. 2pp, mimeo. *ACGA/Smith 13. Dated
17th May.

2023 ------ The chairman's interview. Toronto. 3pp,
mimeo. *ACGA/Smith 13. On recruiting, blood donors
etc. Dated 19th January.

2024 ------ Children's desperate plea! Toronto. (1p)
mimeo. *ACGA/Smith 13. Dated 14th April.

2025 ------ First things first. Toronto. 3pp, mimeo.
*ACGA/Smith 13. Dated 18th April.

2026 ------ Personal notes. Toronto. 3pp, mimeo.
*ACGA/Smith 13. Dated 5th March. 'Well my little
boy, what do you want to be?' 'A survivor'.

2027 ------ The Toronto conference. Toronto. 3pp, mimeo.
*ACGA/Smith 13. Dated January 8th. Referring to a
conference called for 21st January to organize a
Toronto CASD in addition to the national committee.

2028 ------ The weekly bulletin: National Committee re-
organizes. Toronto. 3pp, mimeo. *ACGA/Smith 13.

2029 Communist Party of Canada. A democratic front for
Canada: reports, speeches, resolutions, of the Dominion Executive Committee held on 3-6 June 1938 at
Toronto. Toronto: New Era. 138pp, errata slip
containing missing section (page 23 between paragraphs 2 and 3). *BVAUS/WB31f.2b OHMA2482 OTURS/
RSK. Contains articles by Tim Buck, Sam Carr, Stewart Smith, J.B. Salsberg, Norman Freed, Fred Rose,
Dave Kashtan plus resolutions.

2030 ------ History of the Canadian people. (Toronto).
18pp, mimeo. *OTURS/RSK.

2031 ------ Make your vote count for democratic national
unity. For social security. For peace and democracy.
Regina. (4pp). *SSA/G332.1.

2032 ------ Material to assist students of trade unionism.
Toronto: Toronto Labor College. 28pp, mimeo. *OTURS/
Salsberg T10-24.

2033 ------ Peace must prevail! Regina. (1p) broadside.
*SSA/G71.1.

2034 ------ Stop Hitler! Regina. (1p) broadside. *SSA/
G71.2.

2035 Communist Party of Canada. Submission to the Royal
Commission on Dominion-Provincial Relations, April
1938. (Toronto). 124pp. *OTURS/RSK. See also 2037
below.

2036 ------ The tasks of the Communist Party of Ontario
in the struggle for jobs, recovery, democracy and
peace. Proceedings of the second Ontario convention
of the Communist Party, Toronto October 8,9,10, 1938,
Don Hall. Toronto. 60pp, mimeo. *OTURS/RSK.

2037 ------ Toward democratic unity for Canada. Submission of the Dominion Committee to the Royal Commission
on Dominion-Provincial Relations: revised. Toronto.
123pp. AEU BVIV NFSM OOA OOP QMM *BVAUS/WB31f.2a
OKQS OTURS/RSK. Prepared under the editorship of
Stewart Smith. Revised after submission as 'it was
found that in chapter 11 the share of capitalists in
the national income had been underestimated'.

2038 ------ What is communism? Reading material. np.
(c1938). 13pp, mimeo. *BVAUS/WB31f.2c. Includes
a radio interview with Earl Browder. Possibly issued
in New York.

2039 Conference on the Padlock Law. Conference on the
Padlock law and civil liberties of all progressive
and democratic organizations to unite the people of
Toronto against the threat to Canadian democracy.
Toronto. (1p) broadside. *OTPB/1938 Padlock.

2040 ------ Resolutions. Toronto. (4pp). *OTURS.

2041 CCF. Brief submitted by the council of the Alberta
CCF clubs to the Royal Commission on Dominion-Provincial Relations. (Edmonton). (14pp). *OOA/CCF75.

2042 ------ The CCF debt adjustment and land policy.
Regina. 6pp. *OOA/CCF321 SSA/Gl.1937.2 and 1938.4
SSUS/CCF.

2043 ------ The CCF federal election programme adopted
by the national convention held in Edmonton, July
28 and 29, 1938. Ottawa. (4pp). *OOA/CCF310 and
536 SSA/G2.1938.4.

2044 ------ Election broadsides. As an example of the
kinds of broadsides issued for election purposes the
following are known for 1938:
Bank robbers get billions!
Beware trickery in election news.
The depression and unemployment started under capit-
alism.
Don't be fooled again.
Exploiting the farmer.
Liberals launched depression!
Liberals plan wage-cuts!
Liberty loving Liberals, their debt adjustment act.
Millionaires plot railway steal.
Slave camps for youth: millions for big shots.
Tweedledum and Tweedledee.
What the profiteering system does for you!

What's the difference? Grit and Tory?
Who owns Canada. Various sources, mostly OOA/CCF.

2045 CCF. A handbook to the Saskatchewan CCF: platform
and policy. Regina. 35pp. *OOA/Coldwell 59 and
CCF70, 109 and 320 SSA/Gl.1938.30 SSUS/CCF.

2046 ------ Is social credit coming or going? What is it
doing and who is it doing it for? Regina. (4pp).
*SSA/Gl.1938.10.

2047 ------ Study course: group one. Lesson 1. The history of the CCF. 8pp. 2. The growth of the provincial
platform. 9pp. 3. The CCF land policy. 9pp. 4. Regina manifesto by J.S. Woodsworth. 6pp. 5. Growth of
the federal platform. 4pp. Regina. all mimeo.
*OOA/CCF72 SSA/Gl.16-20.

2048 ------ Study course: group two. Lesson 1. How to
conduct a public meeting. 4pp. 2. How to be an
efficient chairman. 4pp. 3. How to be an efficient
secretary. 2pp. 4. Mechanics of organizing. 7pp.
5. Beating the machine. 10pp. Regina. all mimeo.
*OOA/CCF72 SSA/Gl.21-25.

2049 ------ Study course: group three. Lesson 1. The
technique of democratic self-government, part 1. 4pp.
2. (the same) part 2. 4pp. 3. History of Canadian
political parties, part 1. 4pp. 4. (the same) part 2.
6pp. 5. The Canadian constitution: Dominion-provincial
powers. 4pp. Regina. all mimeo. *OOA/CCF72 SSA/
Gl.26-30.

2050 ------ Study course: group four. Lesson 1. The basic
reason for the failure of capitalism by G.H. Williams.
2. The growth of monopoly under capitalism by Grace
MacInnis. 3pp. Co-operation and socialism by G.H.
Williams. 3pp. 4. A planned economy, part 1 by G.H.
Williams. 5pp. 5. (the same) part 2 by G.H. Williams. 7pp. Regina. all mimeo. *OOA/CCF72 SSA/Gl
31-34.

2051 ------ You and I must act for peace: Japanese aggression in China and Canada's position: what Canada
must do. Ottawa. (4pp). AEUS/CCF XIII-23 OOA/CCF
310, 326 and 540 and Woodsworth 16.

2052 Dallet, Joe. Letters from Spain. Toronto: New Era.
62pp. *BVAUS/WB43f.4a OKQS OTURS/RSK. With brief
introductory articles by William Z. Foster, Earl Browder, Tim Buck, Steve Nelson and John Williamson.
Dallet was first political commissar of the Mackenzie-
Papineau battalion.

2053 Deachman, R.J. Whither democracy: Canadian problems
have been discussed lately over CBC: the opposing
viewpoint was presented by Sir Edward Beatty. (?Tor-
onto). 4pp, mimeo. *OOA/Woodsworth 12. See 2010
above.

2054 The Democratic Control League. (Program). Regina.
(4pp). *SSA/G321.1.

2055 Douglas, T.C. Speeches on unemployment relief; farm implements committee; farmers creditors arrangement act; delivered in the House of Commons during the session of 1938. Ottawa: J.O. Patenaude. 16pp. *SSA/G2.1938.3.

2056 Dubé, Evariste. What's behind the Padlock law? Toronto: New Era. 19pp. AEU *BVAUS/WB42f.1a OTURS/ RSK.

(2057) Duncan, A.S. Unemployment relief in the prairie provinces 1930-37. Unpublished MA thesis, McGill University. 190pp.

2058 Farmer, S.J. The yellow dog contract: an exposé. Winnipeg: CCF. (4pp). *OOA/CCF318.

(2059) Farrow, Norman Douglas. Political aspects of the united farmer movement in Ontario. Unpublished MA thesis, University of Western Ontario.

2060 The Federationist. Gasoline and government: pertinent paragraphs about petroleum: an analysis of the effect of private ownership in industry. Vancouver. (c1938). (6pp). *BVAUS/Garrison 1-9.

2061 Forkin, J. No penalty on poverty. Winnipeg: (?Communist Party - Clarion). 16pp. *OTURS/RSK. Based on a radio address. Beaver penny series.

2062 Fort William and Port Arthur Trades Councils. Programme: Labor day celebrations, Monday September 5th, 1938. Fort William. 24pp. *OTAR/1938/54. Contains articles by P.M. Draper and John P. Burke.

2063 Fowler, Bertram B. The Lord helps those...how the people of Nova Scotia are solving their problems through co-operation. New York: Vanguard. x, 180pp. *OOAL.

2064 Friends of the Mackenzie-Paineau Battalion in Spain. They defend world democracy: what are you doing for them? Toronto. (6pp). *ACGA/Smith 13 *OTURS/RSK.

2065 ------ They fought for Canada - in Spain. Help rehabilitate them. Toronto. 6pp, illus. *OOA/CCF157.

2066 Gowan, Elsie Park. The shop in Toad lane: a play in four scenes. Edmonton: Alberta Cooperative Wholesale Association. 16pp. AEU *ACGA/CCF24. On the Rochdale pioneers.

2067 Guyot, Raymond. Youth wants peace and brotherhood. Toronto: Young Communist League. (c1938). 12pp. *OHMA3151 OTURS/RSK.

2068 Hannam, H.H. What has happened to the purchasing power of the Canadian farmer since 1928? (Toronto): (United Farmers of Ontario). (c1938). (4pp). *ACGA/Coote 4.

2069 Howe, Peter. State medicine for Saskatchewan. Regina: CCF. (2pp), broadside. *SSA/G1.1938.17.

2070 International Woodworkers of America, BC Coast District Council No. 1. Death stalks B.C. woods! Vancouver. (4pp). *T.

2071 Johnson, J.C. Expulsion of members from trade unions.
np: Labour Research Institute. pp78-100. Publications of the Industrial Law Research Council.

2072 J(olliffe), E.B. It can be done. New Zealand is
doing it! Why doesn't Canada do the same? Toronto:
CCF. 4pp. *OHMA2349.

2073 Kardash, William. I fought for Canada in Spain.
Toronto: New Era. 30pp. *BVAUS/WB43f.4a OTURS/RSK.
Foreword by Salem Bland. Timely Topics 3.

2074 Kashtan, William. The road to happiness. Toronto:
(Young Communist League). 39pp. *BVAUS/WB31f.1
MWPL OOA/CCF542 OTURS/RSK. Main report to the 8th
national convention of the Young Communist League of
Canada, 27-30 May 1938.

2075 Keen, George. The organization of a consumers co-
operative. Brantford: Cooperative Union of Canada.
16pp. *OTP.

2076 Lakeview Defense Committee. Your unemployed cannot
work miracles! The Lakeview cases - why we appeal.
(Toronto). (1p) broadside. *OTURS/RSK.

2077 ------ Why the Lakeview arrests?? Shall we starve
in silence? Shall we slowly die dumb? Shall we know
the reason why? Toronto. (4pp). *OOA/CCF49 OTURS/
RSK. The case concerned eight people charged with
unlawful assembly and assaulting a relief officer
over the question of food allowances. Secretary of
the committee was A.E. Smith.

2078 League for Social Reconstruction. Brief submitted
to the Royal Commission on Dominion-Provincial Relations. (Montreal). 34pp, mimeo. *OOA/CCF168
OTURS. Reissued as 2079 below.

2079 ------ Canada - one or nine? The purpose of confederation. Brief submitted to the Royal Commission
on Dominion-Provincial Relations. Montreal. 32pp.
OH OOP QMSS *OOA/CCF536 and Underhill 52 OTURS/RSK
SSUS/Can.History.

2080 ------ Democracy needs socialism. Toronto: Thomas
Nelson. x, 154pp. *OTP.

2081 ------ Manifesto. Toronto. (4pp). BVIP OKQ *SSA/
G105.2

2082 ------ Pioneers in poverty: some facts for western
Canadians today. Winnipeg. 72pp. *BVAUS/Mac31Af.32
OOA/CCF538 OTURS/RSK. Peel 3633.

2083 The Libertarian Group of Toronto. The first of May.
Toronto. (c1938). (4pp). *OHMA.

2084 Litvinov, Maxim. Czechoslovakia and the world crisis.
Toronto: New Era. 15pp. *OHMA OTURS/RSK.

2085 Lumber and Sawmill Workers Union. Timber: reports
and minutes of the second annual convention, local
2786. (Toronto). 48pp. *OTURS/RSK. Convention
held at Port Arthur, 17-19 December 1937. President
was Bruce Magnuson, later leader of the Ontario
Communist Party.

2086 MacDonald, Mrs Colin. Cash or credit? Antigonish:
St Francis Xavier University. 8pp. *NSHP/HDC.

(2087) McDonald, C.P. The co-operative movement in Nova
Scotia. Unpublished MA thesis, McGill University.

2088 MacInnis, Angus. Speeches on old age pensions, workers right to organize, social credit, delivered in
the House of Commons on Fberuary 28, March 18 and 29,
1938. Ottawa: J.O. Patenaude. 16pp. *BVAUS/Mac42
f.4 SSA/G2.1938.1.

2089 ------ Speeches on Spanish embargo, (and) the Quebec
padlock law delivered in the House of Commons on May
26 and 31, 1938. Ottawa: J.O. Patenaude. 10pp.
*BVAUS/Mac27f.44.

2090 ------ and Grant MacNeil. Economic conditions reviewed: addresses on the address in reply to the
speech from the throne delivered in the House of
Commons on February 7 and 10, 1938. Ottawa: J.O.
Patenaude. 11pp. *BVAUS/Mac27f.44 NSHD/H1.

2091 Mackintosh, Margaret. Canada and the ILO: February
1, 1938. Ottawa: League of Nations in Canada. 12pp.
*OOL.

2092a------ An outline of trade union history in Great
Britain, the United States and Canada: with special
emphasis on the causes leading to the present division in the Canadian labour movement. Ottawa: Dept
of Labour. 30pp, mimeo. *AEPAA/Farmilo 1.

2092b------ as above. 31pp. *OOL

2092c------ as above, slightly revised, 1942. *OOL

2092d------ as above, reissued 1946. *MWPA/Russell 1.
Extended from an address given at the Canadian Institute of Economics and Politics, Lake Couchiching,
12 August 1938. Brief additions were made in 1942
and 1946 to bring the information up to date.

2093 Marsh, L.C., A. Grant Fleming and C.F. Blackler.
Health and unemployment, some studies of their rel-
ationships. Toronto: Oxford University Press for
McGill University. 243pp. *OONL.

2094 Mooney, Geo. S. Co-operatives today and tomorrow.
A Canadian survey. Montreal: The Survey Committee.
189pp. *(Own copy).

2095 National Childrens Council. May-day and your child.
Toronto. (c1938). (4pp). *OHMA. An appeal to
keep children out of school on May day. The NCC is
'co-ordinating all activities of working-class childrens organizations in Canada.'

2096 Paterson, Robert A. The shorter working day. Unpublished BA Hons thesis, McMaster University. (iii), 70pp, biblio. *OHMA.

2097 Prevost, Harold. The new untouchables. Ontario's welfare problems. Toronto: CCF. 16pp. *AEUS/CCF XIII-6.

2098 Provisional Anti-Fascist Council. News bulletin: united front against fascism in the streets of Toronto, Canada!! New York. (1p), broadside. *T.

2099 Provisional Committee for Anti-fascist Action. Crush fascism with labor action! Keep the black shirt gangsters out of Toronto. Toronto. (1p), broadside. *OTPB/1938 Anti-fascist. Recorded in OTPB as League for a Revolutionary Workers Party.

2100 Queens University. Industrial retirement plans in Canada. Kingston: Industrial Relations Section. 115pp. *OKQ. Bulletin 1.

2101 ------ The right to organize: recent Canadian legislation. Kingston: Industrial Relations Section. 20pp. *OOA/Woodsworth 10 OKQ. Bulletin 2.

2102 Regina Labor-Progressive Association. Public nominating convention: only unity can win. Regina. (4pp). *SSA/G518.1. Includes platform and constitution. This is not the later Labor-Progressive Party.

2103 Reuel, Doris Catherine. Trade unionism in Canada (1921-1936). Unpublished BA Hons thesis, McMaster University. (iii), 105pp, biblio. *OHMA.

(2104) Richards, A.E. Agricultural co-operation in Canada. Ottawa: np. 18pp. OOAG. Prepared for the 5th International conference of agriculture economists, Macdonald College, 26 August 1938.

2105 Rose, Fred. Fascism over Canada: an exposé. Toronto: New Era. 47pp. AEU BVAU SSU *AEPAA/Brown 6-90 OHMA 2757 OTURS/RSK. Timely Topics 1.

2106 Ryerson, S. The present situation in Quebec. Toronto: Communist Party of Canada. 3pp, mimeo. *OTURS/ RSK. Summary of a report 2 March 1938.

2107 ------ (ed). What Montreal needs - now! A program of municipal reform. (Montreal): Communist Party of Canada. 32pp. *OTURS/RSK. The author was provincial secretary of the Communist Party of Quebec.

2108 Scott, F.R. Canada today: a study of her national interests and national policy. London(Eng): Oxford University Press. xii, 163pp, tables, biblio. *MWPL OONL. Prepared for the British Commonwealth Relations Conference, 1938.

2109 Sims, Thomas C. A reply to Sir Edward Beatty. Toronto: New Era. 15pp. AEU BVIV NBSM *OHMA1901 OOA/ CCF179 OTURS/RSK. Sims was editor of the *Daily Clarion*: the reply concerns Beatty's speeches in favour of railway amalgamation.

2110 Single Tax Association of Canada. Canada's economic
maladies, their cause and cure: being the brief submitted to the Royal Commission on Dominion-Provincial
Relations. Toronto: Hunter Rose. 36pp. BVAU BVIP
OH OOL QMBM QQL *OOP.

2111 Single Unemployed Committee. Tourist guide! See
Vancouver first? Vancouver. (2pp), broadside. *T.
'...in the various sections of the city we have slums
...swap your car for a bull-dozer and blast your way
to the natural beauties of the interior.'

2112 (Single Unemployed Committee). We are hungry! Vancouver. (1p), broadside. *T.

2113 Smith Stewart. Has Chamberlain saved peace? Toronto:
Communist Party of Canada. 27pp. *BVAUS/Mac42f.3a
OHMA2455 OTURS/RSK. Part of a speech to the Ontario
convention, 9 October 1938.

2114 ------ Jobs and security the main issue of the day.
Toronto: New Era. 15pp. *BVAUS/WB43f.18b.

2115 ------ The main centre of extreme reaction in Canada
today: the Hepburn-Duplessis alliance. (Toronto):
(Communist Party of Canada). 8pp, mimeo. *OKQS
OTURS/RSK.

2116 ------ Make civic democracy work for Toronto. Toronto: np. 8pp, mimeo. *OTURS/RSK. Address to Ward
5 ratepayers association, 6 December 1938.

2117 ------ A manual on party branch work. Toronto:
Communist Party of Canada. (c1938). 23pp. *BVAUS/
WB31f.2b OHMA3109 OKQS OTURS/RSK.

2118 ------ A reply to George McCullagh. Toronto: New
Era. (c1938). 23pp. AEU BVIP *BVAUS/WB31f.2a
OTURS/RSK.

2119 ------ War! Our government must take a stand! Toronto: (Communist Party of Canada). (4pp). *OHMA
oturs/RSK. Prepared as a radio address, but not
delivered.

2120 ------ Whither Canadian democracy? The communist
position. Toronto: Communist Party of Canada. (4pp).
*OOA/CCF542 OTURS/RSK. See 2010 above.

2121 Standard International Railway Unions. Amalgamation
- whether called 'unification' or 'compulsory co-operation' - don't let it catch us napping! Winnipeg.
8pp. *OOA/CCF179. Second in a series: others not
traced.

2122 Stapleford, Frank N. After twenty years: a short
history of the Neighbourhood Workers Association.
Toronto. 60pp, illus. OH *OTP.

2123 Tarr, E.J. and F.R. Scott. After Munich: where do
we go from here? Winnipeg: np. 24pp. *London
School of Economics Library.

2124 Thorburn Miners and Citizens. Brief submitted on

behalf of the miners and citizens of Thorburn, Nova Scotia, to the government of Canada and the government of Nova Scotia. Thorburn. 36pp, mimeo. *NSHPL. Regarding the closure of Thorburn mine and reopening another.

2125 Thorez, Maurice. France of the people's front and its mission in the world. Toronto: New Era. 128pp. BVIV *OHMA OTURS/RSK.

2126 Tompkins, J.J. The future of the Antigonish movement. Antigonish: Rural and Industrial Conference. 3pp, mimeo. *OOA/CCF148.

2127 United Church of Canada. A brief on social security by the Commission on Economic and Social Research presented to the Royal Commission on Dominion-Provincial Relations, April 1938. (Toronto). 12pp, mimeo. *OOA/Good 19.

2128 United Farmers of Alberta. Addresses and report to the convention, Edmonton, 1938. (Edmonton). 32pp. *SSA/G291.29.

2129 (anon). The walrus and the carpenter: platform of the get-rich-quick social cordite party...Mr Walrus, president; Mr Carpenter, sec'y-treas. Calgary: World News. (c1938). (4pp). *OTURS.

2130 Wardrope, Geo., C.M. Ross and C.W. Cox. The case against railway amalgamation. Port Arthur: np. 14pp. *OOA/CCF179. Three addresses: Ross and Cox were mayors of Fort William and Port Arthur.

2131 Weaver, Geo. W. How to organize and conduct discussion groups. (Vancouver): CCF. 15pp, mimeo. *OOA/CCF109.

2132 Webster, Arnold. Peace! The CCF policy for peace at home and abroad. A radio address. Vancouver: Commonwealth. (c1938). 24pp. BVIP *BVAUS/Mac42f.3A.

2133 Williams, G.H. A statement on co-operation by the leader of the Saskatchewan CCF. (Regina): CCF. 2pp mimeo. *OOA/CCF393.

2134 Woodsworth, J.S. Speeches on the workers right to organize and unemployment relief. Ottawa: J.O. Patenaude. 8pp. BVIV *ACGL/PDbl OTURS/RSK.

2135 Workers Educational Association. Annual report for the session 1937-38 presented at the annual convention held in the city of Oshawa, Ontario, August 27th, 1938. Toronto. 19pp, mimeo. *T.

2136 Young Communist League. China unites. Toronto. (c1938). 13pp, mimeo. *OHMA3128.

2137 ------ For life with a purpose - to make our country free, happy and strong - join the Young Communist League! Toronto. (4pp). *OHMA.

2138 ------ Our statement of purpose. Toronto. 16pp. *OHMA3122 OTURS/RSK. Includes by-laws.

2139 Young Communist League. Rally to prevent war: all
     out to Massey Hall International Youth Day, September
     6. Danger! Death ahead! - Defend Ethiopia! - Join
     the struggle for the preservation of peace! Toronto:
     (c1938). (4pp). *OHMA.

2140 ------ The road to happiness. Report from the 8th
     national convention. Toronto. 39pp. OONL *BVAUS/
     WB31f.2a.

2141 ------ Souvenir program, 8th national convention.
     Toronto. (24pp). *OTURS/RSK. Contains brief art-
     icles by Tim Buck, 'M' (probably Leslie Morris) and
     others, photographs and biographical articles.

1939

2142 Arkell, H.S. A national policy for agriculture.
     (?Winnipeg): United Farmers. 10pp, mimeo. *OOA/
     Good 16.

2143 Baird, Irene. Waste heritage. Toronto: Macmillan.
     (x), 329pp. *OONL. Novel of labour and the unemp-
     loyed in the 1930's in Vancouver, including the Post
     Office sitdown strike.

2144 Becker, Michel. Up from the shadows. Antigonish:
     St Francis Xavier University. 36pp. NBFL NSHPL
     OTP *OTMCL. Translated by Arthur Albrecht. The
     story of the Rochdale pioneers.

2145 Bradwin, E.W. Frontier College. np. 3pp. *OOA/
     Frontier 179. Reprinted from the Journal of Adult
     Education (USA), June 1939.

2146 British Columbia, Dept of Labour. Narrative history
     (with appendices) of unemployment relief from 1931-
     1937. Victoria. (c1939). 10pp plus 6pp appendices,
     mimeo. *BVAUS/Mac55Af.24.

2147 Brown, W.G. What is the alternative to the present
     social order? Saskatoon. 7pp. *OOA/MacPhail 3.

2148 Buck, Tim. Dunning's budget: what does it mean to
     you? Toronto: New Era. 21pp. NBSM *OHMA2401 OKQS
     OTURS/RSK.

2149 ------ Finland and the Soviet Union. Montreal:
     Contemporary. 33pp, mimeo. *BVAUS/Mac40f.4a OTURS/
     RSK.

2150 ------ The people want peace! Montreal: Contemporary.
     (4pp). *ACGA/Smith 14 OTURS/RSK.

2151 ------ The west and the federal election. Toronto:
     New Era. 21pp. AEU BVIP BVIV *OHMA1485 OKQS OTURS/
     RSK SSUS. Peel 3667. Radio speech in Winnipeg,
     sections of which were censored, but here printed in
     full.

2152 Canadian Committee to Aid Spanish Refugees. Report of Miss Jean Watts, our delegate at the recent conference of the Office International pour L'Enfance, on conditions in the refugee camps in France, May 25 1939. Toronto. 4pp, mimeo. *ACGA/Smith 13. Information bulletin 1.

2153 ------ Eyewitness report by Nan Green. Toronto. 3pp, mimeo. *ACGA/Smith 13. Information bulletin 3.

2154 ------ New camp on the Ile de Re. Toronto. (2pp), mimeo. *ACGA/Smith 13. Information bulletin 4.

2155 ------ News from Spain. Toronto. (4pp), mimeo. *ACGA/Smith 13. Information bulletin 7.

2156 ------ Odyssey of our Spanish children. Toronto. 4pp, mimeo. *ACGA/Smith 13. Bulletin 5. Other bulletins not traced.

2157 Canadian Committee to Aid Spanish Democracy. Summary of the minutes of the national conference, April 22, 1939. Toronto. 9pp, mimeo. *ACGA/Smith 13. 'These minutes will be followed by a complete printed report covering the whole life-time of the Committee.' Not found.

2158 Canadian League for Peace and Democracy. The relative military and economic resources of the democracies and the Axis powers: make peace inevitable. Toronto. 10pp, mimeo. *OOA/CCF168 OTURS/RSK SSA/McNaughton.

2159 Canadian Welfare Council. Recommendations to the Hon. the Minister of Labour, January 26th, 1939, following the conference held January 24th and 25th. (?Ottawa). 17pp, mimeo. *OOA/MacPhail 5. On relief training, migrants etc.

2160 Coady, M.M. Masters of their own destiny: the story of the Antigonish movement of adult education through economic cooperation. New York: Harper. xii, 170pp. *OOAL OONL.

2161 Coldwell, M.J. Coldwell replies to new democracy plea at annual convention. Ottawa: CCF. (2pp), broadside. *SSA/G2.1939.3.

2162 ------ Speeches on war, 1939 - Canada's policy and war budget, delivered in the House of Commons on Saturday, September 9 and Tuesday 12. Ottawa: J.O. Patenaude. 8pp. *SSA/G2.1939.7.

2163 Communist Party of Canada. Draft constitution and by-laws. (4pp). *OOA/CCF393. Special supplement to the Party Builder April, 1939.

2164 ------ Enemies within our gates. Regina. 4pp. *SSA/G175.1. On profiteering.

2165 ------ Financial statement and introductory letter from Tim Buck. Toronto. 4pp. *BVAUS/WB31f.2c. Printed and sent 'to public figures'.

2166 ------ Materials on questions of party training.

(Toronto). 33pp, mimeo. *OTURS/Salsberg T-10.24. Discusses the philosophical forerunners of Marxism, dialectics, social consciousness etc.

2167 Communist Party of Canada. What is democratic unity? (Saskatoon). (1p), mimeo. *OOA/CCF393. Designed to quell rumours that the Communists will support the Liberals.

2168 CCF. Canada and the war. The CCF position. Ottawa. (8pp). BVIP *BVAUS/Mac43f.17 OKQS OOA/CCF326 (3 copies) OOAL OTURS/RSK SSA/G2.1939.1 SSUS/CCF. Back cover has the CCF statement on Canada in the present crisis issued 9 September 1939.

2169 ------ The CCF and private property. Ottawa. (2pp). *ACGL/PDbl OOA/CCF536 SSA/G2.nd.1 and G3.Man.4.

2170 ------ The CCF federal election program. Ottawa. (c1939). 4pp. *SSUS/CCF JC197.

2171 ------ Membership book. Halifax. 16pp. *NSHD/J6 Includes constitution, duties etc.

2172 ------ The real situation in Saskatchewan. Toronto. (2pp). *OOA/CCF49.

2173 ------ Strengthen trade unions. Ottawa. (2pp). *OOA/CCF310 SSA/G2.1939.4 SSUS/CCF.

2174 ------ Towards the dawn: the CCF federal platform explained. Ottawa. 31pp. *ACGL/PDbl AEUS/CCF XIII 29 BVAUS/Mac30f.8 OHMA1527 OOA/CCF310 OTURS/Woodsworth. Issued in February and reissued with slight changes in June (SSA/G2.1939.5). A broadside with the same title was also issued.

2175 ------ Who owns Canada? What happens to promises after election? The CCF has the answers. Ottawa. (8pp). *ACGL/PDbl BVAUS/Mac30Af.12 OOA/CCF298 and 310 SSA/G2.1939.6.

2176 Deachman, R.J. John L. Lewis is a bluffer. Ottawa: Labor Review. (4pp). BVIP OOL *ACGL/PDh2.

2177 ------ Whither bound. An answer to the coupons of Mr George McCullagh of the Globe and Mail. Ottawa. 5pp, mimeo. *OOA/Woodsworth 14. For the equitable distribution of income and cooperation between labour and industry.

2178 Dimitrov, G. War: what for? Montreal: Contemporary. 36pp, mimeo. *BVAUS/WB43f.17(i).

2179 Dutt, R. Palme. The war and the people. Toronto: New Era. 15pp. *BVAUS/Mac43f.17 OTURS/RSK.

2180 Egger, John. The United States of the World. Edmonton. 46pp. *OOA/CCF316. Endorsed by the Committee of the Workmen's Foreign Affairs Society.

2181 Ewart, J.S. Has Canada the right to declare neutrality? Ottawa. 27pp plus 7pp supplement issued after the declaration of war, mimeo. *AEUS/CCFXIII-45.

2182 Filion, Gérard. L'union catholique des cultivateurs ...ce qu'elle est...ce qu'elle a fait...ce qu'elle fera. Montreal: Union Catholique des Cultivateurs. 48pp. QQL *OOL.

2183 Forsey, Eugene. Canada and Alberta: the revival of Dominion control over the provinces. London (Eng): Politica. pp 95-123. *OOA/Woodsworth 20. Offprint from June 1939 issue.

2184 German, R.O. Address at co-operative conference 14 March, 1939, Edmonton. Edmonton: Alberta Dept of Trade and Industry. 12pp. *SSUS/Coops.

2185 Grauer, A.E. Labour legislation: a study prepared for the Royal Commission on Dominion-Provincial Relations. Ottawa: np. (x), 292pp, mimeo. *OONL.

2186 Halldorson, Salome. Women! Do you want to end depression and war? Do you want to establish prosperity and peace? The power is yours! (Winnipeg). 8pp. *OOA/MacPhail 3.

2187 Hambleton, George. The press and the refugee problem. Ottawa: Canadian National Committee on Refugees and Victims of Political Persecution. 5pp plus 1p accompanying letter, mimeo. *ACGA/Smith 13.

2188 Hannam, H.H. The countryside is mobilizing to place returns from farming on a par with other industries. Toronto: United Farmers of Ontario. (4pp). *SSA/G292.25.

2189 Herridge, W.D. The new democracy: address delivered under the auspices of the Toronto District Labor Council, Wednesday 28 June 1939. Toronto: New Democracy Organizing Committee. 16pp. AEU BVIP OKQ OTU SRL SRU *OHMA2718 SSA/G.178.1.

2190 Industrial Workers of the World. Minutes of the sixth general convention of the IWW (Canadian administration) April 17-19, 1939 at 592 Main St, Winnipeg. np. 12pp, mimeo. *BVAUS/IWW.

2191 Korol, M. Why does Hitler want Ukraine? Winnipeg: Canadian-Ukrainian Youth Federation. 32pp. *OTURS/RSK.

2192 Lautenschager, S. The bombing of Chungking. Toronto: Canadian League for Peace and Democracy. 5pp, mimeo. *OOA/CCF168.

2193 McAuslane, A. and Winnipeg and District Trades and Labor Council. Facts about the Estevan strike (and) A statement of the Estevan dispute. Winnipeg. (4pp). *SSA/G229.1.

2194 McDougall, John L. The Canadian railway problem: a discussion of wages and working conditions of employees in train and engine service. Submission to the Special Committee of the Senate, March 21, 1939. Toronto: Citizens Group for Railway Action. 14pp. OOP OTMCL *OOA/CCF179 and Woodsworth 12.

2195 MacInnis, Angus. Unemployment: can we end it?
Ottawa: J.O. Patenaude. 14pp. *BVAUS/Mac43Af.12
OOL SSUS/JL197.

2196 Mackintosh, Margaret. Workmen's compensation in Canada. Geneva: ILO. 32pp. *OOL. Reprinted from the
International Labour Review Vol.XL/1 July 1939.

2197 MacPhail, Agnes. National organization for agriculture. Farm conference day, United Farmers convention
November 21, 1939. (Toronto): United Farmers (of Ontario). 7pp, mimeo. *OOA/MacPhail 3.

2198 Morgan, Lorne T. The origins and development of fas-
cism. Toronto: Workers Educational Assn. 24pp.
*BVAUS/Mac40f.8a OTURS/RSK. Reprinted from H.A.
Innis (ed) *Essays in political economy in honour of E.J.
Urwick* (1938) and later incorporated into part I of
Fascism from origins to maturity. See 2451 below.

2199 Morris, Leslie. The story of Tim Buck's party 1922-
1939: to commemorate the 17th anniversary of the
founding of the Communist Party of Canada. Toronto:
New Era. 31pp. BVIP BVIV OKQ OTP SRL *BVAUS/WB31f.1c
OHMA2722 OOA/CCF542 OTURS/RSK SSUS/SpColl.

2200 Mullen, D.B. and A.M. Allen. The case against amalgamation. Edmonton: Edmonton Local Conference Committee of all Railway Employees. 16pp. *OOA/CCF179.
An interview: Mullen was Minister of Agriculture in
Alberta. No 3 in a series of radio broadcasts in
opposition to the proposals of Sir Edward Beatty for
amalgamating the Canadian railway system.

2201 Noseworthy, J.W. Education - a national responsibility. Toronto: Canadian Forum. 15pp. *OHMA1937.
Forum pamphlets 1.

2202 Ontario Federation of Unemployment. Reports, proceedings and constitution, sixth annual convention, Toronto April 20-21, 1939. Toronto. 44pp, mimeo.
*OTURS/RSK.

2203 Pearson, George S. A statement by the Minister of
Labour on the strike of the Pioneer Mines Limited,
employees and on the 'Industrial Conciliation and
Arbitration Act' December 14th, 1939. Victoria: C.F.
Banfield. 5pp. *BVAUS/Mac34f.10 OOL.

2204 Queens University. Vacations with pay in Canadian
industry. Kingston: Industrial Relations section.
82pp. Bulletin 3. *OKQ.

2205 Quinn, Jack (ed). The five-year plan big business
style of Sir Edward Beatty for amalgamation of the
railroads. Port Arthur: Communist Party of Canada.
(6pp). *OTCPA.

2206 Rose, Fred. Spying on labor. Toronto: New Era.
44pp. BVIP *BVAUS/WB32f.6 OKQS OTURS/RSK.

2207 Rowley, William Philip. Poems of struggle. np. 20pp,
mimeo. *OOA/Woodsworth 20.

2208 St Francis Xavier University. Learning through study clubs. Antigonish. (c1939). 11pp. *OOA/CCF552.

(2209) Saint-Martin, Albert. Frankenstein or consumers! Montreal: The Consumers League. 14lpp. BVIP QMBM.

2210 Sandwell, B.K. Should we admit refugees? Toronto: Canadian National Committee on Refugees. (1p) broad-side. *OTURS. Text of a broadcast over CBL.

2211 Scott, F.R. A policy of neutrality for Canada. New York: Council on Foreign Relations. 17pp. OKQ *BVAUS/Mac43f.17 OOA/CCF538. Reprinted from Foreign Affairs, January 1939.

2212 ------ Recent developments in New Zealand. (Ottawa): CCF. 8pp. *OOA/CCF173.

2213 Smith, Stewart. The horse and the jockey: more in reply to Mr George McCullagh. Toronto: New Era. 30pp. AEU OKQ *BVAUS/WB31f.2a OTURS/RSK. Also printed as 'The jockey and the horse'.

2214 ------ Who is double-crossing peace? Toronto: Communist Party of Canada. (4pp). *OKQS OTURS/RSK.

2215 Stalin, Joseph. From socialism to communism in the Soviet Union. Toronto: New Era. 63pp. BVIP *OHMA OTURS/RSK. Report to the 18th Congress CPSU.

2216 Stapleford, Ernest W. Report on rural relief due to drought conditions and crop failures in western Canada 1930-37. Ottawa: Dept of Agriculture. 130pp. *SSUS Peel 3703.

2217 Stephen, A.M. War in China...what it means to Canada. Vancouver: China Aid Council and National Salvation League. 24pp, illus. *BVAUS/WB43f.5a OHMA2748.

2218 Telford, Gertrude S. What happened to David Jones? Regina: CCF. 46pp. *OOA/Klein 17 SSA/CCF Sask.151.

2219 Tingley, Gerald Everett. Organization and policy of trade unions in the coal mining industry of Nova Scotia. Unpublished MA thesis, McMaster University 105pp. *OHMA.

2220 United Farmers of Canada. Manifesto. Willingdon (Alta). 14pp. *OOA/CCF316.

2221 Valleau, O.W. Training of youth in self-liquidating work and wages projects. Melfort (Sask). (4pp). *SSA/G1.1939.3.

2222 Warshaw, Leo. Report on wage and unemployment cond-itions in Canada. Toronto: Workers Educational Assn. 11pp, mimeo. *E.

2223 Williams, Fred C. The open road and other poems. (Creelman, Sask). 38pp. *OOA/Woodsworth 20. Poems in praise of Woodsworth and other 'social protests'.

2224 Williams, G.H. Problems confronting the retail mer-chants of western Canada. Radio broadcast Wednesday 4th January 1939. Regina: CCF. (4pp). *SSA/G11939.1.

2225 Williams, G.H. Social democracy in Canada. Regina.
55pp. OTP QMS SRL *ACGA/CCF29 MWPA/Ivens 6 OHMA
1560 OOA/CCF321 and 323 and 539 SSA/G1.1939.2 SSUS
JL197. An attempt 'to give an understandable explanation of *This socialism* which the CCF movement in Canada are endeavouring to bring into being.'

2226 Woodsworth, J.S. and others. Canada's road to peace.
Ottawa: J.O. Patenaude. 38pp. *ACGL/PDbl BVAUS/Mac
43f.3a and 27f.44 SSA/G2.1939.2 SSUS/JL197. Others
include: M.J. Coldwell, T.C. Douglas, Grant MacNeil,
Angus MacInnis, P.J. Rowe.

2227 ------ Speeches on war, 1939 - Canada's policy and
war budget delivered in the House of Commons on Friday, September 8 and Tuesday September 12, 1939.
Ottawa: J.O. Patenaude. 10pp. *SSUS/JL197.

2228 ------ Your members speak. Ottawa: J.O. Patenaude.
42pp. *ACGL/PDbl BVAUS/Mac27f.43 and 30f.11 SSA/
G2.1939.8 SSUS/JL197. Others include: M.J. Coldwell,
Angus MacInnis, T.C. Douglas, G.C. MacNeil, P.G. Rowe,
A.A. Heaps.

2229 Woodworth, Kenneth. Canadian youth comes of age.
Toronto: Ryerson. 28pp. *OTURS/RSK. Contains also
a brief on a national youth administration prepared
by the national committee of the Canadian Youth Congress and submitted to the federal Minister of Labour
3 March 1939.

2230 Workers Educational Association. The trade unionist's
handbook. Toronto. (c1939). 47pp. *OTP OTURS/RSK.
Compiled by Bora Laskin.

2231 Young Communist League. Canadian youth fights for
peace. (Toronto). 16pp, mimeo. *OHMA. Various
pagination, includes YCL statement on conscription,
just and unjust wars, first imperialist war etc.
Our Canada no. 2.

2232 ------ Our Canada. (Toronto). 18pp, mimeo. *OHMA
Four outlines for discussion groups - Canada and its
people and Glimpses of Canada's past (3 parts).

1940

2233 All-Canadian Congress of Labour. Proposed amendments
to the constitution submitted by the executive board
for consideration at the tenth convention Toronto,
September 9, 1940. Ottawa. 14pp. *OOA/CCF79. To
change to the Canadian Congress of Labour.

2234 Arnold, Mary Ellicott. The story of Tompkinsville.
New York: Cooperative League. (viii), 102pp, illus,
diags. *OOAL. Cooperative housing in Nova Scotia.

2235 Bain, Roderick Grant. Consumers co-operation in Nova
Scotia. Unpublished MA thesis, Acadia University,

Wolfville. (v), 95(96)pp, biblio. *NSWA.

2236 Barber, Clarence Lyle. Unemployment relief in Saskatchewan. Unpublished honours thesis, University of
Saskatchewan. (i), 81(82-83)pp, biblio. *SSUS.

2237 Brown, W.G. Unity means victory! Saskatoon: United
Reform Movement of Saskatoon. 4pp. *OOA/MacPhail 3.

2238 Buck, Tim. The truth about Finland and USSR. Regina:
Communist Party of Canada. (c1940). 16pp, mimeo.
*SSUS/Communism.

2239 ------ and Stewart Smith. A letter to Toronto electors. (Toronto): Communist Party of Canada. (2pp),
broadside, mimeo. *OTURS/RSK.

2240 Canadian Civil Liberties Union. The war and civil
liberty. Montreal. (c1940). 6pp. OONL *OTURS/RSK.
Concerning the War Measures Act.

2241 Canadian Labor Defense League. On guard for civil
liberty: what the War Measures Act means to you; an
analysis of the War Measures Act and the Canada defence regulations. Toronto. 15pp. *BVAU.

2242 ------ Speakers notes: in defence of civil liberties.
Toronto. (c1940). (4pp). *OTURS/RSK.

2243 Canadian Seamens Union. An appeal to all leaders of
the trade union movement: to all heads of labor organizations: to all friends of labor. Toronto. 2pp,
mimeo. *OTURS/RSK.

2244 ------ Our case before the board: brief submitted
to the Board of Conciliation and Investigation on
the dispute between various shipping companies and
their employees. Toronto. 39pp. *OTURS/RSK.

2245 Canadian Tribune. John Milton or Dr Goebbels, which?
Toronto. (1p), broadside. *T.

2246 Canadian Wheat Pools. The wheat pools and western
community life. An account of some of the ways in
which the wheat pools have endeavoured to assist the
prairie community toward a happier and fuller manner
of living. Saskatoon. 34pp. *SSA/G299.1. see Peel
3424.

2247 Canadian Youth Congress. 5 point program for youth.
Toronto. (4pp), mimeo. *OTURS/RSK.

2248 ------ What do you think? Facts please. Conscription, civil liberties, profiteering, youth conditions.
Toronto. 16pp. *E.

2249 Cohen, J.L. Regulation 21 (Defence of Canada regulations). Toronto: Civil Liberties Assn. 14pp.
*OKQS OOA/CCF147 OTURS/RSK. Regulation 21 provided
for detention without trial. This pamphlet deals
almost exclusively with the case of 'Pat' Sullivan,
President of the Canadian Seamens Union.

2250 Coldwell, M.J. and others. The CCF in Parliament,
1940. Addresses. Ottawa: J.O. Patenaude. 33pp.

*BVAUS/Mac27f.44 and 30f.3 OHMA OOA/Woodsworth 20
SSA/G2.1940.4. Others include: T.C. Douglas, P.E.
Wright, G.H. Castleden, Clarence Gillis, A.M. Nich-
olson, Angus MacInnis.

2251 Coldwell, M.J. and others. Fighting for democracy
on all fronts. Ottawa: E. Cloutier. 43pp. *BVAUS/
Mac27f.44 OHMA1531 SSA/G2.1940.6. Others include
P.E. Wright, Clarence Gillis, Angus MacInnis, A.M.
Nicholson, G.H. Castleden and T.C. Douglas.

2252 ------ ,T.C. Douglas and Angus MacInnis. Money before
men. Ottawa: J.O. Paenaude. 15pp. *BVAUS/Garrison
1-6 SSA/G2.1940.9. Inside title: Mobilization of
national resources.

2253 Communist Party of Canada. Federal election manifesto:
to save Canada from catastrophe, to speed the end of
the slaughter, withdraw Canada from the war! Vote
for peace, vote communist. Ottawa(probably Toronto).
22pp, mimeo. *BVAUS/Smith CP OKQS.

2254 ------ One year of war: what next? Toronto. (2pp),
broadside. *OOA/CCF393.

2255 ------ Questions and answers on the Communist Party.
(Toronto). (c1940). 26pp, mimeo. *OTURS/RSK.
On the 'imperialist war'.

2256 CCF. The CCF and social credit. Vancouver. (4pp).
*BVAUS/Mac30Af.14. Leaflet 2.

2257 ------ CCF election program. Ottawa. (4pp). *OOA/
CCF310 SSA/G2.1940.2 SSUS/CCF. Issued in different
centres across the country.

2258 ------ The farmer has been betrayed. Regina. (2pp).
*SSA/G1.nd.11 and G2.1945.6.

2259 ------ Labor and urban security. Regina. (4pp).
*OOA/CCF70.

2260 ------ Save democracy at home. Ottawa. (4pp).
*OOA/CCF310 and 539.

2261 ------ Time for a change. Ottawa. (8pp). *ACGA/
CCF29 OOA/CCF310 and 539 OTURS/Woodsworth.

2262 ------ Victory needs planning. Toronto. (4pp).
*OKQS. Forward Canada 1.

2263 ------ Ward Two CCF news. Toronto. 4pp. *OOA/CCF
320.

2264 Co-operative Trading Associations. Annual conference
Bessborough Hotel, Saskatoon, June 25th and 26th,
1940. Saskatoon. 30pp, mimeo. *OOA/Good 12. Includes address by W.C. Good.

2265 Co-operative Union of Canada. An expanding economy:
co-operative solution of our economic problems.
Brantford. (4pp). *OOA/CCF546.

2266 Corbett, Jos. Avoid fascism in Canada (and) The
'national government' farce. Shaunavon(Sask): Shaun-

avon Standard. (2pp), broadside. *SSA/G2.1940.10.
Both reprinted from the *New Commonwealth* 15 Feb 1940.

2267 Deacon, William Arthur. Sh-h-h...here comes the
Censor! An address to the Ontario Library Assn, 26
March 1940. Toronto: Macmillan. 16pp. OKQ OOAL
OONL QMBM *OHMA1416. Against any form of censorship.

2268 Fellowship for a Christian Social Order. Christian
action and the profit system. Toronto. 15pp, mimeo.
*OOA/Foresy 15.

2269 Freeman, J. Morton. The demands of god today. Toronto: Fellowship for a Christian Social Order. 14pp,
mimeo. *OOA/Forsey 15. God demands socialist economic planning.

2270 Good, W.C. An open letter to Mr H.G. Wells. np.
7pp, mimeo. *OOA/Good 12.

2271 Hannam, H.H. One organization for Canadian agriculture. Toronto:(United Darmers of Ontario). 5pp,
mimeo. *OOA/Good 16.

2272 ------ Pulling together for 25 years. Brief story
of events and people in the united farmers movement
in Ontario, 1914-1939. Toronto: United Farmers of
Ontario. 64pp. MWP OH OOA OTP SSU *SSA/G292.6.

2273 Harris, J.C. Conscription for peace. Nelson: Useful
Peoples Party. 52pp. *OHMA1708. Extensively revised edn of no. 1952 above.

2274 Hodgson, G.W. A study of Canadian male minimum wage
legislation. Unpublished MA thesis, McMaster University. (iv), 97pp, biblio. *OHMA.

2275 Industrial Workers of the World. Minutes of the 7th
general convention (Canadian administration) April
29/30, Port Arthur. np. (8pp), mimeo. *BVAUS/IWW.

2276 International Woodworkers of America. Proceedings
of third annual convention, BC district council,
Vancouver January 3rd and 4th, 1940. Vancouver.
65pp, mimeo. *BVAUS/Mac34f.22.

2277 Irvine, Wm. Let us reason together: an appeal to
Social Crediters and CCF'ers. Edmonton. 14pp.
*ACGL OOA/CCF310 and 323 SSA/G.501.5 SSUS/JL197.

2278 ------ The trail of a truth twister: an answer to
'The records that tell the story'. Edmonton: (?CCF).
47pp. *ACGL OOA/CCF316 and 541. Peel 3727. The
records tell the story was issued by the Social
Credit government in Alberta.

2279 Jolliffe, E.B. Letter to a social democrat. Toronto:
CCF. 8pp, mimeo. *OOA/CCF393 and Underhill 44 (in
very fragile condition). Anti-communist.

2280 King, W.L. Mackenzie. Labour and the war: two sig-
nificant anniversaries: broadcast. Ottawa: J.O.
Patenaude. 10pp. OOP *OOAL OOL. The anniversaries
are Labour day and the start of world war II.

2281 Lambert, R.S. This freedom: a guide to good citizenship in time of war. Toronto: Canadian Assn for Adult
Education. 15pp. *OOA/CCF197. Deals with civil liberties, defence of Canada regulations etc.

2282 Lawson, William T. The Soviet Union and Finland:
facts and documents. Toronto: New Era. 47pp.
BVIP *BVAUS/Mac40f.4a OTURS/RSK.

2283 McKean, Fergus. I take my stand...let the people
decide: an open letter. Vancouver: Communist Party.
(4pp). *BVAUS/Smith CP.

2284 Mackintosh, W.A. Wage policy in war time. Kingston:
Queens University School of Commerce. 16pp. *OOL.

2285 MacPhail, Agnes. Convict or citizen? The urgent
need for prison reform. Toronto: CCF. 15pp. OKQ
OOP OTURS *AEUS/CCFXIII-2 OHMA2877 OOA/CCF320 (2
copies) and 536.

2286 ------ Prison reform. (Ottawa): CCF. (c1940). 16pp,
mimeo. *OOA/CCF174.

2287 Marsh, Leonard C. and Charlotte Whitton. Administrative implications re unemployment insurance, employment services and unemployment aid. Ottawa: Canadian
Welfare Council. (c1940). 20pp. BVAU MWP *OKQ.

2288 ------ The Canadian working population: an analysis
of occupational status divisions and the incidence
of unemployment. Unpublished PhD thesis, McGill
University. 495pp.

2289 ------ Canadians in and out of work: a survey of
economic classes and their relation to the labour
market. Toronto: Oxford University Press for McGill
University. xxii, 503pp, appendixes, index. *OKQS
OONL.

2290 (May Day). Join the May day parade. Vancouver: May
Day Committee. (1p), broadside. *T.

2291 ------ May day celebration souvenir program. Vancouver: np. (4pp). *T. Songs and historical notes.

2292 Molotov, V.M. Socialism means peace: report to the
Supreme Soviet of the USSR. Toronto: (Canadian Tribune). 11pp, mimeo. *OTURS/RSK.

2293 Morgan, Lorne T. The state and economic life in
fascist Italy. Toronto: University of Toronto Quarterly. pp 428-451. *BVAUS/Mac40Bf.8A. Reprint
from vol. IX July 1940.

2294 Morris, Leslie. The CCF's betrayal. (Toronto):
Communist Party of Canada. (c1940). 29pp. BVAUS
*OHMA1843 OTURS/RSK. The betrayal was their rejec-
tion of the 1934 manifesto clause opposing war.

2295 Nicholson, A.M. An address on living conditions in
northern Saskatchewan delivered in debate on the
War Appropriation Bill. Ottawa: J.O. Patenaude.
4pp. *SSA/G2.1940.8.

2296 Nicholson, A.M. Speech on the budget delivered in the House of Commons on July 3rd and July 4th, 1940. Ottawa: J.O. Patenaude. 4pp. *SSA/G2.1940.1.

2297 Nielsen, Dorise W. Democracy must live! The collected addresses. Toronto: Canadian Tribune. 62pp. OH OKQ OTP SSU *ACGL/Communist BVAUS/WB39f.2a OHMA 1919 OTURS/RSK SSA/G.189.1.

2298 ------ (On wages and general policy.) Toronto. 14pp. *OTURS/RSK. Proof copy only; no final published copy located.

2299 Paterson, William. The progressive political movement 1919-1930. Unpublished MA thesis, University of Toronto. (iv), 191(192-206)pp, no biblio. *OTUAR.

2300 Queens University. The economic welfare of Canadian employees: a study of occupations, earnings, hours and other working conditions, 1913-1937. Kingston: Industrial Relations Dept. 144pp. *OKQ. Bulletin 4.

2301 Richards, A.E. Farmers co-operative business organizations in Canada, 1938-39. Ottawa: Dept of Agriculture. 8pp. *OOA/Avison 9. Reissued for various years.

2302 Royce, Mario V. The contribution of the Methodist church to social welfare in Canada. Unpublished MA thesis, University of Toronto. (iv), 304pp, biblio. *OTUAR.

2303 St Francis Xavier University. What can the women do? Antigonish. 46pp. *NSHP OOA/MacPhail 3.

2304 Salsberg, J.B. The war situation and Canadian labour: the role and tasks of the trade union movement. Toronto: (Communist Party of Canada.) 47pp. *BVAUS/WB 43f.17 OTURS/RSK.

2305 Smith, W. Warren. A survey of unemployment: a study of its causes, effects and solutions, together with an analysis of unemployment in Canada. Unpublished Hon.BA thesis, McMaster University. (ii), 116pp, biblio. *OHMA.

2306 Socialist Labor Party of Canada. Prosperity via socialism. Toronto. (c1940). (4pp). *SSA/G259.1.

2307 ------ Socialist principles vs. parliamentary bickering. Toronto: (c1940). (4pp). *SSA/G259.2.

2308 ------ What means this strike? Toronto. (c1940). (4pp). *SSA/G259.3.

2309 Spencer, H.E. Banking and credit: a study. Edmonton: CCF. (c1940). 15pp. *ACGL/Pdbl AEUS/SpColl. BVAUS/Mac39f.2 OOA/CCF316 SSA/G3.Alta.1.

2310 Two Former Affililates *(sic)* Inland Boatmens Union. Halt 'Dictator Jamieson': save our union movement! What's behind the reactionary anti-labour policy and bureaucratic, hairsplitting, witch-hunting tactics of the Jamieson-Bengough-Showler dictatorship. Vancouver:

Inland Boatmens Union, International Woodworkers of America. (4pp). *T.

2311 United Electrical Workers. Unionism at work: collective bargaining agreement Phillips Electrical Works Ltd and local 510 UEW. Toronto. (24pp). *OTURS/RSK. A sample entry. There are many hundreds of these agreements filed in various archives.

2312 UFO-Labor Political Association. Re-elect Agnes MacPhail UFO-Labor candidate in Grey-Bruce. She has proven her worth. (Toronto). (4pp). *OOA/Heaps 1. Contains editorial, policy and extracts of statements.

2313 Wisdon, Jane. Glace Bay looks ahead: some notes and suggestions arising from a preliminary study of community problems and welfare services, made at the request of the town council of Glace Bay. Ottawa: Canadian Welfare Council. 22pp plus chart, mimeo. *OOAL.

2314 Workers Educational Association. Study courses: cooperation. (a) In cooperation: bulletins 1-10. (b) Consumers cooperation, series 1, part 2 studies 1-5. (c) Credit unions, studies 1-5, all mimeo. (d) Consumer education, bulletins 1-4. Toronto. (c1940). *OTP.

2315 ------ Agricola study association: political science study outline, bulletins 1-14. Toronto. (c1940). *OTP.

2316 Young Communist League. Youth want(s) peace! An important and timely message for young Canadians. Toronto. 4pp, mimeo. *BVAUS/WB31f.2c.

1941

2317 Anti-Fascist Mobilization Committee for Aid to the Soviet Union. Help seal Hitler's doom! Vancouver: (4pp). *T.

2318 ------ Manifesto. Vancouver. (4pp). *BVAUS/Smith CP OTCPA. Cover has a program for a rally on 30 July.

2319 Bellan, Ruben C. Relief in Winnipeg: the economic background. Unpublished MA thesis, University of Toronto. 226pp, map. (pp 124-126 omitted in numbering, p 223a inserted). biblio. *OONL.

2320 Brewin, F.A. Labour and the war. Toronto. 20pp. *OONL. Behind the headlines 5.

2321aBuck, Tim. A national front for victory. np (possibly New York). 32pp. *BVAUS/Mac43f.17 OTURS/RSK.

2321b------ (the same). (?Toronto): Communist Party of Canada. 23pp. *MWPA/CCF35 OKQS OTURS/RSK.

2321c------ (the same) Vancouver: Workers Publishing. 13pp. *BVAUS/WB31f.2a

2322 Canada. Canada's war emergency training programme
for 1941. Repprt of the inter-departmental committee
on labour co-ordination. Ottawa: Edmond Cloutier.
12pp. *AEPAA/Farmilo 1.

2323 ------ Dept of Labour. Canada's wartime wages policy. Ottawa: Edmond Cloutier. 6pp. *OOL.

2324 Canadian Congress of Labor. Labor and the church.
Ottawa. 3pp. *OTURS/RSK. An invitation to the
church for active support of the CCL.

2325 Canadian Federation of Agriculture. Manifesto of
the Canadian farmer. (?Toronto). 11pp. *ACFL/PDg
CCA OOAL.

2326 Canadian Federation of Agriculture. What share of
the national income does the farmer get? Ottawa.
16pp. BVIP *AEUS/CCFXIII-33.

2327 Canadian Youth Congress. Where do we stand? A declaration of aims for Canadian youth today. Toronto.
(4pp). *OTURS.

2328 Cecil-Smith, E. Red ally: an estimate of Soviet life
and Soviet power. Toronto: Adam. 127pp. AEU BVAUS
OONL *OTURS/RSK. Handy Library 2. A very superficial
public relations effort.

2329 Charpentier, Alfred. La Confédération des Travailleurs Catholiques du Canada Inc. Ses oeuvres et ses
aspirations. (?Québec). 16pp. AEU QMBM QMSS *OKQS.
Tract 1: 20éme anniversaire de fondation de la CTCC.

2330 Cohen, J.L. Collective bargaining in Canada: an examination of the legislative record and policy of the
government of the Dominion of Canada. Toronto: Steel
Workers Organizing Committee. 93pp. *SSUS/Labour.

2331 Coldwell, M.J. and Angus MacInnis. Defence of Canada
regulations: Labour conditions. Reprints of speeches
delivered in the House of Commons, session 1940-41.
Ottawa: E. Cloutier. 13pp. *AEPAA/Farmilo 1 BVAUS/
Mac43f.17 OOA/CCF147 SSA/G2.1941.1.

2332 Committee for the Release of Labor Prisoners. They
fought for labor - now interned! Winnipeg. 32pp.
*BVAUS/WB32f.3 OTURS/RSK. Foreword by Dorise Niel-
sen. Written in part by Norman Penner. Relates to
those interned under section 21 of the defence regs.

2333 Communist Party of Canada. Fighter's note book.
(?Toronto). (106pp). *OTURS/RSK. Distributed by
the Soldier's Committee, CPC. Contains 8 questions
and answers, blank pages, address pages, 1942 calendar.

2334 ------ Forward to victory over fascism. (Toronto).
(1p), mimeo. *OOA/Forsey 15.

2335 CCF. The CCF in the legislature, 1944. Regina.
78pp. *SSA/G1.1941.1. Similar records were issued
in 1942, 28pp *SSA/G1.1942.1: 1943, 31pp *BVAUS/Mac
30Bf.21 SSA/G1.1943.1 and 1944, 40pp *OOA/CCF69 SSA/
G1.1944.5.

2336 CCF. A new order shall arise: statements on the pol-
icy of the CCF in the present struggle against the
Nazis and Fascists, consisting of an address by M.J.
Coldwell, (and) policy resolutions adopted by the
1940 national convention. Ottawa. 24pp. BVIP OTP
*BVAUS/Mac30f.8 MWPA/Brigden 7 OKQS OOA/CCF302
OTURS/RSK SSA/G2.1940.11 SSUS/JL197.

2337 ------ Notes for speakers. Regina. (63pp), mimeo.
*SSA/G1.1941.3.

2338 Cooperative Union of Canada. The co-operative movement in Canada. Brantford. (4pp). *OOA/CUC223.

2339 ------ The essential principles of the co-operative
movement. Brantford. (4pp). *OOA/CCF546 and CUC223.

2340 Donaldson, L.J. Canada for all Canadians: a practical programme of prosperity for all the people.
Halifax: Royal Print. 119pp. *OONL.

2341 Dutt, R. Palme. Turning point for the world. (Toronto): (New Era). 24pp. *BVAUS/Mac43f.18 OTURS/RSK.

2342 Good, W.C. A world without war. President's address
annual congress of the Co-operative Union of Canada,
Regina, June 23 and 24, 1941. (Regina): CUC. 11pp,
mimeo. *OOA/Good 12 and 19.

2343 Haythorne, George V. and Leonard C. Marsh. Land and
labour: a social survey of agriculture and the farm
labour market in central Canada. Toronto: Oxford
University Press for McGill University. xxii, 568pp.
*OTP.

2344 Herbert, C.H. Spike that price right! Montreal:
Workers Educational Association. 8pp. *BVIP.

2345 International Labor Office. The Rowell-Sirois report:
a Canadian reaffirmation of the democratic faith in
social progress. Montreal. 30pp. *ACGL/PDb Labor
OOL OTURS/RSK.

2346 International Typographical Union. 85th convention,
August 16th to 23rd, 1941, Vancouver. Vancouver.
(98pp). BVIP BVIPA *BVAA.

2347 Irvine, William. The strategy of victory. np.
(8pp). OH *BVAUS/Mac39f.7.

2348 James, F. Cyril. Control of prices and wages: a Canadian experiment. Winnipeg: Universal Life Assurance
and Annuity Co. 14pp. *OKQS.

2349 Johnstone, A.R. Labor's privileges. Toronto: Canadian Congress Journal. 4pp. *OOA/CCF79. Against
a campaign to close 'beverage rooms'.

2350 Kardash, W.A. Manitoba's program for total war.
Winnipeg: Workers Election Committee. 31pp. *BVAUS/
WB43f.17 MWPL OKQS OTURS/RSK.

2351 Lamberton, H.R. The principles of consumers co-operation. Saskatoon: Cooperative Union of Canada.
24pp. *SSUS/Coops.

2352 Lawson, William T. For all out war against Hitler Germany! Toronto: Communist Party of Canada. 4pp. *OTURS/RSK. Copy bears pencilled note 'revd. 27.x. 41' but revised edn not traced. Contains also an appeal to remove the ban on the Communist Party.

2353 League for Social Reconstruction. Poor man rich man. Montreal. (24pp). BVIP OTP OTURS SRL *ACGA/Coote 10 OHMA1783 OOA/CCF538 and Forsey 8 OOAL. Graphs and charts prepared from material collected under the direction of Eugene Forsey.

2354 Logan, H.A. Canada's control of labour relations. Toronto: Canadian Assn for Adult Education. 29pp. *OOA/CCF544. Behind the Headlines vol 2, no.2.

2355 MacInnis, Angus and Clarence Gillis. Labour policies and the war effort. Ottawa: E. Cloutier. 16pp. *BVAUS/Garrison 1-6 and Mac27f.44 SSA/G2.1941.2 SSUS/JL197.

2356 McTavish, Duncan. The rainbow in the cloud. London (Ont): Jos.Corbett, Brotherhood of Railway Carmen of America. 6pp. *OOA/CCF192. 'A christian social order in our time.'

2357 Manitoba, Dept of Agriculture. Cooperation in theory and practice. Winnipeg. 32pp. *OOA/MacPhail 3.

2358 Mootashed, Marie Emma Ellen. The real earnings of employed workers in Canadian industry, 1917-1938. Unpublished MA thesis, Queens University. vii, 145pp biblio. *OKQ.

2359 National Council for Democratic Rights. Our fight for freedom. Toronto. 32pp. *MWPA/CCF35

2360 Nielsen, Dorise. A people's movement: a message to the Canadian people. Toronto: Tribune. 7pp. *OTURS/ RSK.

2361 Peto, E.J. Wheat marketing. Winnipeg: Manitoba Commonwealth. (4pp). *OOA/CCF318.

2362 Pritchett, Harold J. An appeal for CCF labor unity. Vancouver: (CCF). (4pp). *BVAUS/Smith CP.

2363 Queens University. The war-time wage policy of the Dominion government. Kingston: Industrial Relations Centre. 16pp. *OKQ.

2364 Ridley, Hilda. The post-war woman. Toronto: Ryerson. vi, 39pp. OH OKQ OOP OTP *OONL.

2365 (?Salsberg, J.B.) A wartime labor policy: for united all-out war effort. by J.B. Toronto: Canadian Tribune. 32pp. *OTURS/RSK.

2366 Scott, F.R. Canada and the United States. Boston: World Peace Foundation. 80pp, biblio. *London School of Economics Library.

2367 Smith, Stewart. Shall the past divide us now? (Toronto): (Communist Party of Canada). 14pp. OHMA1888 OTURS/RSK.

2368 Smith, Stewart. The supreme issue of the hour: an historic turning point. (Toronto): (Communist Party of Canada). 6pp, mimeo. *OTURS/RSK. The historic turning point was the German attack on the Soviet Union.

2369 Thomson, J.S. Co-operation and the future. Address at the annual convention of the Saskatchewan section of the Co-operative Union of Canada, Regina, June 26, 1941. (Regina): Cooperative Union of Canada. 6pp, mimeo. *OOA/Good 12.

2370 ------ The new opportunity for co-operation and other selected addresses. Saskatoon: Cooperative Union of Canada. 64pp. *SSUS/Coops.

2371 Trades and Labor Congress of Canada. Government wage control and related matters. Ottawa. 26pp. *OOL.

2372 Voorhis, Jerry. Democracy in action. Regina: Co-operative Union of Canada. 19pp. *SSA/G49.8. Reprinted from the Congressional Record.

2373 Winch, Harold E. and the Economic Relations Committee of the CCF. Summary of CCF brief submitted to the Workmen's Compensation Royal Commission (Justice Sloan, presiding), August 4, 1941. (Vancouver): (CCF). 28pp. BVIP *BVAUS/Mac43f.19 OOA/CCF326. Cover title: CCF presents the case for compensation.

1942

2374 Adamson, A. (ed). Homes or hovels? Toronto: Canadian Assn for Adult Education. 48pp. *OOA/CCF544. Behind the Headlines vol. 3 no. 5.

2375 Aircraft Conference, Fort William, Ontario, May 24th, 25th and 26th, 1942. (Toronto). 17pp, mimeo. *OOA/CCF60. A conference of Ontario trade unions.

2376 Anselm, Sr.M. The Antigonish idea and social welfare. Antigonish: St Francis Xavier University. (c1942). 16pp. *NSHP/HDC.

(2377)British Columbia. Report of the commissioner, the Honorable Mr Justice Gordon McG. Sloan, relating to the Workmen's Compensation Board, 1942. Victoria: Charles F. Banfield. 245pp. BVIP.

2378 Buck, Tim. Back up the boys who fought at Dieppe. Open a second front now! Toronto: Communist-Labor Total War Committee. (4pp). *OHMA.

2379 ------ Canadian labour and the war: radio address broadcast over station CJOR, Vancouver, 3 December 1942. Vancouver: Communist-Labor Total War Committee. 6pp. *BVAUS/Smith CP.

2380 ------ 1942 - the decisive year of the war: organize Canada for total war! (Toronto): (Communist-Labor

Total War Committee). 64pp. *OHMA2447 OTURS/RSK.

2381 Buck, Tim. Tim Buck answers critics...calls for lifting of Communist ban! Toronto: National Council for Democratic Rights. (4pp). *OTURS/RSK SSA/G293.3 Speech at Don Hall for the 71st birthday of A.E. Smith

2382 ------ Tim Buck's appeal: vote 'yes' on the plebiscite. Toronto: Tim Buck Plebiscite Committee. 12pp. *OTURS/RSK. The plebiscite on lifting the ban on the Communist Party.

2383 ------ Tim Buck issues urgent call for second front now! Toronto: Communist-Labor Total War Committee. (4pp). *ACGL/PE.Communist OHMA OTURS/RSK OTURS/RSK. Not the same text as 2378 above.

2384 ------ Unite the nation for all-out war effort! (Toronto): Communist Party of Canada. (4pp). *BVAUS/Mac31f.2c OTURS/RSK.

2385 ------ The way forward to total war: lessons of the plebiscite: smash the fascists in Quebec. Toronto: Tim Buck Plebiscite Committee. 20pp. *BVAUS/WB43f. 17(iii) OHMA2426 OKQS OTURS/RSK.

2386 Burwash, Gordon. Social security: the New Zealand plan. Winnipeg: (CCF). (6pp). *OOA/CCF318 and 539. Leaflet 2.

2387 Cameron, Zita O'H. Over the back fence. A chat with co-op members. Antigonish: St Francis Xavier University. 16pp. *NSHP/HDC.

2388 ------ The study clubs way of adult learning. Antigonish: St Francis Xavier University. 19pp. *NSHP. 'First published 1939' - not traced.

2389 Canada Future. Show...Canada future. Experiment in planning meetings. 1942--progress report no.1. (Ottawa). 122pp, mimeo. *OOA/CCF109. 'An independent group of people working under the general name of Canada Future' - socialist in tone.

2390 Canadian Congress of Labor. Memorandum submitted to the Dominion government. Ottawa. 17pp. *BVAUS/Mac 32f.3 (lacking covers) OOA/CCF192. Deals generally with legislative policy affecting labour. Produced virtually every year.

2391 ------ Labour's plan for production of vital concern to every citizen of Canada. Ottawa. 3pp. *OOL.

2392 Canadian Seamens Union. A victory program for Canada's inland and deep sea shipping. Toronto. 18pp. *OTURS/RSK. Prepared for presentation to the federal government.

2393 Canadian Tribune Civil Liberties Bureau. Why the delay? Why is the ban not removed from the Communist Party? Lift the ban! Build unity in Canada! An appeal to the Parliament of Canada and to the Special Committee on this question. Toronto. 8pp. *ACGA/Smith 12 OTURS/RSK. Signed A.E. Smith.

2394 Carter, Dyson. Men, machines and microbes. Winnipeg: Contemporary. 123pp. BVIP MWP MWU SRL *BVAUS/WB42f. 29b(i).

2395 ------ Russia's secret weapon. Winnipeg: Contemporary. 41pp. BVIP MWU OOP OTP QQL SRL *BVAUS/WB42f.29b(ii) MWPA/Ivens 6 OHMA1496 SSUS/Comm. The secret weapon is science.

2396 Civil Liberties Association in Toronto. Represent- ation to the Select Committee of the House of Commons on the Defence of Canada regulations. Toronto. 8pp. *OTURS/RSK.

2397 Coldwell, M.J. Address over a national radio network at 10.00pm on Tuesday, April 21st, 1942. Ottawa: Director of Public Information. 7pp, mimeo. *OOA/ CCF148.

2398 ------ Chairman's address at the national convention, tenth anniversary CCF, July 27, 1942. (Ottawa): CCF. 4pp, mimeo. *AEUS/XIII-56 OTURS.

2399 ------ Go to the polls: address on the issues of the plebiscite. (Ottawa): Director of Public Information. 8pp. *BVAUS/Mac27f.44 MWPA/Brigden 7 OOA/CCF148 (2 copies) and 326 (3 copies) OTAR/1942/25 SSUS/JL 197.

2400 ------ How safe is your insurance? Regina: CCF. 4pp. *ACGL/PDbl OOA/CCF70 SSA/G1.1944.24 and G2.1941.3. Cover title: Will your life insurance be safe with the CCF in power?

2401 ------ Speeches on Mobilization Act amendment to repeal section 3 providing limitation in respect of service overseas, delivered in the House of Commons, Thursday June 11 and Tuesday, July 7, 1942. Ottawa: E. Cloutier. 10pp. *MWPA/Ivens 6 SSA/G2.1942.6.

2402 ------ and others. The CCF and total war. Ottawa: E. Cloutier. 23pp. *ACGA/CCF29 MWPA/Ivens 6 SSA/ G2.1942.1. Speeches in the 1942 session by Gillis, Douglas and Noseworthy.

2403 Communist Party of Canada. Alderman Eddy and the communists. Saskatoon. (1p) broadside. *SSA/G333.3.

2404 ------ Resolution of the national party conference, February 1942. (Toronto). 18pp. *OKQS OTURS/RSK.

2405 ------ Vote: Yes in the plebiscite! Organize demo- cracy for total war! Appeal of the Communist Party adopted by the February national conference at Ottawa. (Toronto). 8pp. *OOA/CCF148. See also 2382 above.

2406 CCF. The first ten years 1932-1942. Commemorating the tenth anniversary of the CCF at the seventh nat- ional convention, Toronto, July 27, 28, 29, 1942. Ottawa. 64pp. ACGL OOAL OOP SRU *AEUS/CCFXVII-22 BVAUS/Mac30f.3 MWPA/Russell 1 OTURS/RSK SSA/G2.1942. 3 SSUS/JL197 Peel 3791. Includes: J.S. Woodsworth by Bruce Hutchison, biographies and illus.

2407 CCF. For victory and reconstruction: CCF policy
     statement adopted at the national convention, 1942.
     Ottawa. (8pp). BVIP NSHPL OOP OTU *ACGL/PDbl AEUS/
     CCFXIII-20 OKQS OOA/CCF310 SSA/G2.1942.5 SSUS/CCF.

2408 ------ Meet the CCF. Vancouver. 15pp. MWPA/CCF39
     OOA/CCF316. Revd edn 1944, 16pp. *BVAUS/Mac30Af.3b
     OOA/CCF537 SSA/G3.BC.6 SSUS/JL197.

2409 ------ Proceedings: Trade union conference, Toronto
     July 25th, 1942. Convened by the Trade Union Comm-
     ittee, CCF Ontario. Toronto. 21pp, mimeo. *OOA/
     CFAW52 and CCF60.

2410 ------ Victory and reconstruction. (Ottawa). 6pp,
     mimeo. *OOA/Underhill 45.

2511 ------ Victory and reconstruction: CCF national pro-
     gram, 1942. Study outline. Vancouver. 65pp, mimeo.
     (various pagination throughout). *OOA/CCF188 SSA/
     G3.BC.11.

2412 Co-operative Union of Canada. A scare put into pri-
     vate enterprise: a hue and cry against co-operatives.
     Brantford. (7pp). *OOA/CCF546 and CUC223 SSUS/Coop.

2413 Davies, R.A. and Andrew J. Steiger. Soviet Asia.
     New York: Dial. xiii, 15-384pp. *OTURS/RSK.

2414 Delaney, Ida Gallant. Shopping basket economics.
     Antigonish: St Francis Xavier University. (c1942).
     39pp. *NSHP/HDC.

2415 Dominion Communist-Labor Total War Committee. Only
     the second front now will keep faith. Toronto.
     (6pp). *OHMA.

2416 ------ Resolved for victory: resolution of the Nat-
     ional Workers Total War Conference, Toronto, May 30-
     31, 1942. Toronto. 31pp. *OTURS/RSK.

2417 ------ Smash Hitler in two-front war! On the off-
     ensive for Canada's national survival! Appeal of
     the National Communist-Labor Total War Conference
     held in Toronto, May 30-31, 1942. Toronto. (4pp).
     *OKQS OTURS/RSK and Woodsworth 54.

2418 Douglas, T.C. Speech on the address in reply to the
     speech from the throne, delivered in the House of
     Commons, Thursday, February 12, 1942. Ottawa: E.
     Cloutier. 10pp. *ACGL/PDbl SSA/G2.1942.7.

2419 ------ and others. Food for freedom at parity prices:
     CCF speaks on wheat legislation in the House of Comm-
     ons, March 1942. Ottawa: E. Cloutier. 24pp. *SSA/
     G2.1942.4 SSUS/JL197. Others include: P.E. Wright,
     A.M. Nicholson, G.H. Castleden, M.J. Coldwell.

2420 Fellowship for a Christian Social Order. Canada's
     Japanese. Vancouver. (c1942). 11pp. *BVAUS/Smith
     Japanese.

2421 ------ Meet socialism. Toronto. (c1942). 12pp,
     mimeo. *OTURS.

(2422) Garneau, Charles-Edouard. Conciliation et arbitrage dans les conflits du travail. Unpublished MA thesis, Université Laval. 38pp.

(2423) Graham, C.R. Unemployment insurance in Canada. Unpublished MA thesis, McGill University. 216pp.

2424 Grantham, Ronald. Some aspects of the socialist movement in British Columbia, 1898-1933. Unpublished MA thesis, University of British Columbia. (iii), 242(245)pp, biblio. *BVAUS. Appendix reprints some platforms.

2425 Hoadley, George. What's cookin'? A witches brew or a national tonic? The national health is the concern of all. Toronto: Workers Educational Association. 12pp. OOL OTP *OOA/CCF554.

2426 International Labour Office. Labour conditions in war contracts, with special reference to Canada, Great Britain and the United States. Montreal. 59pp. OH OKQ QQL *SSUS/Labour. Studies and reports Series D, no. 23.

2427 International Union of Mine, Mill and Smelter Workers. Kirkland Lake: a statement. Kirkland Lake. 6pp, mimeo. *OOA/CCF188.

2428 Irvine, W. Can capitalism survive the war? Edmonton: (c1942). 24pp. BVIP BVIV OH *ACGL BVAUS/Mac39f.7 OTURS/RSK. Peel 3869.

2429 ------ Tribute to Mr J.S. Woodsworth: address delivered at memorial service, Vancouver, March 29, 1942. (Edmonton): np. 5pp. *OOA/CCF309 SSA/G501.9.

2430 Ivens, William. Can capitalism fight a total war? Winnipeg. (c1942). 2pp, broadside. *OOA/CCF318.

2431 Jewish Council for Allied Victory. A call to action! To the Jewish people of the world. Materials of the second Soviet Jewish Anti-Fascist Conference, Moscow May 1942. Winnipeg. 32pp. *OTURS/RSK. Canadian introduction and postscript.

2432 Kardash, Wm. A. Hitler's agents in Canada. Toronto: np. 32pp. ACU BVIP OOP OTP SRL *OHMA2448 OTURS/RSK. An attack on the Ukrainian National Federation of Canada as being basically a fascist organization.

2433 ------ 1942 year of victory. Toronto: Dominion Communist-Labor Total War Committee. 29pp. *OHMA 1633 OTURS/RSK.

2434 King, W.L.M. Labour and the war: an address to the American Federation of Labor, 1942 convention, Toronto, October 9th, 1942. Ottawa: E. Cloutier. 11pp. OKQ OONL OOP OTP OTU QQL SSU *OOL.

2435 Kuczynski, J. and M. Witt. The economics of barbarism: Hitler's new economic order in Europe. Toronto: Progress. 64pp. BVIV *BVAUS/Mac40f.5a OHMA1626.

2436 Labour Youth Federation of Canada. Constitution and

statement of purpose. Toronto. 20pp. *OTURS/RSK.

2437 Labour Youth Federation of Canada. Draft program (submitted to the) initiative conference, Sunday April 5th, Toronto. Toronto. (8pp). *T.

2438 ------ Report of proceedings of the National Constituent Convention held at the Royal York Hotel, Toronto, September 5, 6 and 7, 1942. Toronto. 39pp, mimeo. *OTURS/RSK.

2439 ------ Young Canada - forward to victory! Toronto. 32pp. *OTURS/RSK.

2440 League of Canadian Croats, Serbians and Slovenes. Help to the Soviet Union from Croatians, Serbians, Slovenians in Canada. Toronto. 67pp. *OTURS/RSK. Bilingual. Included with the notes on each centre is information on the Yugoslavs living there. Mainly a record of contributions.

2441 Little, Elliott M. Commonsense in labour relations: an address to the Canadian Manufacturers Assn, Toronto, 8th June, 1942. Ottawa: Director of Public Information. 19pp. NSHPL OH OKQ OOL OONL OOP *OTAR/1942/29.

2442 ------ Facing realities: an address delivered before the Canadian Congress of Labour, Ottawa September 15, 1942. Ottawa: Wartime Information Board. 15pp. OKQ OOP *OTAR/DL Pamphlets 1.

2443 ------ Labour responsibilities in wartime: an address delivered before the Trades and Labour Congress of Canada, Winnipeg, August 25th, 1942. Ottawa: Director of Public Information. 15pp. OKQ OOL OONL SRL *OTAR/DL Pamphlets 1 OTURS/RSK.

2444 Lower, A.R.M. and J.F. Parkinson. War and reconstruction: some Canadian issues. Addresses given at the Canadian Institute on Public Affairs, August 15 to 23, 1942. Toronto: Ryerson. xiv, 106pp. *OONL. Includes: Reconstruction: problems of the transition period within Canada by Leonard C. Marsh; Agriculture in the reconstruction period by H.H. Hannam; Labour in the war and post-war by David Lewis; Labour problems in Quebec by Roger Brossard.

2445 MacInnis, Angus. Labor: servant or partner? A review of orders-in-council affecting labor, 1940-42. Vancouver: CCF. (4pp). *BVAUS/Mac32f.1 OHMA1857 OOA/CCF537 SSUS/JL197.

2446 Macpherson, James A. and Wm. Halina. Mobilize Alberta for Canada's war effort: statement issued on the plebiscite in answer to a number of requests from Albertans who supported Communist Party candidates. Vote 'yes' for national unity, for total war to defeat Hitler in 1942! Edmonton: Edmonton Council for Democratic Rights. (4pp). *OTURS/RSK.

2447 Merritt, Ronald. Agricultural co-operation in Ontario. Unpublished BAHons thesis, McMaster University (ii), 111pp, biblio. *OHMA.

2448 Mertanen, P. and W. Eklund. The illegal Finnish Org-
     anization of Canada, Inc. Sudbury: Vapaus. 16pp.
     *OTURS/RSK. In the form of a letter to the Minister
     of Justice (Louis St Laurent) protesting the ban on
     the Finnish Organization of Canada.

2449 Michael, Sr. Marie and Ida Delaney. The woman speaks
     her mind: two addresses given at the staff conference,
     St Francis Xavier University. Antigonish: St Francis
     Xavier University. 16pp. *NSHP OHMA2717.

2450 Millard, C.H. Victory needs steel. Toronto: Steel
     Workers Organizing Committee. 24pp. *BVAUS/Mac41f.2.

2451 Morgan, Lorne T. Fascism: from origins to maturity
     in theory and practice. Toronto: Workers Educational
     Assn. 36pp. *BVAUS/WB40f.8a(i) OHMA1669 OTURS/RSK.
     Part I previously published as no. 2198 above.

2452 Nash, Walter. Social security in New Zealand: excer-
     pts from an address before the Special Committee on
     Reconstruction and Re-establishment at Ottawa, May 22
     1942. Regina: CCF. 6pp. *ACGL/PDbl OOA/CCF321 SSA/
     G1.1944.17 SSUS/CCF. Also published in Winnipeg,
     *OTURS/RSK.

2453 National Council for Democratic Rights. Brief account
     of proceedings of a conference held at the Royal York
     Hotel, Toronto, May 17th, 1942. Toronto. 4pp, mimeo
     plus covering letter plus 1p plan of action. *SSA/
     G293.5.

2454 ------ Brief presented to the Hon J.E. Michaud, M.P.
     and the Parliamentary committee of 15 reviewing the
     Defence of Canada regulations. Toronto. 9pp, mimeo.
     *OTURS/RSK.

2455 ------ A fighter for freedom, Fergus McKean interned
     anti-fascist, why is he interned? Vancouver. (c1942).
     (4pp). *T.

2456 ------ For democracy and victory: lift the ban on the
     Communist Party. Toronto. (4pp). *OHMA.

2457 ------ Government must remove the Communist ban!
     Toronto. (4pp). *OHMA SSA/G293.1.

2458 ------ The great issue democracy: more than lifting
     Communist ban at stake! A statement: Premier King
     urged to repudiate Mr St Laurent's attack on democracy.
     Toronto. (4pp). *OHMA SSA/G293.2. OTURS/RSK.

2459 ------ Hail anti-fascist releases! Vital issue of
     democracy still at stake: lift ban on Communist Party.
     Toronto. 25pp, mimeo. *OTURS/RSK.

2460 ------ Information bulletin: Toronto barrister calls
     for drastic change in Defense of Canada regulations.
     Toronto. (2pp), mimeo. *SSA/G293.6. The barrister
     is D. Goldstick.

2461 ------ Interned and imprisoned anti-fascists, now

released. 1939-1942. Toronto. 25pp. *OOL.

2462 National Council for Democratic Rights. Make democracy work for victory! Toronto. 6pp. *OTURS/RSK
SSA/G293.7. Urging people to vote yes in the plebiscite.

2463 ------ Memorandum submitted to the Honourable Louis
St Laurent, K.C., M.P. Minister of Justice. Toronto.
12pp, mimeo. *OOA/CCF147 OTURS/RSK. A short synopsis of delegates and proceedings of the national
conference followed by the memorandum.

2464 ------ Petition of anti-fascist internees. (Tor-
ronto). 2pp, mimeo. *OTURS/RSK.

2465 ------ Statement on release of Tim Buck. Toronto.
(1p) broadside. *SSA/G293.4. Signed by A.E. Smith
and Beckie Buhay, General and Executive Secretaries.

2466 (National Foremens Institute). Reprinted from sabotage: how to guard against it. A manual for industrial
workers, supervisors and executives. (?Toronto).
12pp. *OTAR/DL Pamphlets 1. Reprinted from a manual
by Harry Desmond Farren (USA).

2467 Nicholson, A.M. Speech on curtailing of liquor con-
sumption delivered in the House of Commons, Monday
June 1, 1942. Ottawa: E. Cloutier. 4pp. *SSA/G2.
1942.2.

2468 Nielsen, Dorise W. A call to action! (Saskatoon):
Farm Emergency Conference. (c1942). (4pp). *SSA/
G262.1.

2469 ------- Food for victory. Saskatoon: The Western
Farmer. 20pp. *OHMA1939 OTURS/RSK.

2470 Office and Professional Workers Organizing Committee.
The first Canadian bank strike: the facts Banque Can-
adienne Nationale strike. Toronto. 22pp. *OOL
OTURS/RSK SSUS/Labor.

2471 Pelland, L. Nouvelle économie de demain. Unpublished
MA thesis, University of Ottawa. viii, 124pp.

2472 Power, Terrence. Steel unionism in eastern Canada.
Unpublished BA thesis, St Francis Xavier University.
(i), 27pp, biblio. *NSHPL.

2473 Quebec Committee for Allied Victory. The case for
the second front now. Montreal. 11pp. *OHMA3129
OTURS/RSK.

2474 Queens University. Trade union agreements in Canadian industry. Kingston: Industrial Relations Centre.
177pp. *OKQ.

2475 Roberts, Leslie. Canada for the offensive. Winnipeg:
Contemporary. 59pp. *OHMA3155.

2476 Roper, Elmer and William Irvine. Personal message.
Edmonton: CCF. 4pp. *OOA/CCF337. Platform of CCF-
Labor and biography of Roper by Irvine.

2477 Rose, Fred. Hitler's 5th column in Quebec. Toronto:
Communist-Labor Total War Committee. 60pp. AEU MWU
OOP OTP QMBM QMBN SRL SSU *BVAUS/WB40f.8A OHMA2476
OKQS OOA/Klein 17 OTURS/RSK.

2478 Samuel, Emery. On guard Canadians! The fascist enemies menace our families, homes and country! (Montreal): (Communist Party of Canada). 32pp. *OTURS/
RSK. Secretary of the Quebec provincial committee.

2479 Scott, F.R. The plebiscite vote in Quebec. Toronto:
Canadian Forum. 8pp. OKQ QMBM QMBN QQL *OHMA1572
OOA/CCF148 and 326 OTURS/RSK.

2480 Shcherbakov, A.S. Smashing Hitler's blitzkrieg.
(Montreal): (Communist Party of Canada). 16pp.
*E. Introduction by Fred Rose.

2481 Shoults, W.A. Democratic science movement - philosophy. np. (c1942). (32pp), mimeo. *OTURS/RSK.
Anti-capitalist, pro-labour, nationalization etc.

2482 Smith, A.E. Communist illegality and the new Minister
of Justice. Toronto: National Council for Democratic
Rights. 26pp. OKQ OOL *MWPA/CCF35 OOA/CCF542
OTURS/RSK.

2483 ------ Remove the ban! The communists are making
a vital contribution to the war effort. An appeal
to parliament. Toronto: National Council for Democratic Rights. 16pp. *OTURS/RSK.

2484 ------ Should the Communist Party be illegal? Toronto: National Council for Democratic Rights. 16pp.
*OOL OTURS/RSK.

2485 Society for the Study of Russia. The USSR at war:
50 questions and answers. Toronto: Progress. 48pp.
*OHMA. Produced by the American-Russian Institute
in New York.

2486 Stepler, D.H. Family allowances for Canada? Toronto:
Canadian Association for Adult Education. 32pp.
*OOA/CCF544. Behind the Headlines vol.3 no. 2.

2487 United Electrical, Radio and Machine Workers of America, district 5. We produce for the second front
and victory. Toronto. 32pp. *OHMA OKQS OTURS/RSK.
Includes rules for production councils and a special
Canadian plan.

2488 Vaillancourt, Emile. Strange loyalty: a practical
lesson in Canadian history. With an introductory
letter by M.J. Coldwell, MP. Montreal: np. 12pp.
*BVAUS/Mac41f.15A OTURS/RSK.

2489 Ward, Leo R. Nova Scotia: the land of co-operation.
New York: Sheed and Ward. xiv, 207pp. *OONL.

2490 Winnipeg Council for Allied Victory. Clothing campaign for Russia. Winnipeg. (4pp). *OTURS/RSK.

2491 Woodcock, George. New life to the land. London(Eng):
Freedom Press. 32pp. AEU BVAU BVIV *own copy.

2492 Young Communist League. Everything for the fighting front! (Toronto). (c1942). 28pp. *OTURS/RSK.

2493 ------ Join the armed forces! Toronto. (4pp). *BVAUS/WB31f.1a.

1943

2494 Alberta Farmers Union. Manifesto. (Edmonton). 13pp. *ACGL/PDg AFU.

2495 Bogomolets, Alexander and Pavlo Tychyna. Soviet Ukraine and Ukraino-German nationalists in Canada. Toronto: Ukrainian Canadian Assn. 27pp. OOP OTP *OTURS/RSK. Replying to a memorandum presented to the Canadian government by A. Hlynka, MP, on behalf of the 'Ukrainian Canadian Committee' which demanded the separation of the Ukraine from the USSR.

2496 Brewin, F.A. A trade union act for Ontario. (Toronto): CCF. 4pp, mimeo. *OOA/CCF60.

2497 Browder, Earl. The decisive turn in the war: address at the Philharmonic Auditorium in Los Angeles. Toronto: Ontario Communist-Labor Total War Committee. 6pp, mimeo. *OHMA.

2498 Buck, Tim. Canada in the coming offensive. Toronto: Dominion Communist-Labor Total War Committee. 40pp. AEU MWU *BVAUS/WB43f.17(i) OHMA2404 OKQS OOA/CCF 542 OTURS/RSK.

2499 ------ Canada needs a party of communists. Toronto: National Committee to Convene a Communist Constituent Convention. 30pp. BVAS BVIP MWU *AEUS BVAUS/WB31f. 2b and Smith CP OHMA2421 OKQS OOA/CCF542 OTURS/ RSK.

2500 ------ For victory in the war and prosperity in the peace. Toronto: Spadina Riding Labor Committee. 16pp. *BVAUS/WB43f.17(i) OTURS/RSK.

2501 ------ A labor policy for victory. Toronto: Dominion Communist-Labor Total War Committee. 90pp. AEU BVIP BVIV MWU SSU *BVAUS/WB43f.17 OHMA2415 OKQS OTURS/RSK. Contains a supplementary brief on Quebec by Evariste Dubé. Originally mimeographed for submission to the National War Labour Board, 27 May 1943 (mimeo, 49pp).

2502 ------ 1944 - year of victory: a New Year's message. Toronto: Labor-Progressive Party. 8pp. OTU *OHMA 3112 OTURS/RSK. Also published in Vancouver, 6pp. *BVAUS/WB31f.4.

2503 ------ The people must act now! Toronto: (Labor-Progressive Party). 15pp. AEU *BVAUS/WB31f.2a OHMA 3123 OKQS OTURS/RSK. On the release of prisoners and for lifting the ban on the Communist Party.

2504 Buck, Tim. Victory through unity: report to the constituent convention of the Labor-Progressive Party. Toronto: (Labor-Progressive Party). 64pp. MWU *BVAUS/WB31f.3b OKQS OTURS/RSK SSA/G27.1943.1.

2505 Cameron, Colin. Money and the war. Comox: Comox District Free Press. 12pp. *T.

2506 Canada, Dept of Labour. Wartime orders in council affecting labour. Ottawa: E. Cloutier. 111pp, plus (4pp) appendixes. *OOA/CCF166. Revd edn.

2507 Canadian Congress of Labour. Bill 91: political action by labour. Edmonton. (3pp). *OOA/CCF192. Bill 91 dealt with general labour issues.

2508 ------ Memorandum submitted to the House of Commons Committee on Reconstruction and Re-establishment, July 15, 1943. (Ottawa). 16pp. *OOA/CCF192.

2509 Canadian Federation of Agriculture. Health on the march...national health insurance for Canada. Toronto. 31pp. MWU OONL SRL SSU *OOA/MacPhail 4.

2510 Canadian Tribune. The case for labor. Toronto. 45pp. *BVAUS/WB43f.18B OHMA3136 OTURS/RSK.

2511 Carr, Sam. The face of the enemy. Toronto: Progress. 64pp. *BVAUS/WB40f.8a(ii) OHMA OTURS/RSK. An attack on Nazism.

2512 Carter, Dyson. Booze the saboteur. Winnipeg: Contemporary. 27pp. *BVAUS/Mac41f.9 OTURS/RSK. Not an appeal for prohibition, but a proposal that distilled liquor be classified as a drug.

2513 ------ So that man may prosper. Winnipeg: Contemporary. 32pp. MWP OKQ SRL *BVAUS/WB41f.16 MWPA/ Ivens 6 OHMA1497 OOA/MacPhail 3 SSUS/Comm.

2514 ------ Stalin's life: at last the true story. Winnipeg: Contemporary. 50pp. MWU OTP QMM SRL *BVAUS/ Mac38f.19 OOA/CCF542 OTURS/RSK.

2515 Cassidy, Harry M. Social security and reconstruction in Canada. Toronto: Ryerson. x, 197pp. *OHMA1645.

2516 Charpentier, Alfred. Directives et orientations: rapport moral. Québec: Confédération des Travailleurs Catholiques du Canada. 16pp. QMSS *OOL.

2517 Clement, F.M. Reconstruction of agriculture in Canada. Address to the 7th annual meeting of the Canadian Federation of Agriculture held at the Palisser Hotel, Calgary, January 27th to 30th, 1943. Ottawa: Canadian Federation of Agriculture. 14pp. *OHMA 1424. Partly on adopting the principles of organized labour by agriculture.

2518 Coady, M.M. and others. The Antigonish way: a series of broadcasts over CBC. Antigonish: St Francis Xavier University. 78pp. BVIV NFSM OKQ OONL OOP *NSHP/HDC.

2519 ------ Blueprinting post-war Canada. Quebec: Culture. pp161-171. *NSHP/HDC. Reprinted from Culture no. 4.

2520 Coldwell, M.J. For a living democracy. Radio address delivered over CBC network, Friday January 22, 1943. Ottawa: CCF. 14pp. *AEUS/CCFXIII-4 BVAUS/Mac43f.17 OHMA1519 SSA/G2.1943.5 SSUS/JL197.

2521 ------ Speech on social security and the budget, delivered in the House of Commons on March 4 and 9, 1943. Ottawa: E. Cloutier. 15pp. *SSA/G2.1943.12.

2522 ------ What does the CCF stand for? Ottawa: CCF. 12pp. *ACGL/PDbl OHMA1522 OOA/CCF126, 310 and 540 SSA/G2.1943.17 SSUS/JL197.

2523 ------ and others. Aluminum. Speeches on the Shipshaw Power Development, and the Arvida expansion, of the Aluminum Company of Canada delivered in the House of Commons June 14, 15 and 17, 1943. Ottawa: E. Cloutier. 24pp. *BVAUS/Mac27f.43 OOA/Coldwell 62 and Klein 17 OTURS/RSK and Woodsworth 54 SSUS/JL 197. Others are Stanley Knowles and J.W. Noseworthy.

2524 ------ Planning for victory and security: speeches by CCF members. (Ottawa): (E.Cloutier). 32pp. *BVAUS/Mac27f.43 MWPA/Ivens 6 SSA/G2.1943.10. Others are P.E. Wright, A.M. Nicholson, G.H. Castleden, T.C. Douglas.

2525 ------ The time is now! Speeches by CCF members delivered in the House of Commons February and March 1943. Ottawa: E. Cloutier. 32pp. *AEUS/CCFXIII-11 BVAUS/Mac27f.44 OTURS/RSK SSA/G2.1943.15 SSUS/JL 197. Others are Angus MacInnis (Labour and the CCF); T.C. Douglas (Social ownership and co-operatives); Stanley H. Knowles (Social security); J.W. Noseworthy (Rehabilitation and wage policy) and Clarence Gillis (The rights of armed forces and the workers of Canada. Some of these were issued separately.

2526 Communist Party of Canada. For a total war effort - defeat Arthur Meighen! Toronto: (c1943). (4pp). *OTURS/CPC.

2527 CCF. Books are weapons: reading list. Ottawa. (28pp), mimeo. *OTURS/RSK.

2528 ------ The Canadian heirarchy speaks out on social reconstruction. An exact reprint of the official statement of the Archbishop and Bishops of the Roman Catholic church in Canada and editorial comment from *The Canadian Register*. Regina. (4pp). *OOA/CCF321 and 536 SSA/G1.1943.2 SSUS/CCF.

2529 ------ CCF program for British Columbia. Vancouver: 22pp. *BVAUS/Mac 30Af.10 OOA/Coldwell 59 and CCF316 SSUS/JL197. Amended in 1944 (27pp) and 1945 (30pp).

2530 ------ CCF program for Saskatchewan. Regina. 12pp. *OOA/CCF70. Amended in 1944 and 1948 (20pp).

2531 ------ CCF representation to the National War Labour

Board. Ottawa. 16pp. OTU *AEUS/CCFXIII-1 BVAUS/
Mac32f.3 OHMA1533 OOA/CCF310 and 536 OTAR/1943/61
SSA/G2.1943.2 SSUS/JL197. Presented by Clarence
Gillis, Angus MacInnis and David Lewis on 12th May
1943: mimeo, 12pp. *OOA/CCF192.

2532 CCF. CCF views on the Japanese question. Vancouver.
(4pp). *BVAUS/Smith Japanese.

2533 ------ The farmers program: the CCF program for agriculture in Ontario. Toronto. 4pp. *MWPA/CCF39 OOA/
MacPhail 3.

2534 ------ How the CCF got started. (Regina). 4pp,
mimeo. *SSA/G1.1943.3. Reissued as *The birth of a new
social order* by the NDP in 1972.

2535 ------ Profiteering: second world war style. Vancouver. 4pp. *BVAUS/Mac41f.2 OOA/CCF316.

2536 ------ Unity through the CCF: CCF rejects Communist
splitting tactics. Ottawa. (4pp). *ACGL/PDbl OOA/
CCF393 and 540 OOA/Klein 17 SSA/G2.1944.17 SSUS/CCF.

2537 ------ What the CCF will do. Toronto. 4pp. *OOA/
CCF320 OTURS/RSK.

2538 Cooperative Commonwealth Youth Movement. Constitution
and hand book. Regina: CCF. 14pp, mimeo. *SSA/G19.3
Reissued in 1944 (14pp) and 1945 (23pp). *G19.6.

2539 Co-operative Union of Saskatchewan. The principles
of consumers co-operation. Regina. (c1943). 24pp.
*SSA/G49.1. Consumers cooperation series 1.

2540 Davies, Raymond Arthur. This is our land: Ukrainian
Canadians against Hitler. Toronto: Progress. 158pp,
illus. *BVAUS/Mac38f.18M OHMA3134 OTURS/RSK.

2541 Deachman, R.J. Compulsory collective bargaining.
How it affects labor, the farmer and the consumer.
(?Ottawa). 12pp. BVIP OTP QMBM *BVAUS/Mac39Af.14
OOL.

2542 Delaney, Ida Gallant. Show cash. Antigonish: St
Francis Xavier University. 15pp. *NSHP/HDC.

2543 Dhami, Sadhu Singh. The Sikhs and their religion: a
struggle for democracy. Vancouver: Khalsa Diwan Society. 31pp. ACG AEU BVIP OTP *BVAUS/Mac41f.14 and
Young OTURS/RSK.

2544 Dominion Conference of Communist-Labor Total War Comm-
ittees. Resolutions adopted at the conference held in
Toronto January 16-17, 1943. Toronto. 16pp, mimeo.
*OHMA.

2545 Douglas, T.C. Budget speech: social ownership vs
free enterprise: CCF and the cooperatives: speech
delivered in the House of Commons on March 22nd, 1943.
Ottawa: E. Cloutier. 8pp. *MWPA/Ivens 6 OKQS SSA/
G2.1943.1.

2546 ------ Speech on Dieppe operations - policy for agriculture in wartime delivered in the House of Commons

on Wednesday, February 17, 1943. Ottawa: E.Cloutier.
8pp. *SSA/G2.1943.14.

2547 Douglas, T.C. Speech on man-power delivered in the
House of Commons on Thursday June 3, 1943. Ottawa:
E. Cloutier. 4pp. *SSA/G2.1943.9.

2548 Easton, David Gerald. Social and political aspects
of unemployment insurance in Canada. Unpublished
MA thesis, University of Toronto. (iv), 250pp,
notes, no biblio. *OTUAR.

2549 (Ellis, Russel). Rumblings in a plate mill. Collected by the gangs. Edited by no. 5323. (?Sydney):
np. 41pp. *NSHD/H2. Pen portraits of workers.

2550 Farmilo, Alfred. Workmens compensation implications
of the Beveridge report. np. 6pp. *AEPAA/Farmilo
4. Address given at the 29th annual meeting of the
International Assn of Industrial Accident Boards and
Commissions, Harrisburg, Pa. 25-27 October 1943.

2551 Ferneyhough, Beatrice. Women in industry: a study
of Canada's labor power problems. Toronto: Ontario
Communist-Labor Total War Committee. 6pp, mimeo.
*OHMA.

2552 Forsey, Eugene A. The royal power of dissolution of
Parliament in the British commonwealth. Toronto:
Oxford University Press. xx, 316pp. *OOP.

2553 Freed, Norman. Speech on post-war reconstruction.
Toronto: Ontario Communist-Labor Total War Committee.
4pp, mimeo. *OHMA.

2554 Gibbon, J. Murray. Songs of freedom. Ottawa: Royal
Society of Canada. pp77-111. *OTAR. Reprinted from
Transactions, third series, section II, vol.XXXVII.
Very little on Canadian songs.

2555 Gillis, Clarence and Stanley H. Knowles. Canada and
the plight of Jewish refugees: speeches delivered in
the House of Commons on July 9 and 12, 1943. Ottawa:
E. Cloutier. 8pp. *OOA/CCF180 and Klein 17.

2556 ------ Canada's labor problems and the war. Speeches
delivered in the House of Commons March 11 and April
6, 1943. Ottawa: E. Cloutier. 12pp. *BVAUS/Mac27f.
43 OOA/CCF537.

2557 ------ Letter from home: from a soldier of 1914-19
(sic) to a soldier 1939-194? Toronto: Canadian Forum.
32pp. OOP OTP OTU *OOA/CCF310, 326 and 537 SSUS/JL
197. Fwd by M.J. Coldwell.

2558 Graydon, Gordon, M.J. Coldwell and Brooke Claxton.
Education and government: abridged texts of three
addresses given before the Quebec Provincial Assn
of Protestant Teachers, Montreal, October 8, 1943.
Ottawa: E. Cloutier. 30pp. MWU OOP QMU *MWPA/Ivens
6.

2559 Heaps Engineering (1940) Ltd. The future of industry?
Open letter to political groups. Edmonton: Social

Credit Board. 15pp. *OHMA2368. Contains a reply
from David Lewis, CCF national secretary (pp6-9).

2560 International Labour Office. Social security planning
in Canada. The Marsh report and proposed insurance
legislation. Montreal. 26pp. AEU OH OHM SRU *OTURS/
RSK.

2561 International Union of Mine, Mill and Smelter Workers,
local 598. Victory program. Sudbury. 14pp. *OTURS/
RSK. Contains a 20-point program ranging from union
recognition to housing.

2562 Ivens, William. Canada---whither bound? Winnipeg.
(c1943). *ACGA/CCF29 MWPA/Ivens 4 OOA/CCF318 SSA/
G502.1. Reprints most of the Regina manifesto with
comments and additional material.

2563 Kardash, W.A. Manitoba and the war: an address in
reply to the speech from the throne. Winnipeg: Workers Election Committee. 16pp. *OTURS/RSK.

2564 Keen, George. The history of the co-operative movement in Canada. Brantford: Co-operative Union of
Canada. (c1943). 6pp. *OOA/CCF546 SSUS/Coop.

2565 King, Carlyle. Study outlines: the Saskatchewan CCF
provincial policy. (Regina): Cooperative Commonwealth
Youth Movement. 16pp, mimeo. *ACGA/CCF12 AEUS/XI-4
OOA/CCF70.

2566 ------ What is democratic socialism? Ottawa: CCF.
31pp. AEU BVIP BVIV NSHPL OTP *BVAUS/Mac30f.8 MWPA/
CCF39 OHMA1541 OOA/CCF323 and 540 OTURS/RSK SSA/
G.1943.18 SSUS/JL197.

2567 Knowles, Stanley H. Speech on the address in reply
to the speech from the throne delivered in the House
of Commons, Wednesday February 3, 1943. Ottawa: E.
Cloutier. 7pp. *BVAUS/Mac27f.43.

2568 ------ Speech on social security delivered in the
House of Commons on Wednesday March3, 1943. Ottawa:
E. Cloutier. 8pp. *SSA/G2.1943.11.

2569 Labor-Progressive Party. Constitution and by-laws.
Toronto. 16pp. BVIP OONL *BVAUS/WB31f.3 OKQS
OTURS/RSK.

2570 ------ Manifesto adopted at the first national convention, Toronto, August 21st and 22nd, 1943. Vancouver. (4pp). *BVAUS/WB31f.3c and Smith CP.

2571 ------ Manifesto. Toronto. 48pp. *BVAUS/WB31f.3a
OHMA3159 SSUS/Comm. Resolutions of the first national
constituent convention. Cover title: Resolutions of
the LPP.

2572 Manifesto unity...victory...prosperity. Toronto.
8pp. *BVAUS/WB31f3b OHMA3137 OKQS OTURS/RSK.

2573 Laidler, Harry W. (ed). The third freedom. Freedom
from want. New York: League for Industrial Democracy.
96pp. *OOA/CCF552. Contains, inter alia, Canadian
labor mobilizes for economic security by F.H. Underhill

2574 Landy, A.   Marxism and the woman question.   Toronto:
Progress.   64pp.   BVAS OTP *BVAUS/WB32f.2b   OTURS/RSK.

2575 Lazarus, Morden.   Design for state medicine.   Preliminary proposals for the socialization of the health
services of the Dominion under co-ordinated democratic
control.   Toronto: Canadian Forum.   14pp.   OTURS
*ACGA/CCF29   MWPA/CCF39   OOA/CCF320.

2576 Leslie, Kenneth.   The Nazarene carpenter and the
Soviet Union.   Toronto: Fellowship for a Christian
Social Order.   6pp.   *BVAUS/Mac42f.27A.

2577 Lewis, David.   For a people's victory.   Ottawa: CCF
12pp.   OOP OTP *MWPA/CCF39   OHMA1781   OOA/CCF310 and
537 and Klein 17   SSA/G2.1943.6   SSUS/JL197.

2578 ------ and Frank Scott.   Make this your Canada: a
review of CCF history and policy.   Toronto: Central
Canada Publishing.   223pp. *OHMA1574   OTURS/RSK.
Foreword by M.J. Coldwell.   Includes texts of the
Regina manifesto and For victory and reconstruction
(adopted in 1942).

2579 Macdonald, A.B.   Co-operative and labour unions.
Winnipeg: Prairie School for Social Advance and the
Peoples Cooperative.   (c1943).   4pp.   *MWPA/CCF33.

2580 MacInnis, Angus.   Speeches on the address and reconstruction and re-establishment delivered in the House
of Commons, February 12th and 25th, 1943.   Ottawa:
E. Cloutier.   12pp.   *BVAUS/Mac27f.43.

2581 McKean, Fergus.   British Columbia's contribution to
victory.   Vancouver: BC Communist-Labor Total War
Committee.   26pp.   *BVAUS/WB31f.1c   OTURS/RSK.

2582 Macklin, I.V.   Broadcasts on religion, economics,
politics.   Edmonton.   64pp.   *ACGA/CCF29   OOA/CCF316.
Foreword by William Irvine.   Social gospel, socialism,
farmer and labour questions etc.

2583 Macpherson, James A.   Keep faith with our fighting
sons!   Edmonton: Alberta Communist-Labor-Farmer Committee for Total War.   34pp.   *OTURS/RSK.

(2584)Marsh, Leonard C.   Full employment for post-war Canada;   what it means and what it requires.   Parts I
and II and summary.   Ottawa: (Canadian Welfare Council).   16pp.   OOU   (not found).

2585 ------ Report on social security for Canada.   Ottawa:
E. Cloutier.   145pp.   *OKQS.

2586 Merkur, Paul.   The free Germans to the German people.
Toronto: Ontario Communist-Labor Total War Committee.
4pp, mimeo.   OHMA.

2587 Morgan, Lorne T.   The permanent war or homo the sap.
Toronto: Workers Educational Association.   64pp.
*BVAUS/Mac31f.38c   MWPA/CCF39   OHMA1642   OTURS/RSK.
An economic satire supported by statistics that what
is needed for economic security is a state of perman-
ent war.

2588 Morris, Leslie. Whose war? A reply to the Liberal Party's Winnipeg Free Press. Winnipeg: Labor-Progressive Party. 46pp. MWU OKQ OTP *BVAUS/WB43f.17 (iii) OTURS/RSK.

2589 National Council for Canadian-Soviet Friendship. Abstracts of addresses delivered at the Congress for Canadian-Soviet Friendship November 12, 13 and 14, 1943. Toronto. 19pp, mimeo. *OTURS/RSK.

2590 Nicholson, A.M. Speech on the address in reply to the speech from the throne delivered in the House of Commons, Thursday February 11, 1943. Ottawa: E. Cloutier. 8pp. *MWPA/Ivens 6.

2591 Noseworthy, J.W. Speech on the address in reply to the speech from the throne delivered in the House of Commons on Monday February 8, 1943. Ottawa: E. Cloutier. 4pp. *MWPA/Ivens 6.

2592 Ontario. Proceedings of the Select Committee regarding collective bargaining between employers and employees. Toronto: Kings Printer. 13 vols, mimeo. *OTAR.

2593 Ontario Communist-Labor Total War Committee. Submission to the Select Committee of the Ontario legislature on collective bargaining. (Toronto). 8pp, mimeo. *OHMA.

2594 ------ Lay-offs are not necessary...It is high time that labor's role and labor's rights be fully recognised! Toronto. (4pp). *OHMA.

2595 ------ This is no time for labor to strike! Toronto. 4pp. *OHMA OTURS/RSK.

2596 Ontario Woodsworth Memorial Foundation. Woodsworth memorial meeting. Toronto. (c1943). 24pp. OTURS *OHMA1559 OOA/CCF198. Includes The legacy of Woodsworth by Kenneth McNaught and Recollections by Stanley Knowles.

2597 Partridge, C.H. The progress of man: the spirit of man versus the machine. Lindsay: Wilson and Wilson. x,256 (ii), i-xiv pp. BVIV OH OTP *OONL. Co-operation - religious in tone.

2598 Queens University. Recent Canadian collective bargaining agreements. Kingston: Industrial Relations Centre. 133pp. *OKQ.

2599 ------ The right to organize: recent Canadian legislation. Kingston: Industrial Relations Centre. 7pp. *OKQ.

2600 Roper, Elmer E. First CCF speeches in the Alberta legislature on the speech from the throne and the budget. Edmonton: CCF. 20pp. *OOA/CCF76.

2601 Ryerson, S.B. The dissolution of the Communist International. Toronto: Ontario Communist-Labor Total War Committee. 3pp, mimeo. *OHMA.

2602 Ryerson, Stanley B. French Canada: a study in Canadian democracy. Toronto: Progress. 254pp. *OTURS/RSK. Foreword by Evariste Dubé.

2603 St Francis Xavier University. Mobilizing for enlightenment. Antigonish. 28pp. *NSHP/HDC.

2604 Salsberg, J.B. Let Ontario blaze the trail to victory and post-war prosperity. Toronto: St Andrew Labor Election Committee. 16pp. *OHMA1900 OTURS/RSK.

2605 Saskatchewan. Report of the Commission on employer-employee relations. (Regina). 64 plus 3pp, mimeo. *SSA/EC.5.25.

2606 Shaw, L.R. and S.H. Knowles. Sold down the Saguenay: the story of aluminum and Shipshaw. Ottawa: CCF. 16pp. OH OTP *BVAUS/Mac41f.2 OKQS OOA/CCF539 SSA/G2.1943.13. Victory and Reconstruction series 2.

(2607) Sirken, I.A. Wartime labour problems and policies. Unpublished MA thesis, McGill University. 137pp.

2608 Stalin, J. On the war and the second front in Europe. Toronto: Progress. 15pp. *OTURS/RSK.

2609 Stevenson and Kellogg. Work, wages and workers...are they consistently related? In Canada, the answer generally is 'no'! Montreal. (4pp). *OOAL. Written essentially to sell their job evaluation program.

2610 Thomson, Watson. 'I accuse': a call to arms against the enemy within. Winnipeg: Contemporary. 34pp. MWU OH OOP OTP SRL *OTURS/RSK.

2611 Toronto May Day Conference. All out on May day: victory rally Sunday May 2nd. Speakers J.W. Buckley, Fred Collins, George Harris, Tim Buck. Toronto. (4pp). OHMA.

2612 Trades and Labour Congress of Canada. Submission to the Select Committee on labour appointed by the Legislative Assembly of Toronto. (Ottawa). 18pp, mimeo. *AEPAA/Farmilo 4.

2613 UAW-CIO. Organize for victory: proceedings of the first UAW-CIO farm implement conference, Hamilton, February 21st, 1943. Toronto. 24pp. *OTURS/RSK.

2614 United Farmers of Alberta. Program of the junior branch, July 1943-June 1944. (Calgary). 32pp. *AEPAA/Inf.file Alta.pol.II. Rather empty program: most pages blank for recording minutes.

2615 ------ Report of the twenty-fifth farm young peoples week, Edmonton, June 3-10, 1943 also 25th annual convention junior branch. Calgary. 20pp. *AEPAA/Inf.file Alta.pol.II.

2616 United Jewish Refugee and War Relief Agencies. The free press of Canada: its editorial opinion about the plight of Jewish refugees. Montreal. 48pp. OOP *OTURS/RSK. Facsimile extracts from various newspapers.

2617 Vancouver Island Joint Labour Conference. Apathy the workers enemy. Victoria. (c1943). (4pp). *BVAUS/Mac32f.3. Leaflet 3.

2618 Victoria Trades and Labour Council. Victoria labour annual: Labour day edition. Victoria. 16pp. *OOA/ Bengough 3. Articles by Geo. A. Wilkinson, George S. Pearson, Charles Mudge, Percy Bengough etc.

2619 Whitton, Charlotte. The dawn of ampler life. Some aids to social security. Toronto: Macmillan. vi, 154pp. *NSHD/J4 OOP.

2620 Woodcock, George. The centre cannot hold. London: Routledge. 44pp. AEU BVAU OTU SSU *own copy. Poems: includes Poem for Michael Bakunin, Speech from the dock, Poem for Garcia Lorca, Ferdinand Lassalle etc.

2621 ------ Railways and society: for workers control of railways. London: Freedom Press. 31pp. QMM *own copy.

2622 Young, E.J. Wartime wages policies: a brief presented to the National War Labour Board on May 24th, 1943. Toronto. 8pp. *OOAL.

1944

2623 Alberta Farmers Union. Action program: parity prices, adequate markets, income tax revision, freight rate revision, education, health, recreation. Edmonton. (c1944). 11pp. *ACGL/PDg1.AFU SSA/G290.4.

2624 Amalgamated Building Workers of Canada. Canadian workers: face the facts now: work, wages and security versus depression, doles and degradation. Which? Edmonton. (c1944). (8pp). *ACGL/PDh2.

2625 Ammon, Lord. Newfoundland: the forgotten island. London: Fabian Society. 29pp. *HI uncat C10. Fabian Research series 86.

2626 Anderson, Violet. Canada and the world tomorrow. Toronto: Ryerson. xi, 159pp. *OONL.

2627 Association of Canadian Individualists. This is a challenge! Vancouver. (5pp). *BVAUS/Mac31Af.22 Semi-anarchist.

2628 Beaulac, Romulus. Co-operation en Saskatchewan. (?Saskatoon): np. 108pp. ACG AEU OOA QMBM SRU *OOAL.

2629 Bengough, Percy. Victory what then? Address to the 48th convention of the American Academy of Political and Social Science, Philadelphia, April 15th, 1944. (Ottawa): Trades and Labour Congress of Canada. 11pp mimeo. *OOA/Bengough 1.

2630 Black, Norman F. A challenge to patriotism and statesmanship. Toronto: Christian Social Council of Canada. 16pp. BVIP OONL OTP *BVAUS/Mac41f.14 OOA/ CCJC 3. On the Japanese Canadians.

2631 Bradley, C.P. Democracy today and tomorrow. Think ...or sink! Saskatoon: Citizens Educational Group. (c1944). (4pp).

2632 Brady, Alexander and F.R. Scott (eds). Canada after the war: studies in political, social and economic policies for post-war Canada. Toronto: Canadian Institute of International Affairs. ix, 342pp. tables, biblio. *OONL.

2633 Brewin, F.A. Labour legislation. (Ottawa): CCF. 9pp, mimeo. *OOA/CFAW52.

2634 BC Shipyard Conference. Report of conference on post-war reconstruction and rehabilitation. Vancouver. 56pp. *BVAUS/Mac43Af.17 OTURS/RSK. The conference was organized into panels on housing, labour, agriculture etc. Executive members included H. Herridge, Fergus McKean, C.G. MacNeil & others.

2635 Bryce, William and Stanley H. Knowles. Speeches on the address in reply to the speech from the throne delivered in the House of Commons February 3 and 8, 1944. Ottawa: E. Cloutier. 11pp. *MWPA/Ivens 6 SSA/G2.1944.2.

2636 Buck, Tim. After the war - depression or prosperity? Toronto: Labor-Progressive Party. 12pp. BVAS BVIP *AEUS/SpColl BVAUS/WB43f.17(i) OKQS OTURS/RSK SSA/G27.1944.1 SSUS.

2637 ------ Canada and the Soviet Union...allies and friends in war and peace. Toronto: Labor-Progressive Party. 8pp. BVIV *OHMA3118 OKQS OTURS/RSK SSUS.

2638 ------ Canada's choice - unity or chaos. Toronto: Labor-Progressive Party. 47pp. BVAS BVIP BVIV MWU *AEUS/Spcoll BVAUS/WB31f.3b OHMA2410 OKQS OTURS/ RSK and Woodsworth 54 SSUS.

2639 ------ For a Liberal-Labor coalition government in the coming Dominion elections. (Toronto): Labor-Progressive Party. (4pp). *OTURS/RSK.

2640 ------ What kind of government? Liberal-Labor coalition vs Tory reaction. Toronto: Labor-Progressive Party. 16pp. BVIV *AEUS BVAUS/WB31f.3b and 3c OHMA3113 OKQS OTURS/RSK.

2641 ------ What we propose: Liberal-Labor coalition vs Tory reaction. Toronto: Labor-Progressive Party. 16pp. *OTURS/RSK.

2642 Buhay, Michael. Fred Rose: a short life history. Montreal: Fred Rose Election Committee. 19pp. *OTCPA.

2643 Canada, Dept of Labour. Report on the administration of Japanese affairs in Canada 1942-1944. Ottawa. 53pp. *OOAL.

2644 Canadian Association of Social Workers. Brief on social security and the public welfare services in Ontario: submitted to the Committee on Social Security and Reconstruction of Ontario. (Toronto). 21pp, mimeo. *OOA/MacPhail 5.

2645 Canadian Congress of Labour. Constitution, including by-laws of local chartered unions, labour councils and provincial federations. (Ottawa). 36pp. *OTURS/RSK. Amended 1944, 1953, 1954 etc.

2646 ------ Local union handbooks: Ottawa. 1. The shop stewards job: 2. The case for union security and the check-off: 3. Point of order: 4. Handbook on union agreements: 5. Education: the road to freedom: 6. The UIA, its rights and obligations. *OTP.

2647 ------ Political action by Canadian Labour. Ottawa. 15pp. *AEUS/CCFXIII-9 MWPA/Ivens 6 OTURS/RSK.

2648 Canadian Federation of Agriculture. Submission to the Prime Minister of Canada and members of the government. Ottawa. 11pp, mimeo. *OOA/Good 16. A general review of concerns.

2649 Canadian Seamens Union. The CSU and you: no. 2 d'une serié CCU et vous. Montréal: CSU. 15pp. *BVAUS/Mac32f.15a OTURS/RSK. French text, cover and drawing captions in English.

2650 ------ Submission to the government of Canada dealing with certain aspects of Canadian maritime shipping, which are, in our opinion, of urgent importance in the present crucial hour of the war and in the post-war period of reconstruction. Ottawa. 16pp. *OTP OTURS/RSK.

2651 ------ We stand for unity: official reply of the CSU to demands put forward by Seafarers International Union officers as conditions for affiliation. Toronto. 14pp. *BVAUS/Mac32f.15a OTURS/RSK. Concerning the 'communist tendencies' of the CSU.

2652 Canadian-Soviet Friendship Society. Second annual congress 17-19 November 1944. Toronto. 48pp plus inserted illus. *OTURS/RSK. Includes list of officers with John David Eaton as Vice-President.

(2653) Carter, Eva. Thirty years of progress: history of the United Farm Women of Alberta. (Calgary): (J.D. McAra). 45pp. ACGL, not found.

2654 Central Winnipeg Committee of the Prairie School for Social Advance. Brief supporting the proposal for collective land settlement. Winnipeg. 21pp, mimeo. *SRA/Douglas 619. 'Not a final draft. A version will be distributed in printed form' - not located.

2655 Chinese Canadian Assn. A brief prepared in conjunction with a petitition to the government of the province of British Columbia and the Dominion of Canada for the granting of the franchise of Canadian citizens of Chinese descent in the province of British Columbia.

Vancouver. (c1944). (4pp). *BVAUS/Mac41f.14.

2656 Civil Liberties Assn. An appeal for justice: the case of the seized properties of the Ukrainian Labour-Farmer Temple Assn. Toronto. 32pp. *OHMA1676 OTURS/RSK. Notes that some 60,000 books were destroyed or pulped supposedly on the grounds that they were 'communistic or subversive'.

2657 Cohen, J.L. The Dosco empire vs. the people of Canada. Submission by union counsel to the inquiry by Commissioner, the Honorable W.F. Carroll, established by the government of Nova Scotia. Toronto: United Steelworkers of America. 31pp. BVIP *BVAUS/Mac33f.16.

2658 Coldwell, M.J. Address at the Friends Meeting House, Washington, D.C. January 16, 1944. (Washington): (Friends). 4pp. *OOP.

2659 ------ Address (at the 8th national convention), Montreal, November 29, 1944. (Ottawa):CCF. 6pp, mimeo. *AEUS/CCFXIII-38 OOA/CCF13.

2660 ------ Address to the General Alumnae Assn of Queens University, Montreal branch, Friday March 31, 1944. (Ottawa): CCF. 5pp, mimeo. *OOA/Coldwell 67 and CCF145.

2661 ------ Aluminum was and is a monopoly. Speech delivered in the House of Commons 21 February 1944. Ottawa: E. Cloutier. 8pp. *OOA/CCF536 and 537 SSA/G2. 1944.3.

2662 ------ ,T.C. Douglas and A.M. Nicholson. Banks for the people. Speeches delivered in the House of Commons during the debate on the Bank Act amendment bill, May 8 & 9, 1944. Ottawa: E. Cloutier. 15pp. *OOA/Coldwell 67.

2663 ------ Billions for peace: speech delivered in the House of Commons, Thursday June 29 1944. (Ottawa): E. Cloutier. 8pp. *BVAUS/Mac27f.43.

2664 ------ The British Commonwealth and the post-war world. London (Eng): Empire Parliamentary Assn. 20pp. BVIP SRL *OOA/Coldwell 67.

2665 ------ Canada's foreign policy. (Ottawa): CCF. 6pp, mimeo. *OOA/CCF201 OTURS/RSK.

2666 ------ Canadian progressives on the march: the story of the rise of the CCF. New York: League for Industrial Democracy. 32pp. OOL OTP SRL *BVAUS/Mac30Af.3b MWPA/CCF39 OHMA2343 OOA/CCF552 OTURS/RSK SSUS/JL 197. Address plus manifestos.

2667 ------ A Canadian statesman frankly warns Americans concerning world trends. Washington: US Govt Printing Office. 4pp. *OOA/Coldwell 67. Same as 2658 above, reprinted from the Congressional Record into which it was read by Hon. John M. Coffee.

2668 ------ , J.W. Noseworthy and Stanley H. Knowles. Chemicals: synthetic rubber. Speeches delivered in

the House of Commons March 1944. (Ottawa): (E. Cloutier). 20pp. *BVAUS/Mac27f.43 MWPA/Ivens 6 SSA/
G2.1944.5.

2669 Coldwell, M.J., Clarence Gillis and Angus MacInnis.
CCF examines government policy. Speeches delivered
in the House of Commons, February 1944. (Ottawa):
(E.Cloutier). 16pp. *BVAUS/Mac27f.43 MWPA/Ivens 6
SSA/G2.1944.4.

2670 ------ Equal service for total war: speech on the
reinforcement crisis delivered in the House of Commons on November 27, 1944. Ottawa: E. Cloutier. 7pp.
*MWPA/Ivens 6 SSA/G2.1944.12.

2671 ------ and others. The farmer in the post-war world.
Ottawa: E. Cloutier. 32pp. *OOA/MacPhail 3 SSA/G2
1944.7. Speeches by Wright, Burton, Douglas, Nicholson and Castleden.

2672 ------ and T.C. Douglas. A plea for democratic government: speeches delivered in the House of Commons
on Wednesday and Thursday February 9 and 10, 1944.
Ottawa: (E. Cloutier). 15pp. *SSA/G2.1944.11 SSUS/
CCF.

2673 ------ Speech at Elrose, Saskatchewan April 11, 1944.
Farmers and labour have the same objective. (Ottawa):
CCF. 6pp, mimeo. *OOA/Coldwell 67.

2674 ------ Speech before an agricultural rally, Arthur,
Ontario, April 29, 1944. (Ottawa): CCF. 5pp, mimeo.
*OOA/Coldwell 67.

2675 ------ We are on the offensive. Speech in the House
of Commons Thursday February 10, 1944. Ottawa: E.
Cloutier. 8pp. *ACGL/Pdbl OOA/CCF537 and 540 SSA/
G2.1944.19.

2676 ------ Your Victory Bonds and your bank account.
Regina: CCF. 4pp. ACGL/PDbl MWPA/CCF39 OOA/CCF
70 and 540 SSA/G1.1944.22.

2677 CCF. Action on the home front! The CCF in the BC
legislature. Vancouver. 40pp. *OOA/CCF316 and 536.

2678 ------ After the war---together, organized labor and
the CCF must---win the peace! Vancouver. 4pp.
*OOA/CCF316.

2679 ------ Big shots fight CCF. $100,000 trust fund
backs high pressure propagandist. Toronto: New
Commonwealth. 4pp. *OHMA2363 OOACCF320. An attack
on Gladstone Murray, former general manager of CBC,
who ran the anti-CCF propaganda campaign.

2680 ------ Canada's first socialist government - what
will it do? (Winnipeg). (22pp, approx). 11 lessons
in *OOA/CCF64, but incomplete.

2681 ------ Constitution of the CCF Ontario section.
Toronto. 18pp. *OTURS/RSK. Amended 1946 etc.

2682 ------ The CCF and education in Saskatchewan. Regina. (4pp). *ACGL/PDbl MWPA/CCF39 OOA/CCF70, 321

and 536   SSA/G1. 1944.1.

2683 CCF.   The CCF and social ownership.   Regina.   (4pp).
*ACGL/PDbl   MWPA/CCF39   OOA/CCF70, 321 and 536   SSA/
G1.1944.2.

2684 ------   The CCF and social services.   Regina.   (4pp).
*ACGL/PDbl   MWPA/CCF39   OOA/Coldwell 59 and CCF70,
321 and 536   SSA/G11944.2.

2685 ------   The CCF and your insurance policy.   Halifax.
4pp.   *OOA/CCF29 and 536.

2686 ------   CCF land policy: read it!   remember it!
support it!   Regina.   4pp.   *MWPA/CCF39   OOA/70, 321
and 536   SSA/G1.1944.6.

2687 ------   The CCF platform, federal and provincial,
abbreviated by William Irvine.   Edmonton.   2pp,
broadside.   *OOA/CCF316 and 536.

2688 ------   CCF policy for victory and peace.   Regina.
(1p), broadside.   *SSA/G1.nd.6.

2689 ------   The CCF policy on money.   Regina.   (8pp).
*AEPAA/Brown 36   MWPA/CCF39   OOA/CCF126, 322 and 536
SSA/G1.1944.8.

2690 ------   A CCF quiz.   Vancouver.   16pp.   *OOA/CCF316
and 536.

2691 ------   The farmer and the CCF.   Regina.   8pp.   *OHMA
2356   OOA/CCF537   SSA/G1.1944.13 and G2.1945.5.

2692 ------   Farmers remember what you got: drudgery,
debts, poverty: what the monopolists got: abundance
out of your toil, profits on your debts, the real
wealth of Canada.   The CCF will change this.   Edmonton.   (4pp).   *OOA/CCF537.

2693 ------   Federal election manifesto adopted by the
eighth national convention, Montreal, November 29,
30 and December 1, 1944.   Toronto.   17pp, mimeo.
*OOA/CCF220   SSA/G3.Ont 15.

2694 ------   Federal election manifesto.   (Ottawa).   12pp,
mimeo.   *OOA/CCF125.

2695 ------   Here's to your health: the CCF has a plan.
Ottawa.   16pp.   *OOA/CCF537.

2696 ------   If I were a Liberal or a Conservative I
wouldn't talk about the Japanese!   Vancouver.   4pp.
*OOA/CCF316.

2697 ------   The increased safety of Victory Bonds and
bank accounts under the CCF.   Halifax.   (4pp).
*OOA/CCF537.

2698 ------   Labor and urban security.   Regina.   (4pp).
*SSA/G1.nd.16.

2699 ------   Labour political action pays big dividends
to Canadian workers.   Saskatchewan's new labour laws
CCF government guarantees union security, collective
bargaining, two weeks vacation with pay.   Toronto.

(4pp). *OHMA2357 OOA/CCF60, 320 and 537.

2700 CCF. Let the record speak! Regina. 8pp. *OOA/CCF 70, 321 and 537 SSA/G1.1944.14.

2701 ------ Manual: CCF victory campaign 1944: for the assistance of CCF candidates and speakers. Vancouver. (67pp), mimeo, variously paged. *OOA/CCF316.

2702 ------ March with the CCF. (Toronto). 4pp. *OKQS.

2703 ------ Marching home to what? CCF post-war program for Canada's fighting men and women. Ottawa. 24pp. OTP OTU *ACGL/PDbl BVAUS/43f.17 and 30Af.12 OHMA1586 OOA/CCF310, 326 and 537 and Klein 17 SSA/G1.1945.6 and G2.1944.9 SSUS/CCF and JL197.

2704 ------ A memorandum concerning plans for the rehab- ilitation of the personnel of the Canadian armed forces. Ottawa. 6pp plus 7pp appendix, mimeo. *OOA/ CCF2.

2705 ------ Meet the Liberal underground 1939-43. Regina. (4pp). *SSA/G1.1945.3.

2706 ------ A people's program for Canada: summary of CCF election manifesto adopted at the national convention Montreal, December 1944. Winnipeg. (4pp). *OOA/126 318 and 538.

2707 ------ Planning for freedom: a presentation of prin- ciples, policy and program. 16 lectures. Toronto. 180pp. *ACGA/CCF29 BVAUS/Mac30f.8 OHMA1590 OKQS OOA/CCF538 OTURS/RSK SSA/G3.Ont.9 SSUS/JL197. Lectures include The nature of economic planning by Frank Scott; Freedom and the CCF by George Grube; Socialized health services by T.F. Nicholson; Comm- unity planning and housing by P.A. Deacon; Marching home to what by Clairie Gillis; Social ownership, Dominion and provincial by E.B. Jolliffe; Social ownership, municipal and cooperative by William Denn- ison; The CCF policy on money by Eugene Forsey; Nat- ural resources by David Cass-Beggs; The farmer and the world of tomorrow by T.C. Douglas; Labour legis- lation by Andrew Brewin; A program for education by J.W. Noseworthy; Dominion-provincial relations by F.H. Underhill; Canada's foreign policy by M.J. Cold- well; The structure of the CCF by David Lewis and Social security by members of the Ontario CCF Welfare Committee.

2708 ------ Program for British Columbia. Vancouver. 26pp. *BVAUS/Mac30Af.10 SSA/G3.BC9.

2709 ------ Program on seed grain repayments. Regina. 4pp. *ACGL/PDbl MWPA/CCF39 OOA/CCF70, 321 and 536 SSA/G1.1944.11.

2710 ------ Report of proceedings 3rd annual CCF trade- union conference, July 16, 1944. (Toronto). 18pp, mimeo. *OOA/CFAW52.

2711 ------ Saskatchewan plans for progress. A summary

of legislation passed at the special session of the Saskatchewan legislature October 19 - November 10, 1944. Regina: Bureau of Publications. 40pp. *OOA/CCF69.

2712 CCF. Social security. CCF lecture series. (Ottawa). 8pp, mimeo. *OOA/CCF201. pp 5-8 has The social utilities by Anne Clare Park.

2713 ------ Socialism and co-operatives. Regina. (4pp). *BVAUS/Mac43f.1 MWPA/CCF39 OOA/Coldwell 59 SSA/G1.1944.8 SSUS/CCF and JL 197.

2714 ------ Teachers salaries and CCF policy in Nova Scotia. Halifax. 5pp. *OOA/CCF29 and 539.

2715 ------ The unions and the CCF: what the labor movement will gain by political action. Vancouver. 4pp. *MWPA/CCF39 OOA/316, 320 and 539.

2716 ------ Wartime provincial program. St John. (c1944). (4pp). *OOA/CCF34 and 318.

2717 ------ What is the CCF? Toronto. (4pp). *MWPA/CCF39 and Ivens 6 OHMA1558 OOA/CCF126 and 320 OTURS/RSK SSA/G2.nd.12. Various edns and dates.

2718 ------ What the Liberals have not told you! Regina. (4pp). *SSA/G2.1945.23.

2719 ------ Who voted for total war? Ottawa. (c1944). (1p), broadside. *OTPB/Coldwell 1945 SSA/G2.nd.13.

2720 ------ Youth faces the future: youth calls for comradeship, constructive work, courageous citizenship. Are YOU in the CCF youth movement. Regina. (4pp). *OOA/CCF70.

2721 Cooperative Commonwealth Youth Movement. Constitution and handbook. Regina. 14pp, mimeo. *ACGA/CCF24.

2722 ------ Work, wisdom and well-being in the post-war years. A brief submitted to the Canadian Youth Commission. Regina. 12pp. *OOA/CCF540 SSA/G.19.9.

2723 Co-operative Union of Canada. Submission to the Canadian government. 11pp plus 2pp appendix, mimeo. *OOA/Good 12. Regarding the taxation of co-ops.

2724 (Craig, W.). Report of the President: 11th convention Division 4, Railway Employee's Dept A.F. of L., Winnipeg, 1944. Montreal: Railway Employees. 38pp. *MWPA/Russell 1. First convention since 1938.

2725 Creed, George E. Money: master or servant? The democratic way to full employment. Toronto: League for Economic Democracy. (ii), vi, 273, i-xpp. ACG AEU BVIV NSHPL SRU *OOP.

2726 Davies, Raymond Arthur. Arctic Eldorado: a dramatic report on Canada's northland - the greatest unexploited region in the world - with a workable four-year plan. Toronto: Ryerson. 97pp. *OONL.

2727 Davies, Raymond Arthur. Canada and Russia, neighbours and friends. Toronto: Progress. 111pp, illus,
biblio. *BVAUS/WB42f.25a OHMA3121.

2728 Dexter, Grant. The conscription debates of 1917 and
1944: an analysis. Winnipeg: Winnipeg Free Press.
10pp. BVIP OKQ OOP QMU *OONL.

2729 Donaldson, L.S. Christianity and the CCF. Halifax:
CCF. (2pp). *OOA/CCF536. A radio broadcast.

2730 Douglas, T.C. Toward a united Canada. A radio address, September 20, 1944. Ottawa: CCF. (8pp).
*OOA/CCF310 and 539 SSA/G2.1944.15.

2731 ------ Where's the money coming from? Radio address
broadcast February 3, 7, 8, 9, 1944. Regina: CCF.
(4pp). *ACGL/PDbl OHMA2351 OOA/CCF70, 310 and 540
SSA/G1.1944.23 and G2.1944.20. CCF broadside issued
in 1945 with the same title, *SSUS/CCF.

(2732) Dubensky, A. Some aspects of labor problems in Canadian post-war industry. Unpublished MA thesis,
McGill University. 196pp.

2733 Elliott, J.A. Industrialized agriculture. Brief
presented to the Saskatchewan Rehabilitation Council
and Saskatchewan Consultation Committee on Co-operative Farming. (Saskatoon): United Farmers of Canada.
(c1944). 8pp. *SSA/G37.42 SSUS/UFC.

2734 Fairley, Barker. Art - Canadians, for the use of.
Toronto: Canadian Affairs. 19pp. BVIP SRL *OHMA3154.

2735 Fellowship for a Christian Social Order. Constitution.
Toronto. 5pp, mimeo. *OOA/Forsey 15.

2736 Fines, C.M. The first CCF government in action.
Address at the 8th CCF national convention. Ottawa:
CCF. (8pp). *ACGA/CCF29 BVAUS/Shepherd 4-5 OOA/
CCF310 and 537.

2737 Forsey, E.A. Memorandum on private international
trade arrangements. Ottawa: Canadian Congress of
Labour. 16pp, mimeo plus 1p letter of distribution
from Stuart Jamieson. *OOA/CCF145.

2738 ------ Reply to 'Social suicide'. (?Ottawa): (The
Citizen). (1p) broadside. *OTURS. Part II only
headed 'The first part of this article appeared in
the Citizen yesterday'. Reply to the anti-CCF propaganda leaflet by B.A. Trestrail.

2739 Fowler, Bertram B. Nickels built the factories.
Antigonish: St Francis Xavier University. (4pp).
*OOA/CCF546.

2740 Freed, Norman. A million dollars of your money must
be saved: radio speech over CKCL Monday, April 3rd
1944. Toronto: (?Labor-Progressive Party). (4pp).
*OTURS/RSK.

2741 German Anti-Fascists in Britain and Canada. The rise
and fall of Hitler fascism. Toronto: Ryerson. 64pp.

BVIP NBSAM *BVAUS/WB40f.8A(i)   OHMA2449.

2742 Gillis, Clarence. Marching home: plans for the rehabilitation of the personnel of the Canadian armed
forces. (Ottawa): CCF. 12pp, mimeo. *AEUS/CCFXII-40.

2743 Good, W.C. National co-operative unity: the importance of co-operative consolidation. (Brantford):
Cooperative Union of Canada. (8pp). *OTP.

2744 Gordon, W.E. Christianity, socialism and the CCF.
(Selkirk, Man.). (c1944). (4pp). *OOA/CCF64.

2745 Health Study Bureau. Health can be planned: four
broadcasts on health planning from national farm
radio forum broadcasts December 6-27, 1943. Toronto.
30pp. *OOA/CCF551.

2746 Hill, A.T. The future of western Ontario. Port
Arthur: Labor-Progressive Party. 24pp. *BVAUS/WB
31f.3a OTURS/RSK. Abridged report and resolutions
adopted at the western Ontario regional conference
9 April 1944.

2747 Irvine, William. CCF aims. Edmonton: CCF. (2pp).
*OOA/CCF76, 316 and 536.

2748 ------ The CCF policy. Edmonton: CCF. (2pp).
*OOA/CCF76.

2749 ------ CCF provincial policy: what the CCF will do
for Alberta. Edmonton: CCF. (c1944). 28pp. *SSA/
G3.Alta.10 SSUS/CCF.

2750 ------ Security or abundance: the people must choose.
Winnipeg: Contemporary. 42pp. SRL *ACGA/Spencer 1
BVAUS/Mac43f.17 MWPA/Brigden 7 OHMA1720 OOA/CCF539
OTURS/RSK SSA/G501.7 SSUS/JL197.

2751 Ivens, William. Series of broadsides: 1. The CCF and
its rivals. *SSAG3.Man.3 2. Evolution versus revolution. *SSA/G3.Man.6 SSUS/CCF. 3. Is world war III
inevitable? 4. Our democratic tradition. 5. Socialism: democratic or totalitarian. 6. Socialism does
not mean bureaucracy. 7. There is no real difference
between Liberals and Tories. 8. What's the matter
with capitalism? 9. New social order dawning. *OOA/
CCF296 and 318. 10. What is the basic program of the
CCF. *SSUS/CCF. Winnipeg: author in cooperation with
the CCF.

2752 Jamieson, Laura E. and W.W. Lefeaux. Budget debate:
speeches, session 1944. Vancouver: CCF. 29pp. *T.

2753 Japanese Canadian Committee for Democracy. In the
matter of the War Services Electors Bill (no.135 of
1944) section 5 regarding certain amendments to section 14.ss.2 of the Dominion Elections Act, 1938 and
in the matter of the proposed disenfranchisement of
British subjects and Canadian citizens in Canada:
brief. Toronto. 10pp, mimeo. *OOA/CCJC 1f.1.

2754 Johnson, Hewlett. The secret of Soviet strength.
Winnipeg: Contemporary. 50pp. *BVAUS/Mac38f.18.

2755 Johnson, Hewlett. Socialism and the individual. Toronto: Progress. 52pp. MWU OKQ OTU SRL *BVAUS/ Mac43f.2 OHMA3107.

2756 Jolliffe, Edward B. Family allowances: national need or political football? Toronto: CCF. 8pp. *OOA/ CCF57, 308 and 320 and MacPhail 3 OTURS/Woodsworth 29 SSA/G2.1944.6.

2757 ------ A new deal for the Ontario farmer. Toronto: CCF. 8pp. *MWPA/CCF39 OOA/CCF537.

2758 ------ Social ownership - dominion and provincial. (Toronto): (CCF). 13pp, mimeo. *AEUS/CCFXIII-35 OOA/MacPhail 3.

2759 King, Carlyle. Education for a peoples peace. np. (?CCF). 6pp. *BVAUS/Mac40f.1 BVAUS/Shepherd 4-5 SRA.

2760 Knowles, Stanley H. Speeches on old age pensions and on post-war civil aviation delivered in the House of Commons March 13, 20, 1944. (Ottawa): E. Cloutier. 15pp. *BVAUS/Mac27f.43 MWPA/Ivens 6.

2761 Labour Party (of Great Britain). Report of the conference of British and Dominion Labour parties held at St Ermin's hotel and Transport House, London SW 1 September 12th to 27th, 1944. London. 129pp, mimeo. *OOA/CCF112. Contributions from M.J. Coldwell, C. Gillis, David Lewis, F.R. Scott and P.E. Wright.

2762 Labor-Progressive Party. Set of leaflets on different topics but all with the headline 'Forward Alberta' and numbered as follows: 1. Farm policy of the LPP. 2, Wipe out Alberta's slums. 3. and 4. not found. 5. A labor code for Alberta. 6. Where is the money coming from? 7. Coal and Alberta's future. 8. A health plan for Alberta. 9. Lest we forget (on the CCF leaders). Edmonton. each (4pp). *OTURS/RSK.

2763 ------ A new deal for the Yukon: on the highway to a new Canada. Whitehorse. (6pp). *BVAUS/Smith CP.

2764 ------ Notes on imperialist character of Canadian economy: new data on imperialism: notes on international cartels: Canadian holdings in foreign countries. Timmins. (c1944). 7pp, mimeo. *OHMA.

2765 ------ Program. Toronto. 46pp. BVIP OKQ *BVAUS/ WB31f.3a OHMA1792 OTURS/RSK SSUS/Comm.

2766 ------ Questions and answers about the LPP. Montreal. 6pp. *OTURS.

2767 ------ The status of Canada. np. (c1944). 9pp, mimeo. *OTURS/RSK. Stated to be 're-issued' but source not given nor found.

2768 Labour Youth Federation of Canada. Youth proposes - physical fitness, minimum wage laws, child labour laws. Toronto. 8pp. *OTURS/RSK.

2769 Lasserre, Henri. The communities of Tolstoyans and

their significance for the co-operative movement of today. Toronto: Rural Cooperative Community Council and Canadian Fellowship for Cooperative Community. 31pp. *BVAUS/Mac38f.17 SSUS/Coops.

2770 League of Nations Society in Canada. The League of Nations in the post-war world: a letter to the Hon. W.L. Mackenzie King, M.J. Coldwell, J.H. Blackmore and the Hon. John Bracken with replies from the Hon W.L. Mackenzie King and M.J. Coldwell. Ottawa. 12pp. *OTURS/RSK.

2771 Lenin, V.I. The teachings of Karl Marx. Toronto: Porgress. 54pp. AEU BVIP BVIV NSHPL *BVAUS/WB38f.16 OTURS/RSK. Contains 12pp introduction by Tim Buck.

2772 Lewis, David. Farmer-labor unity: the experience of the CCF. Yellow Springs (Ohio): Antioch Review. pp166-176. *OOA/CCF308. Offprint from Summer 1944.

2773 Logan, H.A. Report on labour relations. Halifax: Kings Printer. 98pp. OTP *OOL.

2774 ------ The state and collective bargaining. Toronto: University of Toronto. pp476-488. *OOL. Offprint from the Canadian Journal of Economics and Political Science.

2775 Lucas, Louise. Women and the banks. Regina: CCF. 4pp. *OOA/CCF70 and 540 SSA/Gl.1944.25.

2776 MacInnis, Angus. Progress demands social ownership; speech delivered in the House of Commons Friday March 10, 1944. (Ottawa): E. Cloutier. 6pp. *BVAUS/Mac 27f.43 MWPA/Ivens 6.

2777 MacInnis, Grace and Angus. Oriental Canadians - outcasts or citizens? Vancouver: Federationist. 20pp. BVIP BVIV OOP OTP *BVAUS/Mac41f.14 OHMA1582 OOA/ CCF316 and 538 and CCJC/1-3 SSUS/JL197.

2778 Magnuson, Bruce. Ontario's green gold. Toronto. 36pp. OTP *BVAUS/Mac41f.16 OTURS/RSK. On forest resources.

2779 Molnar, E.F. Religion and labor relations: an outline for panel discussions together with a preamble on some dialectical principles necessitating a common front. Calgary: Religion and Labour Council. 22pp. *OTURS/RSK.

2780 Morris, Leslie. Forward Ontario: unity for victory, peace and prosperity. Toronto: Labor-Progressive Party. 20pp. OKQ SSU *BVAUS/WB31f.3b OHMA1848 OTURS/RSK. Keynote speech to the 1st Ontario convention of the LPP.

2781 ------ 22 reasons why Drew must go: coalition can do it! (Toronto): Labor-Progressive Party. (2pp). *OKQS OTURS/RSK.

2782 Murry, John Middleton. The dilemma of democracy. (Winnipeg): (Prairie School for Social Advance). 5pp, mimeo. *AEUS/PSSA.

2783 National Council for Canadian-Soviet Friendship.
March to progress. Toronto. (c1944). 20pp. *BVAUS/
WB42f.25a OHMA1935 OTURS/RSK.

2784 ------ Second annual congress of Canadian-Soviet
Friendship November 17-18-19, 1944, Toronto. Toronto.
(48pp), illus. *OHMA/3197 OTURS/RSK.

2785 ------ Summary of proceedings, Congress of Canadian-
Soviet frienship. Toronto. 16pp, mimeo. *OOA/Good
19.

2786 National Farm Radio Forum. Planning for plenty.
Series of five pamphlets. Toronto. 1. Planning,
prices and controls. 13pp. 2. Planning for health.
18pp. 3. Planning farm credit (not found). 4. Planning for rural living. 16pp. 5. PLanning reaches
the family farm. 16pp. OH *OOA/CCF154.

2787 National Interchurch Advisory Committee on Resettlement of Japanese Canadians. Planning resettlement
of Japanese Canadians. Toronto. (6pp). *OOA/CCJC3.

2788 Neruda, Pablo. Let the rail splitter awake. Vancouver: Labor-Progressive Party. (c1944). 24pp.
AEU OTP *BVAUS/Mac41f.9a OHMA OTURS/RSK.

2789 Nicholson, T.F. Socialized health services. (Ottawa): CCF. 8pp, mimeo. *OOA/CCF201.

2790 Nicholson, William B. Democratic Russia. Calgary:
np. 52pp. *BVAUS/DK OTURS/RSK. Written in 1940
as the result of a pre-war visit, but failed to find
a publisher then because of the Nazi-Soviet pact.

2791 Nielsen, Dorise. New worlds for women. Toronto:
Progress. 112pp. BVIP OOP OTP QMBN SSU *ACGL/PE
Comm. BVAUS/WB32f.2b MWPL OHMA1926 SSA/G189.2
OTURS/RSK.

2792 Noseworthy, J.W. A programme for education. (?Tor-
onto): CCF. 11pp, mimeo. *AEUS/CCFXIII-46.

2793 Novak, Louis. Czechoslovakia before and after Munich.
(Toronto): A group of Czechoslovak refugees. viii,
120pp. AEU BVIV MWP NSHPL OH OKQ OONL SSU *OTURS/
RSK.

2794 Ontario. Activities and responsibilities of the
Ontario Department of Labour including an explanatory
address on hours of work and vacations with pay act.
Toronto: T.E. Bowman. 54pp. *OTAR/1944/63.

2795 Penner, Jacob. Next elections: what kind of coalition?
Liberal-Labor coalition vs. Tory reaction. Winnipeg:
Labor-Progressive Party. 16pp. *MWPA/CCF35.

2796 Powell, E.R. The medical quest. Regina: State Hospital and Medical League. 97pp. BVIP MWP OOP OOU
SRL SRU *ACGA/CCF29.

2797 Prairie School for Social Advance. Announcing...the
introductory session and planning conference of the
Prairie School for Social Advance. Farmers, indust-

rial workers, all people interested. Winnipeg. (4pp). *AEUS/PSSA.

2798 Prairie School for Social Advance. Brief supporting the proposal for collective land settlement presented to the Hon. J.H. Sturdy, Minister of Reconstruction and Rehabilitation. (Winnipeg). 21pp, mimeo. *AEUS/PSSA.

2799 ------ Labor weekend. (Topic: Beyond the labor code: preparing for the post-war emergency and opportunity). (Winnipeg). 23pp, mimeo. *AEUS/PSSA.

2800 ------ Proceedings of the first session and conference held at Saskatoon, 16-23 July 1944. (?Winnipeg). 72pp, mimeo. *AEUS/PSSA OTURS/RSK SSA/G540.1. With an enclosed leaflet: Not by bread alone by Watson Thompson, issued by the school. (4pp).

2801 ------ Short report of the first session and conference held at Saskatoon. (Saskatoon). (3pp), mimeo. *AEUS/PSSA. See 2800 above for full report.

2802 ------ and the Needle Trades Council. Labor's decisive hour: first labor forum. (Winnipeg). 7pp, mimeo. *AEUS/PSSA.

2803 Priestley, Norman F. Farmers should organize. Calgary: United Farmers of Alberta. (c1944). (8pp). *ACGA/UFA3.

2804 Proctor, Irwin. The CCF and the banks. Halifax: CCF. (2pp). *NSHP.

2805 Queens University. The closed shop: a study of the methods used by unions to attain security. Kingston: Queens University Industrial Relations Centre. 85pp. *OKQ.

2806 Rose, Fred. Le masque tombe: discours prononcé le 3 juillet 1944 à la Chambre des Communes d'Ottawa. Montréal: Part-Ouvrier-Progressif. 13pp. QMBM *OTURS/RSK.

(2807)------ La menace du chaos: le complot tory contre le Canada. Montréal: (Parti-Ouvrier-Progressif). 13pp. QMBM.

2808 Ryder, Norman B. The economic theory of socialism. Unpublished BA thesis (hons). McMaster University. 103pp, biblio. *OHMA.

2809 Ryerson, S.B. Drew, Dorion, Duplessis contre le Canada-français. Causeries électorales du Parti-Ouvrier-Progressif. Montréal: Parti-Ouvrier-Progressif. 10pp. QMBM *OTURS/RSK.

2810 ------ Two peoples, one land, one future. Toronto: Labor-Progressive Party. 9pp. *BVAUS/WB31f.3c OHMA2445 OTURS/RSK SSA/G27.1944.3.

2811 Sarkin, Sidney. Man of the people Michael Buhay: a short life history. Montreal: (?Labor-Progressive Party). 15pp. *OOA/Kaplansky.

2812 Saskatchewan. Saskatchewan plans for progress.
Regina: T.H. McConica. 40pp. *BVAUS/Mac30Bf.21
OHMA1591 OOA/CCF554. Also issued in 1945.

2813 Scott, F.R. The constitution and the post-war world.
Toronto: Macmillan. 28pp. *OTP.

2814 ------ Cooperation for what? United States and
British Commonwealth. New York: American Council
Institute of Pacific Relations. 64pp. OH OONL OOP
QMBM SRL *OOA/CCF309. IPR Pamphlet 11.

2815 ------ The Montreal Star and the CCF: another monopoly at work. Montreal: CCF. (4pp). *OHMA2135.
Largely a letter sent by Scott to the Montreal Star
which they refused to publish.

2816 Shipyard General Workers Federation. First annual
convention: proceedings. Victoria. 40pp. *BVAUS/
Mac34f.24.

2817 Sims, Charles. The keys to speedy victory: Canada,
the Moscow conference and post-war progress. Toronto:
Labor-Progressive Party. 20pp. MWU *BVAUS/WB31f.3c
OHMA3152 OTURS/RSK.

2818 Smith, Stewart. Handbook of Labor-Progressive Party
education (for the guidance of clubs and club executives). Toronto: Labor-Progressive Party. (4pp).
*OHMA OTURS/RSK. Endorsed by the Ontario convention.

2819 ------ Manual on club work. Toronto: Labor-Progressive Party. (4pp). *OHMA OTURS/RSK.

2820 Socialist Party of Canada. The socialist manifesto.
Winnipeg. 41pp. AEU *BVAUS/Mac30Af.2b OTURS/RSK.

2821 Stalin, Joseph. Order of the day: the speeches and
important orders of the day. Toronto: Progress.
126pp. MWP OH SSU *BVAUS/WB38f.19 OHMA.

2822 Strike at the Royal York: a study in deception.
(Toronto): np. (4pp). *BVAUS/Mac34f.16.

2823 Thomson, Watson. Power to the people. (Regina):
Saskatchewan Dept of Education. 20pp. Four broadcasts. *AEUS/PSSA.

2824 Trades and Labor Congress of Canada. Constitution
and by-laws. Toronto. 36pp. *OTURS/RSK. Contains
also platform of principles.

2825 ------ Diamond jubilee: sixtieth annual convention.
Reports of the Executive Council, provincial executives, federations of labor and fraternal delegates
to the American Federation of Labor. Toronto. 96pp.
*BVAUS/Mac33f.12.

2826 ------ Memorandum presented to the Dominion government, Friday February 25th, 1944. Ottawa. 8pp.
*SSUS/Labour.

2827 Turner, A.H. A co-operative centenary. Regina:
Dept of Co-operation and Co-operative Development.
9pp. *SSUS/Coop.

2828 Ukrainian Canadian Cultural Group. Canadians on the march (Canada united). Yorkton. 52pp. OOP OTP QMBM *OTURS/RSK Peel 3880. First in a series of radio broadcasts under the general title Canada United over CJGX.

2829 Underhill, Frank H. James Shaver Woodsworth, untypical Canadian. An address delivered at the dinner to inaugurate the Ontario Woodsworth Memorial Foundation, King Edward Hotel, Toronto, Saturday October 7th, 1944. Toronto: Ontario Woodsworth Memorial Foundation. 34pp. *BVAUS/Mac39f.2a MWPA/CCF39 OHMA 2867 OOA/CCF326 and 540 OTURS/RSK SSA/G436.3.

2830 UAW-CIO. Why bosses fight unions. Toronto. (c1944). (1p) broadside. *OTURS/RSK.

2831 UE (ie United Electrical Workers). For victory, security and progress in 1944 - the year of transition. Toronto. 16pp. *BVAUS/Mac43Af.17.

2832 ------ To win the peace: the UE plan for Canadian prosperity in the post-war. Toronto. 24pp. *OTURS/ RSK and Woodsworth 54.

2833 Vancouver Island Joint Labour Conference. Report: regional convention on rehabilitation. Victoria. 42pp. BVIP *BVAUS/Mac42f.25.

2834 Walters, Melda L. Old age pensions. Halifax: CCF. (2pp). *OOA/CCF538.

2835 Wilson, Idele L. Union security. Toronto: Workers Educational Assn. 64pp. OTP SRL *BVAUS/Mac42f.1 OTURS/RSK. Originally published as a research bulletin in 1943 called 'The closed shop' and now revised with additional data.

2836 Woodcock, George. Anarchy or chaos. London: Freedom Press. 124pp. AEU SSU *OKQ.

2837 ------ Homes or hovels: the housing problem and its solution. London: Freedom Press. 33pp. BVAU BVIV QMM *own copy.

2838 Young, Fred M. The CCF and education in Nova Scotia. Halifax: CCF. (4pp). *OOA/CCF536.

2839 ------ The CCF and the small business man. Halifax: CCF. (1p). *OOA/29 and 536.

1945

2840 Alberta Livestock Co-operative. Alberta Co-operative leaders. Edmonton. 54pp. *ACGL Peel 3897B. Biographies.

2841 Alberta Wheat Pool. A submission to the Royal Commission appointed by order in council on the 16th day of November 1944, to inquire into the subject of the

Income War Tax Act and the Excess Profits Tax Act, 1940 and co-operative corporations, associations and societies under the chairmanship of the Honorable Mr Justice McDougall. (?Edmonton). 38pp plus 11pp appendixes, mimeo. *OOA/Good 14.

2842 Archibald, Harry G. Speech on the address in reply to the speech from the throne delivered in the House of Commons, September 13, 1945. Ottawa: E. Cloutier. 7pp. *T.

2843 Boilermakers Political Action Committee. (In support of proposals by the BC Federation of Labor to the provincial government). Vancouver. (4pp). *BVAUS/ Smith CP.

2844 Brewin, F.A. First steps of a CCF government. Fall lecture series 1945. (Ottawa): (CCF). 7pp, mimeo. *OOA/CCF310 and 320.

2845 Buck, Tim. Atomic diplomacy, a threat to world peace. Toronto: Labor-Progressive Party. 29pp. BVIP BVIV *AEUS/Spcoll BVAUS/WB31f.3b MWPA/Russell 1 OHMA 2412 OKQS OTURS/RSK SSUS.

2846 ------ The Crimea decisions and your future. Toronto: Labor-Progressive Party. 18pp. *BVAUS/WB31f.3d OHMA2402 OTURS/RSK.

2847 ------ For union security, labour partnership. Tim Buck demands immediate action by King government. Toronto: Labor-Progressive Party. (4pp). *BVAUS/ WB31f.3e.

2848 ------ A letter to you: LPP armed services special. Toronto: Labor-Progressive Party. (4pp). *BVAUS/ WB31f.3e.

2849 Cahan, Jacqueline Flint. A survey of the political activities of the Ontario labor movement 1850-1935. Unpublished MA thesis, University of Toronto. iii, 96 (101)pp, biblio. *OHMA3201 OTUAR OTURS/RSK.

2850 Cameron, Colin. Forestry...BC's devasted industry. Vancouver: CCF. (c1945). 15pp. *BVAUS/Mac40f.6b and Young OOA/CCF316.

2851 Canada, Dept of Labour. Labour legislation in Canada: a historical outline of the principal Dominion and provincial labour laws. Ottawa. 33pp. *MWPA/Russell 1.

2852 Canadian Affairs. Party election statements. Ottawa: E. Cloutier. 30pp. *OOA/CCF126 and 310. Includes CCF pp21-26 and LPP pp29-30.

2853 Canadian Congress of Labor. Hey Joe! What's going on here? (Ottawa). (c1945). (4pp). *SSUS/Labour. In favour of a forty hour week.

2854 ------- Proposed amendments to Wartime Labour Relations Regulations (Order in Council PC.1003) adopted by the Executive Council. Ottawa. (4pp). *OOA/CCF 166. See 2855 below.

2855 Canadian Congress of Labor. Report of the special committee of the Executive Council on PC.1003 and PC.9384. Ottawa. 8pp. *OOA/CCF166. PC. 1003 was the Wartime Labour Relations Regulations and PC.9384 the Wartime Wage Control Order.

2856 Canadian Co-operative Implements Ltd. Questions and answers about CCIL. Winnipeg. 15pp. *OOA/CCF154.

2857 Canadian Co-operative Wool Growers. Brief presented to the Royal Commission on the Taxation of Co-operatives. (Toronto). 6pp, mimeo. *OOA/Good 14.

2858 Canadian Livestock Co-operative. Brief presented to the Royal Commission on Co-operatives. Moncton. 19pp, mimeo. *OAA/Good 14.

2859 Canadian Seamens Union. A national shipping policy for Canada: a permanent merchant marine for an expanding Canadian economy and full employment. Toronto. 18pp. OONL OTP *OTURS/RSK.

2860 Carr, D.B. An evaluation of the social work of the United Church of Canada since union. Unpublished BD thesis, University of Alberta. (v), 160pp, biblio. *AEUS/1945-6.

2861 Carter, Dyson. Industries for the prairies: challenging facts about chemurgy! A letter... Winnipeg: Labor-Progressive Party. 14pp. *BVAUS/Mac41f.2 OTCPA.

2862 ------ Sin and science. Toronto: Progress. 124pp. AEU OKQ OTU SRL *BVAUS/WB42f.29b(ii) OHMA1495.

2863 ------ So you can't have health? Toronto: Progress. 95pp. BVIP OTP SRL *BVAUS/WB40f.8 OHMA1498.

2864 Cassidy, Harry M. Public health and welfare reorganization: the postwar problem in the Canadian provinces. Toronto: Ryerson. xiv, 464pp. *OTP. A sequel to 'Social security and reconstruction in Canada.'

2865 Charpentier, Alfred. Syndicalisme ou politique. Québec: Confédération des Travailleurs Catholique du Canada. 16pp. QMBM *OKQS OOL.

2866 Cheshire, S.W. Consumer co-operation: a brief study of the Rochdale plan. Toronto: CCF. (5pp). *AEUS/ CCFXIII-26 OHMA2872 OOA/CCF320.

2867 Chown, E.B. The committee plan of action for co-operatives. Winnipeg: Manitoba Co-operative Wholesale. (c1945). 30pp. *OOA/CCF546.

2868 Coldwell, M.J. Jobs and homes for peace: speech delivered in the House of Commons Monday, September 10, 1945. Ottawa: E. Cloutier. 8pp. *BVAUS/Garrison 1-5 and Mac27f.43 MWPA/Ivens 6.

2869 ------ Left turn, Canada. London (Eng): Gollancz. 192pp. *OONL. US edition (1946) xv, 247pp.

2870 ------ and others. Planning for peace. CCF proposals. Speeches on the establishment of an international organization for the maintenance of peace and security, delivered in the House of Commons, March 20, 22 and 26, 1945. Ottawa: E. Cloutier. 22pp. *ACGA/Hutchison BVAUS/Mac27f.43 MWPA/Ivens 6 OOA/ CCF 538. Others include Percy Wright, J.W. Noseworthy Stanley H. Knowles.

2871 Communist Party of Canada. What the communist party stands for. Vancouver. (4pp). *BVAUS/Smith CP. Refers to itself as 'the newly formed Communist Party of Canada' and attacks both the CCF and Labor-Progressive Party policies.

2872 Confédération des Travailleurs Catholiques du Canada. Programme de la CTCC pour l'après-guerre. Québec. 10pp plus 10pp English (bilingue). *OOL.

2873 Conroy, Patrick. Production through labour-management. Ottawa: E. Cloutier. 25pp. *OOL.

2874 Contemporary Publishers. International treasury of left wing humour. Winnipeg. 92pp. *OHMA1520 OOA/ CCF551.

2875 ------ Masterpieces of labor humor. Winnipeg. 92pp. *OOA/CCF552. Scraping the barrel - largely the same as 2874 above.

2876 Co-operative Committee on Japanese Canadians. Brief: re patriation of Japanese Canadians. Toronto. 5pp, mimeo. *OOA/CCJC 1.

2877 CCF. Activities for CCF units. 1. General plan. 2.Study groups. 3. Lecture series. Toronto. 6pp, mimeo. *OOA/CCF201.

2878 ------ Agriculture on the prairies: the CCF approach. Winnipeg. 4pp. *OOA/CCF318 SSA/G3.Man 1.

2879 ------ Are you afraid? of poverty - of unemployment - of relief lines - below-cost farm prices - world war III. The CCF will remove these fears. Edmonton. (4pp). *OOA/CCF536.

2880 ------ Brief to be presented to the Royal Commission on Co-operatives. (Vancouver). 6pp, mimeo. *OOA/ CCF148.

2881 ------ Brief to the Royal Commission on Co-operatives. (Winnipeg). 6pp, mimeo. *OOA/CCF316.

2882 ------ Can I keep my farm? Toronto. (2pp). *OOA/ CCF320.

2883 ------ Conservative and Liberal objections answered. Ottawa: Peoples Publications. (4pp). *ACGL/PDbl BVAUS/Mac30Af.12 OOA/CCF126 and 310.

2884 ------ The CCF has the answer. Calgary. (4pp). *OHMA1532 OOA/CCF536.

2885 ------ A CCF quiz. Edmonton (and other centres). 27-28pp. *ACGL/PDbl AEUS/CCFXIII-32 BVAUS/Mac30A f.4c OKQS OOA/CCF320 OTURS/RSK SSA/G1.1944.21 SSUS/CCF. Cover title: What is it: Who is it: What will it do?

2886 CCF. Dear Mr Ilsley: an open letter to the Minister of Finance from a prairie farm woman. Regina. (4pp). *OOA/CCF70, 322 and 536 SSA/G2.1945.30.

2887 ------ Election leaflets issued in Alberta, 1945. 1.Are you afraid? 2. A rich nation. 3. Farmers remember what you got. 4. What does he want? 5. People of Alberta, wake up to what our oil can mean to us. 6. Read these facts about this Canada. 7. This is murder. All published in Edmonton, 4pp. *OOA/CCF 316.

2888 ------ Election leaflets published in British Columbia, 1945. 1. The people of BC - together. 2. Why split labor's vote? 3. Farmers! here is tomorrow. 4. Sign your contract on October 25th. 5. Lady! did you say you weren't interested in politics? 6. Farmers and the CCF. 7. Women must use votes. 8. What do you want? All published in Vancouver, mostly 4pp. *OOA/CCF316.

2889 ------ Election leaflets published by the national CCF, 1945. 1. Clipped again! 2. Here's your ballot Jackson! It's up to you Sue! 3. Impossible, there's no such animal. 4. Jack Brown, veteran. 5. Labour and the CCF. 6. Marching home. 7. A message from M.J. Coldwell. 8. No mystery to this robbery. 9. War teaches Canada to plan for peace. 10. Who benefits from soaring prices? All published Ottawa, mostly 4pp. *OOA/CCF316.

2890 ------ Elementary discussions on economics and politics prepared by the Educational Committee. Toronto 8pp, mimeo. *OOA/CCF320.

2891 ------ Federal election issues: - New Zealand, a planned economy. Ottawa. 11pp, mimeo. *OOA/CCF173.

2892 ------ For victory and reconstruction. Programme of the CCF, Prince Edward Island section. (Bedeque). 6pp. *OOA/CCF32 and 321.

2893 ------ Forward Manitoba! CCF program. Winnipeg. 4pp. *OOA/CCF64 and 318.

2894 ------ Humanity first! What the CCF government has done in Saskatchewan. Regina. (16pp). *BVAUS/Mac 30f.8 MWPA/CCF39 OOA/CCF537 SSA/Gl.nd 13 and G2. 1945,7 SSUS/JL197.

2895 ------ Labour - victim or partner? Toronto. (4pp). *AEUS/CCFXIII-18 OOA/CCF320 OTURS/RSK.

2896 ------ Let there be no blackout of health. Regina. (4pp). *MWPA/CCF39 OOA/Coldwell 59 and CCF537 SSA/ Gl.1944.15.

2897 ------ Nazi methods used in Canada: Drew's gestapo spearheads national anti-labour drive. Montreal. (4pp), bilingual. *OOA/CCF537.

2898 ------ New Zealand prospers under CCF-type rule.

Halifax. (1p). *OOA/CCF29

2899 CCF. Notes for (district) organizers. (Toronto).
12pp, mimeo. *OOA/CCF320, lacking pp 5-8 incl.

2900 ------ Notes on labour legislation in Saskatchewan.
Regina. 12pp, mimeo. *OOA/CCF69.

2901 ------ Opportunity for Canadians - the CCF way.
Regina. (4pp). *OOA/CCF70 SSA/G1.nd.21 and G2.
1945.13.

2902 ------ Program for British Columbia, 1945. Vancouver. 30pp. *BVAUS/Mac30Af.10 OOA/CCF316. Amended
1953, 12pp, *OOA/CCF536.

2903 ------ Program for Nova Scotia. (Halifax). 12pp,
mimeo. *OOA/CCF28.

2904 ------ Property and the CCF. Ottawa. (2pp). *OOA/
CCF539 SSA/G2.1945.15.

2905 ------ Provincial platform Prince Edward Island.
4pp. *OOA/CCF32 and 321.

2906 ------ Report of election campaign conference.
Toronto. 12pp, mimeo. *OOA/CCF57.

2907 ------ Security with victory: CCF manifesto, Dominion general election, 1945. Adopted by the eighth
national convention, Montreal, November 29,30 and
December 1, 1944. Ottawa. 31pp. OTP *ACGL/PDbl
BVAUS/Mac30Af.8a OHMA1569 OKQS OOA/CCF417 and 539
and Coldwell 59 OTURS/RSK SSA/G2.1945.16 SSUS/JL
197. Also issued as a 4pp leaflet.

2908 ------ Sensational legislation! by the CCF government in Saskatchewan. Regina. 4pp. *ACGL/PDbl
OOA/CCF69, 70 and 539 SSA/G1.1946.4 SSUS/CCF.

2909 ------ Socialized health services. A plan for Canada. The preliminary recommendations of the planning
committee for health services. Toronto. 54pp, mimeo.
OH *BVAUS/Mac41f.5 OOA/CCF323 and 539 OTURS/Woods-
worth 58 SSA/G3.Ont.14. Principal author was Dr T.
F. Nicholson. Reprinted and edited by Morden Lazarus, Toronto, Ontario Woodsworth Memroial Foundation
1976. 78pp.

2910 ------ This is what has been done for labor by the
CCF government of Saskatchewan. Regina. (4pp).
*OOA/CCF70 and 539 SSA/G1.1948.17.

2911 ------ This might be Canada! Regina. (4pp). *SSA/
G2.1945.17.

2912 ------ To the lady who says: 'but I'm not interested
in politics!' Ottawa. (2pp). *OOA/CCF539 SSA/G2.
1945.18. See also 2888 above, no. 5.

2913 ------ We can build security. Ottawa. (4pp).
*SSA/G2.1945.19.

2914 ------ What capitalism does to Canadians: takes
away their jobs, their homes. Regiments them into

soup kitchens. The CCF will provide jobs - homes - food - health. Edmonton. (4pp). *ACGL/PDbl OOA/ CCF126 and 540.

2915 CCF. What is the LPP really after? Look at the record of the Canadian communists in six simple stages. Ottawa. 4pp. *OOA/CCF393 and 540 SSA/G2.1945.21.

2916 ------ What kind of labour political action??? (Windsor). (4pp). *OOA/CCF57 and 540. An endorsement of the TLCC program for post-war reconstruction.

2917 ------ What will the CCF do for us? Toronto. (4pp). *OOA/CCF320 and 540.

2918 ------ Why an election now? A CCF challenge to Tory arrogance. Toronto. (4pp). *OOA/CCF320.

2919 ------ Work for all in a land of plenty. Ottawa. (4pp). *ACGL/PDbl BVAUS/Mac30Af.12 OOA/CCF540.

2920 Cooperative Commonwealth Youth Movement. CCYM annual provincial convention, August 11th and 12th: report: Young people of the world unite. (Toronto). 5pp, mimeo. *OOA/CCF350.

2921 La Cooperative du Madawaska Lttée. Submission to the Royal Commission on Cooperatives. Edmunston. 8pp, plus 10pp appendixes, mimeo. *OOA/Good 14.

2922 Co-operative Elevator Associations and Manitoba Pool Elevators. Summary of the submission of 180 local co-operative elevator associations and Manitoba pool elevators to the Royal Commission on the Taxation of Cooperatives, 1945. (Winnipeg). 20pp, mimeo. *OOA/ Good 14.

2923 Co-operative Union of Canada. Co-operative movement protection against private monopolies: impressive evidence. Brantford. (4pp). *OOA/CUC223.

2924 ------ Royal Commission on Co-operatives: introductory submission. (Ottawa). 13pp, mimeo. *OOA/CCF148 and Good 14.

2925 ------ Special release. Ottawa. April-July 1945. Four special releases made during the hearings of the Royal Commission on Taxation of Cooperatives. 1. 7pp, 2. 3pp, 3. 7pp, 4. 5pp, all mimeo. *OOA/CCF 148 and Good 13.

2926 Cooperative Union of P.E.I. Submission to the Royal Commission on Co-operatives. Charlottetown. 12pp plus 3pp appendixes. *OOA/Good 14.

2927 Davies, Raymond Arthur. Inside Russia today. Winnipeg: Contemporary . 92pp. MWP OKQ SRL SSU *BVAUS/ Mac38f.5c OTURS/RSK. A journey on the 'lend-lease' route to Russia and back.

2928 Douglas, T.C. The case against disallowance: giving the Saskatchewan government's stand on the proposed disallowance of three acts passed in 1944 by the provincial legislature. Regina: Bureau of Publications. 15pp. SRL *BVAUS/Mac30Bf.21 OOA/CCF69.

2929 Douglas, T.C. Public health: speech in the budget debate Wednesday March21, 1945. Regina: T.H. McConica. 20pp. *SSUS/Shortt/ Douglas.

2930 ------ Saskatchewan and reconstruction. Address and the Saskatchewan government presentation to the Dominion-Provincial Conference on Reconstruction. Regina: Bureau of Publications. 24pp. ACG BVIP OOP OTP *BVAUS/Mac30Bf.21 OHMA1617 OOA/CCF539 SSUS/ Shortt/Douglas.

2931 Farm Supply Purchasing Co-operatives. Brief submitted by the farm supply purchasing cooperatives in the province of Ontario, featuring the Oxford farmers cooperative produce company, Ilderton-Middlesex farmers cooperative, Ayr district cooperatives. Toronto. 27pp, mimeo. *OOA/Good 14.

2932 First Cooperative Packers of Ontario, Barrie. Brief presented to the Royal Commission on Taxation of Co-operatives. (Toronto): Ontario Cooperative Union. 9pp. mimeo. *OOA/Good 14.

2933 Forsey, Eugene. Reconstruction: the first steps. Ottawa: Canadian Congress of Labour. (c1945). 20pp. OH OOP OTP *BVAUS/Mac43f.17 OOA/Forsey 16 OTURS/ RSK SRA/Douglas 619(16-8). Mainly on public ownership.

2934 Fowke, Edith and A.G. Watson. Democracy and the Japanese Canadian. Toronto: Fellowship of Reconciliation. 8pp. *MWPA/Brigden 7 OHMA1549 OOA/CCJC 3.

2935 Francis, W.B. and others. Royal Commission on Co-operatives. Outline of argument on behalf of certain cooperative associations. (?Ottawa): np. 80pp plus 2pp list of associations, mimeo. *OOA/Good 16. A similar brief was submitted on behalf of 'certain credit unions'.

2936 French, Doris. Canada tomorrow: a report of the CCYM. (Ottawa): CCYM. 15pp, mimeo. *OOA/CCF346 and 536 SSA/G20.1.

2937 Gillis, Clarence, Angus MacInnis, Stanley Knowles and M.J. Coldwell. The Ford strike: labour's struggle for union security. Speeches delivered in the House of Commons, Monday November 5, 1945. Ottawa: E. Cloutier. 15pp. *BVAUS/Garrison 1-5 MWPA/Russell 1 OOA/CCF537.

2938 Good, W.C. President's address: national congress, Co-operative Union of Canada, Winnipeg November 26-28, 1945. (?Ottawa): Cooperative Union of Canada. 5pp, mimeo. *OOA/Good 13.

2939 Grube, G.M.A. The LeBel report and civil liberties. Toronto: Canadian Forum. 16pp. SRL *BVAUS/Mac41f. 14 OHMA1547 OOA/CCF320 and 537 OTURS/RSK. The LeBel report investigated charges by the Ontario CCF leader, E.B. Jolliffe, regarding 'anti-subversive' activities by the provincial police and the political use made of the results.

2940 Hanson, Frank G. CCF action! A weekly presentation of important measures implemented by the CCF government of Saskatchewan from the time it took office July 10, 1944 until the present. Regina: CCF. (1p), broadside. *SSA/G1.nd.2.

2941 Harvey, Hugh H. Co-operative community centres. Part I. Guide to probable development. Regina: Dept of Cooperation and Cooperative Development. 28pp. OTP *HI. Uncat. C350.

2942 Havelock, Eric. The party and the public: a report on the Ontario provincial election of June 4, 1945. Toronto: CCF. 5pp plus 6pp, appendix. *OOA/Underhill 44.

2943 Health Study Bureau. Review of Canada's health needs and health insurance proposals. Toronto. 42pp. AEU BVAU BVIP OH OTU QQL *OOP.

2944 Hull, J.T. Co-operatives and income tax. Brief presented to the Royal Commission on the Taxation of Cooperatives at Winnipeg, February 5th, 1945. Winnipeg: Manitoba Pool Elevators. 15pp. *SSUS/Coops.

2945 Irvine, William. Is socialism the answer? The intelligent man's guide to basic democracy. Winnipeg: Contemporary. 95pp. AEU NSHPL OKQ SRL *ACGL BVAUS/Mac43f.2 MWPA/CCF39 OHMA1723 OOA/CCF323 OTURS/RSK SSA/E501.4 SSUS/JL197. Cover has additional subtitle: The key to jobs for all-economic security and a more abundant life.

2946 Ivens, William. CCF will ensure greater liberty for all: politicians parade 'bogey man' of regimentation. Winnipeg: CCF. (c1945). 4pp. *BVAUS/Webster 9-3 OOA/CCF318.

2947 Jamieson, Laura E. Women dry those tears. Vancouver: CCF. 35pp. BVIP OTP SRL *BVAUS/Mac32f.2 MWPA/CCF39 OHMA1540 OOA/CCF198 and 540 SSA/G3.BC.16 SSUS/JL197.

2948 Johnson, D.L. and B.R. Richards. Official CCF policy is wrong. Vancouver: Labor-Progressive Party. (4pp). *BVAUS/WB31f.4. Statement made by CCF MLA's in the Manitoba legislature.

2949 Jolliffe, E.B. Ontario at the cross-roads! Toronto: CCF. 7pp. *OOA/CCF320 and 538.

2950 Kennedy, Douglas Ross. The Knights of Labor in Canada. MA thesis, University of Western Ontario. (v), 127pp, tables, biblio. Later published by the University in 1956. *OONL.

2951 Kerr, T. Ainslie. Canada's co-ops. Toronto: Ryerson. 58pp. *BVAUS/Mac39f.17 OHMA1628.

2952 King, Carlyle. A discussion guide to William Irvine's 'Is socialism the answer?'. Regina: (CCF). 8pp. *ACGL BVAUS/Mac43f.1 OHMA1543 OOA/CCF310 SSA/G1.

1947.4. SSUS/JL197.

2953 King, Carlyle. Education for dynamic democracy.
Toronto: CCF. (4pp). *BVAUS/Mac40f.1 MWPA/CCF39
OHMA2353 OOA/MacPhail 4 and CCF 310, 320 and 537.

2954 Labor-Progressive Party. A better Canada to fight
for, to work for, to vote for. Toronto. 31pp.
AEU BVAS *ACGL/PE Communist BVAUS/WB31f.3b MWPA/
Russell 1 OHMA1798 OKQS OOA/CCF542 OTURS/RSK
SSUS/Comm. Electoral program.

2955 ------ Forward BC to jobs - homes - security: defeat
the Tory-Liberal coalition by a coalition of progress:
a call to the citizens of BC from the third provincial convention of the LPP. Vancouver. 4pp, mimeo.
*BVAUS/WB31f.3d and Smith CP.

2956 ------ The labor code that Garson killed! Read the
story behind the Kardash bill. Winnipeg. 15pp.
*MWPA/CCF33.

2957 ------ The LPP and post-war Canada: excerpts from
speeches and reports at the LPP national conference
10-16 August 1945. Toronto. 104pp. AEU BVAS BVIP
OKQ *BVAUS/Mac31f.8 OHMA OTURS/RSK. Contains re-
port by Tim Buck and speeches in discussion by Sam
Carr, Leslie Morris, Fred Rose, Stanley B. Ryerson,
Stewart Smith, Gui Louis Caron, Henry Binder and
William Kashtan.

2958 ------ An open letter to Premier John Hart from the
LPP. Vancouver. 3pp, mimeo. *BVAUS/WB31f.3d.

2959 ------ Public demonstration! Fight for jobs. End
unemployment in Vancouver. Vancouver. (4pp). *T.

2960 ------ Summary of proceedings: second annual Ontario
convention, Toronto March 24-25, 1945. Toronto.
10pp, mimeo. *OTURS/RSK.

2961 ------ Toronto LPP convention, St Regis Hotel -
Sunday January 21st, 1945. Toronto. 12pp total,
separately paged sections. *OTURS/RSK.

2962 Laidler, H.W. (ed). Forty years of education: the
task ahead. New York: League for Industrial Democracy. 56pp. *OOA/CCF552. Contains: The CCF, the
League and Canadian progressives by Frank Scott.

2963 MacDonald, A.B. Credit unions in the Maritimes.
Halifax: Nova Scotia Credit Union League. 3pp, mimeo.
*OOA/CCF148.

2964 ------ Picking your pockets: how cartels cut Cana-
dian income. Toronto: CCF. 16pp. *AEUS/CCFXIII-8
OHMA1580 OOA/CCF320 OTURS/RSK SSA/G3.Ont.8 SSUS/
JL197.

2965 MacDonald, Donald. The Roman Catholics and the CCF.
Halifax: CCF. *OOA/CCF539.

2966 MacInnis, Angus. Peace demands fundamental social
changes: speech delivered in the House of Commons

Wednesday, September 12, 1945. Ottawa: E. Cloutier.
7pp. *BVAUS/Garrison 1-6 and Mac27f.43 MWPA/Ivens 6.

2967 McKean, Fergus. Statement on behalf of the LPP at
a meeting of the Vancouver Labor Council, June 26,
1945. Vancouver. (2pp), mimeo. *BVAUS/Smith CP.

2968 Manitoba Co-operative Associations. Brief submitted
on behalf of the major co-operative organizations in
the province of Manitoba by J.T. Hull. (Winnipeg):
Manitoba Pool Elevators and others. 21pp, mimeo.
*OOA/Good 14.

2969 Manitoba Pool Elevators. Brief to the Royal Commission on Co-operatives, April 1945. Verbatim report
of the submission and the examination of W.J. Parker,
President. Winnipeg. 95pp. *MWPA/CCF33.

2970 Milne, J. The meaning of social evolution. Winnipeg:
Socialist Party of Canada. 8pp. *AEUS/Spcoll.
BVAUS/Turner 1 OHMA OTURS/RSK.

(2971) Molnar, E.F. Can organized religion, organized labor,
agriculture and industry join their power toward win-
ning the peace? The new approach; preliminary comments on the new approach by Walter Marshall Horton.
Calgary: Religion and Labor Council. 54pp. SRU.

2972 Morris, Leslie. A letter to every Ontario LPP member. Toronto: Labor-Progressive Party. 4pp.
OTURS/RSK. On the revisionist line of Earl Browder.

2973 ------ Report to the second annual Ontario convention of the LPP, Toronto March 24,25 1945. Toronto:
LPP. 24pp, mimeo. *OTURS/RSK pp 1-18 only.

2974 ------ Time for action! Premier Drew must call the
Ontario legislature into special session at once!
Toronto: LPP. (4pp). *OTURS/RSK. To deal with un-
employment as war contracts are cancelled.

2975 ------ You are invited... Toronto: Labor-Progressive Party. 29pp. *BVAUS/WB31f.3a OHMA1833 OKQS
OOA/CCF542 OTURS/RSK SSUS/Spcoll.

2976 National Council for Canadian-Soviet Friendship.
Goebbels is not dead! Toronto. (24pp). *OTURS/
RSK. Also published under the title 'The book the
Nazis like', also *OTURS/RSK.

2977 ------ Soviet agriculture. Toronto. 32pp. BVIP
*BVAUS/Mac39f.1 OTURS/RSK.

2978 Norman, Howard. What about Japanese Canadians? Vancouver: Vancouver Consultative Council for Cooperation
in Wartime Problems of Canadian Citizenship. 31pp.
*BVAUS/Mac41f.8 OOA/CCJC 3.

2979 Okanagan Society for the Revival of Indian Arts and
Crafts. Native Canadians: a plan for the rehabilitation of Indians submitted to the Committee on Reconstruction and Re-establishment, Ottawa. Oliver
(BC). 20pp. *BVAUS/Mac41f.1

2980 Ontario. Community action for post-war jobs. Toronto: Kings Printer. 19pp, mimeo, illus. *OTU.

(2981)------ Report of the Board of Arbitration arranged
by the Honourable Charles Daly, Minister of Labour
to deal with certain disputes between Canada Packers
Ltd and Local 114, United Packinghouse Workers of
America. Toronto: Kings Printer. 11pp. Not seen.

2982 ------ Report of the Royal Commission appointed
May 28th, 1945, to investigate charges made by Mr
Edward B. Jolliffe, K.C. in a radio address on May
24th, 1945. Toronto: Kings Printer. 62pp. *OTL.
See also 2939 above and note thereto: the LeBel Comm-
ission.

2983 Ontario Cash Mutuals. Submission to the Royal Commission on Co-operatives. Toronto. 48pp plus 2 amended pages, mimeo. *OOA/Good 14.

2984 Ontario Co-operative Union. General brief on co-operative law and development in the province of Ontario
submitted to the Royal Commission to enquire into the
Taxation of Cooperatives. Toronto. 25pp, mimeo.
*OOA/Good 14.

2985 Ontario Credit Union League. Royal Commission to
enquire into Taxation of Co-operatives. (Toronto).
6pp, mimeo. *OOA/Good 14.

2986 Ontario Producer and Marketing Co-operatives. Brief
submitted to Royal Commission to inquire into Taxation of Co-operatives. (Toronto). 3pp, mimeo.
*OOA/Good 14.

2987 Ontario Urban Consumer Cooperatives. Brief to the
Royal Commission to inquire into Taxation of Co-operatives. (Toronto). 7pp, mimeo. *OOA/Good 14.

2988 Palmer, R.A. (comp). Monopolies. (Ottawa): Co-operative Union of Canada. 5pp, mimeo. *OOA/CCF148.

2989 Paynter, Joe. Know your facts then vote: the workingman's guide to Canadian facts, BC edition. Vancouver:
(?author). 78pp. BVIP OH OOL OTP QQL *BVAUS/Mac41f.2

2990 Peto, E.J. A co-operative farm plan. Winnipeg: np.
(8pp). *MWPA/Ivens 6 OOA/CCF318 SSUS/Coops.

2991 ------ The Peto co-operative farm plan for post-war
re-establishment. Winnipeg: Promotional Advisory
Board. 6pp, mimeo. *OOA/CCF148.

2992 Priestley, Norman F. Progress in co-operation. Calgary: United Farmers of Alberta. (c1945). 15pp.
*ACGA/UFA3.

2993 Prince Rupert Fishermen's Co-operative Association.
Submission to the Royal Commission on Taxation of
Co-operatives, Ottawa. Prince Rupert. 11pp, mimeo.
*OOA/Good 14.

2994 Queens University. Union security plans: maintenance
of membership and the check-off. Kingston: Industrial
Relations Centre. 59pp. *OKQ.

2995 Richards, B.R. and D.L. Johnson. Statement in the Manitoba legislature, March 1st 1945. (Winnipeg): (?authors). 2pp, mimeo. *OOA/CCF394. See 2948 above issued by the Labor-Progressive Party. The statement concerns unity of the left.

2996 Rose, Fred. Fred Rose in Parliament: he won respect for Cartier. Montreal: Fred Rose Election Committee. 46pp. *OTURS/RSK. Excerpts from speeches.

2997 Rural and Industrial Cooperatives of Eastern Nova Scotia. Efficient marketing in the Maritimes. (Halifax). (c1945). 8pp, mimeo. *OOA/CCF148.

2998 Ryerson, S.B. Le Canada français: sa tradition, son avenir. Montreal: Ed. la Victoire. 149pp. AEU BVAU OOP OOU QMBM QMBN QQL *OTURS/RSK. Started as a translation of 2602 above, but effectively a new book. 'D'abord, au lieu de faire traduire le texte anglais, ce qui aurait été vite fait, j'ai préféré le remanier d'un bout à l'autre et l'écrire à nouveau en bonne partie.'

2999aSt Francis Xavier University. The social significance of the co-operative movement. A brief for presentation to the Royal Commission on Taxation of Co-operatives. Antigonish. 32pp, mimeo. *OHMA2716 OOA/ Good 14.

2999b (the same). 28pp. *NSHP/HDC. 'The first in a series to be published later as a book: The co-operative movement in the Maritimes.'

3000 Saskatchewan. Saskatchewan plans for health. Regina: Dept of Public Health. 16pp. *OTARS/1945/26.

3001 ------ The seed grain dispute: the Saskatchewan viewpoint. Regina: Bureau of Publications. 24pp. *BVAUS/Mac39f.1 OHMA1573 Peel 3951.

3002 ------ Submission to the Royal Commission on Co-operatives. Regina: Dept of Co-operation and Co-operative Development. 16pp, mimeo. *OOA/Good 14.

3003 ------ Suggestions regarding co-operative action by women. Regina: Dept of Co-operation and Co-operative Development. 6pp. SSUS/Coops.

3004 Saskatchewan Co-operative Producers Ltd. Submission to Commission on Taxation of Co-operatives. Regina. 16pp, mimeo. *OOA/Good 14.

3005 Scott, F.R. Socialism in the Commonwealth. Toronto: Canadian Institute of International Affairs. (9pp). *OHMA1571 OOA/CCF309, 323 and 539 SSA/Gl.1945.4. Offprint from vol. 1.

3006 Shields, E.J. History of trade unionism in Nova Scotia. Unpublished MA thesis, Dalhousie University. (ii), ii, 119pp. *NSHD.

3007 Sioui, Jacques. War...peace in Canada. The invader responsible for the death of the patriot Louis Riel.

Innocence...and...silence. What success will crown the efforts of the patriot who implored the chiefs of our nation to rise and unite in assembly at Ottawa? (Loretteville, Que.): np. 26 plus 27pp, bilingual. *SSA/G282.3.

3008 Smith, Stewart. The battle of housing. Toronto: Labor-Progressive Party. (c1945). 8pp. *OHMA1910 OTURS/RSK.

3009 ------ Heroes need new clothes! Toronto: Labor-Progressive Party. (c1945). 8pp, illus. *BVAUS/Mac43Af.15 OHMA3124 OKQS OTURS/RSK. On the inadequacy of the clothing grant given to discharged veterans.

3010 Socialist Labor Party of Canada. Twentieth century democracy. Toronto. (c1945). (4pp). *BVAUS/Mac 31Af.18.

3011 Stewart, Alistair. Speech on the address in reply to the speech from the throne delivered in the House of Commons on Thursday September 13, 1945. Ottawa: E. Cloutier. 4pp. *MWPA/Ivens 6.

3012 Surrey Co-operative Association. Submission to the Royal Commission on Co-operatives and Taxation. Cloverdale (BC). 11pp, mimeo. *OOA/Good 14.

3013 Trades and Labor Congress of Canada. Memorandum presented to the Dominion government Monday April 23rd 1945. Ottawa. 16pp. *SSUS/Labour.

3014 Ukrainian Canadian Association. The truth about the Ukrainian 'refugees' in Germany. Toronto. 24pp. OH OOP *BVAUS/Mac38f.18M OTURS/RSK. Largely an address by D.Z. Manuilsky at the conference of teachers of the western Ukraine, Lwow, 6 January 1945.

3015 UE. Welcome home. Toronto. 23pp. *OTURS/RSK.

3016 United Farmers of Canada and the Alberta Farmers Union. Farmers action program. Edmonton. (c1945). 16pp. *SSA/G37.31.

3017 United Farmers Co-operative Co. Ltd. Brief presented to Royal Commission on Taxation of Co-operatives. (Toronto). 5pp, mimeo. *OOA/Good 14.

3018 United Grain Growers. Presentation to the Royal Commission on Co-operatives. (?Winnipeg). 41pp, mimeo. *ACGL.

3019 United Mine Workers of America. Submission to the Royal Commission on Coal. Sydney. 71pp plus 2pp summary, mimeo. *OTURS/RSK.

3020 University of Ottawa Social Centre. Cooperatives and taxation: a brief to the Royal Commission on Cooperatives. Ottawa. 41pp, mimeo. *OOA/Good 14.

3021 Wilson, Idele L. Citizen trade unionist. Toronto: Workers Educational Assn. 19pp. BVIP OH OOL OTP *OTURS/RSK.

3022 Wilson, Idele. A gateway to the future: the St Lawrence seaway and power development, a plan to increase employment, industrial expansion, foreign trade.
Toronto: United Electrical, Radio and Machine Workers
of America, district 5. 14pp. *BVAUS/Mac42f.10.

3023 Woodcock, George. Anarchism and morality. London:
Freedom. 16pp. AEU BVAU *own copy.

3024 ------ What is anarchism? London: Freedom. 13pp.
BVAU *own copy.

3025 Workers Educational Association. Paying the shot
for what? Toronto. (6pp). *OHMA.

3026 Wright, Jim. It sure works! Saskatoon: United
Farmers of Canada. 20pp. *SSA/G37.43. What works
is co-operative farming.

3027 (Zuken, Joseph). Joseph Zuken - citizen. Winnipeg:
Labor-Progressive Party. 16pp. *OTCPA.

1946

3028 Aboriginal Natives of the Fraser Valley and Interior
Tribes of British Columbia. Submission (to the)
special joint committee of the Senate and the House
of Commons to consider revision of the Indian act...
to substantiate documents now lodged in Parliament
by recognized incorporated native organizations.
np. 6pp, mimeo. *BVAUS/Mac41f.1.

3029 Alberta Farmers Union. The Alberta Farmers Union
vs. The Canadian Pacific Railway and the Railway
Association of Canada. Edmonton. (4pp). *BVAUS/
Young.

3030 ------ Calling all farmers! Let's face the facts.
Edmonton. (1p), broadside. *ACGL/PDg/AFU.

3031 ------ Instructions and guidelines on organizing
strike action for parity prices. Edmonton. 8pp.
*ACGA/Nesbitt ACGL/PDg/AFU.

3032 ------ and United Farmers of Canada. Farmers action
program. Edmonton. 16pp. *SSUS/UFC Peel 4093.

3033 ------ Strike action brief presented to the Dominion
cabinet in August 1946. (Edmonton). (2pp), mimeo.
*OOA/CCF74.

3034 ------ What we have gained from our non-delivery
strike staged September 6th to October 6th, 1946.
Edmonton. 7pp. *OTURS/RSK.

3035 Alberta Federation of Labor. Proposed constitution.
Calgary. 15pp. *AEPAA/Farmilo 4.

3036 Black, Norman F. and W.H.H. Norman. Save Canadian
children and Canadian honour. Vancouver: Vancouver

Consultative Council for the Study of Problems of
Citizenship. (4pp). *BVAUS/Smith/Japanese OOA/
CCJC 3.

3037 Buck, Tim. Canada on the threshold of a new era.
Toronto: Labor-Progressive Party. 14pp. AEU BVIP
BVIV *BVAUS/WB31f.3c OHMA2405 OKQS OTURS/RSK SSUS.

3038 ------ For peace, progress, socialism. (Toronto):
(Labor-Progressive Party). 104pp. BVIP OOP QMM
*BVAUS/WB31f.3b OHMA3132 OOA/CCF546 OTURS/RSK
SSUS. Contains main report and summary of discus-
sions by Buck, plus the main resolutions, 2nd nation-
al convention LPP.

3039 ------ Palestine, what is the solution? Toronto:
Labor-Progressive Party. 16pp. AEU BVIP *BVAUS/
Mac41f.7c OHMA2416 OTURS/RSK SSUS.

3040 ------ Twenty-five years of Communist activity in
Canada: text of a lecture. (Toronto): Labor-Progressive Party. 14pp, mimeo. *OTURS/RSK.

3041 ------ Wages and inflation: a reply to Donald Gordon.
Toronto: Labor-Progressive Party. 29pp. BVIP BVIV
SRL *BVAUS/WB31f.3d OHMA2141 OKQS OTURS/RSK SSUS.
Donald Gordon, chairman of the Wartime Prices and
Trade Board, had warned that increasing wages was a
direct cause of inflation.

3042 ------ What's behind the spy hysteria? The answer.
Vancouver: Labor-Progressive Party. (4pp). *BVAUS/
WB31f.3c OTURS/RSK.

3043 Buhay, Beckie. Canada must launch crusade for peace:
King-Tory plot imperils nation! Study outline on
political report 2nd national convention LPP. Toronto: Labor-Progressive Party. 5pp, mimeo. *OTURS/RSK.
The political report was given by Tim Buck; see 3038
above.

3044 Campbell, Alfred C. The double squeeze: how farmer
and worker are robbed by monopoly. Toronto: Labor-
Progressive Party. (c1946). 8pp. *OHMA/3149 OTURS/
RSK.

3045 ------ (comp.) LPP national housing campaign: club
discussion notes for speakers and educational directors. (Toronto): Labor-Progressive Party. (c1946).
12pp, mimeo. *OTURS/RSK.

3046 Canada. Report of the Royal Commission appointed to
investigate the facts relating to and the circumstances surrounding the communication by public officials
and other persons in positions of trust of secret and
confidential information to agents of a foreign power.
Ottawa: Edmond Cloutier. 733pp. *OTURS/RSK.

3047 Canadian Association for Adult Education. Is there
freedom of the press in Canada? Toronto. (5pp).
*OTURS/RSK.

3048 ------ Probing our prejudices. Toronto. (6pp).
*OHMA3127.

3049 Canadian Association for Adult Education. What is the social responsibility of labour? Toronto. (6pp) *BVAUS/Mac32f.1.

3050 Canadian Brotherhood of Railway Engineers. Report on activities of the secretariat submitted at the fiftieth anniversary convention of the International Transportworkers Federation, Zurich, Switzerland, May 6 to 12, 1946. Ottawa. 116pp. *SSUS/Labour. Cover title: International Transportworkers Federation: a report.

3051 Canadian Federation of Agriculture. The President's address, London, Ont. Ottawa. 16pp. *OTURS/RSK.

3052 Canadian Welfare Council. Dominion-Provincial relations and social security. Ottawa. 27pp. *NSHD/J4.

3053 Carter, Dyson. Atomic dollars. Winnipeg: Frontier. 66pp. BVIP *BVAUS/WB39f.1f.

3054 ------ A scientist takes his place:...explains why he joined the LPP. Toronto: Labor-Progressive Party. 15pp. AEU BVIP *BVAUS/WB42f.29b(ii) OHMA3147 OTURS/RSK.

3055 Coldwell, M.J. and others. Calling Canadians forward. Speeches by CCF members delivered in the House of Commons March 1946. Ottawa: E. Cloutier. 32pp. *BVAUS/Mac27f.43 MWPA/Ivens 6 OOA/CCF536. Others are Stanley Knowles, J.W. Burton, A.M. Nicholson, Angus MacInnis, E.B. McKay, Clarence Gillis.

3056 ------ Statement on foreign policy. Issued at the close of the meeting of the CCF national council. (Ottawa): CCF. (1p), with added statement on domestic policy, 3pp, mimeo. *OOA/Coldwell 69.

3057 Contemporary Publishers. Vital reading. Winnipeg. 24pp. *OOA/CCF554 OTURS/RSK. Includes: Free enterprise exposed by William Irvine: Psychology of the Russians by Raymond Arthur Davies: Marshal Tito today by Howard Fast and Must we have revolution by Sidney and Beatrice Webb.

3058 Cooperative Committee on Japanese Canadians. From citizens - to refugees. It's happening here! Toronto. (4pp). *OOA/CCJC 3.

3059 ------ Memorandum for the members of the House of Commons and Senate of Canada on orders in council PC 7355, 7356, 7357 for the deportation of Canadians of Japanese racial origin. Toronto. 6pp. *OOA/CCJC 3.

3060 ------ Our Japanese Canadians: citizens not exiles. Toronto. (4pp). *OOA/CCJC 3 and CCF310 and 538.

3061 CCF. An announcement: CCF correspondence course. First term January-April 1947. Ottawa. 3pp, mimeo. *OOA/CCF306 and 536.

3062 ------ CCF in Parliament: 1946 session. Ottawa. 4pp. OTU *OHMA1530 OOA/CCF114 and 536.

3063 CCF. The CCF indictment of liberalism. Vancouver.
(4pp). *BVAUS/Mac30Af.14.

3064 ------ The CCF says houses now! Ottawa. (4pp).
*OKQS.

3065 ------ Answers to the 'Fallacy of socialism'. Toronto. (c1946). 4pp, mimeo. *OOA/CCF56. The 'Fallacy of socialism' was a leaflet distributed by the
Ontario Progressive Conservative Assn.

3066 ------ A battle brewing! - The Saskatchewan CCF government gave you the Farm Security Act - the action
of the Liberal federal government threatens to take
it away. Regina. (4pp). *SSA/G1.1946.1.

3067 ------ CCF members - protect your democracy. Calgary. (c1946). (2pp) broadside. *OOA/CCF316. On
the division in the CCF between J.E. Cook and others.

3068 ------ The farmer and the CCF: CCF farm policy planned by practical farmers. Toronto. (4pp). *ACGL/
PDbl OOA/CCF57, 70, 126, 319, 321 and 537 SSUS/CCF.

3069 ------ Farmer meets worker. Toronto. (18pp), mimeo.
*OOA/CCF56 and 537. Report of a Farmer-Labour Conf-
erence.

3070 ------ Members handbook for Saskatchewan. Regina.
64pp. *SSA/G1.4. Also issued in 1947, 64pp *SSA/
G1.4 and 1948, 1949, ea. 64pp *SSA/G1.6 and 1957,
1958, 1959, 1960 ea. 11pp, *SSA/G1.6. and 1952 *OOA/
Coldwell 59.

3071 ------ Memorandum on international socialist co-operation submitted to the International Conference of
Socialist Parties, November 8-10, 1946. Ottawa. 2pp,
mimeo. *OOA/CCF184.

3072 ------ New rules needed - make your protest heard!
Regina. (4pp). *SSA/G1.1946.2. Relates to the Dominion-provincial conference.

3073 ------ Report of CCF literature conference, Woodsworth House, Toronto March 17th, 1946. (Toronto).
8pp, mimeo. *OOA/CCF57 and 320. The second such
annual conference.

3074 ------ Social credit and CCF. Federal election
issues. Ottawa. 6pp, mimeo. *OOA/CCF323 SSA/G.
Ind. 29.

3075 ------ Study outline for Planning for Freedom.
Ottawa. 33pp, mimeo. *MWPA/CCF39 OOA/CCF188, 323
and 538 SSUS/JL197.

3076 ------ Why should I be interested in politics? Toronto. (4pp). *OOA/CCF320 and 540.

3077 Cooperative Commonwealth University Students. Minutes
of conference of university students interested in
furthering work of the CCF held in Ottawa, March 16
and 17, 1946. 14pp, mimeo, separately paged sections.
*OOA/CCF338.

3078 Cooperative Commonwealth University Students. Minutes CCUF convention held in Toronto December 29, 30, 31, 1946. Ottawa. 11pp, mimeo. *OOA/CCF338.

3079 Cooperative Commonwealth Youth Movement. CCYM convention report October 12, 13 1946 in Woodsworth House. (Toronto). (20pp), mimeo. *OOA/CCF350.

3080 ------ Minutes of the eighth CCYM national convention, Regina August 5 and 6, 1946. Regina. 35pp, mimeo. *OOA/CCF345.

3081 ------ CCYM members handbook for Saskatchewan. Regina. 20pp. *OOA/CCF345 SSA/G.19.2.

3082 ------ National constitution. (Ottawa). 2pp, mimeo. Revised in 1948, 1950, 1952, 1954. *OOA/CCF345.

3083 Cooperative Union of Canada. The CUC: building the future now. Ottawa. 20pp. *OOA/CCF546 SSUS/Coop.

3084 ------ Submission re Income Tax War act. Ottawa. 4pp, mimeo. *OOA/Good 13. Follows the recommendations of the Royal Commission on Co-operatives.

3085 Crate, Charles. Report on conditions in the North West Territories with particular consideration of the Yellowknife area. (Ottawa): (CCF). 10pp, mimeo. separately paged. *OOA/CCF87. Contains: CCF action in Parliament (suggestions) and Political factors and suggestions for CCF organization in Mackenzie district. Considerable controversy attached to Crate who was said to have been leader of the Canadian Union of Fascists and editor of *The Thunderbolt* before the war (when he was very young), but who had apparently had a change of heart.

3086 Davies, Raymond Arthur. Odyssey through hell. New York: L.B. Fischer. 236pp. AEU OH *OKQ.

3087 Després, Jean-Pierre. Le mouvement ouvrier canadien. Montréal: Fides. (c1946). 205pp, biblio. *OONL. Publié sous les aupices du Département des relations industrielles de la Faculté des sciences sociales de Laval.

3088 Dillon, E. Macaulay. Current trends in Canadian labour relations. Toronto: np. 15pp. *SSUS/Labour.

3089 Dymond, William R. The movement for labour-management co-operation in industry. Unpublished MA thesis, University of Toronto. (i), vi, 318pp, appendixes of model constitutions etc, biblio. *OTUAR.

3090 Foster, William Z. Elements of a people's cultural policy. Toronto: (Labor-Porgressive Party). 11pp. *OHMA3150.

3091 Fowke, Edith. The CCF approach to women's problems. A radio play. (Ottawa): CCF. 9pp, mimeo. *SSUS/ CCF.

3092 ------ Japanese Canadians. Toronto: Cooperative Committee on Japanese Canadians. 8pp. *OHMA1550 OOA/CCJC 3.

3093 Freeman, George E. Wage bargaining in the newspaper industry. Unpublished MA thesis, University of Toronto. 82pp, appendix, no bilio. *OTUAR.

3094 Good, W.C. Industrial conflict: a study of some fundamentals and of some remedies. Toronto: Ryerson. vi, 51pp. BVIP MWP OH OOL OOP STP SRL SSU *OONL.

3095 Grimshaw, Josephine. Problems and policies of labour and management in the automobile industry in relation to prices, competitive conditions and industrial structure. Unpublished MA thesis, University of Toronto. xvii, 327pp, tables. *OTUAR.

3096 Guillet, Edwin C. Free education to the limit of ability. Section B: adult education. Brief presented to The Royal Commission on Education. (Toronto): approved for presentation by Council of Toronto district (7) of the Ontario Secondary School Teachers Federation. 51pp, mimeo. *OOA/CCF114.

3097 ------ Life insurance without exploitation. The state can provide it at half the cost. Toronto. 136pp. *BVAUS/Mac41f.7.

(3098) Hannam, H.H. Canadian farmers and the future. Ottawa: CBC. 2pp, mimeo. OOAG.

3099 Hanson, Frank G. March of freedom: how mankind's struggles with economic forces have produced the CCF. Regina: Service. 90pp, illus. OOP OPAL OTU SRL SRU *BVAUS/Mac30f.4 MWPA/CCF39 OHMA1545 OOA/CCF114, 310 and 323 SRA/CCF Sask.13 SSUS/JL197.

3100 Hunt, Leslie. Well, vet, what now. Toronto: (Labor-Progressive Party). 13pp. *BVAUS/WB31f.3b OTURS/RSK. Dealing with unemployment and returned veterans.

3101 International Woodworkers of America (110) district 1. Final negotiations bulletin, 7 May 1946. Vancouver. (4pp). *T

3102 Ivens, William. Is CCF socialism a threat to freedom? Winnipeg: (CCF). (4pp). *OOA/CCF310.

3103 Jolliffe, E.B. Address to 13th annual convention, December 10, 1946, Hamilton. Toronto: CCF. (4pp). *OOA/CCF49.

3104 King, Carlyle. Study outline based upon 'Make this your Canada'....an indispensable aid for CCF discussion groups. (Ottawa): CCF. 15pp, mimeo. *OOA/CCF 310.

3105 Knight, Roy R. Speech on education during the budget debate delivered in the House of Commons on Tuesday July 9, 1946. Ottawa: E. Cloutier. 7pp. *SSA/G2. 1946.2.

3106 Knowles, Stanley. Canada and the UNO: Britain shows the way: friendship with the Soviet Union. A speech on the address in reply to the speech from the throne delivered in the House of Commons 19 March 1946.

Ottawa: E. Cloutier. 8pp. *BVAUS/Mac27f.43 OOA/ CCF308.

3107 Labor-Progressive Party. Act now! Defeat the plans of the railway monopolists to rob the west. Winnipeg. (4pp). *SSA/G27.1947.1.

3108 ------ A call to action! Issued by Western Farm Conference, Regina August 11, 1946. Regina. (4pp). *SSA/G27.1946.2.

3109 ------ Constitution. Toronto. 24pp. *OKQS OTURS/ RSK.

3110 ------ LPP national housing campaign: club discussion notes for speeches and educational directors. Toronto. 12pp, mimeo. *OTURS/RSK.

3111 ------ Let's get back to sanity. An appeal to the people of Canada. Toronto. (4pp). *AEPAA/Inf.file Alta.Pol II BVAUS/WB31f.3c.

3112 ------ Milk: what you must make Drew do! Toronto. 8pp. *OTURS/RSK. Ten cent milk and free milk for school children.

3113 ------ Preliminary draft of a statement of aims and principles: 2nd national convention, LPP, June 1946. (Toronto). 20pp, mimeo. *OTURS/RSK.

3114 ------ The report of proceedings 4th annual provincial convention, BC-Yukon LPP, Vancouver, November 15-18, 1946. 71pp, mimeo. *T.

3115 ------ Second national convention -- organizational statements. (Toronto). (14pp), mimeo. *OTURS/RSK.

3116 ------ The trade unions in the struggle for peace and a higher standard of life: 2nd national convention June 1-5, 1946. (Toronto). 11pp, mimeo. *OTURS/RSK.

3117 ------ Week-end course: Canada - the fight for peace and security. Toronto. 19pp, mimeo, separately paged. *OHMA.

3118 Laidlaw, Alexander. The Antigonish movement in wartime. Philadelphia: American Institute of Cooperation. pp359-365. *NSHP/HDC. Reprinted from 'American Cooperation 1942-1945'.

3119 Laidler, H.W. (ed). A program for labor and progressives. New York: League for Industrial Democracy. 48pp. OOL *OOA/CCF552 SSUS/JL197. Contains: The United States and Canada in the atomic age by M.J. Coldwell; Changing the social order in Saskatchewan by Gladys Strum and a short contribution by David Lewis.

3120 Lang, Bert W. Strikes cause loss of pay and jobs through dictatorship via communist-socialist revolution? The remedies are 1. Sound-equitable labor laws: 2. Speedy-impartial settlement of disputes. Toronto. 19pp. *BVIP. As confused as the title suggests; perhaps intended to be anti-labour.

(3121)Lavoie, Gilles. Les pratiques déloyales dans les conflits ouvriers: Etats-Unis, Canada, Québec. Unpublished MA thesis, Laval University. 81,(5)pp, biblio.

3122 McCuaig, D.J. Speech on agricultural economy delivered in the House of Commons, Thursday May 9, 1946. Ottawa: E. Cloutier. 7pp. *SSA/G2.1946.1.

3123 Macdonald, Alex. Canada and the cartels. (Ottawa): (CCF). 6pp, mimeo. *AEUS/CCFXIII-49 OOA/CCF145.

3124 MacInnis, Angus. Citizenship for all Canadians. A speech delivered in the House of Commons on May 13 and 14, 1946. Ottawa: E. Cloutier. 7pp. *BAUS/Mac27f.43 MWPA/Ivens 6.

3125 ------ Expand production, raise wages - avoid depression. Speeches in the House of Commons on the address in reply to the speech from the throne, March 22, 1946 and on the debate on the loan to Britain, April 15, 1946. Ottawa: E. Cloutier. 8pp. *MWPA/Ivens 6.

3126 ------ Speech on old age pensions: lower age - increased amount - no means test, delivered in the House of Commons on Wednesday April 10, 1946. Ottawa: E. Cloutier. 4pp. *BVAUS/Garrison 1-5 MWPA/Ivens 6.

3127 MacInnis, Grace. It's up to you! How you can be an active citizen through the CCF. Ottawa: CCF. 15pp. BVIP *ACGL/PDbl BVAUS/Mac30Af.4b OHMA1579 OOA/CCF 300, 310 and 537 SSA/G2.1933.2 SSUS/JL197.

3128 McKean, Fergus. Communism versus opportunism: an examination of the revision of Marxism and the communist movement of Canada. Vancouver: Communist Party of Canada. 291pp. AEU BVAU BVIP MWU NSHPL OHM SSU *OKQS OTURS/RSK. Former provincial leader of the LPP (in BC), resigning in August 1945.

3129 Mackintosh, Margaret. The Canadian labour movement: an historical analysis. Ottawa: Canadian Welfare. 11pp. BVIP NSHPL OOAG OOL QMU QQL SRL *OOL OTURS/RSK.

3130 McLean, Lachlan. The CCF: an analysis of 1. Political trends. 2. Organization - as they affect the public relations of the party. Vancouver: (?CCF). 45pp. *OOA/CCF86.

3131 MacLeod, A.A. Palestine and you! Toronto: (Labor-Progressive Party). (c1946). (4pp), bilingual English and Yiddish. *OHMA.

3132 Madge, Helen L. The single tax in Canada. Unpublished BA thesis, McMaster University. (iii), 71pp, biblio. *OHMA.

3133 Morris, Leslie. The big Ford strike. Toronto: Labor-Progressive Party. 8pp. OKQ *BVAUS/WB34f.16 OHMA 1851 OTURS/RSK. The strike was Sept-Dec 1945.

3134 Morris, Leslie. The people vs. Premier Drew: an argument for a coalition government. Toronto: Labor-
Progressive Party. (c1946). 8pp. *OKQS OTURS/RSK.

3135 Mosher, A.R. Labour strikes a blow for tolerance.
Toronto: Canadian Congress of Labour. (3pp).
*OTURS/RSK. Regarding religious and racial discrim-
ination.

3136 National Federation of Labour Youth. Submission to
the Dominion government of Canada April 15th, 16th
and 17th, 1946. Toronto. 20pp, mimeo. *OTURS/RSK.
Seven sections including Employment, wages and working conditions; veteran's rehabilitation; health,
recreation and physical fitness; education and training; civil liberties etc.

3137 Native Brotherhood of British Columbia. Submission
to the provincial government. Vancouver. (c1946).
4pp, mimeo. *BVAUS/Mac41f.1. On education, health
and welfare and citizenship.

3138 Ontario Co-operative Union. General brief presented
to the chairman and members of the Royal Commission
on Education in the province of Ontario. Toronto.
6pp, mimeo. *OOA/Good 13.

3139 Ontario Woodsworth Memorial Foundation. Toward the
future: shaping an idea at Woodsworth House. Toronto.
16pp, illus. BVIP OTURS *AEUS/CCFXIII-30 OHMA2879.

3140 Peel, Bruce Braden. R.M. 45. The social history of
a rural municipality. Unpublished MA thesis, University of Saskatchewan. (xi), 407 (408-427)pp, biblio
with separate album of photographs. *SSUS.

3141 Purcell, Gillis. Wartime press censorship in Canada.
Unpublished MA thesis, University of Toronto. (iv),
156pp; appendixes of official censorship regulations,
directives etc as separate volumes. *OTUAR. World
War II only, no biblio.

3142 Queens University. A selected bibliography on industrial relations. Kingston: Industrial Relations
Centre. 77pp. *OKQ.

3143 Roebuck, Arthur W. Civil liberties: an address at
Convention hall, Chateau Laurier, Wednesday May 15,
1946. Ottawa: Civil Liberties Assn. 7pp, mimeo.
*OOA/CCF147.

3144 (Rose, Fred). You are on the jury in the Fred Rose
case...(Montreal): Fred Rose Defence Committee.
2pp. *OTURS/RSK. Includes statement by Rose.

3145 Rush, Maurice. V-day in the woods: the significance
to labour of the woodworkers strike victory. Vancouver: (Labor-Progressive Party). (11pp). *BVAUS/
WB31f.3b OTURS/RSK. Woodworkers strike May 1946.

3146 Ryerson, S.B. Notes on how to study for students
group leaders, instructors. Toronto: Labor-Progressive Party. (12pp), mimeo. *OHMA OTURS/Salsberg 24

3147 Ryerson, Stanley B. A world to win: an introduction
to the science of socialism. Toronto: Progress.
94pp. BVAU BVIP NFSM OKQ OOL OTP SRU SSU *OHMA2130
OKQS OTURS/RSK. Revised edn. issued 1950, 137pp.
*OOA/CCF542.

3148 St Francis Xavier University. For study and action.
Series of 32 broadcasts under this general title,
starting 5 October 1945 weekly until 31 May 1946.
Antigonish. each 6pp. *NSHP. The broadcasts cover
co-operation, unions, socialization etc etc. The
NSHP set is incomplete.

3149 Salsberg, J.B. The battle is on - for jobs and security. Toronto: Labor-Progressive Party. 29pp.
BVIP *BVAUS/WB31f.3d MWPA/CCF39 OHMA1903 OTURS/RSK.

3150 ------ Labor's fight for a better Canada: problems
on the eve of the 1946 conventions of Canada's labour
union congresses. Toronto: Labor-Progressive Party.
8pp. *BVAUS/WB31f.3c OHMA1902 OTURS/RSK.

3151 Saskatchewan Commonwealth. An adventure in journal-
ism. Regina. (6pp). *OOA/CCF321. Archive copy
wrongly dated 1943.

3152 Saskatoon Trades and Labour Council. Annual: 38th
Labor day celebration. Saskatoon. 48pp. *SSA/G101.1
Also 39th, 1947. 48pp, *SSA/G101.1.

3153 Shipley, Erwin Thompson. Unemployment in Canada,
Great Britain and the United States. Unpublished
MA thesis, Acadia University. (iii), 149pp, biblio.
*NSWA.

3154 Shipyard General Workers Federation. Constitution:
amended at 3rd annual convention, Victoria October
19-20, 1946. Victoria. 40pp. *BVIPA.

3155 Sims, Charles. Greetings, northern neighbour! Toronto: Labor-Progressive Party. (4pp). *OTURS/RSK.
The northern neighbour is the USSR.

3156 Slavic Youth Council. Forward for our future! Reports of the World Youth Conference. Toronto. 51pp.
*OTURS/RSK. Speeches of the Slavic delegates, res-
olutions and constitution of the conference.

3157 Smith, Stewart. The red bogey. Toronto: Labor-Progressive Party. 32pp. *BVAUS/WB31f.3d OHMA2127
OKQS OOA/CCF542. An attack on hysterical anti-
communism.

3158 Somerville, Henry. A course of social science: first
year. Toronto: Canadian Register. 76pp. *OTURS/RSK.
First published 1936 - not found.

3159 ------ Employers and workers: studies in industrial
relations and vocational organization. Toronto: Canadian Register. 110pp. OOL QQLA *OTURS/RSK. 'Seeks
a regulation of economic life by a system of vocational organizations or guilds.'

3160 ------ Public planning and free enterprise: studies

in social reconstruction. Toronto: Canadian Register. (c1946). 100pp. *OTURS/RSK. Discusses CCF program, co-operation etc.

3161 Somerville, Henry. Social studies for Canadians. Toronto: Catholic Register. (iii), 84pp. *OTURS/ RSK. A continuation of 3158 above.

3162 Stewart, Alistair. Citizenship - a bill of rights - the meaning of democracy: a speech delivered in the House of Commons on Tuesday, April 9, 1946. Ottawa: E. Cloutier. 7pp. *MWPA/Ivens 6.

3163 Tanner, Pattie. Minority groups vs. Canadian public. A mock trial. Toronto: UN Society in Canada. 24pp, mimeo. *OOA/CCJC 3.

3164 Toronto District Labor Council. Reply to the Hon. Humphrey Mitchell, Minister of Labor, Ottawa. (An open letter) re price control monthly bulletins. Toronto. (4pp). *OTPB/Buckley.

3165 Trades and Labor Congress of Canada. Memorandum presented to the Dominion government, Tuesday 4th April, 1946. Ottawa. 9pp. *OOL.

3166 Turgeon, Gray. The lesson of the Nuernberg trials. Vancouver. 10pp. *OOA/CCF316. The lesson is in setting the state above the individual.

3167 Union of Saskatchewan Indians. Special joint committee of the Senate and the House of Commons appointed to examine the Indian act: submission. (?Regina). 66pp, mimeo. *BVAUS/Mac41f.1. Status of chiefs and councillors, education, welfare: recommendations.

3168 United Farmers of Alberta. Strike news letter by central strike committee. Edmonton. (2pp), mimeo. *SSA/G290.6.

3169 Vancouver Consultative Council. Orders in council threaten your citizenship! Vancouver. (4pp). *OOA/CCJC 3 OTURS/RSK. On the deportation of Japanese Canadians.

3170 Waisglass, Harry Jacob. Teamwork in action: the story of the joint consultation at the Howard Smith Paper Mills, Cornwall, Ontario. Toronto: Workers Educational Assn. 24pp. *OOL.

3171 Western Canada Federation. Western Canada federation: federation of the western provinces: freedom from domination by Ottawa: free trade with the United States: frontiers extended to the Arctic: full utilization of the port of Churchill. Saddle up! The west is going places! Even the North Pole is our territory. Saskatoon. (c1946). 16pp. *SSA/G149.1. Peel 3485.

3172 Winnipeg and District Trades and Labor Council. Labor day annual, 1946. Winnipeg. 36pp. *MWPA/ Russell 1.

3173 Wismer, Leslie E. Go left young man. Toronto: Bell-man. 127pp. BVAU OH OOL OOP OTU SRL *OOA/CCF537 SSUS/Comm.

3174 Woodcock, George. William Godwin: a biographical study. London: Porcupine. x, 266pp, biblo. *own copy.

1947

3175 Alberta Farmers Union. AFU freight rate brief. Pre-sented in protest to the application by the railway companies for a 30% increase in the tolls and rates. Edmonton. 4pp. *ACGL/PDg AFU.

3176 ------ Federal government resolution passed at the convention December 1st to 5th, 1947. (Edmonton). 9pp, mimeo. *OOA/CCF74.

3177 ------ Constitution. Calgary. 16pp. *AEPAA/Farm-ilo 4.

3178 American Council on Education. A study of national history textbooks used in the schools of Canada and the United States. Washington. 81pp. *L. Detailed tables of Canadian content in US history textbooks and vice versa.

3179 Bishop, Gordon H. A brief history of trade unions in Gananoque, Ontario. Kingston: United Steelworkers of America (c1947). 4pp, mimeo. *OOL.

3180 Boite, K.L.J. Industrial relations in the Maritime provinces. Unpublished MA thesis, Dalhousie Univer-sity. (iii), ii, 54 (58)pp. *NSHD.

3181 Buck, Tim. Canada's path to peace and security. Toronto: Labor-Progressive Party. 33pp. AEU BVIP OPET OTP *BVAUS/WB31f.3d OHMA2422 OKQS OTURS/RSK.

3182 ------ Europe's rebirth: an eyewitness account. Toronto: Progress. 97pp. AEU BVAS BVAU OLU QQLA SSU *OHMA3120 OKQS OTURS/RSK.

3183 ------ Where are we heading to? Let's get back to sanity! An appeal to the people of Canada. Toronto: Labor-Progressive Party. (4pp). *OHMA.

3184 Buhay, B. Imperialism: the final stage of capitalism. (Outline). Toronto: Labor-Progressive Party. (c1947). 9pp, mimeo. OHMA OTURS/Salsberg T10-24.

3185 Burton, J.W. and others. The farmers fight...for a Dominion marketing bill. CCF members speak: delivered in the House of Commons, Friday, March 14 and Monday March 17, 1947. Ottawa: E. Cloutier. 12pp. *BVAUS/ Mac27f.43 OOA/CCF299 SRA/CCF Nat.70. Others are P.E. Wright, A.M. Nicholson, T.J. Bentley, William Bryce, F.S. Zaplitny.

3186 Canada, Dept of Agriculture. A directory of co-operative business organizations in the province of
Ontario. Ottawa. 43pp, mimeo. *OOA/Good 13. Issued
jointly with the Ontario Department of Agriculture.

3187 Canada, Dept of Labour. Report on the re-establish-
ment of Japanese in Canada, 1944-1946. Ottawa: E.
Cloutier. 30pp, appendix of statistics. *OOA/CCJC 3
OOAL.

3188 Canadian Congress of Labour. A report on economic
conditions in Canada. Ottawa. 12pp. *SSA/G160.17.

3189 Canadian Seamans Union. The seamen's answer to J.A.
Sullivan. Montreal. 14pp. *OTURS/RSK. On Sullivan's expulsion from the presidency of the union.

3190 Carroll, W.F. In the matter of the appointment of
an Industrial Dispute Inquiry Commission between the
Dominion Coal Co (and others) of Nova Scotia and their
employees as represented by the United Mine Workers
of America, district 26. Halifax. 5pp, mimeo.
*OOA/CCF147. Justice Carroll was the commissioner.

3191 Chambers, Edward J.S. Should the earnings of co-operative associations be made subject to federal income tax? Unpublished MA thesis, University of British Columbia. vii, 148pp, biblio. *BVAUS.

(3192) Chapman, H.E. and S.E. Medland. Progress of cooperative farming in Saskatchewan. Regina: Dept of Cooperation and Co-operative Development. 15pp. Peel
4029, not seen.

3193 Clarke, Nelson. We fight for socialism: keynote
speech at third annual convention Saskatchewan Labor-
Progressive Party, Saskatoon November 2, 1946.
Saskatoon. 15pp. *OTURS/RSK.

3194 Coldwell, M.J. and others. Rescue refugees as free
Canadians. CCF members speak: delivered in the House
of Commons Monday, May 5 and Monday June 2, 1947.
Ottawa: E.Cloutier. 15pp. *BVAUS/Garrison 1-5 and
Mac27f.43 MWPA/Ivens 6 OOA/CCF299 SSUS/JL 197.
Others are Clarie Gillis, J.W. Burton, Angus MacInnis,
F.S. Zaplitny, Gladys Strum.

3195 ------ Speech on the peace treaties. Ottawa: E.
Cloutier. 7pp. *OOA/CCF299.

3196 ------ Speeches on the address and the Geneva agree-
ments delivered in the House of Commons, Tuesday 9
December, 1947. Ottawa: E. Cloutier. 12pp. *BVAUS/
Young.

3197 CCF. Co-operatives: dicussion leaders notes. Vancouver. 7 plus 9pp, mimeo. *OOA/CCF188.

3198 ------ Investing in our children: some facts about
the nursery-school and day-nursery movement in Ontario. Toronto. 6pp, mimeo. *AEUS/CCFXIII-34.

3199 ------ No! No! a 1,000 times no...'On the record'.
Toronto. (4pp). *BVAUS/Mac30Af.12 OHMA2360 OOA/

CCF320.

3200 CCF. Ontario CCF first-term program. Toronto.
(4pp). OHMA2354 OOA/CCF320 and 538.

3201 ------ The people's business - Saskatchewan government insurance - a story of progress. Regina: Saskatchewan Government Insurance Office. (4pp). *OOA/
CCF322.

3202 ------ People's vote in the legislature. Edmonton.
15pp. *ACGA/Spencer 2 SSA/G3.Alta 5 SSUS/CCF.

3203 ------ Program for Ontario: Ontario section fourteenth annual convention Toronto October 23-24-25
1947. Toronto. 36pp plus 4pp blank. *OOA/CCF48
and 320.

3204 ------ Provincial program. Edmonton. (6pp).
*OOA/CCF75 and 76.

3205 ------ Publicity handbooks (How to handle publicity).
Toronto. 13pp. mimeo. *OOA/CCF320.

3206 ------ Report of the conference of British Commonwealth Labour Parties held at Victoria College,
University of Toronto, Toronto, Canada, September 4
to September 11, 1947. Ottawa. 41pp, mimeo. *OOA/
CCF112 and 310. See also 3213 below.

3207 ------ Report of officers to 1947 provincial con-
vention CCF British Columbia-Yukon section, Vancouver
April 11, 12, 13. 1947. Vancouver. (4pp). *OOA/
CCF316.

3208 ------ Report of Ontario CCF women's conference,
Woodsworth House, Ottawa, May 30, 31, 1947. Toronto.
7pp plus 2pp financial report, mimeo. *OOA/CCF208.

3209 ------ Report to the people. Vancouver. (4pp).
*OOA/CCF316 and 539.

3210 ------ 7 steps to labor advance in Saskatchewan.
Regina: Bureau of Publications. 18pp. *OOA/CCF322.

3211 ------ The story of the CCF national office. Ottawa.
(4pp). *OOA/CCF539.

3212 ------ (Study courses). Course 1. CCF group activities in a community, 29pp. 2. Educational techniques
in CCF group activities, 54pp. 3. History and function of trade unions in Canada, 96pp. 4. Agriculture,
before, during and after the war, 37pp. 5. Socialism
with freedom, 50pp. (Ottawa). All mimeo. *OOA/CCF
114.

3213 ------ Week-end conference of British Commonwealth
Labour Parties with United States and Canadian labour,
farm and co-operative representatives. Victoria College, Toronto...September 6 and 7, 1947. (Ottawa).
14pp, mimeo. *OOA/CCF310. See also 3206 above.

3214 Cooperative Commonwealth University Federation.
Report of the second national convention, McGill University, Montreal, December 29, 30 and 31, 1947.

(Toronto).   (10pp), mimeo.   *OOA/CCF338.

3215 Cooperative Commonwealth Youth Movement.   Report of
the third annual convention of the Ontario section,
Woodsworth House, August 30, 31 and September 1.
(Toronto).   (36pp), mimeo.   *OOA/CCF350.

3216 Co-operative Union of Canada. Submission to the government of Canada.   Ottawa.   12pp, mimeo.   *OOA/
Good 13 and CCF148.   Asking for amending legislation
to the housing, veteran's lands and income war tax
acts.

3217 Co-operative Union of Saskatchewan.   The Antigonish
way.   Regina.   72pp.   *SSA/G50.23.

3218 ------ The Saskactchewan co-operative facts.   Regina.
4pp.   *K.

3219 Cotterill, Murray.   Lessons from the history of
unions in other lands.   (?Ottawa):   CCF.   11pp,
mimeo.   *AEUS/CCFVIII-1.   Acknowledges that 'most
of the material has been taken from Dr Franz Neumann,
European trade unions and politics.'

3220 Cummings, H.R.   Inflation, depression and national
economy.   Rimouski.   34 plus 34pp, bilingual.   *OOP.

3221 Després, Jean-Pierre.   Le Canada et l'Organisation
International du Travail.   Montréal: Fides.   273pp,
biblio.   *OONL.

3222 (Dewhurst, Alf).   Communists in the woods and mills
of British Columbia.   (Vancouver):   (Labor-Progressive
Party).   (c1947).   17pp.   *OTURS/RSK.   Designed to
show the part played by Communists in the trade
union movement in BC.

3223 Douglas, T.C.   In debate on the speech from the
throne, Saskatchewan legislature.   Regina: Thos. H.
McConica.   33pp.   *OTURS/RSK.

3224 ------ Reports on Saskatchewan CCF government.
Vancouver: CCF.   6pp.   *OOA/CCF316 and 358.   An
address delivered in Vancouver.

3225 Dutt, R. Palme and others.   We speak for freedom.
London (Eng): Communist Party of Great Britain.   96pp.
*OTURS/RSK.   Conference of Communist Parties of the
British Empire.   Contains a report on Canada by Tim
Buck, pp41-46 and a closing speech pp86-88.

3226 Elliott, Robbins Leonard.   A study of the Canadian
labour press (1867-1947).   MA thesis, University
of Toronto.   (iii), 152pp.   *NSWA.   The annotated
directory, pp42-129 was later published in the *Canadian Journal of Economics and Political Science*, May 1948.

3227 Freed, Norman.   The fight for labor unity and independent political action.   Toronto: Labor-Progressive Party.   7pp, mimeo.   *OTURS/RSK.

3228 Hannam, H.H.   Address before the Dominion-provincial
agricultural conference, Ottawa, December 3, 1947.

Ottawa: Canadian Federation of Agriculture. 4pp, mimeo. *OOA/Good 16.

3229 Inter-Provincial Farmers Union Council. Look! Read! and learn! Report to its members on wheat policy. (?Saskatoon). 14pp. *SSA/G37.76.

3230 ------ Memorandum (to ministers of the Dominion government), April 10th, 1947. (?Edmonton). 8pp, mimeo. *OOA/CCF74. The Council comprised the United Farmers of Canada, Saskatchewan section, the Alberta Farmers Union and dealt principally with prices.

3231 Irvine, William. Fight for economic freedom: speech delivered in the House of Commons. Ottawa: E.Cloutier. 8pp. *OOA/CCF299 SSA/G2.1947.3.

3232 Ivens, William. Social credit: sense or nonsense? What is offered by technocracy? Jehovah's Witnesses? Communism? The CCF?. Winnipeg: Manitoba Commonwealth. 24pp. *BVAUS/Mac31f.20 OOA/CCF541 OOA/Heaps 2 SSA/G3.Man.14 SSUS/CCF.

3233 Jolliffe, E.B. The Hydro and Dr Hogg: text of a broadcast over CFRB Thursday January 30. (Toronto): (CCF). 4pp plus 2pp, mimeo. *OOA/CCF.

3234 Khalsa Diwan Society. A report of correspondence and documents relative to negotiations between 1929 and 1947, culminating in domiciliary rights being accorded to 210 members of the Indian community by the Dominion government. Vancouver. 27pp. BVIP *BVAUS.

3235 ------ Report on Dominion, provincial and municipal franchise for the Hindus in British Columbia. Victoria. 27pp. BVAU BVIP *OOAL.

3236 Knowles, Stanley. Old age pensions: CPR pension rights: adequate allowances for non-pensioned veterans widows. A speech on the address in reply to the speech from the throne delivered in the House of Commons, Monday March 10, 1947. Ottawa: E. Cloutier. 8pp. *OOA/CCF308.

3237 ------ Stanley Knowles moves that the old age pension be increased to $50 a month. Ottawa: E. Cloutier. 8pp. *OOA/CCF299.

3238 ------ $30 a month at age 70 is an insult. The fight for security goes on. Ottawa: E. Cloutier. 8pp. *OOA/CCF299 SSA/G2.1947.5.

3239 Labor-Progressive Party. Notes on Marxism and Canadian politics. (?London, Ont). (c1947). (29pp), mimeo. OHMA. Has index which bears no relation to the actual contents.

3240 ------ So it can't happen here? (?Sydney): Cape Breton Regional Committee. (c1947). (4pp). *OTURS/RSK. On the violation of trade union liberties.

3241 ------ Unite and sing! A collection of workers songs. (Vancouver). (c1947). 32pp. *AEUS/Sp.Coll.

3242 Laidlaw, Alex. Maritime co-ops: three articles on
the cooperative movement in the Maritime provinces.
Antigonish: St Francis Xavier University. 23pp.
*NSHP/HDC.

3243 Lazarus, Morden. Here's to your health. Toronto:
CCF. 16pp. OTURS *OHMA1575 OOA/CCF56, 320 and 537.

3244 Leiterman, Douglas S. Trade unionism in the Canadian
merchant navy. Unpublished BA thesis, University of
British Columbia. 98pp. *BVAUS.

3245 Lenin, N. The state: a lecture delivered at the
Sverdlov University July 11, 1919. Toronto: Labor-
Progressive Party. 12pp, mimeo. *OHMA OTURS/Sals-
berg T10.24.

3246 Lewis, David. Political action through the CCF.
Ottawa: CCF. (4pp). *ACGA/CCF29 OHMA1558 OOA/
CCF538.

3247 Lipset, S.M. The rural community and political leadership in Saskatchewan. Toronto: Canadian Journal
of Economic and Political Science. pp410-428. *OOA/
Underhill 44. Offprint from vol. 13 no. 3.

3248 Lysenko, Vera. Men in sheepskin coats: a study in
assimilation. Toronto: Ryerson. viii, 312pp, biblio.
*OTP. The Ukrainians in Canada: includes a short
section on early socialists.

3249 McCandless, G.P. The company union: its place in
the labour picture. Unpublished Hons BA thesis,
McMaster University. (viii), 167pp, biblio. *OHMA.

3250 MacInnis, Angus. Senior citizens need higher pensions at a lower age without means test. Speeches
on old age pensions delivered in the House of Commons June 19 and 26, 1947. Ottawa: E. Cloutier.
10pp. *SSUS/JL197.

3251 MacInnis, Grace. Report of discussion groups Ontario
CCF Womens Conference, Woodsworth House, Ottawa May
30, 31, 1947. Ottawa: CCF. 6pp, mimeo. *OOA/CCF
208.

(3252) Marlak, C.F. A labor history of Niagara frontier
(1846-1917): containing an introduction consisting
of conditions prior to 1846. Unpublished PhD thesis
Ottawa University. Not found.

3253 Marshall, John. Milk subsidies are necessary!
Winnipeg: Peoples Cooperative Ltd. 13pp. *SSUS/
Co-ops.

3254 Miller, Minerva. Trotskyism: from opposition to
assassination. Vancouver: Labor-Progressive Party.
4pp, mimeo. *OHMA.

(3255) Mindes, E. Confederation of Catholic workers of
Canada. Unpublished MA thesis, McGill University.
156pp.

3256 Ottawa Civil Liberties Association. The civil rights

of public servants: a tentative study. Ottawa. 8pp plus (9pp) appendix, mimeo. *OOA/CCF147.

3257 Priestley, Norman F. UFA Co-op: progress in cooperation; a discussion of the principles and practice of cooperation with especial reference to the work of UFA Central Cooperative Association, the business organization of the United Farmers of Alberta. Calgary: United Farmers of Alberta. (c1947). (16pp). *OTU.

3258 Robinson, Carmita Bernice. Machinery for the prevention of labor disputes. Unpublished MA thesis, Acadia University. (ii), 117pp, biblio. *NSWA.

3259 (Rosenberg, Louis). Who owns Canada? An examination of the facts concerning the concentration of ownership and control of the means of production, distribution and exchange in Canada by Watt Hugh McCollum. Ottawa: Woodsworth House. 103pp. *ACGA/CCF29 BVAUS/ WB41f.15a MWPA/CCF39 OHMA1668 OOA/CCF540 OTURS/ RSK SSUS/JL197. Rewritten edition of no.1783 above.

3260 (Ryerson, S.B.) The LPP and the arts: a discussion bulletin by S.B.R. (Toronto): Labor-Progressive Party. 6pp, mimeo *OHMA (lacks last page) OTURS/ RSK.

3261 ------ What is socialism? An introductory course. Toronto: Labor-Progressive Party. 17pp, mimeo. *OHMA OTURS/RSK.

3262 Salsberg, J.B. The trade unions in the struggle against the economic crisis and the menace of war. Co-report to the national committee meeting, May 21-23, 1947. Toronto: Labor-Progressive Party. 13pp, mimeo. *OHMA.

3263 Sandwell, B.K. The state and human rights. Toronto: Canadian Assn for Adult Education. 16pp. *OOA/CCF 544. Behind the Headlines vol. 7 no. 2.

3264 Saskatchewan Federation of Labour. Removal of price control and subsidies leading Canada to economic recession. Regina. 6pp. SRL *SSA/G114.21.

3265 Socialist Labor Party. Begin now! Toronto. (4pp). (c1947). *OTURS/RSK.

3266 Stimpfle, Carl J. Address at district 5 convention held in Stony Plain, June 28th, 1947. (Edmonton): Alberta Farmers Union. 7pp, mimeo. *OOA/CCF74.

3267 Strum, Galdys. Speech on old age pensions - nutrition and the milk subsidy delivered in the House of Commons, Friday March 7, 1947. Ottawa: E. Cloutier. 7pp. *OOA/CCF299 and 309.

3268 Sullivan, Pat. (Resignation statement.) (Ottawa): np. 6pp, mimeo. *OOA/CCF393. No title; opening reads 'I am making this document public...'

3269 Tito. The people's front. Toronto: Progress. 32pp. *OTURS/RSK.

3270 UAW-CIO. Ottawa car strike news. Ottawa. (4pp).
*OOA/CCF543.

3271 ------ The true story of the Ottawa car strike.
Ottawa. (4pp). *OOA/CCF188 OOL.

3272 United Farmers of Canada. Rural romance: a story of
the Saskatchewan farmers movement and its objectives.
Saskatoon. 10pp. *SSA/G37.82.

3273 United Jewish Peoples Order. 20 years progressive
fraternalism in Canada. Toronto. 58pp. *OTURS/RSK.
Main reports and resolutions of the 2nd national
convention, Montreal, June 1947.

3274 United Mine Workers of America. Memorandum to the
Dominion Coal Board. Glace Bay. 26pp plus 1p
summary. *OOA/CCF147. Recommending the coal industry become a public utility and dealing with social
problems.

3275 Vancouver Consultative Council for Study of Problems
of Citizenship. The Japanese-Canadian situation
today. Vancouver. (4pp). *BVAUS/Smith/Japanese.

3276 Winch, Harold E. Report to trade unions on BC labor
legislation. Vancouver: CCF. 4pp. *OOA/CCF316.

3277 Woodcock, George. The basis of communal living.
London (Eng): Freedom. 44pp. BVIV *own copy.

3278 Wright, Jim. Veteran reviews strikes present and
Past. Glace Bay: United Mine Workers of America
district 26. (4pp). *OOA/CCF188.

3279 Yates, S.W. The Saskatchewan Wheat Pool; its origin,
organization and progress, 1924-1935; with some reference to the Alberta and Manitoba pools and to the
pools central selling agency. Edited by A.S. Morton.
Saskatoon: United Farmers of Canada. vi, 218pp,
illus. *SSA/G37.83 Peel 4079.

1948

3280 Amalgamated Lithographers of America. A candid review of the contract negotiations between the Canadian Lithographers Assn and the AL of A. Toronto.
8pp. *OOL.

3281 Andras, A. Labor unions in Canada: how they work
and what they seek. Ottawa: Woodsworth House. 86pp.
*BVAUS/Mac32f.3 OHMA2396 OOA/CCF537 OONL SSUS/
JL197.

3282 Bellamy, Edward. The parable of the coach. Regina:
CCF. (4pp). *MWPA/CCF39 OOA/CCF70 SSA/Gl.nd.25.

3283 Bengough, Percy. Bengough backs seamen! Address
delivered to the 7th biennial convention of the Canadian Seamens Union in Toronto, February 24, 1948.

Montreal: Canadian Seamens Union. (3pp). *OOL.
See also 3287 below.

(3284) Bengough, Percy. Danger ahead. Montreal. 4pp.
Mentioned but not found.

3285 ------ President's address to the 63rd annual convention of the Trades and Labor Congress of Canada,
Victoria, BC, October 11-16, 1948. (Ottawa): Trades
and Labor Congress of Canada. 7pp. *OOA/Bengough 1.

3286 ------ Speech at labour conference held Wednesday,
May 12th, 1948 at Labour Temple, Toronto. (Ottawa):
Trades and Labor Congress of Canada. 6pp, mimeo.
*OOL.

3287 ------ Statement: the case of the Canadian Seamens
Union. Montreal: Canadian Seamens Union. 3pp, mimeo.
*OOA/Bengough 1 OOL. On the troubles between the
CSU and the Canada Steamship Lines. See also 3283
above.

3288 Bird, John. Leading personalities of the CCF convention. Ottawa: Ottawa Evening Citizen. 12pp.
*MWPA/CCF39 OOA/CCF537 SSUS/JL197. Biographies
of Coldwell, Scott, Lewis and Knowles.

3289 Bjarnason, Emil and Bert Marcuse. The case of the
dwindling dollar. What is happening to the cost of
living; wages; prices; profits. Vancouver: Trade
Union Research Bureau. 28pp. BVIP OPAL OTP *BVAUS/
Mac31f.32a OHMA1456.

3290 Bone, Enid Turner. Foundation fund, National Council
of Women of Canada: necessity of establishing this
fund: founding of fund - June 1926: brief history of
the succeeding years to date. np: National Council
of Women of Canada. (c1948). (8pp). *OONL.

3291 Brewin, F.A. A review of property claims. Toronto:
Cooperative Committee on Japanese Canadians. (4pp).
*OOA/CCJC 3.

3292 Buck, Tim. Canada: the communist viewpoint. Toronto:
Progress. 288pp. *OKQS OTURS/RSK SSUS.

3293 ------ Keep Canada independent: a new national pol-
icy. Toronto: Labor-Progressive Party. 20pp.
*BVAUS/WB31f.3c OHMA2400 OKQS OOA/CCF542 OTURS/
RSK.

3294 ------ A letter to the party. (Toronto): Labor-
Progressive Party. (4pp). *OTURS/RSK.

3295 Buckley, J.W. Price control - labour's viewpoint.
Toronto: University of Toronto Commerce Club. pp25-
30. *OTPB/Buckley. Reprinted from *The Commerce
Journal* vol 2 no. 8.

3296 Buhay, Beckie. The fight for the party: educational
outline. (Toronto): Labor-Progressive Party. 6pp,
mimeo. *OTURS/RSK.

3297 ------ Handbook of LPP club education. Toronto:

Labor-Progressive Party. 15pp, mimeo. *OHMA OTURS/ RSK.

3298 Buhay, Becky. Quarantine the profiteer! Restore price controls! Facts and notes... Toronto: Labor-Progressive Party. 4pp, mimeo. *OTURS/RSK.

3299 ------ Woman and the fight for peace and socialism. (Toronto): Labor-Progressive Party. 24pp, mimeo. *OTURS/RSK.

3300 Canada. Report of the Canadian government delegates to the thirtieth session of the International Labour Conference, Geneva June 19 to July 11, 1948. Ottawa: E. Cloutier. 86pp. *OHMA2521.

3301 Canadian Brotherhood of Railway Employees. The Canadian Brotherhood of Railway Employees and other transport workers 1908-1948. Forty years of progress. Ottawa. 36pp. BVIP MWP NSHPL OH OOL OTP QMBM *NSWA.

3302 Canadian Committee of the World Federation of Democratic Youth. Journey for peace. Toronto. (c1948) 20pp. *BVAUS/Mac42f.3A.

3303 Canadian Congress of Labour. A national labour code. Ottawa. 31pp. *OOA/CCF192.

3304 Canadian Seamans Union. The CSU and you: the case for free trade unionism. Montreal. (c1948). 30pp. *OOL OTURS/RSK.

3305 Carter, Dyson. What's wrong? Toronto: Progress. 45pp. OTP *BVAUS/WB39f.27 OTURS/RSK.

3306 Coldwell, M.J. Am I my brother's keeper? Ottawa: CCF. 12pp. *ACGA/CCF29 BVAUS/Mac30Af.4b MWPA/CCF 39 OHMA2792 OOA/CCF536 OOA/Klein 17 OTURS/RSK. An address given previously under the title 'The political implications of the Christian faith.'

3307 ------ If the CCF wins the next election. London (Ont): Quarterly Review of Commerce. 8pp. Offprint from the review published by the University of Western Ontario. *BVAUS/Young.

3308 Community Planning Association of Canada. What is the government doing about housing? Ottawa. 24pp. *OOA/CPAC 3.

3309 CCF. Act now! tell Ottawa prices must be held. Ottawa. (2pp), broadside. *OOA/CCF536.

3310 ------ The big question answered about the CCF in Saskatchewan. Regina: CCF. 16pp. BVIP *ACGA/CCF25 BVAUS/Mac30f.21 OOA/CCF321 OTURS/RSK SSA/G1.1948.1 SSUS/JL197.

3311 ------ CCF handbook. Ottawa. 100pp. AEU BVIP NSHPL OOP *MWPA/CCF39 OHMA1535 OKQS OOA/CCF536 OTURS/RSK SSUS/JL197. First national handbook.

3312 ------ CCF songbook, selected by CCF Songbook Committee. Vancouver. (35pp), mimeo. *BVAUS/Mac43f.4 Contains 11 songs by CCF members and traditional songs of protest and of labour.

3313 CCF. For Saskatchewan's children. Regina. (4pp).
*SSA/G1.1948.5.

3314 ------ The Petersens of Saskatchewan. Regina.
(16pp). *SSA/G1.1948.9. Cartoon story of the Saskatchewan government record.

3315 ------ Political confusion and religious scandal.
Ottawa. (2pp) broadside, bilingual. *ACGA/CCF29
OOA/CCF297 SSA/G2.1948.9.

3316 ------ Producer control in milk marketing. Toronto.
32pp. *OOA/CCF320 and 539.

3317 ------ Program for Ontario: CCF Ontario section
fifteenth annual convention. Toronto. 26pp plus
5pp advts. *OOA/CCF48 OTURS/RSK.

3318 ------ Provincial program Alberta section CCF.
Edmonton. 6pp. *OOA/CCF316, 536 and 540.

3319 ------ Religion and the CCF. Regina. (c1948).
(4pp). *SSA/G1.nd.27.

3320 ------ Security for all. Ottawa. 63pp. *ACGA/CCF
29 ACGL/PDbl BVAUS/Mac30Af.8a OKQS OOA/CCF417 and
539 OTURS/RSK SSA/G2.1949.9. CCF first term program
adopted at Winnipeg, August 1948.

3321 ------ Security for farmers: your stake in farm
marketing. Toronto. (4pp). *OHMA2352 OOA/CCF320
and 539.

3322 ------ A short short *(sic)* but important story about
agriculture. Regina. (4pp). *OOA/CCF70 SSA/G1.
1948.13.

3323 ------ Social welfare and health under a CCF government. Regina. (4pp). *AEUS/CCFXIII-16 OOA/CCF70
and 539 SSA/G1.1948.15.

3324 ------ Social welfare in Saskatchewan. Regina.
24pp. *OOA/CCF322.

3325 ------ The story of the Alberta CCF 1932 to 1948
and 1948 provincial convention program, Palliser
Hotel, Calgary, November 19th and 20th. (Edmonton).
72pp. *ACGA/CCF12 OOA/CCF316 Peel 4086.

3326 ------ Summary of legislation passed by Saskatchewan
provincial legislature 1944 to 1947. (Regina).
(147pp), mimeo. *SSA/G1.1947.3.

3327 ------ They'll ask you...1. Is the CCF democratic?
2. Will the CCF mean regimentation? 3. Will the CCF
destroy initiative? 4. Will the CCF endanger my sav-
ings? 5. Is the CCF Communistic? 6. About the CCF
and religion. 7. About the CCF and personal possess-
ions. 8. About the CCF and farm ownership. Here are
the answers. Ottawa. 16pp. BVIP NSHPL *ACGA/CCF29
ACGL AEUS/CCFXIII-17 BVAUS/Mac30Af.4c MWPA/CCF39
and Brigden 7 OHMA1566 OKQS OOA/CCF539 OTURS/RSK
and Woodsworth 29 SSA/G2.1948.5 SSUS/JL197.

3328 CCF. Time for a change! (Edmonton). 16pp. *OOA/
CCF539 SSA/G3.Alta.8.

3329 ------ What do you want? Toronto. (16pp). *BVAUS/
Mac30Af.4c OHMA1564 OOA/CCF57, 70, 320 and 540
SSA/G2.1944.18. Published in different centres.

3330 CCF Elect Carling Committee. The case for Sudbury.
(Sudbury). 19pp. *AEUS/CCFXIII-22 OTURS/RSK and
Woodsworth 29. On the expulsion by the CCF of their
former MPP.

3331 Cooperative Commonwealth University Federation.
Report of the third national convention, Woodsworth
House, Ottawa, December 29-30, 1948. (Saskatoon).
12pp, mimeo. *OOA/CCF338. Note: Cover title states
'third', inside heading says 'second'.

3332 Cullinane, Eugene. The catholic church and socialism.
Regina: CCF. 8pp. ACG SRL *SSA/G1.nd.8 SSUS/CCF.
For the 'new socialism' and anti-communist.

3333 Douglas, T.C. A humanitarian budget: address in the
budget debate, 1948. Regina: T.H. McConica. 18pp.
*OOA/CCF60, 537 and 539.

3334 ------ Religion and the CCF. Edmonton: CCF. (4pp).
*OOA/CCF539.

3335 ------ This thing called freedom. Regina: CCF.
(4pp). *OOA/CCF70, 322 and 539 SSA/G1.1948.19
SSUS/CCF.

3336 Douglas, William O. Labor's opportunity: a speech
at the 1948 CIO convention: presented in Canada by
the United Steelworkers of Canada. Toronto. (8pp).
*OTURS/RSK.

3337 Endicott, James G. A call to peace. Toronto: Canadian Peace Congress. 15pp. *BVAUS/Mac42f.3a OHMA
1614 OTURS/RSK. Keynote address to the peace conference, December 1948.

(3338)Farmers Union and United Farmers of Canada. Farmers
action program of Alberta. 16pp. Peel 4093. Not
found.

3339 Forsey, Eugene.(ed). Canada in a new world: addresses
given at the Canadian Institute on Public Affairs,
1947. Toronto. 75pp. *OOA/Forsey 8 OTURS/RSK.
Addresses by B.K. Sandwell, Leopold Infeld, Dorothy
Fosdick, Escott Reid, Kenneth Wilson, M.J. Coldwell,
Donald Fleming, A.F.W. Plumptre and H.M. Cassidy.

3340 Hayes, Gordon P. Nova Scotia and coal. Unpublished
BA hons thesis, Acadia University. (iii), 58(60)pp.
biblio. *NSWA. Includes labour relations etc.

3341 Interprovincial Farmers Union Council. Memorandum
to government, March 1948. (?Edmonton). 4pp, mimeo.
*OOA/CCF74.

3342 Johnson, Hewlett. The Dean speaks. Toronto: Canadian Peace Congress. 32pp. *BVAUS/Mac42f.3a OHMA

1718 OTURS/RSK. Foreword by J.G. Endicott. Issued at the time of the Dean's North American tour. Contains his address, and interview by Endicott and press quotations.

(3343)Johnson, T.A. The needle trades in Winnipeg: a study in trade unions. Unpublished MA thesis, University of Manitoba. 135pp. Not seen.

3344 Knowles, Stanley. Speech on the right to old age security delivered in the House of Commons on Tuesday, March 2, 1948. Ottawa: E. Cloutier. 10pp. *BVAUS/Mac27f.43.

3345 Labor-Progressive Party. For Canada peace and democracy! Against Wall St, war and fascism! The draft resolution of the national executive of the LPP. Toronto: Canadian Tribune. (4pp). *OTURS/RSK.

3346 ------ The LPP program: people before profits. Vancouver. (c1948). (6pp). *BVAUS/WB31f.3c.

3347 ------ Marx, Engels, Lenin: 100 years. Program Lenin memorial meeting. Vancouver. (14pp). *BVAUS/ Mac38f.16.

3348 ------ A signpost to the future: this program of the LPP shows how unity can keep Saskatchewan out of the Liberal ditch and on the highway to progress. Regina. (c1948). (6pp). *SSA/G27.1948.1.

3349 Lipset, S.M. Political participation and the organization of the CCF in Saskatchewan. Toronto: Canadian Journal of Economics and Political Science. pp191-208. *OACGL/PDbl. Offprint from vol.XIV vol.2.

3350 Lund, Nelson. The ABC of the new world based on Bellamy's forecasts. Bowsman River (Man). 62pp. ACGL *OTURS/RSK. Printed in the USA, almost certainly by Haldeman-Julius. Some copies have a special foreword, mimeo and signed by the author, tipped in.

3351 McCutcheon, Wilfred Whyte. Economic organization and development of the United Farmers Co-operative Company, Limited. Unpublished MSc thesis, University of Toronto. (iv), 168pp plus by-laws; biblio. *OTUAR.

3352 MacKay, Dean R. A survey of labour relations in the metal-mining industry of British Columbia. Unpublished MA thesis, University of British Columbia. (vi), ix, 149pp., biblio. *BVAUS.

3353 Magnuson, Bruce. Prosperity or austerity, which way Canada? Sudbury: Lumber and Sawmill Workers Union. (6pp). *OTURS/RSK. Intended as part of a regular radio series but banned by CKSO, November 1947.

3354 Morgan, Nigel. British Columbia betrayed: why the LPP proposes a CCF government. Vancouver: Labor-Progressive Party. 15pp. BVIPA *BVAUS/WB31f.3b OTURS/RSK.

3355 Morris, Leslie. Ten big lies answered. Port Arthur: Labor-Progressive Party. (c1948). (2pp). *OHMA

OTURS/RSK. Reprinted from the *Canadian Tribune*.

3356 Morton, W.L. The social philosophy of Henry Wise Wood, the Canadian agrarian leader. np: Agricultural History. pp114-123. *AEUS/Rutherford. Offprint from Agricultural History 22.

3357 Nasir, George. Fifteen poems. Winnipeg: Dahl. 16pp. AEU NBSAN OKQ OTMCL SSU *E. On socialist and labour themes.

3358 National Council for Canadian-Soviet Friendship. Nailing the big lie. Toronto. (7pp). *BVAUS/Mac 31f.35 OHMA1927 OTURS/RSK. The big lie is Igor Gouzenko's book *This was my choice*.

3359 National Federation of Labor Youth. Membership book. Toronto. (8pp). *OTURS/RSK. Contains preamble, constitution and by-laws.

3360 National Japanese Canadian Citizens Association. Submission to the Royal Commission on Japanese Canadian property. Toronto. 33pp, mimeo. *OOA/CCJC 1.

3361 ------ Submission to the Prime Minister and members of the government in the matter of certain wartime measures affecting persons of Japanese ancestry. Toronto. 15pp, mimeo. *OOA/CCJC 1.

3362 Ontario Provincial Federation of the Trades and Labor Congress of Canada. To the delegates attending the second annual convention of the Ontario provincial federation, Labor Temple, Toronto January 16-18, 1948. Toronto. 7pp. *OTPB/Buckley.

3363 Penner, Norman. Soldiers or citizens? Toronto: National Federation of Labor Youth. (c1948). 11pp. *OHMA2051 OTURS/RSK. On the employment problems facing school-leavers.

3364 Piroshko, Michael. (collector). Harvest of ideas. Vancouver. 48pp. *BVAUS/Mac44 OHMA2053. Miscellaneous collection of thoughts from various writers. See 1553 above.

3365 Potofsky, Jacob, Emil Mazey and Joseph Curran. Why CIO expelled Mine, Mill: report of the committee to investigate charges against the International Union of Mine, Mill and Smelter Workers. (Toronto). (c1948). 12pp. *OTURS/Woodsworth 29. The members of the investigating committee were all from the CIO executive.

3366 Probe, J.O. Speech on federal aid to education delivered in the House of Commons, Monday 19 April 1948. Ottawa: E. Cloutier. 4pp. *BVAUS/Young.

3367 Revolutionary Workers Party. Against Wall Street and the Kremlin: manifesto of the 2nd World Congress of the Fourth International. Toronto: Workers Press. 48pp. OOL *OHMA2216 OTURS/RSK.

3368 Roback, Leo. Justice in Quebec: the truth about the St Jerome trial. Ottawa: Civil Rights Union. 7pp, mimeo. *OOL. The trials of Madeleine Parent, Kent Farley and others.

3369 Ryerson, Stanley B. Why be a doormat? Toronto: Labor-Progressive Party. 16pp. *BVAUS/WB31f.3d OHMA1908 OOA/CCF542 OTURS/RSK. An attack on US economic domination.

3370 Salsberg, J.B. Put teeth in our labor laws: a call for united action to smash Tory employer's provocations. Toronto: Labor-Progressive Party. (c1948). 7pp. *OTURS/RSK.

3371 Sharp, Paul F. The agrarian revolt in western Canada. A survey showing American parallels. Minneapolis: University of Minnesota Press. ix, 204pp, biblio. *SSUS/Shortt. Peel 4128.

3372 Shipyard General Workers Federation. How to organize the job. (Vancouver). (c1948). 29pp. *BVAUS/Mac 33f.10.

3373 Socialist Party of Canada. The Russian revolution: its origins and outcome. Winnipeg. 52pp. *BVAUS/ Mac30Af.2b OHMA OTURS/RSK. Largely an attack on Soviet communism.

3374 Stewart, Willard W. The single tax in Saskatchewan. Unpublished MA thesis, University of Saskatchewan. vi, 90(95)pp, biblio. *SSU.

3375 Toye, E. Harold. Trifling with destiny. Toronto: Religion-Labour Foundation. (c1948). 76pp. QQL *OKQS OTURS/RSK. Foreword by C.H. Millard.

3376 United Farmers of Canada. The United Farmers of Canada vs The Canadian Pacific Railway and the Railway Association of Canada. Saskatoon. (4pp). *SSA/G 37.107.

3377 Woodcock, George.(ed). A hundred years of revolution: 1848 and after. London (Eng): Porcupine. 286pp. AEU BVAU BVIV OKQ OPET SSU *OONL.

3378 ------ The writer and politics. London (Eng): Porcupine. vi, 7-248pp. *OONL.

3379 Woodsworth, J.S. Toward socialism. Selections from the writings of J.S. Woodsworth edited by Edith Fowke. Toronto: Ontario Woodsworth Memorial Foundation. 48pp. *BVAUS/Mac43f.20 OHMA1553 OOA/CCF326 OTURS/ RSK SSA/G436.2 SSUS/JL197 Peel 4136.

3380 Woodworkers Industrial Union of Canada. Save the woodworkers from company unionism. (Vancouver). (1p), broadside. *BVAUS/Smith CP.

1949

3381 Anderson, Frederick Woodley. Some political aspects

of the grain growers movement, (1915-1935) with particular reference to Saskatchewan. (Short title: Farmers in politics 1915-1935). Unpublished MA thesis University of Saskatchewan. (iv), 203pp. *SSUS.

3382 Bengough, Percy and John W. Buckley. An informed membership will strengthen democracy and defeat domination. Ottawa: Trades and Labor Congress of Canada. 7pp. *OOA/Bengough 1. On the attempted domination by the AFL. Contains the slogan 'Co-operation yes - domination no!

3383 Benton, S. Bruce. A study of the Saskatchewan Labour Relations Board. Unpublished BA hons thesis, University of Saskatchewan. (v), 131, i-lxxiii, (132-36)pp. biblio. *SSUS.

3384 Bjarnason, Emil and Bert Whyte. The BC election and you: the case for public ownership. Vancouver: Labor-Progressive Party. (13pp). BVIP *BVAUS/WB 31f.3c.

3385 Buck, Tim. Block the police state plot. Toronto: Labor-Progressive Party. 8pp. AEU BVIP BVIV MWU OTP *BVAUS/WB31f.3c OHMA2411 OTURS/RSK SSUS. On the 'Lacroix bill' introduced into the House by an 'independent Liberal' to outlaw the LPP among other similar measures.

3386 ------ A Canadian people's national policy. (Toronto): Labor-Progressive Party. 22pp, mimeo. *OTURS/RSK.

3387 ------ On the suicide pact. Toronto: Labor-Progressive Party. 8pp. *BVAUS/WB31f.3c OHMA2417 OKQS OTURS/RSK. The suicide pact is NATO.

3388 Buhay, Beckie. For Canada, peace and democracy. Course for week-end schools based on the main resolutions, February 1949, national convention of the LPP. Toronto: Labor-Progressive Party. 6pp, mimeo. *OTURS/RSK.

3389 Canada, Dept of Labour. Joint consultation in service industries. Ottawa: E. Cloutier. 15pp. *OOL.

3390 Canada, Royal Canadian Mounted Police. Law and order in Canadian democracy: a series of 20 lectures on crime and police work in Canada. Ottawa: E. Cloutier. 227pp. *OTURS/RSK. Deals, among other things, with treason (Riel); sedition (Winnipeg General Strike and Tim Buck); Communism (1931 trial of the Communist leaders); public disturbances and riots (Doukhobors).

3391 Canada, Dept of National Defence. Report on certain 'incidents' which occurred on board HMC ships Athabaskan, Crescent and Magnificent and other matters concerning the Royal Canadian Navy, made to the Minister of National Defence by a Commission. Ottawa: E. Cloutier. 57pp. *OOAL. These were technically mutinies.

3392 Canadian Committee for a Bill of Rights. The Senate speaks: a bill of rights for all Canadians. Toronto. 7pp. *OTURS/RSK.

3393 Canadian Congress of Labour. Education: the road to freedom. Ottawa. OOL *OTURS/RSK.

3394 Canadian Federation of Agriculture. Farmers meet the cabinet. Ottawa. 14pp. *ACGA/CCF25. Issued annually from 1949 on.

3395 Canadian Seamans Union. The 'Tridale' strike. Wellington (NZ): New Zealand Strike Committee CSU. 21pp. *T.

3396 Carter, Dyson. Land without capitalists: 32 years of the USSR. Toronto: Progress. 29pp. AEU BVIP BVIV *BVAUS/Mac38f18k OHMA2954 OTURS/RSK.

(3397)Chan, Victor O. The Canadian Knights of Labor with special reference to the 1880's. Unpublished MA thesis, McGill University. Not seen.

3398 Chisholm, Brock and C. Fred Bosworth. The people's health. Toronto: Canadian Assn for Adult Education. 19pp. *OOA/CCF544. Behind the Headlines vol 9 no 2.

3399 Coldwell, M.J. The nation's business. Ottawa: CCF. (6pp). *ACGL/PDbl BVAUS/Mac27f.26 OOA/CCF537.

3400 ------ Speech on the address in reply to the speech from the throne delivered in the House of Commons on January 31, 1949. Ottawa: E. Cloutier. 8pp. *BVAUS/ Garrison 1-5 OOA/Coldwell 60.

3401 ------ Speech on the alleged combine in the flour milling industry delivered in the House of Commons on November 7, 1949. Ottawa: E. Cloutier. 6pp. *BVAUS/Garrison 1-5.

3402 ------ Speech on the budget delivered in the House of Commons on March 31, 1949. Ottawa: E. Cloutier. 8pp. *BVAUS/Garrison 1-5 and Mac27f.43.

3403 ------ Speech on the proposed North Atlantic Treaty delivered in the House of Commons on March 28, 1949. Ottawa: E. Cloutier. 7pp. *BVAUS/Mac27f.43 OOA/ Coldwell 60.

3404 CCF. Brief on Labour Relations Act of Ontario. Toronto. (c1949). 13pp, mimeo. *OTURS.

3405 ------ Nova Scotia CCF provincial platform as adopted by the CCF annual convention November 1948. Halifax: Maritime Commonwealth. (2pp). *OOA/CCF28.

3406 ------ Organizational guide. Ottawa. 18pp. NSHPL OTV *OOA/CCF536 SSA/G2.1949.2.

3407 ------ Provincial convention program, Masonic Temple, Edmonton. Edmonton. 38pp. *OOA/CCF316.

3408 ------ Provincial platform for Manitoba as adopted at the fourteenth annual convention, July 1949. (Winnipeg). 7pp, mimeo. *OOA/CCF62 and 318.

3409 CCF. Review of legislation, June 1949. Regina.
(35pp). *OOA/CCF70 and 539 SSA/G1.1949.2.

3410 ------ Saskatchewan CCF members handbook. Regina.
61pp. *OOA/CCF345.

3411 ------ Speakers notes. Ottawa. 195pp. AEU BVIV
OOP SRL *BVAUS/Mac30f.15 OOA/Klein 17 and CCF536
and 539 OKQS OTURS/RSK SSA/G2.1949.10 SSUS/CCF.

3412 ------ Talking about unions at a women's conference
on organized labour held in Woodsworth House, Toronto,
December 2 and 3, 1949. Toronto. 32pp, mimeo.
*OTURS.

3413 ------ Think it over... Toronto. (6pp). *OOA/CCF
320 and 539 SSA/G2.1949.11.

3414 ------ What's ahead for agriculture. Ottawa. (4pp).
*OOA/CCF539 SSA/G2.1949.12. Farm program.

3415 Cooperative Commonwealth University Federation.
CCUF convention Kingston, 1949. Ottawa. 15pp,
mimeo. *OOA/CCF338. Fourth convention.

3416 Cooperative Commonwealth Youth Movement. Report on
the meeting of the CCYM national council, Ottawa,
October 29th-30th, 1949. Ottawa. 24pp, mimeo.
*OOA/CCF343.

3417 Co-operative Union of Saskatchewan. Co-op handbook.
Regina. (112pp). *SSA/G50.5.

3418 Crysler, Alfred C. Labour relations and precedents
in Canada: a commentary on labour law and practice
in Canada. Toronto: Carswell. viii, 504pp. *OONL.

3419 Douglas, T.C. Canadians find security with freedom:
CCF in Saskatchewan builds towards cooperative order.
New York: League for Industrial Democracy. 31pp.
BVIP OOL OOP OTP SRL *OOA/CCF552 OTURS/RSK SRA/CCF
Misc 48. Foreword by M.J. Coldwell.

3420 ------ Forward with security. Speech in debate on
the speech from the throne, Saskatchewan legislature,
1949. Regina: T.H. McConica. 38pp. *OTURS/RSK.

3421 Ellis, A.C. and J.S. Burton. A brief to the Royal
Commission on National Development in the Arts,
Letters and the Sciences presented by the CCUF at
Saskatoon, Saskatchewan, Tuesday, October 18, 1949.
(Saskatoon): Cooperative Commonwealth University
Federation. 6pp, mimeo. *OOA/CCF151 and 342.

3422 Gillis, Clarie. Speech on decentralization of industry delivered in the House of Commons, January 31
and February 1, 1949. Ottawa: E. Cloutier. 8pp.
*BVAUS/Young.

3423 Johnson, Hewlett. Design for peace! Vancouver:
National Council for Canadian-Soviet Friendship.
(16pp). BVIPA *BVAUS/Mac31Af.35.

3424 Kashtan, William. You and the depression. Toronto:
Labor-Progressive Party. 31pp. BVIP BVIV SRU *BVAUS/

Mac39f.20a   OHMA1629   OKQS   OTURS/RSK.

3425 Knowles, Stanley.   The case for a railroad retire-
ment act.   Speech delivered in the House of Commons
Thursday April 28, 1949.   Ottawa: E. Cloutier.   4pp.
*BVAUS/Mac27f.44   OOA/CCF308 and Klein 17.

3426 Labor-Progressive Party.   Constitution.   Toronto.
31pp.   *OKQS OTURS/RSK.   Amended 1949.

3427 ------   Important lessons and new tasks.   Resolution
on the lessons of the Toronto civic election, 1949.
Toronto.   5pp, mimeo.   *OTURS/RSK.

3428 ------   An open letter to the members of Canada's
Parliament: is peace treason?   Toronto.   (1p), broadside.   *OOA/Coldwell 60.   On NATO vs the UN.

3429 ------   Statement of the National Cultural Commission
of the LPP.   (Toronto).   60pp, mimeo.   *OTURS/RSK.

3430 ------   Toronto and Yorks conference, September 1949.
Toronto.   12pp, mimeo.   *OTURS/RSK.

3431 Lapierre, Ada Marion.   Some aspects of social legislation in Canada.   Unpublished MA thesis, Acadia
University.   viii, 189pp, biblio.   *NSWA.

3432 Lazarus, Morden.   Planned health services.   A lecture
Ottawa, March 23, 1949.   (Ottawa): (CCF).   11pp,
mimeo.   *OOA/CCF127.

3433 MacDonald, Malcolm A.   Changes in wage structure in
Canada (1939-1946).   Unpublished BA thesis, McMaster
University.   (iii), 89pp, biblio.   *OHMA.

3434 McHenry, Dean E.   The impact of the CCF on Canadian
parties and splinter groups.   np: The Journal of
Politics.   pp365-395.   *BVAUS/Mac30Af.3b.   Offprint
from vol II.

3435 MacInnis, Angus.   Speech on a program of social security for Canada delivered in the House of Commons
on October 3, 1949.   Ottawa: E. Cloutier.   6pp.
*BVAUS/Mac27f.43.

3436 ------   Speech on the address in reply to the speech
from the throne delivered in the House of Commons,
3 March 1949.   Ottawa: E. Cloutier.   7pp.   *BVAUS/
Garrison 1-5.

3437 ------   Speech on National Housing Act amendment delivered in the House of Commons on 31 October 1949.
Ottawa: E. Cloutier.   4pp.   *BVAUS/Garrison 1-5.

3438 McNaught, K.W.   J.S. Woodsworth and a political party
for labour 1896-1921.   np: Canadian Historical Review.
pp123-143.   *AEUS/CCFXIII-12   MWPA/Brigden 7   OOA/
Coldwell 62 and CCF309.   Offprint from June 1949.

(3439)Mills, J.C.   Study of the Canadian Council of Agriculture 1910-1930.   Unpublished MA thesis, University
of Manitoba.   iii,226pp.

3440 Mollberg, Carl Morgan.   Minimum wage regulation in

Saskatchewan. Unpublished BA hons thesis, University of Saskatchewan. (i), vi, 114pp, biblio. *SSUS.

3441 Morris, Leslie. Peace is in your hands. Toronto: Progress. 29pp. BVIP OKQ SSU *BVAUS/WB42f.3a OHMA 1844 OTURS/RSK.

3442 National Federation of Labor Youth. Towards singing tomorrows. Toronto. 40pp, mimeo. *BVAUS/Mac43f.4 OHMA2549. Songs.

3443 Nielsen, Dorise. 80 million speak for peace. Toronto: Womens Committee for Peace Action. 31pp. AEU BVIP BVIV OTP SSU *BVAUS/WB32f.2a OHMA1940 OTURS/RSK.

3444 Priestley, Norman F. Time for expansion. Calgary: United Farmers of Alberta. (4pp). *ACGA/UFA 3.

3445 Queens University. The conciliation and arbitration of labour disputes in Canada. Kingston: Industrial Relations Centre. 68pp. *OKQ.

3446 Ryerson, Stanley B. Which side are you on? A question for Messrs Coldwell, Lewis and Millard. Toronto: Labor-Progressive Party. 8pp. BVIP *AEUS/ Sp.coll BVAUS/WB31f.3c and 4 OHMA2446 OTURS/RSK.

3447 Scott, F.R. Le CCF et la centralisation: un pays - deux cultures. Ottawa: CCF. (4pp). *SSA/G2.1949.5.

3448 ------ Dominion jurisdiction over human rights and fundamental freedoms. Ottawa: Canadian Bar Review. pp497-536. OH QMU *OOAL. Offrpint from vol XXVII no 5.

3449 ------ La médicine sociale. Montréal: Université de Montréal. pp57-68. *OOA/CCF39. Reproduit de la Revue Médicale, vol 1 no 2. Also as an offprint in English from the Canadian Association of Medical Students and Internes, vol VIII no 3.

3450 Smith, A.E. All my life: an autobiography. Toronto: Progress. 224pp. *OTURS/RSK.

3451 Thatcher, W. Ross. The Asbestos strike: speech delivered in the House of Commons 4 April 1949. Ottawa: E. Cloutier. 3pp. *OHMA.

3452 Weaver, Geo. W. Economics for workers: an analysis of social economy. Vancouver: Boag Foundation. 94pp. BVAUS/Mac4f.17 and 39f.27 OTURS/RSK.

3453 ------ History for workers. North Surrey. 77pp. BVIP *BVAUS/Young.

3454 Weir, John. Slavs. Toronto: Canadian Slav Committee. 47pp. BVIP OH OKQ OPET OTP *BVAUS/Mac41f.14 OHMA 1811 OTURS/RSK.

3455 Young, Rod. Speech on an Alberta oil and gas pipe line to Vancouver delivered in the House of Commons on April 29, 1949. Ottawa: E. Cloutier. (2pp). *BVAUS/Mac27f.44.

3456 Young, Rod. Speech on the Atlantic pact delivered in the House of Commons 29 April 1949. Ottawa: E. Cloutier. 4pp. *BVAUS/Mac27f.44.

3457 ------ Speech on price control with remarks of Mr Gardiner and Mr Harkness delivered in the House of Commons on February 18, 1949. Ottawa: E. Cloutier. 4pp. *BVAUS/Garrison 1-5.

3458 ------ Speech on unemployment - housing, social services, merchant marine delivered in the House of Commons on March 4, 1949. Ottawa: E. Cloutier. *BVAUS/Garrison 1-5.

1950

3459 Alberta Co-operative Union. Alberta co-operatives and farm organizations. Edmonton. 55pp. *OOAL.

3460 Association for Civil Liberties. A brief to the Premier of Alberta. Toronto. 16pp. *OTURS/RSK. On racial discrimination.

(3461) Betcherman, P. Unions and wage rates in the newsprint industries of Quebec and Ontario 1909 to 1948: a method of assessing the influence of labour unions on wage rates as exemplified by the Canadian newsprint industry. Unpublished MA thesis, McGill University.

3462 Bjarnason, Emil and Bert Marcuse. Wages and the cost of living. Vancouver: Trade Union Research Bureau. (14pp). BVIP *BVAUS/Mac31f.37 OOA/Endicott 15 OTURS/RSK.

3463 Bristow, Dudley Alexander. Agrarian interest in the politics of Ontario: a study with special reference to the period 1919-1949. Unpublished MA thesis, University of Toronto. (v), 270pp, biblio, appendixes of federal and provincial election results. *OTUAR.

3464 Buck, Tim. Let Canada act to save world peace: act to stop the Korean war. (Toronto): Labor-Progressive Party. (2pp), broadside. *OTURS/RSK.

3465 ------ On Korea: a letter to the Prime Minister (and) Let Canada act to save world peace (3464 above). Toronto: Labor-Progressive Party. 16pp. *BVAUS/Mac 41f.8b OHMA2418 OKQS OTURS/RSK.

3466 ------ The Yankee occupation of Canada. Toronto: Labor-Progressive Party. 16pp. BVIP OPAL *AEUS BVAUS/WB42f.25a OHMA1486 OKQS OTURS/RSK SSUS.

3467 Buckley, J.W. Trade unionism in Canada. An address at the summer school of the International Chemical Workers Union at the WEA Labour College, Port Hope, June 24, 1950. (Toronto): Workers Educational Assn. 7pp, mimeo. *OTPB/Buckley.

3468 Canadian Congress of Labour. Tenth anniversary convention: declaration of positive economic philosophy. Winnipeg. 8pp. *OOA/CCF192.

3469 ------ Report of executive council tenth anniversary convention, Winnipeg, Manitoba, September 25, 1950. Ottawa. 32pp. *OOA/CFAW 50.

3470 Canadian Slav Committee. People, be vigilant!... that this shall never happen again. New secret documents about Nazi plans for the extermination of the Slavic peoples. Toronto. (c1950). 15pp. *BVAUS/ Mac40f.8a OTURS/RSK.

3471 ------ To all Slavic Canadians: unite and act to save peace: manifesto, reports and decisions of the first Canadian Slav Congress, Toronto 29-30 June and 1 July 1950. Toronto. 64pp. *OOA/Endicott 15 OTURS/RSK.

3472 Coldwell, M.J. Speech on the address in reply to the soeech from the throne delivered in the House of Commons 20th February, 1950. Ottawa: E. Cloutier. 8pp. *BVAUS/Garrison 1-5.

3473 ------ Speech on Korea delivered in the House of Commons, September 1, 1950. Ottawa: E. Cloutier. 7pp. *BVAUS/Mac27f.44 OTURS/Woodsworth 54.

3474 Committee for a Democratic Far Eastern Policy. Facts on the Korean situation. Toronto: Progress. 16pp. *OHMA1502 OTURS/RSK. Same text as a New York pamphlet called 'Facts on the Korean crisis'.

3475 CCF. Brief presented to the Ontario Royal Commission on Forestry by the Ontario section of the CCF. (Toronto). 14pp, mimeo. *OOA/CCF320. Includes a supplementary brief on the special problems of southern Ontario.

3476 ------ History of the CCF. (Ottawa). (c1950). 4pp, mimeo. *OOA/CCF315.

3477 ------ How to organize for an election. Toronto. 10pp, mimeo. *OOA/CCF320.

3478 ------ The key to freedom! A labour code designed to protect, not to enslave, the workers of B.C. Vancouver. (c1950). 6pp, mimeo. *BVAUS/Mac34f.19.

3479 ------ Program for Ontario: CCF Ontario section sixteenth annual convention, Toronto April 6-7-8 1950. Toronto. 40pp. *OOA/CCF319 and 539.

3480 ------ Study outline on socialism today. Ottawa. 15pp, mimeo. *BVAUS/Mac30f.17 OOA/CCF539.

3481 ------ Why farmers support the CCF. Regina. 8pp. *ACGA/CCF25 BVAUS/Mac39f.1 OOA/CCF322 OTURS/RSK SSA/G1.1949.3.

3482 Cooperative Commonwealth Youth Movement. Socialism in our time. Minutes of the tenth CCYM national convention, Vancouver July 24-26, 1950. (Ottawa).

49pp, mimeo. *OOA/CCF345.

3483 Cooperative Commonwealth Youth Movement. Statement
of policy adopted at tenth national convention.
Ottawa. (2pp), broadside. *OOA/CCF345.

3484 Donaldson, L.J. Wanted: vital religion in politics.
CCF principles agree with Christian ideals. Halifax.
16pp. NSHPL SSU *BVAUS/Mac42f.27 OOA/CCF540 OTURS/
RSK.

3485 Douglas, T.C. A budget for progress: speech in the
budget debate on the speech from the throne. Regina:
T.H. McConica. 19pp. *OOA/CCF539.

3486 Endicott, James. Watchman - what of the night? Toronto: Canadian Far Eastern Newsletter. 8pp. *BVAUS/
Mac42f.27a OTURS/RSK.

3487 Fort William Natural Resources Development Board.
The crisis in Ontario's forests! Fort William. 11pp,
mimeo. *OOA/CCF312. An attack on the agreement between the Ontario government and Marathon Paper Mills.

3488 ------ Enemies of the forests! Fort William. 13pp,
mimeo. *OOA/CCF312. An attack on Long Lac Pulp and
Paper and Kimberley-Clark.

3489 ------ Private interests, part of a huge forest monopoly, are ruining the forests with single purpose
operations. Fort William. 7pp, mimeo. *OOA/CCF312.
An attack on Abitibi.

3490 Francis, Anne. The rights of women. Toronto: Canadian Assn for Adult Education. 19pp. *OOA/CCF544.
Behind the Headlines vol 10 no 4.

3491 Fraser, Blair. The saintly failure who changed Canada. (Toronto): Maclean's. (c1950). (4pp). *OOA/
CCF198 and 309. A Maclean's Flashback (J.S. Woodsworth). Reprinted from a previous article.

3492 Friends of the Forest. Ontario's forests: your prosperity and life. Quotations from, and analysis of,
the Report of the Ontario Royal Commission on Forestry. London (Ont). 26pp. *OOA/CCF312.

3493 Gelinas, Pierre. Les communistes, les catholiques
et la paix. (Toronto): (Part-Ouvrier Progressiste).
(c1950). 16pp. *OTURS/RSK.

3494 Hamilton, Richard K. A study of Canadian old age
pension planning. Unpublished BA thesis, McMaster
University. (i), iii, 118pp, biblio. *OHMA.

3495 Harwood, Willa Ruth. A survey of Canadian immigration policy, its development and effect with special
reference to prevailing Canadian attitudes on the
subject. Unpublished MA thesis, McMaster University.
vi, 130pp, biblio. *OHMA.

3496 Hopwood, V.G. Science and art and the basis and
superstructure. (Toronto): (?Labor-Progressive Party)
(c1950). 5pp, mimeo. *OHMA.

3497 Knowles, Stanley. The abolition of the means test from the old age pension. Speech delivered in the House of Commons on Monday March 6, 1950. Ottawa: E. Cloutier. 8pp. *BVAUS/Mac27f.43 OOA/CCF308.

3498 Labor-Progressive Party. Crisis on the Canadian campus. Toronto. 16pp. *BVAUS/WB31f.3b OHMA3162.

3499 ------ Prairie farmers organizing against CPR-trusts squeeze. Winnipeg. (1p), broadside. *OKQS.

3500 ------ Unite for peace and Canadian independence! Draft resolution: fourth national LPP convention. Toronto: Canadian Tribune. (4pp). *OTURS/RSK. Different text (same title) from resolution actually adopted.

3501 ------ United action for peace: report and proceedings, seventh annual convention of the BC Yukon district LPP. Vancouver. 44pp, mimeo. *BVAUS/WB31f.3e.

3502 ------ Who wants war? Toronto. (c1950). (16pp). *BVAUS/Mac43f.17 OHMA3143 OTURS/RSK.

3503 League for Democratic Rights. (Constitution). (Toronto). 3pp, mimeo. *OTURS/RSK.

3504 Lefeaux, W.W. Economics:(lecture 1): social economy: lectures 2, 3 and 4. Vancouver: np. (c1950). (3) plus 3 plus 4 plus 3pp. *BVAUS/Young.

3505 Lipset, S.M. Agrarian socialism: the CCF in Saskatchewan. A study in political sociology. Berkeley and Los Angeles: University of California Press/ Toronto: Oxford University Press. (xx), 315pp. *OONL Peel 4207.

3506 (MacDonald, A.B.). Co-operatives: labour's next opportunity. Ottawa: Cooperative Union of Canada. (c1950). 40pp. *MWPA/CCF33.

3507 McDonald, Donald G. Twenty years of trade unionism in Canada. A survey of the inter-war oeriod 1919- 1939. Unpublished MA thesis, Acadia University. (v), 88(92)pp, biblio. *NSWA.

3508 McGuire, J.E. The International Confederation of Free Trade Unions for a world of social justice, freedom and peace. Ottawa: Mutual. 16pp. BVIP NSHPL OH OOP *OTURS/RSK. Includes a manifesto.

3509 McHenry, Dean E. The third force in Canada: the CCF 1932-1948. Berkeley and Los Angeles: University of California Press/Toronto: Oxford University Press. viii, 351pp, biblio. *OONL.

3510 MacInnis, Angus. Speech on Canada's trade situation delivered in the House of Commons on February 28, 1950. Ottawa: E. Cloutier. 4pp. *BVAUS/Mac27f.43.

3511 ------ Speech on government motion for committee on old age security delivered in the House of Commons on March 24, 1950. Ottawa: E. Cloutier. 7pp. *BVAUS/ Garrison 1-6 and Mac27f.43.

3512 MacInnis, Angus. Speech on social security: an app-
eal for a national program delivered in the House of
Commons 17 April 1950. Ottawa: E. Cloutier. 6pp.
*BVAUS/Garrison 1-5.

3513 McMaster, T.A. Beyond collective bargaining. Winnipeg: Manitoba Teachers Society. 100pp. *MWP.

3514 McNaught, K.W.K. James Shaver Woodsworth: from
social gospel to social democracy (1874-1921). PhD
thesis, University of Toronto. (v), 274pp, biblio.
*OTUAR.

3515 Magnuson, Bruce. No wage cuts! No lay-offs! An
open letter to workers in the pulp and paper industry.
(Toronto): (Labor-Progressive Party). 8pp. *OTURS/
RSK. 'Work and wages for Canadian workers must take
priority over dividends and American war policy.'

3516 Masters, D.C. The Winnipeg general strike. Toronto:
University of Toronto Press. xvi, 159pp, illus.
No biblio. *OONL.

3517 Montague, John Tait. Trade unionism in the Canadian
meat packing industry. Unpublished PhD thesis, University of Toronto. 267pp, biblio. *OTUAR.

3518 Morrison, James A. Labor management relations in
the coal mining industry of Nova Scotia. Unpublished
MA thesis, Acadia University. (v), 112(114)pp, biblio. *NSWA.

3519 National Federation of Labor Youth. You and your
future. Toronto. (c1950). (16pp). *BVAUS/Mac43f.
22 OTURS/RSK. A recruiting pamphlet (for NFLY).

3520 Nesbitt, Leonard D. Save our soil. Calgary: Alberta
Wheat Pool. 24pp. OONL *ACGL OOA/CCF312.

3521 Ontario. Report on the Workmens Compensation act;
report of the Honourable Mr Justice Roach, commissioner, appointed to inquire into and report upon,
and to make recommendations regarding, the Workmens
Compensation act upon subjects other than detail
administration, May 31, 1950. Toronto: Kings Printer.
125pp. *OTL.

3522 Ontario Federation of Labour. Memorandum: the legislative proposals as submitted to the Prime Minister
and members of the cabinet of the government of Ontario. Toronto. 6pp, mimeo. *OOA/OFL 8.

3523 Roberts, Thomas C. The story of the padlock law.
Toronto: League for Democratic Rights. (c1950).
(32pp). SSU *BVAUS/WB42f.1a OOA/Endicott 15 OTURS/
RSK. Quotes text of the act.

3524 Rodd, Roscoe S. Our heritage of liberty. Toronto:
League for Democratic Rights. (c1950). 12pp.
*OHMA1895 OOA/Endicott 15 OTURS/RSK.

3525 Rolph, William Kirby. Henry Wise Wood of Alberta.
Toronto: University of Toronto Press. xii, 235pp.
*OONL. See also 3356 above.

3526 Salsberg, J.B. Jobs! Jobs! Jobs! Toronto: Labor-
Progressive Party. 16pp. AEU SSU *BVAUS/WB31f.3a
OHMA1911 OTURS/RSK. Includes 1950 LPP program.

3527 Simcoe County Federation of Agriculture. Community
farming: co-operation as a new method of organizing
the farm business. np. 12pp. *OOA/Avison 10.

3528 Sims, Charles. Where is the CCF going? Toronto:
Labor-Progressive Party. 14pp. BVIP OPAL *BVAUS/
WB31f.3a OHMA1912 OTURS/RSK.

3529 Socialist Labor Party. The high cost of living.
Toronto. (4pp). *OTURS/RSK.

3530 Stuart, Ronald S. The problem of unemployment in
Canada 1929-1939. Unpublished BA thesis, McMaster
University. (ii), v, 155pp, biblio. *OHMA.

3531 Swan, James B. The CCF. Unpublished MA thesis,
Acadia University. v, 150(155)pp, biblio. *NSWA.

3532 Toronto Peace Council. Peace, pen and paper. Toronto. (16pp). *OHMA3144 OOA/Endicott 15 OTURS/
RSK. Poems, excerpts and graphics prepared by a
group of writers and artists.

3533 Trades and Labor Congress of Canada. An historical
review 1873-1949. Ottawa. 20pp. *AEPAA/Farmilo 4.

3534 ------ Memorandum presented to the Dominion government Thursday, March 9th, 1950. (Ottawa). 24pp.
*OOA/Bengough 1. Social security, price and rent
control.

3535 Valleau, O.W. Government insurance is a thriving
business. Regina: np. (c1950). 4pp. *OOA/CCF300.

3536 Vancouver Peace Assembly. You can actually prevent
war: Newspapers kill truth about peace. Vancouver.
(c1950). (2pp), broadside. *BVAUS/Smith CP. The
Stockholm peace appeal.

3537 Woodcock, George and Ivan Avakumovic. The anarchist
prince: a biographical study of Peter Kropotkin.
London: T.V. Boardman. 463pp. *OONL.

3537A Wu Hsiu-Chuan and Tim Buck. China stands for peace:
(and) Canada must recognize China. Toronto: Canadian
Tribune. 8pp, illus. *BVAUS/WB31f.2c.

1951

3538 Alexander, K.L. A study of collective bargaining in
the Canadian labour movement with special emphasis
on the development and use of trade agreements.
Unpublished MA thesis Acadia University. v, 211pp.
*NSWA.

3539 Andras, Abraham. The social cost of intolerance.
Montreal: Canadian Labour Reports. 8pp. *BVAUS/

Mac41Bf.14. First published in *The Commerce Journal*
Toronto, 1951. Hann 2776.

3540 Bloomer, N.S.J. Labour-management relations in the
steam railway industry. Unpublished MA thesis, Dalhousie University. iv, 151pp. *NSHD.

3541 Bouvier, Emile. Patrons et ouvriers. Montréal: La
section des Relations Industrielles de l'Université
de Montréal. 209pp. *OONL. Etudes série A no 1.
Translated, without acknowledgement to the French
edition, as *Neither right nor left in labour relations*,
Study series B no 1.

3542 ------ Unemployment insurance in Canada 1940-1950.
Montreal: Industrial Relations section, University
of Montreal. 16pp. Bulletin 1. *OONL.

3543 Buck, Tim. CCF in Saskatchewan. Vancouver: Labor-
Progressive Party. (1p), broadside. *BVAUS/WB31f.4

3544 ------ Fight for peace - as for life! Toronto:
Labor-Progressive Party. 48pp. AEU BVIP *BVAUS/WB
42f.3a OHMA2423 OTURS/RSK SSUS.

3545 ------ We fight for Canada. Toronto: Labor-Progressive Party. 19pp. AEU BVIP BVIV *BVAUS/WB31f.3c
OHMA2146 OKQS OTURS/RSK. On the Garson amendments
to the criminal code to legalize telephone tapping,
searching without warrants etc.

3546 (Canadian Congress of Labour). Facts about prices
before - after price control. (Ottawa). 10pp, mimeo.
*OOA/CFAW50.

3547 Canadian Trade Union Delegation to the Soviet Union.
We were there: report. Toronto. 64pp. *OTURS/RSK.

3548 Carter, Charlotte and Dyson. We saw socialism. Toronto: Canadian-Soviet Friendship Society. 176pp.
AEU BVAU BVIP MWP OKQ QMU SSU *OTURS/RSK.

3549 Coldwell, M.J. Speech on international affairs delivered in the House of Commons on October 22, 1951.
Ottawa: E. Cloutier. 7pp. *BVAUS/Mac27f.43.

3550 ------ Speech on the Korean crisis delivered in the
House of Commons. Ottawa: E. Cloutier. 7pp.
OTURS/RSK.

3551 Congress of Canadian Women. Women on the march...
for freedom, equality and peace. Toronto. 16pp,
illus. *OHMA OOL OTURS/RSK. Contains keynote
speech of Mrs Rae Luckock (President) to the 2nd
all-Canadian conference; notes on the Congress, list
of offciers, secretaries of local chapters etc.

3552 CCF. The CCF in the world today: a preliminary draft
of a statement of CCF principles. Regina. (4pp).
*SSA/G2.1951.1.

3553 Cooperative Commonwealth University Federation. Min-
utes of the fifth CCUF national convention, Toronto
October 27 and 28, 1951. Ottawa. 8pp, mimeo. *OOA/
CCF338.

3554 Council of Progressive Jewish Organizations. To all
delegates at the plenary session of the Canadian Jewish Congress. (Toronto). (2p), broadside, bilingual.
*OOA/Klein 20. On the expulsion of the progressive
organizations from the Congress.

3555 Croteau, J.T. Cradled in the waves: the story of a
people's co-operative achievement in economic betterment on Prince Edward Island, Canada. Toronto: Ryerson. x, 149pp. *OOAL.

3556 Douglas, T.C. Bread or bombs. Speech in the debate
on the speech from the throne, Saskatchewan legislature, 1951. Regina: T.H. McConica. 19pp. *ACGL/
PDbl OOA/CCF536 and 539 OTURS/RSK.

3557 ------ Co-operation among fishermen: a radio address.
Regina: T.H. McConica. (8pp). *OOA/CCF308.

3558 Dowson, Ross. The CCF: our tasks and perspectives.
(Toronto); Revolutionary Workers Party, Canadian sec-
tion of the Fourth International. 24pp, mimeo.
*OOA/CCF393.

3559 Endicott, James. None shall make them afraid: an
address at the National Assembly to Save Peace.
Toronto: Canadian Far Eastern Newsletter. 8pp.
*OHMA1619 OOA/Endicott 1 OTURS/RSK SSA/McNaughton
H11.

3560 Endicott, J.G. Make peace triumph over war. (Toronto): National Assembly to Save Peace. 8pp. SRL
*BVAUS/Mac42f.3a OHMA1620 OOA/Endicott 1 OTURS/
RSK SSA/McNaughton H11. Includes 6 proposals for
peace action.

3561 Endicott, Mary Austin. My journey for peace. Toronto. 24pp. SRL *BVAUS/Mac38f.5c OHMA1618 OOA/
Endicott 1 OTURS/RSK SSA/McNaughton H11.

(3562)Fort William Natural Resources Development Board.
The case of the Great Lakes Lumber Shipping Ltd.
Strangulation! Fort William. 6pp. OOAG.

3563 Fowke, Edith. They made democracy work: the story
of the Cooperative Committee on Japanese Canadians.
Toronto: Cooperative Committee on Japanese Canadians.
(c1951). 32pp. AEU NSHPL OH OKQ OOP QMBM QMU SSU
*BVAUS/Mac41f.8 OHMA2870 OOA/CCJC 1-2 OTURS/RSK.

3564 Good, W.C. Which way peace? Toronto: Ryerson. (iv),
32pp. MWU OH OONL OOP SRL *MWP.

3565 International Union of Mine, Mill and Smelter Workers.
How high are living costs? The IUMMSW and UE Radio
and Machine Workers of America expose the deficiencies
of the Dominion Bureau of Statistics cost of living
index. (Toronto). vii, 151pp. BVAU BVIP OHM QQLA
SSU *NSHPL.

3566 Irvine, William and Elmer Roper. A personal message. Battle River-Camrose: CCF. (c1951). (4pp).
*SSA/G3.Alta.12.

3567 Jolliffe, E.B. Text of a radio address on provincial affairs, Monday, April 30th 1951 over a provincial network of the CBC. (Toronto): (CCF). 5pp, mimeo. *OOA/CCF308.

3568 Knowles, Stanley. The nations business: (given) over CBC, Thursday May 22nd 1951. (Ottawa): (CCF). 6pp, mimeo. *OOA/CCF308.

3569 Labor-Progressive Party. Constitution. Toronto. 31pp. *OTURS/RSK OKQS.

3570 ------ Danger! The American oil trust threatens the peace and freedom of Saskatchewan. Break its evil grip! End graft in high places. Saskatoon. (4pp). *OTCPA.

3571 ------ Platform for progress: the LPP proposes. Winnipeg. 8pp. *OTURS/RSK.

3572 ------ Report on the second national cultural conference of the LPP held in Toronto May 12-13 1951. Make the arts serve the cause of peace! Toronto. (8pp), mimeo. *OHMA.

3573 Laidler, H.W. World cooperation and social progress. New York: League for Industrial Democracy. 38pp. *OOA/CCF552. Contains brief contribution from M.J. Coldwell.

3574 League for Democratic Rights. Strike penalty - ten years in jail! Toronto. (8pp). *ACGA/Smith 14 BVAUS/Mac32f.3 OHMA OOA/Endicott 15 OTURS/RSK.

3575 ------ What is the League for Democratic Rights? (Toronto). 2pp, mimeo. *OTURS/RSK.

3576 McEwen, Tom. He wrote for us: the story of Bill Bennett, pioneer socialist journalist. Vancouver: Tribune. 161pp. *OTURS/RSK.

3577 MacFarlane, J. (compiler). Quintet: a symposium: CCF foreign policy. What it is and four different viewpoints on what it should be. Toronto: Cooperative Commonwealth Youth Movement. 32pp. *OHMA1595. The four views are pacifist by Beth Dickman; Marxist by Douglas Carr; third force by Peter Macdonald; and world federalist by Hanna Newcombe.

3578 MacInnis, Angus. Speech on control of price delivered in the House of Commons 10 April 1951. Ottawa: E. Cloutier. 7pp. *BVAUS/Garrison 1-5.

3579 National Conference to Defend Liberty. Resolutions adopted at the national conference called to defend liberty, extend democracy, and fight for rights. Toronto. (1p), mimeo. *ACGA/Smith 13.

3580 Ontario Federation of Labour. Memorandum: the legislative proposals as submitted to the Prime Minister and members of the cabinet of the government of Ontario. Toronto. (4pp). *OOA/OFL 8.

3581 Park, Libbie and Frank. Moscow - as two Canadians

saw it. Toronto: Canadian-Soviet Friendship Society.
94pp. AEU OONL OPET SSU *BVAUS/WB38f.5c OHMA1929
OTURS/RSK.

3582 Regina Peace Council. What about Korea? Regina.
(c1951). 8pp. *BVAUS/Mac41f.8B OOA/Endicott 12
OTURS/RSK.

(3583) Reynolds, R.P. Public policy with respect to the
settlement of labour disputes in the Canadian railway industry. Unpublished PhD thesis, Massachusetts
Institute of Technology. viii, 253pp. OONL.

3584 Rodd, Roscoe. Freedom! - the people's prerogative:
address at the national conference of the League for
Democratic Rights. Toronto. 11pp, mimeo. *OTURS/
RSK.

3585 Scott, F.R. New horizons for socialism. Ottawa:
Woodsworth House. 16pp. AEU BVIP NSHPL *BVAUS/Mac
30Af.4b OHMA1570 OOA/Coldwell 61 and CCF538 OTURS/
RSK SSA/G2.1951.3 SSUS/JL197.

3586 Sims, Charles. Tim Buck fighter for peace and socialism. Toronto: Labor-Progressive Party. 16pp.
AEU BVIP *BVAUS/WB39f.2a(ii) OHMA1913 OTURS/RSK.

3587 Smiley, Donald Victor. Canadian labour and the law.
Unpublished MA thesis, University of Alberta. (iii),
156pp. *AEUS.

3588 Stewart, Charles M. Stop big business profiteering
in food: it can be done. Excerpts of CKLG radio
address. Vancouver: Labor-Progressive Party. (c1951).
(3pp). *OTURS/RSK.

3589 Underhill, F.H. Booklist on 'Fifty years of socialism'. Toronto: Ontario Woodsworth Memorial Foundation. (c1951). 8pp, mimeo. *OTURS/RSK SSUS/JL197.

3590 United Electrical Workers. Security conditions:
findings of Rev Allan Ferry, union nominee on an
arbitration board concerning R. Stevens and Canadian
General Electric Co. Toronto. 16pp. *OTURS/RSK.
On the transfer of Stevens to 'unclassified' work.

3591 Weir, John. Bard of Ukraine: an introduction to
the life and works of Taras Shevchenko. Toronto:
Association of United Ukrainian Canadians, National
Jubilee Committee. 64pp. *OTURS/RSK.

3592 Winnipeg and District Trades and Labor Council.
Labor day annual, 1951. 32pp. *MWPA/Russell 1.

3593 Wismer, Leslie E. Workers way to a fair share as
carried forward by the Trades and Labor Congress
of Canada. Montreal: Trades and Labor Congress of
Canada. 118pp. *OTURS/RSK. A history of the Trades
and Labor Congress.

3593a ------ Proceedings of the Canadian labor union congresses 1873-1877. Ottawa: np. 101pp. *OOL.
Summary of reports of the early years.

1952

(3594) Adams, Robert McDonald. The development of the United Steelworkers of America in Canada 1936-1951. Unpublished MA thesis, Queens University. 233pp. OKQ missing.

3595 Allan, Ted and Sydney Gordon. The scalpel, the sword: the story of Dr Norman Bethune. Boston: Little, Brown. (xvi), 336pp, aphorisms, biblio. *OTURS/RSK.

3596 Bjarnason, Emil. What price gold? Vancouver: Trade Union Research Bureau. (c1952). 7pp. *OTURS/RSK.

(3597) Bolduc, Yvon. Organisations ouvrières et droit syndical fédéral; une étude portant sur l'influence de deux Congrès ouvriers (Le Congrès des Metiers et du Travail du Canada et le Congrès canadien du Travail) sur le droit syndical fédéral de 1872-1950. Unpublished MA thesis, Université de Montréal. 166pp.

3598 BC Peace Council. Destroy the bombs not the people. Vancouver. (c1952). 4pp. *OTURS/RSK.

3599 Brown, W.G. Competition and co-operation. (Saskatoon): Consumers Cooperative Refineries. (c1952). (8pp). *SSUS/Coops.

3600 Buck, Tim. Thirty years 1922-1952: the story of the Communist movement in Canada. Toronto: Progress. 224pp. *BVAUS/Mac39f.16 OHMA2428 OKQS OTURS/RSK.

3601 Canadian Congress of Labour. Memorandum submitted to the federal government March27, 1952. Ottawa. (4pp). *OOA/CFAW 49. On labour attachès, price and rent control, national labour code etc.

3602 ------ Interim report of proceedings, twelfth regular convention, September 22-26, 1952. Ottawa. (4pp). *OOA/CFAW 49.

3603 Canadian Peace Congress. Documentation on bacteriological warfare. Toronto. 33 plus (2)pp, mimeo. *OOA/Endicott 11.

3604 ------ National conference call for peace, arms reduction and trade. Toronto. (4pp). *C.

3605 Canadian-Soviet Friendship Society. Report of the national convention. Toronto. 48pp. *BVAUS/WB42f. 25a OTURS/RSK. Speeches, resolutions, program.

3606 Coldwell, M.J. The North Atlantic Treaty Alliance and Korea. Speech delivered in the House of Commons on March 6, 1952. Ottawa: E. Cloutier. 8pp. *BVAUS/Mac27f.43 OOA/Coldwell 60 and CCF537.

3607 ------ Speech on social credit delivered in the House of Commons 11 December 1952. Ottawa: E. Cloutier. 8pp. *OOA/CCF541. Largely an attack on the anti-semitism of Social Credit.

3608 Congress of Canadian Women. Constitution and bill
of rights for Canadian women. Toronto. 11pp.
*OTURS/RSK. Adopted 11 March 1950, amended 1952.

3609 CCF. CCF seeks a world plan to banish poverty and
hunger from the face of the earth. Toronto. (2pp),
broadside. *OOA/CCF298 SSA/G1.nd.7.

3610 ------ Facts about CCF government in Saskatchewan -
an unequalled record of achievement and efficiency!
Regina. 24pp. *BVAUS/Mac30f.21 OHMA1528 OOA/CCF
322 and 554 SSA/G1.1952.2. Various editions with
texts some of which are the same, some different.

3611 ------ $5 millions too much: that's what you're
paying for automobile insurance. Edmonton. (4pp).
*OOA/CCF573.

3612 ------ The future belongs to Saskatchewan. Regina.
(16pp). *SSA/G1.1952.15. Cartoons of CCF record.

3613 ------ Progress in power. Regina. (4pp). *SSA/
G1.1952.5 SSUS/CCF.

3614 ------ Provincial convention program IOOF Hall,
Edmonton December 5-6, 1952. 20pp. *OOA/CCF75.

3615 ------ What about Saskatchewan oil? Regina. (4pp).
*SSA/G1.1952.13.

3616 ------ What we desire for ourselves...we wish for
all. Regina. 14pp. *OOA/CCF540 SSA/G1.1952.8.

3617 ------ Yes, I've joined the CCF and I'll tell you
why. Ottawa. (6pp). *OOA/CCF540 SSA/G2.nd.15.

3618 ------ Yours for humanity, security and progress.
Regina. (4pp). *SSA/G1.1952.10.

3619 Cooperative Commonwealth University Federation.
Minutes of the sixth national convention, Toronto,
December 28 and 29, 1952. Ottawa. 21pp, mimeo.
*OOA/CCF338.

3620 Cooperative Commonwealth Youth Movement. Peace -
freedom - socialism. Minutes of the eleventh national convention, Toronto, August 3, 4 and 5, 1952.
(Ottawa). 50pp, mimeo. *MWPA/CCF26 OOA/CCF345.

3621 Douglas, T.C. A big budget for a big job: speech
in the debate on the budget. Regina: T.H. McConica.
21pp. BVIV *OOA/CCF539.

3622 ------ Security, development, expansion: speech in
the debate on the speech from the throne. Regina:
T.H. McConica. 19pp. BVIV OOP *OOA/CCF539.

3623 Endicott, James G. I accuse! Toronto: Peace Review,
Canadian Peace Congress. 34pp. BVIP OPET *BVAUS/
Mac43f.17 OOA/Endicott 12 OTURS/RSK SSA/McNaughton
H11. On germ warfare in Korea.

3624 ------ Strength through peace. Do everything to
unite, nothing to divide. Opening address to the
national conference for peace, arms reduction and

trade, Massey Hall, Toronto, May 10-11, 1952. Toronto: Canadian Peace Congress. (4pp). *OOA/Endicott 13 OTURS/RSK.

3625 Erickson, Carl. An immediate peace in Korea! A paper delivered at the third BC peace conference in Vancouver, April 19 and 20, 1952. Vancouver: BC Peace Conference. 4pp, mimeo. *BVAUS/WB31f.2c.

3626 Freed, Norman. Canada's war budget: made in USA. Four thousand dollars a minute for armaments. Toronto: Labor-Progressive Party. 16pp. *BVAUS/Mac43 f.17 OHMA1615 OTURS/RSK.

(3627) French, J.K. A survey of labor relations legislation in Canada - federal and Ontario. Unpublished MSc thesis, Massachusetts Institute of Technology. viii, 108pp.

3628 Gardner, Ray. The Japanese peace treaty. Vancouver. 15pp. *BVAUS/Mac41f.8 OOA/Endicott 15 OTURS/RSK. On Japanese and German rearmament.

3629 ------ Wanted for murder: S.S. Brigadefuhrer Kurt Meyer. Vancouver. (c1952). (10pp). *BVAUS/Mac40 f.8a. OTURS/RSK. Against the proposal to release for new military duties a Nazi war criminal sentenced to death (commuted to life imprisonment) for the murder of Canadian troops.

3630 Genkind, Ethel Ostry. Our goal is peace. Toronto: Congress of Canadian Women. 18pp. BVIP *BVAUS/Mac 32f.2 OOA/Endicott 15 OOL OTURS/RSK.

3631 Greening, W.E. Paper makers of Canada: an history of the paper makers union in Canada. (Three Rivers): International Brotherhood of Paper Makers. (ii), 96pp. *NSWA OONL.

3632 International Union of Mine, Mill and Smelter Workers. Voices of freedom at the national convention, special session, Denman auditorium, Vancouver, February 1st, 1952. Vancouver. (8pp). *BVIPA.

3633 Kashtan, William. Jobs through peace. Toronto: Labor-Progressive Party. 16pp. *BVAUS/WB42f.3a.

3634 King, Carlyle. The place of the CCYM in the CCF. (Regina): CCF. (4pp), mimeo. *OOA/CCF344.

3635 Labor-Progressive Party. Canadian independence and people's democracy. Toronto. 29pp. BVAS OKQ SSU *BVAUS/WB31f.3c OHMA1796 OOA/CCF542 OTURS/RSK.

3636 ------ For peace and disarmament in 1952. Toronto. 5pp. *OHMA OTURS/RSK.

3637 ------ Our country betrayed! Save Canada! The LPP has a new program for all Canadians who love peace, national independence and democracy. Toronto. (4pp). *OHMA.

3638 ------ Peace: trade: jobs: BC election manifesto. Vancouver. (4pp). *BVAUS/WB31f.3c.

3639 League for Democratic Rights. A bill of rights -
not abolition of rights! Toronto. 3pp, mimeo.
*ACGA/Smith 14.

3640 ------ Protect our democratic rights: the history
of Bill H-8; insist that Parliament reject the
'police state' proposals in Bill H-8...act now. A
bill of rights not abolition of rights. Toronto.
16pp. *OTURS/RSK.

3641 ------ Radio script. Toronto. 7pp plus (1p)
corrections. *ACGA/Smith 14. The revision of the
criminal code.

3642 ------ Your rights and freedoms in danger. Toronto.
16pp. *OPET OTURS/RSK.

3643 Levitt, Kari and others. The story of Canada's heroes. Part I, Karl Marx: Part II, Mackenzie and Papineau: Part III, Louis Riel. Toronto: National Federation of Labour Youth. 12 plus 20 plus 17pp, mimeo.
*OTURS/RSK.

3644 MacInnis, Angus. Speech on health insurance and war
veterans allowances delivered in the House of Commons
on December 9th and 11th. Ottawa: E. Cloutier. 10pp.

3645 Morrison, Jean. Adventure in Berlin. Toronto: Youth
Friendship League. 26pp. *BVAUS/Mac40f.7c OHMA3161
OTURS/RSK. Record of the 3rd world festival of youth
held in Berlin.

3646 Nesbitt, Leonard D. The case against the speculative
marketing of grain. Calgary: Alberta Wheat Pool.
11pp. OONL SRL *OOA/CUC224 OTURS/RSK.

3647 Noseworthy, J.W. Speech on national health insurance
delivered in the House of Commons on November 25,
1952. (Ottawa): (E. Cloutier). 7pp. *OOA/CCF201.

3648 Pare, Jean. Non à la conscription à la guerre. Montréal: Conseil de Montréal pour la Paix. 16pp. *OOA/
Endicott 15 OTURS/RSK.

3649 Roper, Elmer E. A call to action: address at annual
convention of Alberta CCF in the IOOF Hall, Edmonton
5 December 1952. Edmonton. 7pp. *ACGA/CCF29.

3650 Scott, F.R. Publishing false news. np: Canadian
Bar Review. pp37-47. *OOA/Coldwell 61. Offprint.

3651 Socialist Labor Party of Canada. Peace - security -
freedom - can be won. Toronto. (4pp). *OTURS/RSK.

3652 ------ What socialism means: peace, plenty and freedom for you! Toronto. (c1952). (4pp). *OTURS/RSK.

3653 Socialist Party of Canada. The capitalist. Winnipeg.
(3pp), mimeo. *BVAUS/Mac30Af.2a. No.2 of a series.

3654 ------ Charity. Winnipeg. (3pp), mimeo. *BVAUS/
Mac30Af.2a. No. 9 of a series.

3655 ------ The class struggle. Winnipeg. (3pp), mimeo.
*BVAUS/Mac30Af.2a. No. 4 of a series.

3656 Socialist Party of Canada. Depression! Winnipeg. (3pp), mimeo. *BVAUS/Mac30Af.2a. No. 5 of a series.

3657 ------ Labor Party. Winnipeg. (3pp), mimeo. *BVAUS/Mac30Af.2a. No. 10 of a series.

3658 ------ Politics. Winnipeg. (4pp), mimeo. *BVAUS/Mac30Af.2a. No 6 of a series.

3659 ------ The socialist. Winnipeg. (3pp), mimeo. *BVAUS/Mac30Af.2a. No. 1 of a series.

3660 ------ Wages. Winnipeg. (4pp), mimeo. *BVAUS/Mac30A f.2a No. 7 of a series.

3661 ------ The worker. Winnipeg. (3pp), mimeo. *BVAUS/Mac30Af.2a. No. 3 of a series.

3662 ------ World worth while. Winnipeg. (3pp), mimeo. *BVAUS/Mac30A f.2a. No. 8 of a series.
This series first published jointly with the World Socialist Party of the US, mostly 2pp leaflets, HI Uncat. C150: reissued in above format 1958-59.

3663 Togliatti, Palmiro. The only correct path for mankind. Toronto: Progress. (12pp). *BVAUS/WB39f.16 OTURS/RSK. Facsimile of his *For a lasting peace, for a people's democracy.*

3664 Toronto Writers Group. We write: a selection of work. Toronto. 48pp, mimeo. *OTURS/RSK, defective. Includes Margaret Fairley, Mary Holmes, Ray Lowther, Nancy Doyle etc.

3665 Trades and Labor Congress of Canada. Memorandum to the government of Canada. Ottawa. 47pp. *OOA/Bengough 1. Social security, housing, price control, taxation, national labour code etc.

3666 Underhill, F.H. Reading list for Canadian socialists. Toronto: Ontario Woodsworth Memorial Foundation. 15pp, annotated. *AEUS/CCF XIV-3 BVAUS/Mac43f.1 OHMA 2874 OOA/CCF310.

3667 United Electrical Workers. Labor accuses Duplessis! Toronto. (c1952). 22pp. *OOL OTURS/RSK.

3668 United Fishermen and Allied Workers Union. The case for the fishermen: why all who depend on fishing to earn a living should come under the protection of the BC Compensation act. Vancouver. 9pp. BVIP *BVAUS/Mac40f.4b.

3669 Wood, William Donald. Unionization of office workers in Ontario. Unpublished MA thesis, Queens University. ix, 134pp, biblio. *OKQ.

3670 (Yanovsky, Avrom). 12 litho prints. Toronto: np. 12 prints plus (2pp) foreword. *BVAUS/WB31f.21. Foreword by Tim Buck; prints signed Avrom.

3671 Young, Frederick John Lenane. The limits of collective bargaining in the Canadian automobile industry. Unpublished MA thesis, Queens University. vi, 166pp, biblio. *OKQ.

1953

3672 Bengough, Percy R. Address opening the 68th annual convention of the Trades and Labor Congress of Canada. (Ottawa). 9pp. *OOA/Bengough 1.

3673 Boyle, George. Father Tompkins of Nova Scotia. New York: P.J. Kennedy. xiv, 234pp. *OOAL.

3674 Bright, L.J. Co-operation history and philosophy. Regina: Co-operative Union of Saskatchewan. 75pp. OOP SRL *OOAL. Foreword T.C. Douglas.

3675 Buck, Tim. Beat the threat of depression. Toronto: Labor-Progressive Party. 18pp. ACU AEU BVIP BVIV OPET *BVAUS/WB39f.20a OHMA2408 OKQS OTURS/RSK SSUS.

3676 ------ Canada for her people. Toronto. Labor-Progressive Party. 32pp. *AEUS BVAUS/WB31f.3b OHMA 2406 OKQS OTURS/RSK SSUS.

3677 ------ Canada for her people not for Wall St.: a federal election message. (Port Arthur): Labor-Progressive Party. 4pp. *OTURS/RSK. Includes a program of development for north-western Ontario.

3678 ------ New horizons for young Canada. Toronto: Progress. 31pp, illus. AEU BVAS BVIP BVIV *BVAUS/ WB43f22 OHMA2424 OKQS OTURS/RSK SSUS.

3679 ------ An open letter to members of Parliament. Regina: Labor-Progressive Party. (4pp). *AEUS OHMA2419 OKQS OTURS/RSK. On the criminal code amendments.

3680 ------ Put Canada first! Toronto: (Labor-Progressive Party). (4pp). OHMA OTURS/RSK. On Korea and against selling out Canada to the USA.

3681 ------ Support Churchill's proposal for a meeting with the Soviet Union! Toronto: Labor-Progressive Party. (4pp). *OHMA OTURS/RSK.

3682 Canadian Congress of Labour. Brief submitted to the Senate standing committee on Canadian trade relations. Ottawa. 18pp, mimeo. *OOA/CFAW49.

3683 ------ The Congress memorandum: submitted to the government on March 6, 1953. Ottawa. (6pp). *OOA/ CFAW49.

3684 ------ The Congress memorandum: submitted to the government on December 10, 1953. Ottawa. 8pp. *OOA/CFAW50. Mainly international affairs.

3685 ------ Labour's program for political action: a handbook for PAC members and union officers. Toronto. 14pp. OOL *OOA/CFAW50.

3686 ------ A memorandum submitted to the Unemployment Insurance Advisory Committee, Ottawa, July 14, 1953.

Ottawa. (2pp). *OOA/CFAW49.

3687 Canadian Congress of Labour. Submission to the House of Commons Special Committee on Bill 93 (revision of the criminal code). Ottawa. 6pp. *OOA/CFAW49. The revision deals with treason, sabotage, desertion, sedition, criminal breach of contract, mischief, peaceful picketing etc.

3688 Canadian Congress of Labour. Memorandum submitted to the House of Commons Committee on Broadcasting, April 28, 1953. Ottawa. 17pp, mimeo. *OOA/Forsey 9.

3689 Civil Rights Union. Its a free country - isn't it? You can help keep Canada free. Toronto. Folded leaflet designed to open out as a poster with a declaration of rights. *OTURS/RSK.

(3690) Collins, F.L. The impact of the railway brotherhoods on the Canadian National Railways. Unpublished MA thesis, McGill University. 304pp. Not seen.

3691 Committee for the Rights of Canadian Children. Health insurance now! Toronto. (c1953). 7pp. *OTURS/RSK.

3692 Congress of Canadian Women. Declaration on the rights of Canadian women. Toronto. (c1953). (6pp). *OTURS/RSK.

3693 CCF. Democratic organization of the CCF. (Ottawa). 4pp, mimeo. *OOA/CCF315 and 536.

3694 ------ Organizational guide. Ottawa. 18pp. *ACGL/ PDbl BVAUS/Mac30f.1b OOA/Klein 17 SSUS.

3695 ------ Program for Ontario: nineteenth annual convention, Toronto, April 2-3-4, 1953. Toronto. 40pp. *OOA/CCF48.

3696 ------ Provincial convention program: IOOF Hall, Edmonton, December 3,4,5, 1953. Edmonton. 20pp. *OOA/CCF75.

3697 ------- Report of special convention CCF (Ontario section), November 20 and 21, 1953, Toronto. (Toronto). 5pp, mimeo. *OOA/CCF319 and 350. To elect a new provincial leader.

3698 ------ Speakers notes. Ottawa. 72pp, mimeo. *BVAUS/Mac30f.15 OKQS OOA/CCF536 OTURS/RSK.

3699 ------ Understanding the CCF. Vancouver. 6 booklets in one folder as follows: 1. How the CCF began by Grace MacInnis: 2. The CCF today by Jessie Mendels: 3. The Regina manifesto by J.M. Thomas: 4.'Socialism' by Alex MacDonald: 5. Socialism and democracy by Frank Snowsell: 6. Know the CCF program by Frank McKenzie. *BVAUS/Mac30Af4c OOA/CCF 316. Each 10-13pp.

3700 ------ Understanding our economy. Vancouver: Boag Foundation. 6 booklets as follows: 1. The economy we live in by Colin Cameron: 2. Boom or bust by Stu

Jamieson: 3. The role of co-operatives by Harold
Daykin: 4. Money and jobs by Harold Daykin: 5. Some
social credit fallacies by Harold Daykin: 6. The
welfare state by Grace MacInnis. *BVAUS/Mac39f.27
OOA/CCF316 lacking no.6.

3701 ------ What's the difference? Toronto. (4pp).
*OOA/CCF320 and 540.

3702 Cooperative Commonwealth University Federation.
Minutes of the seventh CCUF national convention,
Montreal December 28 and 29, 1953. Ottawa. 25pp,
mimeo. *OOA/CCF338 and 345.

3703 Cooperative Commonwealth Youth Movement. Building
the CCYM. Ottawa. (c1953). 12 plus (6)pp, mimeo.
*OOA/CCF344.

3704 ------ Socialism in our time: CCF program for youth.
Ottawa. 26pp, mimeo. *OOA/CCF350.

3705 Corry, J.A. Civil liberties in trying times. Fredericton: University of New Brunswick. 16pp. NSHPL
OKQ OONL OKQ QQLA *NSHDS/J4.

3706 Davies, William. Portrait of Mr A.D. Dunnville
(Ont). 22pp. *OOA/Endicott 15. A.D. stands for
Average Democrat.

3707 Douglas, T.C. Program for progress: speech in the
debate on the speech from the throne. Regina: T.H.
McConica. 27pp. BVIV *OOA/CCF539 SSUS/Shortt.

3708 Endicott, Mary Austin. Five stars over China. Toronto. xvi, 19-464pp. *OONL.

3709 Freed, Norman. Study course on J.V. Stalin's class-
ical work 'Economic problems of socialism in the
USSR'. Toronto: Communist Party of Canada. 16pp.
*OHMA OTURS/RSK.

3710 Heckman, John H. Trade with Canadian cooperatives.
Washington: US Dept of Agriculture. 20pp. *HI.

3711 Jolliffe, Edward B. What we have in view...Toronto:
CCF. 38pp. *AEUS/CCFXIII-31 BVAUS/Mac30f.21 OOA/
CCF308 and 320 and Underhill 45.

3712 Labor-Progressive Party. Draft brief to Royal Commission. Regina. 26pp. *OTURS/RSK.

3713 ------ High cost of university education a national
concern. Brief submitted by national committee of
LPP student clubs to the 1953 conference of the National Federation of Canadian University Students.
Toronto. 6pp. *OTURS/RSK.

3714 League for Democratic Rights. It's a crime! To
strike, to picket, to speak freely in the proposed
new criminal code now before Parliament. Defeat the
repressive laws: keep Canada free. Toronto. 15pp.
OPET SSU *OOA/Endicott 15.

3715 ------ It's still a crime! To speak freely, to
strike, to picket, in the new Bill (no.7) revising

the criminal code. Toronto. 16pp. OKQ OPET *OHMA 1784 OTURS/RSK.

3716 MacInnis, Angus. Speech on external affairs with special reference to Korea and Formosa delivered in the House of Commons on 12 February 1953. Ottawa: E. Cloutier. 8pp. *BVAUS/Garrison 1-6.

3717 ------ Speech on groups who need help: evils of combines delivered in the House of Commons on November 25 and 26. Ottawa: E. Cloutier. 8pp. *BVAUS/Mac27 f.43 and Garrison 1-5.

3718 MacInnis, Grace. J.S. Woodsworth, a man to remember. Toronto: Macmillan. xvi, 336pp, index. *OTURS/RSK.

3719 McKinlay, Clare Mary. The Honorable Irene Parlby. Unpublished MA thesis, University of Alberta. vi, 125pp, appendixes, biblio, photographs. *AEUS.

3720 Macpherson, C.B. Democracy in Alberta: the theory and practice of a quasi-party system. Toronto: University of Toronto Press. xii, 258pp. *OONL.

3721 Macquarrie, Lachlan B. Some consequences of continuous unemployment: a study of social problems of 46 men in receipt of unemployment insurance at the Toronto local office of the Unemployment Insurance Commission during May and June 1950. Unpublished MSW thesis, University of Toronto. (vi), 81pp, biblio. *OTUAR.

3722 Morris, Leslie. Towards communism. Toronto: Labor-Progressive Party. 30pp. AEU BVIP OPET *BVAUS/WB 31f.3d OHMA1837 OKQS OTURS/RSK SSUS.

3723 National Federation of Labor Youth. The state: a study outline in five parts. Toronto. 17pp, mimeo *OTURS/RSK.

3724 Neatby, Hilda. So little for the mind. Toronto: Clarke Irwin. x, 384pp, biblio notes. *OONL.

3725 Oesterling, Kjeld and Norman Freed. Peace, freedom and you. Prague: Peace and Socialism. 30pp. *OTURS/RSK.

3726 Ontario. Proceedings and report of the select committee appointed by the Legislative Assembly to enquire into civil liberties and rights with respect to the Indian population of Ontario, and matters relevant thereto. Toronto: Queens Printer. 2 vols. *OTL.

3727 Prang, Margaret. Some opinions of political radicalism in Canada between the two world wars. Unpublished MA thesis, University of Toronto. 284pp, biblio. *OTUAR. A study of the views of four Canadian periodicals: The Canadian Forum, Saturday Night, The Christian Guardian - The New Outlook, The Catholic Register.

3728 Prince,Cyril. A double victory: for peace and wages. Windsor: Labor-Progressive Party. (c1953). 11pp. *OTURS/RSK.

3729 Rodd, Roscoe S. Keep Canada free. Civil Rights
Union anniversary dinner, Saturday December 12th,
1953. (Toronto): Civil Rights Union. (8pp). *OHMA.
Contains also declaration of rights of Canadians.

3730 Roper, Elmer E. They shall walk and not faint.
Edmonton: CCF. (6pp). *ACGA/CCF29.

3731 Scott, F.R., R.A. McKay and A.E. Ritchie. The world
war against poverty. Toronto: University of Toronto
Press for the Royal Society. 32pp. BVAU OH OKQ
OOP OTU *OONL. Technical assistance and economic
aid through the UN; the Colombo plan.

3732 Socialist Labor Party. Banish the cause of fear.
Toronto. (3pp). *OTURS/RSK. Fear of global war.

3733 ------ Stalinism exposed: the greatest fraud in
history. Toronto. (c1953). (4pp). *OTURS/RSK.

3734 Stanton, George. Where is the CCF going? Toronto.
(c1953). 4pp. *C.

3735 Toronto Committee to Secure Clemency for Julius and
Ethel Rosenberg. An appeal to your conscience.
Must the Rosenbergs die? Toronto. (4pp). *OHMA.

3736 Trades and Labor Congress of Canada. An historical
review 1873-1952. Ottawa. 24pp, illus. *OTPB/
Buckley.

3737 ------ Memorandum to the government of Canada.
(Ottawa). 36pp. *OOA/Bengough 1. Social security
and labour legislation.

3738 (USSR). Canadian workers look at the Soviet Union:
statements made by two Canadian trade union delega-
tions which visited the Soviet Union in 1951 and
1952. Moscow: Foreign Languages Publishing House.
95pp. *OONL.

3739 United Electrical. The 521 story at Canada Wire.
Toronto: UE local 521. 40pp. *OTURS/RSK.

3740 Wallace, J.S. All my brothers. Toronto: New Frontiers. 20pp, illus. AEU BVAU *OHMA3196.

3741 Workers Educational Association. Golden jubilee
1903-1953. Toronto. 56pp, illus. *OTURS/RSK.
Mainly the history of the WEA in Canada.

1954

3742 Aseltine, Herschel E. Churchmen and workmen. Hamilton: Christian Labour Assn of Ontario. 19pp.
*HI Uncat C300.

3743 Beausoleil, Gilles. Wages in Quebec and Ontario.
Ottawa: Canadian Congress of Labour. 50pp, tables.
BVAS BVAU NSHPL OOL OOP OTU SSU *OHMA2324 OONL.

3744 Bengough, Percy R. Opening address 69th annual con-
vention, Regina, Sask. August 23rd 1954. (Ottawa):
Trades and Labor Congress of Canada. 8pp. *OOA/
Bengough 1.

(3745)Bisaillon, J.J. History of trade unions in Canada.
Unpublished MA thesis, Columbia University. 69pp.
Not seen.

3746 Bouvier, Emile. Guaranteed annual wage: a modified
system. Montreal: Industrial and Labour Relations
Publications. 52pp, biblio. *OHMA2542. Translated
reprint from 'Relations' April, May, June 1953.

3747 BC Federation of Labour. Submission: representation
on the Board of Industrial Relations. Vancouver.
7pp. *BVIP.

3748 Brotherhood of Railroad Trainmen. Negotiations manual. (Ottawa). 140pp. BVAU MWU NSHPL OKQ OOL *OOP.

3749 Buck, Tim. Every Canadian worker can have a job: we
can beat the Made-in-USA depression. Labor day message of Tim Buck. (Toronto): Labor-Progressive Party.
(4pp). *OTURS/RSK.

3750 ------ Never again! We shall not break faith with
our 100,000 war dead. (Toronto): Labor-Progressive
Party. 2pp, mimeo. *OTURS/RSK.

3751 ------ Put Canada first! Toronto: Labor-Progressive
Party. 46pp. AEU BVIP BVIV OOP *BVAUS/WB31f.3b
OHMA2407 OKQS OTURS/RSK SSUS.

3752 Canada, Dept of Labour. Six broadcasts on apprenticeship. Ottawa: E. Cloutier. 29pp. *OOA/Bengough 3.
Includes 'What is a journeyman' by Bengough.

3753 Canadian Congress of Labour. What did they pay for
your vote? Toronto. 4pp. *OOA/CCF315.

3754 Canadian Labour Reports. These are your rights under
federal and provincial fair employment practice legislation. Montreal. 10pp. *OOA/CCF543.

3755 Canadian Peace Congress. Canadian security vs. German militarism...plan adopted by an enlarged meeting
of the executive held at Toronto December 8, 1954,
with the participation of representatives from Quebec
and of a number of affiliated national organizations.
Toronto. (i), 4 plus 2pp, mimeo. *OHMA.

3756 ------ What people are saying about the H-bomb.
Toronto. (c1954). 4pp, mimeo. *BVAUS/IWW.

3757 Castleden, G.H. Speech on Canada needs leadership
delivered in the House of Commons 14 April 1954.
Ottawa: E. Cloutier. 7pp. *SRA/CCF National 63.

3758 Cheolin, Mor. Recognize China. Edmonton: Committee
for the Recognition of China. 8pp. *BVAUS/WB31f.29.

3759 Coldwell, M.J. Speech on international affairs delivered in the House of Commons on 29 January 1954.
Ottawa: E. Cloutier. 8pp. *SSA/G2.1954.1.

3760 Communist Party of Canada. The issue is survival: put Canada first. Election statement. Edmonton: (c1954). (4pp). *ACGL/PE Communist.

3761 Congress of Support for Negotiated Peace. Declaration to the nation. Toronto. 2pp. *OOA/CCF145.

3762 CCF. How to organize for a federal election. Toronto. 52pp, mimeo. *OOA/CFAW53 and CCF320.

3763 ------ How to organize for a provincial election. Toronto. 20pp, mimeo. *OOA/CCF57.

3764 ------ Humanity first: the CCF program. Ottawa. 46pp. BVIV OOP OTU SRL *ACGA/CCF29 OOA/CCF130 and 417 SSA/G2.1951.2 SSUS/CCF OKQS.

3765 ------ Looking to the future. Program adopted by the 20th annual convention held in Toronto on May 22 23 and 24, 1954. Toronto: Ontario section. 40pp. *OOA/Coldwell 59 and CCF537 OTURS/RSK.

3766 ------ Looking to the future: a statement of the CCF program for Ontario approved by the provincial council for submission to the annual provincial convention. Toronto. 13pp, mimeo. *OOA/CCF319. Preliminary version of 3765 above.

3767 ------ Price control by monopolies. Edmonton. (c1954). (4pp). *ACGA/CCF29.

3768 ------ Program for Newfoundland. (St Johns). (1p) *OOA/CCF25.

3769 ------ Program for Newfoundland as adopted by the provincial convention held at Bay Roberts, November 5 and 6, 1954. (St Johns). (8pp). *OOA/CCF318.

3770 ------ Ten years of progress 1944-1954: ten years of CCF government: ten years of achievement. This is the record. It speaks for itself! (Regina). 18pp. *BVAUS/Mac30f.21 OOA/CCF70 and 539 OTURS/ Woodsworth 29 SSA/G1.1954.4 SSUS/CCF.

3771 Cooperative Commonwealth Youth Movement. Minutes of CCF youth Ontario section, annual convention, Toronto May 1 and 2, 1954. (Toronto). 16 plus 6pp, mimeo. *OOA/CCF350.

3772 ------ Peace - freedom - socialism: minutes of the twelfth national convention Edmonton, Alberta, July 26 and 27, 1954. Ottawa. 40pp, mimeo. *OOA/CCF346

3773 Davis, Richard E. The unfinished task of social welfare in Canada. Ottawa: Canadian Welfare Council. 16pp. *OONL.

3774 Douglas, T.C. Ten years of progress! Speech in the debate on the speech from the throne. Regina: T.H. McConica. 20pp. *BVAUS/Mac30f.22 OOA/CCF539 SSUS/ Shortt.

3775 Endicott, James G. Will they drop the hydrogen bomb? Toronto: Toronto Peace Council. (4pp). *OHMA OTURS/ RSK.

3776 Engelmann, Frederick Charles. The Cooperative Commonwealth Federation of Canada: a study of membership
participation in party policy-making. Unpublished
PhD thesis, Yale University. (iii), vi, 262pp, biblio.
*OOAL. Appendix of who's who in the CCF.

3777 Fistell, Harry. Discussion of the Soviet lesson:
does the LPP slander, frame-up and expel critical
members? A contribution from an LPP member who was
slandered, framed and expelled for criticism. Toronto. 8pp. *OKQS OTURS/RSK.

3778 Gardner, Ray. 600 million friends - for Canada.
Vancouver: BC Peace Council. (16pp). *T. For the
recognition of China.

3779 ------ The truth about the hydrogen bomb. Vancouver:
BC Peace Council. (14pp). *BVAUS/WB39f.1f. Originally published in the Peace Review, Toronto, and
reprinted with addtional 4pp added in BC.

(3780)Herlihy, H.M. The collective bargaining policies
of UAW-CIO in Canada. Unpublished PhD thesis, University of Chicago. v, 142pp. Not seen.

3781 Hougham, George Millard. Minor parties in Canadian
national politics 1867-1940. Unpublished PhD thesis,
University of Pennsylvania. vii, 307pp, biblio.
Microfilm.

3782 Labor-Progressive Party. Brief to the Royal Commission on Constitutional Problems. Toronto. 253pp,
mimeo, in 12 sections, each paged separately. *OHMA
3203 OTURS/RSK.

3783 ------ Canadian independence and a people's parliament. Toronto. 32pp. *BVAUS/WB31f.3b and 31f.3d
OHMA1799 OKQS OTURS/RSK. Program adopted at the
5th convention, March 1954.

3784 ------ Education finance in British Columbia: submission to the Honourable Ray Williston, Minister
of Education, Victoria, BC. Vancouver. 14pp plus
3pp appendix. *BVAUS/WB31f3d.

3785 ------ Proceedings of the 5th Ontario convention
meeting at Toronto May 15-16, 1954. Toronto. 8pp,
mimeo. *OKQS OTURS/RSK.

3786 ------ Stop the betrayal of Canada! Unite for peace
and Canadian independence. Draft resolution for the
fifth convention. Toronto: Canadian Tribune. (4pp).
*OTURS/RSK.

3787 Loosmore, Thomas Robert. The British Columbia labor
movement and political action, 1879-1906. Unpublished
MA thesis, University of British Columbia. (i), iii,
219, xxxviii pp, illus, biblio. *BVAUS.

3788 MacDonald, Donald C. Politics: a moral challenge.
A message to the people of Ontario. Toronto: CCF.
(4pp). *OOA/Coldwell 59 and CCF320 and 538.

3789 National Federation of Labour Youth. Constitution:
for life with a purpose. (Toronto). (c1954). 10pp,
mimeo. *OTURS/RSK.

3790 News-Facts. Trade with the Soviet Union - here are
the facts! Toronto. 17pp. *BVAUS/WB43f.10 OTURS/
RSK.

3791 Normandin, Paul. The padlock law theatens you!
Montreal: Civil Liberties Union. 22pp. AEU BVIV
OKQ OTMCL SSU *BVAUS/WB42f.1a OHMA1933 OTURS/RSK.

(3792)Panting, G.E. A study of the United Farmers of Manitoba in 1928. Unpublished MA thesis, University of
Manitoba. viii, 281pp. Not seen.

3793 Saskatchewan. Labour in Saskatchewan. Regina: Bureau
of Publications. (c1954). (16pp). *OTURS/RSK.

3794 Socialist Labor Party of Canada. Unemployment---
why? Toronto. (4pp). *OTURS/RSK.

3795 Stewart, Alistair. Colonialism means war: a speech
delivered in the House of Commons 28 May 1954. Ottawa: E. Cloutier. 7pp. *SRA/CCF Nat.64.

3796 Szöke, Istvan. We are Canadians: the national group
of Hungarian-Canadians. Toronto: Hungarian Literature
Assn. 95pp. *OHMA1904 OTURS/RSK.

3797 Trades and Labor Congress of Canada. Memorandum to
the government of Canada. (Ottawa). 36pp, *OOA/
Bengough 1 and OFL 8. Health and unemployment insurance, housing, labour legislation etc.

3798 ------ and Canadian Congress of Labour. Agreement
between the Trades and Labor Congress of Canada and
the Canadian Congress of Labour, Ottawa, November 18
1954. Ottawa. 7pp. *OOA/CFAW51. On 'raiding'.

3799 ------ Joint submission to the government of Canada:
unemployment. Ottawa. 15pp. *OOA/OFL 10.

3800 United Electrical. Report from Canada to the international UE 19th convention 27 Sept - 1 Oct 1954.
np. 13pp, mimeo. *OTURS/RSK.

3801 United Jewish Peoples Order. They are marching again!
Montreal. 28pp. *OOA/Endicott 15 OTURS/RSK. On
German rearmament.

3802 Winnipeg Free Press. Protecting our birthright. Disallowance or bill of rights? Winnipeg. 20pp. *OOA/
Underhill 44.

1955

3803 Bilan, Ivan. Social security of employees. Winnipeg:
Ukrainian Labour Committee and Ukrainian Workers Org-
anization. 24pp. *OONL. Title page in English and
Ukrainian, but text entirely in Ukrainian.

3804 Birney, Earle. Down the long table. Toronto:
McClelland and Stewart. (vi), 298pp. *OONL. Novel
of the 1930's relating to the Communist and Trotskyist
organizations.

3805 Boutilier, Danny W. Rockin' chair rhymes. (?Amherst).
np. 48pp. NSHPL *NSHD. Known as 'the poet of the
pits' - a double-edged appellation. Very few of the
poems have anything to do with labour.

3806 Brewer, James L. The anti-communist peril of Waldo
Frank. Halifax: New Christian Books. 12pp. *NSHD.

3807 Buck, Tim. A new deal for the provinces and municipalities - submission to the conference of federal
and provincial governments. Toronto: Labor-Progressive Party. 17pp, mimeo. *BVAA OHMA3194 OTURS/RSK.

3808 Canadian Congress of Labour. Memorandum submitted
to the government 15 December 1955. Ottawa. 7pp.
*OOA/CFAW50.

3809 ------ Submission to the labour legislation review
committee, Dept of Labour, Nefoundland. Ottawa.
17pp, mimeo. *OOA/CFAW49.

3810 ------ 25 questions and answers. Ottawa. 9pp.
*OOA/CFAW49. Why join a union and similar questions.

3811 Charlton, H.M. (Annie). A rebel: poems, prose and
selections. (Victoria). 7pp, mimeo. *BVIPA.
Includes early reminiscences c.1900.

3812 Christie, Edward A. The Presbyterian church in Canada and its official attitude toward public affairs
and social problems 1875-1925. Unpublished MA thesis,
University of Toronto. (i), iii, 319pp, biblio.
*OTUAR. Appendix: Report of special committee to
consider resolution re social unrest (1919).

3813 Coldwell, M.J. A brief autobiography and record of
public service. Regina: CCF. (c1955). (4pp).
*SSA/G2.1935.1. (possibly misreading of 1955).

3814 ------ The challenge of the hydrogen bomb. (Ottawa):
CCF. (4pp). *ACGL/PDbl SSA/G2.1955.2.

3815 Communist Party of Canada. Speak out now for peace,
neutrality and disarmament! Vancouver. (c1955).
(4pp). *BVAUS/WB42f.3a.

3816 CCF. Bosses siren song: where is the CCF going?
Toronto: George (Paddy) Stanton. (c1955). (4pp).
*OTURS/RSK. An inquiry into the decline of CCF sup-
port in the 1948, 1951 and 1955 provincial elections.

3817 ------ The history and organization of the CCF in
the provincial constituency of Humboldt 1933-1954.
Regina. 7pp. *SSA/G1.1954.2.

3818 ------ Policy for British Columbia. Vancouver.
11pp. *OOA/CCF86.

3819 ------ Program for action. Vancouver. (2pp), broadside. *OOA/CCF316.

3820 CCF. Program for Ontario: 21st annual convention,
Toronto April 7-8-9 1955. Toronto. 50pp. *OOA/CCF
319. Includes constitution.

3821 ------ Progress: a survey of Saskatchewan government activity. Regina: Bureau of Publications.
Various editions in pages up to 96pp. *OOA/CCF322.

3822 CCF 'Box 16' Committee. Our CCF movement is in peril.
Vancouver. 3pp, mimeo. *OOA/Coldwell 59. Refers to
Rod Young being accused of promoting a left-wing
splinter group in BC.

3823 Cooperative Commonwealth Youth Movement. The CCF
presents--a program for youth. Ottawa. (4pp). *OKQS.

3824 Douglas, T.C. Saskatchewan faces the future: speech
in the debate on the speech from the throne. Regina:
L. Amon. 19pp. BVIV SRL *OOA/CCF539 SRA/CCF Sask
325 SSUS/Shortt.

3825 ------ Saskatchewan's industrial development: speech
in the debate on the budget. Regina: L. Amon. 21pp.
ACGL *BVAUS/Mac30f.22 OOA/CCF539 SRA/CCF Sask 326
SSUS/Shortt.

3826 Farmers Union of Alberta. FUA jubilee day: the organized farmer. Edmonton. 24pp. *K.

3827 International Union of Mine, Mill and Smelter Workers.
Canadian constitution as adopted by the Canadian
constituent convention, Rossland BC in July 1955 and
referendum vote, November 29, 1955. Toronto. 72pp
OHMA. Amended in 1958, 1959 and 1963.

3828 Ivens, William. Prismatic picture of hydro-electric
power development in Manitoba: past, present, future.
Winnipeg. *OOA/CCF64. This copy a bound typescript
of 265pp, prepared for publication but ? published.

3829 Kashtan, William. Unity! Will organized labor's
dream come true? Toronto: Labor-Progressive Party.
16pp. *BVAUS/WB31f.3a OTURS/RSK. On the agreed
mergers between the AFL and CIO,and CCL and TLCC.

3830 King, Carlyle and T.C. Douglas. With a vision in
our minds of a society based on peace, justice and
equality for all mankind. Reports of progress toward a cooperative commonwealth to the 20th annual
CCF provincial convention, 1955. Regina: CCF. 8pp.
*SSA/Gl.1955.1.

3831 Labor-Progressive Party. A new deal for provinces
and municipalities. Toronto. 14pp, mimeo. *OTURS/
RSK. Not the same text as 3807 above.

3832 ------ The rising tide of democratic Canadianism and
the fight to put Canada first. Report of the national
cultural commission to the fourth national cultural
conference, Toronto 8,9, and 10 April 1955. Toronto.
11pp, mimeo. *OHMA OKQS OTURS/RSK.

3833 ------ United people's action can prevent BC Electric
grab of natural gas distribution. Resolution adopted

by provincial conference, Saturday May 28, 1955.
Vancouver. 5pp, mimeo. *BVAUS/WB31f.3e.

3834 League for Democratic Rights. A civil rights act
for BC. Vancouver. (8pp), mimeo.

3835 Lewack, Harold. The quiet revolution: a study of the
Antigonish movement. New York: Student League of
Industrial Democracy. 20pp. MWP *OOA/CCF554.

3836 Lewis, David. A socialist takes stock. Toronto:
Ontario Woodsworth Memorial Foundation. 12pp.
*BVAUS/Mac42f.1 OTURS/RSK SSUS/JL197.

3837 Macklin, I.V. Have they turned their back to the
Bible? Grande Prairie (Alta). 66pp. ACG OOP OTU
*OOA/CCF541. An attack on social credit.

3838 McLachlan, Alexander and others. The stone, the axe,
the sword and other Canadian poems. Toronto: New
Frontiers. 32pp. *OTURS/RSK. Introduction by J.S.
Wallace; the first in a series. The other poets re-
presented are Isabelle Valancy Crawford, Archibald
Lampman and Peter McArthur.

3839 Meyers, Robert. Spirit of the post road: a story of
self-help communities. (?Winnipeg): Federation of
Southern Manitoba Co-ops. viii, 151pp. *OOAL.

3840 Morris, Leslie. Canada and Geneva: new hope for
world peace. Toronto: Labor-Progressive Party.
16pp. OKQ OPAL SSU *BVAUS/WB42f.3a OHMA1850 OTURS/
RSK. Geneva meeting between Eisenhower, Bulganin,
Eden and Faure.

3841 ------ You are wrong, Mr Pearson! Remilitarizing
the Nazis puts Canada in danger. Toronto: Labor-
Progressive Party. 16pp. BVIP OKQ *BVAUS/WB40f.8a
OHMA1855 OTURS/RSK.

3842 Morris, Vera. Parents are important. Toronto: National Cultural Committee, United Jewish Peoples Order.
30pp. *OTURS/RSK. Errata slip tipped in.

3843 Naas, Bernard G. and Carmelita S. Sakr. American
labor union periodicals: a guide to their location.
Ithaca: Cornell University Press. xv, 175pp. *OONL.
Includes some Canadian.

3844 Ontario Federation of Labour. Talking points: for
use in the coming Ontario provincial elections. Toronto. 17pp plus 7pp appendix. *OOA/Coldwell 59.

3845 ------ and Trades and Labor Congress of Canada.
Joint submission on unemployment insurance and health
insurance. (To the government of Ontario). (Toronto).
11pp, mimeo. *OOA/OFL 8.

3846 ------ Memorandum presented to the Prime Minister
and members of the executive council of Ontario.
(Hamilton). 29pp. *OOA/OFL 8

3847 Parker, Seymour. Union participation: a study in
culture and personality. PhD thesis, Cornell Uni-

versity. 363pp. Microfilm. A study of small communities in the Maritime provinces.

3848 Powrie, Thomas L. Labour and population in Saskatchewan: a study of changes in farm labour utilization
and of farm population growth in Saskatchewan from
1896 to 1951. Unpublished MA thesis, University of
Saskatchewan. (v), 163, xlviii, (164-167), biblio.
*SSUS.

3849 Rhodes, D. Berkeley. The Star and the new radicalism:
1917-1926. Unpublished MA thesis, University of Toronto. viii, 199pp, biblio. *OTUAR.

3850 Schonning, (E)gil. Union-management relations in
the pulp and paper industry of Ontario and Quebec,
1914-1950. Unpublished PhD thesis, University of
Toronto. (viii), 277(283)pp, biblio. *OTUAR.

3851 Schulz, J. Rise and fall of Canadian farm organizations. Winnipeg. 119pp. ACG BVAU BVIP OH OOP OTP
OTU *MWPA/Brigden 7.

3852 Sullivan, J.A. (Pat). Red sails on the Great Lakes.
Toronto: Macmillan. 189pp. *OTURS/RSK. The Communist Party and the Canadian Seamans Union.

3853 TCL-CCL Unity Committee. Report and recommendations
constituting a draft agreement for a merger of the
Canadian Congress of Labour and the Trades and Labor
Congress of Canada. (4pp). *OOA/CFAW 51.

3854 ------ Report and recommendations submitted to the
70th annual convention of the Trades and Labor Congress of Canada, May 30th, 1955, Windsor, Ontario.
Montreal. 11pp plus 11pp, bilingual. *OOA/Bengough 1.

3855 United Electrical, Radio and Machine Workers of America. Jobs for Canadians from Canadian power and industry. Toronto. 47pp. *OTURS/RSK. Submission to
the federal government in support of the Canadian
members call for public hearings on Canadian electrical manufacturing industries.

3856 Workers Benevolent Association of Canada. Constitution and by-laws. Winnipeg. 114pp. *OTURS/RSK.
Adopted in 1944, and amended.

1956

3857 Alberta Federation of Labor. Merger convention. The
Alberta Federation of Labor; Industrial Federation
of Labor of Alberta. September 17th-20th 1956 at
the Masonic Temple, Edmonton, Alberta, Edmonton.
16pp. *AEPAA/Farmilo 3. Mostly portraits.

3858 ------ Seminar in advanced labor education, November
5th to 12th, 1955. Edmonton. 69pp. *AEPAA/Farmilo
3. Includes articles by A. Andras, Stuart Jamieson.

3859 Brown, Homer G. and Muriel J. New China as we saw
it. St Marys (Ont). 27pp. BVIP OHM OTU OOP *BVAUS/
Mac38f.20 OOA/Endicott 1 OTURS/RSK.

3860 Bryden, Ken. What is the CCF? A brief explanation
in question and answer form of the origin, nature
and aims of the CCF. Toronto. 16pp. AEU BVIP
*OOA/CCF540 OTURS/RSK SSA/G3.Ont.17. Also 10pp,
mimeo. *BVAUS/Mac30Af.43 and OOA/CCF57 and 320.

3861 Canadian Labour Congress. Constitution. (Montreal).
35pp. *OTURS/RSK.

3862 ------ Departments. Ottawa. (20pp). *OONL.

3863 ------ Farmer labour program: a farm fair project
for 1956. Ottawa. 7pp, mimeo. *OOA/CFAW51.

3864 ------ Interim report of proceedings, founding convention, Toronto, Ontario, April 23-27, 1956. Ottawa.
6pp. *OOA/CFAW51.

3865 ------ Political education program. Ottawa. 33pp.
*OOA/CCF543.

3866 ------ Principles and policies...the founding convention of the Canadian Labour Congress held in Toronto in April 1956 approved and confirmed these principles and policies. Montreal. (11pp). *OHMA2515
OOA/CFAW52 and CCF192.

3867 ------ Proposed constitution of the Canadian Labour
Congress submitted to the first constitutional convention. Montreal. 12pp. *OOA/CFAW51. See also
3861 above.

3868 ------ The shop steward: a manual designed to give
shop stewards a working knowledge of their duties
and responsibilities. Ottawa. 42pp. *OONL.

3869 ------ Submission to the Royal Commission on Broadcasting. April 15th, 1956. Ottawa. 26pp, mimeo.
Together with: Supplementary submission, 27 September
1956. 13pp, mimeo. *OONL.

3870 Canadian Peace Congress. An appeal to work together
for disarmament. Toronto. (4pp). *OHMA.

3871 Carrothers, A.W.R. A study of the operation of the
injunction in labour-management disputes in British
Columbia 1946-1955 with particular reference to the
law of picketing. Toronto and Montreal: CCH Canada.
xxviii, 276pp. *OONL.

3872 Coldwell, M.J. Is the Communist empire cracking?
Excerpts from a speech at a meeting sponsored by the
English Forum of the Workmens Circle, Montreal, Dec-
ember 14, 1956. (Ottawa): (CCF). 7pp, mimeo. *OOA/
CCF337.

3873 Colquette, R.D. The first fifty years: a history of
United Grain Growers Ltd. Winnipeg: The Public Press.
viii, 309pp, appendix of directors, illus. *SSUS/
Shortt.

3874 CCF. The bunk! in Liberal speeches. How much would their promises cost? Where would they get the money? Regina. (4pp). *OOA/CCF536 SSA/G1.1956.2.

3875 ------ Do you see the whole picture? Toronto. (c1956). (8pp). *OOA/CCF 320.

3876 ------ Election program 1956. Halifax. (4pp). *OOA/CCF318.

3877 ------ The fable of the pump. Toronto. 4pp. *OOA/CCF56, 320 and 537.

3878 ------ Farm power in politics. Regina. 5pp. *OOA/CCF541 SSA/G1.1956.5.

3879 ------ The farmer's share in prosperity. Regina. 8pp. ACGA/CCF29 OOA/CCF537 SSA/G2.1957.6.

3880 ------ Labour and politics. Toronto. 11pp, mimeo. *OOA/CCF320.

3881 ------ Program for industrial development. Halifax. (4pp). *OOA/CCF318.

3882 ------ Program for Manitoba. Winnipeg. (4pp). *OOA/CCF536.

3883 ------ Quick facts for Saskatchewan voters! Saskatchewan leads with the CCF. Regina. 38pp. *OOA/CCF322 and 541 OTURS/RSK SSA/G1.1956.3 SSUS/CCF.

3884 ------ Should we grab or pass the platter? Ottawa. 4pp. *OOA/CCF36 and 539 SSA/G2.1956.1.

3885 ------ Taxes aren't squeezing the farmer! On the average taxes are lower and less a burden on the land in Saskatchewan! Regina. 14pp. *SSA/G1. 1960.9.

3886 ------ What sort of labour laws do we need? Halifax. (4pp). *OOA/CCF318.

3887 ------ Yours for humanity, security and progress. Regina. (c1956). (8pp). *SSA/G1.1956.4.

3888 ------ 1956 Winnipeg declaration of principles of the CCF. Montreal. 4pp. Also published in Ottawa. AEU BVIP OTP OTURS *ACGA/CCF29 MWPA/CCF39 OHMA1537 OOA/CCF536 and 540.

3889 Cooperative Commonwealth Youth Movement. Minutes of the thirteenth CCF youth national convention, Winnipeg July 29 and 30, 1956. Ottawa. 27pp, sections separately paged. *OOA/Coldwell 59.

3890 Crossman, R.H.S. Address to the fourteenth national convention of the CCF, Winnipeg, August 1st, 1956. (Ottawa). 12pp, mimeo. *OOA/CCF337.

3891 Douglas, T.C. In defence of freedom: speech in the debate on the speech from the throne. Regina: L. Amon. 28pp. *OOA/CCF539 SSUS/Shortt.

3892 ------ Program fulfilled: in the budget debate 1956. Regina: L. Amon. 21pp. SRL *SSUS/Shortt.

3893 Embree, David Grant. The rise of the United Farmers of Alberta. Unpublished MA thesis, University of Alberta. iii, 295pp, biblio. *AEUS.

3894 Fawcett, George. The free enterprise post office: a fable. Toronto: CCF. (8pp). *OHMA1551 OOA/CCF 56 and 537.

3895 International Union of Mine, Mill and Smelter Workers. Brief to the Royal Commission on Canada's economic prospects. (Toronto). 61pp plus 5pp appendix, mimeo. *OHMA3195.

3896 Irving, John A. Prairie ideals and realities - the politics of revolt. Kingston: Queens Quarterly. (13pp). *OTURS/RSK. Reprinted from vol lxiii no 2.

3897 Keen, George. The birth of a movement: reminiscences of a co-operator. (?Toronto): (?author). 62pp. OH OKQ OPET OTP SRL *OOP.

3898 Labor-Progressive Party. Appendices to the brief submitted to the Royal Commission on Canada's Econ-omic Prospects. Toronto. 139pp, mimeo. *OTURS/RSK.

3899 ------ Canada's future: submission to the Royal Commission on Canada's Economic Prospects. Toronto: Ryerson. 48pp. *BVAUS/WB31f.3c OHMA1797 OTURS/RSK.

3900 ------ Jobs - peace - security. Regina. (c1956). (4pp). *SSA/G27.1958.1.

3901 ------ Open discussion on all party questions. Tor-onto. 4pp, mimeo. *OKQS OTURS/RSK.

3902 ------ Resolution on the organization of the pre-convention discussion. Toronto. 2pp, mimeo plus accompanying letter. *OTURS/RSK.

3903 ------ Resolution on the 20th congress of the Comm-unist Party of the Soviet Union (adopted by the nat-ional committee of the LPP, May 21, 1956). (Toronto). (2pp), mimeo. *OHMA.

3904 ------ Submission to the Royal Commission on Tele-vision Broadcasting. Toronto. 12pp plus 7pp oral remarks, mimeo. *OTURS/RSK.

3905 Lazarus, Morden. Oil and turmoil. Toronto: Ontario Woodsworth Memorial Foundation. 54pp. AEU BVAUS NSHPL OH OOP OTP *OTURS/RSK SSUS/JL197 OKQS.

3906 League for Democratic Rights. Submission to members of the Legislative Assembly of British Columbia re: civil rights act for BC. Vancouver. 4pp, mimeo. *OTURS/RSK.

3907 Logan, H.A. State intervention and assistance in collective bargaining: the Canadian experience 1943-1954. Toronto: University of Toronto Press. viii, 176pp. *OONL.

3908 MacDonald, Donald C. Forest resources. Toronto: CCF. 7pp, mimeo. *OOA/CCF320.

3909 MacEachern, William. Fourteen days as an old age pensioner. Toronto: Toronto Star. 38pp. *OOA/CCF 315.

3910 MacInnis, Angus. Speech on motion to censure Mr Speaker, delivered in the House of Commons. Ottawa: E. Cloutier. 4pp. *BVAUS/Garrison 1-6.

(3911) Mayne, Don James. Trade unions and schism in Canada. Unpublished MA thesis, University of Pennsylvania. viii, 117pp, biblio.

3912 Morgan, John S. The new look in welfare. Toronto: Ontario Woodsworth Memorial Foundation. 20pp. AEU BVIP OH OTP QMBM QQL *BVAUS/Mac42f.31 OOA/CCF538 OTURS/RSK SSA/G436.5 SSUS.

3913 Morgan, Nigel. British Columbia needs a new forest policy! Vancouver: Labor-Progressive Party. 18pp. *BVAUS/WB31f.3d OTURS/RSK. Synopsis of a brief submitted to the Royal Commission on Forestry.

3914 Ontario Federation of Labour. Memorandum presented to the Prime Minister and members of the executive council of Ontario. 29pp. *OOA/OFL 8. Labour relations act, workmens compensation etc.

3915 Pemberton, Gwen. Health. Toronto: CCF. 8pp, mimeo. *OOA/CCF320.

3916 Roper, Elmer E. Text of an address to a public protest meeting held in the IOOF Hall Edmonton, April 3, 1956. Edmonton: (CCF). (4pp), mimeo. *ACGA/CCF 29 OOA/CCF337. Against building the trans-Canada pipeline.

3917 Ryga, George. Song of my hands and other poems. Edmonton. 86pp. *OTURS/RSK.

3918 Saskatchewan Federation of Labour. Legislative submission to the government of the province of Saskatchewan, Regina, Monday December 17, 1956. (Regina). 14pp, mimeo. *OOA/CCF70. Hours of work, minimum wages, workmens compensation, housing etc.

3919 Scotton, Clifford A. A brief history of Canadian labour. Ottawa: Woodsworth House. 36pp. *BVAUS/ Mac30Af.3b OOA/CCF543 OTURS/RSK. Concentrates on the principal national labour federations.

3920 Smith, Stewart. Marxism and the cult of the individual. Toronto: Labor-Progressive Party. 27pp, mimeo. *OHMA.

3921 ------ Party structure, principle of party organization and party leadership. Toronto: Labor-Progressive Party. 14pp, mimeo. *OHMA OTURS/RSK.

3922 Stewart, Peg and Miller. Socialism. Toronto: CCF. 9pp, mimeo. *OOA/CCF320.

(3923) Trades and Labor Congress of Canada, now the Canadian Labour Congress. Labour mobility. Ottawa: E. Cloutier. 11pp. Not found.

3924 United Electrical. 20th annual convention, November 1-4, 1956. (Toronto). 45pp, mimeo. *OHMA3101.

3925 United Jewish Peoples Order. Statement of aims and purposes. (Toronto). 3pp, mimeo. *OTURS/RSK.

3926 United Steelworkers of America. What price steel? Toronto. 10pp. *OOA/CCF315. Taken from their brief to the Royal Commission on Canada's Economic Prospects.

(3927)Veres, L.J. History of the United Automobile workers in Windsor 1936-1955. Unpublished MA thesis, University of Western Ontario. vii, 180pp.

3928 Wallace, Joe. Hi sister, hi brother! Toronto: New Frontiers. 36pp. *BVAUS/Mac41f.9a OHMA3130 OTURS/ RSK. Poems.

3929 Woodcock, George and others. Papers of the Shaw festival. Vancouver: University of British Columbia. 56pp. *OOA/Underhill 26. Includes Shaw's politics by David C. Corbett.

3930 ------ Pierre-Joseph Proudhon. London (Eng): Routledge and Kegan Paul. (xii), 292pp, biblio. *own copy.

3931 Wright, Jim F.C. Prairie progress: consumer co-operation in Saskatchewan. Saskatoon: Modern Press. xii, 228pp. *OONL.

3932 Young, Fred. Saskatchewan. Toronto: CCF. 9pp, mimeo. *OOA/CCF320.

1957

3933 Argue, Hazen. Speech: give the west a square deal! delivered in the House of Commons 21 January 1957. Ottawa: E. Cloutier. 8pp. *SRA/CCF Nat.66.

(3934)Barnes, Samuel Henry. The ideologies and policies of Canadian labor organizations. PhD thesis, Duke University. xii, 286pp.

3935 BC Federation of Labour. Legislative proposals submitted to the ·Hon W.A.C. Bennett and members of the provincial cabinet. (Vancouver). 21pp. *BVIP.

3936 ------ Statement with reference to the present strike of the International Brotherhood of Locomotive Firemen and Engineers against the CPR. Vancouver. 4pp. *BVIP.

3937 Buck, Tim. 1917-1957: forty years of great change: Canada and the great Russian revolution. Toronto:. Progress. 44pp. AEU BVAS BVIP MWU OOP OTP OTU QMM SRU SSU *BVAUS/Mac38f.18j OHMA2143 OKQS OTURS/RSK SSUS.

3938 ------ Keynote speech, sixth national convention

LPP of Canada, April 19-22, 1957. (Toronto): (Labor-Progressive Party). 22pp, mimeo. *OTURS/RSK.

3939 Buck, Tim. Speech to the national committee meeting, October 1956. (Toronto): Labor-Progressive Party. 17pp. *OTURS/RSK.

3940 Canada. Pension plans and the employment of older workers: a report prepared for the the interdepartmental committee on older workers. (Ottawa): Dept of Labour. 57pp. *OOA/CCF315.

3941 Canadian Brotherhood of Railway Employees. Who represents you? Ottawa. (4pp). *OOA/CCF540.

3942 Canadian Labour Congress. Departments. Ottawa. 25pp. *OOA/CCF543.

3943 ------ First meeting of the General Board: summary of proceedings, Montreal May 1-3, 1957. Ottawa. 17pp. *OOA/CFAW51.

3944 ------ In reply---on the invitation of the Civil Service Association of Ontario the CLC attended a series of educational meetings to assist in their consideration of affiliation with the CLC. Toronto. (c1957). 5pp. *OOA/CCF192.

3945 ------ Memorandum to the government of Canada, January 23, 1957. Ottawa. 33pp. *OOA/CFAW51.

3946 ------ Memorandum to the government of Canada, October 21, 1957. Ottawa. 37pp. *OOA/CCF51.

3947 ------ and Interprovincial Farm Union Council. Farmer labour economic aims. Submission to the government of Canada. Ottawa. 29pp. *OOA/CCF543.

3948 Coldwell, M.J. A personal message. Ottawa: CCF. (4pp). *OOA/CCF123 and 538 SSA/G2.1957.8. Mostly pointing out the similarities between Liberal and Conservative policies.

3949 ------ Speech on farm and other economic problems and the trans-Canada pipeline delivered in the House of Commons on October 16,17,18, 1957. Ottawa: E. Cloutier. 16pp. *SSUS/JL197.

3950 CCF. Album souvenir du 25e anniversaire de la CCF. Ottawa. 126pp. BVIV NSHPL OTP *ACGL BVAUS/Mac. OHMA1565 OOA/Woodsworth 37 SSA/G2.1957.5. Some French text, but mostly English and many advts. Contributors include David Lewis, M.J. Coldwell, T.C. Douglas, Angus MacInnis, Thérèse Casgrain, Andrew Brewin etc. Mostly reminiscences.

3951 ------ Let's share prosperity. Regina. 8pp. *ACGA/CCF29 OOA/CCF537 SSA/G2.1957.1.

3952 ------ Program for Ontario: twenty-third annual convention, CCF ontario section, Toronto, April 18-19-20, 1957. Toronto. 48pp. *OOA/CCF59.

3953 ------ Share Canada's wealth! The national CCF program. Ottawa. 8pp. *ACGA/CCF29 ACGL BVAUS/

Mac30Af.8a MWPA/CCF39 OOA/CCF539 SSA/G2.1957.4.

3954 CCF. Speakers notes. Ottawa. 68pp. BVIP OTURS
*BVAUS/Mac30f.15 OOA/CCF536 and 539.

3955 Crysler, Alfred C. Handbook on Canadian labour laws;
a commentary on the legislation of Canada and its
provinces and the decisions of the courts respecting
labour relations and trade unions. Toronto: Carswell.
xxxv, 373pp. *OONL. Revd edn 1969.

3956 Endicott, James G. The impact of the October revolution of 1917 on the international missionary movement. Toronto: Canadian Far Eastern Newsletter.
22pp. *OHMA OOA/Endicott 1 OTURS/RSK. Principally
the effects in China.

3957 Griffin, J.P. We are not ashamed of the gospel.
Regina: (CCF). 11pp. *ACGA/CCF29 OOA/CCF540.

3958 Hall, Frank. Fair employment practices - a good
beginning. A discussion of federal anti-discrimination legislation. Montreal: Canadian Labour Reports.
(c1957). (4pp). *OTURS.

3959 Hood, Wm C. and Anthony Scott. Output, labour and
capital in the Canadian economy. Ottawa: E. Cloutier.
(vi), 513pp. *OONL. Prepared for the Royal Commission on Canada's Economic Prospects.

3960 Ingle, Lorne. Background of the CPR strike (and)
Press release on the strike. Ottawa: CCF. 7pp
plus 1p, mimeo. *OOA/CCF145.

3961 International Union of Mine, Mill and Smelter Workers.
Submission to the government of Canada on the situation in the non-ferrous metal mining industry. Toronto. 7pp. *OTURS/RSK. Mainly on US tariffs.

3962 Interprovincial Farm Union Council. Submission to
the government of Canada. Ottawa. 14pp, mimeo.
*OOA/CCF315.

3963 Jamieson, Stuart. Industrial relations in Canada.
Toronto: Macmillan. xii, 144pp. *OONL.

3964 Kaplansky, Kalmen. Report of the Department of
International Affairs introduced to the first meeting
of the General Board of the Canadian Labour Congress,
Thursday May 2nd, 1957. (Ottawa). 8pp, mimeo. *OOA/
CCF312.

3965 Kaye, V.J. Participation of Ukrainians in the political life of Canada. Ottawa: np. 24pp. *OTU,
catalogued under Kay-Kysilevs'kyj, V.J.

3966 Kitchener-Waterloo and District Labour Council.
Constitution. Kitchener-Waterloo. 16pp. Amended
in 1959, 1961, 1966, 1969.

3967 Knowles, Stanley H. The role of the opposition in
Parliament. Toronto: Ontario Woodsworth Memorial
Foundation. 11pp. *BVAUS/Mac30f.20 OKQS OOA/CCF
339 OTURS/Woodsworth 29 SSA/G436.4 SSUS/JL197.

3968 Labor-Progressive Party. Constitution. Toronto. 32pp. *OKQS OTURS/RSK.

3969 ------ Peace - democracy - people's needs before monopoly profits! For a democratic national policy! Labor-farmer unity can break the grip of the old-line parties! Federal election program. Toronto. (4pp). *OTURS/RSK.

3970 ------ Recognize China: vitalize BC. Vancouver. 15pp. BVIP SSU *BVAUS/WB31f.3b.

3971 ------ Unite at the polls: break the grip of the old-line parties. Toronto. 4pp. *OTURS/RSK. Various issues (see 3969 above) but all bearing the 'break the grip' message.

3972 MacDonald, Donald. The trade unions and NATO. Paris: NATO. 39pp. *OOA/CCF543.

3973 New Brunswick Federation of Labour and New Brunswick Council of Labour. Brief in support of proposed legislation. St John. 15pp. *OOA/CCF543. Labour relations, workmens compensation, injunctions etc.

3974 Northern Translations Service. Peoples capitalism - a new social order? Toronto. 23pp. *OTURS/RSK. Speeches by Soviet authorities.

3975 Ontario Federation of Labour. Report of the committee on labour relations legislation. Toronto. 38pp plus 18pp plus 4pp. *OOA/CCF543 and OFL 8 *OTAR/1957/46.

3976 ------ Submission to the Select Committee on Labour Relations. (Toronto). 18pp. *OOA/OFL 8.

3977 Shaw, Rosa L. Proud heritage: a history of the National Council of Women of Canada. Toronto: Ryerson. 205pp, illus. *OONL.

3978 Thomas, Clive. The National Council of Canadian Labour and the merger. Ottawa: National Council of Canadian Labour. 8pp. *OOL.

3979 Underhill, Frank H. Canada and the north Atlantic triangle. np. 9pp. *OOP. A talk given at Michigan State University and reprinted from the Centennial Review.

3980 ------ Canadian political parties. Ottawa: Canadian Historical Association. 20pp. *OONL.

3981 Watt, Frank William. Radicalism in English-Canadian literature since confederation. Unpublished PhD thesis, University of Toronto. iii, 358pp. *OTUAR.

1958

3982 Adams, Audrey. A study of the use of plebiscites and referendums by the province of British Columbia.

Unpublished MA thesis, University of British Columbia. 250pp, biblio. *BVAUS.

3983 Biderman, Morris. Report of the executive director to the annual United Jewish Peoples Order conference Toronto 6 and 7, December 1958. (Toronto): United Jewish Peoples Order. 18pp, mimeo. *OTURS/RSK.

3984 Blum, Sid. Education, equality and brotherhood: a discussion of human rights education programs in Canada. Montreal: Canadian Labour Reports. 7pp. *OTURS.

3985 BC Federation of Labour. BC labour. Vancouver. 12pp. *BVAUS/Webster 6-7.

3986 (------) Recommendation for the alleviation of un-employment presented to a general meeting of provin-cial members of the Legislative Assembly, federal members of Parliament and the Executive Board and Unemployment Committees of the Vancouver and Dist-rict Labour Council on December 17, 1958. Vancouver. 17pp, mimeo. *BVAUS/Mac32f.9a.

3987 ------ Submission to the Select Standing Committee on Labour, British Columbia Legislative Assembly. Subject matter: unemployment. Victoria. 23pp, mimeo. *OOA/CCF323.

3988 ------ War against the unions: what's it all about? Vancouver. 12pp. *BVIP.

3989 Bronson, Harold. The dangers of NATO. np. (c1958). (1p). *ACGA/CCF29.

3990 Buck, Tim. Canada in the world crisis. Toronto: Progress. 29pp. BVAS BVIP MWU OONL OPAL *AEUS BVAUS/WB31f.3b OHMA2403 OKQS OTURS/RSK SSUS.

3991 ------ Canada's opportunities: report to the national LPP committee 30 August - 1 September, 1958. (Tor-onto): (Labor-Progressive Party). 18pp, mimeo. *OTURS/RSK.

3992 Canadian Association for Adult Education. Unemploy-ment: cause? treatment? cure? Toronto. 24pp. *MWPA/Russell 1.

3993 Canadian Labour Congress. Brief presented to National Winter Employment Conference, Ottawa July 14 and 15, 1958. Ottawa. 7pp, mimeo. *OOA/CFAW 52.

3994 ------ Report of Executive Council to the second constitutional convention, Winnipeg, Manitoba, April 1958. Ottawa. 141pp. *OOA/CCF145.

3995 ------ Resolution passed at CLC convention. (Tor-onto). 2pp mimeo and 4pp printed. *OOA/CCF378. For the formation of a new 'broadly based people's political movement'.

3996 ------ Submission to the Royal Commission on Price Spreads of Food Products. Ottawa. 13pp. *OOA/CCF315

3997 CLC-CCF Joint Committee. A new political party for

Canada: labour - farmer - CCF - Liberal minded individuals: why is it needed? What can it do? What should its program be? How should it be organized? A discussion outline and reference manual for weekend institutes, conferences, study groups etc. (Ottawa). 11pp, mimeo: later printed 40pp. Mimeo edn in *OOA/CCF302; others ACGA/CCF29 OHMA1589 OOA/CCF378 and 538 SSA/G492.8.

3998 Carter, Dyson. The big brainwash. Gravenhurst: Northern Book House. 176pp. BVAU BVIV OTU QMU *OONL.

3999 ------ Rising world: 365 treasures of human thought and deed. Toronto: Northern Book House. 89pp. AEU OOP *OHMA2852 OTURS/RSK. An anthology.

4000 CCF. The agricultural crisis: legislative inquiry shows where the parties stand! Regina. 12pp. *OOA/CCF541 OKQS SSA/CCF Sask.34 SSUS/CCF.

4001 ------ Challenge for Ontario: the CCF provincial program. Toronto. 32pp. *OKQS OOA/CCF320 and 536 OTURS/RSK.

4002 ------ Count the gains since 1944. Regina. (4pp). *OOA/CCF536 SSA/G1.1958.1.

4003 ------ Farmers betrayed again! The fiasco of Conservative farm promises. (Regina): (c1958). (2pp) broadside. *SSA/G2.1958.3.

4004 ------ The farmers fair deal. Winnipeg. (4pp). *OOA/CCF537.

4005 ------ Let's go forward: (the national CCF program). Ottawa. 8pp. BVIP *ACGA/CCF29 ACGL MWPA/CCF39 OKQS OOA/CFAW53 and CCF537 SSA/G2.1958.4 SSUS.

4006 ------ Speakers notes. Ottawa. 52pp. OOP *BVAUS/ Mac30f.15 OOA/CCF539.

4007 ------ Text of resolution passed at CCF national convention, Montreal, July 1958. Ottawa. 4pp. *OOA/CCF315 and 378. Refers to the new party.

4008 ------ Your right to health: what will the medical care plan mean to you? Regina. (c1958). (6pp). *ACGL/PDbl.

4009 Douglas, T.C. Prosperity at home: peace abroad. Speech in the debate on the speech from the throne. Regina: L. Amon. 22pp. *SSAUS/Shortt.

4010 Good, W.C. Farmer citizen: my fifty years in the Canadian farmers movement. Toronto: Ryerson. xiv, 294pp. *MWP.

4011 Griffin, Harold. British Columbia: the people's early story. Vancouver: Tribune. 95pp. *BVAUS/ WB32f.3.

4012 Hardy, L(oui)s-Laurent. Brève histoire du syndicalisme ouvrier au Canada. Montréal: Editions de l'Hexagone. 158pp. *OONL.

4013 Irvine, William.   Live or die with Russia.   (Calgary).
     143pp.   AEU BVIP OONL OOP QMBM SRL *ACGL OOA/CCF537
     OTURS/RSK.   Based on a visit in 1956.

4014 Knowles, Stanley.   Wage policy and full employment:
     an address to the Sarnia branch of the Engineering
     Institute of Canada, October 9, 1958.   Ottawa: Can-
     adian Labour Congress.   9pp.   *ACGL.

4015 Labor-Progressive Party.   The road to socialism in
     Canada.   Toronto.   32pp.   BVIV OKQ *OTURS/RSK.

4016 Lazarus, Morden.   What the ICFTU means to you.   Ott-
     awa: Canadian Labour Congress.   *OOA/CCF?

4017 MacDonald, D.C.   Challenge for Ontario.   Toronto:
     Ontario Federation of Labour.   4pp.   *OTURS/RSK.

4018 MacLeod, Jean.   United Farmer movement in Ontario
     1914-1943.   Unpublished MA thesis, Queens University.
     (iii), 215(219)pp, biblio.   *OKQ.

4019 Montreal Socialist Forum.   Canadian democracy and the
     struggle for socialism: a report of the second meet-
     ing.   Montreal.   28pp.   *BVAUS/Mackenzie OHMA2129
     OTURS/RSK.   Contributors include Henri Gagnon, Ross
     Dowson, Milton Acorn etc.

4020 Ontario.   Report on labour relations, James A. Mal-
     oney QC, Chairman.   (Toronto): (Queens Printer).
     64pp.   *OTURS/RSK.

4021 Ontario Federation of Labour.   In the matter of the
     Anti-Discrimination Commission act, 1958: submission
     to the Hon Leslie M. Frost, QC, Prime Minister of
     Ontario.   Toronto.   4pp, mimeo.   *OOA/CCF315.

4022 ------   Submission to the Premier and other ministers
     of the government of Ontario: legislative proposals,
     1958.   (Toronto).   16pp.   *OOA/OFL8.

4023 ------   Submission to the Royal Commission on Price
     Spreads of Food Products.   Toronto.   16pp plus 3pp
     appendixes, mimeo.   OOP *OOA/CCF315 and OFL8.   Mainly
     on the significance of labour costs.

4024 ------   Supplement to the submission to the Select
     Committee on Labour Relations.   Toronto.   19pp, mimeo.
     *OOA/CCF314 and OFL8.   (see 4020 above).

4025 Park, F.W.   The power and the money.   Toronto: Pro-
     gress.   104pp.   NBSAM OTP *BVAUS/Mac40f.4 OHMA1930
     OTURS/RSK   SSUS/Can Econ.

4026 Picard, Gérard.   Trade union freedom and labour unity
     in Canada.   Report of the national president to the
     CCCL convention, 1958.   Montreal.   38pp, bilingual.
     *OOA/CCF543.

4027 Shipyard General Workers Federation.   Does Canada
     need a merchant fleet? A preliminary survey.   Vic-
     toria.   14pp.   *BVIPA.

4028 Stolt, Richard G.   The western economy and its future
     as seen by Soviet economists.   Montreal: International

Film and Publishing Co. 102pp. QMU SSU *OOP.
Includes Varga, Kuzminov, Mikoyan and Khrushchev.

4029 Summers, David Fowler. The Labour church and allied
movements of the late 19th and early 20th centuries.
PhD thesis, University of Edinburgh. xii, 747pp.
biblio. Contains material on Brandon Peoples church,
Toronto Socialist church, Church of the Social Revolution, Winnipeg Labor church. Reprints J.S. Woodsworth First story of the Labor church and has W.E.S.
James Notes regarding a socialist church in Canada,
and William Ivens, Winnipeg Labor church movement
1918-1924. *MWPA/Summers.

4030 United Jewish Peoples Order. On the struggle for
Marxism-Leninism among Jewish Canadadians. (Toronto).
6pp, mimeo. *OTURS/RSK.

4031 Wild, Roland. Amor de Cosmos. Toronto: Ryerson.
xiv, 145pp. *OONL.

4032 Woods, H.D. (ed). Patterns of industrial dispute
settlement in five Canadian industries. Montreal:
McGill University Industrial Relations Centre.
vi, 397pp. *OONL. The five industries are Alberta
coal, Quebec mens garment, BC construction, Quebec
primary textiles, BC logging and lumber.

1959

4033 Aitken, Hugh J.G. and others. The American economic
impact on Canada. Durham (USA): Duke University
Press. xviii, 176pp. *OONL. Includes The influence
of American labor organizations and policies on Canadian labour by Eugene Forsey.

4034 Anglo-Newfoundland Development Co. Ltd. Turmoil in
the woods: a report on the dispute between the International Woodworkers of America and the Anglo-Newfoundland Development Co Ltd. Grand Forks. 32pp.
BVIP NFSM NSHPL OKQ OOA OOP OTU *OOL. Written from
the company point of view.

4035 Argue, Hazen. Speech in defence of organized labour
taken from a speech delivered in the House of Commons May 7, 1959. (Ottawa): (Queens Printer). (4pp).
*BVAUS/Mac27f.44.

4036 Armstrong, Myrtle May. The development of trade
union political activity in the CCF. Unpublished
MA thesis University of Toronto. vi, 137pp, biblio.
*OTUAR.

4037 Association of Radio and Television Employees of
Canada. Memorandum to the Board of Broadcast Gov-
ernors regarding the regulation of television broadcasting: November 2 and 3, 1959. (Ottawa). 13pp,
mimeo. *OOA/CCF312.

4038 Biderman, Morris. On the situation in the United
Jewish Peoples Order: report to a special joint
meeting of the National Resident Board and the Toronto Executive, 4 May 1959. Toronto: United Jewish
Peoples Order. 6pp. *OTURS/RSK. On their relations
with the Labor-Progressive Party.

4039 BC Federation of Labour. Memorandum in support of
proposed legislation. Vancouver. 23pp. *BVAUS/
Mac32f9a and 9b OOA/CCF315. On American influence,
labour disturbance, investment, unemployment etc.
issued in 1962, 20pp; 1964 17pp; 1966 14pp; 1967
13pp, all BVIP.

4040 ------ A political activity program to attain labour's legislative rights. Vancouver. Folder containing a pamphlet 'Together we will win', instructions on voting, percentages of votes cast, mimeo
articles on political action, Canadian party system
and political structure etc. *BVAUS/Mac32f.9a OOA/
CCF310.

4041 Buck, Tim. Disarmament means peace. Toronto: Progress. 31pp. BVAS BVIP OTP *AEUS BVAUS/WB31f.1b
OHMA2144 OKQS OTURS/RSK SSUS.

4042 ------ Keynote speech to the national convention
of the Labor-Progressive Party. (Toronto). 22pp,
mimeo. *OTURS/RSK.

4043 ------ Our fight for Canada: selected writings 1923-
1959. Toronto: Progress. 407pp. *OKQS OTURS/RSK.

4044 Canadian Labour Congress. Inflation: submission to
the Senate's standing committee on finance. Ottawa.
19pp, mimeo. *OOA/CCF314.

4045 ------ Memorandum to the government of Canada.
Ottawa. 47pp. OOA/CCF315 and CFAW52. Issued in
1960, 44pp and 1961 35pp, *OOA/CCF382; 1962 (March)
49pp *OHMA2516 and December 34pp *OOA/CFAW52.

4046 ------ Point of order: how to conduct a union meeting. Ottawa. (c1959). 29pp. Various dates and
editions. *OOA/CCF543.

4047 ------ Political education information. Ottawa.
194pp. *OOA/CCF378.

4048 ------ Principles and policies: an official summary. Ottawa. 17pp. *OHMA2515 OOA/CCF543.

4049 ------ Submission to the Board of Broadcast Govern-
ors on the proposed television regulations, Ottawa
November 2-3, 1959. (Ottawa). 10pp, mimeo. *OOA/
CCF316.

4050 ------ Submission to the standing committee on ind-
ustrial relations of the House of Commons re Bill
C-43 (an act to amend the unemployment insurance act).
Ottawa. 15pp, mimeo. *OOA/CCF323.

4051 ------ and CCF. Report of the joint national committee. (Ottawa). 5pp, mimeo. *OOA/CCF314.

4052 Carrothers, A.W.R. What happened next: a fable for
today. (Vancouver): np. (7pp). *OOA/Bengough 3.

4053 Clarke, Nelson. Berlin: peace or war? Toronto:
Labor-Progressive Party. 24pp. OPET *BVAUS/Mac40f.
7c OHMA2784 OTURS/RSK SSUS.

4054 Coldwell, M.J. and others. Report of a community
development evaluation mission to India 23 November
1958 to 3 April 1959. (New Delhi): Dept of Community
Evaluation, India. ii, 100pp. revd edn New York:
United Nations Bureau of Technical Assistance Operations, 1960. 101pp. *British Library of Economics.

4055 Committee for the Maintenance, Stabilization and
Improvement of Production and Employment in Canada's
Aircraft Industry (and others). A brief on the Canadian aircraft industry submitted to the government
of Canada. Montreal. 30pp. *OOA/CCF315.

4056 Communist Party of Canada. Constitution. Toronto.
35pp. *OTURS/RSK. Amended at the 7th national
convention of the Labor-Progressive Party.

4057 ------ Resolved: the new party must be a genuine
labor-farmer party. Toronto. (c1959). (4pp).
*OTURS/RSK.

4058 CCF. The CCF welcomes you. Ottawa. 13pp. *ACGA/
CCF29 BVAUS/Mac30Af.4c OOA/CCF434 and 536 SSA/G2.
1959.1.

4059 ------ Report (of a) sub-committee on new party
constitution. (?Ottawa). 13pp. *OOA/CCF315.

4060 Douglas, T.C. Planning for people. Regina: L. Amon.
20pp. SRL *OOA/CCF538 SSUS/Shortt.

4061 Farmer-Labour Co-ordinating Council. Can farmer and
labour co-operate? A report of the Farmer-Labour
Conference Club, Whitesands, June 27 and 28, 1959.
Toronto. 33pp, illus. *OTURS/RSK.

(4062)Feltham, J. The development of the F.P.U. in Newfoundland (1908-1923). Unpublished MA thesis, Memorial University. 172pp. Not seen.

4063 Fines, C.M. and Fred Neibrandt. Hon C.M. Fines bril-
liant defence of CCF fifteen-year regime. Regina:
CCF. (8pp). *SSA/G1.1959.1.

4064 Forsey, Eugene. History of the labour movement in
Canada: reprinted from the Canada Year Book 1957-58.
Ottawa: Dominion Bureau of Statistics. 10pp. *MWPA/
Russell 1.

4066 Greenslade, J.G. (ed). Canadian politics. Speeches
by F.M. Watkins, Stanley Knowles, J.R. Mallory and
H.D. Hicks delivered at Mount Allison summer institute, August 13 and 15, 1959. Sackville: Mount Allison University. 76pp. *NSHD/J4 OONL.

(4067)Hoffman, John D. Farmer-labour government in Ontario
1919-1923. Unpublished MA thesis University of Tor-

onto. OTUAR, missing.

4068 International Railway Brotherhoods. Submission to
the government of Canada. Ottawa. 13pp. *OOA/CCF
315. Legislative proposals on family allowances, unemployment insurance, immigration, national health
insurance, railways etc.

4069 International Union of Mine, Mill and Smelter Workers.
Report of fact finding committee established to in-
vestigate Alistair Stewart's attack on the union.
(Toronto). 29pp. OOL *MWPA/Russell 1.

4070 Irvine, Wm. and Floyd Johnson. President's address:
highlights of the CCF convention, 1959. Edmonton:
CCF. 12pp. *ACGA/CCF29.

4071 King, Carlyle. G.B.S. on literature: the author as
critic. Kingston: Queens University. pp135-145.
*OOA/Underhill 26. Offprint from Queens Quarterly
LXVI Spring 1959.

4072 King, Margaret. Reminiscences. Victoria: np. 27pp.
*BVAUS/Shepherd 4-5. Cover title: CCF.

4073 Knowles, Stanley. Canadians all. An address prepared
for delivery to the Canadian Club of Montreal, Monday
February 23rd, 1959. Ottawa: (Canadian Labour Congress). 10pp, mimeo. *OOA/CCF308.

4074 ------ A new party for a better Canada. Toronto:
Ontario Federation of Labour. (4pp). *OOA/CCF378.

4075 ------ The new party. Address delivered at the annual provincial convention of the Manitoba CCF at
Winnipeg, Friday, November 20, 1959. (Winnipeg): CCF.
14pp, mimeo. *OOA/CCF308.

4076 ------ The new party: a radio talk prepared for delivery at Galt, Saturday February 7th, 1959. (Ottawa):
(New Party). 6pp, mimeo. *OOA/CCF373.

4077 ------ The new political party. Ottawa: (New Party).
7pp, mimeo. *OOA/CCF373. Written for the March 1959
issue of *The Canadian Commentator.*

4078 Labor-Progressive Party. BC needs a jobs program now.
Vancouver. (4pp). *T.

4079 ------ Duplessis must go! Montreal. 18pp. OHMA1794
OTURS/RSK.

4080 ------ Socialism and you: why you should join the
Labor-Progressive Party. Toronto: Progress. 28pp.
*BVAUS/WB31f3a and 43f.2 OHMA1791 OKQS OTURS/RSK.

4081 Lazarus, Morden. Public enterprise in Canada: a review. Toronto: Ontario Federation of Labour. 15pp,
mimeo. *SRL.

4082 ------ (Report to) the OFL-PAC pre-convention meeting, November 1, 1959, Niagara Falls. Toronto: Ontario Federation of Labour Political Action Committee.
6pp plus 1p resolution, mimeo. *OOA/CCF315.

4083a Lewis, David. Address to national seminar of the
new political party delivered in Winnipeg, Friday
August 28, 1956. (Ottawa): (New Party). 8pp, mimeo.
*OOA/CCF373. Also published as:

4083b ------ It's time to lend a hand...Toronto: Ontario
Federation of Labour. (4pp). *ACGA/CCF29 ACGL/PDbc
OOA/CCF378 and 537 OTURS/RSK.

4084 Lloyd, W.S. Proposed New Party issue. (Regina):
CCF. 8pp, mimeo. *OOA/Coldwell 60.

4085 MacDonald, Donald. The Canadian Labour Congress and
the New Party. (Ottawa): Canadian Labour Congress.
3pp, mimeo. *OOA/CCF315.

4086 McNaught, K. A prophet in politics: a biography of
J.S. Woodsworth. Toronto: University of Toronto
Press. viii, 339pp, no biblio. *OTURS/RSK.

(4087)Manhertz, H.E.D. Social security in the Maritimes
1939-1958. Unpublished MA thesis, University of
New Brunswick. vii, 150pp.

4088 Morgan, J.S. Our unemployment insurance system:
does it meet the needs of today? Toronto: Ontario
Woodsworth Memorial Foundation. 24pp. *MWPA/CCF32
OKQS OTURS/RSK.

4089 Morris, Leslie. Labour-farmer political action.
Toronto: Labor-Progressive Party. 23pp. BVIV OPAL
OTU *AEUS BVAUS/WB31f.3a OKQS OOA/CCF542 OTURS/
RSK SSUS.

4090 National Committee for the New Party. Discussion
paper on programme. Ottawa. 19pp, mimeo. *OOA/
CCF315.

4100 Ontario Federation of Labour. Compare! Labour legislation in Ontario and Saskatchewan. Toronto.
(c1959). (4pp). *OTURS.

4101 ------ The Newfoundland story. Toronto. (6pp).
OOL *OOA/CCF543. The woodworkers union and the
attempt by Smallwood to ban it from the province.

4102 ------ Submission to the committee on the organization of government in Ontario. Toronto. 24pp, mimeo.
*OOA/CCF315 and OFL8. Mainly on boards and tribunals.

4103 ------ Submission to the Premier and other ministers
of the government of Ontario. Toronto. 14pp. *OOA/
CCF315 and OFL8. Legislative proposals: unemployment
labour relations, working conditions etc.

4104 Perepelkin, J.J. Doukhobor problem in Canada: a pro-
totype copy of the Hebrew people in Egypt. Translated
and edited by J.E. Podovinikov. (Krestora, BC):
Fraternal Council of the Union of Christian Communities and Brotherhood of Reformed Doukhobors. 76pp.
ACG BVAU BVIP MWP OTU *OTAR/1959/6.

4105 Provincial CCF and Federation of Labour. Report.
np: (CCF). (23pp), mimeo, sections separately paged.
*OOA/CCF314. On the formation of the new party.

4106 Railway Unions Educational Council. Course outline and study material: course description. (Ottawa). 30pp, mimeo. *OOA/CCF323.

4107 ------ Facts about the Railway Unions Educational Council. (Ottawa). 10pp, mimeo. *OOA/CCF323.

4108 Saskatchewan Federation of Labour. Loaded questions and straight answers on labour. Moose Jaw. 6pp. *BVAUS/Mac32f.3 OOA/CCF312 SSA/C114.9.

4109 Scott, F.R. The Canadian constitution and human rights. Toronto: Canadian Broadcasting Corporation. (viii), 52pp. *MWP OKQS OONL OTURS/RSK.

4110 ------ Civil liberties and Canadian federalism. Toronto: University of Toronto Press and Carleton University. 58pp. *OONL.

4111 ------ What does labour need in a bill of rights? Summary of a paper delivered at the Atlantic Provinces Labour Institute conference at Dalhousie University November 16-20, 1959. Halifax: Dalhousie University Institute of Public Affairs. 15pp. ACU AEU BVAU NFSM NSHPL OTP OTU *OONL.

(4112) Smith, S.G.D. Politics and the party system in the three prairie provinces 1917-1958. Unpublished B.Litt thesis, University of Oxford. Not seen.

4113 Trades and Labor Congress of Canada. Memorandum to the government of Canada. (Ottawa). 47pp. *OOA/ Bengough 1. Unemployment insurance, health insurance and labour legislation etc.

4114 United Jewish Peoples Order. Report of the special committee on unity in UJPO. (Toronto). 6pp plus (2pp) covering letter, mimeo. *OTURS/RSK.

4115 Victoria Typographical Union no. 201. 75th anniversary diamond jubilee: 1884-1959. Victoria. 26pp, illus. *BVIPA.

4116 Watt, F.W. The national policy, the workingman, and proletarian ideas in Victorian Canada. Toronto: Canadian Historical Review (c1959). 26pp. *OKQS OTURS/ RSK.

4117 Weir, John. Turning point in history: the seven year plan of the Soviet Union. Toronto: Progress. 30pp. *BVAUS/Mac38f.18b OHMA1813 OTURS/RSK.

4118 Winch, Harold E. Speech on what should be Canada's defence policy delivered in the House of Commons July 2, 1959. Ottawa. 8pp. *BVAUS/Mac27f.44.

4119 Zaplitny, Fred S. Democratic party of Canada. (Ottawa): (New Party). 9pp, mimeo. *OOA/CCF373.

4120 ------ For the sake of discussion...a policy for the New Party. Toronto: Ontario Federation of Labour. (4pp). *OOA/CCF378. Condensed from an article in the Commonwealth.

1960

4121 Archer, John H. The political development of Saskatchewan. (?Saskatoon). 39pp, mimeo. *OTU.

4122 Beach, H.D. and R.A. Lucas (eds). Individual and
group behaviour in a coal mine disaster. Washington:
National Academy of Sciences-National Research
Council. xvi, 160pp. AEU BVAU NSHPL OPET OTP OTU
QMM *NSHDS. The editors and project staff are all
from Nova Scotia.

4123 Bell, Russell. Unemployment. Address delivered to
the provincial government's trade and industry council, September 26, 1960. (Ottawa): Canadian Labour
Congress. 17pp, mimeo. *OOA/CCF382.

4124 Brewin, Andrew and Kenneth McNaught. Debate on defence: two viewpoints on Canadian foreign policy.
Toronto: Ontario Woodsworth Memorial Foundation.
27pp. *OKQ/CCF.

4125 BC Federation of Labour. The effects of automation
and related problems. A brief presented to the Select Standing Committee on Labour. Vancouver. 23pp.
BVIP OTU *BVAUS/Mac32f.9a OOA/CCF308 and 309.
Cover title: What's happening to jobs?

4126 ------ A submission to the Committee on Trading
Stamps. Vancouver. 8pp plus 2pp, mimeo. BVIP OOP
OTU *BVAUS/Mac32f.9b.

4127 ------ Which do you want...this - or this? Vancouver. 11pp. *BVIP. On BC utilities; endorsed by the
CCF.

4128 Buck, Tim. Neutrality now! Canada can stay out of
war! Toronto: Progress. 21pp. BVIV MWU OTP *AEUS
BVAUS/WB31f.1b OHMA2145 OKQS OTURS/RSK SSUS.

4129 Cameron, J.C. and F.J.L. Young. The status of trade
unions in Canada. Kingston: Queens University Dept
of Industrial Relations. (iv), 169pp. *OONL.

4130 Cameron, James M. Industrial history of the New
Glasgow district. New Glasgow. (viii), 48, 32, 20,
24, 40, 16, 32, 32pp, illus. Each chapter paginated
separately. *NSHP.

4131 Canadian Labour Congress. Constitution. Ottawa.
35pp. *OTU.

4132 ------ A policy for full employment: submission to
the Prime Minister's conference on unemployment.
Ottawa. 37pp. *BVAUS/Mac32f.15 OOA/CCF543.

4133 ------ Political policy decision of the 3rd constit-
utional convention, Montreal April 25th to 29th 1960.
Extracts from the report of the Executive Council.
(Ottawa). 4pp, mimeo. *OOA/CCF373.

4134 ------ Position on Canada's foreign and defence

policy. Montreal. (4pp). *OOA/CFAW52.

4135 Canadian Labour Congress. Tell the people: a manual for union publicity and public relations. Ottawa. 50pp. *OTURS.

4136 Canadian Peace Congress. Rally for peace and disarmament. Toronto. 23pp. *BVAUS/Mac42f.3a OOA/Endicott 1 OTURS/RSK. Contains speeches and messages etc from W.E.B. Du Bois, William Irvine, Sean O'Casey, Rockwell Kent, Pablo Casals, James G. Endicott and others.

4137 ------ Shalom aleichem:שלום עליכם: peace - it's in your hands! Toronto. (c1960). 30pp. *OTURS/RSK.

4138 Communist Party of Canada. Disarmament and neutrality. A brief presented to the government of Canada February 13th. Edmonton. 4pp. *OHMA1513.

4139 ------ The road to socialism in Canada. Toronto. 31pp. AEU BVIP NSHPL SRL *BVAUS/WB31f.2a OKQS OTURS/RSK. Not the same as the LPP program.

4140 CCF. The CCF record in Saskatchewan. Regina. 8pp. *SSA/G1.1960.4.

4141 ------ Facts about Saskatchewan growth, 1960. Regina. 32pp. *SSA/G1.1960.7.

4142 ------ More abundant living: CCF program for 1960. Regina. (8pp). *SSA/G1.1960.8.

4143 Douglas, T.C. More abundant living. Regina: L. Amon 20pp. SRL *BVAUS/Mac30Bf.22a SSUS/Shortt. Speech in the legislature.

4144 Forsey, E.A. Labor and automation. Speech to the Ontario Federation of Labour. Toronto: Ontario Federation of Labour. (4pp). *MWPA/Russell 1.

4145 Hartle, Douglas G. Unemployment: cause? treatment? cure? Toronto: Ontario Woodsworth Memorial Foundation. (24pp). *OHMA30393 OOA/CCF323 OTURS/RSK.

4146 Haythorne, George V. Labor in Canadian agriculture. Cambridge: Harvard University Press. (x), 122pp. *OTP.

4147 International Union of Mine, Mill and Smelter Workers. Mine Mill says: the record speakes for itself. Toronto. 31pp. *OTURS/RSK. On the accusations of Communist leadership by the Canadian Labour Congress.

4148 Lefebvre, Jean-Paul. La lutte ouvrière: choix de textes et commentaire. Les pages le plus dramatiques de l'histoire du travail et des travailleurs. Préface de Jean Marchand. Montréal: Les Editions de l'Homme. 96pp. *OONL.

4149 Lewis, David and others. Bill 74: an act to amend the labour relations act: an analysis. Toronto: Ontario Federation of Labour. 23pp. *OOA/CCF543.

4150 Liao Hung-Ying and Derek Bryan. The world belongs

to all. St Marys (Ont): Mrs Homer Brown. 31pp.
*OOA/Endicott 1.

4151 National Committee for the New Party. A new party
for Canada: study paper on programme of the proposed
new political party for Canada. Ottawa. 19pp.
*ACGL/PDc OOA/CCF383, 538 and 539 SSA/G492.7.

4152 ------ Study paper on constitution of the proposed
new political party for Canada. Ottawa. 14pp.
*ACGA/CCF29 ACGL/PDc OHMA OOA/CCF538 and 539
OTURS/RSK. Also 12pp, mimeo *OOA/CCF315.

4153 New Party. Report on policy seminar on the programme
and structure of the New Party. Calgary. 16pp,
mimeo. *ACGL/PDc.

4154 Ontario Federation of Labour. Farmer-labour confer-
ence: a report of the second farmer-labour conference,
Port Elgin, June 18-19, 1960. Toronto. 46pp. *OOA/
CCF538.

4155 ------ Sputniks and Luniks and...the New Party.
Toronto. (4pp). *OOA/CCF539.

4156 ------ Submission to the Premier and other ministers
of the government of Ontario. Toronto. 26pp. *OOA/
CCF314 and OFL8. Legislative proposals - labour relations, working conditions, workmens compensation,
health services etc.

4157 ------ Submission to the Royal Commission on Industrial Safety. Toronto. 29pp plus 1p appendix, mimeo.
*OOA/OFL8.

4158 ------ Submission to Standing Committee on Government
Commissions, government of Ontario under the chairman-
ship of Mr D.A. Evans. Toronto. 7pp, mimeo. *OOA/
OFL8.

4159 Penner, Jacob. The crisis in municipal government.
Toronto: Progress. 24pp. AEU BVIV OOP OTP *BVAUS/
WB31f.1b OHMA2050 OKQS OTURS/RSK SSUS/Comm.

4160 Pentland, H. Clare. Labour and the development of
industrial capitalism in Canada. PhD thesis, University of Toronto. (iii), 454pp, biblio. *OTUAR.

4161 Perkins, B.B. Cooperatives in Ontario - their development and current position. Guelph: Ontario Agricultural College. vii, 137pp. ACU MWU NSHPL *OTMCL.

4162 Ryerson, Stanley B. The founding of Canada: begin-
nings to 1815. Toronto: Progress. 340pp. *OTURS/
RSK. First volume of a two volume history.

4163 Saskatchewan. Progress Saskatchewan 1960. Regina:
Government of Saskatchewan. 75pp. *OHMA1594.

4164 Saskatchewan Labour. Saskatchewan election 1960:
read the facts: organize action: get out to vote.
Regina. 23pp. *SSA/G1.1960.12.

(4165) Schweitzer, Paul R. Unemployment insurance in Canada
1941-58. Unpublished MA thesis McGill University.

4166 Socialist Press. The story of Atterica. Toronto. (c1960). (4pp). *OTURS/RSK.

(4167) Steele, J. The big strike 1909-1910. Unpublished MA thesis, St Francis Xavier University. 95pp.

4168 Steeves, D.G. Compassionate rebel: Ernest G. Winch and his times. Vancouver: Boag Foundation. 227pp, illus. *OONL.

4169 Stewart, Miller. Let the buyer beware: a summary and commentary on the report of the Royal Commission on Price Spreads of Food Products. Toronto: Ontario Woodsworth Memorial Foundation. 20pp. *OHMA2317.

4170 Underhill, F.H. A Canadian political protestant. Toronto: Canadian Historical Review. pp48-53. *OOAL. Reprint from Vol XLI no 1 March 1960: a review of *A prophet in politics* by Kenneth McNaught.

4171 ------ In search of Canadian liberalism. Toronto: Macmillan. xiv, 282pp. *OONL.

4172 ------ and Paul Fox. The radical tradition: a second view of Canadian history. Toronto: Canadian Broadcasting Corporation. 12pp. *OOAL.

4173 UE. Our visit to people's China. Report of first Canadian trade union delegation to visit people's China. Toronto: United Electrical. 28pp. *OHMA1822.

4174 Young, Walter. The New Party - a party of all the democratic left. Ottawa: New Party Clubs. 11pp, mimeo. *OOA/CCF373.

4175 ------ The Peterborough election: the success of a party image. np. (13pp) plus (2pp) appendix. *OOA/CCF373 and 538. Appears to be an offprint from something...

4176 Young Communist League. Constitution adopted by 15th convention of the YCL, May 21-23, 1960. *OHMA2380 OOA/CCF542.

4177 Zylstra, Bernard. Challenge and response: an address delivered to the Christian Labour Association of Canada at the 1960 national convention held in Snelgrove, Ontario on May 7th, 1960. Brantford: Christian Labour Association. 24pp. *OHMA.

1961

4178 Alcock, Norman Z. The bridge of reason. Toronto: Canadian Peace Research Institute. 40pp. *MWPA/ Brigden 7.

4179 Allen, Alexander Richard. Salem Bland and the social gospel in Canada. Unpublished MA thesis, University of Saskatchewan. viii, 236pp, biblio. *SSUS.

(4180) Ayers, Shirley Ann. The locomotive engineers strike

on the Grand Trunk railway in 1876-1877. Unpublished MA thesis, McGill University.

(4181) Baril, Jean. Des relations entre le phénomène de la grève et les principaux indices d'activités économiques. Unpublished MA thesis, Université de Montréal. xi, 152pp.

4182 Bean, Ronald. The 'cooperative wage study' and industrial relations: a Canadian analysis in the steel industry. Unpublished MA thesis, McMaster University (i), v, 180pp, biblio. *OHM.

4183 Bjarnason, Emil. The case of the tearful tycoon: a reply to J.V. Clyne. Vancouver: Trade Union Research Bureau. 16pp. AEU BVIPA NFSM *ACGL/PDh2 BVAUS/Mac 31f.32a OTURS/RSK. The former Hon Mr Justice Clyne became chairman of Macmillan Bloedel and rashly claimed in his annual report that wages were too high.

4184 Blishen, Bernard R. and others (eds). Canadian society: sociological perspectives. New York: Free Press of Glencoe. xvi, 622pp, index. *OONL. Includes: Married women workers by the Dept of Labour; Democratic control in a labour union by Herbert A. Shepard; Co-operative farming as a variant social pattern by Henry Cooperstock; The religious sect in Canadian politics by S.D. Clark; Social structure and political activity by S.M. Lipset etc.

4185 Boyle, Thomas. Justice through peace: a study of labor in its present situation. Toronto: Longmans. viii, 248pp. *OONL.

(4186) Braid, A.F. The role of directors of local cooperatives in Ontario, Canada in continuity and change. Unpublished PhD thesis, Cornell University. xiv, 269pp.

4187 BC Federation of Labour. The conspiracy against the consumer; complete analysis of a social situation for all who work and the effect labour has upon prices and wages. (Vancouver). 12pp. *BVIPA.

4188 ------ The crisis of unemployment. Vancouver. 7pp, mimeo. *BVAUS/Mac32f.9b.

4189 Canadian Labour Congress. The new party and the community. Ottawa. 6pp. *OOA/CCF388 and 538 SSA/G160.9. Leaflet 6.

4190 ------ The new party and the farmer. Ottawa. 6pp. *OOA/CCF388 and 538 SSA/G160.9. Leaflet 3.

4191 ------ The new party and the professional. Ottawa. 6pp. *OOA/CCF388 and 538 SSA/G160.9. Leaflet 5.

4192 ------ The new party and the worker. Ottawa. 6pp. *OOA/CCF388 and 538 SSA/G160.9. Leaflet 2.

4193 ------ The new party and the citizen. Ottawa. 6pp. *OOA/CCF388 and 538 SSA/G160.9. Leaflet 4.

4194 ------ 1961: the historical year for Canadian poli-

tics. Ottawa. 6pp. *OOA/CCF388 SSA/G160.9.
Leaflet 1.

4195 Canadian Peace Research Institute. Charting a course
for peace... Toronto. 12pp. *OOA/VOW8.

4196 Caplan, Gerald Lewis. The Cooperative Commonwealth
Federation in Ontario 1932-1945: a study of socialist
and anti-socialist politics. Unpublished MA thesis
University of Toronto. (i),v, 495pp, biblio. *OTUAR.

4197 Carlin, Robert H. I know Mine Mill...do you? Toronto: United Steelworkers of America. 15pp. *OONL.

4198 Communist Party of Canada. Brief submitted to:
Committee of Inquiry into the Unemployment Insurance
act. Toronto. 7pp, mimeo. *OTURS/RSK.

4199 ------ Submission of the national executive commitee
to the government of Canada: 'No war over Berlin'.
Toronto. 8pp plus 1p appendix, mimeo. *OTURS/RSK.

4200 CCF. How to have a good riding organization. Toronto. 47pp. *OOA/CCF320.

4201 Crysdale, Stewart. The industrial struggle and protestant ethics in Canada: a survey of changing power
structures and Christian social ethics. Toronto:
Ryerson. 193pp, biblio. *OONL.

4202 Currie, Ian Douglas. British Columbia industrial
conciliators: a study in role perception, perform-
ance and conflict. Unpublished MA thesis, University
of British Columbia. i,228, 65, 43pp. *BVAUS.
Appendixes inserted between pp 227 and 228.

(4203)Dallaire, Germain. Les conditions de travail dans
l'industrie de la construction au Canada. Unpublished MA thesis, Université de Montréal. ix, 75pp.

4204 Dewart, Leslie. A catholic speaks on Cuba. Toronto:
Fair Play for Cuba Committee. 6pp. *E.

4205 Douglas, T.C. 'Fair shares for all': speech in the
debate on the speech from the throne. Regina: L.
Amon. 23pp. SRL *ACGA/CCF29 OOA/CCF539 SSUS/
Shortt.

4206 ------ National pride and national purpose. Ottawa:
New Democratic Party. (6pp). *ACGL/PDc OOA/CCF536
OTURS. Television address 18 October 1961.

4207 ------ Speaks on disarmament. Regina: Saskatoon
Committee for Control of Radiation Hazards. (11pp).
*OOA/CCF546.

4208 Edwards, Lionel. The new Cuba. Toronto: Communist
Party of Canada. 31pp. AEU BVIP OKQ *BVAUS/WB39f.19b
OTURS/RSK.

4209 Endicott, James G. A Canadian letter to President
Kennedy. (Toronto): Canadian Peace Congress. 4pp.
*OOP.

4210 Fairley, Margaret (ed). Highways to peace: a challenge to youth. Toronto. 31pp. *OTURS/RSK. On neo-colonialism, armaments, nuclear arms, recording some Canadian opinions. List of national peace movements and their addresses.

4211 Fawcett, George R. Canada's role for peace: a foreign policy for the new party: a third force. (Fort William). (9pp). *OOA/CCF388.

4212 Feldt, Hans. There is no Santa Claus. Penticton. 28pp. *OOA/CCF554. Mainly on the theories of Silvio Gesell, espousing 'free socialism'.

4213 Forsey, Eugene. Economic growth. Guelph: Ontario Agricultural College. 9pp. *OOA/Forsey 8.

4214 ------ Our Canadian party system and political structure of Canada. Toronto: (Canadian Labour Congress). 5pp, mimeo. *OOA/CFAW52.

4215 Fox, Paul and others. Socialism in Canada: a documentary study of the history of left wing politics in Canada. Toronto: Canadian Broadcasting Corporation. 20pp, mimeo. Others include: Wallace Lefeaux, Elmer Roper, David Orlikow, Tim Buck, T.C. Douglas, Frank Underhill, David Lewis, Angus MacInnis etc. *OTURS. Broadcast July 12, 1961.

4216 Irvine, W. and others. The twain shall meet. Edmonton. 175pp. OONL OOP SRL *BVAUS/Mac38f.22 OTURS/ RSK. On a visit to China in 1960.

4217 Kierans, Eric W. Capitalism without capitalists. Toronto: Ontario Woodsworth Memorial Foundation. 12pp. OPET OTU OTURS SSU *OHMA OOA/Underhill 44.

4218 Knowles, Stanley. The New Party. Toronto: McClelland and Stewart. (vii), 136pp. *OOA/CCF538. The second printing adds 30pp appendix of the draft constitution and draft program.

4219 Kovacs, Aranka E. (ed). Readings in Canadian labour economics. Toronto: McGraw-Hill. xii, 268pp, biblio. *NSWA OONL. Includes: The development of a capitalistic labour market in Canada by H.C. Pentland; The growth of labour organization in Canada 1900-1950 by J.T. Montague; The labour link between Canada and the United States by Paul Norgren; International unions and the Canadian trade union movement by J.T. Montague; The movement towards labour unity in Canada: history and implications by Eugene Forsey; Fifty years of labour legislation in Canada by E. Lorentsen; Industrial relations and government policy by S. Jamieson; Wartime labour problems and policies in Canada by B.M. Stewart; Trends in collective bargaining: a study in causal analysis by H.A. Logan; Compulsory conciliation in Canada by A.E. Kovacs; Government conciliation in labour disputes: some recent experience in Ontario by W.G. Phillips; Canadian collective bargaining and dispute settlement policy: an appraisal by H.D. Woods.

4220 Laidlaw, Alexander Fraser. The campus and the community: the global impact of the Antigonish movement.
Montreal: Harvest House. 173pp. *OONL.

4221 League for Socialist Action. What the League for
Socialist Action is, and what it stands for. Toronto. 11pp. OONL *OTURS/RSK.

4222 Mabey, Ernest LeRoy. A history of movements and
efforts for the improvement of Canadian rural life
with a special exposition of rural science in the
public schools of Nova Scotia. Unpublished MA thesis,
Acadia University. (iv), iii, 93pp, biblio. *NWSA.
Deals with the Grange, Patrons etc.

4223 Marsh, Leonard. The alternatives to armaments: ten
paths to peace. (?Toronto): np. 8pp, mimeo.
*OTURS. 'and Betty'(Marsh) inserted in ms.

4224 Morgan, John S. Social security - the next stage.
Toronto: Ontario Woodsworth Memorial Foundation.
20pp. BVIP MWU OH OTP OTU *OOA/CCF539 OKQS SSUS.

4225 Morris, Joe. The shape and structure of the New
Party. Excerpts from an address to the New Party
conference at Calgary, December 11, 1960. Regina:
CCF. 8pp. *OOA/CCF378 and 539 SSA/G1.1960.22.

4226 Morris, Leslie. Communists and the New Party. Toronto: Communist Party of Canada. 22pp. AEU BVIV
OONL SSU *BVAUS/WB31f.1a OKQS OTURS/RSK.

(4227) Myers, J. The Independent Labor Party of Ontario.
Unpublished MA thesis, University of Toronto.
Not found.

4228 Nasir, George. The Congolese infant and other poems.
Winnipeg: np. (14pp). *OHMA. Proletarian poets 1.

4229 National Committee for a New Party. Co-operation
for peace. Ottawa. 9pp, mimeo. *OOA/CCF383.

4230 ------ Draft constitution: the New Party. Ottawa.
15pp. OOL OOP OTU *ACGL/PDc OOA/CCF378 OTURS/RSK
SSA/G492.5.

4231 ------ Draft program: the New Party. Ottawa. 30pp.
AEU OOP *ACGL/PDc OOA/CCF378 OTURS/RSK SSA/G492.6.

4232 ------ A more complete democracy. Ottawa. 4pp,
mimeo. *OOA/CCF383.

4233 ------ New Party club kit. (Ottawa). Containing
14 items including Canada needs a new political party
by R.D. Sparham, 4pp; A letter to women, 2pp; Draft
constitution; Draft program etc. *OOA/CCF378.

4234 ------ Planning for abundance. (Ottawa). 16pp,
mimeo. *OOA/CCF373 and 383.

4235 ------ Security and freedom. Ottawa. 9pp, mimeo.
*OOA/CCF383.

4236 New Democratic Party. The federal constitution of
the New Democratic Party, adopted by its founding

convention Ottawa, July 31-August 4, 1961. Ottawa. 17pp. AEU OOP *OOA/CCF537.

4237 New Democratic Party. The federal program of the NDP: adopted by its founding convention Ottawa. Ottawa. 29pp. *OOA/CCF538 and Underhill 57 OTURS/ RSK SSA/G5.1961.1.

4238 ------ Founding convention NDP Manitoba section, Fort Garry hotel, Winnipeg November 3 and 4, 1961. Report of proceedings. Winnipeg. (51pp), mimeo. *MWPA/CCF4.

4239 New Democratic Youth. The student and the NDP. Ottawa. (6pp). *OOA/CCF539.

4240 ------ NDY convention report, Ottawa August 1961. (Ottawa). 7 plus (8)pp, mimeo. *OOA/CCF468. Proceedings of the founding convention.

4241 Okulevich, G. At the crossroads: for life, for happiness. Toronto: Canadian Slav Committee. 31pp. *BVAUS/Mac41f.14.

4242 Oliver, Michael. (ed). Social purpose for Canada. Toronto: University of Toronto Press. xii, 472pp. *OONL.

4243 Olley, Robert Edward. Construction wage rates in Ontario 1864 to 1903. Unpublished MA thesis, Queens University. vi, 121pp, biblio. *OKQ.

4244 Ontario Committee for the New Democratic Party. Draft constitution of the NDP of Ontario. Toronto. 12pp. *OOA/CCF538.

4245 Ontario Federation of Labour. Submission to the Royal Commission on Labour-Management Relations in the Construction Industry. Toronto. 11p,, mimeo. *OOA/OFL8.

4246 ------ Unemployment in Ontario: a submission to the government of Ontario. Toronto. 18pp, mimeo. *OOA/ OFL8.

4247 Richard, Gerard. Un code du travail du Canada. (Montréal). 10pp, bilingual. QMU *OOA/CCF543.

4248 Pope, W.H. Let Canada lead. (A new defence policy). Montreal: Combined Universities Campaign for Nuclear Disarmament. 16pp. *OHMA2218.

(4249) Rodnèy, W. A history of the Communist Party 1919-1929. PhD thesis, London School of Economics. 412pp.

(4250) Sanscoucy, Bernard. Le conflit industriel dans la législation du travail nord-américaine. Unpublished MA thesis, Université de Montréal. ix, 119pp.

4251 Saskatchewan Federation of Labour. A case for employment in Saskatchewan. Regina. 35pp. OTU SRL *SSUS/Labour.

4252 ------ The case for a 40 hour five day work week law in Saskatchewan. Regina. 12pp. OTU SRL *K.

4253 Schindeler, Frederick Fernand. The formation of the NDP. Unpublished MA thesis, University of Toronto. 120pp. *OTUAR.

4254 Smith, Wm. J. The brotherhood and politics. Ottawa: (Canadian Labour Congress-CCF). 6pp. *OOA/CCF378 and 543.

4255 Sparham, Desmond. New party clubs: final report upon the development of the third section of the movement to found a new political party. (Ottawa): New Party Clubs. 9pp, mimeo plus 5pp list of clubs. *OOA/CCF 378.

4256 United Jewish Peoples Order. Memorandum to Soviet government on Jewish problems. Toronto. (c1961). (4pp). *OTURS/RSK. In Yiddish and English.

4257 Weir, John. The case of Canada's stepchildren. Toronto: Canadian Slav Committee. (c1961). 24pp. BVIV OOP *BVAUS/Mac41f.14 OHMA2126 OTURS/RSK. On discrimination by the Dept of Immigration.

1962

(4258) Anton, F.R. The role of government in the settlement of industrial disputes in Canada. PhD thesis, University of London (Eng). xiii, 386.

4259 Baum, Rainer Carl Robert. The social and political philosophy of trade unions. Unpublished MA thesis University of British Columbia. i, 118pp, biblio. *BVAU.

4260 Bennett, Gladys. Those irrepressible Chinese! Some observations and reflections following a visit to China in 1962. Bracebridge. 31pp. *OOA/Endicott 1.

4261 BC Federation of Labour. Social Credit's anti-labour legislation. Bill 43 and Bill 42. Vancouver. (c1962). (6pp). *BVAA.

4262 Canadian Labour Congress. Brief summary of the fourth constituent convention, Vancouver April 9-13, 1962. Ottawa. 8 plus 8pp, bilingual. *OOA/CFAW52.

4263 ------ Report of executive council to the fourth constitutional convention, Vancouver April 1962. Ottawa. 97pp. *OOA/CFAW52.

4264 Communist Party of Canada. Canada's women: the home, at work, children, equality, peace. Toronto. 24pp. *BVAUS/WB32f.2b and Mac43f.18a OHMA2213 OKQS OTURS/RSK.

4265 ------ Canadians are not expendable! Let us have peace! Let's be masters in our own house! A message to the people of Canada from the 17th national convention of the CPC, 21 January 1962. (2pp), broadside. *OKQS.

4266 Communist Party of Canada. Constitution. Toronto.
39pp. *OTURS/RSK.

4267 ------ Documents of the 17th national convention,
January 19,20,21, 1962. Toronto. 36pp. *BVAUS/WB
31f.3c OKQS.

4268 ------ Let's be masters in our own house: a new policy for Canada - of independence, neutrality, disarmament. Toronto. (4pp). *OKQS OTURS/RSK.

4269 ------ The road to socialism in Canada. Toronto.
32pp. AEU SSU *OHMA2118 OOA/CCF542 OTURS/RSK.

4270 ------ Submission to the Royal Commission on Banking
and Finance. Toronto. 16pp plus 1p appendix, mimeo.
*OTURS/RSK.

4271 ------ Submission to the Royal Commission on Health
Services. Toronto. 12pp, mimeo. *OTURS/RSK.

4272 Douglas, T.C. Address at the 4th convention of the
Canadian Labour Congress, Vancouver 12 April 1962.
Ottawa: Canadian Labour Congress. 12pp, mimeo.
*OOA/CCF543.

4273 ------ and Morden Lazarus. The New Democratic Party:
its aims and program, the Tommy Douglas story, A planned economy, The only effective shelter. Toronto:
United Steelworkers. 14pp. *OOA/CCF543.

4274 ------ Taking his seat in the House of Commons: a
Plan for full employment and economic growth. Speech
delivered in the House of Commons on November 2, 5,
1962. Ottawa: R. Duhamel. 8pp. *OOA/CCF449 and 537.

4275 Forsey, E.A. The debt of our reason: encaenial address Thursday, May 17th, 1962. Fredericton: University of New Brunswick. 8pp plus 8pp, bilingual.
BVAU BVIP NBSAM NSHPL OPET SRL *OOP.

4276 Frank, Mark. Fallup: mankind's new atomic danger.
Toronto: Progress. 50pp. OOP *BVAUS/Mac39f.1F
OHMA1613 OTURS/RSK.

4277 ------ Poison for the young. Toronto: Progress.
48pp. *BVAUS/WB43f.22 OHMA1616 OTURS/RSK. Inquiry
into juvenile delinquency and attack on televised
violence.

4278 French, Doris. Faith, sweat and politics: the early
trade union years in Canada. Toronto: McClelland
and Stewart. (vi), 154pp. *OONL. Largely an account of Daniel John O'Donoghue. No index, no references.

4279 Goldberg, Theodore. Trade union interest in medical
care and voluntary health insurance: a study of two
collectively bargained programmes. PhD thesis, University of Toronto. 2 vols: xiii, 349pp and 350-504.
biblio, volume 2 is appendixes. *OTUAR.

4280 Herman, Emil Edward. Freedom of association and recognition of labour organizations prior to order in

council PC 1003 of 1944. Unpublished MA thesis,
McGill University.

4281 Hunter, W.D.G. The New Democratic Party: antecedents,
policies, prospects. Kingston: Queens Quarterly.
pp361-376. *OHMA2364. Offprint from vol LXIX no 3.

4282 Jagan, Cheddi. Socialism and democracy. Toronto:
Canadian Far Eastern Newsletter. (7pp). *OOA/End-
icott 1. Text of an address in Washington.

4283 Kashtan, William. Stop union raiding. Toronto:
Progress. 30pp. AEU BVIV SSU *BVAUS/WB31f.1b
OHMA1632 OKQS OTURS/RSK.

4284 Kehde, Mary. Labour unions: an introductory course
for individuals and study groups. Text and references completely revised. Ottawa: St Patricks College.
ix, 167pp. *OOP. First printed in 1954 - not found.

(4285) Kurnicki, Pierre J. The personality of a leader in
the creation and in the application of Marxism. Unpublished MA thesis, University of Montreal.

4286 Labor Poets Workshop. Poems for life. Vancouver.
29pp. BVIPA NBSM NSHPL OTP OTS *BVAUS/WB41f.9a(ii)
OKQS.

4287 LeFresne, G.M. The Royal Twenty Centers - the Dept
of National Defence and federal unemployment relief
1932-36. Unpublished MA thesis, Royal Military College. xii, 225pp, biblio. *OONL.

4288 Lloyd, W.S. Doing things together: speech in the
debate on the speech from the throne. Regina: Saskatchewan Legislature. 25pp. *SSUS/JL197.

4289 MacInnis, Malcolm. The New Democratic Party and
planning. Speech delivered in the House of Commons
on October 30, 1962. Ottawa: R. Duhamel. 4pp.
*OOA/CCF537.

4290 McIvor, R. Craig. Recent growth in Canadian co-operatives. Toronto: Canadian Tax Foundation. iii,
23pp. *OPET.

4291 Manitoba Federation of Labour. The reply of organized labour to Justice Tritschler's report re: Brandon Packers strike. Winnipeg. 37pp. *MWPA/Russell
1. The strike started on 29 February 1960; Mr Justice Tritschler's commission was set up 29 June 1960.

4292 Marx, Karl and Frederick Engels. On the Labour Party.
Toronto: Vanguard. 21pp, mimeo. *E.

4293 Mather, Barry. Speech on ways and means in line with
Canada's financial and economic problems delivered
in the House of Commons 24 October 1962. Ottawa:
R. Duhamel. 4pp. *BVAUS/Garrison 1-5.

4294 Meagher, Nicholas. Socialism and socialistic ideas.
Unpublished MA thesis, Dalhousie University. (iii),
iv, 158pp, biblio. *NSHD. Contains a chapter on
socialism in Canada.

4295 Meekison, James David. The forces of demand for British Columbia's mining labour: an analysis of the trends of wage rates and employment of British Columbia's mining industry. Unpublished MA thesis, University of British Columbia. 93pp, biblio. *BVAUS.

(4296) Milnor, A.J. Agrarian protest in Saskatchewan 1929-1948: a study in ethnic politics. PhD thesis, Duke University. ix, 235pp.

4297 Morris, Leslie. The NDP cannot succeed by embracing McCarthyism: Communist Party replies to letter by York Centre NDP candidate Val Scott. Toronto: Canadian Tribune. (1p) broadside. *OKQS OTURS/RSK.

4298 ------ New jobs through new markets: how the cold war causes unemployment. Toronto: Communist Party of Canada. 28pp. AEU BVIV OKQ SSU *BVAUS/WB31f.1b OHMA1846 OTURS/RSK.

4299 ------ Where do we go from here? Toronto: Communist Party of Canada. 23pp. OONL *AEUS BVAUS/WB31f.1b OHMA1836 OKQS OTURS/RSK SSUS/Comm.

4300 Nesbitt, Leonard D. Tides in the west. Saskatoon: Modern Press. (viii), 413(420)pp, illus. *SSUS/Shortt. On cooperation in the prairies with biographical notes.

4301 New Democratic Party. Program for agriculture: a new deal for Canadian farmers and the family farm. Regina. (6pp). *SSA/G5.1962.9.

4302 ------ The right to health: the NDP plan. Ottawa. (6pp). *OOA/CCF539 SSA/G5.1962.8.

4303 Ontario Federation of Labour. Repprt on the labour relations act. Toronto. 7pp. *OKQS.

4304 ------ Report on medicare. Toronto. 7pp. *OKQS.

4305 ------ Report on workmens compensation problems in Ontario. Toronto. 11pp. *OKQS.

4306 ------ Submission to the Commission of Inquiry in the matter of Industrial Standards act. Toronto. 12pp, mimeo. *OOA/OFL8.

4307 ------ Submission to the Committee on Portable Pensions, Bill 165. Toronto. 12pp, mimeo. *OOA/OFL8.

4308 ------ Submission to the Select Committee on Manpower Training. Toronto. 18 plus 4pp, mimeo. *OOA/OFL8.

4309 ------ To: Royal Commission on Health Services. Toronto. 24 plus(4) plus 5pp, mimeo. *OOA/OFL8.

4310 Park, L.C. and F.W. Anatomy of big business. Toronto: Progress. (ii), 271pp, tables and index of companies and persons. *OTURS/RSK.

4311 Parkin, Frank Iorwell. Conflict in the lumber industry. Unpublished MA thesis, University of British Columbia. 92pp, biblio. BVAU.

(4312) Peltier, Jacques. Labor in the transportation industry. Unpublished MA thesis, Ottawa University.
101pp. Not found.

4313 Pennington, Edward James and Ian Walker. The role
of trade unions in social welfare: an exploratory
study of the attitudes of trade union members towards health and welfare services. Unpublished
MSW thesis, University of British Columbia. 137pp.
*BVAUS.

(4314) Pratt, D.F. William Ivens and the Winnipeg Labor
Church. Saskatoon, St Andrews College BD thesis.

4315 Religion-Labour Council of Canada. Constitution as
revised January 1962. (Toronto). 5pp, mimeo.
*MWPA/Russell 1.

4316 Riley, John Norman. The adaptability of consumer
cooperatives to changes in retailing in Canada.
Unpublished MBA thesis, University of British Columbia. 248pp, biblio. *BVAUS.

4317 Sanouillet, Michel. Le séparatisme québécois et
nous/Separatism and the franco-Ontarians. Toronto:
Nouvelles Françaises. 28 plus 28pp, bilingual.
*OONL.

4318 Saskatchewan Federation of Labour. The first fight
for medicare. Regina. 19pp. OH OTU *OOA/CCF549
SSA/G114.10.

4319 Socialist Party of Canada. The Socialist Party of
Canada and the federal election. Winnipeg. (2pp).
*BVAUS/Mac30Af.2a.

4320 ------ War. Winnipeg. (2pp). *BVAUS/Mac30Af.2a.

4321 Steeves, Dorothy G. Builders and rebels: a short
history of the CCF in British Columbia 1932-1961.
Vancouver: BC Committee for the New Democratic Party.
23pp. BVAU *OOA/CCF536 OTURS/RSK.

4322 Stevenson, John A. Political duplicity...the enemy
of democracy. An internationally known journalist
looks at the case of Hazen Argue. Regina: CCF/NDP.
(4pp). *SSA/G5.1962.3. Argue abruptly left the
NDP after his defeat as proposed leader in order to
run for the Liberals.

4323 Trotsky, Leon. Trade unions in the epoch of imperialist decay. Toronto: Workers Vanguard. (13pp), mimeo.
*E.

4324 Tyre, Robert. Douglas in Saskatchewan: the story of
a socialist experiment. Vancouver: Mitchell. (viii),
212pp, illus, no index, no refs. *OTURS/RSK.

4325 Voice of Women. Brief to the Prime Minister. Toronto. 2pp plus 3pp, mimeo, bilingual. *OOA/VOW7.
On disarmament.

4326 ------ Brief to Right Honourable Harold Macmillan
Prime Minister of Great Britain and Northern Ireland.

Toronto. 6pp, mimeo. *OOA/VOW7. On the British
nuclear tests on Christmas island.

(4327) Wargo, Alan John. The great coal strike: the Vancouver Island coal mine strike, 1912-1914. Unpublished MA thesis, University of British Columbia.
Not found.

4328 Weldon, John C. What is planning? Toronto: Ontario
Woodsworth Memorial Foundation. 13pp. *OKQS.

4329 ------ , George W. Cadbury and Michael K. Oliver.
Democratic planning: a symposium. Toronto: Ontario
Woodsworth Memorial Foundation. 36pp. *OKQS.

4330 Woodcock, George. Anarchism. New York: World.
504pp. *OONL.

4331 Woods, H.D. and Sylvia Ostry. Labour policy and
labour economics in Canada. Toronto: Macmillan.
xviii, 534pp, biblio. *OONL.

4332 Zeitlin, Maurice. Labor in Cuba: Castro and Cuba's
communists. Toronto: Fair Play for Cuba Committee.
13pp, mimeo. *E.

1963

4333 Adams, E.G. Disarmament and prosperity for Canada.
Toronto: Canadian Peace Congress. (c1963). 34pp.
*MWPA/Brigden 7 OHMA1454 OTURS/RSK.

4334 Aitchison, J.H. (ed). The political process in Can-
ada: essays in honour of R. MacGregor Dawson. Tor-
onto: University of Toronto Press. (xii), 193pp.
*OONL. Includes Early socialism in Canada by Paul
W. Fox: The paradox of power in the Saskatchewan
CCF 1944-1961 by Evelyn Eager.

4335 Bartlett, Christopher David Sloan. A study of some
factors affecting growth in Ontario cooperatives.
Unpublished MA thesis, University of Toronto. vii,
122pp, biblio. *OTUAR.

4336 Brown-John, C.L. The decision to amend the Dept of
Labour act, 1957. Unpublished MA thesis, University
of Toronto. (i), iii, 19, 11, 11, 21, 3 (2)pp.
*OTUAR.

4337 Buck, Tim. Power: the key to the future. Toronto:
Progress. 23pp. AEU BVAS BVIV *BVAUS/WB31f.1b
OHMA2142 OKQS OTURS/RSK SSUS.

4338 Canada. Industrial enquiry commission concerning
matters relating to the disruption of shipping on
the Great Lakes, the St Lawrence river system, and
connected waters. Report. Ottawa: R. Duhamel. 2
vols. *OOP.

4339 ------ Proceedings and final report of special committee on manpower and employment. Ottawa: R. Duhamel. 64pp. *OOP.

4340 Canadian Peace Congress. A memorandum to the North Atlantic Treaty Organization Council meeting, Ottawa, Canada May 1963. Toronto. (4pp). *OOA/Endicott 1.

4341 Castro, Fidel. Cuba confronts the future. Toronto: Fair Play for Cuba Committee. 24pp. *E.

4342 ------ Cuba's agrarian reform. Toronto: Fair Play for Cuba Committee. 16pp. *E.

4343 ------ Our line is the line of consistent anti-imperialism. Toronto: Fair Play for Cuba Committee. 12pp, mimeo. *E.

(4344)Combined Universities Campaign for Nuclear Disarmament. A select bibliography of inexpensive peace literature. Toronto. 21pp. Not seen.

4345 Communist Party of Canada. Crisis on the railways. Toronto. 25pp. AEU BVIV SSU *OHMA1509 OKQS OTURS/ RSK. The case for publicly owned railways.

4346 ------ No nuclear arms for Canada! Dismantle US bases in Canada! Toronto. (4pp). *BVAUS/WB39f.1F OTURS/RSK.

4347 ------ Submission re: Webb and Knapp (Canada) Ltd Coal Harbour development. Vancouver. 10 plus (5)pp appendix, mimeo. *BVAA.

4348 ------ Submission to the Ontario Committee on Taxation. Toronto. 27pp, mimeo. *OKQS.

4349 CCF/NDP. Workers handbook. Regina. 21pp, mimeo. *SSA/G4.1963.2.

4350 Cowan, John Scott. See no evil: a study of the chaos in Canadian defence policy. Toronto: Annex. 35pp, errata slip. AEU *AEUS. Endorsed by the NDP.

4351 Cox, Cedric and others. Four Canadians who saw Cuba. Toronto: Fair Play for Cuba Committee. 31pp. *OTURS/ RSK.

4352 ------ , Hugh Clifford and John Macey. A suggested socialist manifesto for the New Democratic Party. Vancouver. (4pp). *OTURS/RSK.

4353 Crowe, Harry S. Oligarchy and democracy in Canadian labour unions. np. 20pp, mimeo. *OKQS.

4354 J.D. and C.L.D. The Tripoli program: program of the Algerian revolution. Toronto: Workers Vanguard. 20pp, mimeo. *E.

4355 Dewart, Leslie. Christianity and revolution: the lesson of Cuba. New York: Herder and Herder. 320pp. *OONL. Published in England as *Cuba, church and crisis: Christianity and politics in the Cuban revolution*, 1964.

4356 Douglas, T.C. Jobs - portable pensions, higher living standards, no nuclear weapons: speech delivered in the House of Commons on May 20 and 21, 1963. Ottawa:

R. Duhamel. 7pp. *OOA/CCF449.

4357 Douglas, T.C. Profiteering in sugar must stop.
Speech delivered in the House of Commons 12th November 1963. Ottawa: R. Duhamel. 4pp. *OOA/CCF449.

4358 ------ Stand of New Democratic Party on nuclear
weapons in Canada. Speech delivered in the House of
Commons on January 24, 1963. Ottawa: R. Duhamel.
8pp. *BVAUS/Garrison 1-5 OOA/CCF413, 449 and 537
SSAG5.1963.3.

4359 Fidler, D. and others. The expulsions from the Ontario New Democratic Party: the case for the defence.
A report of a meeting addressed by five of the expelled youth. Toronto: The Committee to Defend Democracy in the NDP. 27pp, mimeo. *OHMA2124 OTURS/
RSK. The expelled speakers were Dick Fidler, Allan
Engler, Jim Onyschuk, John Wilson, Toni Foster with
a comment by Stan Davies.

4360 Finn, Ed. Sweden: where a government believes in
planning. Toronto: UAW Citizenship Dept. (4pp).
*OOA/CCF539.

4361 Fuentes, Carlos. A Latin American speaks to North
Americans. Toronto: Fair Play for Cuba Committee.
14pp, mimeo. *E.

4362 Hood, Wm. C. and John A. Sawyer (eds). Canadian
political science association conference on statistics: papers. Toronto: University of Toronto Press.
(x), 170pp. *OONL. Includes: Regional aspects of
labour mobility in Canada 1956-1959 by H.F. Greenway
and G.W. Wheatley: Some calculations relating to
trends and fluctuations in the post-war Canadian
labour market by Frank T. Denton.

4363 Knowles, Stanley. The proposed Canada pension plan.
Speech delivered in the House of Commons, Thursday
July 18, 1963. Ottawa: R. Duhamel. 8pp. *MWPA/
Brigden 7 OOA/CCF537.

4364 Lamorie, Andrew (pseud: possibly Dyson Carter). How
they sold our Canada to the USA. Gravenhurst: Northern Book House. 102pp. *BVAUS/Mac42f.25a OHMA1788
OTURS/RSK.

4365 Lazarus, Morden. Background notes on labour's political history. Toronto: Ontario Federation of Labour. 37pp, mimeo. OH OTU *OOP.

4366 Lechuga, Carlos. Cuba's road to peace. Toronto:
Fair Play for Cuba Committee. 12pp, mimeo. *E.

4367 Levitt, Joseph. The CCF and French Canadian 'radical' nationalism: a comparison in policy (1933-1942).
Unpublished MA thesis, University of Toronto. (ii),
213pp, biblio. *OTUAR.

4368 Liversedge, Ronald. Recollections of the On-to-Ottawa trek, 1935. Lake Cowichan (BC). (c1963). 174pp,
mimeo. *OHMA1774.

4369 Lloyd, W.S. Developing, diversifying and expanding. Speech in the debate on the speech from the throne. Regina: Saskatchewan Legislature. 37pp. *SSUS/JL197.

4370 MacDonald, Donald. The structure of the CLC. (Ottawa): Canadian Labour Congress. (4pp). *OOA/CCF543.

4371 McDonald, John C. Automation and the changing meaning of work. Ottawa: Dept of Labour. 15pp. *OOA/CCF444.

4372 Magnuson, Bruce. Stop the US power grab. Toronto: Communist Party of Canada. 21pp. AEU BVIP BVIV OKQ *BVAUS/WB3.f.1b OHMA1860 OTURS/RSK.

(4373)Mayer, L.C. The politics of the labour movement in Australia and Canada. Unpublished MA thesis, University of California. 178pp.

4374 Morris, Leslie. Liberal plans and you. Toronto: Progress. 23pp. BVIP OKQ OPAL *AEUS BVAUS/WB31f.1b OHMA1845 OTURS/RSK SSUS/Comm.

4375 New Democratic Party. The federal program of the NDP adopted by its founding convention...and by its second federal convention, Regina 6-9, 1963. Ottawa. 57pp. *OOA/CCF538.

4376 ------ Objectives and principles: Economic planning: Federalism and biculturalism: International: Agriculture. 5 leaflets. Ottawa. (6pp) each. *OOA/CCF537. Contained in one folder.

4377 ------ Program for Ontario. Toronto. 36pp. *OHMA 1592 OOA/CCF 539 SSA/G6.Ont.5.

4378 ------ and CCF. Workers handbook: every member canvass fall, 1963. Regina. 21pp, mimeo. *OOA/CCF540.

4379 New Democratic Youth. Convention report, 2nd federal convention, Regina 1963. Ottawa. 38pp plus 3p constitution. *OOA/CCF478.

4380 Ontario Federation of Labour. Submission to the Commission of Inquiry into arbitration of disputes in hospitals in Ontario. Toronto. 6pp, mimeo. *OOA/OFL8.

4381 ------ Submission to the Select Committee on consumer credit. Toronto. 11 plus (1)pp, mimeo. *OOA/ OFL8.

4382 Sayles, Fern A. Welland workers make history. Welland: Winifred Sayles. 221pp. BVAU BVIV NBSAM OH OKQ OOL *OTURS/RSK. A history of labour in Welland.

4383 Scott, Jack. Jack Scott takes a second look at Cuba. With an introduction by Bert Herridge. Toronto: Fair Play for Cuba Committee. 28pp. OHMA1898 OTURS/RSK.

4384 Seafarers International Union of Canada. The strange conspiracy to destroy the standards and security of Canadian workers. Montreal. (c1963). 28pp, illus. *BVAUS/Mac32f.3 OHMA2211.

4385 Socialist Party of Canada. Free! The best of everything you may want, need or desire...Victoria. 12pp,
mimeo. *T.

4386 Swankey, Ben. Keep Canada out! Vancouver: Canadian
Cuban Friendship Committee. 20pp. AEU BVIPA OKQ
SSU *OHMA2585 OTURS/RSK. Why Canada should not join
the OAS.

4387 Trevena, J.E. Who does pay the taxes? Calgary: Federated Co-operatives. 11pp. *OOA/MacInnis 6.

4388 Trotsky, Leon. The labor party in America. Toronto:
Vanguard. 37pp, mimeo. *E.

4389 United Rubber Workers of America. A brief history
of local 113. (Hamilton). (c1963). 20pp. *OHMA .

4390 Voice of Women. Brief presented to the Prime Minister. Toronto. 4pp, mimeo. *OOA/VOW7. A general
brief on external aid, peace etc.

4391 ------ To Special Committee on Defense. (Toronto).
6 plus 6pp, mimeo, bilingual. *MWPA/Brigden 3.

4392 ------ Fallout monitoring in Canada: brief to the
Minister of National Health and Welfare. Toronto.
23pp. OTMCL OOP *OOA/VOW 7.

4393 ------ Statement to the Special Committee on Defense.
Toronto. 5pp, mimeo. *OOA/VOW 7. Probably the same
text as 4391 above.

4394 ------ Submitted to the government of the province
of Saskatchewan. Regina. 19pp, mimeo. *SSA/G549.1.
On nuclear war.

4395 ------ Why VOW? (Edmonton). 16pp, mimeo. *OOA/
VOW 7.

1964

4396 Bain, George Sayers. The United Packinghouse, Food
and Allied Workers: its development, structure, collective bargaining and future, with special reference
to Canada. Unpublished MA thesis, University of Manitoba. viii, 232pp, biblio. *OOA/CFAW61.

4397 Buck, Tim. Put monopoly under control: a new econ-
omic policy for Canada. Toronto: Progress. 78pp.
AEU NFSM OONL OOP SSU *BVAUS/WB39f.7 OHMA2756 OKQS
OTURS/RSK.

4398 Buller, Grace, Sadie Jordan and David Summers. Books
about labour, economics, people, social philosophy.
Toronto: Ontario Federation of Labour. 12pp.
*MWPA/Russell 1.

4399 Burney, Derek Hudson. Canadian parties and the nuclear arms issue. Unpublished MA thesis, Queens University. (iv), ii, 194pp, biblio. *OKQ.

4400 Cameron, Colin. The hollow budget. Speech delivered in the House of Commons, March 19, 1964. Ottawa: R. Duhamel. 7pp. *OOA/CCF537.

4401 Canadian Peace Congress. From Potsdam to the multi-lateral force. Toronto. 14pp. *OTURS/RSK.

4402 Castro, Fidel. Addresses Congress of American women. Toronto: Workers Vanguard. 24pp. *E.

4403 ------ Declaration of Santiago. Toronto: Fair Play for Cuba Committee. 36pp, mimeo. *E.

4404 Combined Universities Campaign for Nuclear Disarma-ment. The university and social action in the nuclear age. Toronto. 16pp. OHMA1712.

4405 Communist Party of Canada. Automation: the Hamilton prospect. Toronto: Progress. 22pp. *OHMA1523 OTURS/RSK.

4406 ------ 18th national convention Toronto - March 27-28-29-30, 1964: documents. Toronto. 52pp, mimeo. *OTURS/RSK.

4407 ------ Questions for today: two world systems, peace-fu; coexistence, national liberation, workers vs. mon-opoly, transition to socialism. Documents and comm-entary, 1952-1964. Toronto: Progress. 155pp. *OHMA 2752 OTURS/RSK.

4408 ------ Statement on the draft Columbia river treaty. Toronto. 11pp, mimeo. *OKQS.

4409 ------ Submission to the Board of Transport Comm-issioners for Canada in the matter of review respect-ing the Bell Telephone Company of Canada. Toronto. 11pp, mimeo. *OTURS/RSK.

4410 ------ Submission to the Royal Commission on Biling-ualism and Biculturalism. Toronto. 31pp, mimeo. *OTURS/RSK.

4411 Douglas, T.C. Address to fifth constitutional con-vention of the Canadian Labour Congress: Montreal, April 1964. Montreal: Canadian Labour Congress. (4pp) plus (4pp), bilingual. *OOA/CCF449.

4412 ------ War against poverty: harnessing the scientific revolution; Canada pension plan; No nuclear weapons. Speech delivered in the House of Commons February 20, 1964. Ottawa: R. Duhamel. 7pp. *BVAUS/Garrison 1-5 OOA/CCF449 and 537.

4413 Endicott, Norman A. The I.A.D.L. Budapest meeting. Toronto: Canadian Far Eastern Newsletter. 7pp. *OOA/Endicott 1 OTURS/RSK. The IADL is the Inter-national Association of Democratic Lawyers.

4414 Fair Play for Cuba Committee. Report on Canadian students work tour to Cuba: poem by Al Purdy; imp-ressions by Dorothy Steeves. Toronto. 36pp, mimeo. SSU *E.

4415 ------ The real Cuba as three Canadians saw it.

Toronto. 36pp. AEU *OTURS/RSK. The three Canadians are Michel Chartrand, Vernel Olson and John Riddell.

4416 Feinberg, Abraham L. Storm the gates of Jericho. Toronto: McClelland and Stewart. 344pp. *OONL.

4417 Fergusson, Charles Bruce. The labour movement in Nova Scotia before confederation. Halifax: Public Archives. 36pp. BVAS OOA OOL OTU *OTAR/1964/34.

4418 Guevara, Che. Charges the UN to meet challenge of imperialism. Toronto: Fair Play for Cuba Committee. 12pp, mimeo. *E.

4419 Hallett, Mary Elizabeth. W.D. Herridge and the New Democracy movement. Unpublished MA thesis, Queens University. vi, 182pp, biblio. *OKQ.

(4420) Houde, E. Le droit de grève dans les services publics. Unpublished MA thesis, Université Laval. 163pp.

4421 Howe, Wm. D. A national health plan. Speech delivered in the House of Commons on February 25, 1964. Ottawa: R. Duhamel. 4pp. *OOA/CCF537.

4422 Kaplansky, Kalmen. The international responsibilities of the Canadian Labour Congress. Ottawa. (c1964). 5pp. *OOA/Kaplansky.

4423 ------ The role of labour in international co-operation. Ottawa: Canadian Labour Congress. (6pp). *OOA/CCF543 and Kaplansky.

4424 ------ The role of trade unions in the United Nations. Ottawa: Canadian Labour Congress. 8pp. *OOA/Kaplansky.

4425 Kashtan, William. Automation and labor. Toronto: Progress. 27pp. AEU BVIV OKQ OPET QQL *BVAUS/Mac 39f.1d OHMA1709 OTURS/RSK.

4426 Lewis, Stephen. The scientific revolution: a speech on automation (Legislature of Ontario). (Toronto): (NDP). 8pp. *OOA/CCF444.

4427 Lloyd, W.S. Priorities for people: speech in the debate on the speech from the throne. Regina: Saskatchewan Legislature. 32pp. *SSUS/JL197.

4428 McCrorie, James Napier. In union is strength. Saskatoon: University of Saskatoon. 124pp. *SSUS/Shortt. A history of Saskatchewan farmers.

4429 MacGuigan, Mark and Trevor Lloyd. Liberalism and socialism. Toronto: Exchange for Political Ideas in Canada. 27pp. BVAU OKQ OOP OTU QMU *OTURS/RSK. The original version of MacGuigan's paper was an address to the Canadian University Liberal Federation.

4430 Mandel, Ernst. Vive Cuba: impressions de Cuba. Cuba en marche vers le socialisme. Toronto: Fair Play for Cuba Committee. (c1964). 13pp. *E.

4431 Morris, Leslie. Challenge of the '60s: 3 point pro-

gram for Canada. Toronto: Progress. 32pp. AEU
OONL *BVAUS/WB31f.2a OHMA1849 OTURS/RSK.

4432 New Democratic Party. Program: a minimum program
for a new Canadian society. Regina. (c1964). (12pp)
*SSA/G4.1964.8.

4433 ------ The Riverdale story: a by-election campaign.
Toronto. (iv), 40pp. *OOA/CCF539 OOAL SSA/G6.
Ont.16. First by-election won by the NDP.

4434 ------ Various election pamphlets used by the NDP
1963-1965:
Ah, all you politicians are the same: Because Canada
needs a clear sense of national purpose: Medicare -
the facts: Needed in Ottawa - clear thinking: A
new era for agriculture: Nuclear weapons? No: Vote
New Democrat, build a new Canada: Why more and more
Canadians are planning to vote New Democrat: Your
opportunities. Various places, mostly (2-4)pp.

4435 Ontario Federation of Labour. Poverty in the midst
of plenty: poverty in Ontario 1964. Toronto. 58pp.
*OTURS/RSK.

4436 ------ Submission to the Joint Committee on Legal
Aid. Toronto. 5pp, mimeo. *OOA/OFL8.

4437 ------ Submission to Labour Safety Council of Ontario. Toronto. 11pp. *OOA/OFL8.

4438 ------ To the - Medical Services Insurance Enquiry.
Toronto. 10pp. *OOA/OFL8.

4439 Orlikow, David. Canada's brain drain can be stopped.
Speech delivered in the House of Commons on March 20,
1964. Ottawa: R. Duhamel. 4pp. *OOA/CCF537.

(4440)Osborn, E.A. The Ontario Farmers Union as a movement
of farm protest. Unpublished MSA thesis, University
of Guelph. 147pp.

4441 Pelt, Melvyn L. The Communist Party of Canada 1929-
1942. Unpublished MA thesis, University of Toronto.
vi, 192pp, biblio. *OTUAR.

4442 Rich, John. The worker in a changing world. Vancouver: Boag Foundation. 16pp. AEU *BVAUS/Young
MWPA/Russell 1 OOA/CCF543.

4443 Ross, David Phillips. The causes of labour dispute
in Alberta 1955-1962: an analysis of collective bargaining criteria. Unpublished MA thesis, University
of Alberta. xii, 151pp, biblio. *AEUS.

4444 Rowland, Douglas Charles. Canadian communism: the
post-Stalinist phase. Unpublished MA thesis, University of Manitoba. xi, 292, lxpp, biblio.

4445 Ruff, Norman John Robert. Labour unions and the
Canadian political process. Unpublished MA thesis,
McMaster University. (i), iv, 105pp, biblio. *OHMA.

4446 Saskatchewan Federation of Labour. Labour and the
Sask. Trade Union act. Regina. (4pp). SSA/G114.8.

4447 Saskatchewan Federation of Labour. Submission to the Labour-Management Legislative Review Committee of the province of Saskatchewan. Regina. 42pp. *SSA/Gl14.6. Cover title: Why the Trade Union Act is good for Saskatchewan!

4448 Schleifer, Marc. Letter from Havana. Toronto: Fair Play for Cuba Committee. (6pp), mimeo. *E.

4449 Scott, Reid. The case against hanging. Ottawa: R. Duhamel. 4pp. *OOA/CCF476 and 537.

4450 ------ The scientific revolution - blessing or curse? Speech delivered in the House of Commons on February 28, 1964. Ottawa: R. Duhamel. 4pp. *OOA/CCF537.

4451 Summers, David (ed). Should the churches be neutral about co-ops? The report of a consultation sponsored by the Religion-Labour Council of Canada and the National Labour-Cooperative Committee. Toronto. 10pp. *MWPA/Russell 1.

4452 Underhill, Frank H. The image of confederation. Toronto: Canadian Broadcasting Corporation. (x), 84pp, biblio. *MWP.

4453 USSR-Canada Society. Outline of the society's activities. Moscow. 7pp. *OTURS/RSK.

4454 University New Democrats. 1964 conference report, 2nd annual conference central Canada University New Democrats, Hart House, University of Toronto 9 and 10 May 1964. (Toronto). 12pp, mimeo. *OOA/CCF478.

4455 Vickers, Geoffrey. The impact of automation on society. Toronto: Ontario Woodsworth Memorial Foundation. 12pp. *OOA/CCF444 and 537.

4456 Voice of Women. Memorandum to the government of Canada on the occasion of the meeting of the Council of Voice of Women, February 15 and 16, 1964. Toronto. 6pp, mimeo. *OOA/VOW7

4457 ------ Memorandum to the Prime Minister. Toronto. 5pp, mimeo. *OOA/VOW7. Resolutions and comments from the 1963 annual meeting.

4458 Walsh, S. Un politique sociale au lieu d'une politique bourgeoise. Toronto: Communist Party of Canada. 31pp. *OTCPA.

4459 Whitney, Bill, Andrew Joe and Jack Scott. A symposium of three speeches on the recognition of China. Vancouver: NDP. 25pp, mimeo. *OTURS/RSK.

(4460)Williams, Brian C. Canadian-American trade union relations: a study of the development of binational unionism. PhD thesis, Cornell University. ix, 489pp.

4461 Workers Vanguard. Dynamics of world revolution today. Toronto. 44pp. *OTURS/RSK.

4462 Zakuta, Leo. A protest movement becalmed: a study of change in the CCF. Toronto: University of Toronto

Press. xii, 204pp. *OTURS/RSK. Canadian studies in sociology 1.

1965

4463 Beeching, William. The worker student alliance! Toronto: (Communist Viewpoint). (c1965). 13pp, mimeo. *OKQS.

4464 Bjarnason, Emil. Collective bargaining in the coal mining industry of Canada 1825-1938. Unpublished MA thesis, Queens University. vii, 166pp, biblio. *OKQ. Written mainly in 1941.

4465 Blakeney, Allan E. The wrong budget for Saskatchewan. Regina: CCF/NDP. 21pp. *SSA/G4.1965.5.

4466 Borovoy, A. Alan. Human rights and racial equality - the tactics of combat. Toronto: Ontario Woodsworth Memorial Foundation. 16pp. OHMA3095 OKQS OOA/CCF 537 SSUS.

4467 Brewin, Andrew. Stand on guard: the search for a Canadian defence policy. Toronto: McClelland and Stewart. 140pp. *MWP.

4468 BC Federation of Labour. A handbook on the great conspiracy. Vancouver. 12pp. AEU BVIP *OOA/CCF537.

4469 Bruning, Otto H. The life of an illiterate pioneer. Regina: New Times Book Service. (c1965). (ii), 101pp, mimeo. *SSA/A.190. Autobiography including some socialist/communist reminiscences.

4470 Canadian Labour Congress. Farmer-Labour conference: the automated society: good or bad. Report of the sixth conference UAW education centre, Port Elgin June 19-20 1965. Toronto. 39pp. *OOA/CCF444.

4471 Canadian Railway Labour Executives Association. The plot to blame unions for inflation. Ottawa. (4pp). *OOA/CCF475.

4472 Carrothers, A.W.R. Collective bargaining law in Canada. Toronto: Butterworth. lxxxix, 553pp. *OONL.

4473 Castro, Fidel. On Vietnam: two speeches. Toronto: Fair Play for Cuba Committee. 35pp, mimeo. *E.

4474 Chukukere, Edward. The other Congo story. Toronto: Canadian Peace Congress. (8pp). *OOA/Endicott 1.

4475 Clarke, Nelson. Two nations, one country: the Communist proposals for a democratic solution of the crisis of confederation. Toronto: Progress. 29pp. AEU BVIP OPET OKQ *BVAUS/WB31f.1b OHMA1518 OTURS/ RSK.

4476 Cliche, Robert. Canada and the new Quebec. Ottawa: New Democratic Party. 20pp. *OKQS.

4477 Communist Party of Canada. Alberta round-up: is Canada to train police in Vietnam? Edmonton. 8pp. *OHMA2588.

4478 ------ Democracy on the job: a statement on workers rights. Toronto. (c1965). (6pp). *BVAUS/WB39f.11 OTURS/RSK.

4479 ------ The Great Lakes basin and the future of Canada: submission to the International Joint Commission United States and Canada. Toronto. 12pp, mimeo. *OTURS/RSK.

4480 ------ One million jobs: the proposals of the CPC. Toronto. (6pp). *OOA/CCF475.

4481 Crepeau, P-A. and C.B. Macpherson. The future of Canadian federalism/L'avenir du fédéralisme canadien. Toronto: University of Toronto Press. xiv, 188pp. *OONL. Contains contributions from P.E. Trudeau, Jacques Parizeau, Jacques-Yvan Morin, F.R. Scott.

4482 Crysdale, Stewart. Social effects of a factory relocation: a case study of social and political consequences of job displacement. Toronto: Religion-Labour Council of Canada and United Steelworkers of America. 25pp, illus. *MWPA/Russell 1.

(4483) Davies, David Cyril. The development of Canadian socialist thought. PhD thesis, University of Toronto. Not found.

4484 Douglas, T.C. How Canadians can get their country back. Speech to the Saskatchewan provincial convention, 19 November 1965. (Regina): New Democratic Party. 9pp, mimeo. *OOA/CCF449.

4485 ------ $100 a month at 65: speech delivered in the House of Commons, Monday 29 March 1965. Ottawa: R. Duhamel. 4pp. *OOA/CCF449.

4486 ------ Report to the third biennial federal convention NDP, Royal York, Toronto 13 July 1965. (Ottawa): New Democratic Party. 8pp, mimeo. *OOA/CCF449.

4487 Fahrni, Christopher and others. Canadian students in Cuba. Toronto: Fair Play for Cuba Committee. 59pp, illus. *OHMA1938 OTURS/RSK.

4488 Falkenhagen, John Dale. A study of single unemployed men in Hamilton: an examination of data obtained from 88 single unemployed men interviewed in missions in Hamilton. Unpublished MSW thesis, University of Toronto. (i), i, (i)-viii, 115, (ii), 18, ii, (x)pp, biblio. Includes pp16a and 16b in the signature of 18pp. *OTUAR.

4489 Fraser, Blair. The only party nobody's mad at: will the NDP turn Parliament upside down? Toronto: Macleans. (4pp). *OOA/CCF538.

4490 Freeman, E.G. How a New Democratic government would help Ontario's independent businessmen. Toronto: NDP. 6pp. *OHMA1546 OOA/CCF537.

(4491) Godbout, J. Le militant syndical de la Confédération des Syndicats Nationaux: essai sociologique. Unpublished MA thesis, Université Laval. 199pp, biblio.

4492 Godfrey, William Gerald. The 1933 convention of the Cooperative Commonwealth Federation. Unpublished MA thesis, Waterloo University. iv, 151pp, biblio. Microfilm.

(4493) Gonick, C.W. Aspects of unemployment in Canada. PhD thesis, University of California. vi, 224pp.

4494 Grube, George. The New Democratic way. Toronto: NDP. 12pp. *OHMA1548 OOA/CCF538 OTURS/RSK.

4495 Guevara, Che. Socialism and man. Toronto: Fair Play for Cuba Committee. 24pp. *E.

4496 Habermehl, D.N.(ed). The Christian Reformed Church and the neutral labor union: a survey of synodical decisions. Oshawa. 13pp, mimeo. *OOA/Russell 1.

4497 Harding, James. A time for radical politics. Toronto: SUPA. (c1965). pp11-17 (complete). *OKQS.

(4498) Horowitz, Gad. Canadian labour in politics: the trade unions and the CCF-NDP. PhD thesis, Harvard University. v, 455pp.

4499 Howe, William D. Medicare now! Speech delivered in the House of Commons, Wednesday April 7, 1965. Ottawa: R. Duhamel. 4pp. *OOA/CCF537.

4500 Kashtan, William. A new foreign policy is needed. Where is Canada's voice? (Toronto): (Canadian Tribune). (4pp). *OTURS/RSK.

4501 Larsen, Vernon W. The community development council: case studies in success and failure: with a special chapter on implications for rural development by William B. Baker. Saskatoon: University of Saskatchewan. (iv), 64pp. AEU OTU SSU *OONL.

4502 Laxer, James. Centralism, regionalism, continentalism: problems of Canadian nationhood. Toronto: SUPA. (c1965). 11pp, mimeo. *OKQS.

(4503) Lortie, L'évolution de l'action politique de la Confédération des Syndicats Nationaux. Unpublished MA thesis, Université Laval. 98pp.

4504 Lyons, William E. The NDP in the Canadian political system. PhD thesis, Pennsylvania State University. vi, 458pp, biblio. *OONL.

4505 MacDonald, Donald C. The great medicare fight. Toronto. (c1965). 15pp. BVIP QMML *OKQS SSA/G6.Ont.17.

4506 ----- Ontario education. Toronto: New Democratic Party. 7pp. *OOA/CCF538.

4507 MacMackin, Stewart and Harry Arthurs. Topsy: a review of industrial relations in USA and Canada: 6th international churchmen's consultation, Hamilton, Ontario April 30th-May 1st, 1965. np. 22 and 15pp. *MWPA/Russell 1.

4508 McMenemy, John M. Lion in a den of Daniels: a study of Sam Lawrence, labour in politics. Unpublished MA thesis, McMaster University. x, 169pp plus inserted appendix, biblio. *OHMA.

4509 Morgan, J.S. The prospect of welfare. Ottawa: Canadian Public Welfare Association. 8pp. *OH.

4510 ------ and Albert Rose. The unfinished business in social security. Ottawa: Privy Council Office. 24pp. *OKQ.

4511 Morton, Desmond. Automation and unemployment. Toronto: New Democratic Party. 18pp. *OOA/CCF536 OKQS.

4512 ------ The New Democratic Party: the story of its foundation. Ottawa: New Democratic Party. 12pp. *OTURS/RSK.

4513 ------ and others. Part of a team: a handbook for riding executives. Toronto: New Democratic Party. 42pp. *OOA/CCF538.

4514 New Democratic Party. Convention 1965. (Ottawa). 64pp, bilingual. *OOA/CCF 392 and 537.

4515 ------ The federal program adopted by its founding convention Ottawa, July 31-August 4, 1961 and by its second federal convention 1963, and third federal convention, 1965. Ottawa. 82pp. *OHMA1587 OOA/CCF395.

4516 ------ A firm foundation: a handbook for the every member canvass. Toronto. 18pp. *OOA/CCF537.

4517 ------ Getting to know you: a handbook for the public canvass. Toronto. 10pp. *OOA/CCF537.

4518 ------ A handbook on policy: notes for speakers 1965. Ottawa. 127pp. *OOA/CCF538 SSA/G5.1965.6.

4519 ------ Make it a motion: a handbook for better riding meetings. Toronto. 25pp. *OOA/CCF537.

4520 ------ NDP sets goals for Canada: throne speech debate, 1965. Douglas urges planning for abundance, scientific revolution. Ottawa. 8pp. *OOA/CCF538.

4521 ------ The way ahead for Canada. Ottawa. 16pp. *OOA/CCF540 SSA/G5.1965.5.

4522 Ontario Federation of Labour. Brief to the Industrial Inquiry Commission relating to Canadian National Railway 'run-throughs' Winnipeg, Manitoba. Toronto. 26pp, mimeo. *OOA/OFL 8.

4523 ------ Submission to the Inquiry into Civil Rights. Chief Justice McRuer, Chairman. Toronto. 24pp, mimeo. *OOA/OFL 8.

4524 ------ Submission to the legislative committee on aging. Toronto. 11pp, mimeo. *OOA/OFL 8.

4525 ------ Submission to the members of the Workmens Compensation Board of Ontario concerning a need to revise coverage of the Workmens Compensation act of

Ontario for workers affected by ionizing radiation.
Toronto. 15pp, mimeo. *OOA/OFL 8.

4526 Ontario Federation of Labour. Submission to the Ontario Law Reform Commission, Chief Justice McRuer,
Chairman. Toronto. 9pp, mimeo. *OOA/OFL 8.

4527 ------ Submission to the Ontario Workmens Compensation Board concerning industrial deafness. Toronto.
12pp, mimeo. *OOA/OFL 8.

4528 ------ Submission to the provincial committee on
aims and objectives of education in schools of Ontario. Toronto. 30pp, mimeo. *OOA/OFL 8.

4529 ------ Submission to the Select Committee on Conservation Authorities. Toronto. 21pp, mimeo. *OOA/
OFL 8.

4530 Osler, John H. Injunction in labour disputes: an
outline of the law and practice in Ontario. Toronto.
21pp. *OOA/CCF543.

4531 Peitchinis, Stephen G. The economics of labour: employment and wages in Canada. Toronto: McGraw-Hill.
xi, 412pp, biblio. *OONL.

4532 Progressive Workers Movement. (Draft) statement of
principles. Vancouver. (c1965). (8pp). *OKQS.

4533 Ralston, Harry Keith. The 1900 strike of Fraser
river sockeye salmon fishermen. Unpublished MA
thesis, University of British Columbia. xiv, 183pp,
biblio. *BVAUS.

4534 Rotstein, Abraham (ed). The prospect of change: pro-
posals for Canada's future. Toronto: McGraw-Hill.
xx, 361pp. The proposals are by the University League
for Social Reform: authors include Ian Burton, Ramsay
Cook, John H.G. Crispo, Leslie Dewart, Ian M. Drummond,
J. Stefan Dupré, David P. Gauthier, Arthur M. Kruger,
Jospeh E. Laycock, Trevor Lloyd, John T. McLeod, Hugo
Macpherson, Abraham Rotstein, A.E. Safarian, Melville
H. Watkins, Hugh Whalen. *OONL.

4535 Roussopoulos, Dimitris. The student syndrome. Toronto. SUPA. 12pp, mimeo. *OOA/CCF476.

4536 Ryerson, Stanley. The open society: paradox and
challenge. New York: International. 125pp. *OTURS/
RSK. On the stereotyped view of socialism as a
'closed' society and capitalism as an 'open' one.

4537 Sabine, R.W. and others. NDY: organization of New
Democratic Youth Clubs. Regina: NDY. 13pp. *OOA/
CCF538.

4538 Study Commission on the Toronto Newspaper Strike.
Report. Toronto: University of Toronto Students
Administrative Council. 30pp, mimeo. *OHMA1862.

4539 Sudbury Mine, Mill and Smelter Workers Union local
598. A short history of the struggle for the union
at Inco-Falconbridge. (Toronto). (14pp). *E.

4540 Tanner, Thomas William. Microcosms of misfortune: Canada's unemployment relief camps administered by Department of National Defence 1932-1936. Unpublished MA thesis, University of Western Ontario. xi, 145pp.

4541 Trade Union Research Bureau. Who runs BC? Vancouver. 23pp. AEU BVIP *BVAUS/Mac41Af.15A OHMA1828 OTURS/RSK

4542 United Steelworkers of America. Raiders! Raiders! Raiders! Toronto. (c1965). 6pp. *OHMA1820. An attack on the Communist Party.

4543 University of Toronto New Democrats. Ideas and ideals: the practical program. Toronto. (c1965). (15pp), mimeo. *OOA/CCF537.

4544 Westall, Stanley. Morality in government. Toronto: Ontario Woodsworth Memorial Foundation. 25pp. *OKQS SSA/CCF Misc.14.

4545 Wigney, Trevor. The education of women and girls in a changing society - a selected bibliography with annotations. Toronto: Ontario College of Education. 76pp. *OOA/CCF465.

4546 World Federalists of Canada. The facts about the war in Vietnam. Victoria. 8pp. *OHMA2589.

4547 Wright, J.F.C. The Louise Lucas story: this time tomorrow. Montreal: Harvest House. (vi), 137pp. *OONL.

4548 Young, Walter Douglas. The national CCF: political party and political movement. PhD thesis, University of Toronto. 2 vols: iv, 257pp; 258-480(1-23), biblio. *OTUAR.

4549 Young Communist League. Look around: youth...the future, the challenge. Toronto. (c1965). 18pp. *OHMA2381 OTURS/RSK.

1966

4550 Alberta Socialist Caucus in the NDP. A socialist manifesto for the New Democratic Party. Edmonton. (c1966). (6pp). *ACGL/PDc.

4551 Allen, Alexander Richard. The crest and crisis of the social gospel in Canada 1916-1927. PhD thesis, Duke University. xiii, 459pp, biblio. Microfilm.

4552 Archer, David. Labour and politics. Toronto: New Democratic Party. 14pp. *OKQS.

(4553) Babcock, R.H. Trade unions and politics: impact of the American trade-union movement on Canadian labor 1870-1930. Unpublished MA thesis Duke University.

4554 Balawyder, Aloysius. Canadian-Soviet relations 1920-1935. PhD thesis, McGill University. i,234pp, biblio.

4555 Berg, Barbara J. Operation of program 5 in Alberta.
Unpublished MA thesis, University of Alberta. xv,
194pp, biblio. *AEUS. Program 5 of the federal
Technical and Vocational Training act, 1961 for the
unemployed.

4556 Bergren, Myrtle. Tough timber: the loggers of BC,
their story. Toronto: Progress. 254pp, illus,
errata slip. *OONL. Based on interviews with some
of the organizers of the woodworkers union.

4557 Blakeney, Allan E. The juggler's budget. Regina:
CCF/NDP. 22pp. *SSA/G4.1966.1.

4558 Bourgault, Pierre. Révolution: discours prononcé
à la salle de la Fraternité des Policiers, à Montréal. Montréal: Rassemblement pour l'Indépendence
nationale. (c1966). 14pp. *OTURS/RSK.

4559 Bouvier, Emile. L'education coopérative: la formation à un nouveau type d'homme. Ottawa: Conseil
Canadien de la Cooperation. 24pp. *OONL.

4560 BC Federation of Labour. Automation: threat or
promise? Vancouver. 47pp. BVIP OOP *OONL.

4561 ------ Submission on the use of injunctions in
labour disputes. Vancouver. 12pp. BVIP BVIV *BVAU.

4562 ------ Unionism at work. Vancouver. 16pp. *OKQS.

4563 Brookbank, C.R. Causes and issues in current labour
unrest. Montreal: McGill University. 8pp. *OONL.

4564 Brown, Lorne Alvin. Progressivism and the press in
Saskatchewan 1916-1926. Unpublished MA thesis, University of Saskatchewan. iii, 227pp, biblio. *SSUS.

4565 Bryden, Ken and Des Morton. New Democrats look at
the Canada Pension Plan. Toronto: New Democratic
Party. 14pp. *OOA/CCF538.

4566 Buck, Tim, Rae Murphy and Maurice Rush. Vietnam:
eyewitness report. Toronto: Communist Party of Canada. 19pp. *BVAUS/Mac43f.15a OHMA2420 OTURS/RSK.

4567 Cameron, David M. An electoral analysis of democratic socialism in Ontario: CCF-NDP voting patterns,
1934-1963. Unpublished MPhil thesis, University of
Toronto. (iv), 72 plus (89)pp, biblio and tables
by constituency. *OTUAR.

4568 Canada, Dept of Justice. Report to the Minister of
Justice of the Special Committee on Hate Propaganda
in Canada. Ottawa: R. Duhamel. 327pp, illus.
*OTURS/RSK.

4569 Canadian Labour Congress. CLC policy statement:
automation - a national program. Ottawa. (3pp)
plus 3pp, bilingual. *OOA/CCF444.

4570 ------ Memorandum to the government of Canada, 15
February 1966. Ottawa. 57pp. *OHMA2517.

4571 Carter, Dyson. Science and revolution. Gravenhurst:

Northern Book House. iv, 210pp. OOP SRU *OTURS/RSK.

4572 Cherwinski, Walter Joseph Carl. The formative years of the trade union movement in Saskatchewan 1905-1920. Unpublished MA thesis, University of Saskatchewan. (vi), 220pp, biblio. *OOA/Forsey 11 SSUS.

4573 Communist Party of Canada. Constitution. Toronto. 40pp. *OTURS/RSK OKQS.

4574 ------ 19th convention May 21-24 1966. Resolutions, speeches. Toronto. 72pp. *OTURS/RSK.

4575 ------ Socialism and you. Toronto. 31pp. BVIV *BVAUS/WB31f.1a OHMA2117 OKQS OTURS/RSK. Not the same as 4080 above.

4576 ------ Submission to the Standing Committee on Transport and Communications concerning parliamentary bill C-231 in relation to the problem of public transportation in Canada. Toronto. 26pp, mimeo. *OKQS OTURS/RSK.

4577 ------ Together we can win! The rights of labor are paramount in a democracy. Toronto. (6pp). *BVAUS/ WB31f.2c.

4578 Conway, John F. Notes from Carry-the-Kettle. (Winnipeg): Canadian Dimensions. (4pp). *SSA/G389.14. Recording an attempt at adult education on an Indian reserve.

4579 CCF (Sask) NDP. Annual report 31st annual convention 1966. Regina. 16pp. *SSA/G4.3.1966.

4580 Cowan, Jack. The world speaks for peace. Toronto: United Jewish Peoples Order. (c1966). 10pp. *OTURS/ RSK.

(4581) Davidson, Carl. Towards a student syndicalist movement. Toronto: SUPA. (AEU). Not found.

4582 Douglas, T.C. Medicare now! Speech delivered in the House of Commons 19 October 1966. Ottawa: R. Duhamel. 8pp. *OOA/CCF449.

4583 ------ $100 a month at 65: speech delivered in the House of Commons June 30, 1966. Ottawa: R. Duhamel. 7pp. See also 4485 above. *OOA/CCF449.

4584 ------ Parliamentary priorities: $100 at 65, free higher education, a manpower policy, medicare for all, regain control of Canada, peace in Vietnam. Speech delivered in the House of Commons Thursday June 20, 1966. Ottawa: R. Duhamel. 10pp. *OOA/ CCF449 and 537.

4585 Gibson, Julia-Anne Kathleen and others. A study of the philosophy and social welfare policy of the New Democratic Party of British Columbia: a descriptive study of the origins and basic tenets of the NDP and of its significance in social welfare philosophy of the New Democratic movement as it has emerged in BC. Unpublished MSW thesis, University of British Columbia. 193pp.

4586 Gonick, C.W. What every Canadian should know about Vietnam. Winnipeg: Canadian Dimension. (v), (59)pp. *OONL OOA/MacInnis 18. Includes Prospects for peace by Jean Lacontre, and a postscript.

4587 Gray, Stanley. New left - old left. (Winnipeg): np. 11pp, mimeo. *OOA/CCF476.

(4588)Grimson, C.D. The Communist Party of Canada 1922-1946. Unpublished MA thesis, McGill University. iv, 221pp, biblio.

4589 Hikl, Mario. Labour arbitration: a handbook for Canadian Union of Public Employees. Ottawa: Canadian Union of Public Employees. (iv), (iv), 119pp. *OONL.

4590 Kashtan, William. A new course for Canada. Toronto: Communist Party of Canada. 36pp. OONL OPET *BVAUS/ Mac41f.15a OHMA1711 OTURS/RSK.

4591 Kerr, D.G.G. and R.I.K. Davidson. Canada: a visual history. Toronto: T. Nelson. (vi), 170pp. *OONL. Includes Red river insurrection, North-West rebellion, depression and unemployment.

4592 Kruger, Arthur M. Trade unions and collective bargaining in Canada. Toronto: Ontario Federation of Labour. 24pp. *OOA/CCF543. For schools.

(4593)Lewis, David. Compulsory arbitration. Ottawa: (Canadian Labour Congress). 14pp, mimeo. MWU. Not seen.

4594 ------ Speech for peace in Vietnam delivered in the House of Commons on February 1, 1966. Ottawa: R. Duhamel. 8pp. *OOA/Macinnis 18 SSA/G5.1966.1.

4595 Lipton, Charles. Trade union movement of Canada 1827-1959. Montreal: Canadian Social Publications. xiii, 366pp, biblio. *OONL.

4596 Lloyd, Woodrow S. Speaking in debate on the address in reply to the throne speech Saskatchewan Legislative Assembly, February 10, 1966. Regina: CCF/NDP. 19pp. *SSA/G4.1966.2.

4597 MacInnis, Grace. Speech on poverty, production, working mothers delivered in the House of Commons Monday January 24, 1966. Ottawa: R. Duhamel. 7pp. *OHMA 1581.

(4598)Minnis, Jack and Don Roebuck. How to research the power structure. (Toronto): SUPA. Not found.

4599 Morgan, John S. and Melville H. Watkins. The abolition of poverty: two proposals. Toronto: Ontario Woodsworth Memorial Foundation. 16pp. AEU BVIP NSHPL OPET OTURS QQL SRL *OOA/CCF536 OKQS.

4600 ------ Welfare and wisdom. Toronto: University of Toronto Press. vi, 184pp. *OONL.

4601 Morgan, Nigel. The case for a Canadian water policy: a reply to the US plan to take over Canada's water resources. Toronto: Progress. 38pp. *BVAUS/WB41f.1b OHMA2125 OTURS/RSK.

4602 Morton, Desmond. Crisis in car insurance. Toronto:
Ontario Woodsworth Memorial Foundation. 28pp. OH
OTURS *OOA/CCF536 OKQS.

4603 ------ With your help: an election manual, N.D.P.
Ottawa: New Democratic Party. In two editions:
100pp, illus *OTURS and 50pp, illus. OH *BVIP.
The 50pp version has some added material.

4604 Mowat, Farley. Canada's role in Vietnam. Willow-
dale: Conference on Canada's Role in Vietnam. 13pp.
*OTURS/RSK.

4605 New Democratic Party. Agricultural policy of the
NDP of Ontario. Toronto. (2pp). *OOA/CCF538.

4606 ------ Indians: do we care? Toronto. 9pp. *SSA/
G6.Ont.8.

4607 ------ The NDP: the story of its foundation. Toronto. 12pp. *OOA/CCF538.

4608 ------ Thirty-six position papers from the policy
review committee. Toronto. 16pp. *OOA/CCF539.

4609 ------ People first...the new democratic way.
Vancouver. 38pp. *BVAUS/Garrison 1-9.

4610 New Democratic Youth. What is socialism? The debate
in the NDY. Toronto. 25pp, mimeo. *OHMA2215.

4611 Novack, George. Who will change the world: the new
left and the views of C. Wright Mills. Toronto:
Young Socialists. 36pp. *OHMA1932.

4612 Ontario Federation of Labour. Legislative proposals
to the government of Ontario. Toronto. 13pp. *OOA/
OFL8. On taxation, housing etc.

4613 ------ Submission to the government of Ontario: the
matter of injunctions in labour disputes. Toronto.
16pp. *OOA/OFL 8.

4614 ------ Submission to the Hon. H.L. Rowntree, Q.C.
Minister of Labour, province of Ontario. Toronto.
16pp, mimeo. *OOA/OFL 8. Summary of resolutions
adopted at the annual convention.

4615 ------ Submission to the Hon H.L. Rowntree QC, Minister of Labour, regarding apprenticeship and trades-
mens qualifications. Toronto. 5pp, mimeo. *OOA/
OFL 8.

4616 ------ Submission to the National Energy Board on
the matter of the application of Trans-Canada Pipe
Lines Limited for a permit to build a gas pipe line
from a point near Emerson, Manitoba, through the
United States to a point near Sarnia, Ontario. Ottawa. 5pp, mimeo. *OOA/OFL8.

4617 ------ Submission to Royal Commission Inquiry into
Labour Disputes: Commissioner, Honourable Ivan C.
Rand, LL.D. Toronto. 30pp. BVAU *OHMA1659 OOA/
OFL 8.

4618 Ontario Federation of Labour. Submission to the
Royal Commission on the Workmens Compensation act:
Hon. George E. McGillivary, Commissioner. Toronto.
29pp plus 2pp summary. *OOA/OFL 8.

4619 ------ and New Democratic Party. This party is ours:
a handbook of political participation, a joint publication. Toronto. (ii), 12pp. *OTURS.

4620 Park, F.C. and L.C. Canadian neo-colonialism in
Latin America. Toronto: SUPA. 23pp. *OHMA1916.
A reprint of chapter VI of *Anatomy of big business*.

4621 Power, Jeffrey James. Appeal. Hamilton: Local 105
IBEW. 19pp, mimeo. *BVAUS/Mac33f.39 OHMA1921
OTURS/RSK. Against his conviction for contravening
an injunction against picketing Lenkurt Electric, BC.

4622 ------ Injunctions have no place in labour disputes.
Statement to the Appeal Court of BC. Vancouver:
Marine Workers and Boilermakers Industrial Union,
Local 1. 14pp. *BVAUS/Mac33f.3a OHMA1920.

4623 Rioux, Marcel. Youth in a contemporary world and
in Quebec. Toronto: SUPA. (15pp). *OTURS/RSK.

4624 Robin, Martin. Radical politics and organized labour
in Canada 1880-1930. PhD thesis, University of Toronto. ii, 439pp, biblio. *OTUAR.

4625 Russell, Peter (ed). Nationalism in Canada. Toronto:
McGraw-Hill. xx, 377pp. By members of the University
League for Social Reform. *OONL. Authors include
Carl Berger, Craig Brown, Michel Brunet, Maurice
Careless, Stephen Clarkson, John Dales, Alfred Dubuc,
James Guillet, Charles Hanly, Cole Harris, George
Heiman, John Holmes, Stephen Hymer, Ian Macdonald,
Kenneth McNaught, Frank Peers, Abraham Rotstein,
Peter Russell, Donald Smiley, Elizabeth Wangenheim,
Melville Watkins and Frank Watt.

4626 Sherdahl, Raymond Merle. The Saskatchewan general
election of 1944. Unpublished MA thesis, University
of Saskatchewan. viii, 216pp, biblio. *SSU.

(4627) Sherwood, David Henry. The NDP and French Canada
1961-1965. Unpublished MA thesis, McGill University.

4628 Silcox, Peter and Desmond Morton. Agenda for our
cities. Toronto: New Democratic Party. 21pp.
*OOA/CCF536.

4629 Steele, James. Rationale for war in Vietnam: the
Canadian minority judgment in the fourth interim
report of the International Commission for Super-
vision and Control. Toronto: Conference on Canada's
role in Vietnam. (c1966). 22pp. *OHMA1890 OOA/
MacInnis 18.

4630 Student Union for Peace Action (SUPA). Why?? A statement to the movement March 6 - May 19, 1966. Montreal. (13)pp, mimeo. *OOA/CCF476.

4631 Taylor, Charles. Economic independence for Canada.

Toronto: SUPA. 16pp, mimeo. *OOA/CCF478.

4632 Thwaites, J.D. The International Union of Machinists in Canada to 1919. Unpublished MA thesis, Carleton University. 128pp, biblio. *OOCC.

4633 Tihanyi, Eva. An approach to the study of regional labour absorption: the case of Saskatchewan 1941-61. Unpublished MA thesis, University of Saskatchewan. (ii), iv, 158pp, biblio. *SSU.

(4634) Trowbridge, Robert William. War time rural discontent and the rise of the United Farmers of Ontario 1914-1919. Unpublished MA thesis, University of Waterloo. Not seen.

4635 United Mine Workers of America District 26. Presentation to the Premier and members of the cabinet of the government of Nova Scotia. Halifax. 14pp, mimeo. *NSHP. On legislative reform.

4636 University of British Columbia Members and others. On the Canadian involvement in the Vietnam war: an open letter to the 27th parliament and the government of Canada. (Vancouver). 6pp plus 1p list of signatories. *OOA/CCF476.

4637 University of Toronto Committee to End the War in Vietnam. Canada's role in Vietnam. (7pp). *OOA/CCF476. Reprinting articles from the Canada/Vietnam newsletter.

4638 Vant, Thomas Ross. Collective action by engineers. Unpublished MBA thesis, University of Alberta. vi, 130, xxvpp, biblio. *AEUS.

4639 Voice of Women. Brief submitted to the Standing Committee on Health and Welfare. Toronto. 2pp, mimeo. *OOA/VOW 7. Against the criminal code making the advertising and distribution of contraceptives a criminal offence.

4640 ------ Memoire to the government of Canada: presented to the Minister of External Affairs, the Hon. Paul Martin. Toronto. 3pp plus 3pp, bilingual. *OOA/VOW 7. Against the Vietnam war.

4641 Woodcock, George. Civil disobedience: seven talks for CBC radio. Toronto: CBC. 69pp. *OONL.

4642 ------ Variations on the human theme. Toronto: Ryerson. 243pp. *OONL. Stories and essays.

1967

4643 Badgley, Robin and Samuel Wolfe. Doctors strike: medical care and conflict in Saskatchewan. New York: Atherton/Toronto: Macmillan. xii, 201pp. *OONL.

4644 Balawyder, A. The Winnipeg general strike. Toronto:

Copp Clark.   49pp.   *OTURS/RSK.

4645 Bay, Christian.   Civil disobedience: prerequisite to democracy in mass society.   Edmonton: Alberta Young New Democrats.   26pp, mimeo.   *OOA/CCF478.

4646 ------ A free world: deceptive slogan or political aspiration.   Edmonton: Alberta Young New Democrats. 13pp, mimeo.   *OOA/CCF478.

4647 ------ Political and apolitical students.   Montreal: Our Generation (c1967).   *OOA/CCF476.

4648 ------ Student political activism here to stay? Edmonton: Confrontation.   (c1967).   16pp, mimeo. *OOA/CCF476.

4649 Berger, Tom.   The use of injunctions in labour disputes.   Vancouver: BC Federation of Labour.   6pp, mimeo.   *BVAUS/Steeves 4-4.

4650 Blakeney, Allan E.   The backward budget.   Regina: CCF/NDP.   16pp.   *SSA/G4.1967.29   SSUS/NDP.

4651 Bloom, Bernard.   Why Vietnam?   Edmonton: Alberta Young New Democrats.   13pp, mimeo.   *OOA/CCF478.

4652 Brewin, Andrew and David MacDonald.   Report on a mission to Portugal.   Toronto: Canadian Committee for Amnesty in Portugal.   24pp.   OOP *OHMA2797.

4653 BC Federation of Labour.   Unionism in British Columbia.   Vancouver.   (c1967).   16pp.   BVIP OONL *OKQS.

4654 Brody, Bernard.   A description and an analysis of the trade union growth theory and the Canadian aggregate model 1936-1965.   Unpublished MA thesis, McGill University.   x, 218pp, biblio.   p212 omitted in numbering.   Microfilm.

4655 Brotherhood of Railroad Trainmen.   Strength in brotherhood: a story of the Brotherhood of Railway Trainmen.   (Ottawa).   42pp, illus.   BVAU BVIP NFSM OOP *OONL.

4656 Bryden, Kenneth and others.   Continentalism vs. nationalism.   Toronto: Ontario Woodsworth Memorial Foundtion.   29pp.   *OHMA OKQS.

4657 Buck, Tim.   Canada and the Russian revolution: the impact of the world's first socialist revolution on labour and politics in Canada.   Toronto: Progress. 98pp.   *BVAUS/Mac38f.13G   MWP   OHMA2429   OKQS   OTURS/ RSK   SSUS.

4658 Canadian-American Assembly on Nuclear Weapons.   A report...June 15-18, 1967, Toronto, Canada.   Toronto: Canadian Institute for International Affairs.   20pp. *OOP.   Includes 'Curbing nuclear proliferation' by Klaus Knorr.

4659 Canadian Committee for the International War Crimes Tribunal.   International war crimes tribunal.   Toronto.   32pp.   *OTURS/RSK.

4660 Carew, Anthony. Industrial democracy - European developments and their relevance for Canada. Edmonton:
Confrontations. (c1967). 16pp, mimeo. *OOA/CCF475.

4661 Clarke, Phyllis. High prices - who's to blame? Toronto: Canadian Tribune. 7pp. *OTURS/RSK.

4662 Communist Party of Canada. A decent home for every
Canadian: proposals of the CPC to solve the housing
crisis. Toronto: Canadian Tribune. (6pp). *OTURS/
RSK.

4663 ------ Les prochains pas. Montreal. (c1967). 14pp.
*OHMA3079.

4664 ------ The Rand report: a formula for employer dictatorship. Statement of the Ontario Committee CPC.
Toronto. 6pp. *OHMA2375.

4665 ------ Submission to the Royal Commission on Farm
Marketing. Regina. 25 plus 4pp, mimeo. *OTURS/RSK.

4666 ------ What is Commissioner Ivan C. Rand up to?
Some pertinent questions about the Ontario Royal
Commission Inquiry into Labor Disputes: its purposes
and aims. Toronto. 7pp. *OTURS/RSK. Includes a
charter of labor's rights.

4667 Crispo, John H.G. International unionism: a study
in Canadian-American relations. Toronto: McGraw-
Hill. viii, 327pp, biblio. *OONL.

4668 ------ The role of international unionism in Canada.
Washington/Montreal: Canadian-American Committee.
xiii, 59pp. *OONL.

4669 Crysler, Alfred C. Restraint of trade and labour.
Toronto: Butterworth. xxiii, 424pp, biblio. *OONL.

4670 Cusden, Phoebe E. The international traffic in arms.
Toronto: Voice of Women. 4pp, mimeo. *OOA/VOW 7.

4671 Davidson, Carl. University: mental production plant.
Edmonton: Confrontations. 24pp. *OOA/CCF476 & 482.

4672 Den Otter, Andy A. A social history of the Alberta
Coal Branch. Unpublished MA thesis, University of
Alberta. xvii, 221pp, biblio. *AEUS.

4673 Douglas, T.C. End war in Vietnam! Speech delivered
in the House of Commons February 13, 1967. Ottawa:
R. Duhamel. 8pp. *OOA/CCF476.

4674 Dowson, Ross. The coming Canadian revolution. Toronto: Young Socialists. (7pp). *OHMA1471.

4675 ------ The power and dilemma of the trade unions.
Toronto: (League for Socialist Action). 15pp. AEU
BVIV OONL OOP OPAL SRL *OHMA1473 OTURS/RSK.

4676 Endicott, James G. Co-existence, national liberation,
and the communist-christian dialogue. Toronto: (Canadian Far Eastern Newsletter). 8pp. BVIP *OOA/End-
icott 1 OTURS/RSK.

4677 ------ It is time to change Canada's foreign policy:

an appeal to the Prime Minister. Toronto: Canadian Peace Congress. (c1967). (4pp). *OTURS/RSK.

4678 Endicott, Norman A. Confronting the Red Guard. Toronto: Canadian Far Eastern News Letter. (6pp). *OOA/Endicott 1 OTURS/RSK.

4679 Finn, Ed. The NDY and the labour movement. Edmonton: Confrontations. (c1967). 12pp, mimeo. *OOA/CCF475 and 479.

4680 Frank, Andre Gunder, Kenneth Golby and others. Free Hugo Blanco. Toronto: Robert McCarthy. 16pp. *E. Cover title: Hugo Blanco must not die.

4681 Fric, Lawrence. Labour organizations in Canada: their origins, structures and activities. (Winnipeg): (Winnipeg and District Labour Council). 65pp, mimeo. OPAL *MWPA/Russell 1. Prepared for high schools.

4682 ------ The Manitoba wage differential: its trend from 1943 to 1965. Unpublished MA thesis, University of Manitoba. iv, 116pp, biblio. Microfilm.

4683 Graham, John. The American system. Toronto: SUPA. 15pp. *OTURS/RSK.

4684 Groome, Agnes Jean. M.J. Coldwell and CCF foreign policy, 1932-1950. Unpublished MA thesis, University of Saskatchewan, Regina. x, 274pp, biblio. *SRA.

4685 Hamilton, D.F. Historical sketch: trade unions. Toronto: Ontario Federation of Labour. 18pp. *OKQS.

4686 Haynes, R.C. The labour movement and the injunction in British Columbia. Vancouver: BC Federation of Labour. 8pp, mimeo. *BVAUS/Steeves 4-4.

4687 Hill, A.V. Tides of change. (Prince Rupert): Prince Rupert Fishermans Co-op. xii, 279pp. *OONL.

4688 Horowitz, Gad, Charles Taylor and C.W. Gonick. Nationalism, socialism and Canadian independence. Winnipeg: Canadian Dimension. 30pp. OKQ OTU OTMCL SRU *BVAUS/Mac41Bf.15A OOA/CCF446.

4689 Jackson, C.S. UE Canada: 30 years 1937-1967. (Toronto): United Electrical. 41pp, mimeo. *OHMA3102.

4690 Labor Action. Which way for labor? Toronto. (c1967) (4pp). *OOA/CCF475.

4691 Litvak, Isaiah A. (ed). The nation keepers: Canadian business perspectives. Toronto: McGraw-Hill. xiv, 255pp. *OONL. Includes: The government and the economy by T.C. Douglas; How much welfare does social responsibility demand by David Lewis; Unions in the future by Claude Jodoin etc.

4692 Lloyd, Woodrow S. Problems ignored and promises broken - the 1967 throne speech. Regina: CCF/NDP. 19pp. *SSA/G4.1967.30 SSUS/NDP.

4693 Marx, Karl and Frédéric Engels. Sur le parti ouvrier. (Montréal): La Lutte Ouvrière. 21pp, mimeo. *OHMA 1475.

4694 Morton, Desmond and Leon Kumove. Housing: the pre-
      dictable crisis. Toronto: Ontario Woodsworth Memorial
      Foundation. 20pp. AEU BVIP NSHPL OPET OTU QQL SRL
      *BVAUS/Steeves 5-8 OOA/CCF537.

4695 Murphy, Rae. Canada's trade union movement: change
      and challenge. Toronto: Communist Party of Canada.
      31pp. AEU BVIV IBSAM OPET *BVAUS/WB31f.1b OHMA1834
      OKQS OTURS/RSK.

4696 ------ Vietnam: impressions of a people's war.
      Toronto: (Canadian Tribune). 30pp. BVIV NFSM OONL
      OPET *OHMA1832 OKQS OTURS/RSK.

4697 New Democratic Party. The federal program adopted
      by its fourth federal convention, 1967 and by its
      federal council. Ottawa. 52pp. OOP *OOA/CCF395,
      537 and 538.

4698 ------ NDP program: a minimum program for a new Can-
      adian society. Regina. (12pp). *OOA/CCF538.

4699 ------ NDP program for Ontario. Toronto. 77pp.
      *OOA/CCF538.

4700 ------ New Democrats, new Ontario: policies of the
      New Democratic Party. 21pp. *OOA/CCF538 SSA/G6.
      Ont.6. Summary of policies adopted at the third
      provincial convention, October 1966.

4701 ------ Tax reform? A cool look at the white paper
      by Ontario New Democrats. Toronto. (6pp). *OOA/
      CCF539.

4702 Nkemdirim, Bernard Anyaegbulam. The white-collar
      worker goes on strike: a study in union management
      relations and the development of union identification
      among white collars. Unpublished MA thesis, McMaster
      University. vi, 148pp, biblio. *OHMA.

4703 Ontario Federation of Labour. Legislative proposals
      to the Prime Minister and other members of the gov-
      ernment of Ontario. Toronto. 14pp. *OOA/OFL 8.

4704 ------ Submission to the Commission on Constitution
      of Structure, Canadian Labour Congress. Toronto.
      10pp, mimeo. *OOA/OFL 8.

4705 ------ Submission to the Committee on Religious
      Education in the public schools of Ontario. Toronto.
      13pp, mimeo. *OOA/OFL 8.

4706 ------ Submission to Hon Dalton Bales, Minister of
      Labour, province of Ontario. Toronto. 12pp, mimeo.
      *OOA/OFL 8. Summary of resolutions at annual conven-
      tion, Kingston 1966.

(4707) Phillips, P.A. The British Columbia labour movement
      in the inter-war years: a study of its social and
      political aspects. PhD thesis, University of London.
      402pp.

4708 ------ No power greater: a century of labour in
      British Columbia. Vancouver: BC Federation of Labour.

189pp. *OONL.

4709 Powell, Mary Patricia. Response to the depression: three representative womens groups in British Columbia. Unpublished MA thesis, University of British Columbia. 115pp. *BVAUS.

4710 Priestley, N.F. and E.B. Swindlehurst. Furrows, faith and fellowship: the history of the farm movement in Alberta 1905-1966. Edmonton: Alberta Agricultural Centennial Committee. 317pp. *MWP SSUS.

4711 Royle, Anne. Canadian challenge: story behind the Harmac workers struggle for a Canadian union. Vancouver. (c1967). 53pp. BVIP OKQ OOL OOP *OHMA1909.

4712 Russell, Jim. Bureaucracy and one-dimensional man. Edmonton: Confrontations. 20pp, mimeo. *OOA/CCF478.

4713 Scotton, Clifford A. Canadian labour and politics. (Ottawa): Canadian Labour Congress. 40pp. *OHMA1907 OOA/CCF543 OTAR/1967/9 OTURS/RSK.

(4714) Smith, Mary Marcia. The ideological relationship between the United Farmers of Alberta and the CCF. Unpublished MA thesis, McGill University.

4715 Socialist Caucus. Proposals for the 1967 federal convention of the NDP. Toronto. 8pp. *E.

4716 Stolk, Carl. The BC forest industry and the NDP. Monopoly or public ownership? Vancouver: BC NDP Socialist Caucus. (c1967). 28pp, mimeo. *OHMA2123.

4717 Stone, Gladys May. The Regina riot in 1935. Unpublished MA thesis, University of Saskatchewan. viii, 129pp, biblio. *SSUS.

4718 Student Association to End the War in Vietnam. Ottawa's complicity in Vietnam. Toronto. 14pp. *OTURS/RSK.

4719 Student Union for Peace Action (SUPA). Escape from freedom, or, I didn't raise my boy to be a Canadian. Toronto. 12pp. *OONL. For draft dodgers intending to come to Canada.

4720 Unitarian Church of Vancouver. Abortion: a brief. Vancouver. 34pp, mimeo. *BVAUS/Steeves 5-8.

4721 Victoria Committee on Canadian Responsibility in Vietnam. Canada and Vietnam. Victoria. (c1967). 16pp. *OHMA2587.

4722 Voice of Women. A brief presented to the Committee on Religious Education in the Public Schools. (Toronto). 14pp, mimeo. *OOA/VOW 7.

4723 ------ Report: second international conference on peace, Montreal June 1967. Toronto. 45pp. *MWPA/ Brigden 4.

4724 Wallace, Bronwen. The exploitation of experience: some thoughts on the study of literature. Toronto: Hogtown. (c1967). 9pp, mimeo. *OHMA1804 OOA/CCF 478. Publication no. 1.

4725 Ward, Doug. Open decision making. Ottawa: Canadian Union of Students. 4pp, mimeo. *OOA/CCF478.

4726 Wright, Arthur James. The winter years in Cowichan: a study of the depression in a Vancouver island community. Unpublished MA thesis, University of British Columbia. 170pp. *BVAUS.

4727 Youssef, Roleene Maria. Alienation and the new radical movement. Unpublished MA thesis, McMaster University. iv, 136pp. *OHMA.

1968

4728 Akyeampong, Ernest Bugya. Labour laws and the development of the labour movement in Newfoundland, 1900-1960. Unpublished MA thesis, Memorial University. v, 149pp, biblio. Microfilm.

4729 Arthurs, Harry W. Labour disputes in essential industries. Ottawa: Queens Printer. xi, 305pp, biblio. *OONL. Privy Council Study, Task Force in Labour Relations 8.

4730 Benson, Dan and Ann Giles. Community university: or how to drop out, tune in, turn on to education that does not fold, spindle or mutilate. Edmonton: np. 24pp, mimeo. *OOA/CCF478.

4731 (Bethune, N.) In memory of Norman Bethune, the great Canadian internationalist. (?Montreal): The Internationalist. 25pp, mimeo. *OTURS/RSK. The Communist Party of Canada (Marxist-Leninist), originally a Maoist group, but now fervently pro-Albania.

4732 Black, David. As the screw turns. (Ottawa): (Canadian Union of Students). 39pp, mimeo, biblio. *OOA/CCF480. 'An overview of where the money in Canada comes from and where it goes and why various policies and programs in Canada are inadequate.'

4733 Bordo, Jon. Parallel structures and student power. Ottawa: Canadian Union of Students. 5pp. *AEUS.

4734 BC Federation of Labour. Memorandum concerning labour legislation. Victoria. 8pp. *BVIP.

4735 Bronson, H.E. Agricultural policy. (Saskatoon). 2pp, mimeo. *SSA/G.389.11. Pre-Waffle position paper.

4736 Brown, H.R. Towards a revolutionary socialist alliance. (?Saskatoon). 3pp, mimeo. *SSA/G389.8. Pre-Waffle position paper.

4737 Burt, George. Where was George Burt? Windsor: UAW International Union. 52pp. *E.

4738 Canadian Party of Labour Marxist-Leninist. Combat bourgeois ideas. Toronto. (c1968). 39pp, mimeo. *OHMA.

4739 Carrigan, D. Owen. Canadian party platforms 1867-1968. Toronto: Copp Clark. xii, 363pp. *OONL. Includes some United Farmers, CCF and Communist platforms, federal elections only.

(4740) Chisick, Ernie. The early Marxist socialist movement in Manitoba 1901-1926. Hon. History thesis, University of Winnipeg. Not seen.

4741 Christie, Innis and Morley Gorsky. Unfair labour practices: an explanatory study of the efficacy of the law of unfair labour practices in Canada. Ottawa: Privy Council Office. xii, 220pp. *OONL. Task Force on Labour Relations Study 10.

4742 Clarkson, Stephen (ed). An independent foreign policy for Canada. Toronto: McClelland and Stewart. xiv, 290pp. For the University League for Social Reform. Contributors include David Baldwin, Charles Hanly, Peyton Lyon, Denis Stairs, James Steele, Paul Painchaud, Louis Sabourin, Franklyn Griffiths, Thomas Hoskin, Jack Granatstein, Michael Sherman, Harald von Riekhoff, Kenneth McNaught, David Cox, Ian Lumsden, Cranford Pratt, Clyde Sanger, Stephen Hymer, Brian Van Arkadie, Robert McKinnell. *OONL.

4743 Communist Party of Canada. Submission to the federal task force on housing and urban development. Toronto. 10pp, mimeo. *OTURS/RSK.

4744 ------ Submission to the Royal Commission on the Status of Women in Canada. Toronto. 22pp, mimeo. *OTURS/RSK.

4745 Conway, John. The Carter commission and the government of Canada. Edmonton: Confrontations. 4pp, mimeo. *OOA/CCF478.

4746 ------ Karl Marx: ideologue and social scientist. Edmonton: Confrontations. 20pp, mimeo. *OOA/CCF478.

4747 ------ Labour rights and the NDP. (Saskatoon). 3pp, mimeo. *SSA/G389.13. Pre-Waffle position paper.

4748 Council of Canadian Unions. A time for Canada and Canadian workers! Brantford. (4pp). *OHMA1538. For independence from AFL-CIO.

4749 Crysdale, Stewart. Occupational and social mobility in Riverdale, a blue collar community. Unpublished MA thesis, University of Toronto. ix, 417pp, biblio. *OTUAR.

4750 Cutt, James A. A guaranteed income for Canadians. Toronto: Ontario Woodsworth Memorial Foundation. 17pp. *OHMA3094 OKQS SSA/G436.1.

4751 Dalhousie New Democratic Youth. On course unionism. Halifax. 5pp. *OOA/CCF482.

4752 Davidson, Carl. The new radicals and the multiversity. Montreal: Our Generation. pp60-90. *OHMA1624 Reprinted from Our Generation.

4753 Dessouki, Ali. Canadian foreign policy and the Palestine problem. Ottawa: Middle East Research Centre. 47pp. *OTURS/RSK.

4754 Drache, Danny. A strategy for research: the national consciousness and Marxism. Ottawa: Canadian Union of Students. 8pp, mimeo. *OHMA.

4755 Drummond, R. Minerals and mining in Nova Scotia. Stellarton: Mining Record Office. 368pp. *NSHP. Some information on labour. (See page 627 errata)

4756 Engler, Allen. Organizing for workers power! Ottawa: Confrontations. 22pp, mimeo. *OOA/CCF478.

4757 Feinberg, Abraham L. Rabbi Feinberg's Hanoi diary. Don Mills: Longmans. (xii), 258pp. *OONL.

4758 Finn, Ed. Canadian labour in politics: a book review. Edmonton: Confrontations. 7pp, mimeo. *OOA/CCF479.

4759 Forsey, Eugene A. Our present discontents. (Wolfville): Acadia University. 44pp. *OONL. George C. Nolan lectures, 1967.

4760 Goldenberg, H. Carl and John H.G. Crispo (eds). Construction labour relations. (Toronto): Canadian Construction Association. (xvi), 670pp, no index. Includes chapters by Frank Wildgen, R.F. Legget, F. D. Upex, C. Ross Ford, Gérard Hébert, A.W.R. Carrothers, Gérard Dion, H.W. Arthurs, Gordon W. Bertram, Félix Quinet, Samuel Eckler on income, technological change, manpower, training, standards, relations, disputes, collective bargaining, wage structure etc. BVIP NSHPL OKQ *OONL.

4761 Gordon, Kenneth Douglas. Industrial dispute settlement in Canada: the alternatives before us. Unpublished MA thesis, University of Calgary. 145pp, biblio. Microfilm.

4762 Grant, Bill. 'I have a suggestion for the flag, sir ...': political cartoons from The Commonwealth . 55pp. *OOA/CCF537 SSA/G4.1967.8.

4763 Harding, James. An SDU case history. Ottawa: Canadian Union of Students. 6pp, mimeo. *OOA/CCF478.

4764 Higginbotham, C.H. Off the record: the CCF in Saskatchewan. Toronto: McClelland and Stewart. 143pp, no index, no biblio. *OONL.

4765 Hollett, Gerald A. A stroll down memory lane. Amalgamated Transit Union - division 508, Diamond Jubilee 1968. 23pp. *NSHP.

4766 Holtom, Edith. To prevent a third world war: Ottawa scene 1958-1968. Toronto: Canadian Peace Congress. (60pp). OOP *OTURS/RSK. A compilation.

4767 Horowitz, Gad. Canadian labour in politics. Toronto: University of Toronto Press. (xii), 273pp, no biblio. *OTURS/RSK.

4768 Hutchison, Brian. CUS and student unionism. Ottawa:

Canadian Union of Students. 34pp, mimeo. *OOA/CCF 478.

4769 International Brotherhood of Boilermakers, Iron Ship-builders, Blacksmiths, Forgers and Helpers. 70 years of participation in the development of British Columbia. Victoria. (20pp), illus. *BVIPA. Almost entirely photographs.

4770 Kelly, L.A. The case for automation adjustment mechanisms in unemployment insurance. Kingston: Queens University. 25pp. *OHMA2303.

4771 Krauter, Joseph Francis. Civil liberties and the Canadian minorities. PhD thesis, University of Illinois. vi, 220pp, biblio. Microfilm.

4772 Kumar, Pradeep. Variations in the labour share of national income in Canada 1926-1966. Unpublished MA thesis, Queens University. viii, 118pp. *OKQ.

4773 Lawson, W.T. Youth and violence. Victoria: Jim Lawson Memorial Fund. 8pp. BVIP OTP *OHMA1787 OOA/VOW 8 OTURS/RSK. Jim Lawson was the wife of W.T. Lawson.

4774 League for Socialist Action. Organizational character and constitution. Toronto. 16pp. *E.

4775 ------ The status of women in Canada. Toronto. (c1968). 16pp. NFSM NSHPL *OHMA1469 OTURS/RSK. Brief to the Royal Commission with some key reading on the situation of women by Ruth Blake.

4776 ------ Vive le Quebec libre: the socialist viewpoint: statement of the LSA-LSO. Toronto: Vanguard. 24pp. AEU BVAU NSHPL OKQ OOP SRL *OHMA1779 OTURS/RSK.

4777 LePoole, Steven Dolf. A comparative study of wages policies. Unpublished MBA thesis, University of Alberta. vii, 132pp, biblio. *AEU.

4778 Lewis, Stephen. On student power. (?Winnipeg): (?NDP). (c1968). 6pp, mimeo. *OOA/CCF476.

4779 Lloyd, Lewis L. Memories of a co-operative statesman. (?Saskatoon): (Saskatchewan Federated Cooperatives). 80pp. ACU AEU OONL OOP SRL *OTURS.

4780 Lloyd, Trevor and Jack McLeod (eds). Agenda 1970: proposals for a creative politics. Toronto: University of Toronto Press. xii, 292pp. Includes: Our ideological tradition by Trevor Lloyd; The emotional revolution by John Rich; Post-capitalist society by Jack McLeod; Public and private space by John O'Neill; The regulation of broadcasting by Ian M. Drummond; The proliferation of boards and commissions by Peter Silcox; The Economic Council as phoenix by Gilles Paquet; A new national policy by Mel Watkins; Centrifugally speaking by David M. Nowlan; The flexibility of the BNA act by Barry Strayer; What happens to Parliament by Ronald Blair; Toward the democratic class struggle by Gad Horowitz; Public power and ivory power by J.E. Hodgetts; Government as dialogue by Trevor Lloyd. Essays by the University League for Social Reform. *OONL.

4781 MacDonald, Donald C. A foundation tax plan for general municipal purposes. Toronto: NDP. 14pp. *BVIPA.

4782 McGuire, J. and E. Mahood. Programme paper. (Saskatoon). 4pp, mimeo. *SSA/G389.10. Pre-Waffle position paper on the attainment of a socialist society.

4783 New Democratic Party. Brief to the Royal Commission on the Status of Women in Canada. (Ottawa). 13pp, mimeo. *BVAUS/Steeves 5-8.

4784 Northern Neighbours Magazine. Whatever happened in Czechoslovakia? Gravenhurst. 60pp. *OTURS/RSK.

4785 Ontario Federation of Labour. Submission to the Hon Dalton Bales Minister of Labour, province of Ontario. Toronto. 11pp, mimeo. *OOA/OFL 8.

4786 ------ Submission to the Royal Commission on the Status of Women in Canada. Toronto. 32pp plus 7pp appendixes, mimeo. *OOA/OFL 8.

4787 Orr, Allan Donald. The Western Federation of Miners and the Royal Commission on Industrial Disputes in 1903 with special reference to the Vancouver island coal miners strike. Unpublished MA thesis, University of British Columbia. (i), vii, 242pp, biblio. *BVAUS.

4788 Parsons, Howard L. The young Marx and the young generation. Toronto: Progress. 60pp. *OOP.

4789 Popoff, Ellory. Position paper on organization. (Saskatoon). 10pp, mimeo. *SSA/G389.12. Pre-Waffle position paper.

4790 Rankin, Harry. A program for Vancouver. Vancouver: np. 35pp. *BVIPA.

4791 ------ Who pays the shot? for regional government on the lower mainland: some critical views. Vancouver: Harry Rankin Election Committee. 16pp. *OHMA2122.

(4792) Rice, James Richard. A history of organized labour in Saint John, New Brunswick, 1813-1890. Unpublished MA thesis, University of New Brunswick. 169pp, biblio.

4793 Robin, Martin. Radical politics and Canadian labour 1880-1930. Kingston: Queens University Industrial Relations Centre. xii, 321pp. *OONL.

4794 Rodney, William. Soldiers of the International: a history of the Communist Party of Canada 1919-1929. Toronto: University of Toronto Press. xii, 204pp, biblio. *OONL.

4795 Ryerson, Stanley B. Unequal union: confederation and the roots of conflict in the Canadas, 1815-1873. Toronto: Progress. 477pp. *OHMA2771. Second volume of a history of Canada: see 4162 above for vol. 1.

4796 Saskatchewan Federation of Labour. Summary of policies based on resolutions approved at annual conventions 1956 to 1967. Regina. 57pp. *SSA/G114.11.

(4797) Scott, F.R. La déclaration universelle des droits de l'homme: aspects historique et juridique. Montréal: Association canadienne d'education de langue français. 31pp. QMML.

4798 Skebo, Suzanne Michelle. Liberty and authority: civil liberties in Toronto, 1929-1935. Unpublished MA thesis, University of British Columbia. (iv), 180pp, biblio. *BVAUS.

4799 Strong, George W. Canadian military sales to the USA and the Vietnam war. Oakville: Fellowship of Reconciliation. (c1968). 10pp, mimeo. *OHMA1886. Also issued as a 12pp printed pamphlet.

4800 Taylor, Charles. Socialism in the 1970's in Canada. (Ottawa): New Democratic Party. 20pp, mimeo. *OOA/ MacInnis 15.

4801 Thompson, Rich. NDP: convention and caucus. (Saskatoon). 3pp, mimeo. *SSA/G389.15. Pre-Waffle position paper.

4802 ------ Socialism and the NDP. (Saskatoon). 8pp, mimeo. *SSA/G389. Pre-Waffle position paper.

4803 Tran Tam Tinh. Peace in Vietnam: a Roman Catholic Vietnamese priest looks at the war. Translated by Peter Weldon. (Montreal): The He (Our Generation). 41pp. *OTURS/RSK.

4804 University of Toronto Communist Club. Statement: why do the Vietnamese continue to fight the US war machine? Why is the US still in Vietnam? What can we do in Canada and why? Toronto. (2pp), mimeo, broadside. *OTURS/RSK.

4805 Van Loon, Jean Louise. Ideology and structure in the Confederation of National Trade Unions. Unpublished MA thesis, Queens University. xiii, 138pp, biblio. *OKQ.

4806 Vance, Catharine. Not by gods but by people. Toronto: Progress. 65pp. *OHMA2121 OTURS/RSK. The biography of Bella Hall Gauld.

4807 Vietnam Mobilization Committee. (Manifesto): What is the VMC? Toronto. (c1968). (1p), mimeo broadside. *OTURS/RSK.

4808 Ward, Norman and Duff Spafford (eds). Politics in Saskatchewan. Don Mills: Longmans. (x), 314pp, index and appendix of federal and provincial election results. *OONL. Includes: The left wing 1921-1931 by Duff Spafford; The referendum and the plebiscite by Elizabeth Chambers; Votes for Saskatchewan women by June Menzies etc.

4809 Warrian, Peter. Capitalism and underdevelopment in Canada. Ottawa: Canadian Union of Students. 10pp, mimeo. *OOA/CCF478.

4810 Yorkville Diggers. lawlawlawlawlaw...(Toronto).
(c1968). 20pp. *E.

1969

4811 Abella, Irving Martin. The struggle for industrial
unionism in Canada: the CIO, the Communist Party and
the Canadian Congress of Labour 1936-1956. PhD thesis
University of Toronto. vii, 419pp, biblio. *OONL.

4812 Affairs of the Moment. Outline: Canadian involvement
in Vietnam. Ottawa. 6pp plus 7pp appendixes. *OHMA
1451. Appendixes comprise reproduced excerpts from
newspapers, magazines etc.

4813 Allen, Richard. The social gospel and the reform
tradition in Canada 1890-1928. Toronto: University
of Toronto. pp381-399. *OOA/MacInnis 20. Reprinted
from Canadian Historical Review XLIX no 4.

4814 Anderson, L. Focus of appeal in the analysis of political parties and the case of the CCF/NDP. Unpublished MA thesis, University of Alberta. iii, 148pp,
biblio. *AEUS.

4815 Anderson, Matthew S. Bold experiment. Regina. 42pp.
SRL SRU *AEUS. Saskatchewan medical insurance.

4816 Babcock, Robert Harper. The AF of L. in Canada, 1896-
1908: a study in American labour imperialism. PhD
thesis, Duke University. x, 463pp, biblio. *OONL.

4817 Benston, Margaret. The political economy of womens
liberation. Toronto: Toronto Womens Liberation and
Hogtown Press. 11p, mimeo. *OHMA.

4818 Bossin, Bob. Report of the education consultant:
or, I was a wishy-washy social democrat with hippy
tendencies for the CIA. (Toronto). np. (c1969).
15pp plus 9pp appendix. *OHMA. The appendix is
mainly reproductions of articles on the Free University of Toronto.

4819 BC Civil Liberties Association. Censorship: hate
literature: a position paper. Vancouver. 5pp, mimeo.
AEU *OONL.

4820 Buck, Tim. Lenin, a man for all time. Toronto:
Progress. 23pp. *OTURS/RSK.

4821 Byrne, Cyril, Ken MacKinnon and Robin Mathews. The
Waterloo report. Toronto: Graduate Students Union.
17pp plus (13pp) appendixes, mimeo. *OHMA1459
OTURS/RSK. On the 'de-Canadianization' of Canadian
universities.

4822 Canadian Student Movement. Manifesto: serve the
people! Oppose US imperialism! Toronto. 7pp.
*OTURS/RSK. With an added insert on their 2nd nat-
ional conference, 26-31 December, Vancouver.

4823 Cardinal, Harold. The unjust society: the tragedy of Canada's Indians. Edmonton: M.G. Hurtig. x, 173pp. *OONL.

4824 Clarke, Nelson. Revolution and power: Che Guevara. Toronto: Horizons. 9pp, mimeo. *OHMA1507 OTURS/RSK.

4825 Cleveland, John. Radical youth and alternatives for action. Edmonton: Confrontations. (c1969). 8pp, mimeo. *OOA/CCF478.

4826 ------ Student syndicalism: a programme of action. Edmonton: Confrontations (c1969). 22pp, mimeo. *OOA/CCF476.

4827 Committee to Aid the SFU 114. We are not guilty: the facts about the case of the 114 students arrested during the Simon Fraser University occupation, Nov. 1968. Vancouver. (13pp). *OTURS/RSK.

4828 Committee to Defend the Expelled. Stop expulsions in the NDP! The expulsions in the New Democratic Party. Toronto. 16pp. *OHMA1934.

4829 Communist Party of Canada. Constitution. Toronto. 43pp. *OKQS OTURS/RSK.

4830 ------ The fight against poverty: policy statement of the 20th convention, April 4-6, 1969. Toronto. (4pp). *OTURS/RSK.

4831 ------ For a democratic farm policy. Toronto. (8pp) *OTURS/RSK. Statement on national farm policy reprinted for the founding convention of the Union of Working Farmers.

4832 ------ New times - new policies for agriculture. Say no to the task force. Toronto. (4pp). *OTCPA.

4833 Confrontations. A programme for reform: a left document for the Canadian Labour Congress. Edmonton. 11pp, mimeo. *OOA/CCF475. Written by 'several trade unionists'.

4834 Conway, J.F. American imperialism in our educational system. Ottawa: Canadian Union of Students. 5pp, mimeo. *OOA/CCF476.

4835 ------ The NDP: parliamentary party or political movement? Edmonton: Confrontations. (c1969). 8pp, mimeo. *OOA/CCF478.

4836 ------ The new technology demands a new politics. Edmonton: Confrontations. 5pp, mimeo. *OOA/CCF478.

4837 Cooperative Union of Canada and Le Conseil canadien de la Cooperation. A submission respecting proposals for tax reform as tabled in the House of Commons, Friday November 7th, 1969. (Ottawa). 55pp, mimeo. *OOA/MacInnis 6.

4838 Culhane, Claire. Behead and cure: the truth behind Canada's medical aid to Vietnam. Ottawa: Affairs of the Moment. (4pp). *OOA/MacInnis 18.

4839 Dosman, James Arnold Herman. The medical care issue as a factor in the electoral defeat of the Saskatchewan government in 1964. Unpublished MA thesis, University of Saskatchewan. (ii), vi, 171pp, biblio. *SSUS.

(4840) Fournier, Marcel. Histoire et idéologie du groupe Canadien-français du Parti Communiste 1925-1945. Unpublished MA thesis, Université de Montréal. 290pp.

4841 Goldfield, Evelyn, Sue Munaker and Naomi Weisstein. A woman is a sometime thing or cornering capitalism by removing 51 percent of its commodities. Toronto: Toronto Womens Liberation and Hogtown Press. (c1969). 30pp, mimeo. *OHMA1602.

4842 Gonick, C.W. Poverty and capitalism. Winnipeg: Canadian Dimension. 9pp. *OHMA2332.

4843 Halifax Typographical Union Local 130 of the International Typographical Union. A century of progress: organized September 21, 1869. Kentville: Kentville Publications. 48pp. NSHPL *OONL.

4844 Harding, Jim. The strike at SFU. Toronto: Hogtown Press. (8pp). *OONL. SFU - Simon Fraser University.

4845 Hoar, Victor and Mac Reynolds. The Mackenzie-Papineau Battalion: Canadian participation in the Spanish Civil War. Toronto: Copp Clark. (xii), 285pp, biblio. *OONL.

4846 Horn, Michiel Steven Daniel. The League for Social Reconstruction: socialism and nationalism in Canada 1931-1945. PhD thesis, University of Toronto. 2, vii, 568pp, biblio. *OTUAR.

4847 Howard, Dick. French new working class theories. Toronto: Hogtown Press. 18pp, mimeo. *OHMA1727.

4848 Howard, Frank and others. Special debate: it is alleged that present government policy is a denial of fundamental rights to native Indian people. Speeches delivered in the House of Commons 6 March 1969. Ottawa: Queens Printer. 16pp. *OOA/MacInnis 18.

4849 Hyde, Tony. Economics: large question, short answers. Toronto: Hogtown Press. 10pp, mimeo. *OHMA1726 OONL OOA/CCF478.

4850 Kashtan, William. Keynote address 20th convention Communist Party of Canada. (Toronto): Communist Party of Canada. 26pp, mimeo. *OTURS/RSK.

4851 ------ Say no to austerity: full employment without inflation. Toronto: Progress. 16pp. AEU NFSM NSHPL OPET *OHMA1630 OTURS/RSK.

4852 ------ Why Canada should quit NATO. Toronto: Communist Party of Canada. 37pp. AEU BVIV OKQ QQL *OHMA1710 OTURS/RSK.

4853 ------ and others. Defeat the government's austerity program. Proceedings of the central committee meeting, CPC, Toronto October 4-5-6, 1969. Toronto: Communist Party of Canada. 22pp. *OHMA1512 OTURS/RSK.

4854 Kwavnick, David. Organized labour and government: the Canadian Labour Congress as a political interest group during the Diefenbaker and Pearson administrations. PhD thesis, Carleton University.

4855 Lawton, Alma. Urban relief in Saskatchewan during the years of depression 1930-39. Unpublished MA thesis, University of Saskatchewan. viii, 188pp, biblio. *SSUS.

4856 League for Socialist Action. Canada - U$ relations: a socialist viewpoint. Toronto: Vanguard. 19pp. AEU OONL *OHMA1474 OTURS/RSK.

4857 Levitt, Kari. Canada: economic dependence and political disintegration. Winnipeg: Canadian Dimension. (iv), 82pp. NBSAM QMG SSU *OHMA2704 OONL OTURS/RSK.

4858 Lewis, David, Mel Watkins and others. Debate on the resolutions 'For a united and independent Canada' (C-17): 'For an independent socialist Canada' (R-133) NDP federal convention, Winnipeg October 30, 1969. (Ottawa): (?NDP). 21pp, mimeo. *OOA/CCF446.

4859 Lichtman, Richard. The ideological function of the university. Montreal: Our Generation. (c1969). 14pp, mimeo. *OOA/CCF482.

4860 (Ligue des Jeunes Socialistes). Stratégie et organisation pour la juenesse révolutionnaire. Montréal: Editions d'Avant Garde. 36pp. *OHMA1481.

(4861)McAndrew, W.J. Gold mining trade unions and politics: Ontario in the 1930's. Unpublished MA thesis, University of British Columbia. Not found.

4862 McKenzie, Anthony. The rise and fall of the farmer-labor party in Nova Scotia. Unpublished MA thesis, Dalhousie University. (ii), ix, 205pp, biblio. *NSHD.

4863 McMillan, Charles Joseph. Trade unionism in district 18, 1900-1925: a case study. Unpublished MBA thesis University of Alberta. vi, 212pp, biblio. *AEUS.

4864 Magder, Beatrice. The Winnipeg General Strike. Toronto: Maclean-Hunter. 52pp, illus. *OTURS/RSK.

4865 Magnuson, Bruce. What to do about the crisis in our cities? Toronto: Progress. 11pp. AEU BVAU BVIP OOP QQL *OHMA2386 OTURS/RSK.

(4866)Marceau, Claude. Evolution de la conscience ouvrière 1840-1940. Unpublished MA thesis, Université de Montréal. viii, 339pp.

4867 Marx, Karl and F. Engels. Communist manifesto. Toronto: Vanguard. (c1969). 72pp. *BVAUS/Mac38f.15 OHMA2777. Contains also Ninety years of the Communist manifesto by Leon Trotsky and Significance of the manifesto by V.I. Lenin.

4868 Mathews, Robin and James Steele (eds). The struggle for Canadian universities: a dossier. Toronto: New Press. viii, 184pp.

4869 Maxwell, James Douglas. Royal Commission(s) and social change in Canada 1867-1966. PhD thesis, Cornell University. xiv, 496pp, biblio. *OONL.

4870 Mitchell, Don. Agriculture and change in the 70s. Regina: Young New Democrats. (8pp), mimeo. *SSA/G 389.25.

4871 Morton, Desond. Are you fed up about taxes? (most people are). Ottawa: New Democratic Party. (10pp). *OHMA OOA/CCF536 OTURS/RSK.

4872 ------ A basis for discussion: socialism: Canada: seventies. Toronto: New Democratic Party. 31pp. AEU OTP OOP SRL SSU *SSA/G4.1969.1 OOA/CCF539.

4873 ------ A guide to the New Democratic Party. Ottawa: NDPublications. 13pp. *OHMA.

4874 New Democratic Party. The financial crisis in the catholic high schools. Toronto. 16pp. *OHMA OKQS

4875 ------ Municipal program metropolitan Toronto adopted at the Toronto area convention Sept. 6-7th, 1969 and the Scarborough convention Sept. 20th-21st, 1969. Toronto. 46pp. *OHMA.

4876 ------ NDP news: socialism 70. Convention magazine Oct. 28-31, 1969. Ottawa. 68pp. *OOA/CCF401.

4877 ------ Socialism 70. A series of papers prepared as 'thoughtful background' for the 5th convention in Winnipeg as follows: (1) Economic independence and socialism by Melville H. Watkins, 9pp; (2) A policy on broadcasting and film by Bruce Lawson, 13pp; 3. Observations on the substance and machinery of science policy in Canada by G.B. Doern, 14pp; (4) Towards a responsive development corporation by Max Saltsman, 13pp; 5. Poverty and regional disparity by Desmond Morton, 8pp; (6) A guaranteed annual income by Marion Bryden, 5pp; 7. Sports by Bruce Kidd, 16pp; 8. Industrial democracy by Ed. Broadbent, 6pp; 9. A budget of urban problems by Charles Taylor, 11pp; 10. Universities by Steve Langdon, 14pp; Agriculture by Bev Currie, 4pp; 12. Proposal for tax reform by Marc Eliesen, 13pp; 13. The politics of the housing crisis by Desmond Morton, 15pp; 14. Regional economic policy by Marc Eliesen, 23pp; 15. Power by David Lewis, 10pp; 16. Nationalism and the NDP by Ed. Finn, 14pp; 16B. Agriculture in Canada; partner, servant or millstone, 19pp. All mimeo in folder. *OOA/CCF 539.

4878 NDP Alberta Socialist Caucus. A socialist manifesto for the NDP. Edmonton. (c1969). (6pp). *OTURS/RSK.

4879 NDP-Waffle. A socialist program for Canadian trade unionists. Toronto. (c1969). 13pp. *E.

4880 New Democratic Youth. BC Young New Democrats policy 1967-68. Vancouver. 14pp, mimeo. *OOA/CCF478. Also published 1968-69, 16pp.

4881 New Democratic Youth. Information bulletin. Ottawa. 44pp, mimeo. *SSA/G413.1.

4882 Nova Scotia New Democratic Youth. (Manifesto - untitled). (Halifax). 5pp, mimeo. *OOA/CCF480.

4883 Ontario Federation of Labour. Legislative proposals to the government of Ontario. Toronto. 14pp. *OOA/OFL 8.

4884 ------ Submission to Honourable Dalton Bales, QC, Minister of Labour, province of Ontario in regards to the report of the Royal Commission into Labour Disputes in the province of Ontario. Toronto. 17pp. BVAU BVIP BVIV MWU NSHPL OH OTP QMML SSU *OOA/OFL 8. The Rand report.

4885 ------ Communication: report of the tenth farmer-labour-teachers conference. Toronto. 28pp. *OOA/OFL 10.

4886 Ontario Union of Students. The class content of the Rand and Woods report. Toronto. 41pp. *OTURS/RSK.

4887 Ontario Woodsworth Memorial Foundation. Industrial democracy and Canadian labour. Toronto. 74pp. *OTURS/RSK.

4888 David Orton Defence Committee. A case study of repression: the political persecution of Professor David Orton at Sir George Williams University 1967-1969. Montreal. 81pp. *OTURS/RSK.

4889 Ottawa Committee to End the War in Vietnam. Brief to the External Affairs and National Defence Committee of the House of Commons. 10pp, mimeo. *OHMA 1917.

4890 Perly, Caroline. Women in the work force: a class analysis. Ottawa: Canadian Union of Students. 13pp, mimeo. *OOA/CCF477.

4891 Pittman,(sic)Walter. Education for tomorrow. Edmonton: Confrontations. (c1969). 7pp, mimeo. *OOA/CCF 478.

4892 Rankin, Harry and Bruce Yorke. Tenant rights. Vancouver: BC Tenants Organization. 32pp. BVAU OH OOP OTMCL QQL *OHMA2512 OTURS/RSK.

4893 Ray, Don I. Political thought of Canadian Union Students. Ottawa: Canadian Union of Students. 13pp, mimeo. *OOA/CCF478.

4894 Ridgway, Martin James. The Labour Party and the CCF-NDP: a comparative study of policies and policy-making 1945-1968. Unpublished MA thesis, McMaster University. (i), vi, 165pp, biblio. *OHMA.

4895 Ringle, W.F.P. (pseud. possibly Pringle). Political repression in Canadian history. Toronto: Hogtown

Press. (c1969). 24pp, mimeo. AEU BVAU OOA OONL
OOP *OHMA1892.

(4896) Ripton, Reginald Anthony. Engineering unionism: an
analysis of factors influencing acceptance and re-
jection of unionism by employee-engineers. Unpublished MA thesis, McGill University.

4897 Sanguinetti, Sonja Patricia. Common misperceptions
of the events relating to the rise of the protest
movements in the prairies. Unpublished MA thesis,
University of British Columbia. 52pp. *BVAUS.

4898 Shingler, John. The university and society: transformation and liberation. Ottawa: Canadian Union
of Students. 10pp, mimeo. *OOA/CCF478.

4899 Smart, John David. The Patrons of Industry in Ontario. Unpublished MA thesis, Carleton University.
167pp, biblio. *OOAL.

4900 Smith, Marion B. and others. Women in Canadian universities: a brief presented to the Royal Commission
on the Status of Women in Canada. Toronto: Graduate
Students Union. 14pp, plus inserted appendix.
*OTURS/RSK.

4901 Staples, R.S. A road to consumer sovreignty: a description of direct-charge cooperatives. Weston (Ont):
United Cooperatives of Ontario. 14pp. *OOA/MacInnis4

4902 Stolee, Lief Gordon. The parliamentary career of
William Irvine, 1922-1935. Unpublished MA thesis,
University of Alberta. vii, 235pp, biblio. *AEUS.

4903 Thompson, Richard and Don Mitchell. Agriculture policy. Saskatoon: Waffle Caucus NDP. 18pp, mimeo.
*SSA/G389.28.

4904 TSM (ie. Toronto Student Movement). Summer education
June 1 - July 15. Courses: Theories of revolution.
2. Contradictions in Canada. 3. Bourgeois ideology.
4. Student strategy. 5. Cultural oppression. 6.
Worker-student alliance. (Toronto). (7pp), mimeo.
*OHMA.

4905 Unemployed Citizens Welfare Improvement Council.
Brief presented before the Senate Commission on Poverty. Vancouver. 24pp. *OOA/MacInnis 4.

4906 United Jewish Peoples Order. Peace is possible!
Only peace can guarantee the existence of sovereign
rights of the state of Israel. Toronto. (4pp).
*OTURS/RSK.

4907 University of Toronto Communist Club. Guide to radical student politics. Toronto. (c1969). 50pp.
*OTURS/RSK.

4908 Voice of Women. Brief to the Senate of Canada Special Committee on Science Policy, Spring 1969. Toronto. 25pp, mimeo. OTMCL *OONL.

4909 Waffle. For an independent socialist Canada.

(?Saskatoon). 20pp, mimeo, sections separately paged. *OTURS/RSK SSA/G389.5. Contains the Waffle manifesto and supporting resolutions covering socialist foreign policy, extra-parliamentary activity and universities. Same text introduced by the Waffle caucus to the NDP federal convention in Winnipeg, 7pp, mimeo *SSA/G389.6.

4910 Warrian, Peter. Staples, structures and the state: notes on Canadian economic history up to the depression. Ottawa: Canadian Union of Students. 14pp, mimeo. *OHMA1805 OOA/CCF478. Also issued by Hogtown Press.

4911 Wharf, Brian and Michael Wheeler. The neighbourhood information centre: new opportunity for public-private partnership. Ottawa: Canadian Welfare Council. 38pp, mimeo. *OOA/MacInnis 4.

4912 Yankee Refugee Staff. Americans in Canada. (?Vancouver). (c1969). (2pp). *OHMA1808.

4913 Young, Joe. US aggression in Vietnam and Canada's complicity. Toronto: Anti-Vietnam War Movement. 13pp. *OTURS/RSK.

4914 Young, Walter D. The anatomy of a party: the national CCF 1932-61. Toronto: University of Toronto Press. x, 328pp. *OTURS/RSK.

4915 ------ Democracy and discontent: progressivism, socialism and social credit in the Canadian west. Toronto: Ryerson. xiv, 122pp. *OONL.

4916 Young Communist League. Capitalism in crisis: why you should join the YCL. (Toronto). (2pp). *OTURS/RSK.

1970

4917 Abortion Caravan. Brief, May 1970. np. 6pp, mimeo. *OOA/MacInnis 1.

4918 Adell, B.L. The legal status of collective agreements in England, the United States and Canada. Kingston: Queens University Industrial Relations Centre. xxxii, 240pp. *OONL.

4919 Adler-Karlsson, Gunnar. Reclaiming the Canadian economy: a Swedish approach through functional socialism. Toronto: Anansi. xx, 98pp. *OONL.

4920 African National Congress of South Africa Canadian Committee. Special report on underground activities in South Africa. Don Mills. 7pp and inserted leaflet. *OTURS/RSK.

4921 Amyot, Grant. Strategy for academic reform. Edmonton: Confrontations. (c1970). 14pp, mimeo. *OOA/CCF476.

4922 Anderson, Larry M. Dialectics of the university: a preliminary analysis. (Port Arthur): np. (c1970). 12pp, mimeo. *OOA/CCF482.

4923 Atkins, Martha and Maureen Hynes. The hidden history of the female: the early feminist movement in the United States: a history of the rise of women's consciousness in Canada and in Quebec including various tracts on the ideology of women in the working class, the movement for female emancipation and its links with the temperance struggle and with some conclusions drawn concerning the struggle of Canadian women today. Toronto: Hogtown Press. 24 plus 11pp, mimeo. BVAS NBFU OOP OTV *OHMA.

4924 Bahr, Howard M. Disaffiliated man: essay and bibliography on skid row, vagrancy and outsiders. Toronto: University of Toronto Press. xiv, 428pp. *OONL.

4925 Becerra, Longino. Some roots of opportunism. Toronto: Progress. 8pp. *OTURS/RSK.

4926 Bernstein, Judi and others. Sisters, brothers, lovers ...listen...Toronto: New Left Committee. 13pp, mimeo. *OHMA.

4927 Bethune, Norman. The wounds. Guelph: Alive Press. (c1970). 35pp. *OHMA OTURS/RSK. Little Books of Hope series.

4928 Bouvier, Emile. Les coopératives devant les progrès modernes: conférence donnée à l'occasion du 25e anniversaire des Caisses populaires acadiennes, Caraquet, NB, samedi, le 6 juin 1970. Caraquet: L'Union Cooperative Acadienne. 26pp. *OONL.

4929 Brathwaite, J. Ashton. Bitter soul. Toronto: 21st Century. 20pp. *OHMA1458. Poems written by a West Indian serving in the British army and now resident in Canada.

4930 Brewin, Andrew and David MacDonald. Canada and the Biafran tragedy. Toronto: James, Lewis and Samuel. 173pp. *MWP.

4931 Briemberg, Mordecai. A taste of better things: being an account of recent events in the Department of Political Science, Sociology and Anthropology of Simon Fraser University. Toronto: Hogtown Press. 12pp, mimeo. *OHMA1461.

4932 Broadbent, Ed. The Liberal rip-off: Trudeauism vs. the politics of equality. Toronto: New Press. xii, 84pp. *OHMA2132 OOP.

4933 Buck, Tim. Lenin and Canada: his influence on Canadian political life. Toronto: Progress. 133pp. *MWP OTURS/RSK SSUS. Articles and an address.

4934 ------ Looking for answers??? A message to militant unionists from the Communist Party. Toronto: Communist Party of Canada. (3pp). *OTURS/RSK. Title at head of article: What would you do?

4935 Buck, Tim. Taking counsel with Lenin on the problems of our time. Toronto: Progress. (8pp). *OHMA2427 OTURS/RSK. Progress Books Reprint 1.

(4936) Butcher, Dennis L. Rev. Dr Salem Bland: a study of his activities and infleunce in the politics, reform and church and society of Manitoba and western Canada, 1903-19. Unpublished MA thesis, University of Manitoba.

4937 Canada, Dept of Labour. Working mothers and their child-care arrangements. Ottawa: Queens Printer. x, 58pp. *NSHD.

4938 Canadian Liberation Movement. The Americanization of our universities. Part one: The betrayal of our intellectuals. Toronto. (4pp), mimeo. *OOA/CCF476.

4939 Canadian Tribune. Freedom of the press: for whom? - from what? Submission to the Special Senate Committee on the Mass Media, March 1970. Toronto. 11pp. *OTURS/RSK OKQS.

4940 Carter, Charlotte and Dyson. Worker power: dare we win? Gravenhurst: Northern Book House. 217pp. *OTURS/RSK.

4941 Communist Party of Canada. The case for more pay in 1971. Toronto. (4pp). *OTCPA.

4942 ------ 50th anniversary of the Communist Party of Canada. Toronto. 6pp, mimeo. *OTURS/RSK. Comprising a brief history.

4943 ------ Higher wages a must! Toronto. (4pp). *OTURS/ RSK.

4944 ------ 1970 auto negotiations: as assessment: a perspective. Toronto. (4pp). *OTCPA.

4945 ------ The strike in big steel and metal mining 1969. Toronto. (6pp). *OKQS.

4946 ------ Submission to Canadian Transport Commission, Railway Transport Committee concerning application of Canadian Pacific Railway to abandon 'The Canadian' transcontinental passenger service. Toronto. 5pp, mimeo. *OTURS/RSK.

4947 ------ Submission to David Weatherhead MP, chairman, and members of the Standing Committee on Labour, Manpower and Immigration, re: white paper on 'Unemplyment insurance in the 70's. Toronto. 9pp, mimeo. *OTURS/RSK.

4948 ------ Submission to the Special Joint Committee on the Constitution of Canada. Toronto. 30pp, plus 1p addenda in French from le Parti Communiste du Québec, mimeo. *OTURS/RSK.

4949 ------ Submission to the Standing Committee on Finance, Trade and Economic Affairs. Toronto. 8pp, mimeo. *OTURS/RSK. On the Carter commission tax proposals.

4950 Communist Party of Canada. Submission to the Standing Committee on Finance, Trade and Economic Affairs. Toronto. 6pp. *OTURS/RSK. Not the same as 4949.

4951 Conway, John F. The future of our province. (Saskatoon). 3pp, mimeo. *SSA/G389.21.

4952 Cooperative Union of Canada. Brief to the Special Senate Committee on Poverty. Ottawa. 18pp, mimeo. *OOA/MacInnis 6.

4953 Dewart, Robert, John Hamburger and Mike Naemsch. On strike! New College. Toronto: University of Toronto Worker-Student Alliance. 21pp, mimeo. *OHMA.

4954 Douglas, T.C. Bartering our birthright. Speech delivered in the House of Commons in reply to the speech from the throne, 9 October 1970. Ottawa: Queens Printer. 6pp. *OOA/CCF449.

4955 Dowson, Ross. The CCF: our tasks and perspective. 'Internal bulletin' of the Revolutionary Workers Party Canadian section of the Fourth International, July 1951. Ottawa: New Democratic Youth. (c1970). 24pp, mimeo. *OOA/CCF476. Reprinted by the NDY in relation to the Waffle proposals.

4956 Fidler, Dick. Red power in Canada. Toronto: Vanguard. 15pp. *OHMA1472 OTURS/RSK.

4957 Finkel, Al. An analysis of the Manitoba NDP convention. (Winnipeg): (Waffle). 3pp, mimeo. *OOA/CCF446.

4958 Foster, John W. Relationships: robbery, revolution and reconstruction. Toronto: United Church of Canada Committee on Education for Mission and Stewardship. 9pp. *OHMA1608.

4959 Frank, Andre Gunder. The underdevelopment policy of the United Nations in Latin America. Toronto: Hogtown Press. 19pp, mimeo. *OHMA1607.

4960 Free Speech Movement. We want a university. Toronto: SUPA. (c1970). 7pp. *OOA/CCF482.

4961 Friends of Quebec. Report no. 1 - Report of Montreal visit. Toronto. 3pp, mimeo. *OTURS/RSK.

4962 Gough, K. The struggle at Simon Fraser. Toronto: Hogtown Press. 9pp, mimeo. *OHMA1600.

4963 ------ Women in evolution. Toronto: Hogtown Press. 11pp, mimeo. *OHMA1603.

4964 Haggar, George S. Imperialism and revolution in the mideast. Toronto: Tahrir. 32pp. AEU OTU *E.

4965 Hamilton, Douglas F. My years in the labour movement: 1945 from war's end until merger 1957. (Toronto). (c1970). (248pp), mimeo. *OTURS/Woodsworth 58.

4966 Hamilton-Smith, Terence. New Brunswick socialists: poverty and the great leap forward in New Brunswick. Fredericton: NB Socialists. (28pp) plus 2pp manifesto, mimeo. *OTURS/RSK.

4967 Harding, Jim. Canada's Indians: a powerless minority.
Victoria: Social Science Research. 12pp, mimeo.
*OOP. First published by SUPA 1965, not found.

4968 ------ Freedom from for freedom to: ideas for people
in 'free schools'. Saturna island BC: Free School
Press. 8pp, mimeo. *OONL.

4969 Hardy, Helen Margaret. Seasonal unemployment in Canada 1955 to 1970. Unpublished MA thesis, McMaster
University. x, 110pp, biblio. *OHMA.

4970 Harris, W. Eric. Canada's last chance! Canadians
must make a declaration of independence from United
States domination of Canada's economy and guarantee
that independence by making an economic switch to
Europe. Toronto: Savvy. 70pp. *OHMA2120.

4971 Heaps, Leo. The rebel in the house: the life and
times of A.A. Heaps, MP. London (Eng): Niccolo.
(viii), 168pp. *OONL.

4972 Hoar, Victor. The on to Ottawa trek. Toronto: Copp
Clark. 54pp. *OONL.

4973 Interested Citizens of Halifax. Help the fishermen
of Nova Scotia. Halifax. (4pp). *NSHD. On the
fishermens strike.

4974 James, Alice. Poverty: Canada's legacy to women.
Vancouver: Vancouver Womens Caucus. 24pp. *OOA/
CCF553.

4975 Kashtan, William. The fight for democracy and social
advance. Toronto: Communist Party of Canada. 24pp.
BVAUS BVIP NFSM OOP OPET SSU *OHMA1631 OOA/CCF542
OTURS/RSK. On the Quebec crisis and war measures.

4976 Kopperud, Karen and others. Education policy. Saskatoon: Waffle Caucus. 19pp, mimeo. *SSA/G389.29.

4977 Kunin, Roslyn. Labour force participation rates and
poverty in Canadian metropolitan areas. PhD thesis,
University of British Columbia. 92pp. *BVAUS.

4978 Laxer, James. The energy policy game: the politics
of the continental resources deal. Toronto: New
Press. (vi), ii, 72pp. *OONL.

4979 ------ English Canada and Quebec. (Toronto): (Waffle). 4pp, mimeo. *OOA/CCF446.

4980 ------ Lament for an industry. Toronto: Ontario
Waffle. (4pp). *OOA/CCF446.

4981 ------ The student movement and Canadian independ-
ence (and) Part 2: The socialist tradition in Canada.
Winnipeg: Canadian Dimension. (c1970). 16pp. BVIV
*OHMA1786.

4982 League for Socialist Action. Songs of liberation.
Toronto. (c1970). (17pp), mimeo. *OHMA1782.

4983 Levitt, Kari. Silent surrender: the multinational
corporation in Canada. Toronto: Macmillan. xxii,
185pp. *OONL.

4984 Lewis, David. No information to justify War Measures act. Ottawa: New Democratic Party. (4pp). *OOA/ CCF477 and 538.

4985 Lewis, Richard Francis Victor. A comparison between British Columbia and New Zealand labour movements. Unpublished MBA thesis, University of Alberta. v, 120pp, biblio. *AEUS.

4986 Ligue Socialiste Ouvrière. Socialisme et libération de la femme. Montréal: Editions d'Avant Garde. (c1970). 24pp. *OHMA1465.

4987 Lodge, Derek John. The effect of unionism on the level of wages in the Canadian manufacturing sector. Unpublished MA thesis, Queens University. vi, 80pp, biblio. *OKQ.

4988 Louis Riel University Family Co-op. A crisis in the Louis Riel University Family Co-op. (Saskatoon). (c1970). 3pp, mimeo. *SSA/G482.3.

4989 Lumsden, Ian (ed). Close the 49th parallel etc. The Americanization of Canada. Toronto: University of Toronto Press. (viii), 336pp. *OONL. Prepared for the University League for Social Reform. Contains: The Canadian bourgeoisie and its national conscious- ness by D. Drache; Canadianizing American business; the roots of the branch plant by Michael Bliss; For- eign ownership and political decay by C.W. Gonick; Lament for a union movement by I.M. Abella; Canadian defence policy and the American empire by Philip Resnick; All the news it pays to print by John W. Warnock; Oh say, can you see? by Frank Peers; Yes, cultural imperialism too! by Gail Dexter; The uni- versities; takeover of the mind by James Steele and Robin Mathews; Canada and the American science of politics by Ellen and Neal Wood; The dismal state of economics in Canada by Melville H. Watkins; Bind- ing Prometheus by Abraham Rotstein; The alienation of Canadian resources; the case of the Columbia river treaty by Larrat Higgins; Science in Canada - Amer- ican style by Lynn Trainor; Canada's 'national' sport by Bruce Kidd; The Americanization of the Canadian student movement by James Laxer; What can I do right now? by George Martell; Perspectives on un-American traditions in Canada by Gerald L. Caplan and James Laxer; American imperialism and Canadian intellectuals by Ian Lumsden.

4990 MacInnis, Grace. Women in Canada - in society - in public life - in the NDP. Regina: New Democratic Party. 16pp. *OOA/CCF540. Title at head: Toward freedom.

(4991) McKillop, Alexander Brian. Citizen and socialist: the ethos of political Winnipeg 1919-1935. Unpub- lished MA thesis, University of Manitoba.

4992 McMaster Committee to End the War in Vietnam. We can wave or...we can do it. Hamilton. (c1970) 28pp, mimeo. *OHMA2578. Collection of reprints.

4993 Magnuson, Bruce. Unite in struggle for full employ-
     ment: a message to organized labour by Communist
     Party of Canada. Toronto: Communist Party of Canada.
     18pp. AEU BVIP OKQ OOP *OOA/CCF542 OTURS/RSK.

4994 Mann, W.E. Poverty and social policy in Canada.
     Toronto: Copp Clark. xiv, 429pp. *OONL. Includes:
     Poverty and capitalism by C.W. Gonick; Poverty and
     people power by Ann Bowman; Poverty and political
     movements by Maurice Pinard etc.

4995 Marchak, Maureen Patricia. Bargaining strategy of
     white-collar workers in British Columbia. PhD thesis
     University of British Columbia. 292pp, biblio *BVAUS.

(4996)Masters, Jane Elizabeth. Canadian labour press opin-
     ion 1890-1914: a study in theoretical radicalism and
     practical conservatism. Unpublished MA thesis, Uni-
     versity of Western Ontario.

4997 Millar, Frederick David. The Winnipeg General Strike
     1919: a reinterpretation in the light of oral history
     and pictorial evidence. Unpublished MA thesis, Carl-
     eton University. 376(377)pp, biblio. *OOCC.

4998 Mitchell, Don. The New Democratic Party: political
     movement? or parliamentary machine? (?Regina):
     (?Waffle). (c1970). (4pp). *SSA/G389.2.

4999 Moffatt, Gary. History of the Canadian peace move-
     ment until 1969. St Catharines: Grape Vine Press.
     iv, 188pp. *OTURS/RSK.

5000 Morris, Leslie. Look on Canada, now, and see history
     anew, an epoch past and a new life fashioning under
     your hands: Communism, to which all roads lead. Sel-
     ected writings 1923-1964. Toronto: Progress. xxiv,
     216pp. *OTURS/RSK.

5001 Morton, Desmond. Ontario local government in the
     seventies: a basis for discussion. Toronto: New
     Democratic Party. 12pp. *OOA/CCF538.

5002 Morton, Peggy. They are burning, they are burning
     effigies; why, why, why, effigies?. Toronto: Hog-
     town Press. (c1970). 27pp, mimeo. *OHMA1831.

5003 ------ A woman's work is never done or, the produc-
     tion, maintenance and reproduction of labour power.
     (?Toronto): (?Hogtown Press). (c1970). 22pp, mimeo.
     *OHMA1842.

5004 Native Women's Liberation Front. Native movement:
     'Better red than dead'. Vancouver. 20pp. *OOA/
     CCF460.

5005 New Democratic Party. If you can keep your head...!
     Ottawa. (8pp). *OOA/CCF537. On the War Measures
     act.

5006 ------ It's time to act! A brief to the government
     of Saskatchewan on the economic crisis facing the
     province. Regina. 9pp. *SSA/G4.1970.4.

5007 New Democratic Party. The NDP in Manitoba - a government that cares. (Winnipeg). 4pp, mimeo. *OOA/
CCF537.

5008 NDP-Waffle Labour Committee. A socialist program for
Canadian trade unionists. Toronto. 13pp. *OOA/CCF446.

5009 Novakowski, Ken. The NDP in Alberta: a critique.
Edmonton: Confrontations. (c1970). 7pp, mimeo.
*OOA/CCF478.

5010 Ontario Federation of Labour. Brief to the Hon.
Dalton A. Bales QC, Minister of Labour. Toronto.
8pp, mimeo. OONL QMML *OOA/OFL 8.

5011 ------ Legislative proposals to the government of
Ontario. Toronto. 14pp. *OOA/OFL 8. On education,
training, health care etc.

5012 ------ Submission to the government of the province
of Ontario in regard to the Metropolitan Life, Operating Engineers Supreme Court decision. Toronto.
3pp, mimeo. *OOA/OFL 8.

5013 ------ Submission to Dalton Bales, QC, Minister of
Labour in regard to the Labour Relations act 1970.
Toronto. 20pp, mimeo. OONL QMML *OOA/OFL 8.

5014 ------ Submission to the Ontario Law Reform Commission on the subject of Sunday observance legislation. Toronto. 8pp, mimeo. *OOA/OFL 8.

5015 ------ Summary and evaluation of bill 167, An act
to amend the labour relations act. Toronto. 6pp,
mimeo. *OONL OOL.

5016 ------ Summary of policies. Toronto. 32pp. *OONL.

5017 ------ and Canadian Labour Congress. Solution to
pollution: matter of life and death. Report of the
11th farmer-labour-teacher conference. (Toronto).
47pp. *OOA/OFL 10.

5018 (Ontario Waffle). Education in Ontario. (Toronto).
(c1970). 24pp, mimeo. *OOA/CCF476.

5019 Ontario Waffle Movement in the NDP. For a socialist
Ontario in an independent socialist Canada: resolutions prepared for the Ontario NDP convention October
1970. Toronto. 28pp. *OOA/CCF398, 446 and 537.

5020 Palmer, Earl E. Responsible decision-making in democratic trade unions. Ottawa: Queens Printer. vii,
423pp. *OONL.

5021 Peitchinis, Stephen G. Canadian labour economics:
an introductory analysis. Toronto: McGraw-Hill.
x, 491pp, biblio. *OONL.

5022 Pelletier, Wilfred. Two articles. Toronto: Neewin.
(32pp), illus. *OHMA. Comprises: Childhood in an
Indian village and Some thoughts about organization
and leadership.

5023 Rankin, Harry. Pollution: suicide or survival. Van-

couver: np.   24pp.   BVAU OH OPET QQL *OHMA2543
OTURS/RSK.

5024 The Reform Caucus. A programme for reform. Toronto.
(3pp). *OOA/CCF446. Reform Caucus of the Canadian
Labour Congress.

5025 Richmond, Ted. Kanada and capitalism. Montreal:
Our Generation. 44pp, mimeo. OKQ *OONL.

5026 Riddell, John and others. Free Quebec political prisoners. The issues and background. Toronto: Vanguard. 31pp. OOL *OHMA1466.

5027 Roussopoulos, Dimitrios J. (ed). The new left in
Canada. Montreal: Black Rose. 156pp. *OONL. Contributions from James Harding, Richard Price, Richard
Thompson, Nick Ternette, Philip Resnick, Adèle Lauzon,
on the new left in BC, Alberta, Saskatchewan, Manitoba and Quebec respectively.

5028 Rowntree, Mickey and John. More on the political
economy of women's liberation. Toronto: Toronto
Womens Liberation and Hogtown Press. 6pp, mimeo.
*OTURS/RSK.

5029 Russell, Peter Angus. The co-operative government
in Saskatchewan 1929-1934: response to the depression. Unpublished MA thesis, University of Saskatchewan. (viii), 148(152)pp, biblio. *SSUS.

5030 Semple, Wynton. They'll have to start a war or something. Toronto: Hogtown Press. 16pp, mimeo. *OHMA
1884 OOA/CCF476. Relates to jobs for graduates.

5031 Socialist Organizing Committee. Statement. (Vancouver). (c1970). 11pp. *E.

5032 Stevenson, Paul. Nationalism is a reactionary ten-
dency amongst the working class. (Winnipeg): (New
Democratic Youth). (c1970). 3pp, mimeo. *OOA/CCF480.

5033 ------ Program: Manitoba NDY. Analysis of monopoly
control submitted to 1970 provincial convention.
(Winnipeg): (New Democratic Youth). 12pp, mimeo.
*OOA/CCF479.

5034 Stuart, Richard Grey. The early political career of
Angus MacInnis. Unpublished MA thesis, University
of British Columbia. (vi), 237pp, biblio. *BVAUS.

5035 Swankey, Ben. National identity or cultural genocide?
A reply to Ottawa's new Indian policy. Toronto: Progress. 38pp. *OHMA1905 OTURS/RSK.

5036 Taylor, Barbara. Women and capitalism. (?Saskatoon):
(Womens Liberation Movement). 6pp, mimeo. *SSA/G482.
10.

5037 Thompson, R. and H.R. Brown. Social science and the
ideology of the status quo. Toronto: Hogtown Press.
19pp, mimeo. *OHMA1829.

5038 University of Toronto Worker-Student Alliance. Wom-
en's liberation and class politics. Toronto. 8pp,

mimeo. *OHMA.

5039 Victoria and University of Toronto SAC's. Québec in crisis. Toronto. 24pp. *OTURS/RSK. Various articles.

5040 Waffle. What the Waffle is all about: the condition-ing of women: women in the NDP. (?Toronto). 6pp, mimeo. *OOA/CCF446.

5041 Waffle Labor Committee of the NDP. Why is a house so expensive? Winnipeg. (c1970). (4pp), mimeo. *OOA/CCF446.

5042 Watson, Pat and others. '...strong and free...' '...nos foyers et nos droits...' A response to the War Measures act. Toronto: New Press. 41pp. *OTURS/RSK. Others include: Claude Parisée, Peter Desbarats, James Eayrs, George Bain, David MacDonald.

5043 Willis, Ellen. Consumerism and women. Toronto: Toronto Womens Liberation and Hogtown Press. (c1970). 5pp, mimeo. *OTURS/RSK.

5044 Wilson, Leroy John. Perren Baker and the United Farmers of Alberta - educational principles and pol-icies of an agrarian government. Unpublished MEd. thesis, University of Alberta. vii, 144pp, biblio. *AEUS.

5045 Womens Liberation Movement. Abortion is our right! Vancouver. (4pp). *SSA/G483.2.

Undated

5046 Canadian Association of Railway Enginemen. What the CARE have to offer to Canadian Engineers, Conductors and Trainmen. 20 reasons why you should join the CARE. (Winnipeg). (6pp). *OOA/Woodsworth 10.

5047 Canadian Congress of Labour. What is PAC. Toronto. 6pp. *OOA/CCF315. PAC is Political Action Committee.

5048 CCF. Constitutions and by-laws issued by the Ontario Association of CCF clubs. Toronto. 15pp. *OTURS/RSK.

(5049) Cottons Co-op Publishing Co. Songs of socialism. Hann 2390; OHMA. Not found.

(5050) Independent Labor Party. Labor songs. Hann 2394. OHMA not found.

5051 Lie, Haakon. Canada and the Canadian labour move-ment. *OOA/CCF154. 124pp ms with letter 'I under-stand this has been published in Norwegian and was largely made up with the help of the CCF...'

(5052) Stewart, Charles G. Social credit theories exploded. Winnipeg: c. 193- 23pp. Peel 3543. OH AEU not found.

5053 Textile Workers Union of Canada. What next in the textile mills of Ontario? Toronto. (4pp). *OHMA.

5054 Vancouver City Hall Employees Association. Constitution and by-laws. Vancouver. 15pp. *BVAA.

Annual reports

For convenience, and to avoid cluttering the main text, annual reports and reports of annual conventions or conferences that are available in reasonably long runs are listed below. Annual reports, or reports of conventions of relatively short-lived organizations (less than ten years) or those whose reports are very infrequent and irregular will be found listed under the appropriate year in the main bibliography. The listing is alphabetical, and *not* chronological.

5055 **Alberta Federation of Labor. Report of proceedings,** 1914 - 1952 (2nd to 32nd conventions). Conventions did not take place every year. Lacks 1st, 3rd, 5th, 11th, 13th, 15th-18th, 21st, 25th, 28th, 30th, 31st. *AEPAA/Farmilo 1, 2, 4 and 5.

5056 **All-Canadian** Congress of Labour. Report of proceedings, 1928 - 1940, lacking 1928, 1930-34. Microfilm *OOA. See also National Trades and Labor Congress of Canada (1903-08), Canadian Federation of Labour (1909-1927) and Canadian Congress of Labour.

5057 Canada, Dept of Agriculture. Co-operation in Canada. Annual summary 1931- . OOAG.

5058 Canada, Dept of Labour. Annual report of wage rates and hours of labour in Canada. No. 1, 1901-1920, no.2, 1921 then annually. OOL.

5059 ------ Annual report on labour organization. No.1, 1911 through 1970. OOL.

5060 ------ Labour Gazette. Vol. 1 no.1, September 1900 through 1970. OOL.

5061 ------ Review of trade disputes in Canada 1901-1915; *later* Review of industrial disputes in Canada 1916-1917; *later* Strikes and lockouts in Canada 1918-1946; *later* Strikes and lockouts in Canada with information for certain other countries 1947 through 1970. OOL.

5062 ------ Unemployment relief: reports of the Dominion director. No. 1, 1930 to 1940. OOL.

5063 Canadian Congress of Labour. Report of proceedings, 1st to 14th conventions, 1941-1954. Microfilm NSHD. 1st to 15th conventions, 1941-1955. OTU and OOP. There was no convention in 1945. The first convention of the CCL was also the 10th convention of the All-Canadian Congress of Labour.

5064 Canadian Federation of Labour. Report of proceedings 1909-1927, lacking 1918-20 and 1925-27. Microfilm OOA. The CFL was founded on 15th September 1902 as the National Trades and Labour Congress of Canada (q.v.) and at its 6th convention adopted the name of the Canadian Federation of Labour. In March 1927 it was absorbed into the All-Canadian Congress of Labour (q.v.).

5065 Canadian Labour Congress. Report of proceedings, 1956 to date. OONL. The CLC was founded in 1956 by a merger of the Canadian Congress of Labour and the Trades and Labor Congress of Canada (q.v.).

5066 Communist Party of Canada. There are very few records of full proceedings of the CPC. Usually there are records in the form of keynote speeches and the like which will be found under the appropriate year. The following early reports are known: Proceedings of the fourth, fifth and sixth national conventions, 1925, 1927 and 1929. All *OTURS/RSK.

5067 CCF (Cooperative Commonwealth Federation), national conventions. Virtually all national conventions had draft resolutions and sometimes emergency resolutions circulated in mimeo or as printed booklets prior to each convention. Minutes and full reports of the conventions are to be found in *OOA/CCF in the foll- owing boxes in chronological order of date of meeting: 10, 12, 13, 13, 13, 14, 15, 16, 18, 21, 21. These begin with 1934.

5068 CCF Alberta. (Note: More often than should be the case the provincial conventions of the CCF have been wrongly numbered, sometimes hopelessly so. Conseque- ntly they are listed by year in this entry and all those following). 1942 *ACGA/CCF12: 1947 *OOA/CCF316: 1951 *ACGA/CCF12 and OOA/CCF75: 1952 *OOA/CCF75: 1953 *ACGA/CCF12 and OOA/CCF75: 1954 *OOA/CCF19 and 536: 1954 *ACGA/CCF12: 1956 *ACGA/CCF12 and OOA/ CCF75: 1957 *OOA/CCF75: 1959 *ACGA/CCF12: 1960 *ACGA/CCF12: 1961 *ACGA/CCF12.

5069 CCF BC and Yukon. 1934, 1937, 1943 *OOA/CCF79: 1944 *OOA/CCF80: 1945, 1946, 1947, 1949, 1950, 1951 *OOA/ CCF318 with supplementary material in 80: 1952, 1953, *OOA/CCF80: 1954, 1955 *OOA/CCF317: 1956 *OOA/CCF80: 1957, 1958 *OOA/CCF81: 1959, 1960 *OOA/CCF317.

5070 CCF Manitoba. 1945, 1946, 1947, 1949 *OOA/CCF62 and MWPA/CCF3: 1955 *OOA/CCF62: 1956 *OOA/CCF20 and 536 and MWPA/CCF26: 1956 *OOA/CCF62: 1958, 1959 *OOA/CCF4.

5071 CCF New Brunswick. 1944 *OOACCF318.

5072 CCF Nova Scotia. 1939, 1942, 1944 *OOA/CCF28: 1946, 1947, 1952, 1953, 1954, 1955 *OOA/CCF319: 1958 *OOA/ CCF28.

5073 CCF Ontario. From 1950 Ontario conventions consist of programs (usually printed) and reports (usually

5073 mimeographed.)   The program prints all
     proposed resolutions, the report the authoritative
     text of those actually adopted. 1937-1959 inclusive
     *OTURS: 1936 *OOA/CCF10 and Coldwell 58.

5074 CCF Saskatchewan. Saskatchewan continued using the
     name CCF plus NDP long after the formation of the
     New Democratic Party. 1945, 1946, 1947 *OOA/CCF321:
     1952, 1953, 1954, 1955, 1956, 1957, 1958, 1959, 1960,
     1961, 1962, 1963, 1964, 1965, 1966, 1967, 1968, 1969
     all *SSA/G1 and G4.

5075 Cooperative Union of Canada. Annual report. 1942,
     1943, 1944, 1945, 1946, 1947 *OOA/CUC223: 1948 *OOA/
     CUC224.

5076 Fishermens Protective Union of Newfoundland. Journal
     of proceedings. 1909-1919 *OOL.

5077 Manitoba Grain Growers Association. Proceedings and
     resolutions. 1904, 1908, 1910, 1911, 1912, 1913,
     1914, 1915, 1916, 1917, 1918, 1919 *MWPA/UFM18.

5078 National Council of Women of Canada. Report of pro-
     ceedings. 1894-1898. Title changes to Verbatim re-
     port for 1899, then reverts to Report for 1900-1908,
     1910. Then Year book from 1919, 1920, 1923, 1929-
     1968 inclusive. All *OONL.

5079 National Trades and Labor Congress of Canada. 1900-
     1908 *OOA microfilm. Name changed to Canadian Fed-
     eration of Labor.

5080 New Democratic Party. Proceedings of the national
     party are being added to the collection in the CCF
     archive in OOA. Manitoba provincial conventions from
     1962 on are in *MWPA/CCF4 and 5.

5081 Ontario, Dept of Agriculture: Bureau of Industries.
     Volume of excerpts from annual reports 1884-1893
     with details of labour and wages, cost of living,
     labour organizations, strikes and lockouts. Toronto,
     1894. *OTAR.

5082 Ontario, Dept of Labour. Annual report 1920 to date.
     *OTAR

5083 Ontario Dept of Public Works: Bureau of Labour. Re-
     port for the year ending December 31st 1900 to 16th
     report, 1915. *OTAR.

5084 Ontario, Dept of Public Works: Trades and Labour
     Branch. Report of the Trades and Labour Branch incl-
     uding the 29th annual report of the Factory Inspection
     Branch, 1916 to 1919. *OTAR.

(5085) Patrons of Husbandry. Proceedings of the annual
     meeting, Dominion Grange. 1909, 1918, 1920, 1921
     and 1923. Sometime in OTV, now withdrawn. Not found.

5086 Saskatchewan, Dept of Agriculture. Annual report of
     the Bureau of Labour 1911-1920: continued as Annual
     report of the Bureau of Labour and Industries 1921-
     1928: Continued as Annual report of the Dept of Rail-

ways, Labour and Industries 1929-1934: continued as
Annual report of the Bureau of Labour and Public Wel-
fare 1935-1943: continued as Annual report of the
Dept of Labour 1944 to date. SSA

5087 Saskatchewan Federation of Labour. Proceedings and
minutes of the first annual (merger) convention,
1956 and for 1957-1968. *SSA/G114.24.

5088 Sasktchewan Grain Growers Association. Annual con-
ention reports for 1908, 1909, 1913, 1914, 1926
*SSA/G34.3 and for 1920 *SRU.

5089 Trades and Labor Congress of Canada. (1883-1956).
1890 OKQ; 1891 and 1894 QMBM (in French); 1897 OTAR;
1899 OTAR; 1905, 1906 OHMA; 1907 *MWPA/Russell 1;
1909-1925 OOL microfilm; 1926 *OOA/Woodsworth 10;
1928-1946 lacking some issues BVAU; 1929-1946, 1948,
1950, 1951 OHMA. See also Wismer, 3593a above.

5090 United Farmers of Canada (Saskatchewan section).
The first annual convention...1927 and 1928 to 1949
(two conventions in 1932). *SSA/G37.1. See also
5088 above.

5091 United Farmers of Manitoba. Year book 1920-1926,
*MWPA/UFM18. Minutes of annual convention 1927-
1939 (mimeo), *MWPA/UFM 19. See also 5077 above.

Checklist of serials 1870–1970

I am under no illusions about this section of the bibliography and cannot flatter myself that it is in any way
complete, although it is as complete and accurate as I
could make it within the time I had available to work on
it, and is, I think, more comprehensive than previous
lists. To do it full justice, however, would require
many more months of work and it seemed better to publish
such information as I have accumulated and let time and
other expertise add to it.

I have made use of the *Union list of Canadian newspapers
held by Canadian libraries* and the *Checklist of Canadian ethnic
serials* both published by the National Library of Canada
in 1977 and 1981 respectively. If I had had access to
the latter work earlier in my research then I would have
tried to follow its full format entry which seems to me
the most comprehensive I have found. As it is I follow
its format as much as possible (see below).

In addition I have made use of Elliott, Hann, McLaren
and Woodsworth (see the list of bibliographies consulted)
and I have given cross references to the numbers used by
them. I have not given cross references to the two National Library publications as their entries are not numbered and there should be no difficulty in locating titles
in their very thorough indexes.

This list, like the main bibliography, is chronological and alphabetical within each year. Each entry uses
the following format as far as possible:
1. Name of newspaper or serial. 2. Dates of publication
known or (estimated). 3. Place(s) of publication. 4.
Publisher. 5. Sponsor. 6. Editor(s). 7. Frequency of
publication. 8. Preceded and/or followed by. 9. Issues
known and their location.

With regard to titles that are not in Roman lettering
(eg Cyrillic), a transliteration is given which is the
same as any given on the original publication, together
with any translation, even if the transliteration is not
according to contemporary standards or the translation is
not wholly accurate. If these are not given then the title
is transliterated using the Library of Congress system and
a translation provided. In the case of titles provided by
the publication these are separated by a slash /. If I
have provided them they are within brackets ( ).

Where the place of publication varies the places are
separated by a slash / and cited in chronological order.

Where the publisher is merely the title in company
form (eg. The Daily Times published by the Daily Times
Publishing Co.), this has been ignored.

Sponsorship means any work described as an 'offical organ' or 'endorsed by'. Any appropriate quotation or slogan from early issues of the work is also quoted here. Any known but incited affiliation is in brackets.

Editors names are given when known, in chronological order if more than one is known.

The following abbreviations have been used for frequency of publication, taken from the *Checklist of Canadian Ethnic Serials*: ⊘ irregular; d daily; c twice a week; i three times a week; w weekly; e every two weeks; s twice a month; m monthly; b every two months; q quarterly; t three times a year; f twice a year; u unknown or unchecked. A double slash // means all published.

Details of titles preceding or following the serial being consulted will be found in their proper place in the chronology. This is the case with any changes of name unless they are trivial or vary haphazardly between one version and another, even though numbering may continue with the new title. Parts of titles in brackets indicate that the letter, word or words so enclosed were dropped or included at various times.

The same system and location symbols are used as in the main bibliography.

1871

5092 Le Métis. 1871-1881. St Boniface: 'Le journal est destiné à défendre la bonne cause...' Comité de redaction. w. Later Le Manitoba. Numero prospectus 27 mai 1871: vol.I no.2, 8 juin 1871 to vol.XI no. 17, 29 mai 1881// *MWP microfilm.

1872

5093 (The) Ontario Workman. 1872-1875? Toronto: Williams, Sleeth and Macmillan. 'The equalization of all elements of society in the social scale should be the aim of civilization.' Toronto Trades Assembly and Canadian Labor Union. w. Vol.I no.1, 18 April 1872 to vol.I no.52, 10 April 1873 *OOL microfilm. April 1872 to vol.II no.52, whole no. 104, 9 April 1874 *OTAR, microfilm, incomplete. Elliott 2 Hann 1721.

(5094) Standard. 1872. Hamilton: official paper of the nine-hour movement. Hann 1663, not found.

(5095) Western Workman. 1872. London. Hann 1672, not found.

1873–1875 no entries

1876

5096 Canadian Granger. 1876-? London. Devoted to the interests of the Patrons of Husbandry: in essentials, Unity; in non-essentials, Liberty; in all else Charity. m. Vol.II no.5, March 1877. *OONL. Hann 1668.

1877

5097 Secular Thought. 1877-? Toronto: C.M. Ellis. A journal of liberal opinion and progress. J. Spencer Ellis. w. Vol.XX no.15, 17 Oct 1896 to vol.XXV no. 14, 15 Apr 1899 *OONL, scattered issues only. Hann 1727. The issue of 25 March 1899 banned from the mails because of an 'Easter hymn' said to be a blasphemous libel.

1878 no entry

1879

5098 Canadian Workman. 1879-1930? Orillia: John Curran. Official organ of the A.O.U.W. (ie. Ancient Order of United Workmen) in Canada. John Curran. m. Vol.VII no.2, whole no. 74, June 1886 and 27th year no.317, Oct 1905 only *OTAR. Hann 1674. Essentially the organ of a fraternal lodge society.

1880

5099 The Commonwealth. 1880-? Toronto. Speak thy thought if thou believ'st it: in favour of an eight-hour day. A.W. Wright and J.R. Cameron. w. Vol.1 no.2 29 July 1880, no.3, 5 Aug and no.6 26 Aug *OTAR. Hann 1703.

5100 The Trades Journal. 1880-1891. Spring Hill, NS: R. Drummond. Devoted to the interests of the mine, the workshop, the farm. w. Later The Journal. Vol 1, no.5, 4 Feb 1880 to vol.XII no.1, 7 Jan 1891// *OOL microfilm. Elliott 3 Hann 1635.

1881

5101 The Canadian Co-operator and Patron. 1881-? Owen Sound, Ont. Devoted to the interests of the Patrons

of Husbandry. R.J. Doyle. m. Vol.V no.58, July
1886 only *OTAR. Hann 1682.

5102 Le Manitoba. 1881-1926. St Boniface. Chacun le
sien: justice pour tous. w. Formerly Le Métis.
Numbering continues vol.XI no.1, 13 oct 1881 to vol.
LIV no.36 (wrongly numbered 33), 29 juillet 1925
*MWPL microfilm.

1882

5103 Grange Bulletin. 1882-? Owen Sound, Ont. Devoted
to the interest of the Patrons of Husbandry. R.J.
Doyle. m. Vol.1, no.8, April 1882 *OTAR. Hann
1683. Issued concurrently with 5101 above.

5104 Trades Union Advocate. 1882-1883. Toronto: Eugene
Donovan. Published in the interests of trade unionists: non-sectarian, non-political. w. Later The
Wage Worker. Vol.1 no.4, May 1882 to no.45, 8 March
1883// *OOA/TUA. Hann 1734.

1883

5105 The Labor Union. 1883. Hamilton: W.H. Rowe. w.
Later The Palladium of Labor. Vol.1 no.1, 13 Jan
1883 to no.11 24 March. *OOL microfilm. Issues 12
to 30 missing in OOL. Sometime in that period name
became Palladium. Elliott 4 Hann 1659.

5106 L'Ouvrier. 1883-1884. Montréal. Faire du bien aux
classes ouvrières; gratis tous les samedis soirs aux
acheteurs de l'Etendard. Rédacteur en chef 'Papa-Noé'
rédigé par un Comité d'Ouvriers. Numero prospectus
vol.1 no.1 29 nov 1893 *OONL to août 1884 QQS. Papa-
Noé - le premier ouvrier et le premier entrepreneur
dont nous parle l'histoire.

5107 The Palladium of Labor. 1883-1886. Hamilton: Rowe
and Taylor. Devoted to the interests of workingmen
and workingwomen. (W.H. Rowe). w. Formerly The
Labor Union. Numbering continues: no.31, 11 Aug 1883
to fourth year no.43, 18 Dec 1886//? *OOL microfilm.
Elliott 5 Hann 1722.

5108 The Wage Worker. 1883. Toronto: Eugene Donovan.
Published in the interests of labour. w. Formerly
Trades Union Advocate. Numbering continues: vol.1
no.46, 15 March 1883 to no.52 26 April 1883// Publisher retired. Hann 1741.

1884 no entry

1885

(5109)The Industrial News. Victoria. 26 Dec 1885 to 11 Dec 1886. BVIP, not seen. Hann 1808. Possibly not a labour paper.

1886

(5110)Canadian Labour Courier. 1886-1887. St Thomas, Ont. 30 Dec 1886, 13 Jan and 10 Feb 1887. Elgin County Library, St Thomas. Not seen. Hann 1685.

5111 Canadian Labor Reformer. 1886-1892. Toronto: Labor Publishing Assn. We demand all the reform that justice can ask for, and all the justice that reform can give: (Knights of Labor). w. Vol.1 no.1, 15 May 1886 to no.52, 7 May 1887. *OTAR microfilm. Hann 1696. Possibly superseded by The Labor Advocate which has the same slogan.

5112 The Evening Palladium. 1886. Hamilton: W.H. Rowe. d. Vol.1 no.1, 13 Dec 1886 and no.7, 20 Dec//? *OOL microfilm. Hann 1657.

(5113)Labor Record. 1886-1887. Toronto. w. Hann 1712, not found.

(5114)Union Ouvrière. 1886. Montréal. Chevaliers du travail. Not found.

1887

(5115)Le Travailleur Illustré. 1887-? Montréal. Not found.

1888

5116 L'Ouvrier. 1888. Québec: Antoine Langlois. Publié dans l'intérêt de la classe ouvrière. w. 1re année no.1, 20 oct 1888 *OONL à 24 nov 1888 OOU QQL QQS. Une publication qui vise sincèrement à la défense de leurs (les ouvriers) intérêts at à la suppression des abus dont l'ouvrier et très-souvent la victime.

5117 The Voice of the People. 1888-? Prince Albert, Sask. u. Vol.1 no.2, 17 March 1888. *SSA/G93.6.

1889

(5118)Single Tax Advocate. ?1889-? New Westminster, B.C.
December 1889, New Westminster Public Library. Hann
1772, not seen.

5119 The Social Reformer. 1889-? Toronto: Toronto Single
Tax Assn. m. Vol.1 no.1, Nov 1889, vol.II nos. 4,
5, 6, Apr-June 1892 *OTURS.   Hann 1730.

5120 The Voice of the People. 1889-? Kingston: W. Kelly.
Official organ of the People's Political Party. u.
Vol.1 no.1 December 1889 *OONL.

1890

5121aThe Echo. 1890-1898? Montreal: Montreal Typographical Union no.176 in the interest of organized labor.
w. Vol.1 no.2, 31 May 1890 (part only) to no.7, 25
June 1890 and Special Labor edn. 1 Sept 1890// *OONL
Started during the Herald lockout and followed by

5121bThe Echo. Montreal. A journal for the progressive
workman and family newspaper, endorsed by the Dominion Trades and Labor Congress and Central Trades and
Labor Council of Montreal. Vol.1 no.1, 4 Oct 1890
to no.52, 26 Sept 1891 *OONL

5122 The Labor Advocate. 1890-1891. Toronto: Grip Printing. Endorsed by Toronto Trades and Labor Council
and the Knights of Labor. Phillips Thompson. w.
Vol.1 no.1, 5 Dec 1890 to no.44, 2 Oct 1891// *OOL
microfilm. Elliott 6 Hann 1708.

(5123)The Signal and Workmans Advocate. c1890. Truro, N.S.
1890 NSHP. Hann 1645, not seen.

1891

5124 The Journal. 1891. Stellarton, N.S: R. Drummond.
w. Formerly The Trades Journal, later Journal and
Pictou News. Numbering continued: vol.XII no.2, 14
Jan 1891 to no.16, 22 Apr 1891 *OOL microfilm; actually to no.22, May 1891.

5125 The Journal and Pictou News. 1891. Stellarton, NS:
R. Drummond. w. Formerly The Journal. Numbering
continued: vol.XII no.23, 3 June 1891 to vol.XII no.
49, 2 Dec 1891 *OOL microfilm.

5126 The Social Reformer. 1891-? Toronto. Advocates
the rights of humanity. J.L. Dawkins. Vol.1 no.1
Jan 1891 *OTPB. See also 5119 above.

5127 The Vancouver Typographer. 1891-? Vancouver: Union
Printers of Vancouver. u. Vol.1 no.1, 11 Aug 1891
*BVAA. Issued as a souvenir for Labor Day - ? all
published.

1892

5128 The Canada Farmers Sun. 1892-1896. London/Toronto.
Official organ of the Patrons of Industry. George
Wrigley. w. Later Weekly Sun. Vol.1 no.2, 10 May
1892 to 29 July 1896//*OTAR microfilm. Hann 1705.
Published in London until 1894.

5129 The Industrial Banner. 1892-1922. London/Toronto:
Trades and Labor Council. For the right against the
wrong; for the weak against the strong: owned and
controlled by organized labor. Joseph T. Marks/James
Simpson. m. Vol.V no.3, Jan 1897 to vol.XXX no.5
24 Feb 1922 *OOL microfilm, incomplete //? Elliott
7 Hann 1670. 1903 published by the Labor Educational
Assn of Western Ontario; 1904 by the Labor Educational
Assn of Canada; 1905 by the Labor Educational Assn of
Ontario; 1912 moved to Toronto, endorsed by Ontario
Labor Educational Assn and Toronto Trades and Labor
Council.

(5130) The Workman. c1892. St John, N.B: St John Typographical Union. 1892 NBSM. Hann 1613, not seen.

1893

5131 The Free Lance. (1893)-? Ottawa: A labor paper in
the true sense of the term: endorsed by Ottawa Trades
and Labor Council, Knights of Labor and Federal Council of Building Trades. u. Vol.1 no.1, 13 Oct (1893)
vol. 4 no.11, 15 Dec (?1896) *OOL, three issues only.

1894

5132 The Peoples Voice. 1894-1897. Winnipeg: Winnipeg
Trades and Labor Council, in the interests of the
working classes. C.C. Steuart. w. Later The Voice.
Vol.1 no.1, 16 June 1894 to vol.3 no.44, 1 May 1897//
*MWPL microfilm. Elliott 8 Hann 1817.

5133 The Winnipeg Typographer. 1894-? Winnipeg: Winnipeg
Typographical Union 191. u. (1) 3 Sept 1894 *MWPA/
Russell 2. Printed for the first legal Labor day
celebration in Canada, ? all pub. Contains a history
of the union.

1895 no entry

1896

5134 The Weekly Sun. 1896-1919. Toronto. The Patrons
of Industry. w. Formerly the Canada Farmers Sun;
later The Farmers Sun. 5 Aug 1896 to 26 Mar 1919//
*OTAR microfilm. Hann 1705.

1897

5135 The Voice. 1897-1918. Winnipeg. w. Formerly The
Peoples Voice, later The Western Labor News. Vol.
III no.47 (misnumbered, should be 45) 8 May 1897 to
vol.XXVI no.6, 26 July 1918// *OOL microfilm.

1898

5136 Citizen and Country. 1898-1902? Toronto: Social
Progress Ltd. A journal of social, moral (later
omitted) and economic reform: direct legislation is
the common denominator for all fractional reforms:
official organ of the Toronto Trades and Labor Council. G. Weston Wrigley. w. Later The Canadian
Socialist. Vol.1 no.9, 28 July 1898 only *OTAR: vol.
II no.17, whole no.44, 11 March 1899 to vol. III no.
30, whole no. 130, 7 Dec 1900 BVAU microfilm, *OTAR.
Hann 1702. From 15 June 1900 becomes 'the leading
exponent of trades unionism and socialism in Canada'.
Slogan changes to 'For the masses and against social
conditions that perpetuate the classes.' George
Wrigley was former editor of the Canada Labor Courier,
The Farmers Sun and The Templar, and later became
editor of other labour and socialist papers in the
west.

1899

5137 British Columbia Workman. 1899-? Victoria. u.
Vol.1 no.1 20 May 1899 to 2 Sept 1899// BVIP, not
seen. Hann 1807.

1900

(5138) Le Bulletin du Travail. 1900-1903? Québec: Congrès
National des Métiers et du Travail. u. Vol.1 no.1
1900 to (1903) QQA, not seen.

5139 The Independent. 1900-1904? Vancouver. Published
in the interests of the masses. w. Vol.1 no.1 31
March 1900 *OOL: vol.5 no.2, 5 April 1902 to vol.9
no.21, 22 Aug 1904 *OOL microfilm. Elliott 12 Hann
1790. Probably ceased publication from 7 Nov 1903
(4th year whole number 184, should be 185) to 9 July
1904. Issue of 9 July states 'resuming publication'.
Sometime before July 1904 endorsed by the Trades and
Labor Councils of Vancouver and Victoria. Various
issues are misnumbered.

5140 The Labour Gazette. 1900- . Ottawa: Dept of Labour.
W.L. Mackenzie King. m. Vol.1 no.1 September 1900.
Elliott 10. Phillips Thompson was an early labour
correspondent for Toronto.

5141 The Toiler. 1900-1905? Toronto: Trades and Labor
Council. w. Later The Tribune. Vol.II no.14, 14
April 1902 to vol.IV no.52, 9 Dec 1904 *OOL micro-
film. Elliott 9 Hann 1732.

1901

5142 Aika. 1901-1904. Nanaimo BC/Sointula BC. Ed: Matti
Kurikka. w/s. No. 16,23 August 1901 to no.73, 3 Oct
1902 (format changes and numbering recommences) no.1,
1 Nov 1903 to no.14, 1 June 1904. *OOA microfilm.
Book sales offer Finnish translations of Kautsky,
Morris, Sombart etc.

1902

5143 The Canadian Socialist. 1902-1903. Vancouver: Social
Progress Co, endorsed by the American Labor Union.
George Wrigley. w. Formerly Citizen and Country,
later Western Socialist. No. 214 (5th year) 16 Aug
1902 *OOA/CCF184 only. Hann 1786. Later incorporated
with Social Justice (Dec 1902) see 5745 below.

(5144)Labour Review. 1902-? Windsor: Windsor District
Trades and Labor Council. Annual. 1902-1948?
Elliott 11, not found.

5145 Social Justice. 1902. Toronto: Social Progress Co.
Justice for the underdog in the economic struggle
and eventually an equality of opportunity by the removal of all special privileges and franchises. m.
George Wrigley. Vol.1 no.1 Dec 1902 *OONL. Hann
1729. First issue contains Ontario Socialist platform.

1903

5146 The Bond of Brotherhood. 1903-1904? Calgary: James
Worsley and Alfred Palmer: devoted to the organization
and education of the worker: endorsed by Calgary
Trades and Labor Council. w. (Vol.1) no.1, 30 May
1903 to no.55, 18 June 1904 *OOL microfilm. Elliott
13 Hann 1750.

5147 Western Clarion. 1903-1925. Vancouver. Official
organ of the Socialist Party of Canada. i/s. Formerly Western Socialist, numbering continues.
253, 12 May 1903 to 938 July-Aug 1925//*OOL microfilm. Elliott 14 Hann 1803. Banned 8 Oct 1918:
The Red Flag and Indicator (qv) published instead.
Resumed publication 10 Jan 1920.

5148 Western Socialist. 1903. Vancouver. Ed: Geo. Dales,
manager R.P. Pettipiece. w. Formerly Canadian Socialist, later Western Clarion. Numbering continues:
no. 250, 1 May 1903 *OOL, three issues only. Hann
1804.

1904

(5149)Progress. 1904. Victoria: W.E. Peirce. w. Later
The Week. No.1, 16 Apr 1904 to 17 Dec 1904 BVIPA
microfilm, not seen.

(5150)The Week. 1904-1920. Victoria: W.E. Peirce in the
interests of good government, temperance, single tax
and sane socialism. w. Formerly Progress. Dec 1904
to 8 May 1920 BVIPA microfilm, not seen. Hann 1811.

1905

5151 The Clarion. 1905-? Winnipeg: Typographical Union
191: for the 8-hour day. u. Vol.1 no.1, 4 Nov 1905
? all published. *MWPA/Russell 2.

5152 The Tribune. 1905-1906. Toronto: Toronto District
Labor Council. (Fred Perry). w. Formerly The Toiler.
Vol.1 no.1, 9 Sept 1905 to no.52, 1 Sept 1906 *OOL
microfilm. Elliott 15 Hann 1735.

1906

5153 The (BC) Trades Unionist. 1906-1909. Vancouver:

Vancouver Trades and Labor Council. Editorial Committee, chairman R.P. Pettipiece. m. Later Western Wage Earner. Vol.III no.1, January 1908 to vol.III no.12 (should be vol.IV no.1) Jan 1909//*OOL microfilm. Elliott 16 Hann1783. Oct 1908 misnumbered 9, should be 10.

(5154) Provincial Workman. ?1906-1911? Glace Bay. Hann 1620, not found.

1907

5155 Чероний Прапор /Chervoniy (Chervonyi) Prapor (The Red Banner). 1907-1908. Winnipeg: Socialist Party of Canada. Myroslav Stechyshyn. ∅. Later Robochyi Narod. No. 1 (15) Nov 1907 to 8 Aug 1908// OONL *MWPL microfilm. Hann 1928. Described as the first Socialist paper in North America.

(5156) The Review and Labour News. 1907? Fairville, NB. 21 Sept 1907 NBFU. Hann 1601, not seen.

5157 Saskatchewan Labor's Realm. 1907-1908? Regina: endorsed by the Regina Trades and Labor Council: for labor and social reform. Hugh Peat. w/e/m. Later Labors Realm. Vol.1 no.1, 31 May 1907 to 52, 31 July 1908 *OOL microfilm. Elliott 17 Hann 1829.

5158 Svenska Canada-Tidningen/The Swedish Canada News. 1907-1932. Winnipeg: Canada Weekly Printing Co. Nils F:(Felson) Brown. w. June 1907 to Dec 1932 *MWPL microfilm; issues 1917-1919, incomplete *OOA/ Censor 577, 578. The editor, Brown, seems to have been responsible for the 'socialist character' that the censor found objectionable and he was discharged.

5159 Työkansa/The Workpeople. 1907-1915. Port Arthur: Finnish Publishing Co: published in the interests of working people. w/d after 1912. 1910-1915 *OOA scattered issues; 1913-1914 *OTAR, 4 issues only. Elliott 90 Hann 1856.

1908

(5160) L'Action Ouvrière. 1908-1918? Montréal. m. Jan 1914 à oct 1918 QQLA, incomplete.

5161 The Brantford Co-operative News. 1908-1909? Brantford, Ont: Brantford Co-operative Assn. (m). Vol. 1 no.1-3, April 1908 to vol.2 no.1, April 1909 *OOA/ CUC221.

5162 Cotton's Weekly. 1908-1914? Cowansville, Qué: William Ulric Cotton. Editor: W.U. Cotton. w/e.

Formerly The Observer, later The Canadian Forward.
Numbering continued: vol.XXXVIII no.9, 12 Nov 1908
to no.313 (should be 314) 29 Oct 1914//? BVAU OONL
OTMCL OTU, all incomplete *OOL. Elliott 19. The
Observer is not listed here since by Cotton's own
account the paper did not begin to be Socialist until
December 1908. From 28 Oct 1909 volume numbers were
abandoned and continuous numbering started with no.
60, 4 Nov 1909. In October 1914 Cotton turned over
his stock to the Social Democratic Party and reported
that the Weekly 'will likely be moved to Ontario'.

5163 The Lance. 1908-1915. Toronto: Hambly Bros. Published in the interests of working men and women.
w. Vol.II no.54, 22 May 1909 to vol.VII no.358, 27
March 1915//? BVAU *OOL. Elliott 18 Hann 1713.

1909

5164 The Canadian Co-operator. 1909-1947? Brantford:
Co-operative Union of Canada. m. Vols 1-38, 1909
to 1947 OTU, microfilm. Vol.1 no.1, Oct 1909*SSU /
Coops. AEU OLU OOL miscellaneous issues. Elliott
23 Hann 1650.

5165 The Co-operator. 1909-? Hamilton: Canadian Co-operative Concern Ltd. (w). Unnumbered and undated
issues: (no.1?), c. April 1909 *OOA/CUC221, 4 issues
only.

5166 Eastern Labour News. 1909-1913. Moncton: (Percy D.
Ayer). J.C. Merrill. w. Vol.1 no.1, 6 Feb 1909
to vol.V no.42, 15 Nov 1913//BVAU NSHD SRU *OOL microfilm. Elliott 21 Hann 1604.

5167 Labor's Realm. 1909-1910? Regina: Regina Trades
and Labor Council. Hugh Peat. m. Formerly Saskatchewan Labour's Realm. Vol.1 no.1, 1 May 1909 to
no. 12, 1 April 1910//? *OOL microfilm. Hann 1829.

5168 Робочий Народ /Robotchyj(Robochyi) Narod/The Working
People. 1909-1918. Winnipeg: official organ of the
Ukrainian Socialist (Social Democratic) Federation.
Ъ. Vol.IV no.19, 15 May 1912 to 28 Sept 1918//.
*OONL. Incomplete: some missing issues for 1918 in
*OOA/Censor 516. Hann 1964. Microfilm of issues
1909-June 1914 from the Library of Ukrainian Academy
of Sciences, Lvov. Proscribed in 1918. M. Cheritoff,
editor in 1918 was raided, charged and convicted
shortly after the ban. He described himself as 'Amb-
assador of the Bolshevik government in western Canada'
but was apparently backed financially by a local
druggist, Mr Shane. Other editors included Matthew
Popovich and D. Moysiuk.

5169 The Western Wage-Earner. 1909-1911. Vancouver: Vancouver Trades and Labor Council. Jas. H. McVety.

Formerly The (BC) Trades Unionist. Vol.1 no.1, Feb 1909 to vol.II no.12, Jan 1911 *OOL microfilm. Possibly to May 1911. Elliott 20 Hann 1805.

1910

(5170) Portland Coal Miner. 1910-1914? Stewart, B.C. 5 Feb 1910 to Sept 1911 BVIPA, microfilm, not seen. Hann 1778.

1911

5171 The British Columbia Federationist. 1911-1925. Vancouver: Vancouver Trades and Labor Council. R. Parmater Pettipiece. s/w. Formerly The Western Wage Earner, later Canadian Labor Advocate. Numbering continued: 4th year no.47, 18 Nov 1911 to 17th year no.23, 5 June 1925// *OOL microfilm, lacking some issues. Elliott 25 Hann 1779. The sponsorship of the Federated Labor Party of BC was later substituted for that of the Trades and Labor Council. From 2 June 1922 amalgamted with the BC Labor News.

5172 Canadian Labor Party Bulletin. 1911. Toronto. Devoted to the formation and development of a representative labor party in Canada. Ed. Stephenson; assoc. eds. A.W. Puttee and P.D. Ayer. m. Vol.1 no.1, 3 April 1911//? *OTPB. Hann 1694. First issue reports the 2nd meeting of the reorganized Labor Party of Toronto, 2 Apr 1911.

5173 Lunn's Weekly. 1911-1912. Truro, NS: C.W. Lunn, also editor. w. Later Canadian Labor Leader. Vol.1 no.42 12 Oct 1912//*OOL. Hann 1643. After issue 42 title transferred to Canada Labour Publishing Co. Scattered issues apparently in NSHP, not seen.

(5174) Trades Unionist. 1911-? Fort William: Temple Press: devoted to the labor interest in the Twin Cities. w. 25 Aug 1911. Elliott 24 Hann 1653. Not found.

1912

5175 (The) Canadian Labor Leader. 1912-1918. Truro/Sydney N.S. Devoted to the promotion and welfare of organized labor. William G. Newald. w/e. Formerly Lunn's Weekly, later The Labor Leader. Vol.1 no.1, 26 Oct 1912 to no.53 2 Nov 1918//*OOL microfilm. Lacks issues 6-11, Dec-Jan 1912-13. Elliott 26 Hann 1638. Not published from Jan 1913 to Dec 1917.

5176 Direct Legislation Bulletin. 1912-? Winnipeg. (m).
Unnumbered: 30 April 1912 and 31 May 1912 *OTURS all
found.

5177 IWW Strike Bulletin. 1912. Prince Rupert: GTP-Con-
struction Strikers. w. Nos. 5-9 and 11-13, Sept-
Nov 1912. *OOL. Hann 1773.

5178 The Labo(u)r News. 1912-1955. Hamilton. Devoted to
the presentation of current trade union news. Samuel
L. Landress. w/m. Vol.1 no.1, 5 Jan 1912 to Dec
1955//*OOL microfilm. Elliott 22 Hann 1658. Dec
1955 described as being 'fiftieth year' although Aug
1955 says 'forty-eighth year' - in fact should be the
44th year.

1913

(5179) BC Stationary Engineer. 1913-1919. Vancouver: BC
Assn of Stationary Engineers. m. 1913-1919. Elliott
27 Hann 1782, not found.

5180 Bulletin. 1913-1924. Winnipeg: District Lodge 2,
International Assn of Machinists, Specialists and
Helpers. R.B. Russell. m. Later Machinists Bulletin.
Vol.I no.11, July 1913 to vol.VIII no.69, April 1924
*OOL microfilm, incomplete. Elliott 31 Hann 1814.

(5181) Official Journal. 1913-1929. Montreal: Official
organ of the National Assn of Marine Engineers. 1913-
1929. Elliott 28, not found.

(5182) Powerhouse. 1913-? Toronto: Official organ of the
Canadian Assn of Stationary Engineers. m. 1913.
Elliott 30 Hann 1726. Not found.

(5183) Retail Employee. 1913-1916. Vancouver: Official
organ of the Retail Employees Organization of BC.
m. 1913-1916. Elliott 29 Hann 1800. Not found.

5184 The Single Taxer and Direct Legislation Bulletin.
1913-1921? Winnipeg: Single Tax League of Manitoba
and the Direct Legislation League of Manitoba: a
journal of democracy. D.W. Buchanan. m. Vol.III
no.1, June 1915 to vol.IX no.4, Sept 1921 *MWPL,
lacking vol.7 no.1. Hann 1818.

5185 The Square Deal. 1913-1931? Toronto. A journal of
democracy: we claim the earth as the property of the
whole people. Alan C. Thompson and Ernest J. Farmer.
m. Vol.XXVIII no. 242, March 1931 only *OTAR. Scattered issues NBFU. Hann 1731.

1914

(5186) Canadian Plate Printer. 1914-1932. Ottawa: International Steel and Copper Plate Printers Union Local 6. w. Oct 1914-1932// Elliott 34 Hann 1676, not found.

(5187) Quarterly Review. 1914-? Halifax: Official organ of the Canadian Brotherhood of Railway Employees. q. 1914-. Elliott 37, not found.

1915

(5188) Barber. 1915-1917. Toronto: Ontario Journeyman Barbers Assn. m. Feb 1915-1917// Elliott 35 Hann 1687, not found.

5189 Canadian Railroad Employees Monthly. 1915-1929. Halifax/Ottawa: Canadian Brotherhood of Railroad Employees. A.R. Mosher. m. Later Canadian Railway Employees Monthly. Vol.1 no.1, March 1915 to vol. XV no.10, Dec 1929//*OOL. From March 1919 published in Ottawa. Elliott 32 Hann 1624.

(5190) Co-operative News. ?1915-1920? Halifax. u. Hann 1628, not found.

5191 The District Ledger. 1918-1919? Fernie: United Mineworkers of America District 18. w. Vol.1 no.1, 8 Aug 1918 to vol.2 no.2, 8 Aug 1919//? *OOL microfilm. Elliott 42. Note in no.1 'The District Ledger suspended publication on 25 July 1915' - earlier issues not found.

(5192) Free Press. 1915. Brantford: Official organ of the Brantford Trades and Labor Council. Elliott 38 Hann 1652, not found.

(5193) S'vidoma Syla/(Conscious Strength). 1915-1916. Toronto: Ukrainian Social Democratic Party. Ivan Stefanicky. Later Robitnyche Slovo. e/m. 1915-1916. Hann 1883 McLaren 478, not found.

1916

5194 The Canadian Forward. 1916-1918. Toronto: Social. Democratic Party: In the spirit of the proletariat the revolution must first arise. (Isaac Bainbridge). e. Formerly Cotton's Weekly, later The Social Democrat. Vol.1 no.1 new series, 28 Oct 1916 to vol.2 no.18, 24 Sept 1918//suppressed. *OOL microfilm. Elliott 33.

5195 Framåt/(Forward). 1916-? Port Arthur:(Oscar Johnson) m. Vol.2 no.9, Sept 1917 only *OOA/Censor 578. Pro-temperance, anti-conscription. Hann 1854.

5196 The Nutcracker. 1916-1917. Calgary. Ed. Wm.Irvine.
e. Later The Alberta Non-Partisan. Vol.1 no.1, 17
Nov 1916 to no.22, 14 Sept 1917//*ACGL. No. 9 misnumbered 8.

5197 Робітниче Слово /Robitnyche Slovo/The Workers Word.
1916-1918. Toronto: Workers Publishing Assn. J. Ste-
fanitsky (otherwise Ivan Stefanicky). w. Formerly
S'vidoma Syla. 6 Jan. 1917 to 8 June 1918 *OONL,
incomplete. Hann 1880 McLaren 472

1917

5198 The Alberta Non-Partisan. 1917-1919. Calgary. For
the creation of independent thought and action. Wm.
Irvine. e. Formerly The Nutcracker, later The Western Independent. Numbering continued: no.24, 12 Oct
1917 to vol.III no.16, 7 Aug 1919//*ACGL. Hann 1749.

(5199)Arbeyter Tsaytung/(Workers Paper). 1917. Toronto.
Ed. S. Elshtein. b. Hann 1862 McLaren 335, not
found.

5200 Canadian Railroader. 1917-1929. Toronto: Fifth
Sunday Meeting Assn of Canada. q. Vol.I no.1 (Dec)
1917 to vol.XIII, 1929//*OOL. Elliott 54 Hann 1698.
Not to be confused with a travel magazine of the
same name.

5201 The Critic. 1917-1918? Vancouver. Free-lance.
Louis D. Taylor. u. Vol.I no.1, 11 Aug 1917 to
vol.II no.4, 31 Aug 1918 *OOA/Censor608, scattered
issues only. Hann 1788. E.T. Kingsley and F.C.
Wade were contributors.

5202 The Labor News. 1917. Winnipeg: Labor Campaign
Committee. u. Vol.I no.4, 13 Dec 1917 only *MWPA/
Dixon 2. Probably issued only during elections.

5203 The Messenger. ?1917-? Vancouver/Victoria: Social
Democratic Party of Canada, BC Executive. (Phil. R.
Smith). u. Unnumbered: July 1917 and Dec 1917 *OOA/
Censor605. Hann 1794.

5204 The Nonpartisan Leader of Canada. ?1917-? Ed: Sidney
Godwin. w. No.50, 19 Sept 1917 only *OOA/Censor609.

5205 Trade Report of the Ontario Provincial Council United
Brotherhood of Carpenters and Joiners of America.
1917-1924. (Toronto). m. Later Carpenters Monthly
Bulletin. Unnumbered: Sept 1917 (first issue) to
July 1924//*OOL microfilm. Elliott 71 Hann 1733.

5206 Vapaus/(Liberty). 1917-1974. Sudbury. The only
organ of Finnish workers in Canada. Mostly c.
Vol.I no.1, 6 Nov 1917 and nos. 2, 12, 13: vol.II
nos.2, 15, 32, 69, 70 to 75 *OOA/Censor568. Issue
of 4 Oct 1918 destroyed except for two bundles sent

to Port Arthur consequent to an order in council ban-
ning publications in enemy languages. Suspended until
April 1919. Then issues 1921 to 1972 OPAL *OONL
microfilm. Hann 1861 McLaren 92

1918*

5207 The Beaver. 1918-1919. Montreal. Ed: Wm. E. Collier.
w. Vol.I no.1, 13 March 1918 to no.4 13 April 1918//
*OOA/Censor610.

5208 The Eastern Federationist. 1918-1919. New Glasgow:
Pictou County Trades and Labor Council. w. Vol.II
no.1 8 March 1919 to vol.II no.34, 25 Oct 1919//BVAU
*OOL microfilm. Hann 1633.

(5209)Der Einziger/(The Only One). 1918. Toronto. Ed:
Marcus Graham. An anarchist paper: no copies located.

5210 Industrialisti. c1918. Duluth. A Finnish language
paper that had a regular column 'From Canada' and in
1919 reported over 1,500 Canadian subscribers. Banned
in Canada 26 June 1918. *OOA/Censor566 refs.

5211 Labor. 1918-1919? Montreal: Labor Club: a monthly
organ of the rank and file. Isidore Boltuck. m.
Vol.I no.2 May 1918, no.3 and vol.II no.3 March 1919
*OOA/Censor610.

5212 The Marxian Socialist. 1918-? Toronto: Socialist
Party of North America. m. Vol.I no.4 Aug 1918
only *OOA/Censor604. Banned 12 Nov 1918. Hann 1716.

5213 The Red Flag. 1919. Vancouver: Socialist Party of
Canada: a journal of news and views devoted to the
interests of the working class. C. Stephenson. Published 'when circumstances and finances permit'.
Formerly Western Clarion, succeeded by The Indicator.
Vol.I no.1 28 Dec 1918 also 11 Jan 1919; no.2, 18
Jan 1919 *OOA/Censor602: vol.I no.5, 15 Feb 1919 to
no.38, 11 Oct 1919//*OOL, lacking nos.6, 11, 13.
No.32 probably not published, misnumbered. Elliott
49 Hann 1799. According to the RNWMP it was printed
by F.R. Blockberger 'a well-educated man who is promoting Bolshevism' - doubtless a contradiction in
RNWMP terms - and that circulation in April 1919 was
18,000 per week.

5214 Semi-Weekly Tribune. 1918-1919. Victoria: Trades
Union Publishing Committee: official organ of Consolidated Trades Unionism in Victoria: a journal of
social and industrial reconstruction. c. Vol.I no.1
7 Oct 1918 to vol.II no.109, 6 Nov 1919//BVAJ BVIP
OONL QQLA *OOL microfilm. Elliott 44 Hann 1810.

5215 The Social-Democrat. 1918. Toronto: (Social Democratic Party of Canada). (Isaac Bainbridge). u.
Formerly The Canadian Forward. Unnumbered issue 31

Dec 1918//*OOL microfilm. Hann 1728.

5216 Трудовой Народ/(Trudovoy Narod). 1918. Toronto:
(Ukrainian Social Democratic Party). (J.Stefanitski).
(m). Formerly Zemlya i Volya. Nos.1 and 2 only 28
May and 20 June 1918//*OOA/Censor518. Banned by
order in council. Hann 1887.

5217 Western Labor News. 1918-1923. Winnipeg: Winnipeg
Trades and Labor Council. William Ivens. w. Formerly The Voice. Numbering continued: vol.XXVI no.1,
2 Aug 1918 to vol.XXVI no.42, 16 May 1919 followed
by Special Strike Issues (see 5250 below); then vol.
XXVI no.47, 27 June 1919 to vol.XXVII no.47, 18 June
1920*MWPL microfilm. Vol.XXVII, no.48, 25 June 1920
to vol.XXX no.19, 13 April 1923 //?*OOL microfilm.
Elliott 52 Hann 1822. Issued as The Western Star
(see 5251 below) for one issue only, 24 June 1919.

5218 Земля и Воля /Zemla i Wola. 1918. Toronto: (Workers
Publishing Assn). (John Stefanitski). Later Trudovoy Narod. No.1, 1 May 1918//*OOA/Censor518. Banned
16 May.

1919

(5219)The Anarchist(ic) Soviet Bulletin. 1919. (Montreal):
'Robert Parsons' i.e. Marcus Graham. Distributed in
        N.J. by Graham who admitted to distributing
copies in many cities. *OOA/Censor605 refs. See
also 5209 above.

5220 Brandon Trades and Labor Council Strike Bulletin.
1919. Ed: (A.E. Smith). ɡ. Nos.1 to 6, 21 May 1919
to 5 June 1919. 1, 3, 4, 5 *MWPA/Salton: 2 and 6
*OTURS/RSK.

5221 Calgary Strike Bulletin. 1919. Calgary: Central
Strike Committee. Published more or less every other
day. No.1, 30 May 1919 *OTURS/RSK, *MWPA/RvIvens 6;
nos. 2, 3, 5 to 12, 31 May to 24 June 1919 *MWPA/Rv
Ivens 6.

5222 The Camp Worker. 1919. Vancouver: BC Loggers and
Camp Workers Union. W.A. Pritchard. m. Later The
Worker. Vol.I no.1, 26 April 1919 to no.4, 28 June//
*MWPL microfilm.

5223 Canadian Labor Press. 1919-1963. Ottawa/Toronto.
Official organ of the Allied Trades and Labor Council
of Ottawa: endorsed by Hamilton District Trades and
Labor Council, Hamilton Building Trades Council, Kit-
chener Twin Cities Trades and Labor Council and the
Independent Labor Party of Ottawa (to 1929). Wm.
Lodge and others. w/m. Vol.I no.1, 15 Feb 1919 to
vol.45 no.2, Feb 1963//*OOL microfilm, incomplete.
Elliott 46 Hann 1695.

5224 The Citizen. 1919-1953. Halifax. Published with the sanction and under the control of the Halifax District Trades and Labor Council. J.S. Wallace. w. Vol.I no.1, 9 May 1919 to vol.21 no.40 (whole no.1600), 6 Oct 1950//*OOL microfilm. Elliott 61 Hann 1626.

5225 The Confederate. 1919. Brandon: Dominion Labor Party and Trades and Labor Council of Brandon. Editorial Committee. w. Vol.I no.1, 9 Jan 1919 to vol.II no. 52, 31 Dec 1920//*OOL microfilm. Numbering highly erratic: OOL lacks 17, 20-45, 49, 50 (1919) and 1, 8, 9, 12-15, 19, 24, 25 and 27 (1920) if all were published in their proper order. Nos. 21 and 25 1919 in *MWPA/Salton and nos. 32, 37 and 39 1919 in *OOA/Censor605. Elliott 59 Hann 1812.

5226 Edmonton Free Press. 1919-1920. Edmonton: Henry J. Roche: official organ of the Edmonton Trades and Labor Council. w. Later Alberta Labor News. Vol.1 no.1, 12 April 1919 to vol.II no.21, 28 Aug 1920//BVAU OOL SRU *AEPAA. Elmer Roper named as editor 23 Aug 1919. Elliott 51 Hann 1755.

5227 Edmonton Strike Bulletin. 1919. Edmonton: Strike Press Committee. u. Unnumbered: 5 and 11 June 1919 *MWPA/RvIvens 6.

5228 The Enlightener. 1919. Winnipeg: The Press Committee. d. Formerly Western Star. Nos.1 and 2, 25 and 26 June 1919//*MWPA/Russell 1.

5229 The Farmers Sun. 1919-1934. Toronto. Variable. Formerly The Weekly Sun, amalgamated with The New Commonwealth. 2 April 1919 to 4 Jan 1934//? *OTAR microfilm, incomplete after Dec 1930. Hann 1705.

5230 Forum. 1919. Winnipeg. Ed: Nils F:Son Brown. s. Vol.1 no.1, 31 Oct and 2, Nov 1919 *OOA/Censor578.

5231 The Indicator. 1919-1920. Vancouver: Socialist Party of Canada. C. Stephenson. w. Formerly The Red Flag, later Western Clarion. Vol.I no.1, 18 Oct 1919 to no.29, 27 Dec 1919*OOL microfilm. Hann 1789.

5232 Labor Election Bulletin. 1919. Winnipeg: United Labor. Vol.I no.1, 24 Nov 1919//?*MWPA/Manning 1.

5233 The Labor Leader. 1919-? Sydney. Independent in politics and fearless in defence of the common people. w. Formerly Canadian Labor Leader. Vol.1 no.1 11 Jan 1919 to no.43, 1 Nov 1919 *OOL, lacks 7-21, 23-27, 29, 39, 41, 42. Elliott 47 Hann 1639.

5234 The Labor Leader. 1919-1954. Toronto. Published in the interests of International Trade Unionism. w/m. Vol.I no.1, 27 June 1919 to vol.34 no.12, Dec 1953 BVAU QQLA *OOL. Elliott 60 Hann 1711. Strongly anti-communist.

5235 Labor Star. 1919. Vancouver. From the workers viewpoint. E.T. Kingsley. w. (Vol.I) no.1, 16 June 1919 to first year no.8, 20 March 1919//BVAU NSHD SRU *OOL microfilm. Elliott 57 Hann 1791.

5236 The Little Daily: Stella Nova. 1919. Winnipeg.
?d. Vol.1 no.2 only 24 Nov 1919 *MWPA/Manning 1.
Possibly published only for civic elections.

5237 The New Democracy. 1919-1923. Hamilton: New Democracy: devoted to labor unionism, labor politics and
general labor education. Fred J. Flatman. w/m.
Later Canadian Labor World. Vol.1 no.1, 22 May 1919
to vol.IV, no.4, 5 July 1923//*OOL microfilm. Elliott
55 Hann 1660.

5238 The One Big Union Bulletin. 1919. Edmonton: OBU
Provincial Executive Committee of Alberta. ∅.
Vol.I no.1, 25 March to no.3, 18 April 1919.
No.1 *MWPA/RvIvens 6; no.2*OOA/Censor605 and AEPAA/
Farmilo 5; no.3 *OOA/Bengough 4.

5239 One Big Union Bulletin. 1919-1934. Winnipeg: Winnipeg Central Labor Council of the OBU. John Houston.
(w). Later Labor Leader. Vol.I no.1, 12 Aug 1919
to vol.XV no.772, 24 May 1934 *OOL microfilm. Various issues in *MWPA/Russell 1 and *OOA/Censor605.
Elliott 56 Hann 1816.

5240 The Ontario Labor News. 1919. Toronto: Ontario
Provincial Council, International Assn of Machinists.
H. Lewis. s. Vol.I no.7, 1 May to no.11, 1 July
1919. *OOL microfilm. Elliott 50 Hann 1720.

5241 The Searchlight. 1919-1920. Calgary. A labor paper
published in the interests of the workers and around
the coal mines of Alberta and southeastern British
Columbia. w. Vol.I no.1 to no.35, 14 Nov 1919 to
22 Oct 1920//*OOL microfilm. Elliott 63 Hann 1752.

5242 Socialist Bulletin. 1919. Winnipeg: Socialist Party
of Canada. 'Issued periodically'. Nos. 1-7, Jan to
July 1919, lacking no.2 *OOA/Gray 1. Copies damaged
and marked in preparation for the Winnipeg Strike
trials. Hann 1819.

5243 The Soviet. 1919. Edmonton: Socialist Party of Canada Local 1: devoted to the interests of the working
class. e. Vol.I no.1, 7 Feb 1919 to no.17, 15 Aug
1919//*OOL. Banned 9 Sept 1919. Elliott 48 Hann
1757. Issue 2 has an article 'Let us start at once
to build up a new order of society, the co-operative
commonwealth.

5244 The Statesman. 1919. Edmonton: Dominion Labor Party
Edmonton branch. S. Freeman. w. Vol.I no. 21, 26-
29 and 31, 29 Aug 1919 to 31 October *OOA/Censor606.
Hann 1758.

5245 Strike Bulletin. 1919. Vancouver: Central Strike
Committee. d. Nos.1 to 18, 4 June to 26th June
1919 *BVAUS/Mac36f.12B.

5246 Winnipeg Strikers/Workers Defence Bulletin. 1919.
Winnipeg: Defence Committee, Labor Temple. ∅. Nos.
2, 4 and 5, 25 July to 20 Sept 1919 in *MWPA/Russell
1, *OOA/Censor605 and *OOA/Bengough 4. Title varies

with each issue - Strikers Defense Bulletin, Workers Defense Bulletin. NB. Not the same as the special strike edition of Western Labor News.

5247 УкраЇнsькі РобІтничі ВІсти /(Ukrainski Robitnychi Visti)/Ukrainian Labor News. 1919-1937. Winnipeg: Winnipeg Trades and Labor Council. w, varies. Formerly Robochyi Narod, later Peoples Gazette. Vol I no.1, 22 March and no.2, 27 March 1919 *OOA/Censor516 From April 23 allowed to publish but in Ukrainian only and matters of a non-seditious nature. No. 7 3 May 1919 *OOA/Censor516 and also scattered issues up to no.31, 10 Dec 1919. Vol.II no.10, 10 March 1920 to vol.XIX no.208, 31 Aug 1937 *MWPL microfilm. Elliott 58 Hann 1973. According to RNWMP the editors were Matthew Popovich and D. Labay and possibly Navizivskiy. RNWMP also report that Moses Charitonoff received $7,000 from L.A. Martens in the USA to establish a revolutionary paper to be called Novy Vek (not traced).

5248 The Western Independent. 1919-1920. Calgary: official organ of the United Farmers of Alberta Political Assn. Wm. Irvine. w. Formerly The Alberta Nonpartisan. Vol.I no.1 to no.28, 1 Oct 1919 to 14 April 1920//*ACGL.

5249 Western Labor News Special Strike Edition. 1919. Winnipeg: Strike Committee. d. Later Western Star. Nos. 1 to 32, 19 May to 23 June 1919 *OOL microfilm. Also lacking a few issues *OOA/Forsey 1 and *MWPA/Russell 2. Two issues of no.27, regular and extra, on the day of the arrests.

5250 Western Star. 1919. Winnipeg: Winnipeg Trades and Labor Council. Formerly Western Labor News Strike Bulletin, later The Enlightener. No. 1, 24 June 1919//*OOL, one issue only made. Hann 1823.

5251 The Western Union Printer. 1919-1923? Medicine Hat: Executive Officers of the Western Canada Conference of Typographical Unions. B.W. Bellamy. m. Vol.I no.4, 27 Sept 1919 to vol.IV no.12, 31 May 1923. *OOL microfilm. Elliott 70 Hann 1761.

5252 The Winnower. c1919. Toronto: United Women Voters. Isabel Oag. Published 'occasionally'. Undated, unnumbered: two issues in *SSA/McNaughton H27.

5253 The Worker. 1919-? Vancouver: Lumber Workers Industrial Union OBU. E, Lindberg. s. Formerly The Camp Worker. Numbering continued: vol.I no.5, 19 Sept 1919 to no.9, 30 Oct 1919 *OOL microfilm. Lacks no.6. Hann 1806.

5254 The Workers Weekly. 1919-1925. Stellarton, N.S: Pictou County Organized Labor. w. Formerly Eastern Federationist. Numbering continued: vol.II no.1, 7 Nov 1919 to vol.VII no.22, 10 July 1925//*OOL microfilm. Elliott 45 Hann 1637.

1920

5255 Alberta Labor News. 1920-1936. Edmonton: Alberta
Federation of Labor: the official paper of organized
labor in Alberta. Elmer Roper. w/e/m. Formerly
Edmonton Free Press, later Peoples Weekly. Vol.I
no.1, 4 Sept 1920 to vol.XVI no.21, 18 January 1936//
*AEPAA. Elliott 66 Hann 1753.

(5256) The Breeze. c1920. London. w. Later The (Labour)
Herald. See Elliott 68, not found.

5257 Canadian Forum. 1920- Toronto. m. Formerly The
Rebel. Vol.I no.1, Oct 1920. *OONL.

5258 Civil Service Bulletin. 1920-? Edmonton: Civil Service Assn of Alberta. m. Vol.I no.1 1920. Elliott
67 Hann 1754, not found.

5259 The Co-operator. 1920-? Vancouver: Vancouver Co-
operative Society. Henry W. Watts. m. Nos. 1-5,
March-July 1920, then vol.I no.1, Aug 1920 to no.8,
Sept 1920. All *OOA/CUC221.

5260 Defense Committee Newsletter. 1920. Winnipeg: Defence Committee. (J. Law). ⌀. Unnumbered: 2 Feb
and 4 Feb 1920 *SSA/McNaughton H31. Defence is spelt
both ways on the original.

5261 Dollars and Sense. 1920. Toronto: First Civil Science Movement: the function of capital is to serve
labor; the subjection of capital to the needs of
labor is a world-wide job for community practice
experts. No. 1, 1920 *OTURS/RSK. ? all published.

(5262) Jewish Labo(u)r Gazette. c1920. Toronto. w. Hann
1869 McLaren 340, not found.

(5263) The (Labour) Herald. 1920-1921? London. Independent
Labor. w. Formerly The Breeze. 9 Sept 1920 to 29
Dec 1921. Elliott 68 Hann 1671, not found.

(5264) The Organizer. 1920-1937. Vancouver: official organ
of the Amalgamated Postal Workers. Elliott 69 Hann
1795, not found.

5265 UFWO Bulletin. c1920. Toronto: UFWO (i.e. United
Farm Workers of Ontario). (Meta S. Laws). m. Unnumbered, undated, c1920: Jan to Oct (but ? different
years)*SSA/G310.1.

5266 The Union Worker. 1920-1922? St John/Moncton. Pub-
lished in the interests of the organized workers of
New Brunswick. A.D. Colwell. m. Vol.I no.1, Feb
1920 to vol.III no.2 (whole no.25) April 1922//?*OOL.
Elliott 64 Hann 1612. From Sept 1921 published at
Moncton.

5267 The Worker/LeTravailleur. 1920. Montreal: Lumber
and Camp Workers Industrial Union OBU: no.1, 1 May
1920 to no.16, 15 Dec 1920//? BVAU OONL *OOL microfilm. Elliott 65. Bilingual.

(5268)Di Yidishe Arbeyter Tsaytung. c1920. Winnipeg.
Hann 1985, not found.

1921

5269 The Booster. 1921-1953? Toronto: official publication of the Brotherhood of (Canadian Pacific) Employees. m. Vol.IX no.1, Jan 1927 to vol.XXXV no.5 May
1953 *OOL microfilm. Elliott 62 Hann 1668.

5270 The British Columbia Labor News. 1921-1922. Vancouver: Vancouver Trades and Labor Council. H.W. Watts.
w. Vol.I no.1, 29 July 1921 to no.29, 26 May 1922//
BVAU QQLA SRU *OOL microfilm. Elliott 72 Hann 1780.
Amalgamated with the BC Federationist 2 June 1922.

5271 Canadian Labor Party Bulletin. 1921. Winnipeg.
No.5 only *OOA/Woodsworth 10. Hann 1694. Issued
for the federal election 1921.

5272 The Canadian Trade Unionist. 1921-1934. Toronto.
m. Vol.V no.1, Dec 1925 to Dec 1933. BVAU *OOL microfilm. Elliott 73 Hann 1700.

5273 The Communist. 1921. Toronto: published by authority
of the Third (Communist) International in Canada:
official organ of the Communist Party of Canada (Section of the Communist International). m. Later The
Workers World. Vol.I no.1, 1st May 1921: Vol.I no.1
and 2, June and July 1921//*OTURS/RSK. The attribu-
tion to the Third International appears on the May
issue only.

5274 The Communist Bulletin. (1921). Toronto: published
by the Canadian Section of the United Communist Party
of America. Vol.I no.1, undated//*OTURS/RSK. Refers
to an article by Comrade Kavanagh in the Western Clarion supporting the Third International 'received as
we go to press'.

(5275)Federal Union no.66 Newsletter. 1921. Ottawa: Associated Federal Employees of Ottawa. u. Unnumbered:
7 Feb 1921 NBFU. Hann 1681, not seen.

(5276)Harapnyk/(The Whip). 1921-1922. Edmonton. m.
Hann 1900, not found.

5277 The Independent. 1921. Winnipeg: Independent Labor
Party of Manitoba. Editorial Committee (including
F.J. Dixon and Wm. Ivens). e/w. Vol.I no.1 (1 July
1921) and no.5, 2 Sept 1921 *OOA/Woodsworth 10; nos.
20, 23, 26-30, 34, 36 *MWPA/Russell 2.

5278 The Maritime Labor Herald. 1921-1926. Glace Bay.
Devoted to the interest of labor. W.U. Cotton, later
J.B. McLachlan. w. Vol.I no.1, 14 Oct 1921 to vol.
V no.23, 10 July 1926//BVAU SRU *OOL microfilm.
Elliott 74 Hann 1618.

(5279)Saskatchewan Co-operative News. 1921-1926. Regina.
m. Hann 1828, not found.

5280 The Wedge. 1921. Edmonton. Eds: Geo.L. Ritchie
and P.F. Lawson. u. Vol.I no.2, 3 Sept 1921 *AEPAA/
Farmilo 5.

5281 Winnipeg Socialist. 1921. Winnipeg: Socialist Party
of Canada. u. Vol.I no.4, 22 Oct 1921 *OOA/Woods-
worth 10. Possibly issued only for the election.

5282 Workers Guard. 1921-1922. Toronto: New Era, Comm-
unist Party of Canada/Workers Party of Canada (from
Dec 1921). F.J. Peel. w. Formerly The Workers
World. Vol.I no.7, 15 Oct 1921 to vol.1 no.21, 11
Feb 1922 *OTAR microfilm. Hann 1743.

5283 The Workers World. 1921. Toronto: New Era Publishing
Co. w. Formerly The Communist, later Workers Guard.
Vol.I no.1, 17 Aug 1921//*OTURS/RSK. Hann 1744.
Almost all copies of this single issue were seized
by the police.

1922

5284 Canadian Congress Journal. 1922-1944. Ottawa: Tra-
des and Labor Congress of Canada. J.A.P. Haydon. m.
Later Trades and Labour Congress Journal. Vol.I no.1
Jan 1922 to vol.XXIII no.2, Feb 1944//*OOL microfilm.
Elliott 81 Hann 1679.

(5285)Canadian Telegrapher. 1922-1923. Toronto: Commercial
Telegraph Workers Union of Canada. m. Elliott 77
Hann 1699, not found.

5286 Голос Праці/(Holos Pratsi)/ The Voice of Labour.
1922-1924. Winnipeg. m. Vol.II no.10-11, Autumn
1923*OONL. Apr 1922-Feb 1924 MWP. Hann 1940.

5287 Monthly Report Amalgamated Society of Carpenters and
Joiners Canadian District. 1922-1931. Toronto.
m/ß. New Series, unnumbered: Nov-Dec 1922 to June
1931//*OOL microfilm. March to July and Oct 1927
not published; lacking May 1929-Jan1930 ?published,
similarly Feb 1923.

(5288)Ontario Firefighter. 1922-1929. London: official
organ Provincial Federation of Ontario Firefighters.
m. Elliott 79 Hann 1719, not found.

(5289)Postal Journal. 1922-1937. Toronto: Toronto Branch
Dominion Postal Clerks. m. Elliott 78 Hann 1725,
not found.

5290 Le Travailleur. 1922-? Montréal: Secretariat of
Catholic Sundicats of French Canada: L'Action Sociale.
w. Vol.I no.1, Feb 1922 to vol.I no.46, 28 Dec 1922
*OOL microfilm. Suspended Aug 1923 to Jan 1924,
resumed publication, not found. Elliott 82.

5291 Typographical Bulletin/TTU Bulletin. 1922- . Toronto. m. Vol.XIII no.3 March 1941 through 1970*OOL
microfilm, incomplete. Elliott 83 Hann 1736.

5292 The U.F.A. 1922-1935. Calgary: United Farmers of
Alberta. W. Norman Smith. s. Vol.I no.1, 1 March
1922 to vol.XV no.51, Dec 1935//*AEPAA microfilm.

5293 The Worker. 1922. Toronto: Workers Publishing Assn.
Jack Kavanagh, later Maurice Spector, later Mike
Buhay. c. Later Daily Clarion. Unnumbered issue
1 March 1922; vol.I no.1, 15 March 1922*OTURS/RSK
to vol.XV no.850, 28 April 1936//*OOL microfilm.
Elliott 76 Hann 1742.

1923

5294 British Columbia Musician. 1923-1928? Vancouver:
Musicians Union Local 145. Ernest C, Miller. m.
Vol.I no.1, 8 May 1923 to vol.VI no.5, Sept 1928//
*OOL microfilm. Elliott 86 Hann 1781.

5295 The Canadian Labor World. 1923-1931? Hamilton.
We are opposed to the IWW, the OBU and WPC, socialism
and Bolshevism and absolutely opposed to Communism.
(This doesn't leave too much to be in favour of). m.
Formerly The New Democracy: numbering continues:
vol.IV no.5, 2 Aug 1923 to twelfth year no.8, 26
Nov 1931//? *OOL microfilm. From vol.VIII no.1
becomes 8th year no.2. Hann 1655. Religious in
general tone.

5296 The Glow Worm. 1923. Edmonton: Economic Pub. Co:
cooperation instead of competition. Ernest Brown.
b. Vol.I no.1, 13 April 1923 to no.3, 1 July 1923.
Probably all published. *AEPAA/Brown unboxed 430.

5297 Голос-Робітниці/(Holos Robitnitsi)/The Voice of
Workingwoman. 1923-1924. Winnipeg: Proletcult:
Workingwomens Section of the Ukrainian Labor Temple.
m. Later Robitnytsïa. Vol.I no.2, Jan 1924 *OONL.
Hann 1942.

5298 The Labor News. 1923. Timmins: official organ of
the Porcupine Mine Workers Union. ?m. No. 1 and
2, (?July) and Aug 1923. *OOL.

(5299) The Progressive. 1923-1924. Saskatoon. Not found.

1924

5300 Carpenters Monthly Bulletin. 1924-1932? (Toronto):
Ontario Provincial Council: issued in the interests
of carpenters and woodworkers of Ontario. m. Formerly Trade Report. No.1 Aug 1924 to no.58, May-Oct
1932//? *OOL microfilm. Elliott 93 Hann 1701.
Issues from May 1930 hopelessly misnumbered.

5301 The Federated Railwayman. 1924-1969? Montreal.

Division 4 Railway Employees AFL. (Chas. Dickie). m.
Vol.I no.1, May 1924 to vol.XXXV no.1-2-3, Jan-Feb-
March 1969//?*OOL microfilm. Elliott 91 Hann 1792.

5302 דער קאמף/Der Kamf/(The Struggle). 1924-1939. Mont-
real/Toronto. Ed: H. Dubitzky (one issue only); Mike
Buhay. m. Later Der Veg. Vol.1 no.1 to vol.XIV no.
763, 11 Aug 1939//*OONL microfilm. Starts again vol.
I no.1, 1 Jan 1926 when publishing moved to Toronto.
Elliott 87 Hann 1871 McLaren 343.

5303 The Labo(u)r Statesman. 1924-1968. Vancouver: Van-
couver, New Westminster and District Trades and Labor
Council, later BC Federation of Labour. w. No.1, 25
April 1924 to vol.45 no.3, Sept 1969//*OOL microfilm.
Elliott 88 Hann 1793.

5304 The Left Wing. 1924-1926. Toronto: Canadian Section
Trade Union Educational League. Tim Buck. m. Vol.
1 no.1, 1 Nov 1924 to vol.II no.20, July 1926//*OOL
microfilm. Elliott 84 Hann 1714.

5305 Machinist Bulletin. 1924-1928. Winnipeg: District
2, International Assn of Machinists. m/b/q. Formerly
Bulletin. Vol.I no.1, Aug 1924 to vol.III no.4, May
1928//MWP SSU *OOL microfilm. Hann 1815.

5306 Робiтниця /(Robitnytsīa)/The Workingwoman. 1924-1937.
Winnipeg: Workers and Farmers Publishing Assn Ltd:
organ of the women's section ULFTA. s. Formerly
Holos Robitnytsi. Vol.I no.7, 15 June 1924 to vol.
XIII no.15, Sept 1937//?*OONL; vol.VI no.1, Jan 1929
to vol.IX no.20, Dec 1932 *MWPL. Hann 1965.

5307 The Scoop-Shovel. 1924-1931. Winnipeg: Manitoba
Wheat Pool. J.T. Hull. b/m. Later The Manitoba
Co-operator. Vol.I no.1, 2 Sept 1924 to vol.VII no.8
Aug 1931//*MWPL.

5308 La Vie Syndicale. 1924-1941. Montréal: L'Oeuvre de
publicité syndicale: organe des Syndicats Catholiques
Nationaux. m. Later Le Travail. Vol.I no.1, nov
1924 to (vol.XVII no.12), dec 1941//*OOL microfilm.
Elliott 90.

5309 The Young Worker. 1924-1936. Toronto: official organ
of the Young Communist League of Canada. Leslie
Morris. m/b. Later The Advance. Vol.I no.1, June
1924 to vol.XI no.226, 9 May 1936//*OOL microfilm.
Elliott 89 Hann 1746.

1925

5310 The Canadian (Farmer-) Labor Advocate. 1925-1926.
Vancouver: Labour Publishing Co. w. Formerly BC
Federationist: numbering continued: seventeenth year
no.24, 12 June 1925 to eighteenth year no.17, 29 Apr
1926//BVAU SRU *OOL microfilm. Hann 1785. 'Farmer'
dropped from title 24 July 1925 on.

5311 Фармерське Життя /(Farmers'ke Zhyttīa)/The Farmer's
Life. 1925-1940. Winnipeg: Workers and Farmers Publishing Assn. (M. Popovich). w. Vol.I no.1, 1 Apr
1925 to vol.V no.1 (whole no.196), 2 Jan 1929 *OONL
to vol.XVI no.27 (whole no.795), 3 July 1940 *MWPL
microfilm.

5312 Metsätyöläinen/(The Lumber Worker). 1925-1930 and
1932-1935? Sudbury: Lumber and Agricultural Workers
Industrial Union, Workers Unity League. m. Later
Maa-Ja Metsätyöläinen before reverting to Metsätyöläinen. Vol.I no.1, May 1925 to vol.V no.2, June
1930//*OOA/Finnish Organization of Canada 149, incomplete. Resumes (vol.VII) no.8, Aug 1932 to vol.
IX no.3, Apr 1934, plus one double vol.1934-1935
*OOA/FOC 149. Elliott 117 McLaren 87.

5313 The People's Cause. 1925-1928? Toronto: Labor Educational Assn of Ontario: owned and controlled by
organized labor. Jos. T. Marks. w. Later Labour
Review. Sample edn. 20 Apr 1925; free bulletin 27
Apr 1926; unnumbered issues for Oct 1927, 4 Jan 1928,
14 May 1928. *OOL microfilm. Elliott 105 Hann 1723.

5314 The Radiotelegraph Bulletin. 1925-1926. Vancouver:
Commercial Telegraphers Union of America, Canadian
Radio Division 65. m. Later The Communication Worker.
Vol.I no.1 (old series no.12), 30 Nov 1925 to no.2
27 Dec 1925 and 3, Jan 1926//*OOL microfilm. Issue
3 had Communication Worker as a supplement; thereafter
(Feb 1926) the Bulletin is incorporated into The
Communication Worker.

5315 Railway Mail Clerk. 1925-1943. Winnipeg/Ottawa/Cal-
gary: Dominion Railway Mail Clerks. W.S. Osborne.
m. Vol.I no.1, Aug 1925 to vol.XV no.47, June/July
1943//*OOL. Elliott 94 Hann 1751.

5316 The Weekly News. 1925-1934. Winnipeg: Garry Press:
for economic, political and intellectual freedom.
S.J. Farmer. w. Later Manitoba Commonwealth. Vol.I
no.1, 6 March 1925 to vol.VIII no.485, 29 June 1934//
BVAU MWP OONL *OOL microfilm. Elliott 95 Hann 1821.

1926

5317 Canada Forward. 1926-1927? Toronto: the unity of
labor is the hope of the world. Jas. MacA. Conner.
m. Vol.I no.1, 15 Nov 1926 to no.11, Sept-Oct 1927
*OOL microfilm. Lacks no.10. Elliott 96 Hann 1689.

(5318)The Communication Worker. 1926-1933. Toronto.
Hann 1704, not found.

5319 The Communication Worker. 1926-1939. Vancouver/
Prince Rupert: Electrical Communication Workers of
Canada. m. Formerly The Radiotelegraph Bulletin,
later Contact. Vol.I no.1, Jan 1926 to vol.XIV no.9

Oct 1939//*OOL microfilm. No issues published April 1927 to March 1928. Elliott 100 Hann 1787. Issue no.1 is a supplement to the Radiotelegraph Bulletin; from Feb 1926 the Bulletin is incorporated as a supplement in The Communication Worker.

(5320) Druh'Naroda/(The People's Friend). 1926-1930. Edmonton. m. Hann 1898, not found.

5321 The Furrow. 1926-1935. Saskatoon/Winnipeg: (Farmers Unity League): The voice of the bona fide farmer - he who controls the marketing of my produce controls me. G.E. Dealtry. e. (Vol.I no.1) (Feb 1926) and (no.3) (Mar 1926) then vol.I no.4, 25 March 1926 to whole no. 106, 15 June 1935 *OONL microfilm: 30 Oct 1926 to 7 Dec 1936 *SSA microfilm. OONL incomplete. First three issues undated and unnumbered but first issue date-stamped for receipt on 6 February 1926 at RCMP HQ Ottawa.

5322 The Labor Herald. 1926-1930. Toronto. Devoted to the mutual welfare of capital and labor. m/ɸ. Vol.I no.1, 6 Feb 1926 to vol.V no.4, 29 Dec 1930//? BVAU SRU *OOL microfilm. Elliott 99 Hann 1710.

5323 The Woman Worker. 1926-1929? Toronto: Canadian Federation of Womens Labor Leagues (Workers Party of Canada). Florence Custance. u. No.3, Sept 1926 *OOA/CUC223. Elliott 98 Hann 1740.

1927

5324 The Canadian Unionist. 1927-1956. Ottawa: All-Canadian Congress of Labor. W.T. Burford. m. Vol.I no.1, June 1927 to vol.XXX no.3, March 1956//*OOL microfilm. Elliott 104 Hann 1678. After 1956 merged with Canadian Labour.

(5325) Iskra/(The Spark). c1927. Toronto. ɸ. Hann 1868, not found. A Bulgarian paper.

5326 Cвіт Молоді/(Svit Molodi)/The Youth's World. 1927-1930. Winnipeg: Workers and Farmers Publishing Assn. m. Later Boiova Molod'. Vol.I no.1, March 1927 to vol.IV no.5, May 1930//*MWPL microfilm.

1928

5327 The Canadian Labour Monthly. 1928-? Toronto: Workers Publishing Assn. Maurice Spector. m. Vol.I no. 1, Jan 1928. *OTURS/RSK. Elliott 106 Hann 1693.

5328 The Coal Miner. 1928. Nanaimo: Mineworkers Union of Canada. Jos. Gilbert. w. Vol.I (no.1), 3 Feb 1928 *T.

5329 The Labor Campaign News. 1928. Glace Bay: (?United
Mine Workers). u. Vol.I no.1, 27 Sept 1928 *OOA/
Heaps 2.

5330 The Labor Elector. 1928. Calgary: Canadian Labor
Party. u. Vol.I no.1, 1 Dec 1928 *ACGL.

5331 The Young Comrade. 1928-1929? Toronto: official
organ Young Pioneers, branch of the Young Communist
League. m. Vol.II no.25, 1 July 1929. *OTAR.
Elliott 110 Hann 1745.

1929

5332 The Farm Movement. 1929-? Regina: Provincial Press.
s. Vol.I no.1, 2 and 3, Feb and March 1929.
Contain articles by Wm Irvine, J.S. Woodsworth, Agnes
McPhail, M.J. Coldwell etc.

5333 Kanadai (Canadai) Magyar Munkás/Canadian Hungarian
Worker. 1929-1967. Hamilton/Toronto. w. Vol.I
no.1, 16 July 1929 to vol.XXXIX no.22, 28 Dec 1967//
*OONL microfilm, incomplete. Until 20 May 1931 pub-
lished in Hamilton. Hann 1872 McLaren 255.

5334 The Nova Scotia Miner. 1929-1932? Glace Bay: Progressive Miners of Nova Scotia. J.B. McLachlan. w.
Vol.I no.1, 14 Dec 1929 to vol.II no.3, 23 Jan 1932
*OOL microfilm: vol.II no.8, 27 Feb 1932 *OOA/Woods-
worth 11. Elliott 119 Hann 1619.

5335 Punainen Työläinen. 1929. Sudbury. 1929. ?w.
No.1 and 2, 1 and 4 Dec 1929//? *OOA/FOC141.

5336 The Sudbury Worker. 1929. Toronto: Finnish Agitation
and Propaganda Office of the Communist Party of Canada:
workers of the world unite! s. Nos. (1), (2) and 3
Jan and Feb 1929//?*OOA/FOC. Published on the occasion of a charge of seditious libel against Arvo
Vaara, editor of Vapaus.

5337 The Unemployed Worker. 1929-1952? Vancouver: Workers
Unity League of Vancouver, later Vancouver Central
Council, National Unemployed Workers Assn. b/w.
Vol.III no.17, 7 Feb (1931) to vol.IV no.35, 17 June
1932//? *OOL microfilm, incomplete. Elliott 114.

(5338)Union Labourer. 1929. Edmonton: Local 92 International Hodcarriers, Building and Common Labourers.
m. Elliott 107 Hann 1759, not found.

1930

5339 Бойова Молодь/(Boiova Molod')/The Militant Youth.
1930-1932. Winnipeg: Workers and Farmers Publishing

Assn: organ of the youth section of the U.L.-F.T.A.
m. Formerly Svit Molodi. Vol.I no.2, June 1930 to
vol.III no.7, Aug 1932//*OONL microfilm.

(5340)Borba/(The Struggle). 1930-1936. Toronto: Croatian
and Serbian Workers Educational Assn. Tomo Čačić.
m. Later Pravda (Serbian) and Slobodna Misao (Croatian). 15 Jan 1930 to 19 Sept 1936, OONL not found.
McLaren 46.

5341 Bulletin. 1930. Toronto: Central Agitprop Dept of
the Communist Party of Canada. Unnumbered, undated.
April-May no. (?1930) *OTAR/CPC9.

5342 The Canadian Co-operative Official. 1930-1945.
Brantford: Co-operative Union of Canada. ⌀/m. Vol.
I no.1, Dec 1930 to vol.XVI no.10, Dec 1945 *OOA/CUC
220. Frequent double issues after 1931.

5343 (The)(Canadian) Labor Defender. 1930-1935. Toronto:
Canadian Labor Defense League. m. Vol.I no.1, Feb
1930, numbering repeated vol.I no.1 May 1930 to vol.
V no.12, Sept-Oct 1935//*OOL microfilm. Issue of
Feb 1930 *OTAR/CPC4. Elliott 111 Hann 1692. Var-
ious combinations of title names on masthead.

5344 קאַנאַדיער נאדל אַרבעטער/The Canadian Needle Worker.
1930. Toronto: Industrial Union of Needle Trades
Workers of Canada, Workers Unity League. m. Vol.I
no.1, 10 Sept 1930 to no.3, Nov 1930//*OOL microfilm.

5345 Canadian Railway Employees Monthly. 1930-1952.
Ottawa/Montreal/Hull: Canadian Brotherhood of Railway
Employees. M.M. Maclean. m. Formerly Canadian
Railroad Employees Monthly, later Canadian Transport.
Numbering continued: vol.XVI no.1, Jan 1930 to vol.
XXXIX no.3, Mar 1953//*OOL . From Oct 1934 pub-
lished in Montreal; from May 1939 in Hull.

5346 Election Bulletin. 1930. Winnipeg: Communist Party
of Canada Winnipeg Election Committee. u. No.2
(Nov 1930). *OOA/Heaps 2.

(5347)The Hunger Fighter. 1930. Toronto. u. Not found.

5348 The I.L.P. News. 1930. Vancouver: ILP Propaganda
Committee. John Sidaway. m. Vol.I no.1, Feb 1930,
nos.6 and 7, July and Aug 1930 *BVAU/Mac30Af.1.

5349 Labor Progress. 1930. Fort William. Published in
the interests of the working class and the labor
movement of northern Ontario and endorsed by the Independent Labor Party and the Trades and Labor Council
of Fort William. u. Vol.I no.2, 1 March 1930 *OOA/
Heaps 2.

5350 Maa-Ja Metsätyöläinen. 1930-1932. Sudbury. m.
Formerly Metsätyöläinen, later Metsätyöläinen.
Numbering continued: vol.V no.3, July-Sept 1930 to
vol.VII no.7, July 1932//*OOA/FOC149.

(5351)Militant Cooperator. 1930. Port Arthur. Hann 1684,
not found.

5352 L'Ouvrier Canadien. 1930-1931. Montréal: Journal
officiel du Parti Communiste du Canada, section de
l'Internationale Communiste. e. Vol.I no.1, 15 mai
1930 à no.12, oct 1931//?*OONL. No issues 30 Sept
to Dec 1930. Elliott 115.

5353 Toronto Unemployed Worker. 1930. Toronto: Toronto
Unemployed Workers Assn. Unnumbered, March 1930.
*OTAR.

5354 Український Робітник /(Ukrainskyi Robitnyk)/Ukrainian
Worker. 1930. Winnipeg: ILP of North Winnipeg. w.
Nos. 2 and 3,19 and 26 July 1930.*OOA/Heaps 2.

5355 The Western Miner. 1930-1931. Lethbridge: Miners
Section of the Workers Unity League. s/ø. Later
The Canadian Miner. Vol.I no.1, 20 Feb 1930 to vol.II
no.4, 8 Sept 1931//*OOL microfilm. Incomplete.
Elliott 109.

(5356) Workers Unity. 1930-1932. Vancouver: Workers Unity
League. Elliott 113, not found.

5357 The Workers Vanguard. 1930. Winnipeg: Communist
Party of Canada District 7. Unnumbered and undated
Special election issue, nos.(1) and 2 *OOA/Heaps 2
and OOA/Woodsworth 10. Perhaps issued just for the
federal election.

1931

(5358) Proletarsko Delo/(Proletarian Action). 1931-1935.
Toronto. Later Edinstvo. Bulgarian paper, McLaren
38, not found.

5359 Työtön Työläinen. 1931. Vancouver. OONL, not found.

5370 Unemployed Bulletin. 1931-1932? Calgary: National
Unemployed Workers Assn. (w). Vol.I no.5, 9 Oct
(1931) and nos. 7, 8, 13, 19, Oct 1931 to Jan 1932.
*ACGL.

5371 Weekly Organization Letter. 1931-? (Toronto): Communist Party of Canada, Central Organization Dept. w.
No.1, 24 Feb 1931 to no.22, 4 Aug 1931. *OTAR.

5372 (Workers)Unity. 1931-1936? Toronto: Workers Unity
League of Canada: a paper for working men and women.
b. Vol.I no.1, 15 July 1931, and nos. 2, 5, 6, 10,
12 *OOL microfilm; Vol.III (no.1), March 1933 and
(16) may 1933; vol.IV no.21, April 1934 *SRA/Riot 8.
Vol.V no.4, vol.6 nos.12-14, Jan 1935 to Feb 1936
*SRA/Riot 8. Prefix 'Workers' dropped between Apr
and Dec 1934.

5373 York Knitter. 1931. Toronto: York Knitting Mills
Group, Young Communist League. u. No. 13, Sept
1931. *OTURS/RSK.

1932

5374 The Alarm Clock. 1932-1933. Montreal: McGill Labor
Club. Lloyd G. Reynolds. m during the college year.
Vol.II no.2, Dec 1933.*BVAU/Mac31f.12.

5375 Border Cities Labour News. 1932. Walkerville, Ont:
Border Cities Branch Ontario Labour Party. w. Vol.I
no.8, 16 Jan 1932 to no.25, 24 May 1932//*OOL microfilm, lacking nos.9-11. Elliott 121.

5376 The British Columbia Clarion. 1932-1934? Vancouver:
Socialist Party of Canada. H.E. Winch, jr. m. Vol.I
nos.4-7, 9; vol.II nos.1, 2, 5, 6, Dec 1932 to Jan
1934 *AEPAA/Farmilo 2: vol.III, 1 Sept 1934 *OOA/CCF
345.

5377 Calgary Home News. 1932-1933. Calgary. (CCF). Percy
Hill. w. Vol.II no.4, 17 Feb 1933 *ACGL.

5378 Canadian Association (of Railway Running Trades) Review. 1932-1934. Winnipeg: Canadian Assn of Railway
Enginemen, Conductors, Trainmen, Yardmen, Telegraphers
and Dispatchers. m. Formerly Canadian Running Trades
Journal. Numbering continued: vol.I no.7, Aug 1932 to
vol.III no.1, Jan 1934//*OOL microfilm. 'Of Railway
Running Trades' added with vol.II no.5, May 1933.

5379 Canadian Running Trades Journal. 1932. Winnipeg:
Canadian Assn of Enginement, Conductors, Trainmen,
Yardmen, Telegrapher and Dispatchers. m. Later Canadian Association Review. Vol.I no.1, Jan 1932 to
no.6, June 1932//*OOL microfilm. Elliott 116.

5380 Darbininkų Žodis/The Workers World. 1932-1936. Toronto: Lithuanian Workers Assn. w. Later Liaudies
Balsas. Unnumbered: Sept 1932 to 19 Nov (1935) *OONL
incomplete. McLaren 368.

5381 Głos Pracy/Voice of Labor. 1932-1940. Winnipeg/Tor-
onto: Workers and Farmers Assn, later The Polish Peo-
ples Assn. Varies: mostly w. Formerly Budzik, later
Kronika Tygodniowa. Unnumbered: 30 Apr 1932 to 17
Aug 1940//Banned:*OONL, incomplete. Mclaren 387.
Published in Winnipeg until 19 Dec 1936.

(5382) Holos Karpat/(Voice of the Carpathians). 1932-1933.
Toronto: Labour Enlightenment Carpathian Assn. m.
McLaren 451, not found.

(5383) The Labor Herald. 1932-1934. Prince Rupert. Not
found.

5384 Labour Review. 1932-1955? Victoria: Victoria and
District Trades and Labor Council. e. First year
no.1, 1 Apr 1932 to no.7, 1 Sept 1932.*OOL microfilm.
Elliott 122.

5385 Lightning. 1932. Halifax: Workingmens Protective
Political Assn: the genuine labor paper. Roy Leitch.

w. Later Dawn. Vol.I no.6, 22 Oct 1932.*NSHP.

5386 Lumber Worker. 1932. Sudbury: Lumber Industrial Workers Union of Canada, Workers Unity League. m. Vol.I no.1 and 3, Sept and Nov-Dec 1932//*OOL micro-film.

5387 The People. 1932. Vancouver: The Peoples Party (launched by the United Farmers of BC). u. Vol.I no.1, April 1932. *BVAU/Steeves 4-6.

5388 The Pilot. 1932-1933? Moncton: Independent Labor Party: pointing the way to a new social order. J.A. Robinson. m. Vol.I no.1, Sept 1932 *OOA/Woodsworth 10; no.6, Feb 1933 *OOA/CCF12.

5389 The Plunger. 1932. Vancouver: Fishermans Industrial Union of Canada. u. Vol.I no.1 (undated)(June 1932) *OOL. Issue of The Unemployed Worker 17 June 1932 welcomes the appearance of the first issue of the latest addition to the working class press in the district, The Plunger...

5390 Robotnícke Slovo/Workers Word. 1932-1936. Toronto: Czechoslovak Workers Educational Clubs in Canada. Július Húska. m. Formerly Naše Slovo, later Hlas L'udu. Vol.II no.6, 1 June 1932 to vol.V no.59, 28 July 1936//*OONL incomplete.

5391 The Spark. 1932. Toronto: Student League of Canada. Editorial executive committee includes Stanley Ryerson. u. No.2, Dec 1932 *OTAR. Includes a long letter from IV Pol.Sci. student C.B. Macpherson 'I share your views on the impotence of capitalism' but going on to argue that the university students were not members of the proletariat and if they were to be won to Marxism it must be by rational argument.

5392 The Vanguard. 1932-1936. Toronto:organ of the International Left Opposition of Canada; later official organ of the Workers Party of Canada. m. Later Socialist Action. Vol.I no.1, Nov-Dec 1932 to vol. III, new series, no.23, Dec 1936//*OTP microfilm, incomplete.

1933

5393 The Builder. 1933. (Toronto): (almost certainly Ontario provincial Communist Party). m. Vol.I no.1 March 1933//? *OTURS/RSK. All articles are pseudonymous.

5394 The Building Worker. 1933-1936. Montreal: Amalgamated Building Workers of Canada. m. Vol.I no.1, Aug 1933 to no.25, June 1936.*OTURS. ?Elliott 132.

5395 The CCF Clarion. 1933. Toronto: CCF Clubs. e. Vol.I no.1, 2 Sept 1933 *OTURS/RSK; nos.2 and 3, Sept 1933 *OTAR.

5396 The Commonwealth. 1933-1936. Vancouver: CCF, BC.
W.A. Pritchard. w. Vol.I no.1, 17 May 1933 to vol.
IV no.38, 18 Sept 1936//*BVAU, incomplete.

5397 Dawn. 1932-? Halifax: Workingmens Protective Political Assn: let there be light. (Roy Leitch). w.
Formerly Lightning; numbering continued. Vol.I no.7,
29 Oct 1932 to no.9, 12 Nov 1932//?*NSHP.

5398 Farmer-Labor Bulletin. 1933. (?Wynyard, Sask): Farmer-Labor Party, Wadena constituency. u. Vol.I no.1
Jan 1933//? *SSA/G.18.1933.3.

5399 The Heavy Lift. 1933-1935? Vancouver: for all workers
on the waterfront. ⌀. No.14, 10 Nov 1933 to vol.II
no.15, 2 Jan 1935 plus one unnumbered issue 8 July
1935//? *OOL microfilm. Vol.I no.25 not issued.
Elliott 125.

5400 Labor Journal. 1933. Toronto: Relief Workers Union:
a journal for the discussion of labor problems. N.Law.
s. Vol.I no.1, Oct 1933//?*OTAR.

(5401)Needle Worker. 1933-1935. Montreal: Industrial Union
of Needle Trade Workers of Canada. Elliott 124, not
found.

5402 October Youth. 1933. Toronto: Spartacus Youth Club
(4th International). ⌀. Later Young Militant. (no.1)
April 1933 to (no.5) Oct-Nov 1933//*OTP microfilm.

5403 The Power Engineer. 1933. Montreal: Canadian Assn
of Stationary Engineers. (m). Vol.I no.1, Oct 1933
*OTURS.

5404 The (BC) Relief Camp Worker. 1933-1935? Vancouver:
Relief Camp Workers Union (BC District). ⌀. Vol.I
no.30, 20 July 1934; vol.II no.1, 2 Aug 1934, nos. 2,
6, 17; vol.III nos.4 and 11, 9 May 1935.*SRA/Riot 4
and 5. Vol.III no.4 misnumbered vol.I.

5405 Робітничі Вісти /Robitnychi Visty/Labor News. 1933-
1938. Toronto: Canadian section of the Left Opposition, 4th International. m. Vol.I no.1, Nov 1933
to vol.III no.12-13 (whole nos.39-40), 1 July 1935.
Starts third year, new series, no.1, 1 Aug 1935 to
fourth year, new series, nos.13-14 (whole nos.62-63)
28 July 1936//*OTP microfilm. Lacks one issue (May
1936) only. Plus fifth year no.1 (whole no.64) Nov
1937 and sixth year no.1-2 (whole nos.65-66) March
1938 subsequently published separately by another
hand. *OTP microfilm.

5406 Saskatchewan CCF Research Bureau. 1933-1934? Regina.
m. Vol.I nos.2, 3, 8, Aug 1933 to Mar 1934 *OOA/
Underhill 44; no.10, May 1934 *OOA/CCF321.

5407 Steelworker and Miner. ?1933-1951? Sydney: (M.A.
MacKenzie). w. No.356, 12 April 1941 to no.816
(should be 929 - later numbering all incorrect), 6
Oct 1951//?*OOL microfilm. Elliott 126.

5408 Työtön Työlainen. 1933-1934. Toronto. ?s. Vol.I

no.1, 28 Sept 1933 to vol.II no.8, 11 April 1934.
*OOA/FOC 142, incomplete.

5409 The Western Socialist. 1933. Winnipeg: Socialist
Party of Canada. 'Periodically when funds available'.
Vol.I no.1, Oct 1933 to no.3, Dec 1933//? *MWPL micro-
film.

5410 Workers Educational Association of Ontario Bulletin.
1933-1936. Toronto: Workers Educational Assn for
Labour and Social Legislation. F.C. Auld and J. Finkelman. m. No.1 series 1, Feb 1933 *OTURS/RSK; nos.
2-4, 1933-1934 *OTP: later (1935) numbered but without
series and headed 'Labour Research Institute'; later
(1936) volume no.and serial no. added, starting vol.
I no.1 and headed 'Publications of the Industrial
Law Research Council, prepared for the Labour Research
Institute, WEA. *OTURS/RSK incomplete.

5411 Young Militant. 1933-1934. Toronto: Spartacus Youth
Club, (4th International). ɣ. Formerly October
Youth. (Vol.I no.1) Dec 1933 to vol.II no.5, Sept-
Oct 1934//*OTP microfilm.

1934

5412 The British Columbia Labour (Labor) Truth. 1934-1939.
Vancouver: Vancouver National Labour Council. P.E.
Thompson. m. Probably later BC Workers Review.
Vol.I no.1, May 1934 tp vol.VI no.67, Nov 1939//?
*OOL microfilm. Elliott 128. From April 1935 off-
icial organ of Western Canadian Labour, anti-CIO and
violently anti-Communist.

5413 The B.C. Lumber Worker. 1934-1960? Vancouver: LWIU
(i.e. Lumber Workers Industrial Union) WUL. A. Parkin.
w. Vol.IV no.6, 14 April 1934 to vol.VII no.34, 10
May 1938.*OOL microfilm, incomplete. Elliott 133.
Then: published by International Woodworkers of America. s. vol.XXVII no.1, Jan 1960 to vol.XXVII no.4
Feb 1960. *OOL microfilm. Numbering probably continues
from the US edition.

5414 Camp Worker. 1934. Trenton and Kingston: The Camp
Committee, Unemployed Workers in Government Camp.
u. No.1, 1 May 1934 *OTURS/RSK.

5415 The Canadian Toiler. 1934. Toronto: Workers League
of Canada. m. Vol.I no.1, Feb 1934. *OTURS/RSK.

5416 Communist Review. 1934-1935. (Toronto): Communist
Party of Canada. m. No.I, 1 March 1934 to no.9
Jan 1935//? *OTCPA.

5417 East York Workers Bulletin. 1934. East York, Ont.
(Communist Party of Canada). u. Vol.I no.1, Feb
1934. *OTURS/RSK.

5418 Fight Against War and Fascism. 1934. Toronto: Can-

418

adian Youth Congress Against War and Fascism. m.
Vol.I no.1, 23 June 1934//? *OTURS/RSK.

5419 L'Idée Ouvrière. 1934-1937. St-Hyacinthe. Journal
mensuel de la jeunesse ouvrière canadienne-française
(no.1): Journal franchement dévoué aux intérets ouvriers (no.2). Gerard Brady. m. Later L'Homme Libre.
Vol.I no.1, June 1934 to vol.IV no.7, 31 July 1937//
*OOL. Elliott 129.

(5420) The Link-Up. 1934. Vancouver: Workers Unity League.
Not found.

5421 Manitoba Commonwealth. 1934-1952. Winnipeg: Committee representing Winnipeg Trades and Labor Council,
Manitoba Assn of Social Reconstruction Clubs, Manitoba Farmers Section CCF. T.E. Moore. w. Formerly
The Weekly News: numbering continued: vol.IX no.486
6 July 1934 to vol.XV no.852-55, 10 Oct 1941. *OOL
microfilm; 1943-1952 MWU 1944-1952 SRA. From April
1938 published by CCF Manitoba. Elliott 127.

5422 The Maritime Co-operator. 1934-1942? Truro: Co-operatives, Credit Unions and allied institutions: in
the interests of vital education, land, crafts and
Christian co-operatives. George Boyle. s. Vol.IX
1942, scattered issues only *OOA/CUC222.

5423 Midwest Clarion. 1934-1940? Winnipeg. Ed: John Weir.
u. Vol.V no.193, 6 Jan 1940 and scattered issues
only *OTAR. Elliott 130.

5424 The New Commonwealth and The Weekly Sun. 1934-?
Toronto: CCF. w. Vol.I no.5, 18 Aug 1934.*OTURS/RSK.
Elliott 131.

5425 North Star. 1934-1935. Prince Albert, Sask. Ed:
S.W. Yates, H.H. Luke. w. Vol.I no.1, 21 Sept 1934
to vol.III no.4, 24 July 1935//*OOA/CCF295. From
vol.II subheaded 'Saskatchewan's pioneer CCF newspaper'.

5426 The Postal Tribune/Le Tribune Postal. 1934-? Montreal: Montreal Post Office Employees Assn; later Canadian Postal Employees Assn. René Caillaud. m.
Vol.V no.9, April/avril 1938 onwards *OOL partially
microfilmed. Elliott 156.

5427 Ship and Dock. 1934-1935. Vancouver: Longshoremen
and Water Transport Workers of Canada. m/e. Later
Waterfront Strike Bulletin. Vol.I no.1, Dec 1934
to no.16, 5 Sept 1935//*OOL microfilm. e from 20
March 1935.

5428 Socialist Action. 1934. Toronto: (Socialist Party
of Canada). (Fred Hodgson). e. Vol.I no.1, 16
March 1934 *OTURS/RSK.

5429 The Spark. 1934-1935. Vancouver: Young Socialist
League. b. Vol.I no.7, July 1934 *OOA/Lucas 3;
nos.8, 9; vol.II no.1-3, 7, 9; July 1934 to Sept
1935*BVAU/Mac36f.12A

5430 The Voice of the Fishermen(and Cannery Workers).
1934-1935. Vancouver: Fishermen and Cannery Workers
Industrial Union: Workers Unity League of Canada. s.
Vol.I no.1, March 1934 to no.15, 25 Feb 1935 *OOL
microfilm. Lacks 2, 9.

5431 Workers' Bulletin. 1934. (Toronto): Communist Party
of Canada. ∅. No.1, 1 May 1934; no.2, July 1934//?
*T.

1935

(5432)L'Ami du Peuple. 1935-? Montréal: Fédération des
ouvriers du Canada. 1935 QQA, not seen.

5433 Amoeba. 1935. Vancouver: official organ of the CCY
(i.e. Class Conscious Youth), BC section. m. (Vol.I
no.1), 7 Jan 1935, Jan, May; vol.I no.7 (first numbered issue), june 1925 to no.12, Dec 1935//?*BVAU/
Mac35f.1a. Format varies with almost every issue.

5434 The BC Workers News. 1935-1937. Vancouver: Proletarian Publishing Assn. Geo. Drayton. w. Later The
Peoples Advocate. Vol.I no.2, 25 Jan 1935 to vol.
III, no.11 (whole no.115), 26 March 1937//*OOL microfilm. Elliott 134.

5435 CCF News. 1935. Swift Current: CCF. ∅. Vol.I no.1
6 April 1935 and no.2, July 1935 //?*OOA/Lucas 3.

5436 Calgary Typo News. 1935. Calgary: Calgary Typographical Union 449: published in the interest of locked
out printers in the Albertan plant. w. No.1, 15 Jan
1935 to no.32, 16 Aug 1935//?*OOL and MWPL microfilms.
Both incomplete.

5437 The Canadian Association of Railwaymen's Journal.
1935-1952. Winnipeg: Canadian Assn of Railwaymen.
Geo. Salverson. m. Vol.IV no.2, Feb 1938 to vol.VII
Jan 1941, incomplete; vol.XVIII no.6, June 1952*MWPL.

5438 Clarté. 1935-1939. Montréal: Parti-ouvrier progressiste. A Caron et Darment. Vol.I no.1, fév 1935 à
8 fév 1939//*OONL incomplete. 5 dec 1936 to 8 fév
1939 QMU microfilm.

5439 Labor Leader. 1935. Winnipeg: (One Big Union). w.
Formerly OBU BULLETIN. Vol.I no.1, 4 April 1935 to
no.9, 30 May 1935//*OOL microfilm. Elliott 135.
'We take over the goodwill of the OBU Bulletin which
was forced to suspend publication in May 1934.'

5440 Il Lavatore. 1935-1938. Toronto. For the cause of
Italian workers in Canada. w. Numero speciale vol.I
no.1, 4 Dec 1935; vol.I no.1 (repeated) 19 March 1936
to 17 Sept 1938. *OONL. McLaren 310.

5441 Liekki/(The Flame). 1935- . Sudbury: Vapaus: Canad-
an suomalaisten kaunokirjallinen viikkolehti. w.

Unnumbered, 7 Dec 1935 to 28 Dec 1957 *OONL. New numbering 7 Dec 1935 cited. First number identified from RCMP envelope marked 'First edition received... of Liekki...Retain indefinitely'.

5442 The News Bag. 1935. Vancouver: The Commonwealth. Fanny Lou. m. Vol.I no.2, 10 July 1935 and no.4, 10 Sept 1935 *ACGA/Hutchison.

5443 North Toronto CCYM Youth in Revolt. 1935. Toronto: CCYM. ?w. No.(1) undated; nos.3, 14, 17; 6 July to 26 Oct 1935 *OKQS/CCF.

5444 Peoples Champion. 1935. Winnipeg: Selkirk Communist Election Committee. Vol.I no.1, 4 Oct 1935 *OTURS/RSK.

5445 The S.U.U. (ie. Struggle-Unity-Understanding). 1935. Saskatoon: official organ of the Saskatoon Union of Unemployed. u. Vol.I no.2, 7 May 1935 *SSA/G185.1.

5446 Strike Bulletin. 1935. Regina: Relief Camp Strikers Committee. u. No.1, June 1935; unnumbered 26 June 1935, plus one further bulletin 'official statement' all *OTURS/RSK.

5447 Voice of Youth. 1935. Regina: official organ of CCYM Regina. m. Vol.I no.1, Feb 1935//? *OOA/Lucas 3.

5448 Waterfront Strike Bulletin. 1935. Vancouver: Strike Committee V.& DWWA (ie. Vancouver and District Water Transport Workers Assn). d. Formerly Ship and Dock. Vol.I 'Special' 18 Sept 1935 to no.149, 27 Nov 1935//? *OOL. Lacks 128, 129, 134, 135, 148 but numbering erratic anyway.

5449 We Too. 1935. Nanaimo: Progressive Miners of Nanaimo. w. Vol.I no.1, 16 Feb 1935 to no.17, 2 Nov 1935//?*OOL microfilm. Lacks 4, 6, 8, 9, 11-13.

5450 Winnipeg Typo News. 1935. Winnipeg: edited and published in the interests of locked out members of the Winnipeg Typographical Union. w. Vol.I no.1, 17 April 1935 to no.30, 15 Nov 1935//? *OOL microfilm.

1936

5451 Advance. 1936-1937. Toronto. m. Later New Advance. Vol.I no.1 (?Dec) 1936 to no.7, Aug 1937 *OONL. No. 3 repeated, no. 6 omitted.

5452 Bakery Salesmen's News. 1936. Vancouver. u. No.1 29 Sept 1936//?*OTURS/RSK. Strike bulletin, entirely devoted to a speech by Birt Showler.

5453 BC Maritime Worker. 1936. (Vancouver): a group of progressive longshoremen and seaman. ⌀. Vol.I no.4 to no.13, 27 Nov 1936//?*OOL microfilm. Lacks 6,7,8.

5454 CCF Bulletin. 1936. Vancouver: CCF, BC. ⌀. Numbering erratic and missing: 1-7, Jan 1936; 4 and 5

Feb and March 1936*OOA/CCF221, others *BVAU/Mac35f.2.
See 5462 below for another publication.

5455 Daily Clarion. 1936-1939. Toronto. Ed: T.C. Sims.
d. Formerly The Worker, later The Clarion. Numbering
continued: vol.XV no.851, 1 May 1936 to vol.XVII no.
1830, 19 June 1939//*OOL microfilm. Elliott 137.

5456 Canadian/National Seamen's Union Bulletin. 1936.
(?Toronto): National Seamens Union. m. Nos. 1 and
2, 1936, two issues only *OOL microfilm.

5457 The Challenge. 1936. Saskatoon: CCF Youth Movement.
No.4, 28 April 1936 *OOA/CCF221.

5458 Fascism and Reaction in Many Lands and the Struggle
Against It. 1936. (Toronto): Canadian Labor Defense
League. u. No.1, May 1936//? *OTURS/RSK.

5459 The Federationist. 1936-1943. Vancouver: CCF, BC.
w. Vol.I no.1, 21 Aug 1936 to vol.VIII no.13, 4 Nov
1943//*BVAU. Elliott 183. See 5459 above for an
earlier publication by BC CCF.

(5460)Fisherman's Voice. 1936-1937? Vancouver. u. Later
The Fisherman. Elliott 146, not found.

5461 Hlas L'udu/Voice of the People. 1936-1940. Toronto.
The only semi-weekly labor organ in Canada for Slovak
and Czech speaking people. Cyprián Slimák. i/c.
Formerly Robotnićké Slovo, later L'Udove Zvesti.
Numbering continued: vol.V no.60, 29 July 1936 to
vol.IX no.52, 29 June 1940 to 3 July 1940//Suspended.
*OONL microfilm. McLaren 425.

(5462)Industrial Worker. 1936-1937. Toronto: Educational
Labor Press and Radio Bureau of Canada: to promote
sound trade union ideals. m. OOL, not found.
Elliott 141.

5463 The Labour Review. 1936-1958. Ottawa: Canadian
Federation of Labor. m. Vol.I no.1, Dec 1936 to
vol.XIII no.1, Aug 1958 *OOL. Elliott 136.

5464 Liaudies Balsas/The Peoples Voice. 1936- Toronto:
Lithuanian Press Assn: the Canadian Lithuanian working people. w. Formerly Darbininkų Žodis. Numbering
continues: no.163, 19 March 1936 through 1970*OONL
incomplete. McLaren 371.

5465 The Link. 1936-1938. Toronto: Workers Educational
Assn. Drummond Wren. ɓ. Vol.I no.1, Oct-Nov 1936
to no.4, 1938//*OOL microfilm.

5466 New Era. 1936-1938. Weyburn/Regina:CCF. m. Later
Saskatchewan Commonwealth. Vol.I no.1, Feb 1936 to
30 March 1938// AEU OOP *SRA incomplete. Elliott 138.
Published in Regina after 1937.

5467 News and Views. 1936-1937. Regina: CCF Saskatchewan
section. ?w. No volume: nos.1-10 (1936) to Sept
1937//?*SSA/G.1.1.

5468 Pacific Coast News. 1936-1940. Vancouver: Pilot Publishing Co: owned and controlled by fishermen. w. 4th year np.49, 6 July 1939 to 5th year no.27, 1 Feb 1940.*OOL microfilm. As a nice example of parochialism their issue of 7th Sept 1939 has one comment on the outbreak of war: 'War affects canned salmon shipments'. Also subtitled The BC Fishermen's Weekly.

(5469) Peoples Front. 1936. (Toronto): Canadian League Against War and Fascism. Not found.

5470 The People's Weekly. 1936-1952. Edmonton: Later published by the Alberta CCF. Elmer Roper. w/e/m. Formerly Alberta Labor News: numbering continued: vol.XVI no.22, 25 Jan 1936 to vol.XXXIII no.4, 20 Dec 1952//*OOL microfilm. Elliott 97. Merged with The Commonwealth (Regina) from 6 Jan 1945.

5471 The Rural Co-operator. 1936-1939? Toronto: United Farmers of Ontario and United Farmers Coperative Co. H.H. Hannam. m. Vol.III no.8, 11 April 1939 *OOA/ CUC.

(5472) Shipping and Terminals. 1936-1937. Montreal: Canadian Brotherhood of Ships Employees. Elliott 142, not found.

5473 Ship's News. 1936. Vancouver: official organ of the Seafarers Industrial Union. e. Vol.I no.1, 9 Sept 1936 and 2, 24 Sept 1936//?*OOL.

5474 Slobodna Misao/(Free Thought). 1936-1940. Montreal/ Toronto: Croatian Publishing Co. i. Formerly Borba. Numbering continued: vol.VI no.309, 22 Sept 1936 to vol.X no.915, 15 Aug 1940.*OONL, incomplete. McLaren 54.

5475 The Western Farm Leader. 1936-1941? Calgary. Cooperation, public affairs, social progress: published in the interest of the organized farm movement. s. Vol.II no.4, 19 Feb 1937 *OOA/CCF222; vol.III, 11-16, 3 June-19 Aug 1938 *ACGL; vol.II no.18, 17 Sept 1937, vol.VI no.12, 20 June 1941 *SSA/McNaughton J.1. Elliott 139.

5476 Winnipeg Voter. 1936. Winnipeg: Communist Party of Canada. u. No.3, 24 July 1936. *OOA/CCF393.

5477 The Young Communist. (1936). (Toronto): (Young Communist League). m. Reissued in 1940 in plain wrappers titled 'Art Review'. No.1, Sept (1936). *OTURS/RSK.

1937

5478 The British Columbia Constructive. 1937. Vancouver: Vancouver Centre Campaign of the BC Constructives. u. Vol.I no.1, 29 May 1937//?*T. Robert Connell's breakaway party from the CCF.

5479 The Canadian Labour Herald. 1937-1942. Vancouver:
Vancouver Council of the Canadian Federation of Labour. m. Vol.I no.1, Oct 1937 to vol.V no.5, April
1942//*OOL microfilm. Numbering irregular. Elliott
145.

(5480)Civil Servants Digest. 1937. Vancouver: Amalgamated
Civil Servants Assn. m. Formerly Organizer. Elliott 69, not found.

5481 Discussion. 1937- . Toronto: Communist Party of
Canada. Nos. 3, 5, 5, Oct 1937 *OTURS/RSK. Before
many conventions of the CPC this bulletin was re-
vived and numbered afresh each time.

5482 The Fisherman. 1937. Vancouver: Salmon Purse Sein-
ers Union of the Pacific and Pacific Coast Fishermans
Union. e. Formerly Fisherman's Voice. Vol.I no.2,
11 March 1937 through 1970 *OOL microfilm. Format
changes with vo.II no.43, 30 Jan 1940; from 17 March
1945 published by United Fishermen and Allied Workers. Elliott 146.

(5483)Hamilton Steelworker. 1937. Hamilton. Elliott 148,
not found.

5484 L'Homme Libre. 1937-1941. St-Hyacinthe: Gérard
Brady: hebdomadaire de reconquête national et econ-
omique. w. Formerly L'Idée Ouvrière: numbering
continued: vol.IV no.8, 7 août 1937 to vol.VII no.
20, 6 mars 1941//?*OOL microfilm.

5485 Maritime CCF Bulletin. 1937-1939. Moncton: CCF.
Watson Baird. m. Vol.I no.1, Aug 1937 (carbon copies); vol.II no.1, Jan 1938 to vol.III no.5, June
1939//?*OOA/CCF34.

5486 Народна Газета /(Narodna Gazeta)/People's Gazette.
1937-1941. Winnipeg: Workers and Farmers Publishing
Co. d/w. Formerly Ukrains'ki Robitnychi Visti: numbering continued: vol.XIX, Sept 1937 to April 1941.
OONL*MWPL microfilm. Elliott 157.

(5487)New International Bulletin. 1937. (?Toronto): Can-
adian and United States sections of the LWRP (ie.
League for a Revolutionary Workers Party). m.
Not found.

5488 One Big Union Monthly. 1937-1938. Winnipeg: Winni-
peg Central Labor Council of the OBU. m. Vol.I no.1
Dec 1937 to no.11, Oct.1938//? MWPL *OOL microfilm.
Elliott 151.

5489 The People's Advocate. 1937-1939. Vancouver: Proletarian Publishing Assn. w. Formerly the BC Workers News; later The Advocate: numbering continued:
vol.III no.12 (whole no.116) 2 Apr 1937 to whole no.
241, 25 Aug 1939//*OOL microfilm. No volume numbers
after vol.IV no.24, 24 June 1938. Elliott 147.

5490 Правда/Pravda/Justice. 1937-1940. Toronto: Serbian
Publishing Assn. s/w. Formerly Borba. Vol.I no.1
6 Jan 1937 to vol.IV no.123, 14 Aug 1940 *OONL incomplete.

(5491) Revolutionary Youth. c1937. Toronto: Revolutionary Youth League, Youth section of the LRWP (ie. League for a Revolutionary Workers Party). Not found.

5492 Searchlight. 1937-1949. Montreal: Canadian Seamen's Union. J.A.(Pat) Sullivan. Two to three times a month. Vol.I no.1, 1 July 1937 to vol.XIII no.6 4 Aug 1949.//?*OOL microfilm. Elliott 144.

5493 UFC Information. 1937-1948. (Saskatoon): United Farmers of Canada, Saskatchewan section. m. Vol.I no.2, Sept 1937 to vol.XI no.12, Dec 1948 *SSA/G.37.2 incomplete.

5494 Waterfront Organizer. 1937. Vancouver: BC Maritime Workers Joint Policy Committee. s. Vol.I no.1, 1 May 1937 to no.8, 23 Oct 1937//? *OOL microfilm.

(5495) Workers Voice. 1937. Toronto: Canadian section of the League for Revolutionary Workers Party. Not found.

1938

(5496) The CLDL Veteran. c1938. Vancouver. Not found.

5497 The Commentator. 1938-1966. Trail, BC: International Union of Mine, Mill and Smelter Workers. (A.H. Evans). e/m. Vol.I no.1, 2 Nov 1938 to Dec 1966 *BVAU and *OOL microfilm, incomplete. Elliott 191.

(5498) Commercial Fisherman's Weekly. 1939-1945? Vancouver: in the interests of organized fishermen in BC. w. Vol.I no.1, 1939 to c.1945. Elliott 165, not seen.

5499 Friends of the Soviet Union/Societé des Amis Canadiens de l'Union Sovietique: Bulletin. 1938. Montreal. u. No.1, 15 juin 1938//? *OOA/CCF394.

5500 The Mudslinger. 1938-1939? Toronto: National Union of Shovelmen and Operating Engineers Dist. no.1. u. Unnumbered and undated. Probably Dec 1938 to Feb 1939 *OOL microfilm. Dated from date on receipt stamps in OOL.

5501 The New Advance. 1938-1941? Toronto. Ed: Roy Davis. m. Vol.I no.5, March 1938 *AEPAA/Brown 468.

5502 The New Commonwealth Jr. 1938-? (Toronto): The New Commonwealth. e. Unnumbered, undated: two issues in 1938 *OOA/CCF49.

5503 (The Oshawa) Labor Leader/Press. 1938-1941. Oshawa. Independent and progressive. Wm. E. Noble. w. Vol. I no.1, 14 April 1938 to vol.IV no.37, 13 March 1941// *OOL microfilm. No. 37 should be 39. First title The Labor Leader; August 1938 The Oshawa Labor Leader; August 1938 The Oshawa Labor Press. Elliott 153.

5504 Post Office 'Sitdowners' Gazette. 1938. Vancouver:
P.O. Sitdowners. u. Later Victoria Jobless Journal.
Undated (May-June 1938). No.2 *BVAUS/Shepherd 4-5.

5505 Saskatchewan Commonwealth. 1938-1946. Regina: CCF.
m/e/w. Formerly New Era, later (The Prairie New Democrat) Commonwealth: numbering continued: April 1938
to 1946 AEU *SRA. Elliott 138.

5506 Socialist Action. 1938-1942. Toronto: Socialist
Workers League of Canada/Socialist Policy Group (CCF).
∅. Formerly The Vanguard. (Vol.I) no.1, 15 April
1938 to (vol.II)no.6, Sept 1939//suppressed. Some
further underground issues, mimeo, unnumbered up to
June 1942. All *OTP microfilm.

5507 Steel Labor Canadian Edition. 1938-? Indianapolis:
Steel Workers Organizing Committee CIO. m. First
issue of Canadian edition starts vol.III no.12, 23
Dec 1938 through 1970 *OOL microfilm. Elliott 182.

5508 Toronto Garment Worker. 1938-1954. Toronto: United
Garment Workers of America local 253. (m). Vol.IX
no.92, Jan 1946 to vol.XIV no.151, Aug-Sept 1951 *OOL
incomplete. Then published by the Canadian Garment
Workers Union and numbering recommenced: vol.II no.1,
Jan 1953 to vol.III no.5, Dec 1954 *OOL microfilm.
Elliott 154.

5509 Union News. 1938. Sydney: SWOC Local 1064, official
organ of the steelworkers of Sydney. (SWOC-Steel Workers Organising Cttee).Vol.I no.1, 9 April 1938 to no.
15, 23 July 1938//*OOL microfilm.

5510 Victoria Jobless Journal. 1938. (Victoria). w.
Formerly Post Office Sitdowners Gazette. Vol.I no.1
'in reality the fourth edition of the Post Office
Sitdowners Gazette', no date *T.

1939

5511 The Advocate. 1939-1940. Vancouver. Ed: Hal Griffin.
w. Formerly The People's Advocate; later The People:
numbering continued: full no.242, 1 Sept 1939 to vol.
VI no.22 (full no.283), 14 June 1940//*OOL microfilm.
Resumes volume numbering with vol.VI no.1, 19 Jan 1940.

5512 The Beacon. 1939-1940? Toronto: Young Communust
League. ∅. Vol.I no.1, 4 Oct 1939 to vol.II no.18
May 1940 *OTURS/RSK.

5513 The Bridge River Miner. 1939-1940. (Pioneer, BC):
Pioneer Local 308 IUMMSW. W.A. Paterson. s. Vol.I
no.1, 22 Sept 1939 to no.6, 14 Feb 1940//*OOL microfilm. Elliott 163.

(5514)CAIA Union Pilot. 1939-? Toronto: International
Assn of Machinists Lodge 1625. Elliott 166 not found.

5515 CCF Bulletin. ?1939-1940? Kelowna, BC. Ed: Gordon
D. Herbert. u. No.14, 1 Feb 1940 *BVAUS.

(5516)Canadian Chemical Worker. 1939-? Toronto: International Chemical Workers Union. w. Elliott 161, not
found.

(5517)Canadian Full Fashioned Hosiery Workers Bulletin.
1939-1941? Toronto. m. Elliott 164, not found.

5518 The Clarion. 1939-1941? Toronto. Ed: T.C. Sims.
w. Formerly Daily Clarion: numbering continued:
vol.XVII no.1831, 1 July 1939 to 19 July 1941//?
*OOL microfilm. Irregularly numbered after Nov 1939.

5519 Fight Fascism. 1939-? Toronto: League for a Revolutionary Workers Party. s. No.1, 8 March 1939 *T.

(5520)Guild Annual. 1939-? Vancouver:Canadian Merchant
Service Guild. Elliott 168, not found.

5521 Housewives' Report. 1939-? Vancouver: Housewives
League of BC. m. Vol.I no.1, July 1939 and 2, Aug
1939 *BVAUS/Mac35f.1b. Name changed to BC Housewife
after first issue.

5522 LRI Monthly Survey. 1939-1942? Toronto: Labour Research Institute: news and comment on matters of general interest to labour. Vol.I no.1, June 1939
*OTURS/RSK.

5523 The Melting Pot/Polska Sekcja/Українська Секция /
Magyar Szakasz. 1939-1940. Oshawa: SWOC Lodge 1817
(ie. Steelworkers Organizing Committee). w. Vol.II
no.1, 26 Feb 1940 to no.5, 26 March 1940//*OOL Microfilm.

5524 Le Mouvement Ouvrier. 1939-1944? Montréal/Sherbrooke:
(Ligue Ouvrière Catholique): le journal de la famille
ouvrière. m. Vol.III no.1, òct 1941 to vol.V no.12,
sept 1944//?*OOL. Elliott 194.

5525 The Party Builder. 1939. Toronto: Communist Party
of Canada. m. Nos. 7, 8, 9, May-July 1939 *OTURS/
RSK.

5526 Railway Review. 1939-1951. Winnipeg: National Union
of Railwaymen. m. No.1, Dec 1939 to vol.XI no.1,
Mar-April 1951 *OOL. Elliott 120.

(5527)Railway Journal. 1939-? Winnipeg: Canadian Assn of
Railwaymen. m. Elliott 75, not found.

5528 Ships News. 1939. Vancouver: Inlandboatmens Union
of the Pacific. s. Vol.I no.13, 17 April 1939 to
no.24, 27 Oct 1939//?*OOL microfilm.

5529 דער װעג/(Der Veg)/The Road. 1939-1940. Tononto.
w. Formerly Der Kam(p)f: numbering continued: vol.
XIV no.764, 18 Aug 1939 to 9 Aug 1940//*OONL microfilm. McLaren 358. With some English supplements.

5530 Winnipeg Stitcher. 1939. Winnipeg: Winnipeg Cloak
and Dress Makers Union Locals 216, 237 ILGWU. S. Her-
bst and C. Hart. u. Undated and unnumbered: (Sept

1939) to (Dec 1939)*OOL microfilm.

1940

5531 AFU Bulletin. 1940-1949. Edmonton: Alberta Farmers
Union. m. Later Organized Farmer. Vol.VII no.12,
Dec 1947 to vol.IX no.1, Jan 1949//*OOL microfilm.

(5532)ATE Bulletin. 1940-1947? Toronto: Assn of Technical
Employees. Elliott 184, not found.

(5533)Aircraft and Furniture Worker. 1940-1944. Kitchener.
Elliott 170, not found.

5534 BC Workers Review. 1940-1942. Vancouver: later issues endorsed by BC Council of Longshoremen. A.G.
Pearce. m. Probably formerly BC Labor Truth. Vol.I
no.1, Jan 1940 to vol.III no.30, Aug-Sept 1942//*OOL.
Elliott 180. Contains same violently anti-Communist
and anti-CIO line of the BC Labor Truth and is virtually anti-union.

(5535)Belleville Beacon. 1940-1945. Belleville: United
Auto, Aircraft and Agricultural Implement Workers,
Local 426. m. Elliott 171, not found.

5536 The Canadian/Daily Tribune. 1940- . Toronto: a jour-
nal of democratic opinion. A.A. MacLeod. w/d/w.
Vol.I no.1, 20 Jan 1940 through 1970. *OOL microfilm.
Elliott 181. Published by the Communist Party of
Canada. Became Daily Tribune 1 May to 4 Nov 1947,
then reverted to weekly again.

(5537)Christian Fellowship Letter. 1940. Toronto: Fellowship for a Christian Social Order. u. ?later Christian Social Action.

(5538)Christian Social Action. ?1940-1944? Toronto: Fellowship for a Christian Social Order. u.

5539 The Clarion. 1940. Ottawa: Communist Party of Canada, Ottawa district. Unnumbered: 5 Sept 1940 *OTURS/
RSK.

5540 Contact. 1940-1942? (Nakina, Ont): Canadian Communications Union. ฿. Formerly The Communication
Worker. No.1 (Old series vol.XIV no.10), Aug 1940
to vol.I no.10, Aug-Sept 1942 (Old series vol.XV no.5)
*OOL microfilm. Elliott 167.

(5541)De Havilland Aircraft Worker. 1940-1942. Toronto:
United Automobile, Aircraft and Agricultural Implement Workers Local 112. m. Later De Havilland Aircrafter. Elliott 185, not found. The changes of
name of this publication, together with the lack of
reference copies, are very confusing. The most probable sequence is as follows: 1940 to Dec 1941 - De
Havilland Aircraft Worker: Jan 1942 to July 1943 -
UAW-CIO War Worker (De Havilland Edition): Aug 1943

to 1945 - De Havilland War Worker: 1945-1947 ceased
publication: Jan 1947 to Dec 1953 - De Havilland Aircrafter: 1953 to 1958 - Amalgamated Aircrafter: 1958
through 1970 - Aircrafter.

5542 The Monthly Review. 1940. Toronto: Communist Party
of Canada: a journal of theory and practise of Marxism-Leninism. m. Vol.I no.1, March 1940 to no.5
Aug 1940 *OTURS/RSK. Nos.2 to 5 only *OHMA.

5543 The New Lead. 1940- . Toronto: Newspaper Guild of
Toronto. m. Vol.I no.1, July 1940 through 1970 *OOL.
Suspended 1941-1948. Elliott 175.

(5544) Packer. 1940-1946? Montreal: Packinghouse, Butchers
and Allied Food Workers. m. Elliott 174, not found.

5545 Rowley's Mag. (sic). 1940. (Toronto): (pro-CCF).
Ed: William Philip Rowley. m. Successor to The
Record. Vol.I no.1, Oct 1940 *AEUS/CCF.XIII-15.

(5546) SAL Union News. 1940-1944. Toronto: Electrical,
Radio and Machine Workers Local 519. m. Elliott
173, not found.

5547 Searchlight. 1940. Toronto: Canadian Seamens Union.
u. No.1, 15 April 1940 (Strike special). *OOA/CCF
188.

5548 The Spitfire. ?1940-1945? Montreal: Aircraft Lodge
712, International Assn of Machinists AFL. m.
Vol.III no.1, Feb 1942 to vol.VI no.3, 7 June 1945//?
*OOL Elliott 188.

5549 Le Syndicaliste. 1940-1942. Québec: CTCC bulletin
officiel (Confédération des Travailleurs Catholiques
du Canada). m. Vol.I no.1, Dec 1940 to vol.II no.12
Nov 1942//*OOL microfilm. Absorbed into Le Travail.
Elliott 176.

5550 Tiedonantaja. 1940-1942? (Port Arthur): (Labor Progressive Party). b. Vol.I no.5, July 1940 to (vol.
III no.1) Feb 1942 *OOA/FOC141. Incomplete; one
missing issue (vol.II no.5, June 1941) in *OTURS/RSK.

5551 The Young Communist. 1940. Toronto: Young Communist
League. m. Vol.I no.1, March 1940 to no.4, Oct-Nov
1940//*OTURS/RSK. Issued in covers printed 'Art Review'.

1941

(5552) 756 Review. 1941-1943. Vancouver: International Assn
of Machinists, Lodge 756. m. Elliott 187, not found.

5553 The Bison. 1941-? Winnipeg: Manitoba Government
Employees Assn. m. Vol.I no.1, Dec 1941 to vol.III
no.3, Nov 1945. New series starts vol.I no.1, April
1948. *MWPL incomplete.

5554 Canadian Mineworker. 1941-1957. Edmonton: United Mineworkers of America District 18. m. Vol.I no.1, 1 March 1941 to vol.XVII no.4, June 1957//*OOL microfilm. Elliott 192.

(5555)Canadian War Worker. 1941-1944. Ottawa: Canadian Federation of Labour. w. Vol.I no.1 to vol.IV no.10. Elliott 195, not seen.

5556 Congress Labour News. 1941-? (Ottawa): Canadian Congress of Labour. Ø. Vol.I no.1, June 1941 *OOL.

5557 The Excavator. 1941-1942? Toronto: National Union of Operating Engineers. ?m. Unnumbered: Sept 1941, May, June and Dec 1942 *OOL microfilm.

5558 Kirkland Lake Bulletin. 1941-1942. Kirkland Lake: (Local 240). Ø. No.7, 16 Dec 1941. Strike bulletin: the strike began on 18 Nov 1941 to Feb 1942. Only issue located *OOA/CCF188.

5559 Kronika Tygodniowa/Weekly Chronicle. 1941. Toronto: (Polish Democratic Assn in Canada). w. Formerly Głos Pracy. Vol.I no.2, 1 March 1941 to no.44, 20 Dec 1941 *OONL. McLaren 390.

5560 (L'Udové) Zvesti/(People's News). 1941-? Toronto: Zvesti Publishing: victory over fascism. Jozef Duriancik. w. Vol.I no.1, 27 Sept 1941 to vol.IV, Feb 1944 *OONL incomplete. McLaren 428. Name becomes L'Udové Zvesti with vol.II no.23, 6 June 1942.

5561 News Comment. 1941-1950. Ottawa: CCF National Office. Grace MacInnis. s/m. Later Comment. (Vol.I) no.1, 1 March 1941 to vol.X no.8-9, Aug-Sept 1950// *OOA/CCF531. Indexes exist for most volumes; several issues incorrectly numbered.

(5562)Dos Sotsialishtishe Vort/The Socialist Word. 1941-? Toronto: Jewish Socialist Party. McLaren 352, not found.

(5563)Steel. 1941-1944. Vancouver: United Steelworkers of Canada. Elliott 190, not found.

5564 Вестник/Vestnik/Herald. 1941-1942. Toronto. w. Vol.I no.1, 6 Nov 1941 to 30 Dec 1942//*OONL microfilm. McLaren 407.

1942

(5565)Conciliator. 1942. Regina: Local 1, world's first co-operative refinery. w. Elliott 201, not found.

5566 Congress News. 1942-1944. Vancouver: Canadian Congress of Labor at Pacific Coast. e. Vol.I no.1, 5 Sept 1942 to vol.II no.25, 12 Aug 1944//*OOL microfilm. Numbering irregular.

5567 Co-operative Union News Service. 1942-1943? Regina:

Co-operative Union of Canada, Saskatchewan section.
m. Vol.I no.3, 12, June 1942; March 1943 and vol.II
no.2, May 1943 *OOA/Good 12.

5568 Detonator. 1942-1943. Whitby: UE-DIL, Ajax Local.
w. Vol.I no.1, 6 Oct 1942 to no.18, 3 Aug 1943 *OOL
microfilm.

5569 The Effort. 1942-1944? Fort William: Aircraft Lodge
719. m. Vol.I no.1, Feb 1942 to no.9, Dec 1942. *OOL
microfilm. Elliott 186.

5570 Ford Facts. 1942- . Windsor: Ford Local 200, UAW-
CIO. e. Vol.II no.15, 3 Dec 1943 through 1970 *OOL
part microfilm. Suspended publication July 1952 to
Jan 1953. Elliott 208.

5571 The Gazette (inside: Glace Bay Gazette). 1942-1949.
Glace Bay. The only labour-owned daily in Canada.
d. Later The Star. Unnumbered: (1), 21 Sept 1942
to 8 Jan 1949 BVAU *OOL microfilm. Elliott 197.

5572 (The) (Hamilton) Labour Digest. 1942-1953 and 1957-?
Hamilton: Hamilton and District Trades and Labour
Council. m. Vol.I no.1, Dec 1942 to vol.XI no.6,
Dec 1953//?*OOL. Numbering recommences: Vol.I no.1,
Jan 1957 to no.10, Dec 1957//?*OOL. Elliott 198.

5573 Labour Youth Review. 1942. Toronto: Labour Youth
Federation of Canada. m. Vol.I no.2, 1 Aug 1942 *T.

5574 The Marine Worker. 1942-1943? Halifax: IUMSW of
Canada. ⌀. Vol.II no.1, 9 Jan 1943 to vol.II no.7,
July 1943. *OOL microfilm.

(5575) News Letter. 1942. Bartonville, Ont: Ontario Provincial Council, International Union of Carpenters
and Joiners. Elliott 202, not found.

5576 The People. 1942-1944. Vancouver: (Labor-Progressive Party. Hal Griffin. w. Formerly The Advocate;
later The Pacific Advocate. Vol.II no.1, 7 Jan 1943
to vol.III no.39, 30 Sept 1944. *OOL microfilm.
Elliott 205.

5577 Peterboro UE News. 1942. Peterborough: UE. e.
Vol.I no.1, 2 Sept 1942 to no.4, 6 Nov 1942 *OOL
microfilm.

5578 Le Travail (et la Vie Syndicale). 1942. Montréal:
Organe officiel de la Confédération des Travailleurs
Catholiques du Canada. m. Formerly La Vie Syndicale:
numbering continued: vol.XVIII no.1, janvier 1942
through 1970. *OOL microfilm. Elliott 90. Becomes
Le Travail only in Jan 1944.

(5579) Safety Valve. 1942. Montreal: National Union of
Operating Engineers. e. Elliott 199, not found.

5580 Socialist Press. 1942-1947? Toronto: Socialist
Labor Party of Canada. Paul Debragh. m. Vol.VI
no.12 and vol.VII no.1, March and April 1947 *BVAU/
Mac31Af.18.

5581 The UAW-CIO War Worker - De Havilland Edition. 1942-
1943. Toronto: UAW. ⦰. Formerly De Havilland Aircraft Worker; later De Havilland War Worker. Vol.I
no.12, 24 Feb 1943 to no.25, 2 July 1943//*OOL microfilm. Incomplete.

5582 (UAW-CIO) War Worker. 1942-1945? Toronto/Weston:
International Union Local 382. Jack Henson. m.
Vol.II no.4, 4 Sept 1943 to no.14, June 1945 *OOL
microfilm. Incomplete. Elliott 204.

5583 UE(Canadian) News. 1942- . Toronto: UE, District
5 Council. s. Vol.III no.18, 21 Nov 1944 through
1970. Omits 'Canadian' 3 April 1967. *OOL microfilm. Elliott 193.

(5584)Union Digest. 1942-? Moose Jaw: United Packinghouse
Workers of America Local 177. Elliott 200, not found.

1943

(5585)252 Highlights. 1943. Toronto: UAW, Local 252. w.
Elliott 210, not found.

5586 The Amalgamator. 1943-1947? Hamilton/Toronto/Trail:
Amalgamted Unions of Canada: Canadian control of Canadian labour. D.V. Mitchell. m. Vol.II no.1, Jan
1944 to vol.V no.3, April 1947 *OOL microfilm. Elliott 206.

5587 CCF Challenge. 1943. Montreal: CCF Quebec section.
u. Vol.I no.4, Aug 1943.*OOA/CCF39.

5588 The Canadian CO (ie. Conscientious Objector). 1943-?
Montreal: Canadian Pacifist News. b. Vol.I no.6,
Aug 1943 *SSA/McNaughton H23.

5589 Club Life. 1943-1946? Toronto: Labor-Progressive
Party. m. Vol.I no.5, March 1944 and scattered
issues only to vol.III no.1, Jan 1946 *OTURS/RSK.

5590 CCF News. 1943-1959? Vancouver: Federationist.
Jay Powley. w. Formerly The Federationist: number-
ing continued: vol.VIII no.14, 11 Nov 1943 to vol.
XXIII no.12, 23 Dec 1959*BVAUS.

(5591)De Havilland War Worker. 1943-1945. Toronto: UAW.
?m. Formerly UAW-CIO War Worker De Havilland Edition;
later De Havilland Aircrafter. Elliott 185, not found.

5592 The Main Deck. 1943. Vancouver: Boilermakers and
Iron Shipbuilders Union of Canada local 1. Victor
W. Forster. (w). Vol.I no.2, 16 June 1943 to no.20
1 Dec 1943//*OOL microfilm. Elliott 213.

5593 North Trinity News. 1943. Toronto: Labor-Progressive Party. Vol.I no.2, 20 Nov 1943. *OTURS/RSK.

5594 The (UAW-CIO) Oshaworker. 1943-. Oshawa: UAW, Local
222. William Noble. e. Vol.III no.2, 17 Jan 1945

to vol.IV no.18, 20 Nov 1946 *OOL microfilm. Elliott 196.

5595 Prawo Ludu/The People's Right. 1943-1945. Montreal/ Toronto. Polish Labor Committee. m. Vol.II no.1, Jan 1944 to Dec 1944 *OONL. From Oct 1944 published in Toronto.

5596 Record. 1943-1947. Winnipeg: Building Maintenance Union Local 1. H.B. Deimert. m. Vol.I no.1, Dec 1943 to vol.IV no.9, Aug 1947//*OOL. Elliott 214.

5597 (Sudbury) Beacon. 1943-1945. Sudbury: CCL-CIO Local 598. H. Landon Ladd. w. Vol.I no.1, Jan 1943 to 28 Dec 1945. *OOL microfilm, incomplete. Drops 'Beacon' with vol.II no.13, 5 April 1944; stops numbering with vol.III no.17, 10 Aug 1945. Elliott 207.

5598 UAW-CIO War Worker: Brantford-Simcoe Edition. 1943-1945? Brantford: UAW. Jack Crosbie. ⬝. Vol.III no.1, Jan 1945 to no.4, July 1945//?*OOL microfilm.

5599 Dos Vort/(The Word). 1943-1944? Montreal: Labor Zionist Movement in Canada. m. Vol.II no.17, 21 July 1944 *OOA/Klein 18.

5600 WEA Labour Court Survey (Ontario Labour Court). (1943-1944). Toronto: WEA. u. Undated: Vol.I no.1 to no.12 (1943-1944) *OTP.

1944

5601 Alberta Election Campaign Bulletin. 1944. Edmonton: Labor-Progressive Party. d. Nos.1 to 5, 17-21st July 1944.*OTURS/RSK.

5602 BC District Union News. 1944-1955? Vancouver: International Union of Mine Mill and Smelter Workers. Harvey Murphy. m. Vol.I no.2, 28 June 1944 to vol.X no.14, July 1955//?*OOL microfilm. Elliott 222.

5603 The Canadian Seaman. 1944-1945? Vancouver: Deepsea and Inlandboatmens Union (BC),CIO,CCL. G. Bogerd. e. Vol.I no.1, 18 Aug 1944 to no.14, 24 Feb 1945//? *OOL microfilm.

5604 CCYM Quarterly. 1944. Regina: CCYM Saskatchewan. q. Vol.I no.1, 1944 *OOA/CCF346 and SSA/G.19.1.

(5605)Daily Reminder. c1944. (?Toronto): Labor-Progressive Party. Not found.

(5606)Direct Hit. 1944-1945. Winnipeg: Powder and High Explosives Union local 150. Elliott 218, not found.

(5607)Dorothy K Division News. 1944. Transcona, Man: Canadian Brotherhood of Railway Employees. w. Elliott 221, not found.

(5608)Falcon. 1944. Toronto: Federated Assn of Letter Carriers. Elliott 220, not found.

5609 Le Front Ouvrier.1944-54. Laprairie/Montréal/Ottawa. Pour un monde ouvrier plus humaine. Aimé Carbonneau et Joseph Pelchet. w. Replacing Le Mouvement Ouvrier et La Jeunesse Ouvrière. Vol.I no.1, 2 dec 1944 to vol.X no.16, 20 mars 1954//*OOL microfilm.

(5610)Hotel and Restaurant Employee. 1944. Toronto: Hotel and Restaurant Employees, local joint executive board. Elliott 217, not found.

5611 Labor Comment. 1944. Toronto: CCF Ontario section Trade Union Committee. m. Vol.I nos.3 and 4, Sept and Nov 1944 *OOA/CCF60.

(5612)Liberation. 1944-1946. Montreal: United Textile Workers of America. Elliott 216, not found.

5613 (Local) 195 News. 1944-1952? Windsor: International Assn of United Automobile, Aircraft and Agricultural Implement Workers of America. E. Ballantyne. e. Vol.I no.1, 1 Feb 1944 to vol.III no.12, 25 July 1952//?*OOL microfilm. Drops 'Local' Feb 1950. Elliott 211.

5614 Local 439 News. 1944-1951. Toronto: UAW-CIO Local 439. m. Formerly War Worker (3 issues only). Numbering continued: vol.I no.4, June 1944 to vol.VII no.7, 6 Dec 1951. New volume number started vol.I no.1 Feb 1955 to no.6, July 1955 *OOL. Incomplete. Elliott 224.

5615 Maritime Commonwealth. 1944-1952. Halifax: official organ of the Nova Scotia and Prince Edward Island CCF. s. Later Ontario and Maritime News. 21 June 1944 to 12 June 1952 *SRA. Published in Bridgewater to 25 Oct 1945.

5616 National Affairs Monthly. 1944-1956. Toronto: Labor-Progressive Party. Stanley Ryerson. m. Vol.I no.1, April 1944 to vol.XIII no.12, Dec 1956 *OTCPA.

5617 News Bulletin. 1944-1946. (Toronto): Ontario CCF. m. Vol.I no.1, June 1944 to vol.II no.10, May 1946//? *OOA/CCF57.

5618 Les Nouvelles Ouvrières. 1944-1956. Montréal: Congrès Canadien du Travail. m. Vol.V no.1-2, fev 1948 to vol.XIII no.4, avril 1956//*OOL microfilm. Elliott 212.

5619 שטימע אונזער/Unzer Shtime/Our Voice. 1944. Montreal: 'Socialist monthly'. m. Vol.I no.2, Aug 1944 *OOA/ Klein 18.

5620 PA Pacific Advocate. 1944-1946. Vancouver: Peoples Publishing Co. C.A. Saunders. w. Formerly The People, later Pacific Tribune. First issue continues numbering, ie. Vol.III no.43, 4 Nov 1944, corrected in second issue to vol.I no.2, 11 Nov 1944 to vol.II no.15, 8 Feb 1946//*OOL microfilm.

5621 Reconciliation. 1944-1945? Toronto: Fellowship of Reconciliation in the interests of the peace movement.

Albert G. Watson. b. Vol.I no.5, July 1944 and vol.
II no.5, Sept 1945 only *OOA/CCF554.

(5622) Shoe and Leather Worker. 1944. London/Toronto: Shoe
and Leather Workers Union. Elliott 215, not found.

5623 Today. 1944-1946. Toronto: Sponsored by the Thursday Night Club of Toronto (Anglo-Jewish). m. Vol.I
no.1, Nov 1944 to vol.II no.20, Oct 1946 *OONL.

5624 Trades and Labour Congress Journal. 1944-1956. Ottawa: Trades and Labour Congress of Canada. m. Formerly Canadian Congress Journal: numbering continued:
vol.XXIII no.3, Mar 1944 to vol.XXXV no.3, Mar 1956//
*OOL microfilm. Elliott 81 Hann 1679.

5625 Twin Cities Labor Progressive News. 1944. Kitchener-
Waterloo: Labor-Progressive Party K.W. Club. Vol.I
no.5, May 1944 *OTURS/RSK.

5626 The United Worker. 1944-1956. Ocean Falls, BC: Pulp,
Sulphite local 312 and Paper Makers local 360. m.
Vol.IV no.1, 15 Dec 1947 to vol.XII no.4, 7 March
1956//*OOL microfilm.

5627 War Worker. 1944. Toronto: Local 439 UAW-CIO. m.
Later Local 439 News. Vol.I no.1, 9 March 1944 and
no.2, 5 April 1944 (lacking 3)*OOL microfilm.

5628 The Weldor (sic) Craftsman. 1944. Vancouver: Federation of United Weldors, Cutters and Helpers of Canada.
u. Vol.I no.5, March 1944 *BVAUS/Smith CP.

1945

(5629) Allied Labour News. 1945-1946. Kingston/Peterborough.
Allied Labour Council of Peterborough and District.
Elliott 227, not found.

5630 The CFCC Newsletter. 1945. Toronto: Canadian Fellowship for Cooperative Communities. u. No.7, May
1945 *OOA/Good 12.

5631 The (New) Call. 1945-1952? Calgary: Calgary Trades
and Labor Council. George C. Kirke. s. Vol.I no.1,
1 March 1945 to vol.VIII no.4, 26 March 1952//?*OOL
microfilm. Becomes New Call vol.VIII no.2, 27 Feb
1952. Elliott 223.

5632 Canadian Chemical Worker. 1945-1957. Toronto: International Chemical Workers Union district 4. H. Meyer.
s. Vol.III no.9, Oct-Nov 1947 to vol.VI no.6, Oct-Nov
1957//?*OOL microfilm, incomplete. Absorbed by International Chemical Worker, Canadian Edition, Jan 1958.

(5633) Canadian Mariner. 1945-? Montreal: Mercantile Marine Officers Guild of Canada; Canadian Brotherhood
of Marine Engineers; National Seamens Assn of Canada.
Elliott 226, not found.

(5634) Canadian Postman. 1945-? Toronto: Letter Carriers
Union. Elliott 229, not found.

5635 The Canadian Scientist. 1945. Ottawa: Canadian Assn
of Scientific Workers. m. No.3, Dec 1945 *OTURS/RSK.

5636 Canadian Soviet Council/Friendship Society News(Facts).
1945-1956? Toronto: National Council for Canadian-
Soviet Friendship. m. Vol.I no.1, May 1945 to no.61
Dec 1955-Jan 1956 *OTURS/RSK, scattered issues only.
Starts as Canadian Soviet Council News, becomes Canadian Soviet Friendship Society News, then 'Facts'
added sometime between March 1953 and Dec 1955.

5637 Citizen's Forum. 1945-1946? Toronto: Canadian Assn
for Adult Education. u. No.16, 5 March 1946 *OTURS/
RSK.

5638 Cooperative Committee on Japanese Canadians Bulletin.
1945-1948. Toronto. Ed: Hugh MacMillan. ɓ. No.1
10 Dec 1945 to no.12, 10 Dec 1948//*OOA/CCJC 3.

5639 Co-operative Development. 1945-1948. Regina: Dept
of Cooperation and Cooperative Development. m.
Vol.I no.1, Dec 1945 to vol.III no.4, April 1948//
*SSA.

(5640) District Six News. 1945-? Toronto: Canadian Rubber
Workers. Elliott 234, not found.

5641 The Front Page. 1945. Regina: Adult Education Division, Dept of Education: a living newspaper presented by Radio College. Edward Parker. w. Vol.I no.1
13 Oct 1945 to no.10, 15 Dec 1945//*SSA.

5642 Good Government Advocate. 1945. Toronto: A Committee of Toronto Citizens Supporting the Re-election
of Controller Stewart Smith...Unnumbered: Dec 1945
*OTURS/RSK.

5643 The Health Services Review. 1945. Regina: State
Hospital and Medical League. u. Vol.I no.1, May
1945//?ACGA/CCF29.

5644 The (Information) Bulletin of the Council of Canadian
South Slavs. 1945-1946? Toronto. ?m. Vol.I no.3,
15 April 1945; no.9, Oct-Nov 1945 and vol.II no.12,
March 1946 *OTURS/RSK.

5645 Keeping Posted. 1945-1946. Winnipeg: Prairie School
for Social Advance. m. Vol.I no.1, Nov 1945 to no.3
Feb 1946//?*AEUS/PSSA.

5646 Labour Challenge. 1945-1952. Toronto. Ed: D. White-
side. m. Vol.I no.1, 1 June 1945 to vol.VII no.1
(full no.102), April 1952//?*OOL microfilm. Elliott
239. From vol.III no.2 published by the Revolutionary Workers Party, Canadian Section 4th International.
Reverts to being published by Labour Challenge Publishing Co. Aug 1951.

5647 Trade Union Bulletin. (1945-1946). Regina: CCF
Saskatchewan section. u. Undated, nos. 1-7 (1945-
1946) *SSA/G.1.35.

5648 'True' Democracy. 1945-1948? Fredericton: (CCF): The watchdog of the People: politics, economics, health, religion, education. Fred Cogswell, Linden Peebles, J.H. Dunlap and F.W. Hartwick. s. Vol.II no.1, 12 April 1946 to vol.IV no.2, April 1948//? *OOA/CCF276, some numbers and dates incorrect.

(5649) UPWA Local News. 1945. Toronto: Locals 114, 208, 272 and 287, United Packinghouse Workers of America. Elliott 233, not found.

5650 The Yukoner. 1945. Whitehorse: Labor-Progressive Party BC. Vol.I no.1, Nov 1945 *OTURS/RSK.

1946

(5651) ABC of Building and Construction. 1946. Toronto: Building and Construction Workers of Canada. Elliott 235, not found.

5652 Bindery News. 1952-1970. Toronto: International Brotherhood of Bookbinders and Bindery Women local 28. m. Vol.VII no.9, Sept 1952 through 1970 *OOL microfilm, incomplete.

(5653) The Brotherhood News. 1946. Montreal: Canadian Brotherhood of Railway Employees and other workers. Not found.

5654 Canadian Labour Reports. 1946-1959? Montreal: CLC National Committee on Human Rights. S.L. Blum/K. Kaplansky. m. Vol.I no.1, Sept 1946 to vol.XIII no.12, Dec 1958 *OOL microfilm. Lacks Nov 1946; not published Nov-Dec 1956. Vol.XIV no.8-9, Aug-Sept 1959 *OOACCF314.

5655 Civil Rights. 1946-1948? Toronto: Emergency Committee for Civil Rights; later Civil Rights Union. m. Vol.I no.1, 15 Aug 1946 and no.3, 31 Oct 1946 *ACGA/Smith 14.

5656 Classified News. 1946-1947. Hamilton: Locked-out ITU members of Hamilton Spectator. c. Nos.76 to 103, 14 Jan 1947 to 18 April 1947, incomplete. *ACGL.

(5657) Combat. 1946. Montreal. Not found.

5658 Council Notes. 1946. Toronto: Toronto Council for Canadian-Soviet Friendship. u. (No.1) Oct 1946. *OTURS/RSK.

(5659) Fédération Nationale des Gantiers. 1946-? Montréal. Elliott 237, not found.

(5560) Link. 1946-? Port Colborne, Ont: International Mine Mill and Smelters Union local 637. Elliott 232, not found.

5661 The Native Voice. 1946-1968 and 1970-. Vancouver: Native Brotherhood of British Columbia. Jack Beynon.

m.   Vol.I no.1, Dec 1946 to vol.XXII no.8, Nov 1968.
Restarted vol.I no.1, Nov 1970 *BVAUS incomplete.

5662 The Notice Board. 1946. Vancouver: CCF BC-Yukon.
u. Vol.I no.2, April 1946 *BVAUS/Smith CCF/1945.

5663 Pacific Tribune. 1946- . Vancouver: Peoples Publishing Co. Tom McEwen. w. Vol.I no.1, 15 Feb 1946
through 1970. *OOL microfilm. Elliott 231.

5664 (Prairie New Democrat) Commonwealth. 1946 -. Regina:
CCF. w. 1946 through 1970 *SRA. Elliott 138.
Merges with People's Weekly, 7 Jan 1953: Prairie
New Democrat added 1966-1969.

5665 The Spanish Refugee. 1946-1947? Vancouver: Spanish
Refugee Appeal Committee. F.A. Poole. q. Unnumbered
Sept 1946 and Jan 1947 *ACGA/Smith 13.

5666 UAW-CIO Union Dugest. 1946-1947? Brantford: UAW.
m. Unnumbered: Oct 1946 to April 1947 *OOL microfilm.

1947

5667 Across Canada. 1947-1950? Ottawa: CCF National Mem-
bership Bulletin. m. Vol.I no.1, Sept 1947 to vol.
IV no.8, Nov 1950.*SSA/G.2.3: incomplete issues also
OTU and OOA/CCF346, 531.

5668 Daily Tribune. 1947. Toronto: Communist Party of
Canada. d. Formerly and later Canadian Tribune.
1 May to 4 Nov 1947 *OOL microfilm. Elliott 238.

5669 Horizon. 1947-1949. Ottawa: CCYM. Mary Gilchrist.
Ten times a year. Vol.I no.2, May 1947 to vol.II
no.10, March 1949 *OOA/CCF351, incomplete.

5670 Layout for Living. 1947-1950. Ottawa: Community
Planning Assn of Canada. (m). No.1, Feb 1947 to
no.34, April 1950//*OOA/CPA 3, incomplete. May have
restarted in the fall of 1950.

5671 National Educational Journal. c1947. ?Ottawa: (CCYM).
u. Unnumbered, undated c1947//? *OOA/CCF114.

5672 Northern Neighbours. 1947. Toronto: National Council for Canadian-Soviet Friendship. u. Vol.I no.1
15 Feb 1947 *ACGA/Smith 14.

5673 The Ontario Timberworker. 1947-1951. Sudbury/Port
Arthur: Ontario Joint Council of Lumber and Sawmill
Workers Union; United Brotherhood of Carpenters and
Joiners of America. Bruce Magnuson. m. Vol.I no.1
4 July 1947 to vol.V no.6, May 1951//*OOL microfilm.
Becomes bilingual adding Le Bucheron d'Ontario with
vol.II no.4, 20 mars 1948.

5674 Ottawa Car Strike News. 1947. Ottawa: UAW-CIO local
641. Harry Rowe. ?e. Nos. 3 and 4, July 1 and 11

1947 *OOA/CCF188.

5675 Typo Times. 1947. Ottawa: Locked-out Printers of the Ottawa Citizen. ∅. Nos.24 to 36, 2 Jan to 30 April 1947 *ACGL lacking 27 and 32.

5676 The Typo Times. 1947. Vancouver: Vancouver Typo Union 226 on behalf of its locked-out printers. s. Numbered occasionally: no.14, 1 March 1947 to no.18, 25 June 1947, incomplete *ACGL.

5677 Vorwärts. 1947-. Toronto: Sudetenklub: organ deutscher Sozialdemokraten in Canada. ∅. No.1, 1947 to 1972 *OOA/Sudeten 6 and 7.

5678 Western Tribune. 1947. Winnipeg. Ed: Mitch Sago. w. Later The Westerner. Vol.I no.1, 3 May 1947 to no.7, 14 June 1947//*OONL.

5679 The Westerner. 1947-1948. Winnipeg. Ed: Mitch Sago. w. Formerly Western Tribune: numbering continued: vol.I no.8, 21 June 1947 to vol.II no.71, 11 Sept 1948//?*OONL.

5680 The Winnipeg News. 1947-1948. Winnipeg: On behalf of the locked-out printers. Ernest Constable. ∅. Nos.116 to 152 plus 190 and 193, 7 Jan 1947 to 12 Feb 1948 *ACGL, incomplete. Last issue announced for Feb 26, no.195.

1948

5681 The Builder. 1948. Sudbury: Sudbury CCF Labour Committee. u. Vol.I no.1, 11 March 1948 *OOA/CCF59.

5682 CCF Leader. 1948. Sudbury: Sudbury Federal Riding Assn. ?m. Unnumbered: Sept (1948) *OOA/CCF59.

5683 CCUF National Bulletin. 1948-1956. Ottawa. m. Vol.I no.1, 30 Jan 1948 to vol.VIII no.1, Feb 1956// *OOA/CCF342.

5684 The Canadian Far Eastern Newsletter. 1948-? Toronto: James G. Endicott (and editor). e/∅/m. Vol.I no.1, 1 Jan 1948 through 1970. Numbering runs continuously, volume number changes each January. Some numbers incorrect, supplements with some issues. *OOA/Endicott.

5685 The Canadian Woodworker. 1948-1949. Vancouver: Woodworkers Industrial Union of Canada. J.M. Clark. e. Later Union Woodworker. Vol.I no.1, 3 Nov 1948 to no.8, 2 March 1949//*OOL.

5686 Civil Rights Union Information Bulletin. 1948. (Toronto). Civil Rights Union. Unnumbered: 27 Oct 1948 *OTURS/RSK.

5687 LPP Cultural Commission Bulletin. 1948. (Toronto): Labor-Progressive Party. u. (No.1) June 1948 *OHMA

Preceded by an introductory bulletin called The LPP and the Arts (May 1947).

5688 Labour Research. 1948-1959? Ottawa: CLC Labour Research Dept. E.A. Forsey. m. Vol.I no.2, 15 May 1948 to vol.IV no.9, Sept 1959 *OOA/CCF.

5689 Local 598(Mine Mill)News. 1948-1966. Sudbury: Mine Mill and Smelter Workers Union local 598. m. Vol. VIII no.12, 21 July 1955 to 1966: restarted 1972. *OOL microfilm.

5690 National Labour Journal. 1948-. Ottawa: National Council of Canadian Labour. Clive Thomas. m. Vol. I no.1, Oct 1948 through 1970 *OOL microfilm.

5691 SS: The Student Socialist. 1948. Toronto: CCF Club University of Toronto. ⱷ. Vol.I no.3, 28 Feb 1948 *OOA/CCF342.

5692 Steelworkers News. 1948-1955. Galt, Ont: Local unions of Galt, Hespeler and Preston. Ab Aves. m. Vol.I no.1, Mar 1948 to June 1955//?*OOL microfilm. Numbering ceases during run.

5693 Timmins and District CCF-Trade Union Committee. 1948. Timmins. Vol.I no.2, 20 April 1948. *OOA/CCF.

1949

5694 CCL/Canadian Labour. 1949-1956. Ottawa: Canadian Congress of Labour. Jack Williams. m. Later CLC News. Vol.I no.1, Oct 1949 to vol.VII no.6, March 1956//*OOL microfilm. Name switched to Canadian Labour vol.III no.10, July 1952.

5695 (The) Canadian Sailor/Le Marin Canadien. 1949-. Montreal: Canadian District, Seafarers International Union of North America. ⱷ. Vol.I no.1, 25 Oct 1949 through 1970 *OOL microfilm.

5696 Contact. 1949-1951? Ottawa: National Bulletin CCYM. u. Vol.III no.2, Dec 1951 *OOA/CCF344.

5697 De Havilland Aircrafter. 1949-1953. Toronto: UAW-CIO local 112. Jack Rose. m. Formerly De Havilland War Worker; later Amalgamated Aircrafter. Vol.IV no. 1, Jan 1952 to vol.V no.8, April 1953//*OOL microfilm.

5698 The Organized Farmer. 1949-. Edmonton: Farmers Union of Alberta. m. Formerly AFU Bulletin: numbering continued: vol.IX no.2, Feb 1949 (called FUA Bulletin Souvenir Copy): next issue (March 1949) starts Vol.IX no.1 through 1970 *OOL microfilm.

5699 L'Ouvrier de la Chaussure. 1949-? Montréal. Not found.

5700 PEI CCF News Letter. 1949. Crapaud, PEI. m. Vol.

I no.1 and 2, Jan and Feb 1949//?*OOA/CCF32.

5701 The Seafarers Tribune. 1949. Montreal: Seafarers International Union of North America. b. Special editions 15 March 1949 to 10 June 1949//*OOL . See Canadian Sailor no.5695 for later publication by this union: anti-Canadian Seamans Union.

5702 Seamen's Defender. 1949. Toronto: National Seamens Defence Committee. (?no.1) Jan 1949//?*OTURS/RSK.

5703 The Star. 1949. Glace Bay. w. Formerly The (Glace Bay) Gazette. Unnumbered: (1), 15 Jan 1949 to ?5 May 1949//*OOL microfilm.

5704 Transport. 1949-1956. Montréal: Fraternité canadiennes des Employés de Chemin de Fer et Autres Transports. Jacques Déom. m. Vol.I no.1, dec 1949 to vol.VII no.4, avril 1956.*OOL microfilm.

5705 The Union Woodworker. 1949-1950. Vancouver: Woodworkers Industrial Union of Canada. J.M. Clark. e. Formerly Canadian Woodworker: numbering continued: vol.I no.9, 23 March 1949 to no.27, 23 Aug 1950//? *OOL microfilm. The name was changed because of a complaint from Macleans which had a trade paper of the same name.

5706 Yours to Build. 1949-1953? Toronto: UAW-CIO local 984. Vol.V no.3, June 1953 *OTURS/RSK.

1950

5707 CPAC Newsletter. 1950. Ottawa: Community Planning Association of Canada. u. (no.1) Aug 1950 *OOA/ CPAC 4.

5708 Comment. 1950-1959? Ottawa: CCF National Office. m. Formerly News Comment. Vol.I no.1, Oct 1950 to vol.V no.12 (Dec 1955)//*OOA/CCF532. Dating ceases June 1955. Started again in new format, b. Vol. I no.1 (Jan-Feb 1957) to vol.III no.3 (May-June 1959) //?*OOA/CCF532. Most issues from 1955 not dated. Some years indexed.

5709 Community Planning Review. 1950-1955? Ottawa: Community Planning Assn of Canada. Eric Beecroft. (q). Vol.I no.1, 1950 to vol.V no.1, March 1955, incomplete. *OOA/CPAC.

5710 In Gear. 1950. Windsor: Labor-Progressive Party, Windsor-Essex-Kent Region. u. Vol.I no.2, June 1950. *OTURS/RSK.

(5711) IWA News. c1950. Toronto: International Woodworkers of America. Not found.

5712 The Lamp.1950-54. Edmonton: Labor-Progressive Party Miners Club. Vol.IV no.2, June 1954 *OTURS/RSK.

5713 Materials for Thought. 1950. (Vancouver): W.W. Le-feaux: a socialist forum for the alert rank and file; League for Socialist Education. Ed: W.W. Leafeaux. (m). First issue undated, unnumbered: (No.1),(June 1950) and nos.4, 5, 6 Oct-Dec1950*T; no.2 *BVAUS/Mac 39Af.16; no.3 *OOA/CCF86.

5714 National Expansion Drive Bulletin. 1950. Vancouver: CCF BC-Yukon. Laura Jamieson. Nos. 1-8//? no months 1950. *OOA/CCF316.

5715 The Needle Worker. 1950-1953? Toronto: Labor-Pro-gressive Party Needle Trades Club. m. Vol.I no.1, March 1950 to vol.IV no.4 June 1953 (3 issues only) *OTURS/RSK.

5716 PAC-CCL Newsletter. 1950. Toronto: PAC-CCL. m. Unnumbered, undated (no.1) (Jan 1950) to vol.I no. 8-9, Sept/Oct 1950 *OOA/CFAW 50.

(5717) Security through Autonomy. 1950. (Toronto). Not found.

5718 Socialist Thought. 1950-1951. Vancouver: Socialist Fellowship. m. Vol.I no.6, Dec 1950 to vol.II no.2 March 1951 *BVAUS.

5719 The Spark. 1950-1952? Toronto: Labor-Progressive Party Chemical Workers. m. No.6, Oct 1950; vol.III no.3, Nov 1952 *OTURS/RSK.

5720 TUC Bulletin. 1950-1956? Vancouver: CCF Trade Union Committee. m. Vol.II no.6, July-Aug 1951 to vol. VIII no.1, Jan-Feb 1956 *BVAUS/Turner 1.

5721 Union Farmer. 1950-. Saskatoon: Saskatchewan Farm-ers Union. Jim Wright. m. Vol.I no.1 *SSA/G.38.1 vol.II no.12, Feb 1952 *OOA/Endicott 15; vol.IV no. 10, Dec 1953 through 1970 *OOL microfilm.

5722 The Workers Voice. 1950-1954? Toronto: Labor-Pro-gressive Party Stanley Park Club. Vol.I no.4, Sept 1950 and vol.III no.12, March-April 1954 *OTURS/RSK.

1951

5723 Auto Worker(s)(Voice). 1951-? Toronto:(Labor-Pro-gressive Party Auto Club). ?m. Vol.I no.1, June 1951 and no.3, Nov 1951//?*OTURS/RSK.

(5724) Le Chapelier. 1951. Montréal: Union internationale des Travailleurs de l'Industrie du Chapeau et de la Casquette. Not found.

5725 Examiner. 1951-. Ottawa: Customs Excise Union. Vol.I no.1, Jan 1951 through 1970. *OOL microfilm.

5726 Peace Review. 1951-1955? Toronto: Canadian Peace Congress. u. Later Horizons. Unnumbered: Sept-Oct 1951; no.29, Nov 1953 *OTURS/RSK; no.48 June 1955 *OTAR; ceased 15 Sept 1955.

5727 The Protestant. ?1951-? Cambridge, N.S: New Christian Books. Kenneth Leslie. q. Oct-Nov-Dec 1951
*OOA/Endicott 18. Only issue seen; strongly pro-
peace, anti-military 'The stark raving insanity of
the untrammeled US military mind'.

5728 Railroaders Voice. 1951-1956? Toronto: Labor-Progressive Party Eugene V. Debs Club. ?m. Nos.1 and
30 only, Jan 1951, June 1956 *OTURS/RSK.

5729 Ship and Shop. 1951-1967? Vancouver: Marine Workers and Boilermakers Industrial Union local 1. m/ƀ.
Vol.I no.1, 9 March 1951 to Nov 1967//?*OOL microfilm. Stops numbering with vol.X no.1, Feb 1965.

5730 Socialist Bulletin. 1951. Vancouver: Social Science
Forum. u. Vol.I no.2, Nov 1951 *T.

5731 Steel Shots. 1951-. (Hamilton): United Steelworkers
of America CIO local 1005. Cecil M. Lewis. m. Vol.
I no.1, 3 Sept 1951 through 1970 *OOL microfilm.

5732 Textile Labor Canadian Edition. 1951-. New York:
Textile Workers Union of America. Kenneth Fiester.
m. Vol.XII no.10, 19 May 1951 through 1970 (first
Canadian edition)*OOL microfilm.

5733 The Woodworker/Le Travailleur du Bois. 1951-? Port
Arthur: Canadian Union of Woodworkers. Bruce Magnuson. m. Formerly The Ontario Timberworker. Vol.I
no.1, June 1951 to no.3, Sept 1951//?*OOL microfilm.

1952

5734 CCYM News Letter. 1952-1954. Ottawa: CCYM. Ellen
Cammitzer. m. Vol.I no.1, 20 Sept 1952 to vol.III
no.2, 20 Nov 1954//?*OOA/CCF344, incomplete.

5735 The Canadian Packinghouse Worker. 1952-1969. Chic-
ago/Toronto: United Packinghouse Workers of America.
Mary Gilchrist. m. Starts vol.II no.1, Feb 1952
(first Canadian edition), changes to vol.I no.4, May
1952 to vol.XVIII no.3, March 1969//*OOL microfilm.
Place of publication moved to Toronto with vol.III
no.6, June 1954. Following merger of union with the
Amalgamated Meat Cutters the letters 'CPW' added
before title, Oct 1968.

5736 Canadian World Government News. 1952-1954? Saskatoon: World Federalists of Canada. J.C. Arrand.
u. Vol.III no.1, Jan 1954 *SSA.

5737 The Guardian. 1952-. Windsor/Brampton: UAW-CIO
locals 195, 200, 240 and 89. ?m. Vol.I no.1, 29
Aug 1952 to vol.VI no.24, 27 Aug(1958)// Restarted
vol.VIII no.1, 5 Sept 1960 through 1970 *OOL microfilm.

5738 The Guide. 1952-. Hamilton/Sarnia/Rexdale: Christian Labor Assn of Canada. m. No.2, June 1952 through 1970*OOL incomplete. A dispute in 1958-59 led to The Guide being published by the CLA and a new Christian Trade Unions of Canada assn. The old CTUC then adopted the name The Voice.

5739 Hi-Ball. ?1952-1955? Winnipeg: Labor-Progressive Party Railwaymens Club. Vol.IV, no number Sept 1955 and vol. VIII (?no.8), May 1959 *OTURS/RSK.

5740 High Gear. 1952. Toronto: Labor-Progressive Party York Township Section. Vol.I no.1, Feb 1952//? *OTURS/RSK.

5741 New Frontiers. 1952-1956. Toronto. Ed: Margaret Fairley. q. Vol.I no.1, Winter 1952 to vol.V no.2 Summer 1956//?*OONL.

5742 RR News and Comments. 1952-1956. Vancouver: CCF Agricultural Committee. m/ɓ/b. Vol.I no.1, Oct 1952 to vol.V no.1, Feb-March 1956//?*BVAUS/Turner 1.

5743 The Speaker. 1952-1954. Bay Robert, Nfld. The voice of a free people (CCF). Edgar A. Russell. w. Vol.I no.1, 15 Nov .1952 to vol.II no.19, 17 April 1954// ?*OOA/CCF26 incomplete.

1953

5744 The Agitator. 1953. Toronto: CCF Youth, East End. Vol.I no.3, April 1953 *OTURS/RSK.

5745 Amalgamated Aircrafter. 1953-1958. Toronto: UAW-CIO local 112. Formerly De Havilland Aircrafter; later Aircrafter. m. Numbering continued: vol.VI no.1, June 1953 to vol.III no.2, Feb 1958//*OOL microfilm, incomplete.

5746 The Bullet. (1953). Toronto: UAW-CIO local 303. Vol.II no.4, May 1954 *OTURS/RSK.

5747 Campus Comment. 1953-1954? Toronto: based on an affirmation of the principles in the Universal Declaration of Human Rights. John H.R. Lee. e. Vol.I no.1, Sept 1953 to vol.II no.6//? *OOA/CCF342 and 343. Policy changes to one 'based on the principles of democratic socialism'.

5748 Forward. see Vorwarts, no.5677 above, which added an English title.

5749 Ontario Woodsworth Memorial Foundation Monthly Newsletter. 1953. Toronto. m. Vol.I no.1 and 2, Oct and Nov 1953//?*OTURS/Woodsworth 29.

5750 Union Daily Bulletin. 1953. Timmins: United Steelworkers of America. d. No.36, 24 Oct 1953 *OTURS/ Woodsowrth 30. Strike Bulletin.

(5751)Womans Voice. c1953. Toronto: Congress of Canadian Women. Not found.

1954

5752 CCF News - Newfoundland. ?1954-1956? ?St John's: CCF. ∅? Almost all issues undated; no volume numbers. Incomplete set in *OOA/CCF26 from at least May 1954 to April 1956.

5753 Canadian Transport/Transport Canadien. 1953-. Hull/ Ottawa: Canadian Brotherhood of Railway Employees. s. Formerly Canadian Railway Employees Monthly: numbering continued: vol.XXXIX no.4, April 1953 through 1970 *OOL.

5754 The Civic Reporter. 1954. Winnipeg: Labor Election Committee. b. Unnumbered: March/April 1954.

5755 Electric Sparks. 1954. West Toronto: LPP (electical members). Unnumbered: April 1954 *OTURS/RSK.

5756 Hi-Park Forum. 1954. Toronto: LPP High Park. u. Vol.I no.1, May 1954 *OTURS/RSK.

5757 NDEA News Letter. 1954-1964. Ottawa: National Defence Employees Assn. m. Vol.I no.1, Dec 1954 to Oct 1964 *OOL microfilm.

5758 Party Woman. 1954. Toronto: LPP. No.5, June 1954 *OTURS/RSK. Possibly monthly.

5759 Steelworkers Voice. 1954. Toronto: LPP Steel Clubs. u. Unnumbered: Feb 1954 *OTURS/RSK.

5760 The Workshop. 1954. Toronto: LPP. ∅. Vol.I no.1, Feb 1954 and 2, May-June 1954 *OTURS/RSK.

1955

5761 The Blueprint. 1955. Vancouver: LPP Building Trades Clubs. u. Vol.I no.4, Aug 1955 *OTURS/RSK.

5762 CCF News. 1955-1961. Toronto: CCF. True Davidson. m. Scattered issues in *OOA/CCF. Numbering jumps from vol.III no.7 to vol.XXIII no.8, and continues to vol. XXVII (no.7), Aug 1961. Later The New Democrat.

5763 Canadian Marine Engineer/Ingenieur Marin. 1955-1957. Port Arthur and Montreal. (Separate English and French editions): Great Lakes and Eastern District National Assn of Marine Engineers. John Stirling. ∅. Unnumbered: (1), June 1955 to vol.III no.1, July 1957 *OOL microfilm, incomplete.

5764 Focus. 1955-1960? Toronto: Ontario Woodsworth Memorial Foundation. u. Unnumbered: Oct 1955 *OOA/ CCF309; Spring 1960 *OOA/CCF537.

5765 Mine-Mill Herald. 1955-1967. Toronto: International
Union of Mine Mill and Smelter Workers (Canada). m.
Vol.I no.1, Nov 1955 to vol.XIII no.127, July 1967//?
*OOL microfilm.

5766 (Les) Nouvelles (de) NABET/NABET News. 1955-. Montréal: National Assn of Broadcast Employees and Tech-
nicians CLC. (Jiacomo Papa). b. Vol.II no.1, mars
1956 through 1970 *OOL microfilm. Separate English
edition starts Oct 1969, vol.I no.1 concurrently with
vol.XVII no.10 in French and continues with separate
numbering thereafter.

5767 Our Viewpoint. 1955. Vancouver: Labor-Progressive
Party Jewish Committee. u. No.2, June 1955 *OTURS/
RSK.

5768 The Railroader. 1955. Montreal: Labor-Progressive
Party Railway section. Camille Dionne. u. Vol.I
no.1, March 1955 *OTURS/RSK.

5769 The Shipyard Worker. 1955. Montreal: Labor-Progressive Party Shipyard Workers section. Vol.I no.1,
March 1955 *OTURS/RSK.

5770 The Spitfire News. 1955-1963? Winnipeg: Spitfire
Lodge 74. H. Collinson. m. Vol.I no.1 (Oct 1955)
to vol.VII no.3-4, March-April 1963//?*OOL microfilm
incomplete.

5771 Verdun Patriot. 1955. Verdun: Labor-Progressive
Party Club. Alison Lee. u. Vol.I no.2, March 1955.
*OTURS/RSK.

5772 The Workers Vanguard. 1955-. Toronto: affiliated
with the Socialist Educational League (formed in
1955 by expelled members of the CCF and former members of the Revolutionary Workers Party, 4th International). J. Mitchell. m. Vol.I no.1, Dec 1955
through 1970 *OTP.

1956

5773 The Auto Advocate. 1956. Windsor: Labor-Progressive
Party. u. Vol.I no.1, Jan 1956 *OTURS/RSK.

5774 CLC News. 1956-1958. Ottawa: Canadian Labour Congress. Jack Williams. m. Vol.I no.1, April 1956
to vol.III no.4, July-Aug 1958//*OOL microfilm.

5775 Canadian Labour. 1956-. Hull: Canadian Labour Congress. Norman S. Dowd. m. No.1, April 1956 through
1970. *OOL microfilm.

5776 Compass. 1956. Toronto: Labor-Progressive Party
Auto Club. u. Unnumbered: (May 1956) *OTURS/RSK.

5777 Hotel and Restaurant Worker. 1956-63. Toronto: Labor-
Progressive Party Club. b. Vol.I no.2, June 1956 and
3 other issues to vol.VIII no.1, June 1963 *OTURS/RSK.

5778 LPP Farm Bulletin. 1956-1957? Regina: Labor-Progressive Party. b. Nos. 7, 8 and 10, May, Sept 1956
and March 1957 *OTURS/RSK.

5779 Little Neighbour. 1956. Winnipeg: Labor-Progressive
Party Ward 3 Clubs. u. Vol.I no.2, May 1956 *OTURS/
RSK.

5780 (Ontario) Hydro Employees Union (Local) News. 1956-
Toronto: Ontario Hydro Employees Union. Francis K.
Eady. b. Vol.II no.1, Sept 1957 through 1970 *OOL
microfilm. Variations in title.

5781 Socialist (Press) Bulletin. 1956-. Toronto: Socialist Labor Party of Canada. m. One issue only,
*OTURS/RSK. Woodsworth 325.

5782 The Voice of the Farmer. 1956-1968. Winnipeg: Manitoba Farmers Union. K.J. Singleton. m. Vol.I no.1
Oct 1956 to vol.XII no.8, May 1968//*OOL microfilm.

5783 West Kildonan Clarion. 1956-1957? Winnipeg: Labor-
Progressive Party West Kildonan Club. Vol.II no.1,
March 1957 *OTURS/RSK.

5784 Western Pulp and Paper Worker. 1956-1969. Vancouver: Western Canada Council of Pulp and Paper Mill
Unions. O. Braaten. m. Vol.I no.1, April 1956 to
unnumbered June 1969//?*OOL microfilm.

5785 The Wheat City Spark. 1956. Brandon: Labor-Progressive Party Brandon Club. u. Vol.I no.1, May
1956 *OTURS/RSK.

5786 Workers Unity. 1956. Winnipeg: Labor-Progressive
Party Trade Union Committee. u. No.2, May 1956
*OTURS/RSK.

5787 Youth Review. 1956. Toronto: National Federation
of Labour Youth. u. Winter issue (1956) *OTURS/RSK.

1957

5788 The Advocate. 1957. Toronto. For a democratic
left. Harry Fistell. u. Vol.I no.1, April 1957//?
*OTURS/RSK

5789 CCW News Letter. 1957-1967? Toronto: Congress of
Canadian Women. q. One or two issues only, *OOA/VOW.

5790 Gleanings/Glanures. 1957-1966. Montreal: Canadian
Pulp and Paper Workers. m. Later Canadian Pulp and
Paper Worker Journal/Le Journal des Travailleurs des
Pâtes et Papiers du Canada. Vol.I no.1, (April 1957)
to vol.IV no.8, Dec 1966//*OOL.

5791 Ontario Labour Review. 1957-. Toronto: Ontario
Federation of Labour. m/b. Vol.I no.2 through 1970
*OOA/OFL10, incomplete. No volume numbers from Jan
1962.

5792 The Prairie Steel-Worker. 1957. Edmonton: (Canadian Labour Congress). ⌀. Vol.I no.1, 7 March 1957 and nos. 2, 3, 4, May, Sept and Dec 1957//?*ACGA/USWA2.

5793 Press (for Socialism). 1957-1965. (Vancouver): Socialist Committee for the Organization of a Labour Party in Canada. (R.Young). ⌀. (Vol.I no.1),(Feb 1957); vol.I no.2, March 1957 to vol.VII no.11, Feb-March 1965//*BVAUS.

5794 The Social Democrat. 1957. Montreal: Social Democratic Party (CCF). m. Unnumbered: Aug 1957 *OOA/CCF39.

5795 UAW Solidarity Canadian Edition. 1957-. Indianapolis: UAW, AFL-CIO. Ken Fiester. w. Vol.I no.1, 16 Dec 1957 through 1970 *OOL microfilm.

1958

5796 The Aircrafter. 1958-. Toronto: UAW Local 112 (and local 673). Harry Thomas. m. Formerly Amalgamated Aircrafter: numbering continued: vol.III no.3, March 1958 through 1970 *OOL microfilm, incomplete.

5797 CSAC Journal de l'ASCC. 1958-1966. Ottawa: Civil Service Assn of Canada. Jim Shearon. m. Vol.I no.1 June 1958 to vol.IX no.7, July-Aug 1966//*OOL microfilm. Merged with Argus Journal.

5798 The Canadian Democrat. ?1958-1960? Winnipeg: Winnipeg Woodsworth Society. W. Bedwell, D. Swainson, A. Friesen. b. Vol.II no.2 Jan-Feb 1960 *MWPL.

5799 Communist Viewpoint. 1958-1961. Vancouver: University of British Columbia (Communist Club). ⌀. Vol.I no.1, 16 Oct 1958 to 1961 *OONL, incomplete.

5800 Il Lavatore/The Worker/Le Travailleur. 1958-1961? Toronto. Prototipo di un giornale futuro - de un gruppo di operai italo-canadesi vorrebbe iniziare... ⌀. Numero unico dec 1958, numbering starts with sept 1959 *OONL incomplete.

5801 Parkdalian. 1958. Toronto: CCF Social Committee. m. Vol.I no.1, Jan 1958 to no.6, June 1958//?*OOA/CCF57.

(5802)RUEC Newsletter. 1958-? Ottawa: Railway Unions Educational Committee. Not found.

1959

5803 Communist Party Club News. 1959-1960? North Surrey, BC. u. Vol.II no.2, March 1960 *OTURS/RSK.

5804 LPP News Bulletin. 1959. North Surrey, BC: Delta
     Committee, Labor-Progressive Party. u. Vol.I no.1,
     21 Aug 1959. *OTURS/RSK.

5805 (NUPE) Highlights. 1959-1963. Ottawa: National
     Union of Public Employees. ∅. Early issues un-
     numbered: (no.1?), Feb 1959 to vol.II no.6, Aug 1963
     //*OOL.

5806 NUPSE News/UNESP Nouvelles. 1959-1963? Toronto:
     National Union of Public Service Employees. Francis
     K. Eady. m. Vol.I no.4, 1 Feb 1959 to vol V no.7,
     Aug 1963 *OOL microfilm, incomplete.

5807 Ontario LPP Newsletter. 1959. Toronto: Ontario
     Committee LPP. u. Nos. 1 and 2 only, Sept and Nov
     1959//?*OTURS/RSK.

5808 Orbit. 1959. Toronto: Socialist Youth League (LPP).
     u. Vol.I no.2, May 1959 *OTURS/RSK.

5809 The Progressive Student. 1959-1960? Edmonton: CCF
     Campus Club of the University of Alberta. ∅.
     Vol.II no.6, 6 Jan 1960 *OOA/CCF315.

5810 La Revue Socialiste. 1959-1965? Montréal. Pour
     l'independance absolue du Québec et la liberation
     prolétarienne nationale des Canadiens français.
     Raoul Roy. q. No.1, printemps 1959 to no.8, prin-
     temps 1965//?*OONL.

5811 Trainmen News (in Canada). 1959-1968. Ottawa: Bro-
     therhood of Railroad Trainmen. m. Vol.I no.1, 20
     June 1959 to vol.X no.12, Dec 1968//*OOL microfilm.
     Merged with Transportation News Canada.

5812 The Voice. 1959-. Hamilton: Christian Trade Unions
     of Canada. F.P. Fuyschat. m. Formerly The Guide.
     Vol.I no.1, March 1959 through 1970*OOL microfilm.
     See no. 5738 above for more details.

5813 Voice of Labor. 1959-1960? Vancouver: Communist
     Party of BC. u. Vol.II no.1, March 1960 *OTURS/RSK.

1960

5814 The Builder. 1960-1961? Toronto: Communist Party
     of Canada Metro Toronto Construction Workers Club.
     u. Vol.II no.2, June 1961 *OTURS/RSK.

5815 The Canadian Power Plant Worker. 1960-. Toronto:
     Canadian Union of Operating Engineers. James A. Gray.
     m. Vol.I no.1, Dec 1960 through 1970 *OOL microfilm.

5816 L'Eco di Toronto. 1960. Toronto. Il giornale dei
     lavoratori. G.C. Pedoni. u. Vol.I no.1, April
     1960//?

(5817)Mine Mill Research Review. c1960. Toronto. Not
     found.

5818 The New Party Newsletter. 1960-1961. Ottawa: Nat-
ional Committee for the New Party. m. Later New
Democratic Newsletter. Vol.I no.1, Jan 1960 to vol.
II no.5-6, June-July 1961//*OOA/CCF532.

5819 Research Bulletin. 1960. Toronto: UE Radio and
Machine Workers of America. u. Sept 1960 (unnumbered)*OTURS/RSK.

5820 The Western Canadian Lumber Worker. 1960-1965?
Vancouver: International Woodworkers of America Regional Council no.1. s. Formerly BC Lumber Worker:
numbering continued: vol.XXVII no.5, March 1960 to
vol.XXII (sic) no.24, Dec 1965//?*OOL microfilm.
Issue of Dec 1961 wrongly numbered vol.XVII instead
of XXVII and error continued thereafter.

1961

5821 Advance. 1961-1963. Toronto: (Young Communist League). Dave Clark. m. Vol.I no.1, 1 Nov 1961 to
vol.III no.6, July 1963//*OOA/CCF475.

5822 Canada-USSR Association Bulletin. 1961-1963? Toronto. b. Vol.I no.1, May 1961 plus 2 issues to
vol.III no.2, March-April 1963. *OTURS/RSK.

5823 (The) Democrat. 1961-. Vancouver: New Democratic
Party of BC. Jessie Mendels. e. Formerly CCF News.
Vol.I no.1, Nov 1961 *BVAUS/Webster 9-3; vol.III no.
5, to vol.XIV no.6, July 1974 *BVAUS.

5824 Edmonton Steelworker. 1961-1966? Edmonton: United
Steelworkers of America. m. No.1, 31 Oct 1961 to
no.7, 6 Sept 1963 thereafter unnumbered to 20 May
1966 *ACGLA/USWA 1.

5825 Metro Toronto Advocate. 1961-1962? Toronto: Communist Party of Canada, Metro Toronto Committee. u.
Vol.I no.1, April 1961 *OTURS/RSK.

5826 NDY Information Bulletin. 1961-1968. Ottawa: New
Democratic Youth. b. Later Info Bulletin. No.1,
Sept 1961 to June 1968//unnumbered *OOA/CCF478, in-
complete.

5827 The New Democrat. 1961-. Toronto: NDP Eastern Canada. Walter Stewart. m. Formerly CCF News. Vol.I
no.1, Sept 1961 through 1970. *OOA/CCF

5828 Our Generation (Against Nuclear War). 1961-. Montreal. q. Vol.I no.1, Autumn 1961 through 1970.
Omits 'Against nuclear war' with vol.IV.Woodsworth255.

5829 Viewpoint. 1961-. Ottawa: New Democratic Youth.
Bill Piket. m/b. Vol.I no.1, Sept 1961 through
1970. *OOA/CCF.

5830 Voice of Women National Newsletter. 1961-. Toronto.
m/b. No.6-7-8, Feb 1961 to no.29-30, Nov 1963 *MWPA

Brigden 3: vol.II no.3, Spring 1964 to vol.V no.2,
May 1967//?*OOA/VOW 7. Both incomplete. Woodsworth
390.

5831 Voice of Women Saskatchewan Bulletin. 1961-1963?
Saskatoon. Ed: Diana Wright. (q). Vol.I no.1,
June 1961 to vol.II no.1, March 1963 *SSA/McNaughton
H30.

1962

(5832)Alberta Voice of Women Newsletter. 1962-? Edmonton:
Voice of Women. m. Woodsworth 6, not found.

5833 L'Harmonie Syndicale. 1962-1969? Montréal: Fédéra-
tion canadienne des Associations Indépendantes. u.
Vol.VI no.4, Jan-Feb 1967 to vol.VIII no.10-11, July-
Aug 1969 *OOL microfilm.

(5834)L'Indépendance. 1962-? Montréal: Rassemblement pour
l'Independance Nationale. m. Woodsworth 155, not
found.

5835 The Intercom. 1962-1968? Toronto: Office Employees
International Union. ∅. No.8, April 1962 through
1968 *OOA/)PEU 3, incomplete.

5836 The Marxist Quarterly. 1962-1966. Toronto: Progress
Books: to present Communist views on issues of curr-
ent concern. Stanley Ryerson. q. Later Horizons.
No.1, Spring 1962 to no.18, Winter 1966// *own.

(5837)New Left Commentary. 1962-? Montreal: New Left Assn
of the New Democratic Party. m. Woodsworth 238,
not found.

5838 SOS Survival or Suicide. 1962-? Toronto: Canadian
Campaign for Nuclear Disarmament. R.S. Lambert. u.
Vol.(I) no.14, May 1962 *SSA/McNaughton H23.

5839 Young Socialist Forum. 1962-1964? Vancouver/Toronto:
Vanguard Publishing. Later Young Socialist. Single
copy 1964 only seen. Woodsworth 412.

1963

5840 Alberta Labour. 1963-. Edmonton: AJC Publications.
P. Quintin. b. Vol.I no.1, 3 Oct 1963 through 1970.
*ACGL. Ceased numbering with vol.I no.9, 25 Feb
(1964).

5841 Argus. 1963-1966. Ottawa: Civil Service Federation
of Canada. m. Later Argus-Journal. Unnumbered:
Sept 1963 to July-Aug 1966//*OOL microfilm. First
issue of Sept 1963 has title Civil Service Federation
of Canada Newsletter and invitation to find a title.

5842 Canada-Cuba Bulletin. 1963-1965? Toronto: Canada-
Cuba Friendship Committee. 10 times a year. Vol.I
no.1, January 1963 to Nov 1965// *own. Woodsworth 51.

5843 Canadian Dimension. 1963-. Winnipeg. An independent
journal...the product of the post-nuclear generation
of leftist thinkers. C.W. Gonick. b. Vol.I no.1
(Oct-Nov 1963) through 1970. *OONL.

5844 Cuba Newsletter. 1963-? Canada-Cuba Friendship Committee. u. Vol.I no.5, May 1963 *OTURS/RSK.

(5845)L'Indépendantiste. ?1963-? Montréal: Action Socialiste pour l'Independance du Québec. Woodsworth 154
not found.

5846 New Democratic (Party) News(letter). 1963-1968?
Ottawa: NDP. m/b. Vol.I no.1, Nov 1963 to vol.V
no.12, Dec 1968 SSA *OOA/CCF532. Variations in title.

5847 Sanity. 1963-1970. Montreal/Toronto: Canadian Campaign for Nuclear Disarmament. Vol.I no.1 to May
1970// *OTP. Woodsworth 315.

1964

5848 (CUPE) Journal. 1964-. Ottawa: Canadian Union of
Public Employees. m. Vol.I no.1, Oct 1964 through
1970. *OOL microfilm.

5849 Comment. 1964-? Halifax: New Democratic Party of
Nova Scotia. m. Vol.I no.1, Aug 1964//? *OOA/Cold-
well 60.

5850 The Halifax New Democrat. 1964-1965? Halifax: Halifax Federal Constituency Assn of the NDP. m. Vol.I
no.1, 13 Feb 1964 to no.12 March 1965 *OOA/CCF535,
incomplete.

(5851)Native Brotherhood Newscall. c1964. Prince Albert:
Native Brotherhood of Indians and Métis. Woodsworth
223, not found.

5852 (The New Brunswick) New Democrat. 1964-. Moncton:
NDP of NB. (Tom Jones). m. No.1 (June 1964) to
vol.II no.4, April-May, 1971 *OOA/CCF535, incomplete.

5853 Ontario Young New Democrats Newsletter. 1964-1965.
Toronto. A.F. Bowker. m/b. Later Rejoynder. Vol.I
no.1, Dec 1964 to vol.II no.7, Aug 1965//*OOA/CCF480
incomplete.

5854 The Printers Story. 1964. Toronto: Toronto Typographical Union. u. No.1, July 1964 and no.2, 24
July 1964 *OTURS/RSK. Published during the strike.

5855 Progressive Worker. 1964-? Vancouver: Progressive
Workers Movement. Jack Scott. m/q. Vol.I no.1,
Oct 1964 to vol.VI no.1 ('first issue for 6 months')
*OHMA2644

5856 Socialisme. 1964-? Montréal. Revue du socialisme
international et québecois. q. No.1, printemps
1964 to ? *OONL.

(5857)Le Travail du Permanent. 1964-? Montréal: Confédération des Syndicats Nationaux. QMSCN not seen.

1965

5858 Caiman Review. 1965-. Winnipeg: Canadian Assn of
Industrial, Mechanical and Allied Workers. u.
Scattered issues *OOL.

5859 Canadian Postal Worker. 1965-1968. Vancouver: Vancouver Branch Canadian Postal Employees Assn. E.
Jervis Bloomfield. m. Vol.I no.1, March 1965 to
vol.IV no.6, Nov-Dec 1968//*OOL microfilm.

(5860)Canadian Universities Memo. 1965-? Ottawa: Carleton
University Professors (against Vietnam war). Woodsworth 66, not found.

5861 Candor. 1965. Regina: Saskatchewan New Democratic
Youth. m. Vol.I no.1, Nov 1965 and no.2, Dec 1965
//?*SSA/G.516.2; also *OOA/CCF481, incomplete.

5862 The Conference Table. 1965-1967. Kitchener. A journal of discussion and criticism...pertaining mainly
to direct social action and for peace and progress.
Gary Moffatt. m. Vol.I no.1, July 1965 to vol.II
no.12, June 1967//*OOA/CCF478 and OONL.

5863 Freedom Now. 1965. Toronto: Canadian Friends of
SNCC. Vol.I no.4, 6 July 1965//? *own copy.

5864 Left Leaf. 1965. Toronto: Progressive Workers
Movement. u. No.1, 1 July 1965 *OTURS/RSK.

5865 SUPA Newsletter (ie Student Union for Peace Action)⌋
1965-1967? Toronto. Vol.I no.1, April 1965 to vol.
III no.8, June 1967//? *OHMA.

5866 Scan. 1965-1967? Toronto. Ed: Rae Murphy. ?m.
Vol.III no.4, July-Aug 1967 *OTURS/RSK.

1966

5867 Argus-Journal. 1966-. Ottawa: Public Service Alliance of Canada. Jim Shearon. m. Formerly Argus.
Unnumbered: Aug 1966 through 1970 *OOL microfilm.

5868 CSAO News. 1966-. Toronto: Civil Service Assn of
Ontario. ⌀. Unnumbered: Feb 1966 through 1970 *OOL.

5869 Canada Vietnam Newsletter. 1966-1969? Ottawa/Toro-
nto. m. Vol.I no.1, May 1966 to vol.IV no.2, Oct
1969 *own copy. Woodsworth 54.

(5869A)Canadian Alternatives. 1966-? Regina. u. Vol.I
no.1 (March 1966) *own copy.

5870 Canadian Railwayman/Le Cheminot Canadien. 1966-?
Montreal: International Non-operating Railway Unions
in Canada. ⱡ. Formerly Labor. Vol.I no.1, 25 April
1966 through 1970 *OOL, incomplete. Vol.II no.1, 12
Aug 1967 states 'this is the first issue of Canadian
Railwayman'.

5871 Dissent. 1966. Toronto: High School Students Against
the War in Vietnam. Vol.I no.1 to vol.III no.2 (1966)
(undated) *own copies, incomplete. Woodsworth 101.

5872 The Eye-Opener. 1966-1967? Vancouver/Victoria. No.1
5 Dec 1966 to no.4, 21 Feb 1967// *BVAUS.

5873 Horizons. 1966-1969. Toronto: Progress Books. Stanley Ryerson. q. Formerly Marxist Quarterly, numbering continued: no.19, Autumn 1966 to no.28 1969 *own
copies.

5874 Initiatives. 1966-? Edmonton: New Democratic Youth.
u. Vol.I no.1, Nov 1966 *OOA/CCF478.

(5875)Left Report. 1966-? (Ottawa): Left Caucus of the
New Democratic Youth. Woodsworth 184, not found.

5876 The Manitoba New Democrat. 1966-. Winnipeg: Mani-
toba NDP. m/q. Vol.I no.1, Nov 1966 to vol.III no.4
April 1969: format changes and numbering starts again
Vol.I no.1, Summer 1970-. *OOA.

5877 Peace Centre News. 1966-? Toronto: Toronto Peace
Centre. m. Vol.IV no.2 to vol.V no.2 *OOA/CCF480.

5878 The Public Dispute. 1966-? Vancouver: (Peoples
Press). u. Vol.I no.1, (Fall 1966) *OOA/CCF478.

5879 Rejoynder. 1966-1969. Toronto: Ontario New Democratic Youth. m/ⱡ. Formerly Ontario Young New
Democrats Newsletter; later ONDY/OYND Newsletter:
numbering continued: vol.II 1966 to Sept 1969 *OOA/
CCF480, incomplete.

(5880)Student Association to End the War in Vietnam Bulletin. 1966-1968? Toronto. Vol.I no.1, ?1966 to
vol.III no.5, Nov 1968. Not seen.

5881 This Magazine (is About Schools). 1966-. Toronto.
Vol.I no.1, (May) 1966 *Own copy. Woodsworth 357.

5882 Words (International). 1966-1967? Vancouver: University of British Columbia and Simon Fraser University Internationalists. Vol.I no.1, 18 Jan 1966
*own. Woodsworth 403.

1967

5883 The Alberta Democrat. 1967-? Edmonton: Alberta New
Democrats. Ken Novakowski. m. Vol.I no.1, March

1967. *OONL.

5884 Bulletin of the Montreal Centre for Marxist Research.
1967-? Montreal. u. Unnumbered: Dec 1967 *OTURS/RSK.

5885 CTC Bulletin. 1967-. Montreal/Brantford: Canadian
Textile Council. ∅. Unnumbered: Feb 1967 through
1970 *OOL microfilm. Published in Brantford from
Feb 1969.

5886 Canadian Free Press. 1967-1968. Ottawa. ∅. Later
Octopus. Vol.I no.1, Feb 1967 *own copy to vol.II
no.4, July 1968//. Woodsworth 57.

5887 Canadian (Pulp and) Paper Worker Journal/(Le) Jour-
nal des Travailleurs (Canadiens)(des Pâtes et)(du)
Papier(s) (du Canada). 1967-. Montreal: Internat-
ional Brotherhood of Pulp, Sulphite and Paper Mill
Workers. Fernand J. Duberry. q/∅. Formerly
Gleanings/Glanures: numbering continued: vol.IV no.9
Feb 1967 *OOL. As may be evident they had some pro-
blems in deciding just what the title should be.

(5888)Confrontations. 1967-? Ottawa: New Democratic
Youth. Woodsworth 92, not found.

5889 Georgia Straight. 1967-. Vancouver: Georgia Straight
UPS (ie Underground Press Syndicate). Dan McLeod.
e. Vol.I no.1, 5-18 May 1967 through 1970 *BVAUS.
Woodsworth 134.

(5890)Logos. 1967-1970. Montreal. Woodsworth 191, not
found.

5891 The New Society. 1967. Vancouver. m. Embryo issue
(April) 1967; May issue 1967// *BVAUS. Woodsworth
240.

5892 OFL Facts and Figures. 1967-. Toronto: Ontario
Federation of Labour. Annual. Vol.I no.1, Feb 1967,
preceded by 'Some statistical data of interest to
labour' April 1966, to vol.I no.4, Feb 1970; thereafter described as 'fifth edition' etc. *OOA/OFL8
and *OOA/CCF543.

(5893)Peace Research Reviews. 1967-? Clarkson, Ont.
Not found.

5894 Satyrday. 1967-? Toronto. u. No.1, (no date),
1967 *own copy.

5895 Vietnam Protest. 1967-? Vancouver: Vancouver Vietnam Day Committee. u. No.3, Summer 1967 *BVAUS/
Mackenzie.

5896 Viewpoint. 1967-? Toronto: Communist Party of Canada: discussion bulletin. Vol.IV no.1ᴊ *OTURS/RSK.

1968

5897 Alternate Society (Newsletter. 1968-. St Catharines/

Welland/Toronto. Vol.I no.1, 1968. Woodsworth 9 and 10, not found.

5898 Amor de Cosmos. 1968. Victoria. Ed: Frank Cox u. Unnumbered, undated: No.(1) (May 1968); no.(2), (? June 1968)//*BVIPA. For peace, national freedom, democracy and socialism.

5899 Aurora. 1968. Vancouver: Craig Ferry and Donald Hembroff. e. Vol.I no.1, 5 July 1968 and no.2, 2 Aug 1968//*BVAUS.

5900 Canadian Student. 1968-1971. Toronto:Canadian Student Movement. ʃ. Vol.I no.1 (Sept) 1968 to vol.IV no.3, 3 March 1971//?*own copies, incomplete. Woodsworth 64.

5901 Canadians for the NLF (ie National Liberation Front of South Vietnam) Bulletin. 1968-1969? Toronto. m. Vol.I no.1, (Jan) 1968 to vol.II no.1, Feb 1969//? *own copies. Woodsworth 70.

5902 Chingari. 1968-1971. Toronto: Hindustani Ghadar Party Ad Hoc Committee. m. Vol.I no.1, Oct 1968 to vol.IV no.3, Oct 1971//? *own copies, incomplete. Woodsworth 81.

5903 Confrontations. 1968-1971? Ottawa: New Democratic Youth. Harry Edel. b. Vol.I no.1, Dec 1967-Jan 1968 to vol.III no.(4), Aug 1971 *OOA/CCF478.

(5904)Cotopaxi. 1968-. Toronto. Woodsworth 94, not seen.

5905 The Courier. 1968-. Ottawa: Letter Carriers Union of Canada. m. Vol.I no.1, Jan 1968 through 1970 *OOL microfilm.

5906 Federation. 1968-1969? (Halifax): Nova Scotia New Democratic Youth. ʃ. Undated and unnumbered: c. 1968-1969 - four issues in *OOA/CCF480.

5907 The Front. 1968? Richmond, BC. (Vol.I no.1) July (1968)//*BVAUS.

(5908)The Front Line. 1968-? London: Anti-Imperialist Front. m. Woodsworth 130, not found.

(5909)Fulcrum. 1968? Victoria: Socialist Party of Canada. Woodsworth 131, not found.

5910 Halifax Voice. 1968. Halifax: Voice of Women. ʃ (No.1) June 1968, scattered issues, unnumbered in *OOA/VOW. Woodsworth 142.

(5911)Harambee. 1968. Toronto: Afro-American Progressive Assn. Woodsworth 144, not found.

5912 Harbinger. 1968-1972? Toronto. e. Vol.I no.1, (undated) 1968 through 1970 *own copies. Woodsworth 145.

5913 Info Bulletin. 1968-. Ottawa: New Democratic Youth. ʃ. Formerly NDY Information Bulletin. Unnumbered July 1968 through 1970 *OOA/CCF478, incomplete.

5914 Libertarian. 1968. Toronto: Toronto Libertarian

Group. u. Vol.I no.1//? *OTURS/RSK. Woodsworth
187.

5915 Local 1-80 Bulletin. 1968-. Duncan, BC: International Woodworkers of America. Fernie Viala. m.
? first issue from previous title: vol.IV no.1, Jan
1968 to vol.I no.1 (sic) Nov 1969 *OOL microfilm,
incomplete. Numbering erratic.

5916 McGill Student. 1968-1969. Montreal. Ø. Vol.I
no.1, 18 Sept 1968 *own copy.

5917 La Masse. 1968-1970. Montréal: Front de Libération
Populaire. Vol.I no.1, (May 1968) through April 1970.
QMCSN, not seen. Woodsworth 205.

5918 NARP (ie. Native Alliance for Red Power) Newsletter.
1968-1970. Vancouver. Ed: Ray Bobb. Ø. No.1, June
July 1968 to no.5, Feb-March 1970//*BVAUS. Woodsworth 222.

5919 The Nationalist. 1968-1969? Toronto: Nationalist
Canadian Workers Project. q. Vol.I no.4, Dec 1969
*OTURS/RSK.

5920 Octopus. 1968-1970. Ottawa. m. Formerly Canadian
Free Press: numbering continued: vol.II no.5, Nov
1968 to vol.III no.11, Dec 1970//? *own copies.

(5921)The Rebel. 1968. Montreal: American Deserters Committee. b. Woodsworth 299, not found.

5922 Sir George Student. 1968-1969. Montreal: (Communist
Party of Canada: Marxist-Leninist). Vol.I no.1, 19
Sept 1968 to vol.II no.2, 3 Feb 1969//? *own copies.

5923 Spark. 1968-? Toronto: Workers League Canadian
Section of the 4th International. m. Vol.I no.2,
July 1968 and no.4, Sept 1968 *own copies.

5924 The Torch. 1968. Toronto: Local 721 International
Assn of Bridge, Structural and Ornamental Ironworkers.
Vol.II no.4, May 1969 *OTURS/RSK.

5925 Le Travail des Militants. 1958-1970. Montréal: Confédération des Syndicats Nationaux. QMSCN, not seen.

5926 UAE Newsletter. 1968. Islington, Ont: Union of American Exiles. Ø: not more than once monthly. Later
The American Exile in Canada. No.1, Sept 1968 to
no.4, (Dec) 1968*own copies. Woodsworth 14.

5927 The Western Gate. 1968. Vancouver. Ed: Al Birnie.
b. Vol.I no.1, Feb 1968 and no.3, June 1968//*BVAUS.

5928 Yankee Refugee. 1968-1969. Vancouver. West Coast
Newsletter of American Exiles. Ø. No.1, 10 Nov 1968
to no.8, July 1969//*BVAUS.

1969

5929 The Afroasian. 1969. Montreal: (Internationalists)

?m. Vol.I no.l (June) 1969 and no.2, July 1969 *own copies. Woodsworth 2.

5930 The American Exile in Canada. 1969. Toronto: Union of American Exiles. ϕ. Formerly UAE Newsletter: later Amex: numbering continues: no.5 to no.15, May 1969// *own copies. McLaren 3 Woodsworth 14.

5931 Amex. 1969-. Toronto. ϕ. Formerly The American Exile in Canada: numbering continued: (16), Sept 1969 through 1970 *own copies. Mclaren 4 Woodsworth 17.

(5932)Antithesis. c1969-? Montreal: American Deserters Committee. Formerly The Rebel. Woodsworth 21, not found.

5933 BC Newsletter. 1969-1970. Vancouver: Progressive Workers Movement. m. No.l, July 1969 to no.ll, June-July 1970//*BVAUS. Woodsworth 30.

5934 The Barnacle. 1969. Vancouver: UBC Campus Left Action Movement (CLAM). m. Vol.I no.l, Sept 1969 to no.3, Dec 1969//*BVAUS.

5935 Black Liberation News. 1969-1970. Toronto: Black Liberation Front. Vol.I no.l, July 1969 to vol.II no.2, Feb 1970//*OTU. McLaren 16 Woodsworth 42.

5936 Canadian Internationalist. 1969. (Toronto): Canadian Internationalists (Marxist-Leninist Youth and Student Movement). m. Vol.I no.l, Feb 1969 and no. 2, March 1969//? *own copies. Woodsworth 60.

(5937)Canadian Worker. 1969-. Toronto: Canadian Party of Labour. m. Woodsworth 68, not found.

5938 Communist Viewpoint. 1969-. Toronto: Progress Books. b. Vol.I no.l, March-April 1969 through 1970 *OONL. Woodsworth 88. Formerly Horizons.

(5939)The Fourth Estate. 1969-1970. Halifax. Not found.

5940 The Gap. 1969. Vancouver. (q). Vol.I no.l, 21 July 1969 and no.2, 5 Sept 1969//? *BVAUS.

5941 Last Post. 1969-. Montreal. A radical Canadian newsmagazine...to unearth and publish facts which are omitted, ignored or obscured by the commercial press. q, more or less. Vol.I no.l, Dec 1969 through 1970 *own copies. Woodsworth 181.

5942 Literature and Ideology. 1969-. Progressive Books and Periodicals. q. (Vol.I) no.l, Spring 1969 through 1970 *own copies. Woodsworth 189.

5943 Mass Line. 1969-. Ottawa/Toronto: Peoples Publishing House. ϕ. Pre-issue, 4 July 1969; vol.I no.l, 16 July 1969 through 1970 *own copies. Woodsworth 204.

(5944)Mobilisation. 1969-1970. Montréal: Front de Liberation Populaire: Librairie Progressiste. b. Woodsworth 24, not found.

5945 The Mysterious East. 1969-. Fredericton: Rubber
Duck Press. Vol.I no.1, ? 1969.*own copy. Woodsworth 220.

5946 New Canada. 1969-. Toronto: NC Press. m. Vol.III
no.3, July 1972 *own copy. Woodsworth 233.

5947 The New Feminist. 1969-. Toronto. ∅/m. No.1, Nov
1969 to vol.III no.4, Dec 1972 *own copies. Woodsworth 235.

5948 ONDY/OYND Newsletter. 1969-. Toronto: Ontario Young
New Democrats. m/∅. Formerly Rejoynder. No.1, Oct
1969 through 1970 *OOA/CCF480, incomplete.

5949 Le Patriot Rouge. 1969-1970. Montréal: (Communist
Party of Canada: Marxist-Leninist). ∅. Vol.I no.1,
1969 to vol.II no.2, ? 1970//? *own copies.

5950 Pedestal. 1969-. Vancouver: Vancouver Womens Caucus.
∅. Vol.I no.1 to vol.IV no.2, Feb 1972 *OOA/VOW 8.

5951 The Peninsula Student. 1969-? St Catharines: Niagara Youth Movement. m. Unnumbered: Sept 1969
*OHMA.

(5952) Pouvoir Populaire. 1969-? Québec: Front de Liberation Populaire. Woodsworth 280, not found.

5953 Probe Newsletter. 1969-? Toronto: University of
Toronto Pollution Probe. ∅. Vol.I no.1 () 1969;
no.(3), 4 June 1969 *own copies. Woodsworth 285.

(5954) Solidarity. 1969-? Vancouver/New Westminster. u.
Vol.I no.1 1969. Not found.

5955 The Student. 1969-? Toronto: High School Student
Movement. ∅. Pre-issue, 30 Sept 1969; vol.I no.1,
27 Oct 1969//? *own copy. Woodsworth 338.

(5956) This Paper Belongs to the People. 1969-1970. Kingston. Woodsworth 358, not found.

5957 UBC NDP Journal. 1969-? Vancouver: UBC New Democratic Club. Bob Easton. u. Vol.I no.4, Feb 1969
*OOA/MacInnis 11.

5958 US Students Society Newsletter. 1969. Montreal.
Vol.I no.1, 5 Dec 1969//? *own copy.

5959 UTU (Transformation) News Canada. 1969-. Ottawa:
United Transportation Union. m. Vol.I no.1, Jan
1969 through 1970 *OOL microfilm.

5960 The Vancouver Ad-Hoc Committee for the Defense of
the CBC Demonstrators. 1969. Vancouver. No.1,
Aug 1969 *BVAUS.

5961 Vancouver Student. 1969-. Vancouver. Vol.I no.1,
Jan 1969 through 1970 *BVAUS.

5962 Voice of the Unemployed. 1969. Vancouver. Nos.1
and 2 () 1969//?*BVAUS.

5963 Waffle News. 1969-. Ottawa/Toronto. Eds: Krista
Maeots, Tracey Morey. ∅. No. 1, Aug 1969 through
1970 *OOA/CCF446.

5964 Waterloo Student. 1969. Waterloo: Waterloo Students Movement. u. Vol.I no.1, Jan 1969 and no.6, 28 July 1969//?*own copies.

5965 World Revolutionary Youth. 1969. (?Toronto). Vol.I no.1, Jan 1969; no.3, May 1969//*own copies.

5966 Young Communist. 1969-1970. Toronto: Young Communist League. Vol.I no.1 to vol.II no.4, March 1970.*OTURS/ RSK. Woodsworth 410.

1970

5967 Afro-Asian Liberation. 1970. Vancouver: Afro-Asian Peoples Solidarity Movement. Vol.I no.1, (March) 1970 and 2, April 1970 //? *own copies.

5968 Afro-Asian Solidarity. 1970. Toronto:Afro-Asian Peoples Solidarity Movement (Canada-Québec). Vol.I no.1, March 1970 and nos. 2 and 3, June and Dec 1970 //? *own copies.

5969 Carmmunique. 1970-. Toronto: Committee to Aid Refugees from Militarism. b/m. No.1, 18 Nov 1970 through 1970 *own copies.

5970 City Hall. 1970-. Toronto: James Lewis and Samuel. e. Vol.I no.1, 22 Sept 1970 - *own copies.

5971 The Civac Citizen. 1970-. Toronto: CIVAC. b. No.1, April 1970- *own copies.

5972 Community Concern. 1970. Toronto: Just Society Movement. s. Later Just Society. Vol.I no.1, undated (1970) to no.8, 22 July 1970//?* own copies. Woodsworth 90.

5973 Democratic Front. 1970. Vancouver: Vancouver Peoples Democratic Front. Vol.I no.1, 27 June 1970//?*BVAUS.

5974 Guerilla. 1970-. Toronto: an editorial collective. No.1, 5 June 1970- *own copies. Woodsworth 140.

5975 Hamilton People. 1970. Hamilton: Hamilton Peoples Movement. Vol.I no.1, Sept 1970-. *OHMA. Woodsworth 143.

5976 Just Society. 1970-. Toronto. b. Formerly Community Concern: numbering continues: vol.I no.9, Aug 1970 -. Woodsworth 169.

5977 Labor Challenge. 1970-. Toronto. Ed: John Riddell. e. Vol.I no.1, 9 Feb 1970- *OOA/CCF479. Woodsworth 178.

5978 New Leaf. 1970-. Vancouver. An independent paper for an independent Canada. Introductory issue: Oct 1970 - *BVAUS. Woodsworth 236.

5979 Peace Exchange. 1970. St Catharines. u. No. 6, Nov 1970 *own copy. Woodsworth 262.

5980 Peoples Canada Daily News. 1970-. Toronto. ⌀.
Vol.I no.1, 26 Aug 1970 - *OONL.

5981 Peoples War. 1970. (Toronto): October First Branch
of the Communist Party of Canada(Marxist-Leninist).
(No.1), 20 May 1970//?*own copy.

5982 Prairie Fire. 1970-. Regina: Regina Community Media
Project. w. Vol.I no.31, 10-16 June 1970 -*OOA/CCF
481, incomplete. Woodsworth 282.

5983 Rage. 1970. Vancouver: Vancouver Liberation Front,
Vancouver Womens Liberation. No.1 Oct 1970//?*BVAUS.

5984 Red, White and Black Newsletter. 1970. Toronto.
No.1, 26 Feb 1970 to no.4, 27 April 1970*own copies.
Woodsworth 301. Miscellaneous material was usually
distributed with issue, offprints, broadsides etc.

5985 The Resistance and Marshmallow News. 1970. Vancouver: Unemployed Citizens Welfare Improvement Council.
Vol.I no.5, July 1970*BVAUS. A publication of the
Action Committee for Unemployed Youth backed and inverted on to vol.I no.5 above.

(5986)Rising Up Angry. 1970. Toronto. Woodsworth 307,
not found.

(5987)The River Fiddler. ?1970. Regina: Students for a
Socialist Movement. Woodsworth 309, not found.

5988 Saskatoon Womens Liberation Movement Newsletter.
1970. Saskatoon. No.1, Sept 1970//? *SSA/G482.1.
New series starts (March) 1972.

(5989)The Solution. 1970. Victoria/Vancouver. Woodsworth
327, not found.

5990 Student Front. 1970. Vancouver. Vol.I no.1, Jan
1970 *BVAUS.

5991 Sunshiners. 1970-. Vancouver. Vol.I no.1- *BVAUS.

5992 Toronto American Deserters Committee Newsletter.
1970. Toronto. Vol.I () (1970)//? *own copy.

5993 Toronto Citizen. 1970. Toronto. ⌀/e. Vol.I no.1,
6 Aug 1970- *own copy. Woodsworth 361.

5994 The Toronto New Paper. 1970. Toronto: Mark Trent
and Carl Blazina. ⌀. No.1 (Oct) 1970*own copy.
Woodsworth 363.

5995 Toronto Student. 1970. Toronto: Toronto Student
Movement, unit of the Canadian Student Movement.
Vol.I no.1, March 1970//? *own copy. Woodsworth 364.

5996 Toronto Womens Liberation Newsletter. 1970-. Toronto. m. Unnumbered. 1970-. *own copy.

5997 UBC Communist. 1970. Vancouver. No.(1), March
1970//?*BVAUS.

5998 Uphold Peoples Democratic Rights Bulletin. 1970.
Toronto. No.1, 22 Dec 1970 *own copy.

5999 V-Bag. 1970. Vancouver. No.1, Jan-Feb 1970 *BVAUS. Woodsworth 381. V-Bag, ie. Vancouver Black Action Group.

(6000) Velvet Fist. 1970. Toronto. Woodsworth 383, not found.

6001 Voice of the Poor. 1970-. Toronto: Welfare Rights. Vol.I no.1, 21 July 1970 -. *own copy.

6002 (Canadian) Waterfront News. 1970-. Vancouver: International Longshoremens and Warehousemens Union Canadian Area. q. Vol.I no.1 - *BVAUS.

6003 Weathervane. 1970-. Winnipeg: Manitoba Young New Democrats. b. Vol.I no.1, May 1970 - *OOA/CCF479.

6004 Yellow Journal. 1970. Vancouver: Press Gang Publications. e. Vol.I no.1, 23 April 1970 to no.9, 29 Oct 1970//*BVAUS.

6005 Young Socialist. 1970. Toronto: Workers Vanguard. u. Formerly Young Socialist Forum. Vol.I no.1, Sept 1970 *own copy. Woodsworth 411.

6006 Young Worker. 1970. Toronto: Young Communist League. m. Formerly Young Communist. Vol.I no.1, Oct 1970- *OTURS/RSK.

List of bibliographies consulted

Amtmann, Bernard. Contributions to a short-title catalogue of Canadiana. Montreal, Bernard Amtmann, 1971-73. 3 vols.

Arora, Ved Parkash. Louis Riel: a bibliography. Regina, Provincial Library, 1972.

Backhaus, Christine E. Royal commissions and commissions of inquiry in Alberta 1905-1976. Edmonton, Legislature Library, 1977.

Beals, Helen D. A catalogue of the Eric R.Dennis collection of Canadiana in the library of Acadia University. Wolfville, 1938.

Bhatia, Mohan. Canadian provincial government publications: a bibliography of bibliographies. Saskatoon, University of Saskatchewan library, 1971. Revised edition.

Bishop, Olga B. Publications of the governments of Nova Scotia, Prince Edward Island, New Brunswick 1758-1952. Ottawa, National Library, 1957.

Canada. Canadian government publications relating to labour: sectional catalogue No.10 September 1963. Ottawa, Queens Printer, 1963.

Canada. Dept of Labour. Canadian labour papers currently received. Ottawa, various dates.

Canada. Dept of Labour. Canadian labour papers on microfilm. Ottawa, nd.

Canada. Dominion Bureau of Statistics. Historical catalogue of Dominion Bureau of Statistics publications 1918-1960. Ottawa, 1966.

Canada. National Library. Canadiana. Ottawa, from January 1951. Monthly.

Casey, Magdalen. Catalogue of pamphlets in the Public Archives of Canada. Ottawa, F.A.Acland, 1931-32. 2 vols.

Clement, Wallace and Daniel Drache. A practical guide to Canadian political economy. Toronto, James Lorimer, 1978.

Conover, Helen F. A bibliography of bibliographies of trade unions. Washington, Library of Congress, 1937.

Edwards, Margaret H. and John C.R.Lort. A bibliography of British Columbia: years of growth 1900-1950. Victoria, University of Victoria Social Sciences Research Centre, 1975.

Eichler, Margrit. An annotated selected bibliography of bibliographies on women. Ottawa, AUCC Committee on the Status of Women, 1973.

Elliott, Robbins L. The Canadian labour press from 1867: a chronological annotated directory. Toronto, Canadian Journal of Economics and Political Science, May 1948. Vol XIV pp220-245 plus correction p515. A pioneer work on which all later lists must be based.

Evans, Gwynneth. Women in federal politics: a bio-bibliography. Ottawa, National Library, 1975. Bilingual.

Forsyth, Joseph. Government publications relating to Alberta...from 1905 to 1968 and of publications of the government of Canada relating to the province of Alberta from 1867 to 1968. High Wycombe, University Microfilms,(1972). 8 vols. Facsimile of a thesis.

Le Groupe de chercheurs de L'Université du Québec à Montréal. L'action politique des ouvriers québecois (fin du XIXe siècle à 1919): recueil de documents. Montréal, Les Presses de l'Université du Québec, 1976. Bibliographie, 153-176. '(La Groupe) a commencé par un travail de repérage et de dépouillement des sources, la constitution d'une bibliographie et d'une chronologie...'

Gulick, Charles A.,Roy A.Ockert, Raymond J. Wallace. History and theories of working-class movements: a select bibliography. Berkeley, Bureau of Business and Economic Research, Institute of Industrial Relations, 1953. pp287-292 relate to Canada.

Ham, F.Gerald. Labor manuscripts in the State Historical Society of Wisconsin. Madison, State Historical Society of Wisconsin, 1967.

Hann, Russell G.,Gregory S.Kealey, Linda Kealey and Peter Warrian. Primary sources in Canadian working class history 1860-1930. Kitchener, Dumont Press, 1973. Lists 3,347 items divided into 1-1600 mss sources, 1601-1994 newspapers with a chronology chart, 1995-2799 pamphlets, 2800-3347 government documents. Another pioneer work.

Heggie, Grace. Canadian political parties 1867-1968: a historical bibliography. Toronto, Macmillan, 1977.

Henderson, George Fletcher. Federal Royal Commissions in Canada 1867-1966: a checklist. Toronto, University of Toronto Press, 1967.

Holmes, Marjorie C. Royal Commissions and Commissions of Inquiry under the 'Public Inquiries Act' in British Columbia 1872-1942: a checklist. Victoria, Kings Printer,1945.

Horvath, Maria. A Doukhobor bibliography based on material available in the University of British Columbia library. Part I: Books and periodical articles. Vancouver, University of British Columbia Library, 1968. Reference publication No.22. Enlarged and revised edition of Part I together with the supplement (1970) published as reference publication No.38 in 1972: Part III Audio-visual and unpublished writings published as reference guide 43 in 1973.

Isbester, A.F.,D.Coates and C.B.Williams. Industrial and labour relations in Canada: a selected bibliography.

Kingston, Queens University Industrial Relations Centre, 1965. Bibliographical series No.2.

Kehde, Ned. The American left, 1955-1970: a national union catalog of pamphlets published in the United States and Canada. Westport, Greenwood, 1976.

Klinck, Carl.F. Literary history of Canada: Canadian literature in English. Toronto, University of Toronto Press, 1965. Includes *Literature of protest* by Frank W. Watt.

Knight, Rolf. Work camps and company towns in Canada and the United States: an annotated bibliography. Vancouver, New Star, 1975.

LeBlanc, André E. and James D.Thwaites. Le monde ouvrier au Québec: bibliographie rétrospective. Montréal, Les Presses de L'Université du Québec, 1973. The principal bibliography for Québec covering the present work.

Legislative Library, Halifax, Nova Scotia. Nova Scotia Royal Commissions and Commissions of Enquiry appointed by the Province of Nova Scotia. Halifax, 1973.

Lochhead, Douglas. Bibliography of Canadian bibliographies. Toronto, University of Toronto Press in association with the Bibliographical Society of Canada, 1972. Second edition, revised and enlarged. Bilingual.

Lowther, Barbara Joan. A bibliography of British Columbia; laying the foundations, 1849-1899. Victoria, University of Victoria, 1968.

Macdonald, Christine. Historical directory of Saskatchewan newspapers 1878-1950. Saskatchewan, University of Saskatchewan Office of Saskatchewan Archives, 1951.

Macdonald, Christine. Publications of the Governments of the North-West Territories, 1876-1905 and of the Province of Saskatchewan, 1905-1952. Regina, Legislative Library, 1952.

McLaren, Duncan. Ontario ethno-cultural newspapers 1835-1972: an annotated checklist. Toronto, University of Toronto Press, 1973.

MacTaggart, Hazel I. Publications of the Government of Ontario 1901-1955; a checklist. Toronto, University of Toronto Press, 1964.

Mazur, Carol and Sheila Pepper. Women in Canada 1965 to 1975: a bibliography. Hamilton, McMaster University Library Press, 1976. Revised and expanded version of bibliography first published by Cynthia Harrison in 1972.

Morley, Marjorie. A bibliography of Manitoba from holdings in the Legislative Library of Manitoba. Winnipeg, (Queens Printer), 1970.

Morley, Marjorie. Royal Commissions and Commissions of Inquiry under 'The Evidence Act' in Manitoba: a checklist. (Winnipeg), (Provincial Library), 1952. Typescript copy deposited in the National Library.

Neufeld, Maurice F. A representative bibliography of American labor history. Ithaca, Cornell University Press, 1964.

Peel, Bruce Braden. A bibliography of the Prairie Provinces to 1953 with biographical index. Toronto, University of Toronto Press, 1973. Second edition. A major work whose reference numbers are cited in this bibliography.

Peel, Bruce. Early printing in the Red River Settlement 1859-1870 and its effect on the Riel rebellion. Winnipeg, Peguis, 1974.

Provincial Archives of British Columbia. Dictionary catalogue of the library of the Provincial Archives of British Columbia. Boston, G.K.Hall, 1971. 8 vols.

Roberts, Wayne and others. The Hamilton working class 1820-1977, a bibliography. Hamilton, McMaster University Labour Studies Programme, 1978.

Scotton, Anne. Bibliography of all sources relating to the Cooperative Commonwealth Federation, and the New Democratic Party in Canada. (Ottawa), Woodsworth Archives Project, 1977. Not strictly a bibliography but an invaluable compilation of the finding aids to the major collections of CCF and NDP manuscripts.

Shibata, Yuko, Shoji Matsumoto, Rintaro Hayashi and Shotaro Iida. The forgotten history of the Japanese Canadians in the early fishing industry in British Columbia and an annotated bibliography. Vancouver, New Sun, 1977.

Stewart, Charlotte and Renu Barett with Norma Smith. Canadian pamphlets: a subject listing of the holding of McMaster University Library. Part I A-L, Part II M-Z, Part III Index. Hamilton, McMaster University Library. Published as three issues of Library Research News Vol 3 No 6 December 1976, Vol 4 No 1 April 1977 and Vol 4 No 2 July 1977.

Vaisey, G. Douglas. The labour companion: a bibliography of Canadian labour history based on materials printed from 1950 to 1975. Halifax, Committee on Canadian Labour History 1980.

Weinrich, Peter H. A select bibliography of Tim Buck, General Secretary of the Communist Party of Canada 1929-1962. Toronto, Progress, 1974.

Woodsworth, A. The 'alternative' press in Canada: a checklist of underground, revolutionary, radical and other alternative serials from 1960. Toronto, University of Toronto Press, 1972.

Lists of theses consulted

Bruchet, Susan (Jacques) and Gwynneth Evans. Theses in Canada: a guide to sources of information about theses completed or in preparation. Ottawa, National Library, 1978. Bilingual.

Canadian Political Science Association. Theses in Canadian

political studies, completed and in progress. 1971-
Publication irregular. Bilingual.

Carleton University. Theses and research essays accepted
by Carleton University between 1950 and November 1969 and
held in the MacOdrum Library. Ottawa, 1972.

Humanities Research Council of Canada. Canadian graduate
theses in the humanities and social sciences 1921-1946.
Ottawa, Queens Printer, 1951.

McGill University. McGill University thesis directory.
Montreal, 1975-76. 2 vols.

Mills, Judy and Irene Dombra. University of Toronto doc-
toral theses 1897-1967: a bibliography. Toronto, 1968.

National Library. Canadian theses on microfilm: catalogue,
price list. Nos.1-2450. Ottawa, 1969; supplement 1974.
Bilingual.

Université de Montréal. Thèses de doctorat: thèses de
maîtrise. Montréal, nd.

Université Laval. Liste des thèses 1940 à 1965. Québec,
1965.

Université Laval. Répertoire des thèses 1941-1973. Québec,
1973.

University of Ottawa. Catalogue of social sciences and
humanities theses presented at the University of Ottawa.
Ottawa, 1972. Bilingual.

University of Saskatchewan. University of Saskatchewan
postgraduate theses 1912-1973. Saskatoon, 1975.

Wood, W.D., L.A.Kelly and F. Kumar. Canadian graduate
theses 1919-1967; an annotated bibliography (covering
economics, business and industrial relations). Kingston,
Queens University Industrial Relations Centre, 1970.

List of other works consulted

Abella, Irving. The Canadian labour movement 1902-1960.
Ottawa, Canadian Historical Society, 1975. Booklet No 28.

Abella, Irving and David Millar. The Canadian worker in
the twentieth century. Toronto, Oxford University Press,
1978.

Abella, Irving. Nationalism, communism and Canadian labour,
the CIO, the Communist party and the Canadian Congress of
Labour 1935-1956. Toronto, University of Toronto Press,
1973.

Abella, Irving. On strike: six key labour struggles in
Canada 1919-1949. Toronto, James Lewis and Samuel, 1974.

Allen, Richard. The social passion: religion and social
reform in Canada 1914-28. Toronto, University of Toronto
Press, 1971.

Anderson, Jim and others. A political history of agrarian organizations in Ontario 1914-1940 with special reference to Grey and Bruce counties. (Toronto), Chase Press, 1974.

Avakumovic, Ivan. The Communist party in Canada: a history. Toronto, McClelland and Stewart, 1975.

Avakumovic, Ivan. Socialism in Canada: a study of the CCF-NDP in federal and provincial politics. Toronto, McClelland and Stewart, 1978.

Bercuson, David Jay. Confrontation at Winnipeg: labour, industrial relations and the general strike. Montreal, McGill-Queens University Press, 1974.

Bercuson, David Jay. Fools and wise men: the rise and fall of the One Big Union. Toronto, McGraw-Hill Ryerson, 1978.

Bercuson, David Jay (ed). Western perspectives 1: papers of the Western Canadian Studies Conference, 1973. Toronto Holt, Rinehart and Winston, 1974.

Campbell, Colin. Canadian political facts 1945-1976. Toronto, Methuen, 1977.

Committee on Canadian Labour History. Newsletter nos.1-6. Downsview, York University: together with Bulletin nos 1-2 Halifax, Dalhousie University; together with Labour, 1976 to date. Halifax.

Cross, Michael S. The decline and fall of a good idea: CCF-NDP manifestoes 1932 to 1969. Toronto, New Hogtown Press, 1974.

Forsey, Eugene A. The Canadian labour movement 1812-1902. Ottawa, Canadian Historical Association, 1974. Booklet 27.

Halifax Women's Bureau. Women at work in Nova Scotia. Halifax, 1973.

Kealey, Gregory S. and Peter Warrian (eds). Essays in Canadian working class history. Toronto, McClelland and Stewart, 1976.

Kealey, Greg. Working class Toronto at the turn of the century. Toronto, New Hogtown Press, 1973.

McCormack, A.Ross. Reformers, rebels and revolutionaries: the Western Canadian radical movement 1899-1919. Toronto, University of Toronto Press, 1977.

MacEwan, Paul. Miners and steelworkers: labour in Cape Breton. Toronto, Samuel Stevens Hakkert, 1976.

O'Toole, Roger. The precipitous path: studies in political sects. Toronto, Peter Martin, 1977.

Penner, Norman. The Canadian left: a critical analysis. Scarborough, Prentice-Hall, 1977.

Public Archives of Canada. Guide to Canadian ministries since Confederation July 1,1867 - April 1, 1973. Ottawa, 1974.

Roberts, Wayne. Honest womanhood: feminism, femininity and class consciousness among Toronto working women 1893 to 1914. Toronto, New Hogtown Press, 1976.

Scott, Jack. Plunderbund and proletariat: a history of the IWW in British Columbia. Vancouver, New Star, 1975.

Teeple, Gary (ed). Capitalism and the national question in Canada. Toronto, University of Toronto Press, 1972.

Toronto Public Library and Labour Council of Metropolitan Toronto. Labour in society: an introductory list of selected readings and films. Toronto, 1972.

Urquhart, M.C. and K.A.H.Buckley. Historical statistics of Canada. Toronto, Macmillan, 1965.

Appendix I:
prohibited publications 1920

This appendix is in two parts: first is a copy of the consolidated list of prohibited publications prepared by the
Chief Press Censor in 1920. The orthography, information
and order are those of his list and serial publications are
preceded by an (s).

The second part comprises lists of publications reported from different Canadian cities from May 1919 to
January 1920. These publications were not necessarily
prohibited, but they were all clearly considered dangerous,
and were often accompanied by requests for suppression.
Once the war had ended however, the Censor was reluctant
to make further prohibitions. The lists are interesting
in showing the variety and extent of dissemination of radical works.

(s)Ahjo (The Forge), Finnish quarterly: Duluth.
Anarchism and communism. Russian.
A reply to press lies.
Bolshevist declaration of rights.
(s)Brand (Conflagration), Swedish. Stockholm.
Bielyi Terror (The White Terror). Russian: IWW Chicago.
Budushtche Obshrchestvo (The Future Society). Russian:
 Newark, NJ.
(s)Canadian Forward.
(s)The Class Struggle. New York.
(s)Croneca Sloversiva (Revolutionary Chronicle), Italian:
 Lynn, Mass.
(s)Defense News Bulletin. IWW, Chicago.
Die Arbeitlosigkeit (Unemployment) by Goldfarb. Yiddish,
 New York.
Ershter Mai Bulletin (1st May). Yiddish; Winnipeg, Social-
 ist Propaganda League, 1919.
Farmeren og socialismen (The Farmer and Socialism) by Ole
 Hejt. Norwegian. Chicago.
(s)Free Record. Chinese: ?Canton. Anarchist.
(s)Ghadr-Gaddar or Hindustan Ghadr (Mutiny). San Fran-
 cisco.
Gusly (Collection of revolutionary songs). Russian: New
 York.
Gosudarstvo i revolyutzia (State and Revolution) by Lenin.
 New York.
(s)Glos Robotniczy (Voice of the Workers). Polish: Detroit.
(s)Golos Truzhenika (Voice of the Workers). Russian: IWW
 Chicago.

(s)Industrialisti. Finnish: Duluth (IWW).
(s)Industrialisti Joulu. Duluth.
(s)Industrial Worker. IWW: Seattle.
(s)The International. New York.
(s)International Socialist Review. Chicago.
Die Iberbaueng fur der Geselschaft nach'n Krieg (Reconstruction of Society after the War). Yiddish: New York.
(s)Indystriyalist. Ukrainian. IWW: New York.
Industrianaya Respublika v Meksikie. (Industrial republic
 in Mexico). Russian: New York.
(s)Il Nuova-Proletario. Chicago: IWW.
Kolokol (The Bell). Russian. (Presumably should be (s)).
Der Klassenkampf (Class Struggle). Yiddish: Philadelphia.
(s)Khlieb i Volia (Bread and Freedom). Russian: New York.
Kapliamy krovy zapysana istoriya industrialnykh rabotchkh
 mire (In drops of blood is recorded the history of the
 world). IWW: Chicago.
Komu sluzhit soldat (Whom does the soldier serve?) Russian: New York.
(s)Labour. Chinese: Canton?
(s)Labour Defender. IWW: New York.
(s)Lumberjack Bulletin. IWW.
Lasten Kevat 1919. Finnish: Astoria, Oregon.
(s)La Guardia Rossa (The Red Guard). Italian: New York.
Men and mules by W.F. Ries. Girard, Kansas.
(s)Melting Pot. St Louis.
Manifest i programma kommunistitchnoho Internatzionalu
 (Manifest of programme of the Communist International).
 New York.
(s)The Marxian Socialist. Toronto.
Miznnaroniy socyalistytchniy i robitnychiy rukh (The International Socialist and Labour Movement). Ukrainian:
 Cleveland.
Mertvetzy kommuny by A. Kollontai (The dead of the commune)
 Russian: New York.
(s)Molot (The Hammer). Ukrainian: New York.
(s)Nove Evangelie (The New Evangel). Russian: New York.
Novyj Svit. Ukrainian: Montreal.
Naukovi i utopyini sotzializm (Scientific and Utopian soc-
 ialism). Ukrainian: New York.
(s)Naye Welt (New World). Yiddish: New York, IWW.
(s)Nove Svyato (New Holiday). Ukrainian: New York.
(s)Novy Mir. Russian: New York.
Otcherky Russkoi Revolyoutzii (Short history of the Russ-
 ian Revolution) by G.I. Kvasha. Ukrainian: New York.
Organizuites (Organize). Ukrainian: Cleveland.
Osnovni Zasady Komunizmu (Fundamental principles of comm-
 unism) by Engels. Ukrainian: Winnipeg.
O Pokhodzhenie Nashoho Boha (The Origin of our God). Ukr-
 ainian: New York.
Pilsni Rabotchykh (Songs of the Workers). Russian.
Proletarian Revolution in Russia by Lenin and Trotsky.
 New York.
Programa Kommunisty (Bolsheviki) by Bukharin. Ukrainian:
 New York.
Political Parties in Russia by Lenin (from The Class Str-
 uggle). New York.

(s)Rabotchyj Narod (The Working People) ed Popovich. Russian: Winnipeg.

(s)Rabotchyj Narod (The Working People) Ukrainian ed Charitonoff. Winnipeg.

(s)Rabinytchyi Vistnyk (The Workers Herald). Ukrainian: New York.

Retch o Russkoi Revolyoutzi (Lecture on the Russian Revolution). Russian: New York.

(s)Raivaaja. Finnish: Fitchburg, Mass.

(s)Robitnyk. Ukrainian: Cleveland.

(s)Sakenia. Finnish: Fitchburg, Mass.

(s)Seattle Daily Call.

(s)Svoboda. Bulgarian: Chicago.

Der Sotzializmus, seine Ursachen, Ziehlen un Wegen (Socialism, its causes, objects and paths). Yiddish: Chicago.

Soviety Rabotchykh Soldatskikh i Kresyanskikh Deputatov i Nashe Knim Otnoshenie (Soviets of the Workers and Soldiers and Peasant Deputies and our relation towards them) Russian: New York.

Soviet Russia. New York.

(s)The Soviet. Edmonton.

Socziyalizm (Socialism) by E. Kruk. Ukrainian: New York.

(s)Strahdneeks (The Worker). Lettish: Boston.

(s)Svobonaya Rossia (Free Russia). Russian: Chicago.

Teollisen Kansanvallan Kehitys (Development of Industrial Democracy). Finnish: Duluth.

Toverin Toimitsijain Syyttaminen (Official Comrades who have been persecuted). Finnish: Astoria, Oregon.

(s)Trudovaya Misl (Labours Thoughts). Russian: Chicago.

(s)Tie Vapauteen (Road to Freedom). Finnish: New York.

Tschto Bolsheviki Obieschtchaly Narodnu i Tachto Daly Emu (What the Bolshevik have promised the nation and what they have given it). Russian: New York.

To the young workers by A. Karelyn. Russian: New York.

(s)Toveri. Finnish: Astoria, Oregon.

Uroky Revolyoutzi (Lessons of the Revolution) by Lenin. Russian: New York.

(s)Uus Ilm (The New World). Estonian: New York.

Vallan Kamouksellinen. Finnish: Duluth.

(s)Vsemirny Soyuse. Russian: Chicago.

(s)The Week published by W.E. Peirce: Victoria: 'A mass of Bolsheviki, pacifist and radical socialism'.

(s)Western Clarion. Vancouver.

(s)Zemla i Wola. Russian published by John Stefanitski: Toronto.

Zadatchy Proletariata v'Nashey Revolyoutzi (The task of the proletariat in our revolution) by Lenin. New York.

(s)Die Volkstimme (Peoples Voice). Yiddish: Winnipeg.

Vos is Bolshevizm? by B. Hoffmann. Yiddish: New York.

Vappu 1919. Finnish: Astoria, Oregon.

Valon Tiella (The Lighted Road) Finnish: Fitchburg.

Virtually all these publications are described with fine, if somewhat inaccurate, impartiality as being 'Communist' 'Bolshevik' 'Revolutionary' 'Anarchist' or 'Socialist'.

In addition to the specific titles there were blanket prohibitions on all the following:

All publications of the IWW (Industrial Workers of the World); this included all the publications of Charles Kerr of Chicago on the ostensible grounds that they all contained IWW advertisements: all those of the Russian Social Democratic Party; the Russian Revolutionary Group; the Russian Social Revolutionists; the Russian Workers Union; the Ukrainian Revolutionary Group; the Ukrainian Social Democratic Party; the Social Labour Party; the Group of Social Democrats of Bolsheviki; the Group of Social Democrats of Anarchists; the Workers International Industrial Union; the Chinese National League; the Chinese Labour Association.

The following reports were received from different cities:

23 May 1919: Ottawa. Copies of The genesis and evolution of slavery: Historical materialism: The class struggle: The capitalistic class: Western Convention report (of the OBU): The Proletarian: Condemned from the dock: The evolution of industrial democracy: The Soviet and The Red Flag.

29 May 1919: Winnipeg. The Red Flag: The Soviet: The Proletarian: The Revolutionary Age: The Bolshevik and the Soviet: The slave of the farm: The Farm Workman: The right to be lazy: The Confederate, Brandon: The Russian constitution: Lessons of the Russian revolution: Questions and answers on the Bolsheviks: Soviet pamphlet no.76 by Albert Williams: Western Labour News.

18 September 1919: Saskatoon. Fim asimilatziye biz poale Zionizm by Ch. Zhitlowski: Der Yiddisher Arbeiter un die Yiddische bafreiung by A. Wohlimer: and publications of the North West Jewish Socialist Workers Party.

2 October 1919: Toronto. A Toronto Anarchist group circulating Patriotizm i Pravitelstvo by L.N. Tolstoi and Budushtche obshtchestvo.

23 October 1919: Port Arthur. Na Razayya Temy by L.N. Tolstoi: Mortvetzy Kommuny by A. Kollontai: Otcherky Russkoi Revolutyoutzii by I. Kvasha.

3 November 1919: Medicine Hat. Industrianaya Respublica v Meksikie by Senn Zogg: Gosudarstvo Budushtchago by Karl Kautsky: Retch o Russkoi Revolyoutzi by Elize Reklyu: Komu Sluzhit Soldat: Soviety Rabotchykh Soldatskikh i Krestyanskikh Deputatov i nashek nim otnoshenie.

24 October 1919: Der Klassen Kampf by Saul Elstein. Das Freie Wort (Philadelphia): Der Sozialismus, seine Ursachen, Ziehlen un Wegen: Die Arbeitslosigkeit by M. Goldfarb: Die Iberbaueng fur der Geselschaft nach'n Krieg: Wos is Bolshevizm.

January 1920: Ottawa. English titles from originals in Greek. Williams; Questions and answers: Kropotkin; A call to youth: E.J. Tsagarkas; Socialism in theory and practice: Trotsky; The war and the Bolsheviki: George Katsioli; The red danger: I. Ghent; The 8 hour day: The first of May: Ergaticos Agon: The worker and machinery: A.Karelin: To the young labourer: I. Ghent; What we want: I. Ghent; Collectivism.

Appendix II:
non-Canadian publications seized 1931

The following list is of books and pamphlets seized by the
police in August 1931 at the time of the arrest of the
leaders of the Communist Party. Presumably most of them
came from the party headquarters, though some may have
come from the homes of individual members.

Works in English:

American working women in the class struggle. New York,
  Communist Party of the USA.
Anderson, Tom. Socialist Sunday schools. Glasgow, 1918.
Another war coming. New York.
Beer, M. A guide to the study of Marx. London.
Bell, Tom. The movement for world trade union unity.
  Chicago, 1925.
Bennett, A.J. The general council and the general strike.
  London.
Browder, E. Civil war in nationalist China. Chicago,1927.
Brown, W.T. How capitalism has hypnotized society. Chic-
  ago.
Burns, Elinor. British imperialism in China. London,1926.
China in revolt. Chicago, (1927).
Class against class. London, 1929.
Communist International. Fourth congress, abridged. Lon-
  don, 1923.
------ From the fourth to the fifth world congress. Lon-
  don, 1924.
------ Resolutions and theses of the fourth congress.
  London, 1923.
------ Theses and resolutions of the third world congress.
  New York, 1921.
Cook, A.J. The nine days. London.
Craik, W.W. A short history of the British working class
  movement. London, 1919.
De Leon, D. Two pages from Roman history. Glasgow.
Dobb, M.H. The development of capitalism. London.
Dutt, R.P. Empire 'socialism'. London, 1925.
Eleventh plenum of the ECCI. London.
Engdahl, J.L. Sedition! to protest against war...New York.
Foster, W.Z. Organize the unorganized. Chicago.
------ Strike strategy. Chicago, 1926.
Fuernberg, F. Where to begin? How to build a mass YCL.
  New York.
The gains of revolution. London.
Kaplun, S. The protection of labor in Soviet Russia.
  New York, 1920.
Kolontai, A. Communism and the family. New York.
Lafargue, P. The religion of capital. New York, 1918.
Lenin and the youth. London.
Lenin, N. Lessons of the Russian revolution. London,1918.

476

Lenin, N. On the road to insurrection. London.
------ Revolutionary lessons. New York, 1929.
Losovsky, A. The international council of trade and ind-
ustrial unions. New York, 1920.
Lovestone, Jay. American imperialism. Chicago.
Marx, C. Value, price and profit. Chicago.
The militant trades council. London, 1926.
Nearing, Scott. The American empire. New York, 1921.
------ Education in Soviet Russia. New York, 1926.
------ Whither China? New York, 1927.
Postgate, R.W. A short history of the British workers.
London, 1926.
Radek, K. The development of socialism. Glasgow, (1931).
Raid on Arcos Ltd. London, 1927.
Red International of Labour Unions. Resolutions and dec-
isions, 1st world congress. New York (1921).
------ Resolutions and decisions, 2nd world congress.
Chicago, 1923.
------ Resolutions of the 5th world congress. London,1931.
The railwayman's union of the USSR and railway transport.
Moscow, 1928.
Resolutions of the Enlarged Executive, YCI. London, 1926.
The results of two congresses (5th CI and 4th YCI). Stock-
holm, 1924.
Schachtman, Max. 1871, the Paris Commune. Chicago.
The second year of the Workers Party of America: theses,
program, resolutions. Chicago, 1924.
The social significance of fascism.
Spiro, G. Paris on the barricades. New York, 1929.
Stalin, J. Our new tasks. Moscow, 1931.
------ Theory and practice of Leninism. London, 1925.
Starr, Mark. Trade unionism. London, 1926.
Symposium on the programme question. London, 1924.
Theses and resolutions CPUSA, 7th national convention, 1930.
Theses and statutes 3rd CI. Moscow, 1920.
Theses of the CI. London, 1920.
Towards a communist programme. London, 1922.
Trotsky, L. Where is Britain going? London, 1926.
------ Whither Russia? New York, 1926.
Under the banner of militant nationalism. Moscow, 1930.
Varga, E. The decline of capitalism. London, 1924.
Voks. A clash of two systems. Moscow, 1931.
What to read. London, 1923.
Wolfe, B.D. The Trotsky opposition. New York, 1928.
Young Communist International. Between the 4th and 5th
congresses 1924-1928. London, 1928.
------ Resolutions and theses, 3rd Congress, Berlin 1923.
------ Resolutions, 4th congress, Stockholm 1924.
------ The child of the worker. Berlin, 1923.
Young Communist League, GB. January fifteenth.

In Finnish.

Bill Haywood Kirja. New York, 1929.
Jenks, M. Kommunistinen solu. New York, 1929.
Kollontay, A. Työväen oppositsioni. Duluth.
Kolmannen internationalen toisen kongressin päätökset ja
ohjelma. (Helsinki).

Koulukysymys suomen sos-dem. nuorisoliiton ohjelmassa.
  Pori, 1920.
Kujala, J. Orjuudesta vapauteen. Hancock, Mich. 1911.
Lenin. Imperialismi. Superior, Wisc. 1929.
------ Kirjeitä taktiikasta. Kustantaja, 1920.
------ Taistelija, opettaja, johtaja. Superior, 1928.
Marx, K. Ranskan kansalaissota. Superior, 1920.
Neuvosto-venäjän lait. Astoria, Oregon.
Raeus, Magnus. Yli kuoleman kenttien. Worcester, Mass.
Rutanen, M. Joukkovoima. Worcester, Mass.
E.S. Työväenliike ja yhteiskunnallisen elämän johto.
Työväen laulukirja. Superior, 1925.
Vatanen, J.I. Avuttomia. Helsinki, 1913.
Viesti. Vol.I no.2, Worcester, Mass.

French.

Naumov, I.K. Les journées d'octobre. Paris.

German.

Gorki, M. Mit Bomben und Granaten. Berlin.
Halle, Felix. Wie verteidigt sich der Proletarier...
  Berlin, 1929.
Krylenko, N. Weisser und roter Terror. Berlin, 1927.
Losowsky, A. Der Streik. Berlin, 1930.
------ Streiktaktik und Streikstrategie: resolution des
  Strassburger Konferenz. Berlin.
Der Rote Aufbau, vol.IV heft 11. Berlin, 1931.
Rubiner, Frida. Die Grundlagen des Sowjetstaates. Berlin,
  1927.
Das Urteil würder vollstrecht! Der Erschiessung der '48'
  in Sowetrussland und ihre Hintergründer. Berlin.

Russian.

Ілюстробаний робітничо-фармерський календар на переступний рік 1928,
  Вінніпег, 1927
Ленин,Н. Империализм. Ленинград, 1925.
Пугачов,С. Загроза нобоï імперіалістичноï інтервенціï в СРСР. Вінніпег, 1931.
Тадеуш, П.Я. Американская коммуна „сеятель". Москва 1930.
Зыбкобец,А.В. Производственный план коллективного хозяйства.
  Москва, 1930.

Author index

All references are to item numbers, not pages.

500

New Democratic Party (cont)
4521, 4605, 4606, 4607,
4608, 4609, 4697, 4698,
4699, 4700, 4701, 4783,
4874, 4875, 4876, 4877,
5005, 5006, 5007, 5080
New Democratic Party Alberta
Socialist Caucus 4878
NDP Waffle 4879, 5008
New Democratic Youth
4239, 4240, 4379, 4610,
4880, 4881
New Party 4153
Newcomb, D.B. 35
News-Facts 3790
Nicholson, A.M. 2251,
2295, 2296, 2419, 2467,
2590, 2662, 2671, 3185
Nicholson, T.F. 2789
Nicholson, William B. 2790
Nielsen, Dorise W. 2297,
2298, 2360, 2468, 2469,
2791, 3443
Nkemdirim, Bernard A. 4702
No More War Committee 970
No-Party League of Western
Canada 524
Non Partisan League 857
Norman, Howard 2978
Norman, W.H.H. 3036
Normandin, Paul 3791
Norris, William 68
North Star Publishing 1776
Northern Neighbours Maga-
zine 4784
Northern Translations
Service 3974
Northwest Grain Dealers
Assn 1196
Noseworthy, J.W. 2201,
2402, 2523, 2525, 2591,
2668, 2792, 2870, 3647
Nova Scotia 256, 1015,
1161
Nova Scotia New Democratic
Youth 4882
Nova Scotia Teachers Union
858
Novack, George 4611
Novak, Louis 2793
Novakowski, Ken 5009
Nowlan, David M. 4780

O'Boyle, Wm P. 758

O'Brien, C.M. 430
O'Donoghue, D.J. 280, 316
O'Donoghue, J.G. 859
Oesterling, Kjeld 3725
Office and Professional Work-
ers of Canada 2470
O'Hanly, J.L.P. 36. 37
Okanagan Society for the
Revival of Indian Arts and
Crafts 2979
Okulevich, G. 4241
Oliver, Michael 4242, 4329
Olley, Robert E. 4243
One Big Union 759, 760, 761,
762, 763, 764, 765, 766,
767, 768, 860, 861, 862,
863, 928, 971. 972, 973,
974, 975, 976, 1016, 1070,
1071, 1115, 1116, 1162,
1163, 1164, 1165, 1197,
1198, 1199, 1200, 1201,
1202, 1203, 1204, 1241
One of the Bunglers 181
One Who Knows 164
O'Neill, John 4280
Ontario 47, 288, 383, 403,
461, 486, 525, 582, 601,
679, 769, 977, 1017, 1242,
1281, 1461, 1462, 1463,
1550, 1777, 2592, 2794,
2980, 2981, 2982, 3521,
3726, 4020, 5081, 5082,
5083, 5084
Ontario & Quebec Conference
of Typographical Unions
1117
Ontario Cash Mutuals 2983
Ontario Committee for the
New Democratic Party 4244
Ontario Communist-Labor Total War Committee 2593,
2594, 2595
Ontario Co-operative Union
2984, 3138
Ontario Credit Union League
2985
Ontario Federation of Labour
3522, 3580, 3844, 3845,
3846, 3914, 3975, 3976,
4021, 4022, 4023, 4024,
4100, 4101, 4102, 4103,
4154, 4155, 4156, 4157,
4158, 4245, 4246, 4303,
4304, 4305, 4306, 4307,
4308, 4309, 4380, 4381,
4435, 4436, 4437, 4438,
4522, 4523, 4524, 4525,

Title index

In the following title index the initial words 'the, le,
la, les, a, an, un, une' have been disregarded. I know
this is partly contrary to convention, but having experi-
enced the frustration of not knowing whether a title was
'The new deal' or 'A new deal', and having only a 50-50
chance of success (which seldom obeys the laws of chance
anyway), I feel someone has to make a start and eliminate
the illogicality whereby 'the' is disregarded, but 'a' is
not. Note though, that these words have not been disregarded when they occur in the body of the title.
    Where the same title occurs more than once the list-
ing is alphabetical by the author (cited in brackets);
where author and title are identical the sequence is chronological and dated (in brackets).
    Serials are cited in italics.
    Except in the titles of serials all initials are in-
dexed as if expanded: thus CCF as if Cooperative Commonwealth Federation; BC as if British Columbia etc. No dis-
tinction has been made between co-operative and cooperative or labor and labour which appear as if the first were
one word and the second spelt labour.
    Numerals appear first in sequence, then initials, then
full alphabet. Numbers of conventions which have sometimes
been given numerals and sometimes spelled out eg. Minutes
of the 20th convention, Minutes of the twenty-first convention have been cited as if spelled out. Others have been
left in the numerated or spelled out version according to
the version on the title.

514

516

Bureaucracy and one-dimensional man   4712
By-laws   (Brant Farmers Co-op)   653
By-laws   (United Farmers of Ontario) (1921)   953
By-laws   (United Farmers of Ontario) (1923)   1025
By-Laws and sketch of Sandon Miners Union Hospital   354
By-laws approved as amended 1919 (Steam Engineers)   733
By-laws as amended by referendum (Lumber Workers)   1818
By-laws in effect 1 Jan 1918 (Metal Trades)   633
By-laws of the library & reading room   100
By-laws of Victoria branch (Granite Cutters)   479

CAIA Union Pilot   5514
CCF Bulletin   5515
CCF Challenge   5587
CCF Leader   5682
CCF News (Toronto)   5762
CCF News (Vancouver)   5590
CCF News- Nfld   5752
CCL Labour   5694
CCUF National Bulletin   5683
CCW News Letter   5789
CCYM News Letter   5734
CCYM Quarterly   5604
The CFCC Newsletter   5630
CLC News   5774
The CLDL Veteran   5496
CPAC Newsletter   5707
CSAC Journal de l'ASCC   5797
CSAO News   5868
CTC Bulletin   5885
(CUPE) Journal   5848
Caiman Review   5858
Calgary Home News   5377
Calgary rest centre   954
Calgary Strike Bulletin   5221
Calgary Typo News   5436
A call for Canadian justice   574
A call for unity!   1581
Call for western congress against section 98   1496
A call to a politico-socio-economic conference   1119
A call to action   2468
A call to action: address at annual convention (CCF)   3649
Call to action, Canadian Congress for Peace & Democracy
   2013
A call to action issued by Western Farm Conference   3108
A call to action: to all oppressed farmers   1304
A call to action: to all workers on the railroads   1162
A call to action! To the Jewish people of the world   2431
Call to all needle trades workers of Canada   1269
A call to independence   618
A call to peace   3337
Call to the farmers!   99
A call to the people of Canada   1436
A call to the rank and file of the CCF   1497

The Guide 5738
Guide to LSR activities 1975
A guide to the New Democratic Party 4873
Guild Annual 5520

Hail anti-fascist releases! 2459
The Halifax New Democrat 5850
Halifax Voice 5910
Halt Dictator Jamieson: save our union movement! 2310
(The) (Hamilton) Labour Digest 5572
Hamilton People 5975
Hamilton Steelworker 5483
Hamilton strike leaflets 1265
Hamilton labor directory 1919 728
Handbook for speakers 1512
Handbook of Labor-Progressive Party education 2818
Handbook of LPP Club education 3297
Handbook of practical work 950
Handbook of the League for Social Reconstruction 1534
Handbook on Canadian labour laws 3955
A handbook on policy 4518
A handbook on the great conspiracy 4468
Handbook on union agreements 2646
A handbook to the Sask CCF: platform & policy 2045
Hands off Russia! 825
Harambee 5911
Harapnyk/(The Whip) 5276
Harbinger 5912
Hard times in Ontario: a pretty story, certainly 38
Hard times no more 1459
L'Harmonie Syndicale 5833
Harvest of ideas 3364
Has Canada the right to declare neutrality? 2181
Has Chamberlain saved peace? 2113
Have they turned their back to the Bible? 3837
He wrote for us 3576
Health 3915
Health and unemployment 2093
Health can be planned 2745
Health insurance now! 3691
Health on the march 2509
The Health Services Review 5643
Heart of Spain 1922
The Heavy Lift 5399
Hello Canada! Canada's Mackenzie-Papineau battalion 1948
Help Canada's youth in their fight for justice! 1829
Help seal Hitler's doom! 2317
Help Spain make the world safe for democracy 1904
Help the fishermen of Nova Scotia 4973
Help to the Soviet Union from Croatians... 2440
Henry Wise Wood of Alberta 3525
Hepburn's betrayal...what now? 1984
Here's to your health 3243
Here's to your health: the CCF has a plan 2695

In defence of freedom 3891
In reply...on the invitation of the Civil Service Assn 3944
In search of Canadian liberalism 4171
In support of proposals by BC Federation of Labour 2843
In the case of Louis Riel 116
In the clutches of the Cheka 1323
In the matter of the Anti-Discrimination Act 1958 4021
In the matter of the appointment of an Industrial Dispute
 Inquiry Commission 3190
In the matter of the War Services Electors Bill 2753
In the Privy Council: an appeal...appellant's case 1365
In the Privy Council: an appeal...Record of proceedings
 (Young) 1364
In union in strength 4428
Inaugural meeting (Women of Halifax) 245
The increased safety of Victory Bonds 2697
L'Indépendance 5834
L'Indépendantiste 5845
The Independent (Vancouver) 5139
The Independent (Winnipeg) 5277
The independent CCF 1513
The independent CCF BC provincial platform 1541
An independent foreign policy for Canada? 4742
The Independent Labor Party of Ontario 4227
Independent Labor Party's appeal to all labor 917
Indians: do we care? 4606
The Indicator 5231
The indictment: grave charges in the legislature 1886
An indictment of capitalism 1423
Individual & group behaviour in a coal mine disaster 4122
Industrial & craft unionism in Canada 1191
Industrial & economic reorganization 777
The Industrial Banner 5129
Industrial bonds 681
Industrial conflict 3094
Industrial democracy & Canadian labour 4887
Industrial democracy - European developments 4660
Industrial dispute settlement in Canada 4761
Industrial disputes and the Canadian act 635
Industrial disputes in the commercial fisheries 4065
Industrial enquiry commission...relating to the disruption
 of shipping on the Great Lakes 4338
Industrial history of the New Glasgow district 4130
Industrial labour conditions in Canada 1792
Industrial life & immigration report 980
The Industrial News 5109
Industrial occupation of women 773
Industrial organization of labor in Great Britain 760
Industrial peace 468
Industrial relations in Canada 3963
Industrial relations in the Maritime provinces 3180
Industrial retirement plans in Canada 2100
Industrial schools 461
The industrial struggle & Protestant ethics 4201
The industrial union 1661
Industrial unrest 789
Industrial Worker 5462

568

Militant Cooperator 5351
Le militant syndical de la CSN 4491
Military training in Canadian schools 1218
Milk subsidies are necessary! 3253
Milk: what you must make Drew do! 3112
A million dollars of your money must be saved 2740
Millionaires plot railway steal 2044
Mind your own business 1171
Mine-Mill Herald 5765
Mine Mill Research Review 5817
Mine Mill says: the record speaks for itself 4147
Minerals & mining in Nova Scotia 4755
The minimum wage & its proposed application 1873
The minimum wage for women 1263
The minimum wage in Canada 965
A minimum wage of $5,000 a year! 1955
Minimum wage regulation in Saskatchewan 3440
Ministers on trial 135
Minor parties in Canadian national politics 3781
Minority groups vs Canadian public 3163
Misadventures of a working hobo in Canada 1356
The mission of capitalism 640
Minutes of CCF youth Ontario annual convention 1954 3771
Minutes: CCUF convention 1946 3078
Minutes of conference of university students 3077
Minutes of convention to organize Canadian Labor Party 905
Minutes of the fifth annual convention (Can Labor) 1051
Minutes of the fifth CCUF convention 1951 3553
Minutes of the fourth annual meeting Patrons of Industry
 Grand Assn of Ontario 1895 257
Minutes of second annual meeting Grand Assn of Ont 242
Minutes of the seventh CCUF national convention 3702
Minutes of the seventh general convention IWW 2275
Minutes of the sixth annual convention Can Labor Party 1097
Minutes of the sixth CCUF national convention 3619
Minutes of the sixth general convention IWW 2190
Minutes of the third annual convention IWW 1755
Minutes of the third annual meeting Grand Assn of Ont 249
Minutes of the thirteenth CCF youth convention 3889
Minutes of the twenty-first constitutional general con-
 vention IWW 1637
Minutes of third national onvention (CLDL) 1699
Mobilisation 5944
Mobilize Alberta for Canada's war effort 2446
Mobilizing for enlightenment 2603
The modern juggernaut 641
Moncton's labor day celebrations 1919 755
Money and jobs 3700
Money and the war 2505
Money before men 2252
Money: master or servant? 2725
Money power in Canada - capitalism 1597
Monkey sense 1542
Monopolies 2988
Monster demonstration (CLDL 1931) 1380
Monthly Report Amalgamated Society of Carpenters & Joiners 5287
The Monthly Review 5542
The Montreal Star & the CCF 2815

The new party and the worker   4192
New Party Club kit   4233
New Party Clubs   4255
A new party for a better Canada   4074
A new party for Canada   4151
The New Party Newsletter   5818
The new political party (Dominion Labor Party)   720
The new political party (Knowles)   4077
A new political party for Canada   3997
New provincial political platform   856
The new radicals & the multiversity   4752
New rules needed - make your protest heard!   3072
New social order dawning   2751
The New Society   5891
The new technology demands a new politics   4836
New times - new policies for agriculture   4832
The new trail   1355
The new untouchables   2097
New worlds for women   2791
New Zealand prospers under CCF-type rule   2898
The Newfoundland story   4101
Newfoundland: the forgotten island   2625
News and Views   5467
The News Bag   5442
News Bulletin   5617
News bulletin   1831
News bulletin: for youth and democracy   1916
News bulletin: united front against fascism   2098
News Comment   5561
News from Spain   2155
News Letter   5575
News letter: defence claims Crown offered witness $500 to
   give false testimony   805
Next elections: what kind of coalition?   2795
Nickels built the factories   2739
The nine of power   951
Nine years of achievement   1347
Nineteenth convention CPC   4574
N. Lenin: his life and work   891
No conscription   642
No conscription   643
No conscription! uncompromising opposition to military
   despotism   644
No information to justify War Measures act   4984
No mystery to this robbery   2889
No! no! a 1,000 times no   3199
No nuclear arms for Canada!   4346
No penalty on poverty   2061
No power greater   4708
No wage cuts! No lay-offs!   3515
Non à la conscription à la guerre   3648
None shall make them afraid   3559
The Nonpartisan Leader of Canada   5204
North America and the Soviet Union   1902
The North Atlantic Treaty Alliance & Korea   3606
North Star   5425
North Toronto CCYM Youth in Revolt   5443

590

612

Young workers! Sept 8 is our day! 1368
Your members speak 2228
Your money's worth 1251
Your opportunity 4434
Your rights and freedoms are in danger 3642
Your right to health 4008
Your unemployed cannot work miracles! 2076
Your Victory Bonds and your bank account 2676
Yours for humanity, security and progress 3618, 3887
Yours to Build 5706
Youth and fascism 1870
Youth and violence 4773
Youth faces the future 2720
Youth in a contemporary world and in Quebec 4623
Youth of the happy land 1812
Youth proposes - physical fitness, minimum wage laws 2768
Youth Review 5787
Youth want peace 2316
Youth wants peace and brotherhood 2067
Youth's peace policy 1912
The Yukoner 5650

Zemlya i Volya 5218
Zvesti see L'Udove Zvesti

Index of selected organizations

The following short index is intended to give only the
earliest likely dates for researchers interested in a
particular organization. It is not intended to give accurate dates for the founding meetings, first conventions
etc, but simply to be a guide instead of an exhaustive
listing of all the titles in the main bibliography that
might relate to the organization in question. In any
case much research is still needed to pin down all the
dates of the many splinter groups. Bert Robinson wrote
to Harold Winch in February 1933 about Ontario, 'The situation here is hard to understand and harder to convey...'
Multiply that by several provinces forty or fifty years
later and you have some idea of the confusion possible.
Note that the references are to years, not item numbers.

Alberta Federation of Labor (AFL) 1912
All-Canadian Congress of Labor (ACCL) 1927
British Columbia Federation of Labor (BCFL) 1910
Canadian Congress of Labor (CCL) 1940
Canadian Council of Agriculture (CCA) 1909
Canadian Federation of Labor (CFL) 1908
Canadian Labour Congress (CLC) 1874 and 1956
Canadian Labor Defense League (CLDL) 1929

Canadian Labor Party (CLP)   1921
Canadian League Against War and Fascism (CLAWF)   1934
Canadian League for Peace and Democracy   1936
Canadian Socialist Federation   1911
Canadian Socialist League   1893
Communist Party of Canada (CPC)   1919; 1924-1943; 1962
Communist Party of Canada (Marxist-Leninist) (CPC M-L)
 commonly known as 'Maoists'   1968
Cooperative Commonwealth Federation (CCF) 1932.   Note
 that references to a 'cooperative commonwealth' occured
 as early as 1919
Co-operative Union of Canada (CUC)   1909
Dominion Communist-Labor Total War Committee   1942
Dominion Grange (Patrons of Husbandry)   1874
Dominion Labor Party   1918
Farmers Unity League (FUL)   1930
Federated Labor Party   1920
Independent Labor Party of Manitoba (ILP)   1920
Independent Labor Party of Ontario (ILP)   1893
Industrial Workers of the World (IWW)   1905 (USA); mater-
 ial circulated here before the Canadian sections founded.
Knights of Labor (KL)   1869   (USA)
Labor Church   1918
Labor Educational Association   1903
Labor-Progressive Party (LPP)   1943
Labor Representation League   1920
League for Social Reconstruction (LSR)   1932
League for Socialist Action (LSA)   1959
Manitoba Grain Growers Association (MGGA)   1904
National Council for Canadian-Soviet Friendship   1943
National Council of Women of Canada   1894
National Trades and Labor Congress of Canada (NTLCC)   1900
New Democratic Party (NDP) 1961.   Preceded by references
 to a 'New Party'.   Note that the Saskatchewan provincial
 body called itself 'CCF Saskatchewan section of the NDP'
 until 1967-68
One Big Union (OBU)   1919
Ontario Federation of Labour (OFL)   1950
Patrons of Husbandry   1874
Patrons of Industry   1890
Prairie School for Social Advance (PSSA) 1944
Revolutionary Socialist Party   1902
Revolutionary Workers Party   1946
Saskatchewan Federation of Labour   1956
Saskatchewan Grain Growers Association (SGGA)   1905
Single Tax Associations   1890
Social Democratic Party of BC   1907
Social Democratic Party of Canada (SDPC)   1910
Social Democratic Party (SDP)   1911
Socialist Labor Party   1899
Socialist Party of Canada   (SPC)   1904
Socialist Party of North America   1910
Territorial Grain Growers Association   1901
Trades and Labor Congress of Canada (TLCC)   1883
Trades and Labor Councils, various   1890
Trade Union Educational League (TUEL)   1923
United Farm Women of Alberta   (UFWA)   1916

United Farm Women of Manitoba (UFWM)   1918
United Farm Women of Ontario (UFWO)   1918
United Farmers of Alberta (UFA)   1909
United Farmers of Canada (UFC)   1926
United Farmers of Manitoba (UFM)   1918
United Farmers of Ontario (UFO)   1914
Voice of Women (VOW)   1960
Western Federation of Miners   1898
Workers Educational Association (WEA)   1918
Womens International League for Peace & Freedom (WILPF)
 1921 (The Hague)
Workers Party of Canada (WPC)   1921
Workers Unity League (WUL)   1929
Workingmens Protective Association (WPA)   1878
Young Communist League (YCL)   1922

Errata

Through a misreading of my own writing 4755 is entered
chronologically under 1968.   It should be 1918.

The following entries are duplicated:
3045 and 3110
3270 and 5674
5060 and 5140

Entry numbers 4091-4099 and 5360-5369 do not exist.